EPPP Step One Exam Review

Anne S. Klee, PhD, CPRP, completed her graduate work at the Ferkauf Graduate School of Psychology of Yeshiva University, Bronx, New York, and her undergraduate work at Columbia University, New York, New York. After completing predoctoral and postdoctoral fellowships at the Yale School of Medicine, New Haven, Connecticut, she accepted a position at VA Connecticut Healthcare System, where she has worked for the past 20 years in various roles. She is also an associate professor in the Department of Psychiatry at the Yale School of Medicine. Professionally, she is devoted to developing quality, recovery-oriented programs for individuals with serious mental illness, training and supporting the work of peer specialists, and training the next generation of clinicians in the field of psychosocial rehabilitation and engaging them in careers in public mental health. She serves in national and state capacities. She is a former council representative of the American Psychological Association (APA), a Past Chair of the APA Board of Professional Affairs, a past president of Psychologists in Public Service (Division 18) of the APA, a past president of the Connecticut Psychological Association, and the current president of the Connecticut Psychological Association (CPA) Educational Foundation. Dr. Klee is a Fellow of the APA Divisions 18 and 31. She is licensed in Connecticut.

Bret A. Moore, PsyD, ABPP, is a board-certified clinical psychologist and clinical psychopharmacologist in San Antonio, Texas. He is the author and editor of 24 books including *Clinical Psychopharmacology Made Ridiculously Simple* (9th and 10th editions), *Handbook of Clinical Psychopharmacology for Therapists* (9th and 10th editions), and *Child and Adolescent Clinical Psychopharmacology Made Simple* (4th edition). From 2009 to 2017, Dr. Moore wrote the biweekly column, "Kevlar for the Mind," which was published in the *Army Times*, *Navy Times*, *Air Force Times*, and *Marine Corps Times*. He has also written feature articles for *Scientific American Mind*, *The New Republic*, and *Psychology Today*. Dr. Moore is a Fellow of the American Psychological Association (Divisions 18, 19, and 55) and recipient of numerous awards from national and state organizations. His views on clinical and military psychology have been quoted in *USA Today*, *The New York Times*, *National Geographic*, *The Boston Globe*, and *TV Guide*, and on CNN and Fox News. He has appeared on National Public Radio, the British Broadcasting Company, and the Canadian Broadcasting Company.

EPPP Step One Exam Review
THIRD EDITION

Anne S. Klee, PhD, CPRP
Bret A. Moore, PsyD, ABPP

Editors

Copyright © 2025 Springer Publishing Company, LLC
All rights reserved.
First Springer Publishing edition 978-0-8261-9973-7 © 2013; subsequent edition 2018.

No part of this publication may be reproduced, stored in a retrieval system, or transmitted in any form or by any means, electronic, mechanical, photocopying, recording, or otherwise, without the prior permission of Springer Publishing Company, LLC, or authorization through payment of the appropriate fees to the Copyright Clearance Center, Inc., 222 Rosewood Drive, Danvers, MA 01923, 978-750-8400, fax 978-646-8600, info@copyright.com or at www.copyright.com.

Springer Publishing Company, LLC
902 Carnegie Center, Suite 140, Princeton, NJ 08540
www.springerpub.com
connect.springerpub.com

Acquisitions Editor: Jaclyn Koshofer
Content Development Editor: Libby Ornstein
Production Editor: Susan White
Compositor: Thomson Digital

ISBN: 978-0-8261-9021-5
e-book ISBN: 978-0-8261-9022-2
DOI: 10.1891/9780826190222

24 25 26 27 / 5 4 3 2 1

The author and the publisher of this work have made every effort to use sources believed to be reliable to provide information that is accurate and compatible with the standards generally accepted at the time of publication. Because medical science is continually advancing, our knowledge base continues to expand. Therefore, as new information becomes available, changes in procedures become necessary. We recommend that the reader always consult current research and specific institutional policies before performing any clinical procedure or delivering any medication. The author and publisher shall not be liable for any special, consequential, or exemplary damages resulting, in whole or in part, from the readers' use of, or reliance on, the information contained in this book. The publisher has no responsibility for the persistence or accuracy of URLs for external or third-party internet websites referred to in this publication and does not guarantee that any content on such websites is, or will remain, accurate or appropriate.

The Examination for Professional Practice in Psychology (EPPP) is developed by the Association of State and Provincial Psychology Boards (ASPPB). ASPPB does not sponsor or endorse this resource, nor does it have a proprietary relationship with Springer Publishing Company.

Library of Congress Control Number: 2024944121

Contact sales@springerpub.com to receive discount rates on bulk purchases.

Publisher's Note: **New and used products purchased from third-party sellers are not guaranteed for quality, authenticity, or access to any included digital components.**

Printed in the United States of America by Gasch Printing.

Contents

Contributors vii
Preface ix
Pass Guarantee xi

Chapter 1. About the EPPP   1
Anne S. Klee and Bret A. Moore

Chapter 2. Preparation Strategies and Tips   5
Walter Erich Penk and Dolores Little

Chapter 3. Biological Bases of Behavior   11
David Shearer and Tyler R. Reese

Chapter 4. Cognitive–Affective Bases of Behavior   43
Elyssa Scharaga

Chapter 5. Social and Cultural Bases of Behavior   77
Loretta E. Braxton, Jessica J. Fulton, Jennifer Yi,
Stephanie Salcedo Rossitch, and Raha Forooz Sabet

Chapter 6. Growth and Life-Span Development   111
Casey B. Corso, Rebecca Hoppe, Edith Winters,
Laura E. Boylan, and Marcia A. Winter

Chapter 7. Assessment and Diagnosis   155
Megan N. Scott, Lauren Bush, and Scott J. Hunter

Chapter 8. Treatment, Intervention, Prevention, and Supervision   199
Ashley B. Batastini and Ashley C. T. Jones

Chapter 9. Research Methods and Statistics   253
Amy E. Ellis, Nicole Mantella, Brianna Domaceti,
and Luca Hartman

Chapter 10. Ethical, Legal, and Professional Issues   301
Rodney L. Lowman and Linda M. Richardson

Chapter 11. Practice Test   333

Chapter 12. Practice Test: Answers   379

Index   411

Contributors

Ashley B. Batastini, PhD, Associate Professor, Swinburne University of Technology, Hawthorn, Victoria, Australia

Laura E. Boylan, Doctoral Student, Virginia Commonwealth University, Richmond, Virginia

Loretta E. Braxton, PhD, Psychologist, Durham Veterans Affairs Health Care System, Durham, North Carolina

Lauren Bush, PhD, Assistant Professor, RUSH University Medical Center, Chicago, Illinois

Casey B. Corso, PhD, Researcher and Evaluator, Magnolia Consulting, Charlottesville, Virginia

Brianna Domaceti, MS, Graduate Student, PsyD Clinical Psychology, Nova Southeastern University, Davie, Florida

Amy E. Ellis, PhD, Assistant Professor, Nova Southeastern University, Davie, Florida

Jessica J. Fulton, PhD, Chief, Office of Employee Experience, Durham Veterans Affairs Health Care System, Durham, North Carolina

Luca Hartman, MS, Graduate Student, PsyD Clinical Psychology, Nova Southeastern University, Davie, Florida

Rebecca Hoppe, PhD, NIDA T32 Postdoctoral Research Fellow, Arizona State University REACH Institute, Tempe, Arizona

Scott J. Hunter, PhD, Senior Scientific Expert, Neurodevelopment, WCG Clinical Research Solutions, Chicago, Illinois

Ashley C. T. Jones, PhD, Postdoctoral Fellow, Utah State Hospital, Provo, Utah

Rodney L. Lowman, PhD, ABAP, Distinguished Professor Emeritus, California School of Professional Psychology/Alliant International University, Mt. Helix, California

Nicole Mantella, PhD, Psychology Trainee; Psychology Intern, Nova Southeastern University, Davie, Florida; Joseph Maxwell Cleland Atlanta Veterans Affairs Medical Center, Decatur, Georgia

Walter Erich Penk, PhD, ABPP, Professor and Clinical Psychologist (retired), Texas College of Medicine, New Braunfels, Texas

Tyler R. Reese, MD, MPH, FAAFP, Faculty Physician, Madgian Army Medical Center, Tacoma, Washington

Linda M. Richardson, PhD, Consulting Psychologist, Lowman & Richardson Consulting Psychologists, P.C., La Mesa, California

Stephanie Salcedo Rossitch, PhD, Staff Psychologist, Durham Veterans Affairs Health Care System, Durham, North Carolina

Raha Forooz Sabet, Durham Veterans Affairs Health Care System, Durham, North Carolina

Elyssa Scharaga, PhD, Clinical Neuropsychologist, Northwell Health, New York, New York

Megan N. Scott, PhD, Associate Professor of Psychiatry and Behavioral Sciences, Northwestern University Feinberg School of Medicine, Chicago, Illinois

David Shearer, PhD, MSCP, Prescribing Psychologist, Director of Behavioral Sciences, Family Medicine Residency, Gig Harbor, Washington

Marcia A. Winter, PhD, Associate Professor of Psychology, Virginia Commonwealth University, Richmond, Virginia

Edith Winters, Graduate Student, Loyola University Maryland, Baltimore, Maryland

Jennifer Yi, PhD, Staff Psychologist, Durham VA Medical Center, Durham, North Carolina

Preface

Most professions require some type of state or national examination before formal entrance into their respective fields can occur. For example, medicine requires completion of the U.S. Medical Licensing Exam. Prospective lawyers must pass the Bar. Accountants are required to take a test if they wish to become certified. And although it varies by state, to become a teacher, one must successfully navigate a certification exam. The profession of psychology is no different. Before one can practice psychology independently, the EPPP must be passed.

The EPPP is a 225-question examination that focuses on eight content areas: biological bases of behavior; cognitive–affective bases of behavior; social and cultural bases of behavior; growth and life-span development; assessment and diagnosis; treatment, intervention, prevention, and supervision; research methods and statistics; and ethical, legal, and professional issues. It is a comprehensive test that assesses the individual's depth and breadth of knowledge of psychology. The underlying assumption behind inclusion of the exam content is that the questions assess the knowledge base required to successfully function as a psychologist in professional practice (Association of State and Provincial Psychology Boards [ASPPB], 2024). It is not all-encompassing of what an effective psychologist should know, only a mere sampling. (You can find detailed information about the EPPP and the examination process at www.asppb.net.)

The EPPP is arguably one of the most anxiety-provoking milestones associated with becoming a psychologist. Without successful completion, it will delay one's entry into the profession and lead to uncertainty, potential financial strain, and, for some, thoughts of inadequacy and myriad negative emotions. Therefore, the anxiety is understandable. However, it is most often unwarranted and unnecessary. The truth is that the vast majority of individuals pass the test the first time (Schaffer et al., 2012). And for those who do not, most all will pass it in a subsequent attempt. For the reasons mentioned earlier, passing the examination the first time is highly desirable. And the best way to maximize your chances of passing the examination right out of the chute is to adequately prepare.

This third edition of *EPPP Step One Exam Review* provides a comprehensive review of core examination content and includes over 450 sample questions. *EPPP Step One Exam Review* goes beyond merely "teaching the test" through rote memorization. Instead, it covers the eight content domains of the EPPP and their representative knowledge areas in a stepwise, narrative, and review format. Another unique aspect of *EPPP Step One Exam Review* is that it is an edited volume. Consequently, it includes contributions from psychologists associated with some of the top psychology training and internship programs in the United States. The lead contributors are professors, training directors, and practitioners with expertise in the content areas of the chapters they authored. This combined approach is likely familiar to graduate students in psychology as it mirrors how doctoral level courses are commonly taught.

EPPP Step One Exam Review can be used in a variety of ways. We believe that the guide can serve as an instrumental text for supporting traditional systematic study methods or a primary resource for those who are not able to invest in a formalized study program. However, due to the significance of the examination and the amount of material covered, we do not recommend this volume be your only source of preparation. Many students will find the textbook format of the guide useful as a primer at the beginning of the study process or as a "topping-off" review at the end. Questions found at the end of each chapter can serve as a gauge for successful review of the chapter material, and the questions at the end of the text can serve as a review of the entire contents of the book.

Regardless of how you use this third edition of *EPPP Step One Exam Review*, we wish you tremendous success with the examination and your future career as a psychologist. Passing the EPPP and becoming a professional psychologist will be one of the most memorable stages of your professional and personal life. We are glad that we are able to be a small part of that process.

▶ REFERENCES

Association of State and Provincial Psychology Boards. (2024). *EPPP candidate handbook: Examination for professional practice in psychology*. https://cdn.ymaws.com/www.asppb.net/resource/resmgr/eppp_/candidate_handbook/eppp_hdbk_may24.pdf

Schaffer, J. B., Rodolfa, E., Owen, J., Lipkins, R., Webb, C., & Horn, J. (2012). The examination for professional practice in psychology: New data-practical implications. *Training and Education in Professional Psychology, 6*(1), 1–7. https://doi.org/10.1037/a0026823

Pass Guarantee

If you use this resource to prepare for your exam and do not pass, you may return it for a refund of your full purchase price, excluding tax, shipping, and handling. To receive a refund, return your product along with a copy of your exam score report and original receipt showing purchase of new product (not used). Product must be returned and received within 180 days of the original purchase date. Refunds will be issued within 8 weeks from acceptance and approval. One offer per person and address. This offer is valid for U.S. residents only. Void where prohibited. To initiate a refund, please contact Customer Service at csexamprep@springerpub.com.

About the EPPP

Anne S. Klee and Bret A. Moore

▶ INTRODUCTION

Congratulations! By purchasing this book, you have taken a crucial step toward successfully passing the EPPP Step One for licensure in psychology. While your graduate program provided a solid foundation, specific knowledge is needed to pass the examinations. We recommend the use of multiple modalities to prepare for the examination, including the review of this book, materials from your courses, and examination blueprint/test plans; a comprehensive certification examination review course; sample examinations; and the review of the examination bibliography.

▶ ABOUT THIS BOOK

This third edition of *EPPP Step One Exam Review* provides a comprehensive review of core examination content and includes over 450 sample questions. It covers the eight content domains of the EPPP and is written by top professors, training directors, and practitioners in the field of psychology with expertise in the content areas of the chapters they authored.

This book is intended to prepare candidates with the knowledge and competency to pass the EPPP Step One. Both the end-of-chapter Q&A and the 225-question practice test can help to identify gaps and weaknesses in knowledge, as well as reinforce areas of strength, before sitting for the examination.

The *EPPP Step One Exam Review* is *not* intended to replace comprehensive and detailed reading, in-depth studying, or mastery of content. Mastery of the practice questions will help you prepare, but will not be the only material you will need to know or review to pass the examinations.

▶ OVERVIEW OF CERTIFICATION EXAMINATIONS

The EPPP (Part 1—Knowledge) is developed and owned by the Association of State and Provincial Psychology Boards (ASPPB). This exam is the foundational knowledge examination that is presently in place in the United States and Canada as a requirement for licensure as a psychologist. It tests a candidate's general knowledge of psychology, including important psychological theories in areas such as cognition, affect, development, general knowledge of intervention and assessment, research, factors impacting psychological functioning, and many other aspects of the foundational knowledge that psychologists are taught in graduate school (ASPPB, 2024).

The purpose in including the examination content is to assess the knowledge base necessary for successfully functioning as a psychologist in professional practice.

The EPPP (Part 2—Skills) assesses a candidate's use of knowledge in their professional decision-making and activities. The content in this book covers review material for EPPP Step One only.

ABOUT THE CONTENT AND QUESTIONS

The EPPP focuses on eight content areas:

- biological bases of behavior;
- cognitive-affective bases of behavior;
- social and cultural bases of behavior;
- growth and life-span development;
- assessment and diagnosis;
- treatment, intervention, prevention, and supervision;
- research methods and statistics; and
- ethical, legal, and professional issues.

It is a comprehensive test that assesses the individual's depth and breadth of knowledge of psychology. It contains 225 multiple-choice questions, of which 175 are scored and 50 are pretest items, which do not count toward the final score. Each item has four possible responses, only one of which is the correct answer (ASPPB, 2024).

▶ THE ASSOCIATION OF STATE AND PROVINCIAL PSYCHOLOGY BOARDS

The ASPPB was founded in 1961 as an alliance of state, provincial, and territorial agencies responsible for the licensure and certification of psychologists throughout the United States and Canada. Its mission is to support member jurisdictions in fulfilling their responsibility of public protection by providing consistent standards that ensure the competent practice of psychology. The EPPP was created to meet this need (ASPBB, n.d.).

The first EPPP was administered in 1965, and it has since grown to be among the most researched, validated, and defensible professional examinations in all professions. The ASPPB is highly regarded within the professional psychological community and has partnerships with many of the major organizations in psychology (ASPPB, n.d.).

EXAMINATION DEVELOPMENT PROCESS

The ASPPB uses a job task analysis to determine the percentage of examination questions for each of the eight content areas. Those percentages, and the specific subareas for each domain, are then used to build the test specifications (ASPPB, 2024). As such, the examination content should closely reflect what is seen in practice.

EXAMINATION ELIGIBILITY

In order to take the EPPP, candidates must first apply for licensure with the licensing authority/board in the state, province, or territory in which they wish to practice. The requirements for eligibility to sit for this examination vary among the licensing boards. One must contact the appropriate licensing board to verify the requirements and/or individual eligibility (ASPPB, 2024).

APPLYING FOR THE EXAMINATION

Once the licensing authority has approved a candidate to sit for the EPPP, they will enter the candidate's identifying information and authorization into the EPPP online registration system, creating an account for the candidate with ASPPB. The candidate will then be sent emails with instructions to begin the process of registration (ASPPB, 2024).

▶ PREPARING FOR THE CERTIFICATION EXAMINATION

Due to the significance of the examination and the amount of material covered, we do not recommend this volume be your only source of preparation. Other methods of preparation can include a review of materials from your courses and examination blueprint/test plans, a comprehensive certification examination review course, and a review of the examination bibliography, among others.

The ASPPB offers candidates optional sample examinations for a fee. There are two versions of the sample examination comprising retired or unused EPPP knowledge items. For that reason, the ASPPB does not recommend using sample examinations to assess areas where additional study might be needed (ASPPB, 2024). The Q&A in this book can help determine strengths and weaknesses in knowledge and provide remediation through detailed answer rationales.

For practical, in-depth information on preparing for the EPPP Step One exam, see Chapter 2 of this book "Preparation Strategies and Tips." Through the information in that and other chapters, you will come away with the knowledge needed to take the exam with confidence.

▶ SUMMARY

We know that licensing examinations can be the most anxiety-provoking milestones in one's professional career. We hope that this text gives you the knowledge and confidence to pass the EPPP Step One with ease.

For more detailed information about the EPPP Step One, visit www.asppb.net.

▶ REFERENCES

Full reference list available at http://examprepconnect.springerpub.com

Preparation Strategies and Tips

Walter Erich Penk and Dolores Little

▶ INTRODUCTION

Perhaps the most challenging rite of passage for becoming a psychologist is preparing for the EPPP. Taking the EPPP is the last requirement to complete before being licensed and certified. It is the last hurdle to leap before crafting and creating one's career. Herein, we discuss the following in test taking: Deliberate Practice Theory (or the 10,000-hour practice test); Getting Grit; Learning the EPPP Rules; Domains of the EPPP; Improving Working Memory and Executive Functioning; Exercising Body and Mind; Learning from Books, Journals, and Apps in the Internet Age; Preparing through Professional Societies; Learning with Peers and Professionals; and Persevering Until You Pass.

Many changes have taken place that are impacting psychology practices since the second edition of Chapter 2 was written 5 years ago. Salient discoveries are discussed in later chapters of this third edition. However, for Chapter 2, we must underscore how artificial intelligence technologies are improving as we learn more on the internet. New approaches in telehealth, plus electronic medical/psychological record-keeping, with training techniques, have become more complicated. Such new designs and developments were already happening as the COVID-19 pandemic appeared, threatening us all, including those we serve. We see so many changes in the practice of psychology now, 5 years later, as we revise Chapter 2 to reconsider tests needed for expertise in the EPPP.

▶ EPPP—THE TEST

DELIBERATE PRACTICE THEORY OR THE 10,000-HOUR PRACTICE TEST

Goals for testing practices by psychologists include mastering skills to understand, predict, describe, influence, and persuade, in order to improve the quality of life in terms of the physical, emotional, social, and mental well-being of others as well as ourselves. Deliberate practice theory applies to those candidates using the EPPP to become psychologists in the tradition of the 10,000-hour practice rule mastered during 3 years of graduate study combined with 2 years of pre- and postdoctoral practical training for students.

In addition, the EPPP is similar to correlations between practice and performance as trainees receive individualized training from licensed psychologists who teach trainees using deliberate practice theory (cf. Ericsson & Harwell, 2019). The EPPP chapters were written to specify goals so trainees can internally master their practices. Also, trainees are provided practice activities as well as test questions with immediate feedback. Taking the EPPP means feedback trainees receive can revise understandings to improve performance, in keeping with outcomes that Ericsson and Harwell (2019) report in their review of significant effects on practice by performances from training and the EPPP. What is clear is that the EPPP requires both natural endowment and hard work over many years in order to meet and fulfill the requisites to become a psychologist.

What is further clear is that while success in performance on the EPPP may result primarily from the three variables of general abilities, task-specific skills, and work ethics, as one prepares to take the EPPP, it is assuredly time to continue actualizing as much of the *10,000-hour practice rule* as one possibly can. Preparing for the EPPP is not the time to worry about general or task-specific abilities. However, it is time to remain motivated, to stay consistent in studying psychology, and to continue persisting in applying the *10,000-hour* experiences (Robertson et al., 2010).

GETTING GRIT

It is also the time for grit—to access within one's self and to promote one's grit. Grit is defined as personal characteristics of passion and perseverance for achieving one's potential as a person. This also applies to becoming a psychologist. Angela Duckworth published a book in 2016, after the second edition of *EPPP Fundamentals* appeared, operationally defining grit for individuals in general, and using scales to measure grit. Subsequent experiments have been reported assessing grit among psychologists (e.g., Logan et al., 2023). Psychology is both a profession and a science, developed on case studies followed by randomized clinical trials, and the results from these must be applied in everyday living.

Taking the EPPP is a time to practice one's passions and perseverance: one's grit. It is a time when one stands alone, outside the care and comfort of one's colleagues, beyond facilities where one was trained to practice. The EPPP is the needed place for grit, where one alone competes to demonstrate one has mastered the qualifications to be called a psychologist. It is the last step in becoming a psychologist, where one brings together, within one's self, a focus on talent and experience, as well as all of the resources within one's mind and body, to demonstrate that one has, as an individual and as a person, the knowledge and the experience to practice as a psychologist. Therefore, early in the process of preparation, one should learn one's scores on the Grit Scale (Duckworth, 2016). One must learn one's grit scores about personal consistency in interests and personal passion for performance, as applied to psychology, as one strives to increase one's grit to improve one's test-taking strategy for the EPPP.

Also, if inspiration from others is required, one only needs to read about Katalin Karikó. Migrating from Hungary to the United States, she worked in medical laboratories, struggling in her research on biochemical structures of messenger RNA (mRNA). Her experiments kept failing. She was demoted and threatened with deportation, but she kept conducting her research, which, finally, led to discovering solutions for mRNA, which are critical to the rapid development of vaccines against viruses, now saving millions of lives, and leading her to receive the Nobel Prize on October 3, 2023. She inspires us with her grit, by demonstrating her passion and perseverance for her research (www.pennmedicine.org/providers/profile/katalin-kariko).

LEARNING RULES ABOUT THE EPPP TEST TAKING

Restrictions prevail about the extent to which any psychologist can write about and describe the test that comprises the EPPP. Among the first steps taken when getting ready to take the EPPP, each candidate must promise, as part of ethical and legal duties, never to divulge the content of the EPPP test items. Hence, any descriptions provided beforehand must remain in keeping with guidelines and primary source documents that the Association of State and Provincial Psychology Boards (ASPPB) provide. See www.asppb.net for *EPPP Candidate Handbook Part 1 and Part 2*.

The EPPP evaluates knowledge that the most recent practice analysis has determined to be foundational to the component practice of psychology (ASPPB, n.d.-b).

One of the best ways to prepare for the EPPP is to take practice exams. ASPPB offers the Sample Examination for Professional Practice in Psychology Online (SEPPPO; ASPPB, 2024). Through ASPPB, candidates can register and pay to take computer-delivered online examinations of retired questions. There are two versions of the SEPPPO with 100 questions each. Since the questions were constructed for the EPPP and follow test specifications and format, they are most similar to the questions candidates will encounter when they take the actual EPPP (ASPPB, 2024). One may be asked to pay a modest fee; nonetheless, such experiences are informative about the candidate's capacity. Further, it enhances one's experience of taking computerized standardized tests. In addition, such experiences yield important clues about the tasks and goals ahead. While the SEPPO is only 100 questions, unlike the full 225-item EPPP, it gives the candidate a glimpse in how to plan ahead for the 4-hour exam time limit.

In addition, candidates may access "test-taking strategies videos" on Google and relearn previous skills for answering multiple-choice items, like eliminating wrong answers, solving easy items first, coping with tricky words, coping with "all" or "none" answers, and setting a comfortable pace. It is worthwhile for the candidate to review the mechanics of test taking by accessing tutorials on www.google.com and www.youtube.com. Although now may be the Age of Apps, the Age of YouTube, and the Age of the Internet, we all need to recall and practice the test-taking skills we mastered so long ago in our childhood to help us cope with tests as adults.

LEARNING DOMAINS OF THE EPPP

Candidates must not only become acquainted with directions for taking the EPPP, but, further, they must study in advance about domains comprising the EPPP, as described in the chapters of this book. In other words, the EPPP has 225 multiple-choice items. The candidate has up to 4 hours to answer them from an online site, with an extra 15 minutes at the beginning for practice purposes. The EPPP test items are subcategorized into eight areas: (a) biological bases of behavior; (b) cognitive-affective bases of behavior; (c) social and cultural bases of behavior; (d) growth and life-span development; (e) assessment and diagnosis; (f) treatment, intervention, prevention, and supervision; (g) research methods and statistics; and (h) ethical, legal, and professional issues.

Elements comprising each of these eight categories must be studied when preparing for the EPPP, in order to learn and demonstrate expertise in the most recent developments that have been documented as foundational to the science of psychology (see domains in this third edition of *EPPP Step One Exam Review*). These domains are central to the profession of psychology. Each constitutes knowledge, skills, and ethics that candidates must demonstrate as having mastered in order to advance to the level of becoming licensed and certified as a psychologist.

Likewise, in learning about the domains and their elements that are being assessed, the candidate needs to understand how the EPPP items were developed and validated (see ASPPB, n.d.-a; Cynkar, 2007; and Missman, 2023). These highlight the expertise that candidates must achieve to seek licensing as a psychologist in our times. This is an age when many subdoctoral, less-well-trained individuals are seeking legislative support to take over services delivered by psychologists in federal and state healthcare agencies. Candidates mastering the EPPP domains are highly qualified in specific requirements to become psychologists and have learned more prerequisites than subdoctoral candidates who are less skilled in these domains.

IMPROVING THE WORKING MEMORY AND EXECUTIVE FUNCTIONING

Getting grit means you are also reviewing your mastery of learning techniques, such as working memory and executive functioning. Adopting effective test-taking strategies can improve your skills for learning. Cramming for the EPPP, indeed, may yield some positive results for short periods of time; however, what you learn fast, you forget quickly. Psychology is a marathon, not a walk around the block.

Research by psychologists such as Henry L. Roediger, III, PhD, demonstrates that we remember more of what we learn when we distribute our learning over time. We learn by frequently self-testing ourselves about the content that we are learning (see books coauthored by Roediger such as *Make It Stick: The Science of Successful Learning* [Brown et al., 2014]; *Varieties of Memory and Consciousness* [Roediger & Craik, 2014]; *Study Smart* [Soderstrom et al., 2016]; and *Critical*

Thinking in Psychology [Sternberg & Halpern, 2020]). Roediger teaches us to go beyond rereading, summarizing, outlining, and highlighting. Rather, we must also repeatedly test ourselves on the materials we are learning and the results and outcomes from which we practice. Working memory and executive functioning provide better results when we build into our learning tests about the materials we are accessing and findings from the services we have provided.

We learn by repeatedly testing ourselves. This principle, validated now by Roediger and others, is as old as psychology itself. In his 1890 book *Principles of Psychology*, William James taught us, "It pays better to wait and recollect by an effort from within, than to look at the book again" (James, 1890, p. 686). We improve our performance when we increase testing ourselves on the new materials we have just learned. Our mastery of self-testing to improve working memory is just as important for each one of us to do as it is for us to facilitate the performance of others whom we may be training by teaching them to test themselves. Learning is *testing*, as the EPPP reminds us.

EXERCISING THE BODY AND THE MIND

Getting grit as a test-taking strategy means that you exercise both the body and mind. Taking the EPPP is likely to improve when you have mastered relaxation and meditation and are exercising and practicing positive nutrition. Grit means that you master mediation for conflict resolution and cognitive problem-solving skills. Such mastery of mind and body is essential for the practice of psychology in general and, accordingly, for the EPPP. This is because psychology is a field that confronts and copes with stress. Psychology is a discipline where clinicians vicariously experience stress and trauma when providing services for clients who have been stressed and traumatized. Exercise and meditation not only facilitate organization in coping with personal feelings, emotions, stress, and thoughts, but also likewise improve relationships with others. As a consequence, in preparing for the EPPP, the candidate may improve performance by balancing reading and talking with exercising and meditation. Bender and Messner's (2022) book is a recent example of a text that improves professional development in psychotherapies.

Preparing for the EPPP is a matter of organizing one's life around the age-old principle of balancing time to create a sound body in a sound mind—exercise and meditation are needed when preparing for the EPPP. We all must learn how to balance rest and use the brain's default mode for our education. It helps if one goes to the EPPP well-rested and relaxed, as the clinician and researcher, Bessel van der Kolk, teaches us in the 2015 book *The Body Keeps the Score: Brain, Mind, and Body in the Healing of Trauma*. Dr. van der Kolk's classic book—on the *New York Times'* 10 best-selling paperbacks for 289 consecutive weeks in the United States as of this writing—teaches us how to cope with stress and trauma within ourselves and within others. Also, new training in our age of gun violence in the United States and fear of war as Russia fights Ukraine can be found in tutorials on www.google.com, Mastering the Treatment of Trauma (see resources in National Institute for the Clinical Application of Behavioral Medicine at www.nicabm.com /program/treating-trauma-master).

LEARNING FROM BOOKS, JOURNALS, AND APPS IN THE INTERNET AGE

Getting grit for the EPPP means mastering the most recent knowledge about psychology as a profession. Planning beforehand for the EPPP, recalling the emphasis upon "recent" knowledge foundational to psychology, suggests that journals such as the *Annual Review of Psychology* are essential for reading and improving working memory and retention by constantly testing one's self about such content. Also, the ongoing books, experiments, and tutorials, such as those by Dr. van der Kolk in *The Body Keeps the Score* (2015), may facilitate many successful performances on the EPPP.

Regularly reading journals in one's profession is essential for not just preparing for the EPPP but also creating one's career as a psychologist. For the candidate seeking state licensure to practice as a clinical psychologist, journals from the American Psychological Association (APA) and the Association for Psychological Science (APS) are vital (e.g., *Journal of Abnormal Psychology*,

Journal of Consulting and Clinical Psychology, Professional Psychology, American Psychologist, Observer, Perspectives on Psychological Science, Psychological Science, and *Clinical Psychological Science*), as are other journals in one's area of specialized focus (e.g., *Behavior Therapy*).

APA's *Psychological Review* brings those taking the EPPP up to date on recent knowledge about discoveries in psychology. Such learning may be intensified through wellness and mental health apps and thus is useful for candidates, psychologists, and clients (UCSF Department of Psychiatry and Behavioral Sciences, n.d.).

PREPARING THROUGH PROFESSIONAL SOCIETIES

Becoming a psychologist also means that candidates for the EPPP prepare for learning by participating in professional societies. The APA and the APS are rich in providing resources to develop new psychologists. Likewise, state psychological associations, along with societies for specialized practice (e.g., International Society of Traumatic Stress Studies and Association of Behavior and Cognitive Therapies), contain major contributors to the development of the discipline. Professional societies offer student rates for candidates, lowering dues and providing support to prepare for licensing and certification. Newsletters from professional societies, divisions, state associations, and specialty societies are valuable resources for learning fundamentals for domains evaluated in the EPPP (e.g., APA's Practice Directorate).

LEARNING WITH PEERS AND SUPERVISORS

Grit means you form social groups, not just with supervisors but also with peers, from whom to learn not just facts, but categories of principles to practice. Training is important from licensed supervisors, but likewise, there are peer interactions that occur, akin to training in business and industry.

When preparing for the EPPP, one is encouraged to form groups of doctoral candidates to study together; to develop tests to improve working memory; and to practice transferring principles of psychology from one kind of task to another, from one setting to another, from one person to another, and, in 2024, from one's computer at home to computers in homes of clients, in our Age of Telepsychology (see APA [2024]. See also the writings of Marlene M. Maheu, PhD, executive director of the Telebehavioral Health Institute at telehealth.org/maheu-publications, including Telepsychology Best Practices 101 at www.apa.org/career-development/telepsychology.).

Peers are necessary to corroborate the transfer of training, as well as feedback from supervisors and from clients whom the candidate is serving. Staff conferences in facilities training candidates are vital in transferring knowledge from texts to persons.

Getting ready for the EPPP is a blueprint for what one will experience in their professional career, collaborating with peers, supervisors, patients, and with clients. Psychology is preparing. Peers and patients are vital forces in preparation.

Continuing education is a way of living that psychologists undertake once they pass the EPPP. Psychology is a science and a profession that requires perpetual preparation. These are changing times, when the older forms of preparing and continuing education by learning with peers and learning from professional supervisors are being expanded by learning through advances in technology through resources on the internet. It is not just a matter that technology is expanding the resources by which we learn to take the EPPP; rather, in addition, growth in technology means that the candidate must expand their mastery of the domains of psychology from diverse areas, such as computerized medical records, human performance models, neurosciences, skills acquisition, augmented cognition, emotional regulation, change management, and computer sciences, to using mobile devices for increasing access to intelligent agents, apps, games, virtual reality, and synthetic learning environments. The computer, our newest peer, is also our most demanding and challenging peer in the age of telehealth, telepsychology, and apps.

Examples of interactions with peers and supervisors that are nationally available can be found in continuing education webinars. For example, the U.S. Department of Defense provides monthly webinars at no expense for APA members. The University of Texas Health Sciences Center internet and symposia training in San Antonio, led by Katherine Dondanville, PhD, and Alan Peterson, PhD, through STRONG STAR (strongstartraining.org), is another great resource. For professional ethics and forensics, the University of New Mexico Department of Psychiatry and Behavioral Sciences offers free continuing education training at https://continuinged.unm.edu/search/publicCourseAdvancedSearch.do?method=doPaginatedFilter&type=subject&objectId=1008960. Such examples, of which there are many more, provide educational updates on ethics and practices to cope with stress and trauma. This is essential not only in times of COVID-19 but also among U.S military and veterans as their treatment and rehabilitation expand from military hospitals and VA medical centers to community care, which is increasingly being provided by private practitioners.

PERSEVERE UNTIL YOU PASS BASED ON YOUR PASSIONS

Getting grit as an EPPP test-taking strategy means, at the outset, that you plan to keep taking the EPPP until you pass. That means, from the beginning, you plan for the worst possible outcome—not passing. You prepare by learning at the outset what you will do if you do not pass. From the beginning, you create your own personal support services from peers and supervisors. You obtain all of the feedback you are able to. You constantly test the new skills you are learning with peers, supervisors, and clients. You learn the ASPPB rules about the EPPP before you pay your first dollar to participate in Pearson VUE's EPPP. Your main EPPP test-taking strategy is that you will persevere until you pass.

Although not everyone passes, preparation is learning, so nothing is lost by failing. Failing is essential for learning (Gino & Pisano, 2011).

Grit is not only for the prelicensed psychologists-to-be but also for psychologists who are licensed to practice. Preparing for the EPPP is the prototype of the career to come for the professional who wishes to advance in one's discipline, who dedicates their life and living to providing outstanding performance, and who is planning to achieve unusual contributions to the science and to the profession of psychology. Passing the EPPP is the *rite de passage* that one must hurdle to become, to be, and to remain a psychologist.

ABOUT MY COAUTHOR, DOLORES LITTLE, PHD

Dolores Little, PhD, and I first coauthored this chapter in 2013. We continued to write together until Dolores died on September 23, 2022. Dolores graduated with her PhD in psychology from Texas A&M University in 1973. We met at the Dallas VA Medical Center in 1974, when Dolores became the associate chief of staff for academic affairs; in this role she supervised physician interns and residents, as well as nurses and psychologists in training. She then trained at the Audie Murphy Memorial Veterans Medical Center in San Antonio, Texas, to become a VA associate medical center director. Dolores later was promoted to become the first woman to serve as a VA associate medical center director for VA medical centers in Big Spring, Texas; Bedford, Massachusetts; Providence, Rhode Island; and Loma Linda, California. Dolores was also one of the first women to train in psychology at the Lexington, Kentucky VA Medical Center, among the first women to complete a PhD at Texas A&M University, and the first woman to be a VA associate chief of staff for academic affairs. Dolores worked in the VA adding more women to staff and increasing more women veterans for treatment. Dolores is, and remains, in my heart and mind, body and soul, my coauthor, colleague, and collaborator.

▶ REFERENCES

Full reference list available at http://examprepconnect.springerpub.com

Biological Bases of Behavior

David Shearer and Tyler R. Reese

> **BROAD CONTENT AREAS**
> - Biological and neural bases of behavior
> - Psychopharmacology
> - Methodologies supporting this body of knowledge

▶ INTRODUCTION

The biological nature of human behavior is a highly complex, integrated set of physiologic processes existing in the confines of the nervous system. Knowledge of these processes is expanding daily to include new interrelationships and systems that shape the ability to understand normal behavior and abnormal disease processes. This chapter provides core concepts of neuroanatomy, physiology, pathophysiology, and psychopharmacology to aid in providing effective clinical care.

▶ CENTRAL NERVOUS SYSTEM

The brain and spinal cord make up the central nervous system (CNS), the biological core of the human experience. Understanding this system in terms of its functions and dysfunctions requires an understanding of the major structures and their role in the integration of our internal and external experiences.

SPINAL CORD

The human spinal cord is a collection of nerve fibers exiting the brain through the foramen magnum at the base of the skull and proceeding through the vertebral foramen that stack together to form a protected canal. Then, the nerve fibers emerge in segmented distributions that communicate with the organs and muscles of specific body regions. These segmented distributions (30 total) are divided into four general regions from the neck to the sacrum named: cervical (C1–C8), thoracic (T1–T12), lumbar (L1–L5), and sacral (S1–S5).

At each segment of the spinal cord between vertebrae, nerve fibers on the dorsal portion of the spinal cord carry sensory information from the body to the brain. Correspondingly, descending fibers exiting the ventral portion of the spinal cord carry motor information to the muscles (Bican et al., 2013). Since the fibers run in parallel and segment off to areas as they reach them, an injury to the spinal cord often causes a loss of sensation and movement at and below the site of the damage. For example, damage to the upper cervical regions of the spinal cord results in the inability to move the arms and legs (quadriplegia), whereas damage to lower cervical regions results in the inability to move the legs (paraplegia). Incomplete damage to the spinal cord may result in muscle weakness (paresis) as opposed to total immobility (paralysis). In addition to mediating voluntary movement, the spinal cord is also involved in involuntary movements such as reflexes (e.g., the withdrawal reflex from pain; Eli et al., 2021).

BRAIN

Skull and Cranial Meninges

The CNS, and the brain, are guarded by several layers of protection. The most obvious are the skin and then the skull, which is the bone structure forming the cranial vault. Just inside and, in various places, closely attached to the skull is the dura mater. This tough fibrous membrane also spans off the skull to form dividers such as the tentorium cerebelli (the space between the cerebellum and cerebrum) and the falx cerebri, which extends down from the skin in the midline into the longitudinal fissure separating the two hemispheres of the brain. These fibrous dividers provide a location for blood return from the brain called sinuses (Adeeb et al., 2012). Then, closer to the nerve tissues themselves, the arachnoid mater is a thinner and more delicate membrane separated from the dura mater by the subdural space, through which passes a series of veins known to rupture in trauma and cause subdural hemorrhages. Finally, the pia mater, which is the most delicate and highly vascular membrane, closely follows the contours of the brain. The pia mater is separated from the dura mater by the subarachnoid space, which contains a network of arteries, veins, and connective tissue known as trabeculae that can leak with vascular disease of aging or trauma to cause subarachnoid hemorrhages (Kiliç & Akakin, 2008).

Ventricles

Providing both protection and structural support, the internally located ventricular system comprises open chambers and channels filled with cerebral spinal fluid (CSF). This colorless fluid is formed predominantly in the linings of the two large lateral ventricles known as the choroid plexus. Then, the fluid circulates through the lateral ventricles, located internally in each cerebral hemisphere, to the centrally located third ventricle, through the cerebral aqueduct, and into the fourth ventricle in the dorsal brainstem. From there, the fluid flows into the subarachnoid space around the brain and spinal cord where it is passively reabsorbed after its circulation. The CSF maintains the brain's neutral buoyancy and protection from pressure and forces on the cranial vault (Sakka et al., 2011). It also plays still minimally understood roles in protection from infection, regulation of cerebral blood flow, and management of metabolites that diffuse from the brain cells (Pellegrini et al., 2020).

Cerebrum

Gross examination of the human brain reveals fissures (the inward folds) and gyri (the smoothly curved hills), both serving to increase the surface area of the cortex. The cortex forms the outer and most visible layer of the brain, also known as the gray matter, and is microscopically comprised of six layers of cell bodies and interconnections. Although functionally significant for surface area to vascular flow and CSF exposure, the fissures and gyri also form the definitions and boundaries of the major structures of the telencephalon, or cerebrum, which includes the four major lobes (frontal, temporal, parietal, and occipital). Each lobe is represented bilaterally in the right and left hemispheres (Rhoton, 2007).

Frontal Lobe

Located anterior of the largest coronal sulcus, known as the central sulcus, the frontal lobe is the largest of the four lobes, governs output, and is considered the seat of higher cortical and cognitive functioning. Major anatomical subdivisions include the primary motor cortex, premotor cortex, orbitofrontal cortex, and prefrontal cortex. These regions are particularly devoted to attention, cognition, reasoning, problem-solving, and voluntary movement (Rhoton, 2007).

Directly anterior to the central sulcus is the primary motor cortex, which occupies part of the gyrus, running laterally from superior to inferior. This area is crucial in the initiation of motor movements, and all the isolated muscle groups are specifically represented along this gyrus. Moreover, the relative representation in this region corresponds directly to the requisite accuracy of motor control. For example, hands, fingers, lips, and tongue are heavily represented, whereas other regions, such as the trunk and torso, are less so. Damage to this region will produce deficits in motor learning, and more severe forms of lateralized damage will produce hemiparesis (Thompson & Thompson, 2023).

Directly anterior to the primary motor cortex is the premotor cortex, a region dedicated to the initiation and execution of more complex limb movement patterns in conjunction with input from other cortical regions. Mirror neurons located here have been associated with imitation and even empathy and have been the focus of some autism studies (Acharya & Shukla, 2012; Schulte-Ruther et al., 2007; Williams et al., 2001).

The prefrontal and orbitofrontal regions, located anterior to the primary motor cortex, are most often associated with the higher-level cognitive functions also known as the executive functions, which include reasoning, planning, and judgment. Dysfunction in this region has been associated with many disorders, including attention deficit hyperactivity disorder (ADHD) and schizophrenia. Inhibitory control is also most often associated with this region. The frontal lobe injury sustained in the mid-1800s by Phineas Gage, a railroad construction worker, is often considered an illustrative example of classic frontal lobe impairment (Damasio et al., 1994).

As an example of frontal lobe complexity, the inferior lateral region of the left frontal lobe is known as the Broca area. This area has been suggested to be dedicated to the fluent production of oral and written speech, as well as grammar and comprehension of syntax. The dysfunction associated with a lesion here is most often recognized as Broca (or expressive) aphasia (an acquired disorder of language; Fridriksson et al., 2015). However, it must be realized that recent neuroscience efforts have described the challenges in proving simplistic views of areas (Fedorenko & Blank, 2020).

Temporal Lobes

Located inferior to the lateral sulcus, the temporal lobes are divided into the superior, middle, and inferior temporal gyri. The superior temporal gyrus is the site of primary auditory processing, where conscious perception of sound takes place. This region, typically found in the infolded region of superior temporal gyrus, is also known as the Heschl convolutions. Reception of stimuli in this region is considered "tonotopic," which corresponds to individual frequencies detected at the level of the cochlea located in the inner ear. Stimuli arrive here by way of the vestibulocochlear nerves and the medial geniculate nuclei of the thalamus and undergo only partial "decussation," by which the incoming stimuli are transmitted to the contralateral hemisphere for processing. Because of partial decussation, or crossing of fibers, sound stimuli critical for auditory language comprehension will still arrive at the language-dominant hemisphere (Tervaniemi, 2001). Immediately adjacent and posterior to the primary auditory cortex is the auditory association cortex, where sound is further processed. In the language-dominant hemisphere, this region is known as the Wernicke area, which is dedicated to the comprehension of language. Lesions in this region will disrupt not only the ability to comprehend language but also the meaningful expression of language, a deficit known as Wernicke (or receptive) aphasia (Fridriksson et al., 2015).

Parietal Lobes

The parietal lobes are located posterior to the central sulcus and include the site of primary somatosensory processing on the postcentral gyrus. Major neuroanatomical structures also include the inferior and superior parietal lobules. Within the parietal lobes are large regions of the heteromodal cortex, where different sensory modalities are integrated to construct a complete picture. The parietal lobes process visual information along dorsal and ventral pathways from the occipital lobes to help coordinate movements and behaviors with the environment.

Damage to posterior regions of the parietal lobe can result in neglect syndromes such as hemispatial neglect, which is characterized by an inability to attend to features of the environment in the space contralateral to the lesion site (Corbetta & Shulman, 2011).

As noted, primary somatosensory processing occurs on the postcentral gyrus, where "somatotopic" detection of touch, pressure, pain, and temperature takes place. As on the primary motor cortex, regions of the sensory cortex proportionally represent body regions depending on their relative sensitivity; for example, there is a heavy representation of the fingertips, face, and lips. Lateralized lesions here will result in hemisensory loss (loss of sensation on one side of the body; Paff et al., 2021).

Occipital Lobes

Located posterior to the temporal and parietal lobes, the occipital lobes are geographically defined by the parieto-occipital sulcus visible on the medial surface of the hemisphere. Primarily dedicated to visual processing, primary visual processing is located in the region of the occipital pole, posterior to the calcarine sulcus. Primary visual processing is photopic in nature, receiving stimuli from the retina and optic nerve by way of the lateral geniculate nucleus of the thalamus.

Properties such as color and movement are processed at the primary visual, or striate, cortex. They are then sent for further processing and integration along the dorsal stream to parietal regions for processing of object location and along the ventral stream to temporal regions for object identification. These areas adjacent to primary processing, also known as peristriatal regions, are considered visual association areas, which further process and integrate visual stimuli. Lesions in primary visual processing regions result in cortical blindness (Teuber et al., 1960). Other lesions can result in disturbances in color perception and an inability to detect orientation or movement (Gattass et al., 1990; Schmidt et al., 2014). Deficits in the naming and recognition of objects presented visually may be specifically associated with lesions of the temporal lobes, a region of tertiary visual processing (Riddoch & Humphreys, 2003).

SUBCORTICAL BRAIN REGIONS

Hippocampus

The inferior temporal lobe curls in toward the midline and forms a region known as the hippocampus. As part of the limbic system, the hippocampus is critical for memory formation, such as the transfer of memories to longer-term stores. Classically reported cases of hippocampal damage through surgery or encephalitis illustrate the debilitating memory impairments associated with bilateral hippocampal lesions (Neves et al., 2008).

Amygdala

Anterior to the hippocampus, the amygdala is involved with processing emotions. Its interconnections to the midbrain structures make the amygdala an essential component of managing emotional stimuli and the "fight or flight" response (Meisner et al., 2022). The amygdala links emotions to our senses, including odors. It is part of the primary olfactory cortex and is involved in processing olfactory stimuli (Porada et al., 2019).

Thalamus

Located superior to and contiguous with the brainstem is the thalamus. This structure performs the critical relay functions between the cortex and the brainstem. Specific nuclei, or collections of nerve cells, form the specific transmission sites in the thalamus to and from specific cortical regions. Because of these very rich interconnections, the thalamus also performs important attention and perceptual functions.

Basal Ganglia

The basal ganglia is an important subcortical structure comprising a network of complex loops involved in motor output (i.e., descending motor pathways), emotions, cognition, and eye movements. The main components of the basal ganglia include the caudate nucleus, putamen, globus pallidus, subthalamic nucleus, and substantia nigra. The cerebral cortex provides most of the input to the basal ganglia, and the primary outputs of the basal ganglia are sent to the thalamus. Motor abnormalities due to basal ganglia do not involve paresis or paralysis, but rather the coordination and rhythm of movement. These syndromes are referred to as "extrapyramidal syndromes." For example, slow movements (i.e., bradykinesia) or excessive muscle rigidity result from basal ganglia dysfunction. Movement disorders such as Parkinson disease (PD) and Huntington disease result from abnormal activity in the basal ganglia (Buckner et al., 2008).

Brainstem

Comprising the medulla (also referred to as the medulla oblongata), pons, and midbrain, the brainstem forms the core of the brain. The midbrain and its component structures are surrounded by the cerebral hemispheres. Located caudally, or toward the tail, is the pons (or bridge), followed by the medulla, which is essentially contiguous with the spinal cord. Functionally, the brainstem, as a unit, is involved in the control and regulation of autonomic functions and maintaining the body's homeostasis, including breathing, heart rate, temperature regulation, and blood pressure. The reticular formation, including the reticular activating system, plays important roles in alertness, consciousness, and pain. It also plays an important role in regulating the respiratory and cardiovascular systems. Ascending sensory pathways from the spinal cord rise through dorsal regions, whereas descending motor fibers pass through anterior regions of the brainstem (Buckner et al., 2008).

Cerebellum

Attached to the posterior brainstem is the cerebellum. Rich in neurons, the cerebellum is structurally divided into the superior, middle, and inferior cerebellar peduncles. The middle cerebellar peduncle is the only structure visible on surface examination of the brain. The cerebellum comprises a gray matter cortex and subcortical white matter with rich interconnections to cortical regions of the other hemispheres of the brain. Functionally, the cerebellum is most often associated with the regulation of movement, including automatic and rhythmic movements, coordination of the limbs, and postural control. Studies have also associated the cerebellum with cognitive functions such as learning and attention (Helmuth et al., 1997).

The complex coordination processed through cerebellar networks is evident in the autoimmune destruction in multiple sclerosis, which can result in disruption of ocular movements such as nystagmus (a rapid rhythmic eye movement that is particularly enhanced when the gaze is in the same direction of the lesion site). Lesions of the cerebellum can also produce motor incoordination and a characteristic wide-based stance and gait (Roostaei et al., 2014).

NEURONS

Lastly, to make up these individual areas and functions, neuron cells vary in size and shape and are highly specialized to specific functions. A typical neuron consists of a cell body (containing the nucleus), dendrites (short processes emerging from the cell body that receive impulses from other neurons), and axons (longer processes that carry impulses further distances). Axons can range in length from 1 mm to 1 m. Maintaining rapid and protected signals in long axons, a myelin-based sheath surrounds the axon and speeds up transmission. At the end of the dendrites or axons, the synapse is the connection space between two neurons in which chemical and/or electrical communication occurs (Booker & Vida, 2018).

Chemicals known as neurotransmitters are released between cells and exist "presynaptically" by the axon terminal of one neuron and bind to neurotransmitter receptors on the "postsynaptic" neuron, which may then cause postsynaptic excitation or inhibition to the impacted neuron. When postsynaptic excitation reaches a minimum threshold, that neuron then fires an action potential, causing that neuron cell membrane to send the neural signal along its axon. The firing of a neuron is an "all-or-nothing" phenomenon, that is, the strength of neuronal firing does not vary in response to the strength of the input. In other words, a neuron either fires or does not. After a neuron fires, there is a refractory period during which it is unable to fire again until it reestablishes an electrochemically based resting potential state (Susuki & Kuba, 2016). Different neurotransmitters have different effects on cells (excitatory or inhibitory), and the amount of a neurotransmitter that is available for binding to the postsynaptic neuron can be affected by various medications as described in the text that follows.

NEUROTRANSMITTERS

Neurotransmitters are chemicals that transmit signals from one neuron to another and are classified according to their molecular size. Biogenic amines (e.g., acetylcholine [ACh] and serotonin), catecholamines (e.g., dopamine [DA], norepinephrine [NE], and epinephrine), and amino acids (e.g., gamma-aminobutyric acid [GABA] and glutamate) are smaller molecular messengers, whereas neuropeptides (e.g., vasopressin, oxytocin, and substance P) are larger molecules. Neurotransmitters fit into a receptor site like a lock and key, although a variety of neurotransmitters may fit into a single type of receptor (Zillmer & Spiers, 2001). The most significant neurotransmitters in psychopharmacology include NE, serotonin, DA, GABA, ACh, and glutamate (Wegman, 2012).

NE or "noradrenalin" is a catecholamine and functions as a hormone and a neurotransmitter. It is formed in the brainstem at a site called the "locus coeruleus" and is found in the sympathetic nervous system and CNS. It regulates mood, memory, alertness, hormones, and the ability to feel pleasure. Elevated levels may lead to anxiety, whereas low levels may cause depression (Wegman, 2012). NE also underlies the "fight or flight" response and is released into the blood as a hormone by the adrenal gland in response to stress or arousal. It is primarily considered an excitatory neurotransmitter but may result in inhibition in some areas.

DA is also a catecholamine and can be both excitatory and inhibitory. The majority of DA neurons are in the substantia nigra. DA pathways extend to the frontal lobes, basal ganglia, and hypothalamus. Overactivity of DA in the pathway to the frontal lobes has been implicated in schizophrenia, and the loss of DA-producing neurons in the basal ganglia pathway is the underlying cause of PD. Underactivity of DA has also been implicated in ADHD (Wegman, 2012). DA plays a role in emotions, movement, and endocrine functioning, as well as attention, sociability, motivation, desire, pleasure, and reward-driven learning.

Serotonin (5-HT) is a biogenic amine and is primarily inhibitory. It is widely distributed throughout the brain and originates in the raphe nuclei in the brainstem. Pathways extend to the limbic system, and serotonin levels are associated with the regulation of mood, anger, aggression, anxiety, appetite, learning, sleep, sexual functioning, level of consciousness, and pain. Low levels of serotonin are associated with depression, obsessive-compulsive disorder (OCD), and anxiety disorders (Wegman, 2012).

ACh is also a biogenic amine and plays a major role in the parasympathetic nervous system and autonomic nervous system (Zillmer & Spiers, 2001). It is the primary neurotransmitter at the neuromuscular junction (the synapse between neuron and muscle cells) and is involved in movement. Degeneration of ACh in the striatum of the brain is associated with the movement disorder called Huntington disease. ACh also plays a major role in activating the brain through the reticular activating system and regulates alertness and attention. Another cholinergic system involving the hippocampus influences attention, learning, and memory (Zillmer & Spiers, 2001).

GABA is an amino acid and is the major inhibitory neurotransmitter of the CNS. It is widely distributed throughout the CNS but is most concentrated in the striatum, hypothalamus, spinal cord, and temporal lobes. GABA is associated with emotion, balance, and sleep patterns. Low levels of GABA are associated with high anxiety and agitation, and higher levels are associated with a reduction in anxiety (Wegman, 2012). GABA deficiencies are also implicated in epilepsy, and many antiepileptic drugs increase GABA activity.

Glutamate is also an amino acid and is the brain's primary excitatory neurotransmitter. It is widely distributed throughout the CNS. It is a basic building block of proteins and plays an important role in learning and memory (Wegman, 2012). Excessive glutamate causes excitotoxicity (cell death due to excessive stimulation and excitation) and is implicated in cell death following traumatic brain injury and stroke.

▶ PSYCHOPHARMACOLOGY

Psychologists may or may not have prescription privileges, depending on whether they have specialized training, whether prescriptive authority for psychologists is permitted in the state in which they practice, and if they work for some specific departments or agencies of the federal government (Curtis et al., 2023). Additionally, depending on the state in which a psychologist practices, psychologists may legally make recommendations to prescribers regarding psychotropic medication if it is within the scope of their competence. Further, given the ubiquitous nature of the use of psychotropic medication, many psychologists are likely to encounter patients who are concurrently taking medication while participating in a psychological therapeutic intervention. Therefore, it is important for even nonprescribing psychologists to possess a general understanding of psychotropic agents, as well as their risks, potential benefits, and common side effects. Often the psychologist will act as the intermediary between the patient and a prescribing clinician. It is necessary to be able to recognize when an evaluation for psychotropic medication (or for termination of medication) may be beneficial to the patient. Each patient is unique and will have different requirements based on age, sensitivities to medications, personal preferences, and other characteristics. It is helpful to know that medications are often referred to by two names, a brand name and a generic name. The generic name is not capitalized (e.g., fluoxetine) and the brand name is capitalized (e.g., Prozac). In practice, the brand and generic name for a drug can and may be used interchangeably.

PHARMACOKINETICS AND PHARMACODYNAMICS

Psychotropic medications cross the blood–brain barrier and cause physiological and biochemical changes. The mechanism of action (MOA) for these medications is complex. To put it simply, these medications alter the activity of neurotransmitter communication between neurons by doing one or more of the following: disrupting the action of the neurotransmitter at the synapse (thus blocking the action of the neurotransmitter), inhibiting the enzymes that break down neurotransmitters in the synaptic cleft (thus boosting the overall transmission of that neurotransmitter), changing the sensitivity of postsynaptic neurons to neurotransmitters, or increasing the amount of neurotransmitter produced and available at the synapse (Stahl, 2021a).

Psychoactive drugs are able to cause downstream biochemical and physiological changes by binding to receptor sites on neurons and either boosting the action of a particular neurotransmitter system or blocking the action of a neurotransmitter system (Stahl, 2021a). An agonist is a chemical that binds to a receptor site and mimics the activity of a neurotransmitter, thus causing the same downstream effects as that neurotransmitter and boosting the overall system. A partial agonist also binds to a receptor site and mimics the activity of a neurotransmitter but cannot produce 100% of the effect of a full agonist, even at very high doses. An inverse agonist binds to the same receptor site as an agonist but has the opposite effect of full agonists by causing a reduction in the overall efficacy of a neurotransmitter system. An antagonist also blocks or reverses the effect of agonists or inverse agonists, but when an agonist is not present, it has no effect of its own (Stahl, 2021a).

Pharmacodynamics describes the biochemical and physiological effects of drugs on the body. This is often referred to as the MOA of the drug, or, put more simply, how the drug works. Pharmacokinetics describes how the body handles the drug through absorption, distribution, metabolism, and elimination. Sometimes pharmacokinetics is referred to as "what the body does to the drug" in terms of entering the body, moving through, and then out of the body (Benet & Zia-Amirhosseini, 1995). Absorption is the process through which drugs reach the bloodstream. For drugs that are administered orally (by mouth), this absorption occurs mainly in the small intestine and results in the drug's onset and degree of action. A poorly absorbed drug may not reach the minimal effective concentration required in the blood for clinical efficacy. The absorption of a drug can depend on patient-specific factors as well as characteristics of the drug itself (Grogan & Preuss, 2023). The bloodstream serves as the means of distribution of a drug to the site of action. The speed of distribution varies depending on how the drug is administered. For example, drugs taken orally must first travel through the digestive system, whereas drugs injected intravenously have a faster response because they directly enter the bloodstream. When a drug enters the bloodstream, metabolism begins. The body recognizes the drug as a foreign substance and attempts to eliminate it via chemical transformation. Metabolism occurs primarily in the liver and kidney. People metabolize psychotropic agents differently, and the sensitivities and preferences of each individual patient must be considered to get optimum risk–benefit ratios. For example, children and older adults may metabolize drugs differently than young adults, and therefore dosage or scheduling adjustments may be required to achieve the best risk–benefit ratios (Alomar, 2014). Once a drug is in circulation, elimination is predominantly a function of the kidneys and liver. The elimination half-life of the drug is the time it takes for the peak drug concentration to decrease by half during metabolic change and excretion. In the steady state, the rate of elimination is equal to the rate of administration of the drug, which results in a "steady" or consistent concentration of the drug in the blood (Whalen et al., 2014). When a drug is administered at regular intervals or by infusion it can reach a steady state in about 4 to 5 half-lives (Hallare & Gerriets, 2023).

A therapeutic window is defined by the range of a drug dose that can result in desired clinical efficacy without resulting in unsafe side effects. For example, if a drug has a narrow therapeutic window, then there is only a small range of dosages that can result in the desired benefit before it becomes unsafe. A therapeutic index (TI) is the ratio of the amount of the drug that causes the desired benefit to the amount of the drug that produces dangerous side effects. It is more desirable for a drug to have a high TI, as it is a measure of drug safety (McCallum et al., 2014).

Psychoactive drugs can be classified according to the clinical disorders that they treat (e.g., anxiolytics [anti-anxiety], antidepressants, antipsychotics, mood stabilizers, stimulants, and pain medications). Psychoactive drug classes have unique MOAs, differing even among those that treat similar clinical disorders, and all have the risk of side effects and possible drug interactions that must be considered. Psychoactive drugs may be prescribed "on-label" or "off-label." "On-label" prescription of a drug indicates that it is being used for a U.S. Food and Drug Administration (FDA)-approved indication. For example, fluoxetine (Prozac) is FDA-approved for the treatment of major depressive disorder. An example of "off-label" use of fluoxetine would be for the treatment of posttraumatic stress disorder (PTSD). While there is research evidence that fluoxetine can be helpful in the treatment of PTSD, it is not specifically approved for that purpose by the FDA (Kolek et al., 2023). The following section summarizes the primary psychoactive drug classifications, their MOA, and potential side effects.

Anxiolytics

Anxiolytics refer to psychotropic medications that may be used to treat anxiety disorders and can be classified into benzodiazepines and nonbenzodiazepines. Examples of anxiolytics that are benzodiazepines are alprazolam (Xanax), clonazepam (Klonopin), diazepam (Valium), and lorazepam (Ativan).

Anxiety disorders that may be treated with benzodiazepines include generalized anxiety disorder, panic disorder, phobic disorders, adjustment disorder with anxiety, anxiety disorder due to a general medical condition, and substance-induced anxiety disorder. Additionally, some benzodiazepines are used as sleep agents, whereas others may treat seizure disorders, alcohol withdrawal, and other psychiatric disorders (Stahl, 2021b).

Benzodiazepines act through the CNS and cause muscle relaxation as well as sedative, anxiolytic, and anticonvulsant effects. They enhance the action of GABA (which is the primary inhibitory neurotransmitter) and block the rapid release of stress hormones associated with anxiety and panic. These medications are rapidly and completely absorbed after oral administration and distributed throughout the body. Benzodiazepines can be short-, medium-, or long-acting (Stahl, 2021b).

The most significant side effects of benzodiazepines include drowsiness, confusion, feelings of detachment, dizziness, imbalance, and a high potential for tolerance and dependence. When discontinued, benzodiazepines must be tapered slowly to prevent withdrawal symptoms. With regard to drug interactions, benzodiazepines increase the effects of alcohol and other CNS depressants; in particular, the concurrent use of opioid analgesics and benzodiazepines should generally be avoided (Lo-Ciganic et al., 2022). They should be used cautiously in patients with liver disease and avoided in patients with a history of substance abuse (Stahl, 2021b).

Medications other than benzodiazepines are used to treat anxiety; however, they do not provide the immediate relief that benzodiazepines provide (with the potential exception of the antihistamine hydroxyzine). Buspirone is an example of a nonbenzodiazepine anxiolytic. Compared to benzodiazepines, buspirone does not induce tolerance, causes less fatigue, and lacks hypnotic, anticonvulsant, and muscle-relaxant properties (Ingersoll & Rak, 2016).

Gabapentin (Neurontin), an anticonvulsant frequently prescribed for neuropathic pain, is also often prescribed off-label for anxiety. It is generally well-tolerated and abuse/dependence is generally not a concern (Heldt, 2017), although some abuse of gabapentin has been reported (Karavolis et al., 2022). Pregabalin (Lyrica) is another anticonvulsant prescribed for anxiety (Stahl, 2021b).

Hydroxyzine (Vistaril) is an antihistamine that reduces anxiety more than other medications in its class. It is very sedating, so it may not be well-tolerated for daytime use in some patients. Abuse and dependence are not concerns with this medication (Heldt, 2017). Some relief from acute anxiety can occur as quickly as 20 minutes after taking hydroxyzine; however, for optimal benefits, it may require daily dosing for several weeks (Stahl, 2021b). Since the 1990s, benzodiazepines have been increasingly replaced by selective serotonin reuptake inhibitors (SSRIs) and other antidepressants as clinicians' first choice for the treatment of anxiety disorders due to their increased safety, lower side-effect profile, and decreased likelihood of dependence (Asho & Sheehan, 2004). SSRIs include paroxetine (Paxil), sertraline (Zoloft), escitalopram (Lexapro), citalopram (Celexa), fluoxetine (Prozac), and fluvoxamine (Luvox). Other antidepressants used on-label and off-label for anxiety include tricyclic antidepressants (TCAs; e.g., amitriptyline), serotonin–norepinephrine reuptake inhibitors (SNRIs; e.g., venlafaxine and duloxetine), and other antidepressants such as mirtazapine and vortioxetine (Stahl, 2021b).

Barbiturates are medications that were formerly used for sedation and to induce sleep but have now been essentially replaced by benzodiazepines. However, barbiturates such as phenobarbital continue to be used by some providers as a detox medication when treating alcoholism (Weaver, 2017). The side effects of barbiturates are extreme, including tolerance, physical dependency, and very severe withdrawal symptoms. They also enhance the function of GABA in the CNS (Stringer, 2011).

Antidepressants

Antidepressants are a diverse group of medications. Each class has different MOAs. The primary classifications of antidepressants include monoamine oxidase inhibitors (MAOIs), TCAs, SSRIs, NE–DA reuptake inhibitors (NDRIs), SNRIs, and others that may be considered "atypical" antidepressants that do not fit in other classifications. In general, antidepressants are not considered addictive substances (Turki et al., 2023). These medications are used to treat disorders such as unipolar major depression, dysthymic disorder, adjustment disorders, premenstrual dysphoric disorder, and mood disorders due to general medical condition. These medications are also used in the treatment of many anxiety disorders, ADHD, PTSD, and eating disorders (Stahl, 2021b). The use of antidepressants is relatively contraindicated in patients with bipolar disorder, as these medications may induce mania (unless the patient is currently being treated with a mood stabilizer; Stahl, 2021b; Stein et al., 2012). They are also used in the treatment of OCD (Ingersoll & Rak, 2016).

Many antidepressants target a class of neurotransmitters called monoamines, which include NE, serotonin (5HT), and DA. The "monoamine hypothesis" of depression dates back to the 1960s and postulates that depression is caused by abnormal functioning of these neurotransmitters (Mulinari, 2012). Based on this hypothesis, antidepressant medications are thought to increase the availability of these neurotransmitters at the synaptic level. However, a simple deficiency of monoamines at the synaptic level is no longer thought to explain the MOAs of these medications in full (Patterson et al., 2010). Further, antidepressants likely affect many biological systems in addition to neurotransmitter uptake (Mycek et al., 1997).

Tricyclic Antidepressants

These drugs, as indicated in their name, are categorized on the basis of their chemical three-ring structure (Stahl, 2021a). Examples of TCAs include amitriptyline, nortriptyline (Pamelor), imipramine, doxepin (Silenor), and desipramine (Norpramin). Absorption of the tricyclic drugs occurs in the small intestine, and peak blood levels occur within 2 to 8 hours following ingestion (Golan et al., 2008). Tricyclics block the reuptake of serotonin and NE (thus increasing the activity of these neurotransmitter systems by making them more available for binding to postsynaptic neurons); however, the precise MOA of the TCAs is unknown (Stringer, 2011).

TCAs are effective medications and are comparable in efficacy to SSRIs (Anderson, 2000). The TCAs predominantly target the neurotransmitters NE and serotonin. However, these medications have troublesome side effects and patients are more likely to discontinue their use than SSRIs (von Wolff et al., 2013). Side effects of TCAs fall into three categories: cardiac/autonomic, anticholinergic, and neurobehavioral. Orthostatic hypotension (a drop in standing blood pressure) is a common side effect of this medication (Pies, 2005; Stahl, 2021b).

Monoamine Oxidase Inhibitors

While effective as an antidepressant treatment, MAOIs are rarely used today because of potentially serious drug–drug and drug–food interactions. They block the reuptake of monoamine neurotransmitters (serotonin, NE, and DA) by blocking their respective monoamine transporters, thus increasing the levels of these neurotransmitters in the synaptic cleft (Keltner & Folks, 2005). Examples of MAOIs include phenelzine (Nardil) and tranylcypromine (Parnate). The most dangerous side effect of MAOIs is hypertensive crisis, which can occur when an MAOI is taken with food or drugs containing tyramine (Stahl, 2021b).

Selective Serotonin Reuptake Inhibitors

These medications, which block the reuptake of serotonin by selective binding, are especially effective for the treatment of depression with agitation and/or comorbid anxiety. The term *selective* is used because they have a weaker affinity for blocking the action of other monoamines. Examples of SSRIs include fluoxetine (Prozac), paroxetine (Paxil), fluvoxamine (Luvox), sertraline (Zoloft), citalopram (Celexa), and escitalopram (Lexapro; Stahl, 2021a). SSRIs are less likely to cause anticholinergic and cardiac/autonomic side effects than the TCAs; however, possible side effects can include gastrointestinal side effects, headache, sexual dysfunction, insomnia, psychomotor agitation, and occasional extrapyramidal reactions (Wegman, 2012). Serotonin syndrome, a dangerous side effect, can occur when two serotonergic drugs are taken at the same time or when excessively high amounts of a single serotonergic agent are ingested. Symptoms include a change in mental status, shivering, confusion, restlessness, flushing, diaphoresis (sweating), diarrhea, lethargy, myoclonus (muscle twitching and jerks), and tremors. In its extreme form, serotonin syndrome can be fatal (Heldt, 2017).

Atypical antidepressants do not fall into the earlier categories. Some examples are as follows.

NE–DA Reuptake Inhibitors (NDRIs): These antidepressants work by blocking the reuptake of NE and DA. An example of an NDRI is bupropion (Wellbutrin). Bupropion is FDA-approved for smoking cessation. Some common side effects include dry mouth, constipation, nausea, weight loss, insomnia, dizziness, and headaches (Stahl, 2021b).

SNRIs: These medications block the reuptake of serotonin and NE. Examples of SNRIs include venlafaxine (Effexor), desvenlafaxine (Pristiq), levomilnacipran (Fetzima), milnacipran (Savella), and duloxetine (Cymbalta). Some SNRIs are also FDA-approved to treat fibromyalgia. Some common side effects include headache, nervousness, insomnia, sedation, nausea, sexual dysfunction, and sweating (Stahl, 2021b).

Mirtazapine (Remeron): A serotonin-NE antagonist, this atypical antidepressant medication increases both serotonin and NE release by blocking the appropriate autoreceptors. Some common side effects include dry mouth, constipation, weight gain, increased appetite, sedation, dizziness, and abnormal dreams (Stahl, 2021b).

Vortioxetine (Trintellix): The MOA of this atypical antidepressant is complex. It increases the release of neurotransmitters including serotonin, NE, DA, glutamate, ACh, and histamine while reducing the release of GABA. It differs from SSRIs in its multimodal effect of serotonin transport and reuptake. It also theoretically improves cognitive symptoms, which distinguishes it from other antidepressants (Bass & Iliades, 2014). Some common side effects include nausea, vomiting, constipation, and sexual dysfunction (Stahl, 2021b).

Trazodone: This atypical antidepressant is often used to treat insomnia, rather than as an antidepressant (Adams et al., 2017). Trazodone influences neurotransmitters that include serotonin, noradrenaline, DA, ACh, and histamine. Some common side effects include nausea, vomiting, blurred vision, constipation, sedation, dizziness, headache, tremor, and dry mouth (Stahl, 2021b).

Brexanolone (Zulresso): This unique atypical antidepressant is FDA-approved for the treatment of postpartum depression and is considered a neuroactive steroid that predominantly influences the inhibitory neurotransmitter GABA. It is administered as a continuous intravenous infusion over 60 hours. Some common side effects may include sedation, dizziness, dry mouth, flushing, and hot flashes (Stahl, 2021b).

Esketamine (Spravato): This atypical antidepressant is used in conjunction with other antidepressants for treatment-resistant depression. It predominantly works by influencing the neurotransmitter glutamate and its various receptors. It is unusual for antidepressants in that it is administered as a nasal spray. Some common side effects include dissociation, dizziness, sedation, anxiety, lethargy, feeling drunk, numbness, nausea, vomiting, and increased frequency of urination (Stahl, 2021b).

Vilazodone (Viibryd): Vilazodone exerts its antidepressant effect by influencing serotonin receptors in a way that differs from the SSRIs discussed earlier in the text. Some common side effects may include nausea, diarrhea, vomiting, insomnia, dizziness, bruising, and sexual side effects (Stahl, 2021b).

Over-the-counter products: St. John's wort, S-adenosyl methionine, 5-HTP, omega-3 fatty acids, and folic acid have all been shown to have some efficacy in treating depression. Omega-3 fatty acids and folic acid are typically used in conjunction with antidepressants (Preston & Johnson, 2014). However, it is important to note that these alternative remedies can also have negative side effects and adverse drug interactions. For example, St. John's wort can reduce the effectiveness of oral contraceptives, and omega-3 fatty acids can increase the risk of bruising and bleeding, especially when combined with blood thinners (Wegman, 2012). Herbal medicine and dietary supplements are widely used. There is some research that shows efficacy for some of these products, but issues such as potential inaccurate labeling, unsubstantiated claims of benefit, and variable quality controls require consideration (Saper, 2023).

Antipsychotics

Antipsychotics are primarily used to treat schizophrenia, schizophreniform disorder, schizoaffective disorder, brief psychotic disorder, bipolar disorder, and agitation (Pies, 2005). Several neurochemical abnormalities are associated with schizophrenia, but the DA system is the most studied (Patterson et al., 2010). All conventional (or first-generation) antipsychotic medications block DA receptors, whereas atypicals (second- or third-generation antipsychotics) also block serotonin receptors and can influence a variety of additional transmitters (Stahl, 2021a).

Conventional Antipsychotics ("Typical" or "First Generation")

First developed in the 1950s, all of the drugs in this group seem to have equal efficacy but differ in potency and side effects. Examples of conventional antipsychotics include haloperidol (Haldol), thioridazine, molindone, thiothixene, fluphenazine, trifluoperazine, chlorpromazine, loxapine, and pimozide (Preston & Johnson, 2014).

Conventional antipsychotics may cause side effects called extrapyramidal symptoms (EPSs), including parkinsonism, acute dystonia, akathisia, and tardive dyskinesia (TD). Parkinsonism includes bradykinesia (slowed movements), tremor, and rigidity. Acute dystonia involves muscle spasms in the tongue, face, neck, and back. Akathisia is characterized by restless movements and symptoms of anxiety and agitation. Parkinsonism, acute dystonia, and akathisia are often early signs of drug reactions. TD is characterized by abnormal involuntary, stereotyped movements of the face, tongue, trunk, and extremities. Typically, TD is the result of longer-term use of antipsychotics. Unfortunately, this syndrome may be irreversible, even when antipsychotic medications are discontinued (Lehne, 2013). A 2017 FDA-approved medication, valbenazine (Ingrezza), may improve the TD symptoms.

Another potential side effect is neuroleptic malignant syndrome, a rare but life-threatening reaction characterized by catatonia, stupor, fever, and autonomic instability. Additional side effects of the antipsychotics may include orthostatic hypotension, sexual dysfunction, and sedation, as well as anticholinergic effects such as dry mouth, constipation, and difficulty with urination (Lehne, 2013).

Atypical Antipsychotics (Second- and Third-Generation)

Atypical antipsychotics became available in the 1990s. In addition to blocking DA receptors in the CNS, atypical antipsychotics also influence serotonin receptors. Depending on the atypical antipsychotic, they may influence other neurotransmitters such as NE, glutamate, and ACh (Mauri et al., 2014; Patterson et al., 2010). Initially, the atypical antipsychotic medications were thought to be more effective than the typical or first-generation antipsychotics; however, the Clinical Antipsychotic Trials of Intervention Effectiveness, a nationwide clinical trial funded by the National Institutes of Health, revealed that the typical or first-generation antipsychotics may indeed be just as effective as some of the newer atypical antipsychotic medications (Lieberman et al., 2005). The newer atypical antipsychotics produce fewer EPSs than the typical antipsychotics; however, they may cause dangerous metabolic effects such as weight gain, diabetes, hypertension, and dyslipidemia (Lehne, 2013).

There are many atypical antipsychotics available on the market. Some examples include olanzapine (Zyprexa), quetiapine (Seroquel), ziprasidone (Geodon), aripiprazole (Abilify), paliperidone (Invega), iloperidone (Fanapt), asenapine (Saphris), clozapine (Clozaril), risperidone (Risperdal), and cariprazine (Vraylar). All atypical antipsychotics fall into the same classification, but some have slightly different MOAs and influence a variety of neurotransmitters other than DA and serotonin. Ability is unique, as it does not block DA completely, but rather is a partial agonist at the DA receptor. Clozapine is one of the more effective atypical antipsychotics, although it has some significant risks. Fatal agranulocytosis (dangerously low white blood cell count causing decreased ability to fight infection) is a potential side effect of clozapine. Therefore, testing of white blood counts is done on a regular basis. Risperidone is a first-line medication for new-onset schizophrenia and is also well-accepted for the treatment of agitation and aggression in dementia and bipolar disorders. An unfortunate possible side effect of risperidone is hyperprolactinemia leading to gynecomastia (enlargement of breast tissue in males; Heldt, 2017). Risperidone is also FDA-approved for minimizing self-harm in autism and disruptive behavior disorders in children and adolescents (FDA, 2015; Stahl, 2021b; Stringer, 2011).

There is a high level of noncompliance in taking medication as prescribed for persons with psychotic disorders because in some cases the illness precludes insight. Therefore, other methods of dosing antipsychotics were developed. Several are available as rapidly dissolving tablets or long-acting injectables. Some of those available as long-acting antipsychotics include fluphenazine, olanzapine, paliperidone, risperidone, aripiprazole, and haloperidol (Heldt, 2017).

Mood Stabilizers

Lithium was the first mood-stabilizing medication approved by the FDA for the treatment of acute mania and hypomania. It has well-documented efficacy in preventing relapse in bipolar disorder. Lithium's MOA is complex and theoretical. It is suspected to involve NE and serotonin (Wegman, 2012). Lithium has a slower onset of action and a narrow TI (i.e., the therapeutic dose is close to toxic).

Common side effects of lithium include nausea, diarrhea, vomiting, thirst, excessive urination, weight gain, and hand tremor. A reversible increase in white blood cell count frequently occurs with lithium use. Side effects related to chronic use can include hypothyroidism, goiter, and, rarely, kidney damage. Toxicity may result in lethargy, ataxia, slurred speech, shock, delirium, coma, or even death (Wegman, 2012). Drug interactions with diuretics and nonsteroidal anti-inflammatory agents can increase serum lithium levels (Stahl, 2021b).

Antipsychotics and anticonvulsant medications may also be used as mood stabilizers and are considered first-line treatments for bipolar disorder (Wegman, 2012). For example, antipsychotics such as cariprazine, lurasidone (Latuda), quetiapine, aripiprazole, asenapine, olanzapine, risperidone, and ziprasidone are FDA-approved for various phases of bipolar disorder (Stahl, 2021b). Examples of anticonvulsants used as mood stabilizers include divalproex (Depakote), lamotrigine (Lamictal), carbamazepine (Tegretol), and topiramate (Topamax). Anticonvulsants may work by enhancing the actions of GABA, influencing voltage-sensitive ion channels and/or glutamate. All anticonvulsants can cause side effects. One example of a serious side effect of an anticonvulsant medication (lamotrigine) is Stevens–Johnson syndrome, a potentially fatal skin rash (Edinoff et al., 2021).

Opioids (Narcotic Analgesics)

Opium is a residue extracted from the opium poppy and has been used for thousands of years for pain relief and sedation. The term *opioid* refers to natural or synthetic compounds that stimulate opioid receptors. Naturally occurring opioids are called opiates and include opium, morphine, and codeine. Semisynthetic derivatives of opiates include morphine, heroin, Percodan (oxycodone hydrochloride and aspirin), and Dilaudid (hydromorphone hydrochloride). The brain produces its own version of opiates called endogenous opioids; as a result, there are naturally occurring binding sites in the brain called opioid receptors (Shenoy & Lui, 2023). ("Endogenous" refers to substances produced by the human body.)

Opioids are used to relieve intense pain and the anxiety that can accompany that pain. They also induce sleep. Some opiates are prescribed for severe diarrhea or coughs (Stringer, 2011). Opioids are sometimes combined with nonopioid analgesics, such as aspirin and acetaminophen (Percodan and Percocet, respectively). The nonopioid analgesics work well in combination with opioids because these different classes of drugs affect pain pathways via different MOAs (Stringer, 2011).

Long-term opioid use changes the way nerve cells work in the brain, which can lead to withdrawal symptoms when they are suddenly discontinued. These withdrawal symptoms may include diarrhea, vomiting, chills, fever, tearing and runny nose, tremor, abdominal cramps, and pain (Stringer, 2011). Regarding drug interaction, the depressant actions of morphine are enhanced by MAOIs and TCAs (Mycek et al., 1997).

Opioids may be abused for their euphoric effects. Opioid abuse and addiction is referred to as an opioid use disorder (OUD; American Psychiatric Association [APA], 2022). One effective treatment for OUD is called medication-assisted treatment in which a less-addictive opioid replaces the opioid of abuse such as methadone or buprenorphine (Weaver, 2017). Additionally, an opioid antagonist such as naltrexone (Vivitrol) can also be used to treat OUD (Ghanem et al., 2022).

Psychostimulants

Psychostimulants increase prefrontal cortex levels of NE and DA (Stahl, 2021b) and are primarily used to treat ADHD. Some examples of psychostimulants include amphetamine (Evekeo), methylphenidate (Concerta), armodafinil (Nuvigil), and modafinil (Provigil). Methylphenidate- and amphetamine-based medications are most often used for the treatment of ADHD. Armodafinil and modafinil are sometimes also described as wake-promoting agents and are more often used for sleep disorders such as narcolepsy or shift work sleep disorder. Some antidepressants, such as bupropion, are used in the treatment of ADHD because they also enhance the actions of NE and DA in the prefrontal cortex (Preston & Johnson, 2014; Wegman, 2012).

Side effects of the psychostimulants may include insomnia, headache, tic exacerbation, nervousness, irritability, overstimulation, tremor and dizziness, weight loss, abdominal pain or nausea, possibly slow normal growth in children, and blurred vision (Stahl, 2021b). There are numerous potential drug interactions. For example, they should not be used with MAOIs as they may cause a hypertensive crisis (Stahl, 2021b). The risk of misuse, abuse, addiction, or sharing of stimulant medication has prompted the FDA to issue a warning to providers to assess these risks when considering prescribing stimulant medication (FDA, 2023).

Some nonstimulant medications are also used to treat ADHD; however, they may be less effective than stimulants (Krull & Chan, 2023). For example, atomoxetine (Strattera) is a NE reuptake inhibitor with a minor effect on serotonin and almost no effect on DA. Viloxazine (Qelbree) modulates serotonergic activity and moderately inhibits NE. There is very little potential for abuse of these drugs as opposed to stimulant medication. Guanfacine (Intuniv) and clonidine (Catapres) reduce the hyperactivity and impulsivity associated with ADHD rather than increase focus. These medications can be sedating rather than stimulating (Heldt, 2017).

▶ COMBINED TREATMENTS: PSYCHOPHARMACOLOGY AND BEYOND

It is important to note that the psychoactive medications described earlier often complement other nonmedication approaches to treatment for many psychiatric and neurological illnesses. For example, in the treatment of mild depression, cognitive behavioral therapy (CBT), antidepressants, and their combination have been shown to result in equal benefits (Otto et al., 2005). For the treatment of moderate to severe depression, antidepressants used in combination with CBT have been shown to be more effective than either CBT or medication alone (Cuijpers et al., 2009, 2020; Keller et al., 2000). Bright light therapy, some dietary supplements, and exercise may also be beneficial when treating some patients with depression and may be combined with medication. Other approaches that might be combined with antidepressant medication are ketamine, electroconvulsive therapy, transcranial magnetic stimulation, vagal nerve stimulation, and deep brain stimulation (DBS; Bahji et al., 2022; Balchin et al., 2016; Cleare et al., 2015; Gitlin, 2023; Wegman, 2012).

There are some psychiatric conditions for which medication is the first line of therapy, such as bipolar disorder and psychotic disorders. However, even in these cases, adding psychotherapy, psychoeducation, or other psychosocial interventions often improves outcomes. In many cases, combining medication and some form of psychotherapy is an effective strategy. However, there are disorders for which medication is clearly the second line of therapy when compared to psychotherapeutic approaches; for example, adjustment disorders, specific phobias, borderline personality disorder, primary insomnia, anorexia nervosa, and conduct disorder (Muse, 2018; Perlis, 2011). Ultimately, patient preference, tolerance of a particular recommended treatment, and/or availability of the treatment of choice may determine the type of therapeutic approach taken. Pharmacogenomics and pharmacogenetics use the analysis of a patient's genetic makeup to determine how they may respond to certain drugs. Psychiatric pharmacogenomics and pharmacogenetics have already begun to influence how medications are prescribed and are likely to increasingly play a part in how prescribers select medication for their individual patients. There are limitations to the testing, as it is not available for all medications and can be costly (Tantisira & Weiss, 2023).

▶ NEUROIMAGING

The types of brain imaging techniques that can be used to visualize neuroanatomy and assess for neurological disorders are usually divided into "structural" and "functional" imaging techniques.

STRUCTURAL IMAGING

Computed Tomography

Computed tomography, or CT, uses x-ray radiation imaging collected in 360° around the patient and reconstructed with sophisticated computer algorithms into imaging "slices" of the brain (referred to as tomography). The appearance of brain tissues on a CT scan depends on the tissue density. For example, hyperdense tissues, such as bone, appear white, but hypodense tissues, such as the simple fluid CSF, appear black. The middle ground of isodense brain tissues will have shades of gray, whereas cells have a different density than areas rich in axons. Contrary to direct visualization of brain tissue, CT-visualized white matter is slightly darker than gray matter due to its high myelin content. In some instances, material containing iodine is injected into the patient prior to obtaining the CT scan for better visualization of certain tissues. This intravenous contrast material is denser than brain tissue and will therefore appear hyperdense (white) in large blood vessels, areas of increased vascularity, or blood leakage from hemorrhage. CT images are often obtained with and without contrast for comparison. An *enhancing lesion* refers to areas that are absorbing this contrast material and may be indicative of brain neoplasms, abscess, infarct (area of dead tissue resulting from obstructed blood flow), demyelinating disease, resolving hematoma, or vascular malformation (Copen et al., 2016).

Clinically, CT is often used in the ED to detect acute hemorrhage or skull fracture following trauma. Fresh intracranial hemorrhage coagulates almost immediately and shows up as hyperdense (white) areas. Areas of brain cell death from blood flow changes, called acute cerebral infarcts, often cannot be seen with CT without later signs of swelling or fluid changes that change density. CT scans are also useful in the detection of neoplasms (tumors), mass effect through changes to the ventricles, or ventricular enlargement, called hydrocephalus (Diaconis & Rao, 1980).

Magnetic Resonance Imaging

Magnetic resonance imaging, or MRI, was developed in conjunction with sophisticated computer software in the 1980s and uses powerful magnetic fields to make hydrogen atoms align themselves to the magnetic field, which sends out a radiofrequency signal that is captured and analyzed. This makes MRIs ideal to reduce radiation exposure and they provide intensity, or brightness, relative to the tissue composition of hydrogen. Hydrogen is highly present in water and the fat in myelin so that "hyperintense" (brighter) areas may highlight myelinated axons and "hypointense" (less bright) areas could define areas with more cell bodies or other tissues.

Clinically, MRI provides high-resolution imaging with good anatomical detail due to the high contrast between tissues, which is not possible with CT. MRI is the preferred method for detecting small lesions such as plaques found in patients with multiple sclerosis, diffuse neurodegenerative processes, subtle tumors, or chronic hemorrhage. MRI imaging can be even further improved for vascular features using gadolinium intravenous contrast. However, MRI has much higher costs and takes more time to complete and analyze (Lerch et al., 2017).

When comparing which method of cross-sectional imaging to use, CT is preferred in the urgent assessment of head trauma with suspected intracranial hemorrhage, and it is better at visualizing bony structures (e.g., skull fracture). CT is also preferred for patients who have metallic implanted devices, such as a pacemaker, since MRI utilizes high-powered magnets. MRI is preferred in nonurgent situations in which a higher-resolution imaging method is required for better anatomical detail (Blumenfeld, 2010).

Neuroangiography

Neuroangiography is used to visualize the distribution and pathology of blood vessels through the use of intravenous contrast and some imaging techniques, which could include a series of simple x-ray images. It is the gold standard for evaluating vascular diseases in the head, neck, and spine, such as atherosclerotic plaques and other vessel narrowings, aneurysms, and arteriovenous malformation. Angiography can be achieved with CT and MRI utilizing the contrasting mentioned previously. Often, in the setting of a stroke, when an intervention is needed, angiography is often part of an invasive procedure that requires anesthesia (Case et al., 2020). As a specific example of neuroangiography, a Wada test uses amobarbital injected selectively into different cerebral blood flow distributions to localize speech functional areas in presurgical planning in patients with epilepsy who are undergoing brain resection. By localizing specific vessels, the intervention can essentially selectively anesthetize a contralateral hemisphere so that various cognitive functions (e.g., memory and language) can be assessed in that hemisphere (Baxendale, 2009). More technical procedures like this have been partly replaced by functional neuroimaging, which externally identifies brain functional areas.

FUNCTIONAL NEUROIMAGING

Electroencephalography

The electroencephalography (EEG) measures brain activity using a small metal disk placed on the scalp that records the electrical activity of the neurons in the underlying brain area. A collection of these small electrical impulses are amplified and displayed on paper using a chart recorder called an electroencephalograph. EEG is useful in detecting widespread abnormality in brain function in a variety of contexts (e.g., sleep, anesthesia, coma, traumatic brain injury, and epilepsy), but its sensitivity and spatial resolution for detecting brain lesions are poor (Beniczky & Schomer, 2020).

Positron Emission Tomography

Positron emission tomography (PET) uses small amounts of injected radioactive molecules to measure regional cerebral blood flow or specific neurotransmitter distribution patterns. In the most common example, a glucose-like radioactive tracer is taken up in more active brain areas and shows more radioactive signals than in less active areas. However, the brain is always active, so the brain's normal background activity is usually measured first to establish a baseline, which is then "subtracted" from the activity measured during the test (Quigg & Kundu, 2022). PET scans are also useful, most often in research settings, for mapping the distribution of neurotransmitters and identifying brain dysfunction due to stroke, epilepsy, tumor, dementia, and other brain-impairing conditions (Xiang et al., 2023).

Functional MRI

Functional MRI (fMRI) was developed directly from MRI and can detect functionally induced changes from blood oxygenation. The basic idea is that oxygen distribution varies with brain activity and the amount of oxygen in the blood changes the magnetic properties of the blood without having to inject any radioactive materials, such as with PET or CT. Like MRI, fMRI has excellent resolution and provides a detailed structural map while also providing functional information. fMRI can be used to measure the brain's real-time response to motor activities or neuropsychological tests (Sorger & Goebel, 2020).

▶ DISORDERS

APHASIA

Aphasia refers to an acquired disorder of language (as opposed to a developmental language disorder) and can affect expressive speech, receptive speech, reading, and/or writing. Aphasia syndromes can be subdivided into three major classifications: fluent aphasia (in which speech is fluent but there are difficulties with comprehension and/or repetition of words or phrases spoken by others), nonfluent aphasia (in which expressive speech is notable for poor articulation or poor grammar, but comprehension is relatively preserved), and pure aphasia (in which select aspects of language are affected, such as reading [alexia] or writing [agraphia]). Lastly, global aphasia has all aspects of language impairment, including expressive speech, comprehension, repetition, reading, and writing.

An example of fluent aphasia, Wernicke aphasia (also known as sensory aphasia or receptive aphasia), has a primary deficit of inability to understand language. Speech is usually fluent (with normal rate and articulation), but the content of the speech is often nonsensical and meaningless, often containing neologisms (nonwords) or incorrect combinations of words ("word salad"). People with Wernicke aphasia often have poor insight into their deficit and may expect others to understand what they are saying. The ability to repeat what others say is also impaired. The lesion typically associated with Wernicke aphasia is in the left temporal lobe. Another fluent aphasia is transcortical sensory, in which comprehension is poor, but the individual can repeat what others say (unlike Wernicke aphasia). The lesion is usually in the border zones between the parietal and temporal lobes. A last example of fluent aphasia is conduction aphasia in which people can speak normally, but the sole deficit is in the repetition of what others say. Conduction aphasia is considered a "disconnection syndrome" from damage to the arcuate fasciculus (a large white matter tract) connecting the receptive and expressive centers of the Broca area and the Wernicke area.

Of nonfluent aphasia, Broca aphasia (also known as motor or expressive aphasia) is seen when a person speaks in a slow, halting manner, with poor grammar and limited prosody. Only keywords are used, and the use of verbs or connecting words is limited. Damage is usually in the left frontal lobe around Brodmann areas 44 and 45, also known as the "Broca area." Writing is usually slow and effortful. Repetition is also impaired. Auditory comprehension and reading comprehension are relatively preserved. Similarly, transcortical motor aphasia (sometimes referred to as "little Broca aphasia") is seen when a person has the speech issues of Broca aphasia but is able to repeat what others say in a normal fashion. Damage usually occurs in the left frontal areas surrounding the Broca area, leaving the Broca area and its connections to the Wernicke area intact.

Anomic aphasia consists of a focal deficit in naming objects, although the person can adequately produce meaningful speech, comprehend speech, and repeat speech. The angular gyrus is thought to be affected in this type of aphasia; however, some degree of anomia, or problems with word finding, is present in most types of aphasias and is not consistently localized to a particular brain region. In global aphasia, all aspects of language are impaired, including expressive speech, comprehension, repetition, reading, and writing (Kertesz, 1993).

APRAXIA

Apraxia is an acquired disorder of skilled, purposeful movement that is not due to a primary motor or sensory impairment such as paresis or paralysis. For example, a person may not be able to demonstrate how to brush their hair or wave goodbye on command. There are many types of apraxia. In some cases, the action may be carried out accurately but in a clumsy manner, and in other forms of apraxia, the person may commit errors such as performing sequenced actions in the wrong order (such as sealing an envelope before placing the letter inside). The lesion site may vary depending on the type of apraxia but is usually in the left hemisphere.

DEMENTIA

Dementia is a syndrome of decline in cognitive functioning that impairs activities of daily living that is not a feature of normal aging. It has recently been replaced by the term *neurocognitive disorder* in the *Diagnostic and Statistical Manual of Mental Disorders* (5th ed.; *DSM-5*; APA, 2013), but the term *dementia* is applied colloquially to multiple progressive, static, or sometimes reversible disease processes (National Institute of Neurological Disorders and Stroke [NINDS] & National Institute on Aging [NIA], 2021). Notably, dementia is entirely distinct from delirium, which is a cognitive decline that is very acute and potentially reversible. Delirium occurs over hours to days versus months to years for dementia and is marked predominantly by inattention and clarity of focus. Delirium may co-occur with dementia, causing apparent large changes to baseline function and should be assessed and treated by removing underlying physical and cognitive stressors like pain, acute pathologic processes, lack of sleep, and intoxication (Inouye et al., 2014).

Often associated with dementia is mild cognitive impairment (MCI), which captures a functional decline between normal aging and multifunctional declines in dementia. People with MCI do not generally exhibit significant changes in their everyday, functional abilities (Peterson, 1995). Since the conception of MCI, four clinical subtypes of MCI have been defined: amnestic MCI—single domain, amnestic MCI—multiple domains, nonamnestic MCI—single domain, and nonamnestic MCI—multiple domain (Busse et al., 2006). When followed longitudinally, individuals have MCI for an average of 5 years and have significantly increased rates of developing dementia, with conversion rates ranging from 8% to 15% per year, compared to a rate of 1% to 2% per year for the "normal" aging population (Devanand et al., 2008; Peterson et al., 1997). Individuals with amnestic MCI have the highest risk of progressing to Alzheimer disease (AD; Busse et al., 2006).

A variety of psychiatric illnesses can present with dementia-type features (called pseudodementias); a subset of patients with mood disorders and these features may resemble other neurological etiologies of dementia. Individuals with depression may report various cognitive problems in their daily lives, including slowed processing speed, memory problems, and attention problems. The onset of these cognitive symptoms can sometimes be linked to a precise date of onset (perhaps associated with the onset of a life stressor or emotional upset), and the course tends to progress more rapidly than in dementia. Subjective cognitive complaints in depression are typically greater in severity than the actual impairment on testing. Conversely, patients with AD may underestimate their impairments due to poor insight, which is often a hallmark of the later stages of the disease.

Several presenting features can distinguish *organic* dementia from dementia due to depression. First, cortical signs such as aphasia, apraxia, and agnosia are typically absent in depression. Second, depressed patients may exhibit psychomotor slowing and inconsistent effort or attention during neuropsychological testing, rather than primary problems with retentive memory or visuospatial functioning. Cognitive impairments occurring during the acute stages of depression are typically reversible with the treatment of symptoms of depression. However, it is important to note that depression may also co-occur in the early stages of dementia, and cognitive symptoms in this context would be less likely to improve with antidepressant treatments.

Within the true major neurocognitive disorders, AD is the most common cause of a dementia syndrome in those aged 65 and older, with 10% of people over the age of 65 and nearly 50% of people over 85 having the disease (NINDS & NIA, 2021). AD is diagnosed exclusively by clinical presentation, obtained through a detailed clinical history and evaluation of cognitive abilities (McKhann et al., 2011). The *DSM-5* definition is a decline in memory and at least one other cognitive domain with a progressive, steady decline in cognition, but there cannot be evidence of mixed etiology from an Axis I disorder, medical disorder, or delirium (APA, 2013).

Once studied pathologically in the brain, AD shows neuronal loss and atrophy of the cerebral cortex from beta-amyloid plaques (insoluble protein cores) and neurofibrillary tangles (intracellular protein tangles). There is a strong primary impact in the limbic cortex region (e.g., the hippocampus), which is involved in memory as well as the medial temporal areas, including the amygdala, hippocampal formation, and entorhinal cortex. In the later stages of the disease, there are impacts to the basal temporal cortex, parietal–occipital cortex, posterior cingulate gyrus, and frontal lobes. Neurotransmitter changes are also present, with primary dysfunction in the cholinergic neurons, which are involved in learning and memory. The primary motor, somatosensory, visual, and auditory cortices are relatively spared (Devanand et al., 2008).

Sophisticated imaging and biological marker techniques, such as PET and CSF assays, are also being developed to identify the pathological hallmarks of the disease, which develop years before the clinical signs of memory loss appear (Sperling et al., 2011) but have not shown consistent translation to AD (Rabinovici et al., 2017). However, the greatest risk factor for developing AD is age, with most cases of AD being sporadic, although several risk genes have been implicated. The risk gene with the strongest influence is called apolipoprotein E-e4 (APOE-e4). Scientists estimate that APOE-e4 may be a factor in 20% to 25% of Alzheimer cases. There is also a rare form of "familial" AD, which is caused by an autosomal dominant gene and often onsets before the age of 60 (Yin & Wang, 2018).

In AD treatment, there are three groups of medications with specific FDA indications: cholinesterase inhibitors, N-methyl-D-aspartate (NMDA) receptor antagonists, and newer therapies focusing on removing amyloid. The cholinesterase inhibitors prevent the breakdown of ACh and include galantamine, rivastigmine (Exelon), and donepezil (Aricept). These medications typically slow the progression of AD, rather than restore previously lost cognitive functions. Their side effects include weight gain, sedation, and, rarely, seizures (Sharma, 2019). The only NMDA receptor antagonist, memantine (Namenda), works by regulating glutamate, which, in excess, can lead to cell death. Memantine has been shown to slow the progression of disease with side effects including dizziness, headache, and constipation (Stahl, 2011). The last category of AD therapies includes a group of monoclonal antibodies (laboratory-grown human immune proteins) that bind to amyloid in the brain. This stimulates immune responses that reduce amyloid deposits and have been shown to reduce disease progression in short trials (van Dyck et al., 2023).

Cerebrovascular disease (CVD) is the second leading cause of acquired dementia following AD and is caused by multiple infarcts, in either large vessels or smaller vessels, which penetrate deeper in the brain. Dementia due to CVD, also called *multi-infarct dementia* or *vascular dementia*, tends to begin earlier than AD and is more common in men than women. The onset is typically abrupt with a *stepwise* or fluctuating course. Risk factors include hypertension, abnormal lipid levels, smoking, diabetes, obesity, cardiovascular disease, or previous stroke or transient ischemic attacks. CVD may coexist with other causes of dementia, including AD (O'Brien et al., 2003). The types of deficits present in vascular dementia are variable and depend on the nature, type, and extent of the cerebrovascular lesions. Focal deficits may be present, as well as gait disturbance or psychomotor retardation. Depression or mood changes are also common. Cognitive deficits common in vascular dementia include psychomotor processing speed, complex attention, and executive functioning (APA, 2013). Treatments are often preventive, focusing on the underlying risk factors (e.g., smoking cessation, exercise, antihypertensive medications, and dietary modifications), but AD-specific therapies have shown some evidence of slowing the progression (O'Brien & Thomas, 2015).

After accounting for AD and CVD, a number of other major neurocognitive conditions appear as dementia syndromes and deserve mention. Pick disease is a rare form of cortical dementia that is caused by the degeneration of the frontal and temporal lobes of the brain. Pick disease is one specific cause of a heterogeneous group of dementias referred to as frontotemporal dementia (FTD). Pathologically, Pick disease is distinguishable on autopsy by characteristic Pick inclusion bodies usually found in cortical and hippocampal neurons in the frontal and anterior temporal lobes (as opposed to the amyloid plaques and neurofibrillary tangles, which are the hallmark of AD). Dementia due to Pick disease, as well as other types of FTDs, are characterized by personality changes such as behavioral disinhibition, which often occur early in the course of the disease, as well as executive dysfunction and language abnormalities. Memory problems are also present but tend to become more obvious later in the disease (as opposed to AD where memory loss is typically the primary presenting problem). Onset is typically younger than that of AD, occurring between ages 50 and 60. There is no treatment for Pick disease, but the symptoms may be managed with various medications focusing on behavior impact (Heilman & Valenstein, 2003).

Another common dementia syndrome is associated with PD. PD is a progressive neurodegenerative condition that is characterized clinically by tremors, rigidity, bradykinesia (slowed movement), and postural instability caused by the degeneration of the substantia nigra in the basal ganglia and loss of DA. While PD is predominantly considered a movement disorder, patients with PD often have comorbid depression (30%) and dementia syndromes (20%–60%). PD is considered a "subcortical" dementia and may be characterized by deficits in executive functioning, learning and recall aspects of memory, slowed psychomotor speed, and bradyphrenia (slowed thinking). There are typically no cortical disturbances such as aphasia or apraxia (APA, 2013).

Treatment for PD focuses on DA agonists to boost DA systems in the brain. For example, levodopa (L-DOPA), a precursor to DA, works to replace losses from the substantia nigra but unfortunately becomes less effective over time as the disease progresses. DA agonists such as L-DOPA primarily help with the motor symptoms of the disease, but the cognitive symptoms are not improved. Neurosurgery such as DBS uses a surgically implanted device called a neurostimulator to deliver electrical stimulation to block the abnormal electrical signals within the basal ganglia. This type of treatment treats the motor symptoms of the disease and is used with patients whose symptoms are not adequately controlled with medication (NINDS & NIA, 2021).

A less common but unique scenario causing dementia is Huntington disease or Huntington chorea, which is often considered a movement disorder and is caused by a degenerative loss of neurons in the basal ganglia, particularly the caudate nucleus. Cells producing neurotransmitters such as GABA and NE, which normally inhibit the DA pathways, die during the course of the disease, thus creating a hyperactive DA system. It is an autosomal dominant genetic disorder affecting approximately 5/100,000. The defect causes a part of DNA—called a cytosine, adenine, or guanine repeat—to occur many more times than normal. Offspring have a 50% chance of developing this disorder. The disorder typically appears in the third or fourth decade of life. Dementia almost always occurs and is characterized by a decline in memory retrieval and executive functioning, with more severe deficits in memory and global intellectual functioning later in the disease. Behavioral disturbances occur in up to 50% of cases and are often the initial feature of the disease. These behavioral changes may include depression, personality changes, anxiety, irritability, restlessness, or psychosis (NINDS & NIA, 2021). The abnormal movements associated with this disease include "choreiform movements" (frequent, brisk jerks of the pelvis, trunk, and limbs), athetosis (slow uncontrolled movements), and unusual posturing. These motor symptoms often present months to a year after the disease onset. Subtle changes in personality, memory, and coordination are often the first symptoms of the disease. There is no treatment for

Huntington disease. Genetic counseling plays an important role for those with a family history of Huntington disease (McColgan & Tabrizi, 2018).

As a final example, dementia has been seen in some infectious diseases including HIV. HIV causes subcortical dementia by direct pathophysiological changes called AIDS dementia complex or HIV/AIDS encephalopathy. Neuropathological findings include diffuse, multifocal destruction of white matter and subcortical structures, resulting in cognitive, behavioral, and motor symptoms. Cognitive symptoms include forgetfulness, slowness, concentration problems, and problem-solving difficulties. Behavioral manifestations include apathy and social withdrawal as the primary features, although some individuals may experience visual hallucinations, delusions, or delirium. Motor symptoms include tremors, balance problems, impaired repetitive movements, ataxia, and hypertonia. CD4 counts are an important biomarker of HIV disease, and dementia due to HIV disease is more likely to occur as CD4+ count levels fall below 200 cells per microliter. With the advent of highly active antiretroviral therapy, the frequency of dementia due to HIV disease has declined from 30% to 60% of people infected with HIV to less than 20% (Eggers et al., 2017).

CONCUSSION AND TRAUMATIC ENCEPHALOPATHY

Concussion, which is a form of mild traumatic brain injury, is the result of direct or indirect trauma to the head. Although a loss of consciousness may occur, it is not necessary for diagnosis. Even though many diagnostic frameworks have been developed, all require an identified trauma to the head, as well as at least some *alteration* of consciousness, posttraumatic amnesia (or amnesia for the event), or some focal neurological deficit. Most of the literature suggests the presence of concussion-related symptoms for a few hours to several days after the injury. However, a more enduring syndrome of symptoms can occur and is known as postconcussion syndrome (PCS). For most, this syndrome will resolve within the first 3 months. However, there is a smaller group of individuals who can remain symptomatic for over 3 months and, sometimes, up to several years following the injury. PCS can be associated with a triad of somatic, cognitive, and behavioral symptoms. Somatic symptoms can include disordered sleep, fatigue, headaches, sensitivity to light and/or noise, vertigo or dizziness, and/or nausea. Personality/emotional changes can include anxiety, depressed affect, irritability, and/or apathy. Residual cognitive disturbances can include impaired attention and concentration; diminished short-term memory; slowed learning; decreased processing speed; lack of initiation; and poor planning, organization, and problem-solving (Freire-Aragón et al., 2017).

Chronic traumatic encephalopathy (CTE) is a recently defined progressive neurodegenerative disorder linked to a history of head trauma. Dr. Bennet Omalu first documented the presence of CTE upon autopsy in a National Football League football player in 2002 (Omalu et al., 2005). As of now, CTE can only be diagnosed with postmortem examination of the brain. The neuropathology of CTE is characterized primarily by hyperphosphorylated-tau protein (p-tau). This p-tau protein is usually distributed in an irregular, focal distribution around the periventricular regions (Hay et al., 2016). The neuropathology of p-tau is not unique to CTE, although a recent consensus panel funded by the NINDS and National Institute of Biomedical Imaging and Bioengineering (McKee et al., 2016) found acceptable interrater reliability among neuropathologists in discriminating between 25 cases of various tauopathies, including CTE, AD, progressive supranuclear palsy, argyrophilic grain disease, corticobasal degeneration, primary age-related tauopathy, and parkinsonism dementia complex of Guam.

The clinical manifestations of CTE include a broad range of psychiatric, behavioral, and cognitive changes. It remains unclear whether the neuropathological changes associated with CTE result in a specific set of behavioral, cognitive, or emotional symptoms. Current limitations in the study of CTE include the reliance on retrospective reporting of family members to gather associated clinical information postmortem, the lack of prospective studies, and similarities in neuropsychiatric symptoms between CTE and other neurodegenerative and neuropsychiatric disorders (Hanlon et al., 2017).

SEIZURE DISORDERS

A seizure is an episode of an abnormal electrical firing of neurons resulting in abnormal behavior or experience of the individual (NINDS, 2011; Zillmer et al., 2008). The abnormal neuronal firing that occurs during a seizure may result in strange sensations, emotions, behavior, or sometimes convulsions or loss of consciousness. Epilepsy is a condition in which an individual experiences two or more unprovoked seizures. An unprovoked seizure means there is no identifiable cause or trigger. Having a seizure is not the same as being diagnosed with epilepsy. For example, someone may experience an isolated seizure without going on to develop epilepsy. Some children experience *febrile seizures*, in which a seizure occurs in the context of a high fever. However, most children with febrile seizures do not go on to develop epilepsy. Approximately 1% of the U.S. population has experienced an unprovoked seizure or has been diagnosed with epilepsy (NINDS, 2011). There are many causes of epilepsy. Anything that disrupts the normal pattern of neuronal activity may cause a seizure, for example, brain damage, abnormal development, illness, infection, toxins, drugs, or trauma. In about half of the cases of epilepsy, the exact cause is *idiopathic*, or unknown (NINDS, 2011).

There are several classifications of seizures. The first main classification is *generalized* versus *partial* or *focal*. In a generalized seizure, both sides of the brain are affected, resulting in loss of consciousness (or altered consciousness), falls, or muscle spasms. There are several types of generalized seizures. In a *tonic–clonic generalized seizure*, formally known as a *grand mal seizure*, the individual typically loses consciousness and exhibits stiffening of the body and repetitive jerking of the arms and/or legs. In an *absence seizure*, formally known as a *petit-mal seizure*, the person may appear to be staring into space.

Focal seizures, also called *partial seizures*, affect only one part of the brain. In a *simple partial* seizure, the individual does not lose consciousness. A person with a *simple partial* seizure may experience sudden and unexplained joy or anger or may hear, smell, or see things that are not real. In a *complex partial seizure*, the person experiences an alteration or loss of consciousness. A person having a complex partial seizure may display repetitive movements or behaviors, such as blinks, twitches, mouth movements, or more complicated actions. *Temporal lobe epilepsy* is the most common type of recurring focal seizures and may be associated with memory problems due to the involvement of the hippocampus. Some people with partial or focal seizures experience an *aura*, or unusual sensation that warns a seizure is about to happen.

Not all seizures are distinctly partial or generalized. Some seizures may begin as a partial seizure and then spread to the entire brain. In addition, some people may appear to have a seizure, but there is no evidence of seizure activity in their brain. These events are referred to as *nonepileptic seizures*, formally referred to as *pseudoseizures*. The cause of these nonepileptic seizures may be psychogenic in origin, and sometimes people with epilepsy also have psychogenic seizures. It can be difficult to distinguish between epileptic and nonepileptic seizures—careful evaluation and monitoring are required.

Epilepsy is usually diagnosed with EEG monitoring, brain scans, blood tests, neurological or behavioral tests, and a thorough check of medical history. Epilepsy is usually treated with antiseizure medication, although not all individuals with epilepsy respond well to these medications. When medications are not effective in controlling seizures, surgery to remove the affected brain tissue may be considered, depending on the nature and type of seizures.

▶ REFERENCES

Full reference list available at http://examprepconnect.springerpub.com

KNOWLEDGE CHECK: CHAPTER 3

1. The human spinal cord is divided into four general regions called from top to bottom:
   A. Cervical, thoracic, lumbar, and sacral
   B. Sacral, lumbar, thoracic, and cervical
   C. Sacral, thoracic, cervical, and lumbar
   D. Thoracic, lumbar, sacral, and cervical

2. The cerebrum is comprised of four major lobes: the frontal, temporal, occipital, and _____.
   A. Angular lobes
   B. Dorsal lobes
   C. Parietal lobes
   D. Thalamal lobes

3. Wernicke aphasia, compromising one's ability to comprehend language, can occur when there is a lesion in the _____ lobe.
   A. Frontal
   B. Occipital
   C. Parietal
   D. Temporal

4. The _____ is a subcortical brain region responsible for the "fight or flight" response and managing emotional stimuli.
   A. Amygdala
   B. Basal ganglia
   C. Hippocampus
   D. Thalamus

5. A typical neuron consists of which of the following structures?
   A. Cell body, axons, myelin sheath
   B. Cell body, axons, neurotransmitter
   C. Cell body, dendrites, axons
   D. Cell body, synapse, dendrites

6. An electrical-chemical process responsible for communication between neurons is:
   A. Synapses
   B. Neurotransmission
   C. Glia
   D. Gradation

(See answers on the next page.)

1. **A) Cervical, thoracic, lumbar, and sacral**
   The four general spinal regions, starting at the neck and proceeding downward to the sacrum, are the cervical, thoracic, lumbar, and sacral regions. Nerve fibers exiting and entering the spinal cord in these regions send information to the brain from outside the central nervous system (CNS) and from outside the CNS to the brain.

2. **C) Parietal Lobes**
   The parietal lobes are one of four lobes that make up the cerebrum. Among other properties, the parietal lobes are responsible for somatosensory processing including the perception of touch, pressure, pain and temperature. Angular lobes, dorsal lobes, and thalamal lobes are not lobes of the brain.

3. **D) Temporal**
   Wernicke area in the parietal lobe is dedicated to the comprehension of language. Damage to this region may not only cause problems understanding language, but also expressing language as well. The frontal lobe is generally responsible for executive function. The occipital lobe is responsible for vision. The parietal lobe is responsible for processing sensory information such as heat, cold, pressure, and touch.

4. **A) Amygdala**
   The amygdala's interconnections to the midbrain play an important role in "fight or flight" response as well as processing emotional stimuli. The basal ganglia is involved in movement, the hippocampus is involved in memory, and the thalamus is the "relay station" for the brain's sensory information.

5. **C) Cell body, dendrites, axons**
   While neurons can come in many shapes and sizes, the typical neuron is comprised of a cell body which contains the nucleus; dendrites, which are short processes that extend from the cell body and receive impulses from other neurons; and axons, which can be longer processes that send impulses from the neuron to other neurons. Myelin sheath is not generally considered a structure, but rather a layer that surrounds the axon. Neurotransmitters are chemical substances that are released from neurons. The synapse is the space between neurons.

6. **B) Neurotransmission**
   Neurons communicate via an electrical-chemical process that involves multiple structures, which is referred to as neurotransmission. Synapses are the space between neurons. Glia is a type of cell found in the brain that is not directly related to neurotransmission. Gradation is not a term or concept associated with neuronal communication.

7. The body's primary excitatory (versus inhibitory) neurotransmitter is:
   A. Gamma-aminobutyric acid (GABA)
   B. Glutamate
   C. Norepinepherine
   D. Serotonin

8. _____ is a pharmacology term that describes the effect of a drug on the body.
   A. Pharmacodynamics
   B. Pharmacogenetics
   C. Pharmacokinetics
   D. Psychoactivity

9. A patient presents to their prescriber's office complaining that they have experienced an increase in side effects after a small increase to their lithium dose, which is a drug often used to treat bipolar disorder. Lithium is a drug that has a narrow range of blood levels, below which it is ineffective and above which it can be toxic. The prescriber explains to the patient that they may have seen an increase in side effects even after only a minor adjustment to the dose because lithium has a narrow _____.
   A. Drug effect
   B. Efficacy window
   C. Therapeutic range
   D. Therapeutic window

10. A 30-year-old patient has been taking a medication prescribed for acute panic. When a panic attack starts, the patient takes the medication and finds that about 20 to 30 minutes later they feel less anxious and more relaxed. However, over the course of taking the medication for several months, the patient has found that they need a higher dose of the medication to get the same effect they experienced when they first started taking it. Based on this information, you suspect that the patient is most likely taking the following type of medication.
    A. Anticonvulsant
    B. Antidepressant
    C. Benzodiazepine
    D. Stimulant

11. A patient reports to their prescriber that they experience increased sedation when they have a single drink of alcohol around the same time they take their benzodiazepine Xanax for anxiety. The prescriber explains that because alcohol and Xanax both modulate the neurotransmitter _____, she will likely experience increased sedation.
    A. Gamma-aminobutyric acid (GABA)
    B. Serotonin
    C. Norepinepherine (NE)
    D. Dopamine (DA)

(See answers on the next page.)

7. **B) Glutamate**
   Glutamate is both an amino acid and the brain's primary excitatory neurotransmitter. Excessive glutamate activity is implicated in cell death. GABA is the body's primary inhibitory neurotransmitter. Norepinepherine and serotonin are neurotransmitters and responsible for multiple actions, but are not considered excitatory or inhibitory by nature.

8. **A) Pharmacodynamics**
   The pharmacology of a drug can be divided into pharmacodynamics and pharmacokinetics. Pharmacodynamics refers to the effects of the drug on the human body, whereas pharmacokinetics refers to the actions of the body on the drug (e.g., elimination). Pharmacogenetics is the study of how a person's genes impact their response to a medication. The term psychoactivity is unrelated to the broad field of pharmacology.

9. **D) Therapeutic window**
   Drugs with a narrow therapeutic window often require obtaining blood levels from the patient to ensure that the dose of the drug is not too low or too high. The terms drug effect, therapeutic range, and efficacy window are not related to the narrow range between the effective dose of a medication and the toxic dose of a medication.

10. **C) Benzodiazepine**
    Benzodiazepines such as Ativan, Xanax, and Valium can be effective short-term treatments for acute anxiety and/or panic. However, a patient may develop a tolerance to the medication over time, resulting in higher doses of the drug being required to get the therapeutic effect desired. Benzodiazepines carry the risk of dependence and can be dangerous when used in conjunction with other medications that are central nervous system (CNS) depressants such as opioids. Anticonvulsants, antidepressants, and stimulant medications generally do not require dosage adjustments due to the development of tolerance.

11. **A) Gamma-aminobutyric acid (GABA)**
    Benzodiazepines like Xanax influence the specific neurotransmitter GABA as does alcohol. Benzodiazepines and alcohol have no effects on serotonin, NE, or DA.

12. The patient is a 36-year-old diagnosed with schizophrenia and treated with an antipsychotic medication. The patient's positive symptoms of schizophrenia are well managed on the medication, but they have been gaining weight, their blood pressure is elevated, and their primary care physician tells them they are at risk for developing diabetes. These medical issues were not present before starting this medication. Based on the side effects that have been reported, the patient is likely taking which type of antipsychotic?
    A. Atypical antipsychotic
    B. Conventional antipsychotic
    C. Typical antipsychotic
    D. Unconventional antipsychotic

13. A patient is being treated for bipolar disorder and was prescribed quetiapine (Seroquel). After returning home, she researched the medication online. In several instances, the websites she visited made reference to quetiapine as an antipsychotic. Knowing that she is not experiencing any psychotic symptoms or been diagnosed with a psychotic disorder, she immediately called her prescriber and voiced her confusion. The doctor likely explained to her that:
    A. Atypical antipsychotics are used for bipolar disorder as well as psychotic disorders.
    B. She was told that she has a psychotic disorder but must have forgotten.
    C. She is not taking an atypical antipsychotic.
    D. She is confused and should not research medication on the internet.

14. Deciding to manage their depression without medication, a 43-year-old patient purchases the over-the-counter supplement St. John's wort, which has been shown in some clinical trials to be effective for depression. After several months of taking the supplement, the patient noticed no improvement. However, they reported several annoying side effects, including sweating and diarrhea. They visited their primary care provider and voiced concerns about the side effects and frustration that the supplement hasn't been effective. The primary care provider likely told the patient all of the following, EXCEPT:
    A. Over-the-counter supplements are not regulated by a governmental body.
    B. Clinical trials of over-the-counter supplements tend to not be as rigorous as studies conducted on medications.
    C. Since over-the-counter supplements are not regulated, one cannot be certain what ingredients are actually in the supplement.
    D. They have not been taking the supplement long enough.

15. A 16-year-old patient has been started by their psychiatrist on a stimulant medication for an established diagnosis of attention deficit hyperactivity disorder (ADHD). While stimulant medication can be an effective treatment for many patients with ADHD, this class of medication carries the risk of all of the following side effects EXCEPT:
    A. Abdominal pain
    B. Excessive sedation
    C. Irritability
    D. Weight loss

(See answers on the next page.)

12. **A) Atypical antipsychotic**
    While atypical antipsychotics may have less risk of causing extrapyramidal side effects (EPS) and tardive dyskinesia (TD), they may have an increased risk of causing weight gain, prediabetes, hypertension, and high cholesterol. Conventional antipsychotics, also referred to as typical antipsychotics, may cause weight gain, but are not generally known to have the significant level of metabolic effects seen with atypical antipsychotics like quetiapine, risperidone, and clozapine. Unconventional antipsychotic is not a commonly used term in psychiatry.

13. **A) Atypical antipsychotics are used for bipolar disorder as well as psychotic disorders.**
    Several atypical antipsychotics have been approved by the U.S. Food and Drug Administration (FDA) for the treatment of various phases of bipolar disorder. These drugs include cariprazine (Vraylar), quetiapine (Seroquel), aripiprazole (Abilify), and risperidone (Risperdal), and have been approved for this use. The patient could have been told that she has a psychotic disorder and forgot or that she was confused by misinformation on the internet, but this is unlikely.

14. **D) They have not been taking the supplement long enough.**
    The patient has been taking the supplement long enough to see the effects. Over-the-counter supplements are not regulated by a governmental organization, and, as a result, efficacy, safety, and actual ingredients cannot be assured.

15. **B) Excessive sedation**
    Stimulant medication is generally well tolerated, but is known to cause some side effects that can include insomnia, headaches, tic exacerbation, nervousness, irritability, overstimulation, tremor and dizziness, weight loss, abdominal pain or nausea, possibly slowed growth in children, and blurred vision, among others. Sedation is generally not a side effect of ADHD medications.

16. A 27-year-old patient with moderate major depression with cognitive behavioral therapy (CBT) would like to know if adding an antidepressant might be helpful. According to the research in this area regarding moderate depression, combining CBT with an antidepressant:
    A. Has been found to be more effective for some patients than either CBT or medication alone
    B. Is an effective strategy for some disorders, but not for major depression
    C. Is contraindicated
    D. Is generally not advised since the use of medication can interfere with the efficacy of CBT

17. A 31-year-old patient is being treated for a specific phobia. The patient's friend has suggested that they ask their doctor for a prescription of a medication called Xanax (alprazolam) because the friend found it useful in treating their panic disorder. All of the following statements are true, EXCEPT:
    A. Benzodiazepines are not considered a first-line (preferred) treatment option.
    B. Exposure-based therapy approaches are considered first-line (preferred) treatment.
    C. The combination is superior to either medication or exposure-based therapy alone.
    D. The use of benzodiazepine may interfere with the efficacy of exposure-based treatment.

18. Broca aphasia refers to:
    A. Difficulty in expressive language due to a lesion/damage to a region of the brain called the Broca area
    B. Difficulty in receptive language due to a lesion/damage to a region of the brain called the Broca area
    C. Difficulty in seeing colors accurately due to a lesion/damage to a region of the brain called the Broca area
    D. Difficulty in the ability to swallow food due to a lesion/damage to a region of the brain called the Broca area

19. Alexia differs from dyslexia in that it is a/an _____ inability to read typically resulting from a _____.
    A. Acquired; stroke
    B. Congenital; substandard education
    C. Preexisting; poor nutrition
    D. Intermittent; psychological disorder

20. The central nervous system (CNS) is comprised of which of the following structures?
    A. Brain and meninges
    B. Brain and spinal cord
    C. Spinal cord and ventricles
    D. Ventricles and meninges

(See answers on the next page.)

16. **A) Has been found to be more effective for some patients than either CBT or medication alone**
    While there is some evidence that either CBT alone or medication alone can be an equally effective treatment for mild depression, combined CBT and medication has been found to be more effective than either alone for moderate to severe depression.

17. **C) The combination is superior to either medication or exposure-based therapy alone.**
    Most guidelines indicate that the preferred (first-line) treatment for specific phobia is exposure-based therapy with gradual repeated exposure to the feared stimulus. It is thought that the use of a benzodiazepine may interfere with the need for heightened arousal during exposure-based therapy, resulting in less successful outcomes. Combination treatment (using a benzodiazepine and exposure therapy together) has not been shown to be more effective in clinical trials than using exposure therapy alone.

18. **A) Difficulty in expressive language due to a lesion/damage to a region of the brain called the Broca area**
    Broca area is in the left frontal lobe; a lesion or damage to the area can result in difficulty speaking as manifested by speaking in a slow, halting manner, with poor grammar and prosody. Receptive language difficulties are generally associated with the condition Wernicke aphasia. Color aphasia is generally associated with damage to the occipital-temporal region of the brain. The subcortical area called the insula is associated with dysphagia, or difficulty swallowing.

19. **A) Acquired; stroke**
    Dyslexia is a developmental disorder in which the patient has difficulty reading. Alexia, on the other hand, is difficulty or an inability to read (in a person who could previously read) after an injury to the brain such as a stroke or traumatic brain injury. Alexia is not associated with poor education or poor nutrition and is not considering intermittent or a psychosocial related disorder.

20. **B) Brain and spinal cord**
    The CNS is comprised of the brain and spinal cord.

21. A patient begins taking hydroxyzine for anxiety. Since they started taking the medication, they noticed that their environmental allergies have improved. Wondering if there is a connection, they ask their primary care provider if this is just a coincidence. The primary care provider informs the patient that it is not a coincidence because hydroxyzine is a(n):

    A. Antihistamine with anxiolytic properties
    B. Benzodiazepine with antihistaminic properties
    C. Beta-blocker with antihistaminic properties
    D. Serotonergic medication with antihistaminic properties

22. Aphasia syndromes can be subdivided into three major classifications. Which is NOT a classification of aphasia?

    A. Fluent
    B. Nonfluent
    C. Pure
    D. Agraphia

(See answers on the next page.)

21. **A) Antihistamine with anxiolytic properties**
    Hydroxyzine is a potent antihistamine and is effective for relieving allergic reactions. It also has anti-anxiety properties, which is why it is often prescribed for anxiety.

22. **D) Agraphia**
    Fluent, nonfluent, and pure are all major classifications of aphasia. Agraphia is loss of the ability to write.

Cognitive–Affective Bases of Behavior

Elyssa Scharaga*

> ### BROAD CONTENT AREAS
> - Cognitive functions, including sensation, perception, attention, intelligence, and executive function
> - Learning and memory
> - Emotion and motivation
> - Interaction of cognition, emotion, and motivation

▶ INTRODUCTION

This chapter focuses on four content areas: (a) cognitive functions including sensation, perception, attention, intelligence, and executive function; (b) learning and memory; (c) emotion and motivation; and (d) interaction of cognition, emotion, and motivation, including theories with clinical application. This chapter will attempt to summarize the broad content area and highlight notable information. It also includes seminal and recent research in the content areas.

▶ COGNITIVE FUNCTIONS

SENSATION

Sensation is the detection of stimulation, the study of which commonly deals with the structure of sensory mechanisms (e.g., eye) and the stimuli (e.g., light) that affect those mechanisms. The study of both sensation and perception deals with the transduction of physical energy in one's environment into neural energy/signals. Although the five senses (i.e., vision, audition, body senses, taste, and olfaction) are at first glance vastly different, each sensory system is organized in a hierarchical manner. Following neural signals from the point of transduction in sensory receptors (e.g., retina, cochlea, mechanoreceptors [for touch/pain]), through a series of synaptic connections to the primary sensory cortex, the information is first represented very briefly in short-term sensory stores whose capacity has been shown to exceed that of short-term memory (STM; Sperling, 1960). How individuals perceive their external environment is affected by the intensity of the stimulus they encounter and the receptors that transduce (or convert) sensory energy into neural activity. Signal detection theory (Green & Swets, 1966) explains how humans detect external stimuli and how they separate meaningful information from excess "noise." More currently, optimal estimation theory or statistical decision theory, a Bayesian (probabilistic)

---

* Thank you to Matthew Jerram, David Gansler, and Robert Webb for their contribution to the first edition of this chapter.

approach (Parr et al., 2018), has supplanted signal detection theory and is described in the section on perception. Signal detection theory deals with the observation that two individuals confronted with the same stimulus presentation may come to different conclusions, that is, they may not agree on the intensity or presence of a simple stimulus. Disagreement may occur due to differences in discriminability or response bias. Response bias is the propensity of an individual to categorize stimuli as targets rather than foils or "noise" and can be characterized as liberal, neutral, or conservative (Wixted, 2020). For example, a more liberal response bias may be set if failing to identify stimuli could be relatively costly (being alert to all noises in fear of predators in the wild), or the response bias may be set lower (more conservatively) if incorrectly identifying a stimulus as a threat could be costly (wrongly perceiving a person's grimace and apologizing unnecessarily). Discriminability of the stimulus is described by the mathematical function of separation/spread, with separation representing signal strength and spread representing the background noise present during the stimulus presentation. Anyone traveling in a car listening to the local radio has experienced the frustration of reduced signal strength and increased background noise as the vehicle gets farther from the broadcast tower.

PERCEPTION

The complex process known as perception takes into account the contexts in which sensory impressions take place, our previous experiences, and our current psychological state of mind. Perception, rather than sensation, is of most interest to neuropsychologists. Perception deals with the detection and interpretation of sensory stimuli. Walking through a busy intersection in a safe manner requires successful integration of vision, touch, hearing, and perhaps even smell. In order to understand how people make interpretations about external stimuli (e.g., visual stimulus), return to the short-term sensory store of the previous example. It should be kept in mind, however, that the principles of perceptual processing presented here can also be generalized to other sensory modalities. Vision tends to dominate our perceptions and attentional resources, and has even infiltrated our language (e.g., "I see" used as a statement to indicate we understand a concept). In addition, over 50% of the cerebral cortex is involved in processing visual information (Hagen, n.d.). Visual information is contained in the light reflected from objects. Once a visual stimulus has grabbed our attentional resources and enters STM, it will be processed further for its location, shape, object identity, and a number of other features (e.g., color, luminance, direction, and speed of motion). The processing of these distinct visual features will be conducted in hierarchical, functionally segregated, and parallel units of the visual cortex (the occipital lobe and bordering parts of the temporal and parietal lobe [Hilgetag & Goulas, 2020]). There is extensive convergence and divergence across visual areas within the cortex, as stimulus processing proceeds from coarser to finer grained analysis (bottom-up processing) and as they return to coarser levels (top-down processing; Pinel & Barnes, 2021). It is worth elaborating on what is meant by hierarchical and parallel perceptual processing. *Hierarchical processing* means that a perceived stimulus will undergo successive expansion. Specifically for a visual stimulus, this is referring to simple cells responding best to oriented stimuli (e.g., bars, edges), whereas more complex cells will have larger receptive fields and may be selective for orientation but will be more "tolerant" of the exact positioning of stimuli. Later stages will incorporate the identification of an object from a memory store at a later stage. There is integration of visual features (e.g., shape, color, and motion) that occurs simultaneously as processing units gain information. *Parallel processing* relates to the integration that occurs simultaneously by different processing units that gain access to each other's contents. Further, hierarchical processing refers to information being processed and subsequently sent to different neuroanatomical regions for further processing. Therefore, in addition to different types of cells that are responsible for various aspects of perception, numerous neuroanatomical areas are accountable for perceptual processing (Hilgetag & Goulas, 2020).

Going back to the previous example of crossing a busy intersection: Pedestrians need to pay attention to the traffic light (vision), sidewalk (touch), traffic sounds (audition), and perhaps even smell—a gas leak, exhaust fumes, animal feces, and a fire nearby (olfaction). Combining these pieces of information, or *multisensory processing*, will help you cross the street as safely as possible. Multisensory processing has become the foundation when discussing the accuracy of processing sensory information. Specifically, recent literature has supported that multisensory stimulation is advantageous for learning and accurately identifying information (Noppeney, 2021). Multisensory integration requires greater attentional resources than processing a single feature (e.g., processing just vision), is more likely to rely on the activity of the frontal and parietal cortex, and is supported by cholinergic activity (Botly & De Rosa, 2008). Finally, according to Pinel and Barnes (2021), parallel processing was described as simultaneous analysis of a signal in by multiple parallel pathways of a neural network.

ATTENTION

Attention can refer to global states or selective processes (Gazzaniga et al., 2009). Sleep and wakefulness are global states, and wakefulness itself can be divided into inattentive states such as drowsiness or relaxation versus an attentive/alert state. *Attention* can also mean the ability to attend to some stimuli while ignoring others. In this section, the word *attention* refers to its role as a selective mechanism (selective attention), and not as it would be applied to global states. William James's (1890) definition of selective attention applies here: "Everyone knows what attention is. It is the taking possession by the mind, in clear and vivid form, of one out of what seem several simultaneously possible objects or trains of thought. Focalization, concentration of consciousness are of its essence" (pp. 403–404).

Selective attention operates both by facilitation and inhibition of resources. The facilitating effects (i.e., valid cuing in the Posner paradigm) of selective attention have been demonstrated in increased accuracy and speed of target response, increased perceptual sensitivity for discrimination, and increased contrast sensitivity (Kastner et al., 2009). The inhibitory effects of selective attention operating when a stimulus is ignored can be observed in reduction of distractor interference with increased attentional load (Kastner et al., 2009) and by negative priming (i.e., invalid cuing in the Posner paradigm) and inhibition of return. The phenomenon of attentional blindness (Simons & Chabris, 1999) reveals the limits of selective attention. In the classic demonstration of attentional blindness, individuals who are actively tracking an aspect of a sports event fail to notice a person in a gorilla suit walking directly through the game—clearly, attention cannot be directed everywhere.

Attentional Resources

In keeping with the limits of attentional resources, when those are taxed through increased processing load, or by dividing them between two tasks, performance decrements are observed; however, those resources can be increased through practice (Treisman, 2009). Three reasons for limitations in attentional resources (Treisman, 2009) are as follows:

- *Structural interference:* The more similar tasks are, the more they compete for attentional resources. Similar tasks tend to share the same sensory/perceptual modality.
- *General resource:* There is a general limit to the extent of attentional resources. Evidence for this limit can be found even when attention is divided between two noninterfering (i.e., different modalities) tasks and performance decrements occur. These decrements are less than those occurring with high structural interference, but they are still meaningful enough to indicate a drain on a general attentional resource that is occurring.
- *Behavioral coherence:* The unity of our actions places limits on attentional resources in preparing responses.

Attentional Selection

Attention selects for objects and location (Wolfe, 2021), and attributes such as motion (Corbetta et al., 1991), within the visual field. The Stroop effect (Stroop, 1935) is an example of attention to objects (e.g., word identity) taking precedence over attention to attributes (e.g., the color of ink the word is printed in). *Attentional load theory* (Lavie & Tsal, 1994) helps to explain the push–pull relationship of the facilitative and inhibitory mechanisms at work (Pinsk et al., 2004). The theory posits that the degree to which an ignored stimulus is processed depends on the extent of processing required by the attended stimulus. According to *attentional load theory*, reduction of interference caused by distractors is greatest when the processing demands to the attended stimulus are highest.

Attentional Control

Attention can be divided into two broad categories: voluntary and reflexive. Reflexive attention describes when sensory information is "captured" in a stimulus-driven fashion, referred to as a bottom-up mechanism (Treisman, 2009). Stimuli with high survival value, such as the odor of smoke indicating fire, or with high subjective value, such as one's name spoken from across a crowded room, are both quickly brought into the focus of attention, and exemplify the operation of bottom-up attention mechanisms. Voluntary attention is a top-down mechanism that is ascribed to an individual's ability to intentionally attend to something (Gazzaniga et al., 2009). Anne Treisman's conjunction search paradigm (Treisman & Gelade, 1980) is an example of a top-down mechanism. In that paradigm, the participant is to search a broad stimulus array for the only stimulus that satisfies two conditions (e.g., find the letter *O* that is printed in red ink, in an array of *X*s printed in red or *O*s printed in green). Neuroscientists proposed the existence of an attentional control system for top-down aspects of attention, communicating with but distinct from sensory–motor systems, represented in the lateral parietal and frontal lobes. In contrast, stimulus-driven aspects of attentional control (bottom up) may be represented between the amygdala and ventral aspects of the frontal lobe. In day-to-day life, attentional selection occurs among the multitude of stimuli with which we interact, all of which automatically compete for attentional resources. Experimental evidence indicates that stimuli presented at the same time influence one another in a mutually suppressive manner. For example, a stimulus, when presented on its own, activates greater brain activity than when it is presented simultaneously with other stimuli (Moore & Zirnsak, 2017). Evidence is accumulating that the *Gestalt* principles of perceptual organization (i.e., similarity, proximity, and continuity) are part of bottom-up attentional influences (Kastner et al., 2009). Top-down attentional control helps to resolve competition between stimuli by introducing bias toward one stimulus over another.

EXECUTIVE FUNCTIONING

Executive functions consist of capacities that enable a person to engage successfully in independent, purposeful, self-directed, and self-serving behavior (Lezak et al., 2012). Executive functioning is often characterized as being activated in novel or unfamiliar circumstances and are thus contrasted with routinized or more automatic behaviors (Shallice, 1990). For example, they aid in planning, selecting an item from many options, ignoring "noise" and persisting on current tasks, and improving time management (Kolb & Whishaw, 2021). Specific executive functions may involve supervisory attention, working memory, inhibitory control, or social problem-solving. *Working memory*, an aspect of executive functioning, can be described as active memory that temporarily holds data in the mind that can then be manipulated. Initially hypothesized by Alan Baddeley, working memory incorporates a *phonological loop* that preserves verbal information, a *visuospatial scratchpad* to control visual information, and a manager that allocates attention between the data (Baddeley & Hitch, 1974). Latent variable analysis suggests that working memory is a critical component of executive functions, as there is a near perfect correlation of working memory and nonworking memory executive functioning tasks, leading some experts to refer to a unitary underlying construct of executive attention (Cristofori et al., 2019). Thought to be controlled by the premotor and prefrontal regions of the frontal lobe, executive functions are also strongly associated with emotional distress, as frontal lobe dysfunction may be characterized by changes in affect and disinhibitory psychopathology (Reber & Tranel, 2019).

For example, one of the more salient symptomatology in frontal lobe lesions is the loss of divergent thinking, which can be observed on standard intelligence tests. Patients with frontal lobe lesions have often also been found to exhibit a loss of spontaneous speech, quantified on letter or semantic fluency tasks such as the Controlled Oral Word Association Test from the Multilingual Aphasia Examination (MAE; Benton et al., 1994). Risk-taking, perseveration, and rule breaking are also typical features in patients with frontal lobe lesions. Frequently used clinical neuropsychological tests of executive functioning include the Wisconsin Card Sort Test (set establishment and maintenance) and the Stroop Color Word Test (attentional control), which involve inhibiting responses and shifting strategies on visually mediated tasks (Kolb & Whishaw, 2021). Executive functioning has also been shown to play a specific role in geriatric depression (Lezak et al., 2012).

INTELLIGENCE

There are numerous definitions of intelligence, and some of the variability stems from either the anthropologic or educational setting from which the definition arises. Anastasi (1986) emphasizes the individual operating in the environment—"intelligence is not an entity within the organism but a quality of behavior. Intelligent behavior is essentially adaptive, insofar as it represents effective ways of meeting the demands of a changing environment" (pp. 19–20). Raymond Cattell proposed the concepts of fluid and crystal, which John L. Horn later elaborated on. The Cattell-Horn Two Factor Theory (1966) Cattell contends there are two types of cognitive abilities. The first is *crystallized intelligence* in which knowledge depends on particular culture and education. The second is *fluid intelligence* which is free of culture and is independent of formal learning (Horn & Cattell, 1966). For example, fluid intelligence involves abstract thinking and problem-solving, which has been found to decline in later adulthood. Crystalized intelligence was defined as involving knowledge that comes from prior learning and past experiences, such as reading comprehension and vocabulary.

In contrast, Carr (1910) provided a definition emphasizing intellectual processes—"intelligence is the power of using categories, it is knowledge of the relations of things" (p. 232). The differing intelligence theories have had ramifications, and the measures based on them (e.g., Stanford–Binet and Wechsler scales) have been criticized for focusing too much on the types of analytical and sequential thought processes required for academic success, while ignoring creative and practical abilities essential for broader life success (Sternberg, 1999). For example, Howard Gardner viewed intelligence tests as probing the limited range of linguistic, logical–mathematical, and spatial abilities, and so created a theory of multiple intelligences inclusive of musical, bodily-kinesthetics, naturalistic, interpersonal, and intrapersonal abilities (Gardner, 2011). Given the absence of an agreed upon definition, it is reasonable to note one of the better definitions as provided by David Wechsler (1939), "intelligence is the aggregate or global capacity of the individual to act purposefully, to think rationally and to deal effectively with his environment" (p. 3). It should also be noted that although intelligence tests measure a person's cognitive functioning at a certain time point and thus are most beneficial for short-term predictions, they can be gross estimates of premorbid intellectual functioning. Specific intelligence tests that include subtests that can be used to estimate an individual's premorbid functioning are those created by Wechsler (e.g., *Wechsler Adult Intelligence Scale–Fourth Edition* [WAIS-IV] and *Wechsler Intelligence Scale for Children–Fifth Edition* [WISC-V]).

Research-Based Theories of Intelligence

Empirically based approaches to intelligence rely primarily on two kinds of evidence: (a) structural research relying on factor analysis and later hierarchical factor analysis that resolved some of the earlier controversies arising from differences in British and American factor analytic techniques and (b) research on cognitive development across the life span (Flanagan & McDonough, 2018).

One significant recent trend is the integration of the intellectual strains of cognitive neuroscience/neuropsychology with that of cognitive psychology models of intelligence. The Planning, Attention, Simultaneous, and Successive (PASS) model is based on A. R. Luria's three-level theory of higher cortical functions (Luria, 1980) and represents an important alternative to the more purely cognitive British and North American traditions focused on fluid and crystalized intelligence (Naglieri & Otero, 2018). The three levels in Luria's (1980) theory, from the bottom up, are (1) regulation of cortical arousal and attention; (2) receiving, processing, and retention of information; and (3) programming, regulation, and verification of behavior.

Structural Research on Models of Intelligence

Within the first 30 years of research on tests of cognitive ability, it was discovered that all of the tests are positively correlated (Spearman, 1904), and this central tendency has come to be known as the positive manifold. Spearman, a student of Wilhelm Wundt, theorized that each mental ability represented by a mental test was influenced by a general factor and a specific factor, which he designated as lowercase g and s (Spearman, 1927). Thurstone (1938), relying on North American traditions of conducting factor analysis, as opposed to Spearman's British statistical practices, came to a different conclusion when analyzing data on multiple tests of cognitive abilities. According to his theory of primary mental abilities, each of those belonged to between seven and nine ability categories that were independent of a higher-order g factor. Comparatively, Cattell (1941) proposed that g was actually composed of general fluid (Gf) and general crystallized (Gc) ability. Gf was described as a facility for reasoning and adapting to new situations. Gc was described as accessible stores of knowledge. Horn and then John Carroll extended these theories with their extensive work in hierarchical factor analytic models (Carroll, 1993). The three-stratum model is often referred to as the Cattell–Horn–Carroll theory, and the majority of contemporary intelligence tests are based on it (Schneider & McGrew, 2012).

Developmental Research on Models of Intelligence

What does intelligence look like over time? As stated earlier, *crystalized* and *fluid intelligence* have been used as terms to describe cognition across the life span. Crystalized intelligence refers to skills and knowledge that is overlearned and familiar. Vocabulary and knowledge of general information (e.g., who is George Washington?) are examples of crystalized intelligence. Crystalized intelligence accumulates over time and has been demonstrated to improve into the individual's 60s and 70s; older adult populations tend to perform better on these tasks compared to younger adults (Salthouse, 2012). Comparatively, younger adults perform better on tasks requiring fluid intelligence, problem-solving, mental manipulation, and abstract reasoning independent of rote information they have learned. Specifically, fluid intelligence includes the cognitive domains of executive functioning, psychomotor and processing speed, and working memory. It has been found to peak in the 30s and slowly decline with age (Salthouse, 2012).

Gender stereotypes have reinforced that males outperform females in mathematics and spatial tests, and females outperform males on verbal abilities. However, more recent meta-analyses conducted indicate that the U.S. gender differences in mathematics have significantly decreased. Meta-analyses continue to demonstrate males' strength in spatial skills, including 3-D mental rotation. Across multiple meta-analyses in varying verbal abilities, differences between genders were not substantial (Hyde, 2016). In general, sex differences in cognitive abilities are the exception, rather than the rule. Most brains are considered to be "mosaics," in that they have neuroanatomical features that are more common in cisgender males, cisgender females, and features that are common in both. Further, it is unclear how and if structural differences translate into differences in cognitive functioning. Several types of intelligence tests have been created over the years. The most common will be discussed in detail. First, the Stanford–Binet Intelligence Scale, developed by French psychologist Alfred Binet in 1905, was designed to determine a total IQ score. An individual's strengths and weaknesses can be derived from the test; however, based on scoring, they would cancel each other out to create an overall IQ score. The fifth and latest edition of the Stanford–Binet, published in 2003, includes multiple factors of abilities, with added nonverbal subtests, based on critiques that previous versions heavily relied on language skills. This critique is one of the main reasons that the Wechsler Scales were created—in order to remove the bias against individuals with verbal learning disabilities. Another difference between the two main intelligence measures is that the scores for individual subtests are recorded and normed on the WAIS-IV, allowing for the psychologist to better understand an individual's strengths and weaknesses, unlike the overall IQ score calculated in the Stanford–Binet Intelligence Scale (Becker, 2003). An important note to remember is that the majority of the fundamental intellectual demands (e.g., sustained attention, STM, working memory, comprehension) on the subtests of the WAIS-IV can be linked to the general constructs found in the Stanford–Binet (Ackerman, 2017). Overall, both measures are grossly valid predictors of academic achievement in U.S.-based populations.

Applications of Research on Models of Intelligence Tests

Intelligence testing has major educational, occupational, clinical, forensic, and treatment applications. Lubinski's (2004) review of criterion validity revealed *g* covaried 0.70 to 0.80 with academic achievement measures; 0.70 with military training assignments; 0.20 to 0.60 with work performance, with the higher correlations pertaining to the more complex jobs; 0.30 to 0.40 with income; 0.40 with socioeconomic status (SES) of origin; and 0.50 to 0.70 with achieved SES. Intelligence tests aid in identifying individuals with psychoeducational and/or neurodevelopmental disorders (e.g., attention deficit hyperactivity disorder [ADHD], learning disability, autism spectrum disorder, and intellectual disability), and giftedness. Intelligence tests can also be used to provide recommendations for the development of individualized instructional programming and the identification of occupational performance and/or training potential (Flanagan & McDonough, 2018). The major intelligence tests include the WAIS-IV; *Wechsler Preschool and Primary Scale of Intelligence–Fourth Edition* (WPPSI-IV), WISC-V, *Stanford–Binet Intelligence Scales–Fifth Edition* (SB5); *Kaufman Assessment Battery for Children–Second Edition* (KABC-II); *Woodcock–Johnson IV* (WJ-IV); *Differential Abilities Scales–II* (DAS-II); *Universal Nonverbal Intelligence Test–Second Edition* (UNIT-2); *Cognitive Assessment System, Second Edition* (CAS2); and the *Reynolds Intellectual Assessment Scales, Second Edition* (RIAS-2). Intelligence test administration takes anywhere from 1 to 2 hours, not including scoring and interpretation, depending on the evaluator and the patient; therefore, abbreviated versions of tests have been developed to provide reliable and valid estimates of intellectual ability (e.g., *Wechsler Abbreviated Scale of Intelligence–Second Edition* [WASI–II]).

Psychometric Properties and Intelligence Tests

The current major intelligence tests produce composite and specific ability deviation scores, are generally based on standardization samples of 2,000 or more participants stratified by age, and are generally conormed to an academic achievement battery. All report split-half and test–retest reliability, nearly all report convergent validity with at least one other intelligence test, and nearly all report the results of exploratory and confirmatory factor analysis to address construct validity of the more global and specific indices. Split-half reliability for composite scores tends to be above 0.9, with a range from 0.84 to 0.99, with lower reliabilities coming from the youngest samples. Test–retest reliabilities for composite scores range from 0.79 to 0.96. Test–retest reliabilities for subtests display a greater range from 0.38 to 0.9, with speeded tasks tending to produce lower reliabilities. Convergent validity—that is, correlations between the composite scores of major intelligence tests—tends to fall in the 0.70s and range from 0.69 to 0.92.

Bias in Intelligence Testing

Racial differences on intelligence measures are arguably among the most controversial topics in the study of individual differences in cognition in the last century. Nonverbal measures of intelligence were created in an attempt to alleviate culture biases; these include the *Leiter International Performance Scale, Revised* (Leiter-R), which is comprised of a visualization and reasoning battery and an attention and memory battery (Roid & Miller, 1997). The Raven's Progressive Matrices assess an individual's ability to solve complex problems and store and reproduce information and is applicable in a non-English-speaking population.

Research indicates that marginalized groups' differences in cognitive abilities can also be understood as a function of factors such as stereotype threat and the quality and extent of education and acculturation (Fuji, 2018; Rabin et al., 2020). Many cross-cultural clinical researchers recommend using the appropriate ethnic group normative statistics to improve diagnostic accuracy (Rabin et al., 2020). However, other psychologists have raised concerns that the specific group norm approach fails to increase our understanding of underlying psychological and cognitive processes, which could inadvertently encourage belief in a biological basis of ethnic differences in intellect. Instead, therefore, they recommend adjusting cognitive test scores on the basis of degree of acculturation and quality of education (Fuji, 2018). However, how to do that in a standardized manner remains to be determined. For example, there are limited specific ethnic group norms for the neuropsychological assessments currently in use. The WAIS-IV, for example, is one of the most widely used measures of intelligence in neuropsychological and psychological assessments. The WAIS-IV was normed in a grossly Caucasian, North American population. These norms will not easily translate to a U.S. resident born in South America who speaks Spanish as their first language. Additionally, the neuropsychological norms that we do have for Spanish-speaking individuals do not consider the diverse Hispanic cultures (e.g., Spanish, Catalonian, various South American, Mexican). Sternberg (2003) has demonstrated in *Project Rainbow* that measures of practical and creative ability contribute significantly to predicting first-year undergraduate grade point average (GPA) above and beyond Scholastic Assessment Test (SAT) scores. Relative to ethnic differences in SAT and GPA, the *Project Rainbow* practical and creative ability measures reduced ethnic difference gaps, particularly for Hispanic Americans.

LEARNING

Learning is essentially the storage by the central nervous system of information for its retrieval at a later time. There are two types of learning theory. One involves a focus on environmental events that influence behaviors, and the other focuses on changes that take place within the learner (Schwartz & Reisberg, 1991). The dominant learning theory of the early 20th century was based on the work of Edward Thorndike (1898) and Ivan Pavlov (1927). Their findings were known as related forms of conditioning and became the cornerstone of behaviorism. Because behaviorism's conclusions were all based on observable qualities in either the environment or in behavior, it was well suited to studies of animals. In the mid-20th century, as methods of working with human subjects developed, research in social and cognitive approaches began to be gradually more important and was aided by the introduction of the computer. The rise of cognitive psychology was a consequence, although it was a number of years before affect or feelings became acceptable as research topics.

CLASSICAL OR PAVLOVIAN CONDITIONING

Ivan Pavlov was a Russian physiologist working on the problem of what causes salivation. Food in the mouth of a hungry dog was readily seen to produce salivation (a saliva duct was surgically brought outside to make it visible). Pavlov eventually worked out a relationship between smelling meat and salivation, and it became known as classical conditioning. Pavlov described the stimulus–response paradigm in terms of an unconditioned stimulus (US; something to which an organism instinctively responds), an unconditioned response (UR; the instinctive response of the organism to the US), a conditioned stimulus (CS; a stimulus that is not responded to instinctively that is paired temporally with the US), and a conditioned response (CR; an organism's response to the CS that is similar to the UR). The basic paradigm is as follows.

The CS/US → UR until conditioning has occurred, when the UR takes place as soon as the CS appears and the US is no longer needed, and the paradigm becomes simply CS → CR. Pavlov used a metronome as his CS, although we all know him as having rung a bell. He would present the metronome (CS) and follow it with meat powder (US) in the dog's mouth. The dog would salivate (UR) in the course of eating the tiny amount of food. After a few trials, the dog salivated (CR) to the sound.

John B. Watson is known for conditioning Little Albert to fear white rats in very few trials (Watson & Raynor, 1920). Moreover, the fear conditioning generalized to include other white furry objects. More everyday examples might show the acquisition of phobias, or anxiety in response to certain stimuli. Stimuli in these situations are not as simple as Pavlov's. They encompass complex elements of environmental context, such as speaking in front of an audience or driving across a bridge, such that just talking or thinking about doing these things will produce responses of fear and anxiety. Many emotions are attached to contexts that may have occurred in childhood. They often elicit autonomic responses, such as increased blood pressure, heart rate, or galvanic skin response, a method of measuring electrical skin resistance.

In recent years, there has been an extension of classical conditioning as an important mechanism in drug and illness responses. For example, it was found that cues from the environment had a strong effect on response strength in the case of heroin. If a user administered their heroin shots in the same room (i.e., same lighting and furniture) every day, their body would begin an antagonistic response to it as soon as they entered that room. The drug's effect was lessened by this antagonistic reaction, becoming a factor in adaptation (or tolerance), so that higher doses gradually became necessary to achieve the same high. However, if the shot was administered in a new room, the body would not begin reacting as soon (or the conditioned reaction does not occur); thus, the drug had its full effect on the body and an overdose would potentially ensue.

OPERANT CONDITIONING

The basics of operant conditioning were discovered by Edward Thorndike (1898), and he called the relationship "the law of effect" because he found that random behaviors would be repeated only if they were followed by some sort of reward. The term *operant conditioning* was ultimately coined by B. F. Skinner, who was specifically interested in how the consequences of one's actions influenced their behaviors. The basic paradigm of operant conditioning became as follows: CS → CR/US → UR. The paradigm is read as: A stimulus that precedes a behavior that leads to a "satisfying state of affairs" will tend to be repeated. The main difference from classical conditioning is that for CR, the response includes the element of choice, so that the response can be made if it leads to something desired, or one can refrain from doing the response if one does not receive a "reward," or if it leads to something aversive. There are several types of ways to reinforce behavior in operant conditioning. One example is *shaping*, which is when behaviors that are close to the target behavior are reinforced, also known as successive approximations. It involves a process of reinforcing behaviors that are successively closer to the target (desired) behavior. This is used frequently in treatment of patients with autism when teaching them ways to communicate. *Response generalization*, on the other hand, refers to the target response spreading to other stimuli that are similar to the target (that received the reinforcement). Response generalization occurs if a target operant response causes an increase in other responses that are similar to the target response. For example, if you were operantly conditioned to be scared whenever you saw a spider, a response generalization would be that you were then scared when you saw any arthropod. Slightly different generalization, termed *mediated generalization*, is the process of responding to a stimulus not physically similar to the CS, which was not previously encountered in conditioning. Continuing with our example of being operantly conditioned to be scared of spiders, an example of mediated generalization would be when a person is scared of any insect (grasshopper, bee, etc.), when they were only conditioned to be scared of a spider.

Negative outcomes of behavior in operant conditioning are called punishers, but, because they tend to make the CR *less* likely to happen, they *cannot* be called reinforcements. Note that the term *negative reinforcement* has different meanings in the two forms of conditioning: In classical, it increases the CR, whereas in operant it decreases its likelihood. Simply, actions that are followed by positive reinforcement will be strengthened and actions that are followed by punishment will less likely be repeated, or eventually become *extinct*. Negative reinforcements in operant conditioning involve the removal of an unfavorable event after a behavior; thus, a response is strengthened by the removal of something considered unpleasant (e.g., giving a dog a treat to stop it from barking). This is different than a punishment, wherein an adverse event or outcome causes a decrease in the behavior it follows. There are two different types of punishments. Positive punishment is when an unfavorable event/outcome is committed in order to weaken the response it follows (e.g., hitting your dog with a newspaper after it had an accident in the house). Negative punishment occurs when a favorable event/outcome is taken away after a behavior occurs (e.g., taking your child's toy away following misbehavior). In theory, when punishment occurs, the behavior hopefully decreases.

Much of the difference between classical and operant conditioning is whether a behavior is voluntary or involuntary. Specifically for operant conditioning, it involves a degree of choice for the voluntary behavior. In classical conditioning, the animal/human cannot avoid the stimuli since they are under control of the experimenter. Because avoidance was not possible, the animals quickly learned whether the signal (CS) was leading to something good or bad, and CRs became faster than URs. The index of response was the faster reaction time to the CS, or a secretion such as salivation that the animal could not willfully control. In operant conditioning, on the other hand, animals/humans have the voluntary choice to respond or not, and the nature of the consequence influences their decision (rewards vs. punishments). A specific principle that utilizes operant conditioning is the *Premack Principle*, originally theorized by David Premack in 1965. The Premack Principle, colloquially termed "Grandma's Principle," states that a behavior which is done reliably can be used as a reinforcer for a behavior that occurs less frequently. For example, most children enjoy playing outside with friends or spending time using a computer. This behavior happens reliably (frequently), and this behavior can be used as a reinforcer for an activity children like to do less, such as homework, cleaning their room, and so on. Therefore, parents or teachers can use "playtime" activities as a reinforcer to complete their homework or household chores.

REINFORCEMENT SCHEDULE

The learning situation in operant conditioning involves not only what the reinforcement will be, but also how often it is likely to appear—the reinforcement schedule. Skinner proposed several types of reinforcement schedules. If the reinforcer follows every instance of the CS, it is called *continuous reinforcement*. Continuous reinforcement is the fastest way to learn; however, it is not efficient because it requires so many reinforcers. *Extinction* occurs very quickly in this type of schedule after reinforcement has discontinued. But, learning can still occur even if you are not rewarded every time you do a behavior and only in some proportion. For example, a *fixed ratio* is when the schedule varies in proportion (e.g., consistently, every fifth press is rewarded). It is found in human behavior control as piecework, or work on commission, where each piece produced earns a set amount of money. *Fixed ratio schedules* lead to steady response rates. A *variable ratio schedule* is similar to the *fixed ratio schedule*, except that in the variable ratio schedule the ratio requirement changes unsystematically (after a varied number of responses). Pop quizzes illustrate use of this schedule. Both ratio schedules produce high rates of output. *Variable ratio schedules* also lead to high response rates and slow extinction rates.

There are also two common schedules based on the passage of time and not on number of responses. They are known as *interval schedules*. *Fixed interval schedules* are a partial reinforcement wherein reinforcement occurs after a specific interval of time passes. For example, the *fixed interval schedule* between reinforcements will always be 10 seconds. A *fixed interval schedule* leads to intermittent behavior in which response rates remain relatively stable, and then start to increase as the reinforcement time nears and then slows down immediately after the reinforcement is delivered. *Variable interval* has intervals between reinforcements are of an unpredictable length of time. *Variable interval schedules* set an "average" interval size, but they vary unsystematically (e.g., variable interval is 30 seconds, but the intervals could be 2 seconds or 180 seconds). *Variable interval schedules* produce a steady and fast response rate and slow extinction rate. Again, this rate maximizes reinforcement while minimizing work. To summarize, *ratio schedules* occur based on the number of responses from the participant and *interval schedules* provide a reward after a certain amount of time, no matter the response (or work) rate.

▶ MEMORY

Memory is the process of encoding, consolidating, and retrieving information. The measurement of learning is always through the mechanism of memory. Moreover, how something is learned has a strong influence on how it is remembered. This means that perception becomes important as well, for how it is perceived determines how it will be learned and, thus, remembered.

Past memory research reflected the influence of computer advances, as did learning research. The main force was epitomized as "information processing," which broke the neurological process into successive steps and sorted sensory inputs into categories represented by analogous cell groups. Atkinson and Shiffrin (1968) expanded information processing to include three levels: sensory memory, STM, and long-term memory (LTM; Schwartz & Reisberg, 1991). Before defining these terms, we should break down the stages in learning and memory: encoding, storage, and retrieval. Encoding is the initial learning of the information presented. Storage refers to maintaining the memory over a period of time. Finally, retrieval is the process of accessing the information stored in LTM upon request (Baddeley & Hitch, 1974). Sensory memory is now considered too brief to be called memory (Schwartz & Reisberg, 1991). Experience involves a continuous flow of information, but the nervous system is built around discrete impulses, that is, a succession of separate packages of information, and there is a need to transform the information from one form to the other. Sensory memory is based on retaining visual images and auditory inputs for just milliseconds. In turn, these residual images can be used by the visual system. Individuals notice this in the after-image of a flash, when they see a spot everywhere they look. Sensory and analogous motor memory are currently subsumed under STM (Kolb & Whishaw, 2021).

STM represents storage of information that can be retained only for a brief time, and in limited amounts. Put another way, in order to think about something, it has been brought into STM, or "front of mind" consciousness. An example of STM would be trying to remember where you left the coffee mug you were drinking from while reading this chapter. In regard to learning and initial encoding of information, a theory of interference, or *inhibition*, occurs at different levels of learning. *Retroactive interference* is defined as later learning that interferes with information previously encoded (old memories), whereas *proactive interference* is defined as previously learned information that interferes with the ability to learn new or subsequent information (Baddeley & Hitch, 1974). A case of proactive interference would involve a patient who had difficulty remembering a set of words after learning a previous (different) list of words.

LTM refers to all the information that has been learned and is relatively more permanent. It is a vast library of information and comes in three main categories: *declarative*, *implicit*, and *emotional*. *Declarative*, or *explicit*, memory is composed of things one knows (conscious) and it has two types, *semantic* and *episodic*. Semantic memory refers to knowledge of the world, such as facts, meanings, concepts, and rules of culture. These are often learned in school and may require hard work to store (e.g., repetition, index cards, and mnemonics). Episodic memory was proposed by Tulving (1972) and is personal, autobiographical memory. Everyday experiences are recorded here and are connected to other events of the day. These memories are essentially stored automatically and may be why hands-on learning is easier to retain than lecture. The more life is repetitious, the more these memories interfere with each other and result in some loss of sequence and time specificity. Research has evaluated different methods to enhance or increase consolidation and retrieval of information stored in LTM. Although the mechanisms of sleep's role in consolidation is beyond the scope of this chapter, consensus of current research is that sleep optimizes the consolidation of newly acquired information in memory (Brodt et al., 2023). Explicit memory is associated with the temporal lobe, specifically the hippocampus, perirhinal cortex, and aspects of the frontal cortex. Moreover, episodic memory has been found to be linked to the ventral frontal lobe and hippocampus, based on research conducted in patients with damage to these areas. Another type of memory that describes awareness and memory for completing a planned action in the future is called *prospective memory*. An example would be remembering to take your medications in the morning. You can think of prospective memory as "remembering to remember."

Implicit, or *nondeclarative* memory, is unconscious and nonintentional. For example, your ability to perform skills such as riding a bike and speaking are implicit memories. It is encoded in a bottom-up process, or data driven. For example, you can be *primed* with words related to a target word in order to recall the target word. Priming is a form of cueing that involves activating similar brain areas, so the search is more efficient. Damage to the basal ganglia can result in deficits in learned motor skills and habits, whereas damage to the cerebellum has been associated with loss of coordinated movements and responses. Patients with cerebellar lesions are uncoordinated and have difficulty reaching for objects.

Affective memories also rely on bottom-up processing. Emotional memory is available on prompting and stimulating due to the nature of the types of memories stored. It also has the intentional, top-down element of explicit memory in that internal cues that we use to process emotional events can also be used to initiate spontaneous recall (Kolb & Whishaw, 2021). Affective processing picks up the stimulus as a source of threat, and the cognitive system then analyzes it to find out why (Mikels & Reuter-Lorenz, 2019). Neural substrates associated with emotional memory include the amygdala (located in the temporal lobes), which is responsible for the perception and control of emotions. An interesting subset of affective memory has been coined the *Zeigarnik effect*, which states that people (e.g., students, participants) will remember uncompleted or interrupted tasks better than tasks they have completed. The Zeigarnik effect has been used in several older and more recent studies and also has been highlighted in Gestalt psychology. In general, the Zeigarnik effect posits that an interrupted or incomplete task leads to strong motivation and intrusive thoughts about the goal that was left unaccomplished.

An interesting case illustrates the explicit–implicit difference. H.M. experienced seizures as a child, and underwent a corrective surgery, which ultimately damaged his hippocampus and amygdala bilaterally. The hippocampus is the main structure for consolidating LTM, and H.M. could not store anything new, resulting in anterograde amnesia. His wife came to visit often, but each time she was out of the room for more than a few minutes, he greeted her return as though he had not seen her for weeks. In other words, his STM was working, as was his LTM from before his injury, but he had no memory after his injury. While he was able to show improvement on learning lists and mazes in a short session, he was unable to recall seeing them from sessions prior.

▶ EMOTION AND MOTIVATION

Emotions are a central part of the psychological experience and significantly contribute to the motivation of behavior. Generally speaking, psychologists understand emotions to contain the following components: (a) physiological effects (e.g., autonomic arousal, action urges, facial expressions), (b) cognitive appraisals, and (c) subjective feeling of emotions. Motivation involves emotional, biological, social, and cognitive forces that activate behavior.

THEORIES OF EMOTIONAL EXPERIENCE

The concept of emotion is one without a single overriding theory in psychology. Instead, there are several coexisting theories of emotion. To understand the prevailing theories, it is useful to approach them from a historical perspective.

William James was the first psychologist to propose a theory of emotional experience. His theory postulated that changes in physiological sensation are the primary elements of emotional experience (James, 1884). This theory is generally referred to as the James–Lange theory of emotion, as the theory was independently proposed by Carl Lange, a Danish physician. In the simplest terms, the James–Lange theory models emotion as the psychological response to the changes in the physical systems of the body after the presentation of a stimulus. Fear is often used as an example of this model:

1. The individual observes a threatening bear in the woods.
2. The individual has increased autonomic activity (e.g., heart rate and respiration) and runs away.
3. The individual observes their increased autonomic activity (e.g., heart palpitations, sweating) and recognizes that they are running away from the bear.
4. The individual concludes that they are experiencing fear.

The James–Lange theory argued that the physiological reactions were necessary to experience an emotion (e.g., anger, fear)—so much so that it stated that if an individual were asked to imagine a stated emotion, the imagined emotion would be a "bland version" of the real feeling, and that emotions are nearly impossible to be experienced "on demand." Several critiques of the James–Lange theory quickly emerged. Primarily, these critiques focused on the nature and response of the autonomic nervous system. The critiques validly indicate flaws in the theory as a comprehensive model of emotion. Researchers countered the James–Lange theory by applying electrical stimulation. Researchers found that applying stimulation to elicit a physiological response did not result in emotional responses in participants. A significant counterproposal to the James–Lange theory was presented by Walter Cannon and Philip Bard (Cannon, 1931).

The Cannon–Bard theory proposes that the physiological responses associated with emotions are a consequence of experiencing emotion, not a necessary precursor to it. As popularly understood, the Cannon–Bard theory states that one has the psychological experience of emotion, and this experience generates a physiological change. To use the example of the bear, an emotional experience would take the following path:

1. The individual observes a threatening bear in the woods.
2. The individual processes the sensory information and recognizes a threatening situation.
3. The individual experiences fear.
4. The individual begins to experience physiological changes, such as autonomic arousal and an urge to flee.

However, this simplistic formulation of the Cannon–Bard theory neglects the important fact that perhaps the first theory of emotion not only centered the experience within the brain, but identified specific regions involved with the experience. In particular, the Cannon–Bard theory centers emotional experience on the thalamus, an area that we now think of as a sensory relay area and one of many brain regions involved in emotional processing. The theory modeled the process of emotional experience in the following way:

Stimulus ⟶ Cortical processing ⟶ Thalamic processing ⟶ Behavior

Therefore, in contrast to the James–Lange theory, the Cannon–Bard theory requires processing within the brain prior to physiological changes. In terms of the perceived experience, the Cannon–Bard theory postulates that the conscious awareness of an emotional state and the physiological changes associated with that state occur simultaneously, such that the person would note the emotion and the physical changes as parallel, rather than sequential.

The James–Lange and Cannon–Bard theories remained the main models of emotional experience until the 1960s, when Schachter and Singer (1962) published their seminal article, "Cognitive, Social and Physiological Determinants of Emotional State." In this study, they demonstrated that similar physiological experiences would lead to different emotional experiences depending on the context. Through their research results, Schachter and Singer (1962) concluded that individuals must cognitively appraise a situation in order to determine their emotional states; they referred to this as the "two-factor" model of emotion:

Autonomic arousal ⟶ Cognitive interpretation ⟶ Emotion

Subsequently, this model of emotion has been subsumed in the broader term *cognitive appraisal*, which has been the dominant model of emotion since the 1960s.

Lazarus (1966, 1991) developed a sophisticated appraisal model of emotion in which he theorized that each emotional experience arises from how an individual appraises ongoing interactions with the environment. His early work identified two stages of appraisal. In primary appraisal, the valence and threat of the stimulus are identified in a general sense (positive vs. negative; benign vs. stressful). During secondary appraisal, the individual identifies the resources and options that may be available to cope with the stimuli. Both processes combine into the experience of a particular emotion. The coping mechanisms of secondary appraisal may be identified as "emotion focused" (use of internal resources to cope with situation) or "problem focused" (intervention in the environment to solve a problem externally). This distinction has been found to be useful in the study of depression, for instance, in which individuals with depression are more likely to use emotion-focused coping than are those with executive functioning deficits (Segerstrom & Smith, 2019). Later adaptations of this theory by Lazarus (1991) have indicated that each emotion has a particular motivational function. In other words, the appraisal of the relationship between the individual and the stimuli is unique to each emotion experienced. This iteration of the model identifies multiple types of primary appraisal, including goal relevance, goal congruency, and ego involvement. There are also additions to the types of secondary appraisal, including identifying blame, coping resources, and expectations of the future. These adaptations address criticisms of Lazarus's work that suggested his model was a theory of stress response more than a comprehensive theory of emotion.

In response to Lazarus's theory and the primacy of cognitive appraisal models, Zajonc (1980) described a model of emotion that allowed for the experience of affect without cognitive contribution. He challenged the idea that cognition is a necessary component of emotional experience, although he did not conclude that cognition never contributed to emotion.

SOMATIC MARKER HYPOTHESIS

A recent addition to theories of emotion is somatic marker hypothesis, which focuses on the role of somatic and emotional responses in decision-making (Damasio et al., 1996). The somatic marker hypothesis proposed that the physiological responses or somatic markers coming from the body were regulated in the emotion substrates in the brain, more specifically the ventromedial prefrontal cortex. The frontal lobe, and particularly the ventromedial prefrontal cortex, has been documented to manage decision-making and social behavior/interactions, based on case reports of localized injuries. The somatic marker hypothesis proposes a mechanism by which emotional processes can influence behavior, predominantly decision-making. Damasio and colleagues hypothesized that decision-making deficits following ventromedial prefrontal cortex damage result from the inability to draw on emotions to direct future behavior based on past experiences (Damasio et al., 1996).

The central tenet behind the somatic marker hypothesis is that decision-making is influenced by marker signals that arise from multiple levels of operation, both consciously and unconsciously. Marker signals arise in bioregulatory processes (e.g., changes in heart rate, blood pressure, and glandular secretion), and in emotions and feeling. According to the somatic marker hypothesis, the sensory mapping of visceral responses not only contributes to emotions but is also vital for the implementation of goal-oriented behaviors. Subsequently, visceral responses operate by "marking" potential choices as beneficial or detrimental.

Emotional decision-making can significantly affect individuals' daily lives and, accordingly, the somatic marker hypothesis has important clinical implications. In addiction, a deficit in the neural circuitry that subserves the action of somatic markers is implicated in individuals' diminished ability to make favorable real-life decisions.

DIMENSIONAL/BASIC EMOTION MODELS

The determination of the appropriate model to classify and define emotions has focused on two competing theories. One side theorizes that all emotions can be described by a small group of specific emotions—usually referred to as the "basic emotion" model. The other side considers emotions to be a combination of several dimensions of physiological and psychological phenomena—usually referred to as the "dimensional" model. Each model has supporting research evidence and few efforts have been made to reconcile the opposing theories.

The main figure associated with the basic emotion model is Paul Ekman. Ekman and Friesen (1971) reported on the ubiquity of facial expressions related to emotion after studying facial expressions across several cultures. They identified six basic/primary emotions as defined by these facial expressions—happy, sad, surprised, disgusted, angry, and afraid. *Basic emotion theory* holds that these (usually) six emotions are the only emotions humans experience. The basic emotions are "hardwired" into humans at birth. Therefore, "secondary" emotions that might be labeled other than happy, sad, surprised, disgusted, angry, or afraid are, in fact, combinations of some of the six basic emotions and are influenced by cultural factors, among others. One of the main critiques of this theory is that, by setting a low limit on the number of "true" emotions, the theory is not sufficiently flexible to explain the complexity of human emotional experience.

Dimensional models of emotion attempt to incorporate flexibility into a simple model in an effort to provide a broader description of emotional experience. Dimensional models were described early in the development of psychology (e.g., Wundt in 1896), but were not well described and researched until Osgood et al. (1961) began work on the semantic differential. In this work, they had individuals rate their impression of stimuli on a Likert scale between two sematic opposites. Using factor analysis on these data, they identified three factors in the response patterns and they hypothesized that these factors represented the basic dimensions of emotional experience. Further research replicated this finding, although the first two factors were consistently much stronger than the third. Russell (1980) developed the two dimensions of the circumplex model of emotion: *valence*, the pleasantness of a stimulus, and *arousal*, the autonomic arousal in response to a stimulus. This is the dominant dimensional model currently. Much like the basic emotion model, the dimensional model has been criticized for not adequately describing the scope of human emotional experience. Dimensional models that are restricted to two axes, such as the circumplex model, have received similar criticism.

BRAIN SYSTEMS

The limbic system is a system of brain regions that is most commonly associated with emotion. Most of the regions of this system were first described by James Papez in 1937. The limbic system is composed of an interconnected network of structures including the amygdala, olfactory bulb, hypothalamus, hippocampus, mammillary bodies, septal nuclei, orbital frontal cortex, subcallosal gyrus, insular cortex, parahippocampal gyrus, and cingulate gyrus. It is highly interconnected with the endocrine system and autonomic nervous system, particularly in response to emotional stimuli. Together, the limbic system is involved in motivation and reinforcing behaviors, and many of the structures are critical in memory functions. The limbic system has its own input/processing side (including limbic cortex, amygdala, and hippocampus) and an output side (including the septal nuclei and hypothalamus; Rolls, 2019).

In regard to monitoring and regulating emotional responses, the amygdala plays an important role in coordination of behavioral, autonomic, and endocrine responses to emotionally laden stimuli. The amygdala ("almond" in Greek) is located in the anterior temporal lobe, receives inputs from all sensory systems, and is specifically involved in the coordination of responses to stress. LeDoux (2003) has focused much of the attention of emotion-related brain regions on the amygdala through his research establishing the amygdala as the primary center of fear-related processing. The amygdala is reliably observed to activate in response to threatening or fearful stimuli, but not for stimuli related to positive emotions. Patients with lesions in their amygdala have a reduced stress response, in particular for emotional responses. Research protocols wherein the amygdala was stimulated produced behavioral arousal and rage reactions (Berboth & Morawetz, 2021). The hippocampus is another processing structure within the limbic system and it is located in the medial aspect of the temporal lobe. The hippocampus receives reciprocal connections within the cortex in addition to outputs along the fornix. The hippocampus is responsible for understanding spatial relations with the environment and encoding memory, specifically, declarative memories. Established memories are transferred to other areas of the cerebral cortex and have association areas in the frontal lobe and parieto–temporal–occipital association cortex.

Another cortical area that is important for conditioned emotional responses is the prefrontal cortex. The adjacent orbitofrontal cortex has been implicated in the regulation of emotional behavior and is considered to provide an inhibitory influence on impulsive emotional responses (Bechara et al., 2000). It has strong connections with the amygdala and the cingulate gyrus, providing evidence to support this role. Damage to the orbitofrontal cortex is associated with disinhibited behaviors, especially aggressive behaviors. This area of the cortex is also strongly affected by alcohol consumption. Additionally, the prefrontal cortex is highly involved in mood regulation. For example, depression has been associated with increased activity in portions of the frontal lobe (Rudebeck & Rich, 2018). Another cortical structure implicated in mood disorders is the nucleus accumbens, a small cluster of neurons within the basal ganglia. Changes in activity in this region are associated with symptoms of depression (Nestler & Carlezon, 2006) and obsessive-compulsive disorder (Park et al., 2019). The nucleus accumbens has been shown to be particularly important to the process of positive reinforcement and reward and is often identified as the brain's "pleasure center" (LeGates et al., 2018). Research has demonstrated that it is active in response to rewarding stimuli, both physiological (e.g., substances) and psychological (Bayassi-Jakowicka et al., 2022).

THEORIES OF MOTIVATION

Motivation is the internal force that pushes the individual toward action and is generally considered to be composed of three components—arousal, direction, and intensity (Deckers, 2018). Motivation can either be directed toward internal rewards (intrinsic) or toward external rewards (extrinsic). The first theories of motivation focused on instinctual processes, such as Darwin's natural selection model and Freud's model, which postulates that motivation is a function of an organism's attempts to reduce the urge of a biological drive, such as hunger or sexual desire. Currently, instinctual models are not widely used, as they have been found to be too simple to describe most human behavior. Other theories of motivation have focused on drives, needs, and cognitive processes.

Drive Theories
Drive theory revolves around the concept of homeostasis (Bouton, 2007), which is the idea that an organism works to keep a physiological equilibrium. When the equilibrium is upset, the

organism has a need and is then motivated to engage in behavior that will reestablish equilibrium (drive reduction). For example, when the body is depleted of energy, this upsets the internal equilibrium and the organism will seek to find food.

Clark Hull is among the most influential theorists that developed drive theory. He used the term *drive* to refer to states of arousal caused by biological or physiological needs (e.g., hunger, need for warmth, thirst). These are considered *primary drives*—those that are biological and innate. Drives that are learned through experience, such as achieving wealth, are *secondary drives*; they are not innate and do not directly support a biological need. Hull (1943), like other behaviorists, believed that behavior can be explained by conditioning and reinforcement. He developed a formula to describe motivation using habit strength, drive strength, and excitatory potential (how likely is the individual to respond to the stimulus), although it has limited practical utility.

Drive theory has been extensively studied and has found a substantial amount of support. Attachment theorists have identified drive reduction as a mechanism behind attachment behavior in infants (Dollard & Miller, 1950). Zajonc (1965) used drive theory to develop an explanation of social facilitation. However, drive theory falls short in that it does not consider how secondary reinforcers reduce drives. For example, money allows you to purchase primary reinforcers (e.g., food, water, and clothing), but it does not directly reduce the drive itself. However, money continues to act as a powerful reinforcer. Drive theory would suggest a linear relation between these variables, and research has indicated that there is a cognitive component that intervenes in the direct stimulus–response interaction. That is, the response becomes a habit only if it is reinforced and the organism will engage in that response only if it anticipates a positive outcome (Dickinson & Balleine, 1994).

Another consideration around drive theory is the concept of frustration and its impact on motivation. Early research demonstrated that frustration can increase motivation more than reward. By frustration, they refer to thwarted anticipation of rewards and they showed that, in the context of the expectation of a large reward, no reward (or even a small reward) can lead to increased motivation to continue or complete a task. This research in frustration helps to explain paradoxical reward effects, which occur when a reward seems to weaken a response rather than strengthen it (Bouton, 2007).

Need-Based Theories

The most well-known of the need-based theories is Abraham Maslow's hierarchy of needs. Maslow theorized that individuals are motivated to act based on certain needs and that these needs can be understood in a hierarchical fashion: from the most basic physical needs to more abstract intellectual and psychological needs. At its base are physiological needs (e.g., food, water, sleep). Similar to the drive theory, individuals will be motivated to engage in behaviors that fulfill physiological needs. Maslow further hypothesized that individuals will not be motivated to engage in behavior that will fulfill a higher-level need (e.g., social support) until lower-level needs are met. Only then will an individual reach psychological health. Maslow's hierarchy of needs (Maslow, 1970) is listed as follows, from basic to highest levels:

1. *Physiological:* food, water, sleep, and sex
2. *Safety:* shelter, employment, and health
3. *Love/belonging:* friendship and family
4. *Esteem:* self-esteem, achievement, and respect of others
5. *Self-actualization:* morality and creativity

Little research evidence supported Maslow's theory, and it has generally fallen out of favor among motivation theorists. Need-based theories, however, have remained.

Workplace motivation was thought to have two factors: intrinsic and extrinsic motivation (Herzberg et al., 1959). They also delineated motivators, elements such as recognition and work challenges, which provide positive reward and satisfaction, and hygiene factors such as security and status, which reduce motivation in their absence. Atkinson and McClelland developed the need for achievement theory, which postulates that motivation is governed by three considerations—achievement, authority, and affiliation (McClelland, 1965). Achievement is the need to find a sense of accomplishment through advancement and feedback. Authority is the need to lead and to make an impact. Affiliation is the need to be liked and to develop positive social interactions. According to the theory, people have varying degrees of each of the three motivational needs, and this theory is particularly relevant in industrial and organizational (I/O) psychology.

A more recent theory, self-determination theory, focuses on the idea that humans have "inherent growth tendencies" that lead to consistent effort (Deci & Vansteenkiste, 2004). This theory centers on intrinsic motivation and consists of three basic needs—competence, relatedness, and autonomy. Competence is the need to develop mastery. Relatedness is the need to develop relationships with others. Autonomy is the need to have control in one's own life while maintaining relationships with others.

Learning Theories

B. F. Skinner's description of operant conditioning (Skinner, 1938) can also be understood in the context of motivation. Skinner did not agree with Hull that a drive must be reduced in order for learning to occur. Instead, Skinner focused on the extrinsic reward as the motivation for behavior. Although he did not describe his thoughts as a theory, it is easy to understand why his model of behavioral modification informs the understanding of motivation; he took the focus of motivation from the internal forces that instinct and drive theories posit and applied them to the external contingencies of behavior.

Cognitive Process Theories

The most well-known of the cognitive process models is cognitive dissonance theory (Festinger, 1957). According to this theory, when individuals behave in a manner that is inconsistent with their values or beliefs, they will change their beliefs to manage the psychological tension created by the mismatch. This urge to cope with the dissonance generates motivation—either to change one's behavior or to change one's beliefs about the behavior. Most research indicates that people tend toward the latter solution.

Expectancy theory, developed by Vroom (1964), is another attempt to understand motivation, especially in decision-making and formulating expectations about the future. Expectancy theory relies on three components—valence, expectancy, and instrumentality—to understand behavioral motivation. Valence refers to how much one values a particular consequence and will lead an individual to approach or avoid a behavior. Expectancy is the belief that one possesses the resources to achieve a certain goal; instrumentality is the belief that completing a behavior will lead to a predictable outcome. Motivation is understood to be a combination of these three elements—individuals are motivated by a "motivational force" that is the product of the three elements.

▶ INTERRELATIONSHIPS AMONG COGNITION, EMOTION, AND MOTIVATION

The interrelationships among cognition, emotion, and motivation are complex and cut across all areas of human functioning. Many of the observed interrelationships are based on the theories that have been outlined in the rest of this chapter. This section will describe some of the more important contributions to the understanding of these interrelationships.

Albert Ellis was the first psychologist to describe the importance of the interaction of cognition and emotion in normal and abnormal functioning, particularly in disorders like depression. He established rational emotive behavior therapy (REBT), which focused on how thoughts determine emotion. Ellis focused on "self-defeating" thoughts and postulated that these led to maladaptive behavior and pathological emotional states. He felt that helping an individual reduce these irrational thoughts would reestablish healthy emotions and behavior (Ellis, 1976).

Aaron Beck expanded on the influence of cognition on emotion and introduced the concept of automatic thoughts and cognitive distortions and hypothesized that these concepts were primarily responsible for disruptions of normal emotional functioning. Automatic thoughts are a stream of thoughts that we notice and are understood as accurate interpretations of reality by the individual. Automatic thoughts are well-learned interpretations and often interpret reality in ways that are biased, either negatively or positively. This bias is reflected in cognitive distortions (Beck et al., 1979). Cognitive distortions, or negative thinking, can be characterized by certain themes, including: magical thinking (e.g., I know what they are thinking), perfectionism (e.g., unless I do everything perfectly, life is intolerable), all or nothing (e.g., if I am not exceling at my job, I am a failure), and personalization (e.g., a parent feels responsible for their child's poor grades/bullying). Beck theorized that cognitive distortions lead to disrupted mood disorders such as depression.

The theory of learned helplessness (Seligman & Maier, 1967) was developed in explanation of research that found that animals exposed to inescapable pain will eventually stop trying to avoid the pain, even when opportunities to escape were presented. This theory has been considered a possible explanation for depression, as individuals develop a sense that they are unable to escape pain and feel helpless, which eventually leads to depression (Seligman, 1975).

Attributional theory developed from Seligman's work based on research showing that learned helplessness was not a universal phenomenon (Cole & Coyne, 1977). Weiner (1986) developed the concept of attributional style and globality/specificity, stability/instability, and internality/externality. Globality/specificity refers to whether an individual interprets events as a general response or a situation-specific response. Stability refers to the amount to which an individual expects a particular response to be consistent across time. Internality/externality refers to the extent to which an individual believes a result is caused by factors internal to the person or from the external environment.

Evaluative interactions between cognition and emotion have also been used to understand performance and job satisfaction. Equity theory (Adams, 1965) was among the first theories to apply cognitive/emotional interactions to these areas. This theory postulates that individuals assess the rewards from their work. If they feel underrewarded or overrewarded, they experience emotional distress and attempt to rectify these feelings by changing either their evaluations of or contributions to their work.

Goal-setting theory incorporated the fact that humans can plan for and form expectations about the future and that these expectations can assist individuals in reaching peak performance. Humans can set future goals that will then affect their behavior. Goal-setting theory also holds that the individual must have a commitment to the goal in order to maintain motivation. According to Locke (1968), goals affect behavior in four ways:

1. by directing attention,
2. by mobilizing efforts and resources for the task,
3. by encouraging persistence, and
4. by facilitating the development of strategies to complete the goal.

More recently, theories have been developed to understand the role of emotion and cognition in performance. Of particular interest is the role that anxiety (or autonomic arousal in general) plays in performance. The observable effects of anxiety on performance have been described with the Yerkes–Dodson law, which indicates that there is an optimal level of anxiety that will lead to peak performance (Yerkes & Dodson, 1908). If anxiety is too low or too high, performance will be negatively affected. Although the Yerkes–Dodson law describes the impact of anxiety on performance, it does not adequately explain the mechanisms at work.

Two competing theories proposed to understand the role of anxiety in performance are the conscious processing hypothesis and the processing efficiency theory. Conscious processing hypothesis postulates that increased anxiety associated with performance under pressure leads the individual to exert conscious control over a skill or activity that otherwise can be completed with automatic processing (Masters, 1992). This conscious focus on the skill disrupts the normally smooth automatic processing and leads to decrements in performance. Research has been equivocal for this theory (Mullen et al., 2005; Wilson et al., 2007). On the other hand, processing efficiency theory focuses on the effect anxiety has on the cognitive resources available to the individual. Processing efficiency theory predicts that increased stress will reduce the capacity of working memory, thus reducing the available resources to complete a given task (Eysenck & Calvo, 1992). Processing efficiency theory also provides an explanation for maintained or improved performance under pressure by postulating that, concomitant with decreases in working memory, there is an increase in the attention that is directed to the task. Research has generally been more supportive of processing efficiency theory over conscious processing hypothesis (Hardy et al., 2018; Wilson et al., 2007). Processing efficiency theory can account for the additive effects of cognitive anxiety on performance, whereas individuals might put forth great mental effort on tasks they deem more challenging (Wilson et al., 2007). Processing efficiency theory has been applied to test and sport performance anxieties.

Another resource-focused theory is conservation of resources, which postulates that the impact of stress and emotions on performance can be understood as a function of individual and group resources (Hobfoll, 1998). According to this theory, an individual is primarily motivated to build and maintain resources that will protect both the individual and the social system that supports the individual. Resources provide both the means to deal with stress and anxiety and the framework for an individual's appraisal of an event and ability to cope with the event. Individuals who already have reduced resources will be more vulnerable than those who have abundant resources; these vulnerable individuals will show reduced performance in the face of stress due to their depleted resources (von der Embse et al., 2018).

Recent research has also focused on the role of self-talk in performance. Self-talk is the verbalizations (internal or external) that allow individuals to regulate emotions, interpret perceptions, and provide instructions or feedback (reinforcement or punishment). This phenomenon has been associated with cognitive interference theory (Sarason, 1984), which postulates that negative self-talk unrelated to the task interferes with the individual's ability to perform adequately by drawing cognitive resources, such as attention, away from the task. This differs from the more contemporary understanding of self-talk in that current research tends to focus on self-talk related to the task. Self-talk has been a particular focus of research in sports psychology and has generally been found to be a significant predictor of performance, with negative self-talk leading to decrements in performance and positive self-talk to improvements in performance (Hatzigeorgiadis et al., 2011). Interventions to improve performance that incorporate training the individual in positive self-talk have been found to be more efficacious than interventions that do not (Hardy et al., 2018; Hatzigeorgiadis et al., 2011).

▶ REFERENCES

Full reference list available at http://examprepconnect.springerpub.com

KNOWLEDGE CHECK: CHAPTER 4

1. Which of the following statements regarding multisensory stimulation is most accurate?
   A. Multisensory stimulation has no effect on reaction time or learning.
   B. Multisensory stimulus impedes learning.
   C. Presenting stimulus across multiple senses is advantageous for learning.
   D. Stimuli presented across multiple senses becomes confusing, leading to slower reaction time.

2. Which of the following is the best definition of reflexive attention, otherwise called exogenous attention?
   A. A function of being alert and oriented to person, place, and time
   B. Bottom-up processing, wherein information is captured in a stimulus-driven fashion
   C. Feature binding that occurs at later stages of perceptual processing
   D. Top-down processing, wherein an individual actively chooses to attend to stimuli

3. You have just listened to a presentation in a large conference room and are catching up with a colleague while the conference room starts to fill up with the next group. You are in deep discussion with them about a recent case you saw, while you hear another group of individuals across the room mention your name related to research you presented earlier. This ability would be best defined as:
   A. Attentional blindness
   B. Reduction of distractor interference
   C. The cocktail party phenomenon
   D. Wakefulness

4. Which of the following statements does NOT best describe an aspect of executive functioning?
   A. Executive functions are processed in the prefrontal cortex.
   B. Executive functions aid in decision-making.
   C. Executive functions are not related to emotional distress.
   D. The constructs of working memory and executive functions are closely related.

(See answers on the next page.)

1. **C) Presenting stimulus across multiple senses is advantageous for learning.**
   Ongoing and previous research supports that our senses are designed to process simultaneous sensory inputs across multiple modalities in a parallel and reciprocal manner in order for information to be identified correctly and responded to appropriately. Thus, multisensory stimulation is beneficial for both learning and encoding information. Multisensory stimulation has in fact proven to reduce reaction time and enhance learning across domains. Multisensory stimulus significantly enhances association learning and retrieval in multiple domains. As stated before, stimuli presented across multiple domains leads to quicker reaction times. Research has indicated that responses to trimodal stimulus combinations were faster than those to bimodal combinations, which in turn were faster than reactions to unimodal stimuli.

2. **B) Bottom-up processing, wherein information is captured in a stimulus-driven fashion**
   Reflexive attention describes when sensory information is "captured" in a stimulus-driven fashion, referred to as a bottom-up mechanism. These are stimuli with high survival value, such as the odor of smoke indicating fire, and with high subjective value. Reflexive attention facilitates processing in the sensory cortex and can be demonstrated in the Posner paradigm. Being alert and oriented x3 is a function of general mental status, not an aspect of attention. Feature binding is a process that creates an integrated representation of an object. It allows us to memorize separate visual features (e.g., colors, shapes, orientations) and their conjunctions that characterize objects in the visual world. Top-down processing initiates with thoughts, which flow down to lower-level functions, such as the senses. It is guided by higher level cognitive functioning (e.g., executive functioning). Reflexive attention is part of bottom-up processing, wherein stimuli taken into consideration is more basic (i.e., sense) versus more complex (i.e., thoughts).

3. **C) The cocktail party phenomenon**
   The definition of the cocktail party phenomenon is a person's ability to tune their attention to one thing (typically auditory stimuli) from a multitude of stimuli. Attentional blindness is a failure to notice visual stimuli, which is attributed to attentional issues (e.g., focus was on another task) and not visuoperceptual impairment. Distractor suppression is the ability to disregard salient distractors when dealing with task-relevant information. This would be the opposite of being able to hear information from a conversation *outside* of the one you were having. This example is one of being able to attend to multiple stimuli at once, not suppress unrelated information. Wakefulness is the condition of being alert, and not sleepy. While this is absolutely necessary to be able to attend to and engage in conversations, it does not encompass all of the cognitive abilities necessary for these tasks.

4. **C) Executive functions are not related to emotional distress.**
   Executive functions are increasingly important because they are the cognitive domain most strongly associated with emotional distress and may reflect differing facets of underlying frontal lobe dysfunction. Executive functions are processed in the prefrontal cortex, basal ganglia, and thalamus. Executive functions do aid in decision-making, in addition to multitasking, and problem-solving. Working memory and executive functioning are closely related and share an underlying executive attention component, which is strongly predictive of higher level cognition.

5. The clinician is asked to complete an evaluation for a 15-year-old student who moved to the United States during elementary school from a Latin American Spanish-speaking country. They have been noted to have difficulties in history, English, and economics class. They appear to be proficient in English and do not appear to have word reading difficulties. What may be one of the many contributing factors to this student's difficulties?

   A. Biological sex
   B. Capacity to think rationally
   C. Specific learning disorder, with impairment in reading comprehension
   D. Specific learning disorder, with impairment in reading

6. Intelligence in psychology refers to the mental capacity to learn from experiences, adapt, understand abstract concepts, and use knowledge to manipulate one's environment. Which of the following is the only true statement applying to the field of intelligence?

   A. A. R. Luria's three-level theory of neuropsychological function is unrelated to intelligence test development.
   B. Cattell made a major contribution by identifying fluid and crystallized forms of intelligence.
   C. Spearman was a primary mental ability theorist.
   D. Additional types of general intelligence include (but are not limited to) visual and verbal memory (*Gvm*).

7. The clinician works in an inpatient unit for medically complex patients and the treatment team referred an English-speaking patient in their 50's for a potential left ventricular assist device (LVAD) due to end-stage heart failure. The clinician is creating a neuropsychological battery to ascertain their ability to care for the device postsurgery. In addition to testing multiple cognitive domains (e.g., memory, executive functioning, attention, processing speed), what would help round out the evaluation without adding undue burden to the patient?

   A. Abbreviated test of intelligence to determine baseline functioning
   B. Academic achievement assessments such as the Wechsler Individual Achievement Test or the Woodcock-Johnson
   C. Comprehensive intelligence measure, such as the Stanford-Binet Intelligence Scales
   D. Mini Mental Status Exam (MMSE)

8. Which of the following statements regarding bias in intelligence testing is true?

   A. Cross-cultural psychologists only care about a patient's native language.
   B. Increasingly, cross-cultural psychologists view ethnic differences on intelligence tests as a proxy for the effects of quality of education and acculturation.
   C. Intelligence testing is not a predictor of future success/outcomes.
   D. Stereotype threat does not influence test performance.

(See answers on the next page.)

5. **C) Specific learning disorder, with impairment in reading comprehension**
The best choice out of the options was specific learning disorder, with impairment in reading comprehension, as this would cause great difficulties in any class requiring interpreting and extrapolating information from written materials, especially at a high school level. Biological sex, while previously thought to be a predictor for specific cognitive strengths/weaknesses, has not had as much support in recent literature. While historically research has shown some sex differences in cognitive abilities, it would not be one of the main reasons for these broad academic difficulties. Capacity to think rationally is needed in any academic class; however, "rational thought" is not a cognitive construct that we can objectively test for. While a specific learning disorder, with impairment in reading (e.g., dyslexia), can cause academic difficulties in the stated classes, it was noted that this student's word reading in English was at expectations. Social acculturation issues may also be at play; however, that was not one of the answer choices.

6. **B) Cattell made a major contribution by identifying fluid and crystallized forms of intelligence.**
Cattell proposed that the Spearman theory of intelligence was actually composed of general fluid (Gf) and general crystallized (Gc) ability. A. R. Luria's three-level theory of neuropsychological function states that a particular area of the brain usually represents a single "factor" that is the foundation of different systems and supports numerous psychological functions. Luria's diagnostic tests include assessing for intellectual functioning. Spearman developed his two-factor theory of intelligence using factor analysis. The Spearman two-factor theory proposes that intelligence has two components: general intelligence ("g") and specific ability ("s"). Other types of general intelligence, often referred to as the "g's of intelligence," include general memory and learning (Gy) and broad visual perception (Gv).

7. **A) Abbreviated test of intelligence to determine baseline functioning**
As intelligence test administration takes between 1 to 2 hours before scoring and interpretation, depending on the test taker, abbreviated versions of tests have been developed to provide reliable, valid estimates of intellectual ability. These are most useful to assist in abbreviated batteries needed on medical inpatient units. Academic tests are not necessary for this referral question. This patient is not looking for academic accommodations; we need to assess their ability to comprehend the surgery and follow-up care. While a comprehensive intelligence measure would be nice to give, it is not appropriate in the setting in which the patient is being seen. This would place undue burden on the patient and take too long to provide a quick turnaround time to the referring physician. An MMSE would give the psychologist a quick glance at the patient's general cognitive functioning; however, it would not help us determine specific cognitive domains where the patient has deficits.

8. **B) Increasingly, cross-cultural psychologists view ethnic differences on intelligence tests as a proxy for the effects of quality of education and acculturation.**
Research has indicated that minority groups with more exposure to high-quality education performed similarly to the majority ethnicity, compared to those without exposure to higher quality education. Many cross-cultural clinical researchers recommend using the appropriate ethnic group measurement norm to improve diagnostic accuracy. Cross-cultural psychologists have a comprehensive view of patients and take into consideration much more than just a patient's native language. Intelligence testing can be a predictor of future success and general outcomes. It is definitely not the only factor. Stereotype threat theory states that female and minority test takers underperform on cognitive tests, as they experience pressure by negative stereotypes about their group's performance.

9. Protective factors against the deleterious effects of aging include control beliefs, social support, and _____.
   A. Agreeableness
   B. Early retirement
   C. Physical exercise
   D. Religiosity

10. Reinforcing behaviors makes them more likely to occur again. A negative reinforcer is found in _____ and causes response rates to _____.
    A. Classical conditioning; decrease
    B. Classical conditioning; increase
    C. Operant conditioning; decrease
    D. Operant conditioning; increase

11. Pop quizzes are utilized to help promote continuous studying in students. To produce consistent performance over time, one would employ a/an _____ schedule of reinforcement.
    A. Continuous reinforcement
    B. Fixed interval
    C. Ratio
    D. Variable interval

12. Learning rates have been utilized in computer/machine learning. For the fastest learning rates, one would employ a _____ schedule of reinforcement.
    A. Continuous reinforcement
    B. Fixed ratio schedule
    C. Variable interval schedule
    D. Variable ratio schedule

13. A new hire completes their to-do list by Thursday each week, as they know their manager will review completion every Friday. What type of schedule of reinforcement is occurring in this scenario?
    A. Continuous reinforcement
    B. Fixed interval schedule
    C. Fixed ratio schedule
    D. Variable interval schedule

(See answers on the next page.)

9. **C) Physical exercise**
Protective factors against age-related decline in cognitive function include frequency of cognitive activity, control beliefs, social support, and physical exercise. While openness has been shown to be positively correlated with cognitive resilience in some studies, agreeableness, conscientiousness, or extraversion have not shown to be consistently associated with cognitive resilience. Early retirement has been found to cause an increased risk in cognitive decline. While religiosity has some protective abilities, as it adds a purpose to life, community, and social support, it is not thought to be a main contributing factor to prevent cognitive decline.

10. **D) Operant conditioning; increase**
In operant conditioning, negative reinforcement increases the conditioned response. Operant conditioning centers on the idea of reinforcement. Negative reinforcement allows the person or animal to remove the negative stimuli in exchange for a reward. Classical conditioning deals with involuntary responses, so one cannot negatively reinforce a behavior. While this is a good example of operant conditioning; a negative reinforcer would increase response rates, not decrease them.

11. **D) Variable interval**
A variable interval schedule enforces persistence in a behavior over a long period of time due to unpredictability effects where people do not know when they will be rewarded or punished. The advantage of continuous reinforcement is that desired behavior is typically learned quickly, although it is difficult to maintain over a long period of time. A fixed interval schedule of reinforcement does have a high response rate near the end of the interval, although a slower response rate is observed directly after delivery of the reinforcer. The predictability of rewards can decrease motivation over time. Ratio schedules produce high rates of output. That is, they follow the rule that the more the work, the more the reward, or to maximize rewards, one maximizes output. Gambling and lottery games are good examples of a reward based on a variable ratio schedule.

12. **A) Continuous reinforcement**
If the reinforcer follows every instance of the conditioned stimulus, it is called continuous reinforcement, and it is the fastest way to learn. It is especially effective to learn a new behavior. A fixed ratio is the number of times an action must be done in order to receive an award. The weaknesses include postreward pause and quick extinction. Variable-interval involves reinforcement of a target behavior after an interval of time has passed. After the reward has been applied, the frequency of behavior drops. In addition, the predictability of rewards can decrease motivation over time. Variable ratio schedule is a partial schedule of reinforcement in which a response is reinforced after an unpredictable number of responses. While it does make for a high level of motivation, it is not the fastest way to learn since you do not know when the reinforcement will occur.

13. **B) Fixed interval schedule**
A fixed interval schedule leads to intermittent behavior with response rates remaining relatively stable, and then starting to increase as the reinforcement time nears and then slowing down immediately after the reinforcement is delivered. Continuous reinforcement would mean that the to-do list was completed and reviewed each day (or on a consistent basis). An example of a fixed ratio schedule would be if the manager reviewed work after every third task was completed. An example of a variable interval schedule would be the manager checking in on tasks completed every 2 to 5 days.

14. What neuroanatomical structure manages movement and if damaged can cause difficulties in learned motor skills (e.g., walking, turning, and initiating tasks)?
    A. Basal ganglia
    B. Cerebellum
    C. Hippocampus
    D. Thalamus

15. B. F. Skinner, best known for his theory of operant conditioning, argued that _____ creates wanted behaviors.
    A. Extrinsic reward
    B. Intrinsic reward
    C. Meditation
    D. Punishment

16. Working memory is an aspect of executive functioning. Working memory can be best described as:
    A. A component of long-term memory (LTM)
    B. A component of short-term memory (STM) that allows you to manipulate information
    C. Memories you need to work hard to remember
    D. Sensory memory

17. William James and Carl Lange had a theory about emotional experiences. Which statement best describes the critiques of the James–Lange theory?
    A. If you imagine an emotion, your experience will be muted.
    B. One cannot experience an emotion until they experience a physiological response.
    C. Physiological responses are not necessary precursors to the experience of emotion.
    D. You need to see a stimulus in order to experience an emotion.

18. Memory systems that are distinct from each other can be separated by functioning, in addition to neuroanatomical underpinnings. Nondeclarative memory is characterized by being:
    A. Explicit in nature
    B. Memories too painful to recall
    C. Memories we do not know we have
    D. Memories we do not want to talk about

(See answers on the next page.)

14. **A) Basal ganglia**
    Damage to the basal ganglia can result in deficits in learned motor skills and habits. The basal ganglia are associated with procedural learning and voluntary motor movements. Lesions in the basal ganglia can cause significant conditions, including but not limited to dystonia, Parkinson disease, and Huntington disease. The cerebellum maintains motor equilibrium and calibration of movements. While it is essential in maintaining gait, stance, and balance, its primary function is not in learned motor skills. The hippocampus is involved in memory, learning, and emotion. Its primary function is to hold short-term memories and transfer them to long-term storage in our brains. The thalamus is the brain's primary relay system. It also regulates consciousness and alertness.

15. **A) Extrinsic reward**
    B. F. Skinner maintained that none of us has free will and that external rewards are the motivation for behaviors to occur. Intrinsic rewards, or intrinsically motivated activities, were thought to be those for which the reward was in the activity itself. Meditation is a behavior that can help create a calm environment and thus can be seen as a self-regulation strategy for stress management. Punishment would discontinue a behavior according to Skinner, not increase a behavior.

16. **B) A component of short-term memory (STM) that allows you to manipulate information**
    Working memory is an aspect of STM, wherein information is held and later manipulated to provide a response. It allows us to work with information without losing track of the task we are completing. Working memory is not LTM, but an aspect of STM. Working memory requires mental manipulation; it is not an aspect of retrieving old memories. Working memory and sensory memory are both parts of STM. However, sensory memory is very brief, up to a second, while working memory is related to executive functioning and helps retain a small amount of information.

17. **C) Physiological responses are not necessary precursors to the experience of emotion.**
    Critiques of the James–Lange theory focused on the nature and response of the autonomic nervous system. In sum, they stated that the experience of a physiological reaction is not necessary to have an emotional response. They also discussed that various emotions share the same physiological reaction. You can experience an emotion even if you imagine it, based on the James–Lange theory. The theory postulates that emotions stem from your interpretation of your physical sensations. James–Lange theory specifically suggests that emotions occur as a result of physiological reactions to emotions. Critiques did not focus on seeing a stimulus. Critiques focused on the fact that physiological changes occur too slowly to trigger sudden emotion.

18. **C) Memories we do not know we have**
    Nondeclarative memory consists of items the knower is unaware of knowing (implicit) yet can still demonstrate knowledge of them. Explicit memory refers to cases of conscious recollection. Research has shown that emotional content is easier to recall. Nondeclarative memory is procedural (e.g., skills and actions); for example, knowing how to ride a bike. Although there may be memories about these skills that we do not want to talk about, that is unrelated to nondeclarative memory.

19. H.M. was a man who had lost his ability to form new memories. Damage to which structure in his brain was mainly responsible for his cognitive difficulties?
    A. Frontal cortex
    B. Hippocampus
    C. Hypothalamus
    D. Thalamus

20. Which theory of emotion postulates that physiological sensations are the primary element of emotional experience?
    A. Cannon–Bard theory
    B. Circumplex model
    C. James–Lange theory
    D. Two-factor model

21. Emotions are first physiological and then brought into thought/consciousness. The interpretation of emotional experience through cognitive processes is known as:
    A. Cognitive appraisal
    B. Cognitive assessment
    C. Cognitive dissonance
    D. Emotional decision-making

22. Fear is one of the strongest emotions a mammal can feel. Which brain region is the primary center of fear-related processing?
    A. Amygdala
    B. Cingulate gyrus
    C. Hippocampus
    D. Ventromedial prefrontal cortex

(*See answers on the next page.*)

19. **B) Hippocampus**
    A man identified only as H.M. lost the use of his hippocampus and amygdala on both sides of his brain. The hippocampus is the main structure for consolidating long-term memories. The frontal cortex helps us make decisions, multitask, manage our emotions, and organize information. The hypothalamus helps our bodies regulate appetite, weight, and body temperature. It is not directly involved in memory. The thalamus helps relay motor and sensory signals (except smell) to the cerebral cortex. It is also involved in regulating sleep, alertness, and wakefulness. The thalamus is connected to the limbic system, which is involved in processing emotions and the formation and storage of memories, although that is not its primary function.

20. **C) James–Lange theory**
    The theory that postulates that changes in physiological sensation are the primary element of emotional experience is generally referred to as the James–Lange theory of emotion, as the theory was independently proposed by William James and Carl Lange. The Cannon–Bard theory, also known as the Thalamic theory of emotion, proposed that outside events can cause independent emotional and physical responses at the same time. The circumplex model of emotion suggests that the two underlying neurophysiological systems of valence and arousal subserve all emotional states. In addition, it states that there are layered cognitive processes that interpret and refine emotional experience according to salient situational and historical contexts. The two-factor theory of emotion is also known as the Schachter–Singer theory, which proposed that our experiences of emotions depend on both physiological arousal and our cognitive interpretation of the arousal.

21. **A) Cognitive appraisal**
    Schachter and Singer concluded that an individual must cognitively appraise a situation in order to determine their emotional state. This model of emotion has been known by the term cognitive appraisal. Cognitive assessment refers to an evaluation of someone's abilities in various cognitive domains. At times, cognitive assessments will include assessments of emotions, but this is not an individual's interpretation of their emotions. Cognitive dissonance is the feeling of discomfort someone feels when their behavior does not align with their values or beliefs. Emotional decision-making is referring to making decisions based on your emotions and not facts or objective information. Emotional decision-making is neither good nor bad.

22. **A) Amygdala**
    LeDoux established through his research that the amygdala is the primary center of fear-related processing. The amygdala is reliably observed to activate in response to threatening or fearful stimuli but not for stimuli related to positive emotions. The cingulate cortex is an important part of the limbic system. While it does help regulate pain and emotions, it is not the *primary* center for processing fear-related information. Also a part of the limbic system, the hippocampus' primary function is to hold short-term memories and then transfer them to long-term storage. The ventromedial prefrontal cortex's main function is in decision-making and inhibition. It is involved in emotion, reward, motivation, and threat detection. While it does play a role in fear-related emotions, it is not the *primary* center for fear-related information.

23. A parent has been referred to see a psychologist to assist in helping increase their child's participation in household responsibilities, including their homework. They originally promised their child would get $50 a week if they consistently completed the required tasks. However, without discussing with their child, the parent changed the reward to $5 a week. After a month, the parent noticed their child's motivation to complete tasks decreased. The child ultimately discontinued participation in previously agreed upon tasks. What term would be best to describe the reason behind the child's behavior?

    A. Arousal
    B. Drive
    C. Paradoxical reward effects
    D. Valence

24. Aaron Beck's cognitive therapy includes cognitive distortions, automatic thoughts, and _____.

    A. Cognitive bias
    B. Resistance
    C. Self-actualizing
    D. Self-defeating thoughts

25. The clinician was referred a young adult patient with a history of temporal lobe epilepsy (TLE) and concurrent depression. They reported frustration and sadness related to functional difficulties and changes in their cognitive functioning. Specifically, they noted a decline in their memory functioning, making it harder to recall recent conversations and tasks they need to complete. While thinking about how to conceptualize this therapy case, the clinician may want to keep in mind the neuroanatomical area that may be impacted by their TLE. This neuroanatomical substrate is the:

    A. Anterior cingulate cortex
    B. Cerebellum
    C. Heschl gyrus
    D. Hippocampus

26. A psychologist works in a community mental health clinic and is doing a chart review and intake evaluation. The patient is a 45-year-old cisgender male who is referred for difficulties managing his anger both at work and home. The referring primary care provider reported difficulties have been going on for at least 5 years, with an increase in the last several months. Of note, the patient reported he recently increased his alcohol consumption from several beers on a weekend to drinking at least one 6-pack of beer most nights of the week. While conceptualizing this case, which neuroanatomical substrate may be implicated in the patient's presentation?

    A. Anterior cingulate cortex
    B. Hypothalamus
    C. Mammillary bodies
    D. Orbitofrontal cortex

(See answers on the next page.)

23. **C) Paradoxical reward effects**
    Motivation is the internal force that pushes the individual toward action. However, when a person experiences frustration, it can help explain paradoxical reward effects, which occur when a reward seems to weaken a response rather than strengthen it due to preconceived notions of how large the reward would be. The arousal theory of motivation posits that motivation is dictated by specific levels of mental alertness. This would not be the best theory to help understand this child's underlying level of motivation. Drive is related to increased arousal and motivation to achieve a goal or purpose. While drive is certainly involved in the child's initial decision to complete their homework, it was not involved in the child's decision to discontinue participation. Valence refers to the emotional orientations people hold with respect to outcomes or rewards. For example, it can refer to the amount of *want* or *desire* that someone has for an extrinsitic (e.g., money) or intrinsic (e.g., satisfaction) reward. This is related to the child's initial motivation to complete the tasks; however, it is not related to their decision to ultimately discontinue participation.

24. **A) Cognitive bias**
    Cognitive bias is a term Aaron Beck used to describe unhelpful or faulty thinking patterns. These biases were also called *automatic thoughts,* which suggest they were not full conscious thought processes. Resistance refers to a patient's unconscious opposition to exploration of memories, based on Freud's theory. Resistance is also a term used in motivational interviewing. Self-actualizing is one of Maslow's levels in his hierarchy of needs. Self-defeating thoughts are part of rational emotive behavior therapy by Albert Ellis.

25. **D) Hippocampus**
    Seizures, especially ones that start in the temporal lobe, typically affect the hippocampus. The hippocampus is involved in learning, memory, and emotion. Unfortunately, it is particularly sensitive to changes in brain activity. Seizures in the cingulate are rare and cause motor symptoms, fear, laughter, and some personality changes. They are classified as a form of frontal lobe epilepsy, and it is difficult to detect seizure onset from this area. Memory is not a main symptom of frontal lobe epilepsy. The cerebellum is not traditionally associated with epilepsy. However, the cerebellum can play a role in seizure networks and can be a target for treatments. Seizures can arise from the Heschl gyrus, although it is quite rare. Seizures originating in the Heschl gyrus has been called musicogenic epilepsy, wherein seizures are provoked by listening to or playing music.

26. **D) Orbitofrontal cortex**
    The adjacent orbitofrontal cortex has been implicated in the regulation of emotional behavior and is considered to provide an inhibitory influence on impulsive emotional responses. Damage to the orbitofrontal cortex is associated with disinhibited behaviors, especially aggressive behaviors. This area of the cortex is also strongly affected by alcohol consumption. The anterior cingulate cortex is most directly involved in regulating attention, emotion, inhibitory control, and motivation. While these play a role in anger management and consuming high levels of a substance, it is not the best answer out of the available choices. The hypothalamus helps keep our bodies in homeostasis (e.g., normal and balanced state of body temperature, hunger, heart rate, etc.). It acts as a link between the nervous and endocrine systems. The mammillary bodies are part of the limbic system and are involved in recollective memory.

27. A psychologist is working in a college that has a large sports program. They are working with a student athlete who has recently reported difficulties performing at their best on game day. The patient noted increased sadness and frustration due to poor performance and a recent conversation with their coach that they may be benched for the next game. What type of intervention should the psychologist employ to assist in improving the student athlete's performance on the field?

   A. Acceptance and commitment therapy (ACT)
   B. Psychoanalysis
   C. Rational emotive behavior therapy (REBT)
   D. Training in positive self-talk

28. A psychologist is consulting at an elementary school and assisting a teacher to increase students' participation in learning exercises both at home and in the classroom. The teacher has implemented exercises to help increase the positive relationships between the students and between the teacher and the students. What else should they be focusing on fostering in the classroom to improve students' motivation to learn?

   A. Autonomy
   B. Conscientiousness
   C. Engagement
   D. Kindness

29. Which of the following is the BEST definition of signal detection theory (SDT)?

   A. A recurring brain state in which an individual is conscious and responding to the external world
   B. The ability to focus on a particular object for a period of time while ignoring distractions
   C. The observation that two individuals confronted with the same stimulus presentation may come to different conclusions and may not agree on the intensity or presence of a simple stimulus
   D. The failure to notice unexpected but perceptible stimuli in a visual scene when a person's attention is focused elsewhere

(See answers on the next page.)

27. **D) Training in positive self-talk**
Interventions focused on improving an individual's use of self-talk have been found to provide positive improvements in performance. ACT is an action-oriented, evidence-based, psychotherapy which stems from behavior therapy and cognitive behavioral therapy (CBT). While it may be helpful in work-related stressors and general anxiety, it would not be *the best* option for athletic-specific performance coaching. Psychoanalysis is a set of theories and therapeutic techniques to help treat psychological distress by exploring the interactions of conscious and unconscious elements by several techniques including dream interpretation and free association. There is a role for psychoanalysis in sports, as consultants can help explain behaviors that are influenced by unconscious factors. While this is an option, there is limited randomized controlled trial evidence; therefore, this is not the *best* answer out of the choices provided. REBT is a type of CBT that is focused on assisting and improving patients who suffer from irrational beliefs. Research is in its nascent stages for REBT's use in sports performance coaching and therefore not the *best* answer choice here.

28. **A) Autonomy**
Self-determination theory centers on intrinsic motivation and consists of three basic needs—competence, relatedness, and autonomy. Researchers have found that students show a greater intrinsic motivation toward learning when teachers encourage a culture of autonomy. This would include facilitating ways for them to feel supported while they explore and supporting trial and error while implementing solutions to their problems. Conscientiousness is also a great characteristic to help foster in students, as it mediates the relationship between motivation and academic success. Conscientious students have high academic self-efficacy. However, autonomy gives a greater intrinsic motivating factor, and therefore is the best choice. Engagement can be emotional, behavioral, or cognitive in nature. Self-determination theory suggests that students' motivation (i.e., moving from motivation → extrinsic motivation → intrinsic motivation) is enabled by supporting the three universal needs: autonomy, competence, and relatedness. Thus, engagement is not the best answer choice. While kindness is a great foundation for any teacher to help foster emotional connectedness and general engagement with students, it is not a main component of self-determination theory.

29. **C) The observation that two individuals confronted with the same stimulus presentation may come to different conclusions and may not agree on the intensity or presence of a simple stimulus**
SDT is the observation that two individuals confronted with the same stimulus presentation may come to different conclusions and may not agree on the intensity or presence of a simple stimulus. SDT disagreement may occur due to differences in discriminability or response bias. A recurring brain state in which an individual is conscious and responding to the external world refers to wakefulness, which is a recurring brain state in which an individual is conscious and responding to the external world. The ability to focus on a particular object for a period of time while ignoring distractions refers to selective attention. The failure to notice unexpected but perceptible stimuli in a visual scene when a person's attention is focused elsewhere refers to inattentional blindness. For example, individuals who are actively tracking an aspect of a sports event, such as basketball shots, may fail to notice a person in a gorilla suit walking directly through the game.

Social and Cultural Bases of Behavior

Loretta E. Braxton, Jessica J. Fulton, Jennifer Yi, Stephanie Salcedo Rossitch, and Raha Forooz Sabet*

BROAD CONTENT AREAS
- Interpersonal, intrapersonal, and intergroup processes and dynamics
- Theories of personality
- Cultural and individual diversity

▶ INTRODUCTION

Increasing our understanding of how people think, feel, and act is useful in interpreting cultural norms, group dynamics, and interpersonal relationships. Answering questions such as how people explain behavior and events, how people think about groups, what puts people in a more aggressive frame of mind, and what underlies prejudice and stereotypes provides a foundation for competent clinical practice and research. Examining theories focused on understanding how environmental forces impact our behavior and studying evolutionary perspectives about our emotions and mate selection also add to our knowledge base of understanding human behavior. Furthermore, all these social and cognitive processes are inextricably linked to cultural and individual diversity factors. These topic areas are present as we negotiate our daily lives and raise interesting questions about our behavior and the behavior of those around us. As consumers of information, we benefit from learning about fundamental concepts such as error and bias. We learn from each other, and our knowledge is transmitted within our current systems. In this chapter, we review several broad areas, including social cognition, social judgments and interactions, aggression, prejudice, discrimination, implicit bias, group dynamics, social influences on individual functioning, theories of personality, environmental factors, and issues related to cultural bases of behavior.

SOCIAL COGNITION: STRUCTURES AND PROCESSES

Sometimes called impression formation, social cognition is the study of how people make sense of their social world; that is, how we make sense of ourselves, others, and ourselves in relation to others. Social cognition research indicates that the ways we behave and interact in the social world are facilitated by cognitive representations called schemas (Fiske & Taylor, 1991). Schemas are organized patterns of thought and behavior that influence what we attend to and how we absorb new information. Schemas help us organize information in an efficient manner by providing tentative explanations about incoming stimuli and a sense of prediction and control of our

---

* With acknowledgment of Christina Riccardi, PhD, and Samantha Kettle, PsyD, for their contributions to the previous edition.

social worlds. Schemas help us facilitate memory recall, are energy-saving devices, and are evaluative and affective. They are used for evaluation, role-playing, identification, and prediction. For example, when we evaluate individuals who have a certain role, we compare their behavior to our identified schema for that role. Role-playing is the script we use to help us decide how we will behave or how others should be behaving. Individuals are categorized and identified by the roles they have, and role schemas help us place individuals into a certain category by matching their observed behavior with our role schema. We predict the future behavior of individuals once we place them in a specific category/role, and we assume the individual will behave in accordance with our predictions of their behavior.

Types of Schema

Schema research has been applied to four main areas: person schema, event schema, role schema, and self-schema (Fiske & Taylor, 1991). Person schemas are attributes that we use to categorize people and make inferences about their behavior. We assess their skills, competencies, and values to make determinations about their personality traits. Event schemas, often referred to as cognitive scripts, provide the basis for anticipating the future, setting goals, and making plans. The cognitive scripts are the processes or practices we use to approach tasks or problems. Role schemas, often associated with stereotypes, include behavior sets and role expectations. These schemas tell us how we expect individuals in certain roles to behave. Self-schemas are cognitive representations about our self-concept, that is, perceptions of our traits, competencies, and values.

Heuristics

When we are faced with complex problems or incomplete information, we use mental shortcuts to form judgments, draw inferences, or make decisions in a quick and efficient manner. One of the strategies the mind employs to make sense of information or uncertainty is heuristics. Useful in many situations, heuristics are efficient thinking strategies to make things easier by saving us time and energy. However, due to their efficiency, heuristics can lead to errors in judgment and decision-making. There are many types of heuristics, but we will highlight two—availability and representativeness. Availability heuristic is a mental shortcut that comes to mind when an individual is evaluating a topic, decision, or concept, and is based on the notion that the easier information is to recall, the more impact it will have on subsequent decisions or judgments (Tversky & Kahneman, 1973). An example of availability heuristic is overestimating your likelihood of winning the lottery after seeing a television show about other lottery winners. You begin to invest more of your money in lottery tickets after learning about a lottery winner. Another example is that people who read successful stories about building a business are more likely to believe there is ease in taking on such a task. Representativeness heuristic is judging the likelihood of an event based on its resemblance to the typical case rather than base rates. In other words, it is a mental shortcut that helps us make a decision or judgment by comparing information to our typical mental models. However, representativeness heuristic tends to lead to more errors due to the overestimation of the likelihood that something will happen. For example, if given the description of a woman who is intelligent, ambitious, confident, and creative, representativeness heuristic would lead people to assume this woman is a college professor rather than a cashier or secretary, even though the base rate of cashiers and secretaries is much higher than that of college professors.

Models for Social Categorization

People rely on models of social categorization to facilitate their information processing—prototypical and exemplar models. Social objects, people, and events have typical or prototypical variables that represent the category. The more features that are shared in a category, the more efficiently and confidently social objects can be placed into the category. In contrast, exemplar models represent specific and concrete information about a category. Exemplar models represent the extreme instances within an overall general category. We tend to rely on both models—prototypical and exemplar—based on the conditions of information processing.

Attribution of Cause
Attributions provide explanations for behaviors and events. Heider (1958) theorized that people observe, analyze, and explain behaviors with explanations, although people attribute different kinds of explanations to behaviors. He differentiated between two types of causal attribution—dispositional and situational. Dispositional attribution refers to characteristics such as personality traits, motives, and attitudes. Situational attribution refers to social norms, external pressures, random chance, acts of God, and so forth. Heider explained that we tend to overestimate dispositional factors and underestimate situational factors, which is known as the fundamental attribution error.

Attribution Theories
Correspondent Inference Theory
Jones and Davis (1965) introduced correspondent inference theory, which posits that people make inferences about others' behavior when they are looking for a cause of their behavior. People make correspondent inferences by reviewing the context of the behavior. Correspondent inference theory describes how people identify explanations of people's personal characteristics from behavioral evidence. For example, a correspondent inference would be to attribute an individual's frequent anger outburst to an underlying stable trait within the person.

Covariation Model of Attribution
Kelley (1972) introduced the theory of covariation model of attribution, which contends that we assess similarities (covariation) across situations to help us make causal attributions in a rational and logical fashion. Covariation of behavior is assessed using three types of information: consensus information—how other people act in the same situation and with the same stimulus; distinctiveness information—how similarly people act in different situations toward different stimuli; and consistency information—how frequently people perceive the same stimuli and respond the same.

Weiner (1985) proposed a theory of motivation and emotion based on attribution achievement. He posits that attributions people make for success and failure elicit different emotional consequences that are characterized by three underlying causal dimensions: stable and unstable (the cause of the behavior is perceived as fixed [e.g., personality] or changeable [e.g., motivation or effort]; internal and external (locus of control—whether success or failure is attributed internally or externally); and controllable and uncontrollable (control—whether we feel we have any control over the cause).

Bias and Errors in Attributions
While trying to find rational and logical explanations for people's behavior, there is a tendency to fall into biases and errors. Bias occurs when the perceiver systematically distorts what are thought to be correct and logical procedures. Research has found evidence of persistent biases in attribution processes (Fiske & Taylor, 1991). Types of pervasive forms of attribution biases include fundamental attribution error, actor–observer difference, the self-serving bias, and culture bias.

The *fundamental attribution error* is the tendency to overvalue personal/dispositional explanations for behavior while undervaluing situational explanations. Fundamental attribution error is most noticeable when we are trying to explain the behavior of others. For example, if a friend is late to a lunch meeting with you, you are more likely to assume that your friend does not value your time rather than taking into account other explanations of why your friend may be late.

The *actor–observer bias* occurs when we attribute dispositional factors to other people's behavior while attributing situational factors to our behavior. For example, when an individual gets a poor grade on a test, we tend to attribute internal factors such as laziness or failure to study. Alternatively, if we get a poor grade, we tend to attribute it to situational factors that justify the outcome. For example, the test covered materials that were not addressed in the study guide.

The *self-serving bias* is the tendency to attribute dispositional factors for success and external, uncontrollable factors for failure. Sometimes called the self-enhancing bias, it refers to motivational factors that drive us to enhance our self-esteem when we succeed and to protect it when we fail.

The self-serving bias also operates at the group level. There is a tendency to protect the group(s) to which we belong, and research shows that we make attributions based on our group membership. For example, members of individualist cultures tend to engage in more self-serving bias than collectivist cultures.

Confirmation bias is when we search for, interpret, or recall information that confirms our preexisting beliefs or biases. For example, people who support or oppose a particular political issue or theory will seek individuals who support their position and interpret incoming newsfeeds in ways that uphold their existing positions.

The self-fulfilling prophecy is when a prediction causes itself to come true simply due to the fact that a person expects it to come true. For example, a college professor assumes that certain students are not intelligent and provides less positive feedback and more negative feedback, resulting in poorer performance by the students. The Barnum effect is the tendency for individuals to give high accuracy ratings to descriptions of their personalities that they presume are tailored to them. The descriptions are, in fact, vague and general and may apply to a wide range of people. A good example of the Barnum effect is the horoscope.

The illusory correlation is the perception that a relationship exists between variables (e.g., people, events, or behaviors) when only a minor or no relationship exists. A common example is believing there are more shark attacks than there actually are; this belief arises from more attention being drawn to shark attacks than when sharks do not attack (which is less attention grabbing).

Self-categorization is the process of deciding where we want to belong and how this makes a difference from others. The theory asserts that human beings are and act as both individuals and as part of social groups. A person may act as an individual in one context and as a group member in another. There is much flexibility in the way people define and perceive themselves. Individuals establish who they are through self-categorization.

SOCIAL JUDGMENTS AND INTERACTIONS

Social judgments are how we perceive people and social situations and how we form impressions about them. Two concepts are involved in forming impressions: filtering and inference. With respect to filtering, people tend to ignore much of what they see. With inference, people tend to go beyond the evidence in front of them and complete the picture that they filtered or did not see. Filtering prevents us from being overwhelmed by too much information, and inference allows us to complete pictures or stories with incomplete information; however, they also lead us to make errors of judgment. Prejudice and discrimination are normally associated with errors of judgment.

Impression Formation and Management

Impression formation is the process, conscious or subconscious, through which people form a global impression of each other. Asch (1946), based on his studies, found that forming impressions of others involves more than simply combining individual traits. A person's individual traits are seen in relation to each other and not individually. As such, a person's traits are seen as integrated, dynamic, and whole. Research has shown that primacy effect (i.e., information presented first has a greater impact) exists in impression formation. Asch's seminal research on formations of personality impression suggested that when adjectives describing a person are presented in sequence, the first adjectives have more impact than the later ones. The negativity bias is the tendency to give more weight to negative experiences and information over positive or neutral input, even when the negative information is inconsequential.

Some tactics used in impression formation are self-promotion, self-monitoring, and self-handicapping. *Self-promotion* occurs when individuals point out their abilities or accomplishments to be seen as competent by observers. *Self-monitoring* is the ability to regulate behavior to accommodate social situations or facilitate concern for situational appropriateness. People monitor their self-presentations, expressive behavior, and nonverbal affective displays to influence others' perceptions of them. *Self-handicapping* is creating obstacles because the person anticipates failure. The goal is to externalize failure while internalizing success. For example, if a student says, "I'm not going to do well on the biology test because I'm sick," then if the student gets a poor grade, they can blame it on illness instead of a lack of preparation or poor skill development. There are two types of self-handicapping: behavioral and verbal. In behavioral self-handicapping, people physically create obstacles to success. Verbal self-handicapping is orally expressing excuses for failure.

Affiliation and Attraction

Affiliation is the desire to be with others and form social relationships. There are a number of factors that affect how and when people affiliate with one another. Anxiety also increases the tendency to affiliate. In anxiety-provoking situations, social comparison, when we evaluate our opinions and abilities by comparing ourselves to others to learn how to define ourselves or to reduce uncertainty (Festinger, 1954), often leads to affiliation more so than relief from discomfort.

Attraction is a type of affiliation based on "liking." Attraction is affected by a number of factors, including physical attractiveness, proximity and exposure, similarity, reciprocity, self-disclosure, and reinforcement. Gain–loss theory posits that attraction is maximized when an individual's evaluation of a person is at first negative and then changes to positive. Social exchange theory (Blau, 1964) suggests that attraction occurs when the relationship's rewards exceed its costs and when the rewards and costs are reciprocal. People are likely to remain in a relationship when the rewards outweigh the costs and leave a relationship when the costs exceed the rewards. Equity theory also focuses on relationship rewards and costs, but suggests that perceptions of equity in a relationship are more important than the magnitude of costs and rewards.

Organizational Justice

Social exchange theory and equity theory also apply to individuals in the workplace. When an individual forms a relationship with other employees and the organization, the individual is likely to perform in ways that benefit other employees and the organization (Cropanzano & Mitchell, 2005). Further, evidence suggests that fairness in the workplace is associated with higher job satisfaction and performance (Konovsky, 2000; Konovsky & Cropanzano, 1991). Organizational justice refers to an individual's perceptions of fairness in organizations (Greenberg, 1987a), and individuals evaluate the fairness of three types of justice: distributive justice, procedural justice, and interactional justice.

Distributive justice refers to the fairness of outcomes (for a review, see Byrne & Cropanzano, 2001; Greenberg, 1990). Examples of outcomes include tangible distributions (e.g., office assignment, pay) and intangible distributions (e.g., recognition and praise).

Procedural justice refers to the fairness of processes through which outcomes are decided (Konovsky, 2000). Factors in the decision-making process that impact perceptions of fairness are the degree to which employee voice is considered (Folger & Lewis, 1993), appropriateness of performance appraisal criteria (Nathan et al., 1991), and accuracy of information used to decide on an outcome (Greenberg, 1987b).

Interactional justice is the treatment of the individual as decisions are made (Cropanzano et al., 2002); it has two components: interpersonal justice and informational justice. Interpersonal justice is the degree to which the individual is treated with dignity and respect when the decision is being made (Baron, 1993; Bies & Moag, 1986). Informational justice refers to the timeliness, specificity, and truthfulness of the justification or explanation of the decision (Bies, 1989; Bobocel & Farrell, 1996; Bobocel et al., 1997).

Distributive justice is more related to person-level outcomes (e.g., satisfaction with pay), whereas procedural justice is more related to organization-level outcomes (e.g., commitment to the organization; Sweeney & McFarlin, 1993). Procedural justice is the strongest predictor of managerial and organizational trust (Hubbell & Assad, 2005).

Prosocial Behavior

Altruism is the motivation to increase another's welfare. There is debate over the capability of humans to be truly altruistic and place the welfare of others in front of their own. The social exchange theory suggests that altruism exists when benefits outweigh cost. However, others suggest four categories that motivate altruism: altruism to benefit the self (egoism), to benefit the other person (altruism), to benefit a group (collectivism), or to uphold a moral principle (principlism). The empathy–altruism hypothesis suggests that altruism is evoked by the desire to help someone who is suffering. Feelings of concern for the other person are contrasted with personal distress, which leads people to act to reduce the negative emotions, which are experienced when suffering is witnessed.

Bystander effect occurs when individuals are less likely to offer help to a victim when other people are present. In fact, the probability of help is inversely related to the number of bystanders; responsibility is diffused in the presence of other people. One of the most infamous bystander examples is that of Catherine Genovese. On March 13, 1964, as she was entering her apartment building early in the morning in Queens, New York, Genovese was stabbed twice by a man. Genovese screamed for help and although her neighbors heard her, none came to her assistance. A dozen or so people claimed to have seen the attack and admitted they did not want to get involved. It is postulated that a simple phone call to the police would have helped, but everyone assumed someone else would do it. In addition to diffusion of responsibility, Latané and Darley (1970) found two other factors that influence bystander apathy: social comparison and evaluation apprehension. Social comparison occurs when a bystander seeks clarification of proper behavior by monitoring the cues of others. If others are not helping, the individual may surmise the situation is not an emergency and help is not needed. Evaluation apprehension is when the bystander may fear taking action due to embarrassment or social disapproval if the action taken is inappropriate.

AGGRESSION, PREJUDICE, DISCRIMINATION, AND IMPLICIT BIAS

Aggression

Aggression is any form of behavior directed toward the goal of harming or injuring another who is motivated to avoid such treatment (Baron & Richardson, 1994). The frustration–aggression hypothesis proposes that aggression is the result of frustration, which is produced whenever the ability to achieve a desired goal is blocked (Dollard et al., 1939). The objective of aggression is to move the block, but if the block cannot be removed, then aggression may be directed at another object. This theory was modified due to the lack of evidence of a causal relationship between frustration and aggression. Berkowitz (1971) suggested that frustration creates a readiness for aggression; however, expression of aggression requires both anger arousal and the presence of external aggressive cues. In contrast, social learning theory states that aggressive behaviors arise through the observation of others. Research has supported social learning of aggression (e.g., Bobo doll studies; Bandura, 1983). Recent research on the effects of viewing violence in the media has produced inconsistent results; however, the majority of studies conclude that viewing violence increases aggression.

Expression of aggression is affected by a number of factors. Deindividuation refers to the tendency of people to act aggressively when they believe their actions are anonymous. Social roles and expectations are influential in determining aggressive and antisocial behavior. For example, in Zimbardo's prison study (1970), student participants were assigned to roles as either prisoner or guard. Participants strongly adapted to their roles; some of those in the guard condition went as far as to torture those in the prisoner role, many of whom passively accepted the torture. The threat of retaliation often decreases aggressiveness; however, when provocation is coupled with the threat of retaliation, people are more likely to act aggressively—but the aggression may be displaced to someone other than the provocateur.

Prejudice and Discrimination

The field of psychology has long focused on causes, manifestations, and effects of oppression. Prejudice can be defined as an intolerant, unfair, or negative attitude toward an individual simply because of their group membership. Discrimination includes negative, unfair, and often aggressive acts toward members of a particular group. In other words, prejudice includes more of an affective component, whereas discrimination focuses chiefly on the behavioral component.

There are many causes of prejudice and discrimination, including stereotyping and perceived threat. Stereotyping occurs when an individual holds schemas about entire groups that contain oversimplified, rigid, and generalized impressions of members. This is the cognitive component of prejudice. It is important to note that the individual may not be aware of these beliefs, leading to more complex and ambivalent racial expressions sometimes referred to as "aversive racism" (Gaertner & Dovidio, 1986). Another cause may be perceived threat, or when an individual believes that a particular group represents a direct threat to one's well-being.

Although overt racism persists, symbolic (modern) racism is more prevalent. These types of prejudice and discrimination are less blatant and may include rejections of obvious forms of prejudice and discrimination. For example, someone may say "I'm not a racist" but oppose busing, welfare, affirmative action, and other programs, which would counter White privilege. Sue et al. (1997) highlighted the use of racial microaggressions or "brief and commonplace daily verbal, behavioral, or environmental indignities, whether intentional or unintentional, that communicate hostile, derogatory, or negative racial slights and insults toward people of color."

Recent studies have also focused on sexism and heterosexism. The term *homophobia* was coined by Weinberg (1972) to refer to antigay attitudes and behaviors. It may also be used to imply an irrational fear of homosexuality. Heterosexism is an ideological system that denies, denigrates, and stigmatizes among nonheterosexual forms of behavior, identity, relationships, or community (Herek, 1991). Heterosexism contains both individual and cultural components (Herek & Berrill, 1992).

Sexual prejudice refers to negative attitudes based on sexual orientation. Research focused on correlates of sexual prejudice have generally found higher levels of sexual prejudice among heterosexual men, as well as among individuals who are older, have lower levels of education, live in Southern or Midwestern states or in rural areas, or have limited personal contact with homosexuals (Herek, 2000).

Sexism was coined to label discrimination against men or women because of their identified sex. Studies indicate that "81% of 8th to 11th graders, 30% of undergraduates, and 40% of graduate students have been sexually harassed" (Sue & Sue, 2003, p. 407). Furthermore, several research studies have demonstrated that teachers may unwittingly promote sexism by responding differently to female and male students. For example, many studies show that math is considered to be a "male" domain, and communication is labeled differently (e.g., it is more acceptable for boys to interrupt; girls should raise their hands).

Implicit Bias

"Federal laws prohibit discrimination based on a person's origin, race, color, religion, disability, sex, and familial status" (Civil Rights Division, U.S. Justice Department, 2000, para. 1). Thus, overt expressions of prejudice are not only immoral but illegal. Prejudice continues to affect people's lives, although overt expressions have declined. There is a subtler, unintentional form of bias that has drawn attention in recent years—implicit bias, which refers to the internalized and unconscious attitudes and stereotypes that affect our attitudes and behaviors toward people. Characteristics of implicit biases include pervasiveness and malleability. Implicit biases are often inversely related to our explicit or declared beliefs. They are distinct from explicit biases but are not mutually exclusive (Staats et al., 2015).

Methods for Reducing Prejudice and Discrimination

Allport (1954) argues that intergroup prejudice arises from a combination of historical, cultural, economic, cognitive, and personality factors and proposes that because prejudice has multiple determinants, focusing on one will not lead to understanding and resolution of the problem. It is important to note that laws prohibiting discrimination can be effective even when they do not reflect public consensus.

Similar to the belief that aversive racism increases by staying in-group, contact hypothesis states that stereotypes will decrease when contact among members of different groups increases. However, this is not to say that contact alone is enough. People from both groups must have equal status and power and must have opportunities to disconfirm negative stereotypes about members of other groups. Additionally, contact should require intergroup cooperation to achieve mutual goals. This can be particularly challenging due to systematic and cultural components that perpetuate White privilege and heterosexism, and help other dominant groups to stay in power.

GROUP AND SYSTEM PROCESSES

Job satisfaction refers to an individual's attitude about the degree to which they are satisfied or dissatisfied with their job, with satisfaction levels existing along a continuum from favorable to unfavorable (Spector, 2022). According to Spector (2022), job satisfaction can be measured globally (i.e., an overall evaluation of the job) or by facets of the job (e.g., pay, nature of work, supervisor, organization's policies). Satisfaction with different facets of the job vary, and correlations among the job facets are modest (Spector, 1985). Four key areas of job satisfaction are nature of work, organizational context, rewards, and social environment (Locke, 1976). According to Hackman and Oldham's (1976) job characteristic theory, the five core characteristics of jobs are skill variety, task identity, task significance, autonomy, and job feedback. These core characteristics are theorized to impact job performance, job motivation, turnover, and job satisfaction. Job satisfaction is positively correlated with preferable job characteristics (Spector, 2022).

Psychological safety is the shared belief among team members that the workplace is safe for interpersonal risk taking (Edmondson, 1999). Indeed, the common findings across the large set of studies reviewed (especially at the group level) consistently support a relationship between psychological safety and learning studies; this relationship shows that individuals who experience greater psychological safety are more likely to speak up at work. Psychological safety is also associated with increased innovation in the workplace, task performance, employee satisfaction, and employee engagement. In addition, there is a positive relationship between psychological safety and employee commitment (Edmondson & Lei, 2014).

SOCIAL INFLUENCES ON INDIVIDUAL FUNCTIONING

Social influence occurs when an individual's attitudes, thoughts, feelings, or behaviors are affected by others. There are many responses to social influence. For example, people adjust their beliefs, attitudes, and behaviors based on their respect for others who have similar feelings. They also tend to adopt the attitudes of their social group if the majority of members hold particular beliefs. Kelman (1958) identified three effects on social behavior: compliance, identification, and internalization.

Compliance occurs when people change their behavior to obtain a reward or to avoid punishment. They appear to agree with others but actually keep their opposing thoughts and opinions private. Two methods of gaining compliance are the foot-in-the-door technique and door-in-the-face technique. The foot-in-the-door technique is presenting a small request that is difficult to refuse, setting the individual up to give in to a larger, desired request. The door-in-the-face technique is when a larger request that is more likely to be turned down is presented, then a smaller, more reasonable request is presented. *Identification* occurs when there is a behavioral change because of desired acceptance or to identify with another person. An example is when someone is influenced by an individual who is well regarded and respected, like a celebrity. *Internalization* is acceptance of a belief, attitude, or behavior that is expressed publicly and privately. People make changes based on the acceptance of others' beliefs and attitudes or behaviors.

The most common form of social influence is conformity. Conformity occurs when an individual changes a belief or behavior to fit in with a particular group or to meet the expectations of others. Examples of conformity are informational conformity (accepting information from others as evidence), normative conformity (pressure to conform to the positive expectations of others), and peer pressure. People's willingness to conform is affected by group unanimity, group size, group cohesiveness, and ability to express opinions anonymously. Two seminal studies on conformity were conducted by Sherif (1936) and Asch (1951). In a study examining autokinetic effect, the illusion that a light was moving, Sherif found that through social influence, the subjects changed their evaluations of how the light moved to conform to group experiences. Asch demonstrated that people are influenced by others in a group, specifically by how peer pressure impacts conformity. Study participants were given an unambiguous task during which they were asked to match the length of two lines. Confederates provided the wrong responses to the task, and the study participants agreed with them 37% of the time.

Obedience occurs when a person submits to a request of authority. Zimbardo's prison experiments (Haney et al., 1973) tested the effects of social roles on behavior and is an example of study participants' willingness to obey authority figures even in the face of conflicted personal conscience. Reactance occurs when a person feels that their choices or alternatives are being taken away or limited and the reaction is the opposite of what is desired (Brehm, 1972).

Social power is the exertion of influence over another person. French and Raven (1959) provided an early formulation of the bases of social power. They viewed social influence as the outcome of the exertion of social power from one of the five distinct bases: coercive, reward, expert, referent, and legitimate. An opinion or attitude change, usually conformity, was considered an instance of social influence whether it represented a true private change or not. A person's ability to influence someone is the result of two or more bases of power. The more varied the individual sources of power, the greater the ability to influence others.

Minority influence (Moscovici, 1985) occurs when the minority changes the opinion of the majority. Minority influence usually involves a shift in personal opinion. People often comply with the majority for normative reasons (to be liked or avoid punishment) and comply with the minority for informational reasons (e.g., minority has caused them to reevaluate their beliefs). Minority influence more likely occurs when the point of view is consistent, flexible, clear, and aligned with current social trends. Maass and Clark (1988) found that influence is more likely to occur when the majority or minority are a part of the "in-group," as influence is more likely among those who are similar.

Social impact theory (Latané, 1981) provides a framework for understanding outcomes in social situations. This theory posits that the effect of any information source on an individual will increase with three factors: strength of the source of the impact, immediacy of the event, and the number of sources imposing the impact. An impediment to any of these factors will attenuate the impact. A noted weakness of social impact theory is that it depicts people as passive recipients who accept social impact rather than as active pursuers. To expand on social impact theory, Latané and L' Herrou (1996) included group interactions to describe and predict the diffusion of beliefs through social systems. The new focus was called dynamic social impact theory, and it includes four components that influence how group dynamics operate and how ideas are diffused throughout the groups. The four components are consolidation—diversity reduced by minority opinion accepting the majority opinion; clustering—subgroups that emerge and hold differing opinions than the overarching population; correlation—previously disconnected ideas become connected in some way; and principle of continuing diversity—because there is clustering that causes subgroups to emerge, consolidation will not be able to wipe out minority opinion. This view suggests that people influence each other in a dynamic and iterative way.

Persuasion is the process of guiding oneself or another toward the adoption of some attitude by some rational or symbolic means. Cialdini (2001) defines six principles of persuasion that can contribute to an individual's propensity to be influenced by a persuader: reciprocity—return favors and pay back; commitment and consistency; social proof—people do things when they see others doing them; authority—people obey authority figures; liking—people are persuaded by people they like; and scarcity—sense of scarcity generates demand.

Additional theories about attitude change exist. Festinger's (1957) cognitive dissonance theory proposes that people desire consistency between two or more attitudes or between an attitude and a behavior. States of dissonance (or inconsistency) are unpleasant, prompting the person to eliminate the dissonance by changing one's attitude (e.g., changing one's attitude to believe something is more enjoyable when receiving very little compensation for your participation) or acquiring new information that reduces or altogether eliminates the inconsistency (e.g., smoking is bad for one's health but prevents weight gain).

Communication is also a powerful factor influencing attitude change. The elaboration likelihood model (Petty & Cacioppo, 1986) suggests that there are two communication routes to changing attitudes: peripheral and central. The central route focuses on cues relevant to the message and involves careful information processing. The peripheral route focuses on cues not relevant to the message and relies on mental shortcuts. The central route is activated when the message is perceived as important, the speaker is perceived as well-informed, the listener is not distracted, and/or the listener is in a neutral or negative mood. The peripheral route is activated when the message is perceived as unimportant, the speaker is perceived as uninformed, the listener is distracted, and/or the listener is in a positive mood. Not surprisingly, the central route is more likely to result in lasting attitude change.

Other communication factors influencing attitude change include communicator credibility, communication characteristics, and audience characteristics. Communicators are perceived as more credible when they are arguing against their own self-interests, have nothing to gain from persuading the audience, and are not intentionally directing their message to the audience. Additionally, presenting one or both sides of a message can impact how persuasive it is. If the audience is relatively uninformed about a topic, they are more likely to be persuaded by a one-sided argument. If the audience has an informed opinion on a topic, they are more likely to be persuaded by a two-sided message when the audience initially disagrees with the communicator's position and the communicator is relatively well-informed on the topic. Messages that are moderately discrepant (vs. minimally or extremely discrepant) from the audience's opinion are more likely to be persuasive. When two sides of an argument are being presented one after another, the side presented first is more likely to change attitudes (primacy effect); however, if there is time between the two presenting viewpoints, the second message is more likely to have greater impact on attitude change (recency effect).

Audience characteristics impacting the effectiveness of persuasive communication include mood and forewarning. When people are in a positive mood, they want to maintain their positive feelings. Accordingly, when they hear a message while in a positive mood, they are more likely to be persuaded because they are less likely to carefully process the information being presented (Schwarz et al., 1991). However, this finding typically applies only when the message is relatively weak. Strong messages are more likely to persuade persons in a neutral or bad mood (Bless et al., 1990). Forewarning in social psychology refers to the finding that people are less likely to be persuaded by a message if they are told in advance that they will be hearing a persuasive message, especially when the message is personally important to them (Wood & Quinn, 2003). Finally, messages that appeal to fear by attempting to scare audiences are generally not effective unless they also increase the audience's sense of vulnerability and provide information about how to avoid the danger discussed in the message (Freimuth et al., 1990; Keller, 1999).

Communication includes more than just what people say. There are many types of nonverbal communication. Kinesics is the use of body movement, facial expressions, and eye contact (Mehrabian, 1981). Haptics is the use of physical touch, such as handshakes, kissing, and hugging (Hans & Hans, 2015). Paralanguage (or paralinguistics) is the use of vocal tone, pitch, loudness, and rate of speech. Proxemics is the use of space (proximity) and how it relates to relationships people have with others (Hall, 1966). How people communicate with another, both verbally and nonverbally, can differ vastly by culture. In low-context cultures, individuals value what is stated or verbalized (Hall, 1973). They may speak in a straightforward manner and may be more personal and informal across settings. In such cultures, being direct and to the point is highly valued. In high-context cultures, however, individuals place high value on the situation and nonverbal cues, which can alter the meaning of the verbal communication. People may not necessarily verbalize what they mean and rely on nonverbal communication to convey their points. Their language might also be tailored to who they are talking to, and they may rely on hierarchies and rules around formality to adjust their communication. They may also value keeping the peace and being more indirect when sharing difficult messages. Researchers have characterized India, Thailand, Japan, and some Latin American countries as practicing high-context communication, whereas the United States, Germany, and Scandinavian countries act as low-context cultures (Croucher et al., 2012; Hall & Hall, 1990). However, a 2008 meta-analysis analyzing 224 articles in business and technical communications (Cardon, 2008) found lack of support for this model.

People have been using the internet to communicate more easily, and social networking sites (SNSs; e.g., Facebook, Instagram, X) have facilitated this form of electronic communication. With the rise of social media use to communicate with others, there have been concerns raised about potential negative impacts of this increased connectivity, especially in the realm of mental health. One meta-analysis explored the connection between SNS use and depressive symptoms and found a moderate positive association between problematic SNS use and depression symptoms, but only a weak association with time spent using SNS and intensity of SNS use (Cunningham et al., 2021). Another meta-analysis found that there was a small to-medium-effect between depressive symptoms and greater social comparisons on SNS, but the effect sizes for the relationship between SNS frequency of use and time spent with depression were small (Yoon et al., 2019). These findings are consistent in the youth literature (Ivie et al., 2020). It is important to note that, in general, the effect sizes for these effects have been small to medium, and there is great heterogeneity in the effects across studies, so more research is needed to establish whether there is a causal link between social media use and depressive symptoms (Appel et al., 2020; Vannucci et al., 2020).

ENVIRONMENTAL/ECOLOGICAL PSYCHOLOGY

Environment can have a significant impact on individual behavior. Field theory (Lewin, 1936) states that behavior is affected by both the person and concurrently the environment they are in, although their relative importance is different in different cases. Field theory was applied to a number of inter- and intrapersonal behaviors, including conflict, group dynamics, and leadership. Lewin (1931) identified three categories of intraindividual conflict; later, a fourth category was added (Miller, 1944):

Approach–approach conflict occurs when an individual must choose between two equally attractive or positive goals. This type of conflict tends to be the easiest to resolve because both outcomes are appealing.

Avoidance–avoidance conflict occurs when an individual must choose between two equally unattractive or negative goals. This type of conflict is generally difficult to resolve and often leads to inaction, indecision, and withdrawal from the situation.

Approach–avoidance conflict occurs when a single goal has both attractive and unattractive qualities. Individuals experiencing this conflict often feel increased avoidance as they move toward a goal and conversely experience increased desire toward the goal as they decide to move away from it.

Double approach–avoidance conflict occurs when choosing between two goals that both have attractive and unattractive qualities. This tends to be the most difficult conflict to resolve and often results in moving between two alternatives.

TRANSFORMATIONAL LEADERSHIP

The concept of transformational leadership stems from the field of organizational change and was originally introduced by James MacGregor Burns (1978). Burns viewed leadership styles as falling in one of two categories: (1) transactional or (2) transformational. Transactional leadership is focused on an exchange between the leader and the individual(s) the leader serves. However, transformational leadership involves leading with the intent of motivating followers. As a result of this approach, followers may feel inspired to accomplish goals and more invested in the mission of the organization, as well as in their own growth (Bass, 1985; Bass & Riggio, 2010; Burns 1978). A recent meta-analysis (Peng et al., 2021) found that transformational leadership is positively associated with followers being open to and ready for change. This leadership style is also associated with a reduction in negative responses to change.

Research on the impact of environment on behavior has also focused on the effects of crowding. *Crowding* refers to the state of mind that occurs when people are in high population-density situations. The effects of crowding depend on the specific circumstances. Crowding can have positive effects in some situations, and people tend to prefer it at sporting events (e.g., football games), rock concerts, and attention-grabbing movies (e.g., violent or humorous movies). Crowding has been linked with negative performance on complex tasks but has little or no impact on simple tasks. Densely populated residential areas have been linked with increased physical and mental health problems, poor academic performance, juvenile delinquency, and higher mortality rates.

A number of factors that contribute to the effects of crowding have been identified. When people perceive a sense of control, they are better able to handle the stress of crowded situations. Additionally, when people anticipate that an environment will be crowded or when distracted by an event (e.g., games and movies), they experience less stress. The density–intensity hypothesis suggests that differential effects of crowding occur because crowds increase positive experiences and situations and also make unpleasant experiences more negative (Deaux & Wrightsman, 1988). An individual's need for personal space also influences the effects of crowding. Intrusions of personal space commonly lead to anxiety, irritability, and increased aggression. The need for personal space varies with culture, and Americans generally need more personal space than individuals of Latin American, Arab, Greek, and French descent. Men and individuals with high authoritarianism or low self-esteem also report a greater need for personal space.

EVOLUTIONARY PERSPECTIVES ON SOCIAL EMOTIONS, THOUGHTS, AND BEHAVIOR

Evolutionary perspectives on social behavior propose that many thoughts, feelings, and behaviors are partially a result of selective psychological adaptations by natural selection over time (Zeigler-Hill et al., 2015). Thus, evolutionary theory offers a framework for understanding many social behaviors, including mate or partner selection, feelings such as empathy, and prosocial behaviors such as altruism.

Mate Selection

Buss (2007) refers to mating as "differential reproductive success" because of the natural selection that allowed modern humans to inherit the mating strategies of their ancestors. Darwin's sexual selection theory and Trivers's parental investment theory (Trivers, 1972) provide the conceptual framework for the evolution of mating adaptations. Darwin's sexual selection identifies same-sex competition and preferential mate choices as the driving force for mating adaptations. Years later, Trivers added parental investment theory that posits that animals are most selective of mates when the investment in offspring is the greatest. Females were identified as having the greatest investment.

Current evolutionary psychologists disagree about the fundamental mating strategies of humans. Having tackled different challenges in the mating domain, the sexes have emerged with different psychological mating solutions. Buss (2007) describes these psychological differences as "possessing distinct mate preferences, dissimilar desires for short-term mating, and distinct triggers that evoke sexual jealousy" (p. 502). Similarly, Schmitt (2005) outlines human mating strategies that are sex-differentiated and sensitive to context. He explored the temporal context of short-term mating and long-term mating. Schmitt describes four mating strategies: monogamous, polygynous, polyandrous, and short-term.

Monogamous mating occurs when two people (or organisms) choose each other exclusively for reproductive efforts and can be perennial or serial. Members of the opposite sex may choose one partner for life or serially choose different partners but only one at a time. Polygynous mating occurs when one male mates with numerous females, but the females only mate with one male. Polyandrous mating occurs when females compete for access to numerous males, and after mating with an individual male, abandon the male and offspring entirely. Polyandry is not a preferred mating arrangement, as it is found in less than 1% of preindustrial cultures. Short-term mating strategies occur when females mate with multiple males, and males mate with multiple females. These mating pairs tend to be brief and lack exclusivity, though mate preferences for dominance, status, and health remain.

Prosocial Emotions and Behavior

Prosocial behavior occurs when one acts to help another when there is no goal other than to help a fellow person. Empathy is a prosocial emotion that has been researched by Batson (1991), who formulated the empathy–altruism hypothesis. The empathy–altruism hypothesis states that the amount of help we are likely to give without any selfish thoughts is directly in proportion to the amount of empathy we feel for the person; however, if we do not feel empathy for them, we will only help them if the rewards outweigh the costs of helping them. In summarizing how empathy is enhanced, Baumeister and Finkel (2010) report that empathy for another person can be evoked by focusing on another's feelings; by sharing emotions, feelings, and sensations; by valuing another's welfare; and by recognition of kinship, similarity, or closeness. Batson, his colleagues, and his detractors conducted numerous investigations to evaluate the motivations underlying empathy-induced behavior. They asserted that the motivation could be altruistic, egoist, or both. They found that participants in a low-empathy group opted out of helping a confederate when doing so was easy, but helped out half the time when opting out of the situation was difficult. Conversely, the high-empathy group opted to help the confederate whether opting out was easy or difficult. In another series of experiments, Batson et al. (2009) concluded that empathy-induced behavior motivated by the goal of avoiding social or self-punishments for failing to help has consistently supported the empathy–altruism hypothesis.

MAJOR RESEARCH-BASED THEORIES OF PERSONALITY

Personality is a pattern of relatively stable traits and unique characteristics that give patterning and coherence to one's behavior (Roberts & Mroczek, 2008). Personality shapes social behavior, and aspects of one's social environment elicit and constrain the individual's behavior. Understanding personality can help us understand how individuals may be inclined to behave toward people and in particular situations.

Psychoanalytic/Psychodynamic Theories

Within psychology, there are a number of research-based theories of personality. One of the earliest conceptualizations was Freud's psychoanalytic theory. This structural theory comprises three distinct aspects of personality: the id, ego, and superego. The id is present at birth and operates on the pleasure principle. It consists of both life (e.g., self-preservation and sexual gratification/libido) and death (e.g., destruction, anger, and aggression/thanatos) instincts. The id is also thought to be responsible for the primary process of thinking and basic instincts. At 6 months, the ego begins to develop in response to the id's inability to gratify all of its needs. The ego strives to mediate the conflicting demands of the id and reality and defer gratification until appropriate. The id is responsible for secondary process thinking, which is realistic and rational. Between the ages of 4 and 5, the superego emerges and is an internalization of society's values and standards conveyed to a child through reward and punishment. The superego attempts to permanently block the id's socially unacceptable drives and is driven by concepts of right and wrong. An overdeveloped ego occurs when the drive for pleasure is overindulged (overactive id) and can lead to addiction, anger, and other self-harming behaviors. Conversely, an overdeveloped superego (i.e., exaggerated sense of right and wrong) can lead to increased feelings of guilt, anxiety, and eating disorders.

Object relations theory is another psychodynamic theory that grew largely from the work of Klein. This theory emphasizes the process by which an infant assumes their own physical and psychological identity. Objects are conceptualized as internalized images, which assist the unconscious in making sense of people and the environment, most often based on the infant's mother or father. From birth to 1 month, a child is oblivious to the external world, which can be described as normal autism. At 2 to 3 months, an infant is fused with their mother and does not differentiate between "I" and "not-I," which is termed *normal symbiosis*. At this stage, infants mainly view the world as part objects, that is, viewing objects as good and bad and as separate rather than part of the same whole object. When a child reaches 4 months, the separation–individuation phase begins. During this phase, a child takes steps toward separation and sensory exploration. By 3 years, a child develops a permanent sense of self and object, also known as object constancy, and is able to perceive others as both separate and related. Disruption of this process is thought to cause an individual to carry that object in their unconscious during adulthood and expect similar interactions with others. For example, if a child is neglected or abused as an infant, they will expect similar outcomes from others and use that experience to understand their adult relationships.

Jungian theories are based on the work of Jung and conceptualize personality as a consequence of both the conscious and the unconscious mind. The conscious mind is orientated toward the external world. It is governed by the ego and is representative of individual thoughts, feelings, ideas, perceptions, and memories. The unconscious mind contains both the personal and collective unconscious. The personal unconscious comprises experiences that were once recalled but are now repressed and forgotten. The collective unconscious consists of hidden memories that are passed down from one generation to the next. A persona is a public mask that overemphasizes individuality, minimizes the collective psyche, and hides the true nature of the individual. Jung also introduced the notion of archetypes or "primordial images," which cause people to experience and understand certain phenomena in a universal way. The "self" strives for unity among different, and sometimes conflicting, parts of personality, including feminine (anima) and masculine (animus) aspects of personality. Jung proposed that each individual has a personality type based on how they perceive things and how they make decisions. There are four basic psychological functions that contribute to these processes: thinking, feeling, sensing, and intuiting. The function a person uses most frequently is referred to as dominant and may either be extroverted or introverted. The Myers–Briggs type indicator grew out of Jung's personality theory (Myers & Myers, 1995).

Adlerian theory (originally called individual psychology) postulates that basic mistakes originating from faulty perceptions, attitudes, and beliefs lead to myths, which strongly influence personality. Self-defeating perceptions and feelings of inferiority develop during childhood as the result of real or perceived biological, psychological, or social weakness. These beliefs may have been appropriate during childhood but are no longer useful as the person ages. Adler suggested that people strive for superiority due to an inherent tendency toward becoming competent and achieving "perfect completion." Individuals follow a "style of life," which unifies various aspects of the personality. This style is affected by experiences in the family atmosphere during childhood. Thus, birth order is an important component of Adler's theory, and he identified five psychological positions from which children view life: oldest, second of only two, middle, youngest, and only. A healthy style of life includes goals that reflect optimism and confidence, entails contributions to the welfare of others, and includes community feeling (i.e., social interest and a sense of being connected to humanity). An unhealthy (mistaken) style of life includes goals reflecting self-centeredness, competition, and striving for personal power.

Self-psychology theory hypothesizes that an illness or personality disruption is the result of unmet developmental needs. This theory emphasizes the parents' ability to provide a child with factors that lead to a cohesive sense of self or "healthy narcissism." Key factors in healthy personality development include empathy and optimal frustration.

Humanistic/Existential Theories

Although there are a broad range of theories under the umbrella of humanistic and existential approaches, most emphasize subjectivity and self-reflection, particularly the importance of choice and self-determination. The existential view of the mind is based on the principle that humans are alone in the world yet long to be connected with others. Yalom (1980/2020) identified anxiety arising when individuals are confronted with normal life experiences, including death, isolation, meaninglessness, and freedom. An individual's response to these four concerns may be functional or dysfunctional, as existentialists believe that every individual has a capacity of choice and direction in their life. A healthy personality is able to integrate these components, whereas an unhealthy personality becomes overwhelmed by either freedom or limitations and is unable to balance the realities of living.

Person-centered theories are often associated with the work of Rogers. The central concept of these theories is the notion of "self." The whole persona is composed of perceptions of the "I" or "me," and perceptions of the relationship of the "I" or "me" to others, as well as the values attached to these perceptions. Rogers believed that individuals have an inherent need for positive regard from others they depend on. To grow, the self must remain unified and respond to environmental demands as a whole. Rogers identified two parts of the self that develop over time: the ideal self and the self-concept. The ideal self is how the person would like to be, and the self-concept is how the person views themself. Disruptions and conflicts between these parts can be minimized by openness to experience, which leads to a state of congruence and wholeness. If the individual is rigid and unwilling to be flexible in their perceptions, then they will often overgeneralize experiences and have poor reality testing, sometimes leading to various personality disorders.

Gestalt theories postulate that personality consists of self and self-image. The self is the creative aspect of personality that promotes individuals' inherent tendency for self-actualization (ability to live a fully integrated life). On the other hand, the self-image is the "darker side" of personality. Personality depends on the person's early interactions with the environment. Perls emphasized choice and personal responsibility, also including the social circumstance as important. There is often a balance that needs to be created between personal needs and values that are taken due to environmental demands. An introject is a value that is not assimilated into the self and creates conflict within the personality.

Cognitive and Behavioral Theories

Behavioral approaches generally conceptualize personality as a result of mutual interaction of the person or "the organism" with its environment. Skinner developed an operant theory known as radical behaviorism. He believed children do bad things because the behavior obtains attention that serves as a reinforcer. The three-term contingency model or "Stimulus–Response–Consequence Model" was created as a method for analyzing behavior. This model suggests that we do things because of learned consequences, sometimes called contingencies of reinforcement. These contingencies may be positive or negative and may occur whether the behavior does or does not occur.

Social cognitive approaches grew out of behaviorism and social learning theory. Bandura focused on the reciprocal determinism between the interaction of personal factors, behavior, and the environment (Bandura, 1978). In social cognitive approaches, behavior is explained as being guided by cognitions (e.g., expectations) about the world, especially those about other people. Similar to other theories, the person and environment influence each other, yet heavy emphasis is placed on cognitive capabilities. Social cognitive theory emphasizes cognitive processes such as thinking and judgment.

Reality therapy was developed by Glasser and is often categorized as a form of cognitive behavioral therapy. This theory proposes that human behavior is purposeful and originates from within the individual rather than external forces. There are several basic innate needs: four psychological (belonging, power, freedom, and fun) and one physical (survival). A success identity fulfills needs in a responsible manner, whereas a failure identity gratifies a need to be irresponsible.

Trait Theory

Trait theory focuses on the role of specific personality traits. Traits are thought to be relatively stable over time and are defined as patterns of behavior, thought, and emotion. Allport defined central traits as basic aspects of someone's personality, with secondary traits defined as less important. Cardinal traits are the characteristics by which an individual may be recognized. In recent years, there has been a shift to studying group statistics (nomothetic) rather than individual (idiographic) traits.

Interpersonal and Systematic Theory

Interpersonal and systematic theories of personality combine elements of both psychodynamic and cognitive behavioral theories. The common theme in these approaches is the focus on elements external to the individual (e.g., environment and other people) as largely contributing to behavior rather than aspects of personality. Therefore, the social environment, both personal relationships and larger social systems, is of tantamount importance. Often the person's self is defined by various interactions, as noted in the work of Harry Stack Sullivan.

CULTURAL AND INDIVIDUAL DIVERSITY

Culture and individual diversity refers to personal and demographic characteristics that include race, ethnicity, gender identity, sexual orientation, disabilities, socioeconomic status, and age. Cultural and individual diversity implicitly and explicitly influence our sense of self and interactions with the world; they are fluid and complex, changing constantly in subtle and concrete ways. Thus, cultural and individual diversity factors are paramount in attempting to understand the behavior and interacting effectively with people.

Race and Ethnicity

Traditionally, race has implied relatedness through genealogy, biology, and physical traits (e.g., skin color; Quintana 1998), and ethnicity has implied relatedness through shared heritage and culture (Phinney, 1990). However, most social scientists agree that race and ethnicity are social constructs and therefore are malleable categories influenced by historical, political, scientific, and multiple other forces (Shanklin, 1994). Furthermore, it is important to remember that Black/African Americans, Asian Americans, Latin Americans, Native Americans, and other races and ethnicities have distinct within-group and individual differences (Atkinson et al., 1998).

Identity Development

Over the past three decades, various theories on racial and ethnic identity development have emerged. African American identity and White identity development models have been the most frequently studied and will be described in greater detail in the following section. However, based on research supporting similar patterns of adjustment to cultural oppression by minority groups (B. Berry, 1965; Stonequist, 1937/1961), a broader model of minority identity development was developed in an attempt to combine common features of development across populations (Atkinson et al., 1979, 1989, 1998). Sue and Sue (1999) broadened the model to apply to White identity development as well, calling it the Racial/Cultural Identity Development Model (RCID; Table 5.1). The RCID distinguished among five stages that people experience as they attempt to understand themselves in terms of their culture, the dominant culture, and the oppressive relationship among cultures.

TABLE 5.1 Stages of the Racial/Cultural Identity Development Model

Stage 1	Conformity	Positive attitudes toward a preference for dominant cultural values and depreciating attitudes toward one's own culture
Stage 2	Dissonance	Confusion and conflict over the contradictory appreciating and depreciating attitudes that one has toward self and others of the same and different groups
Stage 3	Resistance and immersion	Active rejection of the dominant society; exhibits appreciating attitudes toward self and members of one's own group
Stage 4	Introspection	Uncertainty about the rigidity of beliefs held in stage 3 and conflicts between loyalty and responsibility toward one's own group and feelings of personal autonomy
Stage 5	Integrative awareness	A sense of fulfillment with regard to cultural identity and a strong desire to eliminate all forms of oppression; a multicultural perspective and objective examination of the values, beliefs, and so forth, of one's own and other groups before accepting or rejecting them

Cross (1971, 1991) and Cross and Vandiver (2001) developed the Black Racial (Nigrescence) Identity Development Model. The first version of the model describes a shift from Black self-hatred to Black self-acceptance, which occurs through five stages of identity development: preencounter, encounter, immersion–emersion, internalization, and internalization–commitment. In 1991, a revision reduced the number of stages to four and introduced the idea of "race salience." Racial identity salience is the extent to which an individual's race is currently a relevant part of their self-concept. The model was expanded in 2001 by Cross and Vandiver (see Table 5.2); four stages remained, but the preencounter stage was expanded to include assimilation, miseducation, and self-hatred identities, and the internalization stage was expanded to include two multiculturalist orientations (racial and inclusive).

The White Racial Identity Development Model was created by Helms (1990, 1995) and comprises six distinct phases. Racism is a central part of being White in America and that identity development involves two phases: abandoning racism (statuses 1–3) and developing a nonracist White identity (statuses 4–6). Each phase or status (see Table 5.3) is characterized by a different information-processing strategy, which refers to the methods the individual uses to reduce discomfort related to racial issues.

Gender and Sexual Orientation

Based on the American Psychological Association's (APA, 2012, 2015) definition of terms, sex is a person's biological status assigned before or at the time of birth based on visible characteristics (i.e., external genitalia) and is typically categorized as male, female, or intersex (i.e., a variation

TABLE 5.2 Stages of the Black Racial Identity Development Model

Preencounter stage	Race and identity have low salience. In this stage the person tries to assimilate into the mainstream identity and accepts negative beliefs about Black people; as a result, they are likely to have low self-esteem.
Encounter stage	Exposure to single significant race-related event or series of events leads to racial/cultural awareness and interest in developing a Black identity.
Immersion–emersion stage	Race and racial identity have high salience. Individuals idealize Blacks and Black culture and feel a great deal of rage toward Whites as well as guilt and anxiety about their own previous lack of awareness of race. During the emersion substage, intense emotions subside but individuals reject all aspects of White culture and begin to internalize a Black identity.
Internalization stage	Race continues to have high salience. Individuals in this stage adopt one of three identities: pro-Black, nonracist (Afrocentric); biculturist orientation that integrates Black identity with White or another salient cultural identity; or multiculturalist orientation that integrates Black identity with two or more other salient cultural identities.

TABLE 5.3 Stages of the White Racial Identity Development Model

STAGE	DESCRIPTION	INFORMATION-PROCESSING STRATEGY
Contact status	Little awareness of racism and racial identity and may exhibit unsophisticated behaviors that reflect racist attitudes and beliefs	Obliviousness and denial
Disintegration status	Increasing awareness of race and racism leads to confusion and emotional conflict. To reduce dissonance, person may overidentify with members of minority groups, act in paternalist ways toward them, or retreat into White society.	Suppression of information and ambivalence
Reintegration status	Attempts to resolve moral dilemmas associated with the disintegration status by idealizing White society and denigrating members of minority groups	Selective perception and negative out-group distortion
Pseudoindependence status	Personally jarring event or series of events causes person to question racist views and acknowledge role that Whites have in perpetrating racism; interested in understanding racial/cultural differences but only on an intellectual level	Selective perception and reshaping reality
Immersion–emersion status	Explores what it means to be White, confronts own biases, and begins to understand ways they can benefit from White privilege	Hypervigilance and reshaping
Autonomy status	Internalizes nonracist White identity that includes appreciation of and respect for racial/cultural differences and similarities	Flexibility and complexity

in indicators of biological sex that do not fit the typical definitions for male or female). Gender refers to culturally prescribed attitudes, feelings, and behaviors associated with biological sex.

Gender identity refers to a person's sense of self as man, woman, or other gender. Gender expression is how an individual presents as a man, woman, or other gender in a given culture through physical appearance, clothing choice and accessories, and behaviors. Gender expression may or may not be congruent with socially prescribed gender roles and/or the person's gender identity. In other words, gender persons can vary substantially in their degree of masculinity and/or femininity, and whether or not an individual's gender expression is consistent with socially prescribed gender roles may or may not reflect gender identity. For instance, cross dressing (i.e., wearing clothes, accessories, makeup, and/or adopting a gender expression not associated with one's sex assigned at birth) and drag (i.e., adopting a gender expression as part of a performance) are not necessarily reflective of one's gender identity.

Cisgender refers to persons whose gender identity aligns or corresponds with their biological sex. When an individual's gender identity and biological sex are incongruent, he, she, or they may identify as transgender or gender nonconforming (TGNC). TGNC is an umbrella term referring to persons who express gender atypically across a continuum. Individuals identifying as transgender (or trans) may feel as if they are in the wrong gender, but this perception may or may not correlate with a desire to transition (i.e., process by which a person shifts to a gender that is different from the one associated with his/her/their sex assigned at birth) via sexual medical confirmation procedures (Meier & Labuski, 2013). Individuals who are changing or have changed their bodies through medical confirmation procedures to a gender identity different from the sex assigned at birth are described as transsexual. When an individual who identifies as TGNC is able to blend in with cisgender people without being recognized as TGNC based on their gender expression or role, the individual is described as "passing." Passing may or may not be an aspiration for individuals identifying as TGNC. Another common gender identity term is *genderqueer*, which refers to persons who do not identify fully as either male or female (e.g., may also identify as bigender, pangender, androgyne), neither man nor woman (e.g., genderless, gender neutral, agender), moving between genders (e.g., gender fluid), and/or embodying a third gender. In Native American cultures, the term *two-spirit* is used to describe individuals who identify with both male and female gender roles.

Sexual orientation encompasses one's sexual and emotional attraction to another person and their associated behavior. Research suggests that sexual orientation occurs on a continuum and may be fluid for some people, particularly women. Individuals may be attracted to members of one's own biological sex (gay or lesbian), to members of the opposite biological sex (heterosexual), to both sexes (bisexual), neither (asexuality or lack of sexual attraction to others), or to people who identify as genderqueer or have other gender identities.

One of the most prominent models explaining the impact of stress on sexual minorities is Meyer's (2003) minority stress model. This model demonstrates the various unique stressors sexual minorities face due to their sexual identities, which can have a deleterious impact on their physical and mental health. In particular, the model identifies distal stressors, which are outside events such as instances of discrimination and violence, and proximal stressors, which are internal processes such as internalized homophobia, rejection expectations, and concealment of their minoritized identity. Meyer (2003) argues that the impact of these stressors can be mediated by factors such as social support, individual resilience, and opportunities for positive identification with their sexual identity.

Models of Development

Heterosexual identity is often conceptualized as an invisible identity, given that sexual identity frequently only becomes visible once an individual deviates from heterosexual norms (e.g., Diamond, 2008; Striepe & Tolman, 2003). Accordingly, less attention has been given to heterosexual identity development models; however, several have been proposed (Eliason, 1995; Sullivan, 1998; Worthington et al., 2002). Across all models, heterosexual identity development is assumed to be a relatively effortless process (compared to the identity development of sexual minority individuals), likely as a result of heteronormative privilege (Morgan, 2012).

The earliest models of sexual minority identity development emphasized self-identification with "coming out" as gay or lesbian (Cass, 1979; Coleman, 1982; Troiden, 1979, 1988). These models were primarily based on research with gay men and White individuals. More recent models of sexual orientation identity development (e.g., Dillon et al., 2011; Horowitz & Newcomb, 2001; Savins-Williams, 2001) incorporate multiple dimensions of sexual orientation (such as sexual attraction, sexual behavior, sexual fantasies, emotional preference, social preference, and lifestyle) and acknowledge a temporal aspect of identity (past, present, and future). Regarding the latter, research has demonstrated that sexual orientation identity may change over the life course due to shifts in awareness and to historical and cultural forces (Cohler & Hammack, 2007; Diamond, 2008). Some research suggests that, for persons of sexual minorities, timing between sexual orientation identity stages or milestones is becoming shorter, with self-labels being used similarly at adolescent and emerging adult development stages (Glover et al., 2009); it has been suggested that this condensed timing between stages may be due to sociohistorical forces that are normalizing sexuality identity development for persons of sexual minorities (e.g., Floyd & Bakeman, 2006; Grov et al., 2006).

Disability and Rehabilitation Issues

The Americans with Disabilities Act (ADA; 1991) defines a physical or mental impairment as one that substantially limits one or more of the individual's major life activities; the definition also includes having a history of impairment or the perception of having such an impairment. Disabilities can be both visible (e.g., amputation) and invisible (e.g., traumatic brain injury). The ADA (1991) prohibits employers from discriminating against qualified individuals with mental or physical disabilities. This act states that if a disabled person is able to perform the essential functions of a job, they are considered qualified and the employer must make "reasonable accommodations" as long as those accommodations do not place undue hardship on the employer. The ADA also requires that preemployment measures be directly related to job requirements and prohibits a medical examination prior to an employment offer. If medical examinations are administered, they must be given to all applicants, not just those with disabilities. Drug tests are an exception and not considered a medical exam according to the ADA.

Models of Disability

A number of conceptual models have been proposed to understand and explain disability, including the medical model and the minority (or social) model. The medical model suggests that disability is a problem directly caused by disease, trauma, or other health conditions that require sustained medical treatment provided by professionals. Treatment is focused on adjustment and behavior change that would "cure" the disability. In contrast, the social model views disability as a socially created problem that is the result of loss or limitation of opportunities to take part in the normal life of the community on an equal level because of physical and social barriers (Oliver, 1996). Management of the problem requires social and political solutions that would allow people with disabilities to fully participate in all areas of social life.

ACCULTURATION OF IMMIGRANT, REFUGEE, AND POLITICAL-ASYLUM-SEEKING POPULATIONS

Acculturation is a multidimensional construct that refers to the extent to which an individual changes, adapts, accommodates, or adopts to the values, attitudes, and behaviors of their own group and the dominant or majority group (Kohatsu, 2005). Acculturation is interconnected with other aspects of an individual's identity. Additionally, it is contextually based in that its meaning can change across contexts. For instance, sociocultural and racial environmental contexts can influence the quality of acculturation for people of color. J. W. Berry et al. (1987) proposed four categories of acculturation status:

Integration: A person maintains their own (minority) culture and incorporates many aspects of the dominant culture.

Assimilation: A person relinquishes their culture and accepts the majority culture.

Separation: A person withdraws from the dominant culture and accepts their own culture.

Marginalization: A person does not identify with either their own culture or the majority culture.

Phinney and Devich-Navarro (1997) also proposed a model of acculturation that distinguishes among six categories: assimilated, fused, blended bicultural, alternating bicultural, separated, and marginal. Using these categories, they found that the majority of African American and Mexican American adolescents described themselves as either blended bicultural (strong integrated ethnic and American identities) or separated (only an ethnic identity).

Social-Contextual Issues Related to Culture and Individual Diversity

Privilege is defined as a right or benefit that only belongs to one group. Hays (2001) provides the ADDRESSING acronym (see Table 5.4) to guide understanding of potential areas of holding or not holding privilege within the American power system. Having self-awareness of personal privilege, as well as an understanding of oppressions that exist, are important aspects of being a competent provider of psychological services. Experiences of prejudice and discrimination are a daily reality for individuals who do not hold privilege in these domains. Oppression has often taught people in nondominant groups that it is not safe to self-disclose, and they develop an adaptive level of paranoia. Furthermore, the impact of power and oppression can be magnified when individuals share multiple marginalized identities; Kimberle Crenshaw (1989) coined the term *intersectionality* to describe how individuals' identities (e.g., race, SES, gender) can intersect with one another and lead to multiplied experiences of discrimination and social inequity, which highlighted the inequities of antidiscrimination laws.

TABLE 5.4 The ADDRESSING Acronym

Cultural Influences	Dominant Groups/Hold Privilege
Age and generational influences	30–60 years old
Developmental or acquired Disabilities	Do not have disability
Religion and spiritual orientation	Secular or Christian home
Ethnicity	Euro-American heritage
Socioeconomic status	Middle or upper class
Sexual orientation	Heterosexual
Indigenous heritage	Not of indigenous heritage
National origin	Live in country where born/grew up
Gender	Male; cisgender

Holding privilege (regardless of being aware or unaware) may lead to "ethnocentric monoculturalism." Sue et al. (1998) identified five components of ethnocentric monoculturalism: belief in superiority, belief in the inferiority of others, power to impose standards, manifestation in institutions, and the invisible veil (i.e., assumption that everyone experiences reality and truth). These components reinforce prejudice and discrimination and lead to labeling individuals in nondominant groups as being the ones with problems. This approach is problematic for several reasons and is starting to be challenged by various movements within psychology. One such movement is international or global psychology.

Global psychology is used to imply a worldwide scope, *international psychology* is used when discussing differences among nations, and *cross-cultural psychology* is used to refer to differences among cultures (regardless of within or outside nations). These branches of the field explore cross-cultural comparisons, including power structures, communication, and practice. Exploration may focus on a global issue (such as subjective well-being or gender roles) or compare how different approaches lead to different outcomes. Of note, many scholars have begun to utilize the term *global majority* to more accurately reference Black, Indigenous, and people of color (Lee et al., 2023; Portelli & Campbell-Stephens, 2009). Finally, literature on the area of political differences is vast. In the context of the United States, political differences have become increasingly amplified. This has resulted in animosity between American Democrats and Republicans (Iyengar et al., 2019), which, in turn, can negatively impact collaborative efforts across party lines to address pressing matters impacting the nation. Empathy can play an important role in these dynamics (Santos et al., 2022).

▶ REFERENCES

Full reference list available at http://examprepconnect.springerpub.com

KNOWLEDGE CHECK: CHAPTER 5

1. In making attributions about behavior, we tend to commit biases and errors. Fundamental attribution error is a common bias that states:
   A. The tendency to attribute personal factors for success and external factors for failure
   B. The tendency to attribute personal factors to others' failure and situational factors to personal failure
   C. The tendency to overvalue personal factors and undervalue situational factors when explaining others' behavior
   D. The tendency to undervalue personal factors and overvalue situational factors when explaining others' behavior

2. Zimbardo's prison study (1970) demonstrates which type of social influence?
   A. Informational conformity
   B. Internalization
   C. Obedience
   D. Peer pressure

3. According to Cross and Vandiver's (2001) Black Racial Identity Development Model, which stage of identity development is associated with an awareness and interest in developing a Black identity?
   A. Encounter
   B. Immersion-emersion
   C. Internalization
   D. Preencounter

4. Which of the following is a technique that involves getting a person to agree to a large request by first having them agree to a smaller request?
   A. Bargaining technique
   B. Door-in-the-face technique
   C. Foot-in-the-door technique
   D. Stepping forward technique

5. A therapist who conceptualizes a client's behavior as a result of learned consequences likely ascribes to which theory of personality?
   A. Behavioral
   B. Existential
   C. Humanistic
   D. Social cognitive

(See answers on the next page.)

1. **C) The tendency to overvalue personal factors and undervalue situational factors when explaining others' behavior**
   The fundamental attribution error refers to how individuals tend to overestimate dispositional factors and underestimate situational factors when explaining others' behavior. The actor-observer bias occurs when individuals attribute dispositional factors to other people's behavior while attributing situational factors to their own behavior. The self-serving bias is the tendency to attribute dispositional factors for success and external, uncontrollable factors for failure.

2. **C) Obedience**
   In Zimbardo's prison study (1970), student participants strongly adapted to their assigned roles as either prisoners or guards, which demonstrated their willingness to obey authority figures even in the face of conflicted personal conscience (guards acting aggressively toward prisoners). Informational conformity refers to a form of social influence when individuals accept information from others as evidence. Peer pressure is another form of social influence characterized by direct or indirect influence on peers. Internalization is an effect of social influence on social behavior during which an individual accepts a belief, attitude, or behavior that is expressed publicly and privately.

3. **A) Encounter**
   During the encounter (second) stage of Cross and Vandiver's Black Racial Identity Development Model (2001), exposure to a single significant race-related event or series of events leads to racial/cultural awareness and interest in developing a Black identity. The first stage of the model is the preencounter stage during which race and identity have low salience. The third stage of the model is the immersion-emersion stage during which race and racial identity have high salience. The fourth stage of the model is the internalization stage during which race continues to have high salience and individuals adopt one of three identities: pro-Black, nonracist (Afrocentric); biculturist orientation integrating Black identity with White or another salient cultural identity; or multiculturalist orientation that integrates Black identity with two or more other salient cultural identities.

4. **C) Foot-in-the-door technique**
   The foot-in-the-door technique involves presenting a small request that is difficult to refuse, setting the individual up to give in to a larger, desired request. The door-in-the-face technique starts with a larger request that is more likely to be turned down, followed by a smaller, more reasonable request.

5. **A) Behavioral**
   Behavioral theories of personality generally conceptualize personality as a result of mutual interaction of the person (or the "organism") with its environment. Social cognitive theory of personality emphasizes cognitive processes such as thinking and judgment. Humanistic and existential theories of personality emphasize subjectivity and self-reflection, particularly the importance of choice and self-determination.

6. A graduate school applicant tells their friend that they're nervous because of their upcoming graduate school interviews. When the applicant sees other nervous-looking applicants in the waiting room before their interview, they believe that the other applicants are generally nervous people. This is an example of which of the following?

   A. Actor-observer effect
   B. Projective identification
   C. Self-serving bias
   D. Social comparison effect

7. A new employee with a history of impairment from a traumatic brain injury is completing a medical exam as part of their preemployment process. The Americans with Disabilities Act (ADA; 1991) asserts:

   A. A drug test must be administered as part of the medical exam.
   B. The medical exam must be administered prior to the employment offer.
   C. The medical exam must be administered to all applicants.
   D. The medical exam is only necessary if the employee has a visible disability.

8. A licensed psychologist is treating a client who is struggling to manage work stress. The client received a job offer for a job at a company that is known for prioritizing employee satisfaction and work–life balance; however, this job also pays significantly less than the client's current job. The client has also been considering taking a long vacation with their loved ones but is worried about what the workload will be like after they return from the vacation. The client is likely experiencing what type of intraindividual conflict?

   A. Approach–approach
   B. Approach–avoidance
   C. Double approach–approach
   D. Double approach–avoidance

9. During a couple's therapy session, a licensed psychologist observes one partner using physical touch to comfort their partner and the other partner changing their facial expressions in response. What types of nonverbal communication is the psychologist observing?

   A. Haptics and kinesics
   B. Haptics and paralanguage
   C. Haptics and proxemics
   D. Kinesics and paralanguage

10. A teenage client reports feeling a strong sense of inferiority among their peers during school and extracurricular activities. Their therapist, who practices predominantly in line with Adlerian theory, is most likely to:

    A. Help the teenager develop their sense of empathy and cooperation with peers.
    B. Help the teenager increase their sense of competition with peers.
    C. Place emphasis on the role of conditioning and reinforcement.
    D. Promote exploration of unconscious processes and early childhood experiences.

(*See answers on the next page.*)

6. **A) Actor-observer effect**
The actor-observer bias occurs when individuals attribute dispositional factors to other people's behavior while attributing situational factors to their own behavior. The graduate school applicant is demonstrating this bias as they conclude that other applicants are nervous in the waiting room because they are generally nervous people, while they attribute their own nervousness to the situation (i.e., waiting for the interview). The applicant would be demonstrating the self-serving bias if attributions were being made about successes or failures, more specifically, dispositional factors attributed for personal successes (e.g., "I am smart.") and external, uncontrollable factors for personal failures (e.g., "The interviewers asked irrelevant questions."). Individuals may also be prone to making social comparisons in anxiety-provoking situations; however, this refers to when individuals evaluate their own opinions and abilities by comparing themselves to others. These comparisons are often made to help individuals define themselves or reduce uncertainty.

7. **C) The medical exam must be administered to all applicants.**
The ADA (1991) prohibits administering a medical exam prior to an employment offer. If medical exams are administered, they must be given to all applicants, not just those with disabilities. Drug tests are an exception and not considered a medical exam according to the ADA.

8. **D) Double approach–avoidance**
Double approach–avoidance conflict occurs when choosing between two goals (e.g., finding a new job and taking a vacation) that both have attractive (e.g., improved work–life balance at the job and relaxation during vacation) and unattractive (less pay for the new job and unmanageable workload after vacation) qualities. Approach–approach conflict occurs when an individual must choose between two equally attractive or positive goals. Approach–avoidance conflict occurs when a single goal has both attractive and unattractive qualities.

9. **A) Haptics and kinesics**
Haptics refers to the use of physical touch (e.g., handshakes, kissing, hugging), while kinesics refers to the use of body movement, facial expressions, and eye contact as forms of nonverbal communication. Proxemics refers to the use of space (proximity) and how it relates to relationships people have with others. Paralanguage, also known as paralinguistics, refers to the use of vocal tone, pitch, loudness, and rate of speech.

10. **A) Help the teenager develop their sense of empathy and cooperation with peers.**
Adlerian theory conceptualizes that basic mistakes originating from faulty perceptions, attitudes, and beliefs lead to myths, which strongly influence personality. It further postulates that in childhood, an individual may develop self-defeating perceptions and feelings of inferiority from real or perceived biological, psychological, or social weakness. However, as individuals age, these beliefs are no longer useful. Individuals follow a "style of life," which unifies various aspects of the personality. A healthy style of life is believed to include goals that reflect optimism and confidence, contributions to the welfare of others, and community feeling (i.e., social interest and sense of being connected to humanity). Given this conceptualization, a therapist who practices predominantly in line with Adlerian theory is most likely to encourage the development of goals and progress toward empathy and cooperation with peers as they relate to social interest and connection to others, while also motivating individuals to contribute to the welfare of others. An unhealthy style of life includes goals reflecting self-centeredness, competition, and striving for personal power. A psychoanalytic or psychodynamic therapist is likely to promote exploration of unconscious processes and early childhood experiences. A behavioral therapist is likely to place emphasis on the role of conditioning and reinforcement.

11. In a species of animals, one male mates with numerous females, but the females only mate with one male. This mating strategy is known as:
    A. Monogamous
    B. Polyandrous
    C. Polygynous
    D. Short-term

12. An individual is deciding whether to buy a pair of shoes online. According to Kelley's (1972) theory of covariation model of attribution, which of the following may influence the individual to move forward with the purchase?
    A. Being in an excited and happy mood
    B. Finding an online coupon for the shoes
    C. Reading positive reviews of the shoes by satisfied customers
    D. Viewing a captivating advertisement showcasing the shoes

13. Which theory suggests why an individual may choose to end a relationship when the relationship's costs exceed its rewards?
    A. Equity theory
    B. Gain-loss theory
    C. Social exchange theory
    D. Social impact theory

14. A manager of a team of employees notices that during weekly meetings, team members rarely share their concerns about the work culture, which is characterized by high levels of burnout, competition, and dissatisfaction. When developing activities for a team building workshop, what group process should the manager prioritize?
    A. Autonomy
    B. Job feedback
    C. Psychological safety
    D. Skill variety

15. A pharmaceutical company is developing their marketing materials for a new drug that will be advertised to medication prescribers. What element of their marketing materials is likely to increase their persuasive impact?
    A. A minimally discrepant message
    B. An extremely discrepant message
    C. A one-sided message
    D. A two-sided message

(See answers on the next page.)

11. **C) Polygynous**
    Polygynous mating occurs when one male mates with numerous females, but the females only mate with one male. Short-term mating occurs when females mate with multiple males, and males mate with multiple females. Polyandrous mating occurs when females compete for access to numerous males and, after mating with an individual male, abandon the male and offspring entirely. Monogamous mating occurs when two people (or organisms) choose each other exclusively for reproductive efforts that occur perennially or serially.

12. **C) Reading positive reviews of the shoes by satisfied customers**
    Kelley's theory of covariation model of attribution (1972) contends that individuals assess similarities (covariation) across situations to help us make causal attributions in a rational and logical fashion. Covariation of behavior is assessed using three types of information: consensus information—how other people act in the same situation and with the same stimulus; distinctiveness information—how similarly people act in different situations toward different stimuli; and consistency information—how frequently people perceive the same stimuli and respond the same. Reading positive reviews of the shoes by satisfied customers is in line with consensus information or, in other words, how other people have acted in the same situation (bought the shoes and reported being happy with their purchase) and with the same stimulus (seeing the shoe advertisement online).

13. **C) Social exchange theory**
    Blau's social exchange theory (1964) suggests that attraction occurs when the relationship's rewards exceed its costs and when the rewards and costs are reciprocal. Like social exchange theory, equity theory also focuses on relationship rewards and costs, but it suggests that perceptions of equity in a relationship are more important than the magnitude of costs and rewards. Gain-loss theory suggests that attraction is maximized when an individual's evaluation of a person is at first negative and then changes to positive. Social impact theory is relevant to social influences on individual functioning rather than affiliation and attraction. This theory suggests that the effects of any information source on an individual will increase with three factors: strength of the source of the impact, immediacy of the event, and the number of sources imposing the impact.

14. **C) Psychological safety**
    Psychological safety is the shared belief among team members that the workplace is safe for interpersonal risk taking (such as speaking up about concerns at work). Psychological safety is associated with a range of positive processes and outcomes including increased innovation in the workplace, task performance, employee satisfaction, employee engagement, and employee commitment. Although skill variety, autonomy, and job feedback have been proposed as core characteristics of jobs (i.e., Hackman and Oldham, 1976), prioritizing activities that focus on these characteristics will not necessarily address the discomfort team members have with sharing their concerns with the rest of their team and manager.

15. **D) A two-sided message**
    If the audience has an informed opinion on a topic, they are more likely to be persuaded by a two-sided message when the audience initially disagrees with the communicator's position and the communicator is relatively well-informed on the topic. The audience of medication prescribers is likely to have an informed opinion on prescription drugs. A one-sided message is likely to be more persuasive if the audience is relatively uninformed about the topic. Moderately discrepant messages are more likely to be persuasive compared to minimally or extremely discrepant messages.

16. Which of the following types of organizational justice refers to the fairness of outcomes such as pay, office assignments, and recognition?
    A. Distributive justice
    B. Informational justice
    C. Interactional justice
    D. Procedural justice

17. Sexual prejudice is correlated with:
    A. Higher levels of education
    B. Living in an urban area
    C. Living in Northern states
    D. Older age

18. A classmate moved from Spain to the United States a year ago. More recently, this classmate asks their parents to refrain from speaking Spanish to them when outside of their home. This classmate has also been enthusiastically celebrating most American holidays. With what category of acculturation status is their experience most consistent?
    A. Assimilation
    B. Integration
    C. Marginalization
    D. Separation

19. An individual meets their new neighbor who shares that they used to be a college athlete. They assume that their new neighbor is competitive, disciplined, and physically fit. What type of schema is most likely being activated?
    A. Event
    B. Person
    C. Role
    D. Self

20. According to Freud's psychoanalytic theory, what aspect of personality is driving an individual's desire to eat an extra slice of cake?
    A. Ego
    B. Id
    C. Superego
    D. Thanatos

(See answers on the next page.)

16. **A) Distributive justice**
Distributive justice refers to fairness of outcomes such as tangible distributions (e.g., office assignment, pay) and intangible distributions (e.g., recognition, praise). Procedural justice refers to the fairness of processes through which outcomes are decided. Interactional justice is the treatment of individuals as decisions are made. Informational justice refers to the timeliness, specificity, and truthfulness of the justification or explanation of the decision.

17. **D) Older age**
Research focused on correlates of sexual prejudice have generally found high levels of sexual prejudice among heterosexual men, as well as among individuals who are older, have lower levels of education, live in Southern or Midwestern states or in rural areas, or have limited personal contact with homosexual individuals.

18. **A) Assimilation**
Integration, assimilation, separation, and marginalization are four categories of acculturation status proposed by J. W. Berry et al. (1987). This classmate's attitudes and behaviors are most consistent with assimilation during which an individual relinquishes their culture (asking their parents to refrain from speaking Spanish to them) and accepts the majority culture (enthusiastically celebrating most American holidays). Integration refers to when an individual maintains their own (minority) culture and incorporates many aspects of the dominant culture. Separation refers to when an individual withdraws from the dominant culture and accepts their own culture. Marginalization refers to when an individual does not identify with either their own (minority) culture or the majority culture.

19. **B) Person**
Person schemas are attributes individuals use to categorize people and make inferences about their behavior. This individual is categorizing their new neighbor as a college athlete, which leads to inferences about their skills, competencies, and values to make determinations about their personality traits. Role schemas, often associated with stereotypes, include behavior sets and role expectations. Event schemas, also referred to as cognitive scripts, provide the basis for anticipating the future, setting goals, and making plans. Self-schemas are cognitive representations about our self-concept or, in other words, perceptions of our traits, competencies, and values.

20. **B) Id**
Freud's psychoanalytic theory proposes three distinct aspects of personality: the id, ego, and superego. An individual's desire to eat an extra slice of cake is consistent with the belief that the id operates on the pleasure principle. The ego is thought to possess a mediating role between the conflicting demands of the id and reality, as well as defer gratification until appropriate. Meanwhile, the superego is conceptualized to engage in attempts to permanently block the id's socially unacceptable drives and is driven by the concepts of right and wrong. Thanatos is not conceptualized as an aspect of personality, but rather aggressive instincts present at death that contribute to the id.

21. A patient reflects on a recent therapy session during which they processed the decision to end a long-term relationship. They note that they appreciated their therapist's emphasis on the importance of choice and self-determination. What therapeutic approach is the patient likely remembering?
    A. Behavioral
    B. Cognitive
    C. Humanistic/existential
    D. Psychodynamic

22. A psychology professor asks their students to describe traits they believe dominate their own personalities and traits they believe are situation-specific. With what major theory of personality is this assignment most consistent?
    A. Adlerian theory
    B. Object relations theory
    C. Psychoanalytic theory
    D. Trait theory

23. A licensed psychologist is listening to an audio recording of their supervisee delivering an evidence-based therapy. Throughout the session recording, the psychologist notices that the supervisee frequently proposes examples of values-based activities that tend to cost a lot of money (e.g., traveling). What tool or concept would be most helpful to explore in supervision, specifically in regard to this case?
    A. ADDRESSING acronym
    B. Confirmation bias
    C. Person schemas
    D. Social exchange theory

(See answers on the next page.)

21. **C) Humanistic/existential**
    Humanistic and existential theories of personality emphasize subjectivity and self-reflection, particularly the importance of choice and self-determination; thus, a humanistic and existential therapeutic approach emphasizes the role of choice and self-determination in an individual's life. Behavioral theories of personality generally conceptualize personality as a result of mutual interaction of the person (or the "organism") with its environment. Behavioral therapy places emphasis on the processes of learning and reinforcement, utilizing contingencies to shape behavior. Cognitive therapy predominantly explores the role of cognitions and uses strategies such as cognitive restructuring to help change unhelpful and/or inaccurate beliefs to impact emotions and behaviors. Psychodynamic therapy focuses on unconscious processes as they manifest in an individual's present thoughts and behaviors.

22. **D) Trait theory**
    Trait theory focuses on the role of specific personality traits as traits, defined as patterns of behavior, thought, and emotion, that are proposed to be relatively stable over time. Central traits refer to basic aspects of someone's personality, while cardinal traits refer to the characteristics by which an individual may be recognized. Psychoanalytic theory is comprised of the role of three distinct aspects of personality (the id, ego, and superego) that describe unconscious processes that impact our thinking and behavior. Object relations theory emphasizes the process by which an infant assumes their own physical and psychological identity through objects (conceptualized as internalized images which assist the unconscious in making sense of people and the environment). Adlerian theory postulates that basic mistakes originating from faulty perceptions, attitudes, and beliefs lead to myths, which strongly influence personality.

23. **A) ADDRESSING acronym**
    Hays' ADDRESSING acronym (2001) provides a tool for individuals to explore and understand potential areas of holding or not holding privilege within the American power system. Having self-awareness of personal privilege, as well as an understanding of oppressions that exist, are important aspects of being a competent provider of psychological services. Exploring the ADDRESSING acronym in supervision may be beneficial for the supervisee to increase their self-awareness of their own privileges and how that may impact their provision of therapy (e.g., examples that they use with their clients that may be perceived as inaccessible or unrelatable).

24. An individual observes their family members making statements about a stranger's racial and ethnic identity while at a local event. This motivates the individual to read several books about the role that White individuals have in perpetrating racism. What information processing strategy is most likely being utilized?
    A. Flexibility and complexity
    B. Internalization
    C. Selective perception and negative out-group distortion
    D. Selective perception and reshaping reality

25. According to Meyer's (2003) minority stress model, experiences such as discrimination and violence related to sexual minority identity are conceptualized as:
    A. Distal stressors
    B. Integrative awareness milestones
    C. Proximal stressors
    D. Stages of identity development

(See answers on the next page.)

24. **D) Selective perception and reshaping reality**
    Helms' White Racial Identity Development Model (1990, 1995) is composed of six distinct phases that are characterized by different information-processing strategies, which refers to the methods individuals use to reduce discomfort related to racial issues. First is the contact status stage characterized by little awareness of racism and racial identity, involving information-processing strategies of obliviousness and denial. Second is the disintegration status characterized by increasing awareness of race and racism, leading to confusion and emotional conflict. Individuals in this stage use strategies of suppression of information and ambivalence. Third is the reintegration status characterized by attempts to resolve moral dilemmas associated with the disintegration status by idealizing White society and denigrating members of minority groups, involving strategies of selective perception and negative out-group distortion. Fourth is the pseudoindependence status stage, characterized by a personally jarring event or series of events that cause individuals to question racist views and acknowledge the role that Whites have in perpetrating racism. Strategies of selective perception and reshaping reality may manifest as interest in understanding racial and cultural differences, but only on an intellectual level (e.g., reading textbooks and learning relevant theories). Fifth is the immersion-emersion stage, characterized by exploration of what it means to be White, confrontation of individuals' own biases, and beginning to understand ways they can benefit from White privilege. This stage involves strategies of hypervigilance and reshaping. Sixth is the autonomy status stage, characterized by internalization of nonracist White identity that includes appreciation of and respect for racial and cultural differences and similarities. Strategies in this stage include flexibility and complexity.

25. **A) Distal stressors**
    Meyer's minority stress model (2003) identifies distal stressors, which are outside events (such as discrimination and violence), and proximal stressors, which are internal processes (such as internalized homophobia, rejection expectations, and concealment of minoritized identity).

Growth and Life-Span Development

Casey B. Corso, Rebecca Hoppe, Edith Winters, Laura E. Boylan, and Marcia A. Winter

> **BROAD CONTENT AREAS**
> - Theoretical underpinnings of developmental research
> - Key domains of development and their respective processes
> - Typical and atypical patterns of development across the life span
> - Protective and risk factors that influence developmental trajectories of individuals

▶ INTRODUCTION

Development is, simply put, how an individual changes over time. Development involves growth and change that occur as a means of making an individual better adapted to the environment. This adaptation can occur through enhancement of the individual's ability to engage in, understand, and experience more complex behavior, thinking, and emotions. Development is a relatively enduring component of an individual and encompasses the differences an individual experiences over time cognitively, socially, and emotionally, as well as in language, neurobiological and physical maturation, environment, life experiences, and genetics; development is also inclusive of how these complex aspects interact with one another over time (Beltre & Mendez, 2022). Virtually all developmentalists agree that development involves the constant interplay between biology (nature) and the environment (nurture), occurs in multilayered contexts, and is cumulative and continuous (Sameroff, 2010). The pathway of development over time that connects a person's past to their future is known as a developmental trajectory.

▶ ORGANIZING CONCEPTS, THEORIES, AND MODELS

Developmental science is organized around major concepts. For one, current science recognizes that development occurs as a function of "nature with nurture" (Houmark et al., 2020; Steinberg et al., 2011). While these components used to be seen as opposing forces, it is now widely accepted that development will not occur without both, and they "interpenetrate" each other in that "one's nature changes one's nurture" and vice versa (Sameroff, 2010, p. 9). Indeed, the current consensus among developmentalists is that the biological forces that govern development ("nature") interact with the environmental conditions and with the supports that influence development ("nurture").

Complementary with the interactive "nature with nurture" approach, additional theories and models of development are guided by the following concepts: (a) sensitive or critical periods, (b) continuity and discontinuity, (c) risk and resilience, and (d) the active or passive role of the individual and environment. Each of these concepts focuses more specifically on issues of developmental timing and event impact on one's developmental trajectory, as well as on the relative contributions of the individual ("nature") and environment ("nurture") within and between the domains of development.

Beyond the major organizing concepts, there are six generally accepted stages of development. Each period characterizes major transitions in human development: the prenatal period (conception to birth), infancy (birth to 2 years), early childhood (ages 2–6), middle childhood (ages 6–11), adolescence (ages 11–20), and adulthood (above age 20). Two additional age periods (emerging adulthood, ages 18–25, and geriatric adulthood, ages above 80) have begun to receive attention as individually significant periods of transition. In each of the outlined stages, the age ranges provided only serve as approximations to mark major developmental milestones, and consideration for individual and cultural differences should be recognized.

In this chapter, first we expand on the major organizing concepts of developmental science. Second, we describe major theories, organized by historical and contemporary frameworks. Then, we expand on specific topics and provide definitions, terms, descriptions, and current evidence. As a whole, this chapter takes a life-span perspective, beginning prenatally and continuing through adulthood. Topic sections are primarily organized by developmental domain and secondarily by developmental chronology. Within each domain, subtopics will be addressed. Further, each topic will follow a set organization: (a) introduction to the topic (i.e., definition/explanation), (b) outline of the typical developmental course and/or implications of the topic for typical development, and (c) topical interactions with the environment. Relevant overall concepts and theoretical perspectives that pertain primarily only to that topic are also included, as appropriate. Lastly, consideration for key risk and protective factors is embedded throughout the chapter.

▶ MAJOR ORGANIZING CONCEPTS

The interactive approach (nature and nurture) to development means that development results from the constant interplay of biology and the environment. This approach explains current and future behavior and adaptation as a measured function of individual and environmental characteristics.

The individual is characterized by physical attributes such as genetic, biological, hormonal, and anatomical makeup; descriptive characteristics such as age, sex, gender, or health status; cognitive and social–emotional features such as reactivity; cognitive capacities; motivation; and knowledge accrued over time through experience and learning. While all children come into the world with the set of genes they inherit from their parents (genotype, or the 23 pairs of chromosomes one inherits from one's parents), only a few traits are genetically "determined." The phenotypic characteristics a child develops (i.e., one's observable appearance and characteristics) are the result of interaction between genetic and environmental influences over time (Gottlieb et al., 2006). A child may inherit a genetic tendency to be inhibited, for instance, but whether this leads to painful shyness or quiet confidence depends on the child's experiences.

The environment is characterized by the range of characteristics of the physical and social/relational contexts in which they are situated. These typically include home environments and primary and secondary caregivers such as parents; extended family members, including siblings; other children, including peers and friends; school and educational settings and associated nonparental caregivers, teachers, and other adults; and romantic partners, friends, and coworkers; plus the broader environment, including their caregivers' environments and supports, and the culture, laws, and norms of the whole.

The role of the environment diverges in models that are primarily focused on traits, on the environment, or on the interaction of the two (Sharp et al., 2020). Trait models, also often called medical models, look to predict a later outcome based on earlier status features. Traits can be "innate" (e.g., genetic features or temperamental tendencies) or process-based (e.g., attributes or other features not seen as readily malleable). Trait models are common in personality theory. However, evidence reveals some problems with trait models. For one, trait models are not often predictive of later behaviors, characteristics, or psychopathology (Sharp et al., 2020). In addition, individual traits tend to be situation specific, and trait models do not consider this impact of the situation (Sharp et al., 2020).

Environmental models view development as a function of environmental forces acting continuously on the individual, with rewards and punishments from the environment directly predicting the individual's behavior. Consistent environments are seen as influencing consistent child behavior, whereas if a child's environment changes, so will the child's status and behavior. Modeling and observational learning fit within environmental models. The indirect effects of memories of earlier environmental forces on concurrent and later behavior also fit within this framework.

Still, the interactional approach is dominant in the field (McAdams et al., 2023). Interactional models consider both the individual and environment to have an active role in one's developmental trajectory. As such, characteristics of both the child and the environment must be measured and taken into account to explain current and future behavior and adaptation. Five principles can be drawn from the accumulated research evidence (Steinberg et al., 2011):

1. *Development results from the constant interplay of biology and the environment.*
2. *Development occurs in a multilayered context of interpersonal relationships, social institutions, culture, and historical period.*
3. *Development is a dynamic, reciprocal process wherein each individual takes an active role in shaping their development.*
4. *Development is cumulative; understanding early periods and experiences are critical for predicting future trajectories.*
5. *Development occurs throughout the life span, from birth to death.*

Several subconcepts further organize the understanding of human development. The first concepts described in the following section—namely, sensitive or critical periods, plasticity, and continuity—are more concerned with time, chronology, and developmental trajectories, whereas the latter two, risk/resilience and active/passive roles, are more concerned with the relative characteristics and roles of the individual and environment. However, these may all be at work in any given developmental process and across developmental processes over time.

SENSITIVE OR CRITICAL PERIODS

The concept of sensitive or critical periods encompasses the idea that individuals may have different developmental trajectories depending on the timing of an environmental experience or lack thereof (Bornstein, 1989). If a process, structure, or function is undeveloped at the time of the onset of an environmental experience, the experience may induce or prevent emergence of that process, structure, or function. Without any experience, the process, structure, or function will not develop. If a process, structure, or function is partially developed, experience may maintain, attune, facilitate, or suppress further development. If a process, structure, or function is more fully developed, experience could maintain it, or lack of effective experience could eventuate in loss. For example, in severe cases of neglect, children's development is detrimentally affected in a variety of domains due to a lack of experience. Consider the development of language, which necessitates the child experiencing noise verbalizations, which eventually turn to words and sentences and overall communication reciprocity. Children whose early babbles are not reciprocated or who are not often spoken to by an adult are, as a consequence, not afforded the experience required for language development and will either not develop language as expected, or will develop it with inhibitions or delays. If that process has been developed, say with an older child, cases of neglect wherein a child is not spoken to may instead result in a stagnation or regression of that skill development.

If an aspect of development is subject to a critical period, which also could be called an "all-or-nothing" period, this means that there is a period of growth when something specific must occur (or not occur) if development is to proceed normally. Research findings indicate that there are few truly critical periods in human development in which experience or lack thereof will eventuate in a permanent alteration of a typical developmental trajectory. Most of these appear to be in prenatal development and will be described in relevant sections in the text that follows.

If an aspect of development is subject to a sensitive period, this means that there are times in an individual's development of heightened sensitivity to certain environmental stimuli when a particular experience (or lack of it) has a more pronounced effect—be it positive or negative—on the organism than does the experience at another time. Research supports sensitive periods in several aspects of human development in which experiences can influence developmental trajectories, with the possibility that future experience can further influence that trajectory becoming smaller or requiring more profound experiences. Evidence of such sensitive periods will be described and presented in relevant sections throughout this chapter.

Plasticity

Related to the concept of critical or sensitive periods is the concept of plasticity, or malleability. *Plasticity* can be defined as a sensitivity to the environment engendered by experience, including the capacity of immature systems to take on different functions as a result of experience and the degree to which a developing structure or behavior is modifiable due to experience (Sommer, 2020). Certain aspects of development are more or less fixed and difficult to change, whereas other aspects of development are relatively malleable and easy to change. In the former, the environment may have less influence, or less influence over time, whereas in the latter, the environment can have great influence. However, the notion of sensitive periods also implies that the malleability or plasticity of some aspects of development changes. In other words, it becomes harder to change some aspects over time.

Continuity and Discontinuity

The concept of continuity involves the notion that development is a gradual, continuous process of change, whereas the concept of discontinuity involves the notion that development is punctuated by periods of rapid change and sudden emergence of new forms of thought and behavior. Formal developmental theories that take a discontinuous approach are also called stage theories (Lerner, 1997). Stage theorists suggest development to be discontinuous due to the seemingly sudden jumps in abilities, such as children who begin walking and quickly master the skill. Continuous theorists instead suggest that development is a steady, ongoing process that you cannot fully view as it happens, similar to how one's cells are constantly growing and evolving. Continuous development can be seen as a "zoomed in" understanding of the processes occurring, whereas stage theorists can be seen as taking a more "zoomed out" and broad approach to understanding development.

Risk and Resilience

In human development, a risk is any characteristic that is associated with an elevated probability of an undesirable outcome. A risk factor (e.g., chronic poverty, family violence, maternal depression, substance abuse) is a predictor of an undesirable outcome in a population. The probabilities of such undesirable outcomes are established by studying groups of people. An individual described as "at risk" is a member of a group in which research has shown an elevated probability of the negative outcome under consideration. In contrast, protective factors are conditions or strengths in individuals, families, and communities that help to buffer against risk and promote healthy development and well-being. Resilience can be broadly defined as one's capacity to successfully adapt when facing multisystem processes that challenge or threaten one's function, survival, or development (Masten et al., 2021). Many components of resilience have been found to be fundamental to one's adaptive systems, occurring through coevolved processes that may, in turn, result in transdiagnostic protections against psychopathology (Masten et al., 2021).

Active and Passive Roles of Individual and Environment
Some developmental models are classified by whether they consider individual children or persons and the environment as passive or active agents in development. In a model with a passive child and an active environment, the environment is viewed as controlling the child's behavior and development. Operant conditioning processes fall into this view. This may include behavior modification treatment or parent education or parent guidance programs that aim to alter maladaptive behavior and/or guide parent behavior to shape child behavior. In a model with an active child and a passive environment, the child is viewed as extracting and constructing their knowledge and world. Piaget's cognitive development theory fits within this framework, as the child needs the environment to provide input and construct knowledge, but the environment itself does not play a major role. It is important to note that current science most supports the view of active development; many approaches fit this approach, including transactional, epigenetic, and bioecological models.

MAJOR DEVELOPMENTAL THEORIES

A theory is a broad framework or set of principles and ideas that can be used to guide the collection and interpretation of a set of facts. It describes, explains, and predicts behavior while providing testable hypotheses. Developmental theories are particularly focused on how human beings grow and change over time.

Historical Theories
The major theories with elements addressing human development that tended to dominate developmental science and practice in the earlier phases of the discipline include psychoanalytic and personality theories, learning theories, and cognitive-developmental theories.

Psychodynamic theories, including Freud's theory of psychosexual development and Erikson's theory of psychosocial development, are historically important but no longer drive modern developmental science and practice. Learning theories, including behaviorism, classical and operant conditioning, and social learning theory, continue to play a role in developmental science and practice (Kazdin, 2001), albeit a more limited role pertaining to comprehensive developmental processes. The cognitive-developmental theory of Piaget (1954) continues to influence some aspects of current research and practice, although many of the specific propositions have been dropped or revised in the face of later research evidence.

Piaget's Cognitive-Developmental Theory
Through detailed observations of his own three children and subsequent observations and interviews with other children, Piaget developed his stage theory and changed people's perceptions about the ways in which children think about the world. Children's thinking is not less intelligent than adults', just different. According to Piaget, cognitive development is not governed by internal maturation or external teachings alone; instead, children are "little scientists" who actively construct their cognitive worlds through exploration, manipulation, and trying to make sense of their environment. As children develop from birth through adolescence, they undergo a process of decentralization from an undifferentiated, concrete, perceptual world to one that is increasingly conceptual and able to be symbolically represented. Through adaptation, children build mental structures—called schemas—to organize knowledge, adapt to the world, and adjust to new environmental demands. In the process of assimilation, individuals incorporate new information or experiences into their existing schemas. For example, a child who has learned the word *dog* for a four-legged animal may refer to other animals such as cats, zebras, and elephants as "dogs." In

the process of accommodation, individuals adjust their schema to take into account new information or experiences. Thus, a child learns to fine-tune his "dog" schema to only include animals that are four-legged, furry, and bark. By a mechanism called equilibration, children attempt to create a balance between assimilation and accommodation. The internal search for equilibrium is the motivation for change and helps to explain children's shift from one stage of thought to the next. As a result of these processes, children undergo cognitive change.

Piaget proposed four stages of cognitive development: sensorimotor, preoperational, concrete operational, and formal operational. Individuals progress through the stages in a fixed order, with each stage building on the preceding stage. Moving to the next stage represents a qualitative difference in understanding. During the sensorimotor stage (birth to 2 years), infants learn about themselves and the environment by coordinating their sensory experiences with physical actions. Initially, children primarily use reflexive behaviors, but by the end of the stage they are able to employ complex sensorimotor patterns and simple symbols. The sensorimotor stage is further divided into six substages. During the simple reflexes substage (birth to 1 month), newborn babies use reflexes such as rooting and sucking to coordinate sensation and action. For example, newborns will only suck if there is a nipple placed in their mouths; within a month, they may start to suck when a bottle or nipple is near their mouths, initiating an action that resembles a reflex, and actively organizing their experience. In the second substage—first habits and primary circular reactions (1–4 months)—infants can coordinate sensation with two types of schema: habits (reflexes that are separated from the eliciting stimulus) and primary circular reactions (creation of an event that initially occurred by chance). Thus, infants may suck even when a bottle is not present or try to suck on their fingers again after accidentally sucking them when they were placed near their mouth. The primary focus remains on the infants' bodies; they do not look to the environment. During the third substage—secondary circular reactions (4–8 months)—infants move beyond self-preoccupation and become more object oriented. For instance, an infant may accidentally shake a rattle and then repeat the action because the sound it makes is interesting and satisfying. In the fourth substage—coordination of secondary circular reactions (8–12 months)—infants' actions become outwardly-directed and intentional. They are able to coordinate touch and vision to make hand–eye movements. Thus, for example, an infant might simultaneously examine a rattle visually while exploring it tactilely. Likewise, a baby may intentionally use a stick to bring an attractive toy within reach. During this substage, infants also become more capable of recognizing object permanence, the understanding that objects continue to exist even if they cannot be seen, heard, or touched. In the fifth substage—tertiary circular reactions, novelty, and curiosity (12–18 months)—infants become interested in the various properties of objects. They continually experiment to explore what happens to objects. For example, an infant may choose a block and throw it, slide it across the ground, or hit another object with it so they can observe the consequences of these actions. During the sixth substage of the sensorimotor period—internalization of schemata (18–24 months)—infants develop the ability to use simple symbols and form lasting mental representations. This allows infants to think about concrete events and represent them by using internalized sensory images or words. For example, a child who has never thrown a temper tantrum before sees another child throw a tantrum, retains a memory of this event, and throws a tantrum the next day. In short, the key cognitive-developmental achievement of the sensorimotor period is the ability to create symbolic representations of experiences and the environment.

The second stage of cognitive development in Piaget's theory is the preoperational stage (2–7 years). At this stage, children use mental representations, such as words, images, and drawings, to understand the world and begin to reason. This stage is dominated by egocentric thinking and magical beliefs. The preoperational stage is divided further into two substages, symbolic function and intuitive thought. During the symbolic function substage (2–4 years), young children are able to mentally represent an object that is not present; this is evidenced by scribbling, language use, and pretend play. The "three mountains" task is used to demonstrate egocentrism, or the inability to differentiate one's own perspective from someone else's. For example, a child and a doll sit on opposite sides of a model displaying three mountains of different sizes. When asked to point to the picture of the way the doll sees the three mountains, the child in the preoperational stage points to the picture showing their own perspective, demonstrating that they cannot take the doll's point of view. During this stage, a young child believes in animism, that inanimate objects have lifelike characteristics and are able to perform actions. Therefore, according to a child with preoperational thought, a car is not starting because it is sick or tired, and a piece of furniture must be punished because it is naughty since it hurt the child when he ran into it. Children in the second substage—intuitive thought (4–7 years)—begin to use simple reasoning and ask "why" questions to figure out how the world works.

In the third stage of Piaget's cognitive-developmental theory, the concrete operational stage (7–11 years), children are able to reason logically in specific or concrete examples. Due to their emerging ability to mentally reverse actions, their thinking is no longer controlled by centration (i.e., focusing on one aspect to the exclusion of all others) and they can now understand conservation. Conservation is the comprehension that changing the appearance of an object or substance does not change its basic properties. The beaker test is a task that demonstrates conservation. A child is shown two identical beakers with the same amount of liquid in each. As the child watches, an experimenter pours the liquid from one beaker into another beaker that is taller and thinner than the two identical beakers. When asked which beaker has more liquid, a child in the preoperational stage will point to the taller and thinner beaker, whereas a child in the concrete operational stage will understand that the amount of liquid has not changed in the transfer.

The fourth and final stage of Piaget's theory is the formal operational stage; it appears between 11 and 15 years of age and continues through adulthood. This stage is characterized by abstract, idealistic, and logical thinking. Instead of relying on trial and error, individuals are now capable of hypothetical-deductive reasoning, the ability to develop hypotheses and determine systematically the best way to solve a problem and arrive at a conclusion.

Although Piaget's theory heavily influenced the current field of children's cognitive development, research findings have led to quite a few criticisms and clarifications. Current thinking is that cognitive development is less abrupt and stagelike and more gradual and continuous than Piaget thought. Cognitive development is not necessarily a general process, and new skills in one area may not translate to new skills in another area. Moreover, Piaget may have underestimated children's competence and overestimated adolescents' cognitive abilities. In particular, Piaget placed an overreliance on the physical and motor skills of infants and ignored learning through sensation, perception, and environmental input. Methodologically, Piaget required children to perform complex tasks and answer complex questions. When children are given real-world, less-abstract tasks to complete, they are generally more successful at an earlier age than Piaget predicted. Finally, Piaget did not consider the influence of the environment, individual differences, cultural variations, and social trends on children's cognitive development. Neo-Piagetians believe that Piaget's theory needs considerable revision and they place greater emphasis on children's use of attention, memory, speed, and strategy to process information (Case, 1987, 1999).

Vygotsky's Sociocultural Cognitive Theory
Like Piaget, Vygotsky (1978a, 1978b) believed that children actively construct their knowledge and understanding of the world. However, Vygotsky's theory emphasizes the importance of social interaction and cultural context in shaping children's thinking. For Vygotsky, instruction plays a major role in cognitive development, and this is reflected in his concept of the zone of proximal development (ZPD). The ZPD encompasses the tasks that are too difficult for children to complete on their own but can be learned and accomplished with the guidance of someone more skilled. The lower limit of the ZPD is the level of skill children have while working independently and the upper limit is the level of additional capability the children could reach with the assistance of instructors. Scaffolding refers to the changing level of support instructors—typically adults—provide as they adjust to children's current performance level based on their increasing skill level. Thus, teachers may use a great amount of direct instruction and assistance initially, then offer less guidance as students' competence increases.

Some criticisms of Vygotsky's theory include that it was not specific enough about age-related changes, did not adequately explain how changes in social–emotional abilities translate to cognitive development, and overemphasized the role of language in thinking. Nonetheless, many of Vygotsky's ideas continue to be influential to the ways that development is conceptualized and studied. For example, Rogoff (1990) drew on and expanded Vygotsky's ideas in developing the concept of guided participation in sociocultural activity as contributing to cognitive development.

Contemporary Theories

Drawing from the bases of historical theories, more recent approaches to development shape current research and practice. Although there are many, we focus on several that demonstrate the breadth and depth of contemporary thinking.

Bioecological Systems Theory

The bioecological systems theory (or ecological systems) proposed by Bronfenbrenner (1979, 1986; Bronfenbrenner & Morris, 2006) emphasizes the influence of process, person, context, and time on individual development. Bronfenbrenner described four types of ecological systems nested within each other—the microsystem, mesosystem, exosystem, and macrosystem—as well as the influence of time in the chronosystem (see Figure 6.1). The individual is in the center, and

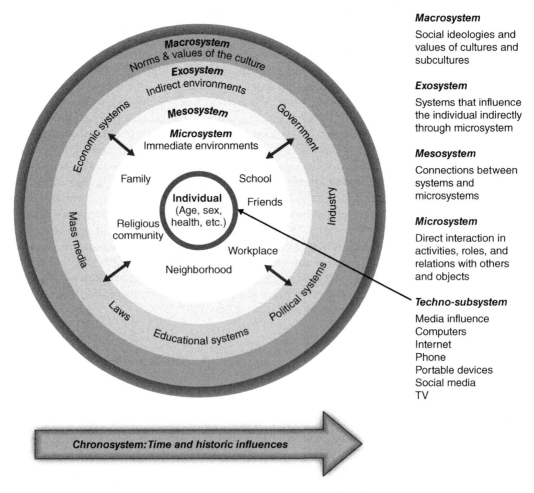

Figure 6.1 Bronfenbrenner's bioecological model of human development.
Source: Adapted from Bronfenbrenner, U., & Morris, P. A. (2006). The bioecological model of human development. In R. M. Lerner & W. Damon (Eds.), *Handbook of child psychology: Vol. 1, Theoretical models of human development* (6th ed., pp. 793–828). John Wiley.

the biological influences of factors such as sex, age, and health that affect development are considered. The microsystem includes all of the settings with which the individual directly interacts as well as the contexts that directly influence development (e.g., family, peers, school, and neighborhood). Individuals actively construct their experiences in these settings and are not merely passive participants. The mesosystem consists of the connections among microsystems, such as the relationship between the family and school or the family and peers. For example, children's education and experiences in school may be influenced by parents' interactions with teachers and the extent of their involvement with the school. The exosystem includes contexts within which the individual does not directly interact but has indirect influences on development. For instance, there may be increased interparental conflict and changes in parent–child interaction patterns when a working parent receives a promotion that necessitates more work-related travel. The macrosystem describes the impact of the broader social context in which an individual lives—including the laws, policies, and ideologies of that culture—on development. Changes in national policies—for example, those related to education, healthcare, and other social services—can impact children's access to resources and thus their well-being and development. The final level of Bronfenbrenner's model is the chronosystem, which represents the developmental patterns and transitions of the individual across time as well as the sociohistorical conditions of that time. Some transitions are expected (e.g., starting formal schooling), whereas others are not predicted (e.g., parent divorce). Historical events such as the COVID-19 pandemic are also chronosystem influences on individual development. For Bronfenbrenner, the nested systems continue to function, albeit within different contexts, throughout the life span. For adults, microsystem settings typically include their home, place of work, and other settings that comprise individuals' most proximal relationships and environments (e.g., religious or recreation organizations). Although the specific nature of changes within the exo- and macrosystems may evolve over time and within the chronosystem from childhood to adulthood, the theoretical structure of the system influences remains stable over time.

Bronfenbrenner's bioecological systems theory (Figure 6.1) is prevalent because it considers both the micro and macro influences on individual development and gives attention to the interactions among environmental systems. The major criticisms of the theory are that it does not sufficiently address biological and cognitive factors, although later formulations of the theory at least partially addressed those concerns (Bronfenbrenner & Morris, 2006). Variants of the theory have been introduced, for example, the phenomenological variant of ecological systems theory (PVEST; Spencer et al., 1997). The PVEST focuses particularly on the social, historical, and cultural contexts in which individuals develop, with emphasis on individuals' environmentally influenced perceptions and appraisals during identity development. Research grounded in PVEST has contributed to the understanding of how racially minoritized youth—particularly Black and African American youth in the United States—develop within systems (Cunningham et al., 2023).

Dynamic Systems Theory

The dynamic systems theory of Thelen (Thelen & Smith, 2006) posits that the child's mind, body, and physical and social worlds form an integrated system that guides mastery of new skills. Any change in one context or domain of development can disrupt the entire system, prompting a reorganization that requires adaptation. In this model, *dynamic* refers to the concept that a change in any part disrupts the current organism–environment relationship. In turn, the disruption leads to active reorganization so that the system's components work together again, but this time in more complex, effective ways. Development is viewed as nonlinear; rather, this perspective often symbolizes development as a web, with branching processes and skills. Dynamic processes are central during transitions.

For example, a child's first steps are highly influenced by physical maturation, as the child's muscles strengthen and balance improves. The change from nonwalker to walker is more than a physical change, however, in that it can disrupt the system both within children and in their broader environments. This prompts a reorganization that leads to more adaptive functioning: The newly walking children receive novel perceptual and cognitive input, as their perspectives are now from an upright stance and they can touch, see, and hear more; this new input will then allow them to adjust their understanding of the world. Moreover, new walkers can now reach something of interest on their own rather than having to wait or signal desire to others. This ability can reinforce their interest in the world, motivation to explore, excitement, and sense of achievement. In the environment, a newly walking child prompts both excitement and nervousness in parents and caregivers. Parents love to see children's first steps, but they also worry about injury and must reorganize their homes by adding stair gates and placing certain items out of reach. Parents may also become more restrictive of children out of concern; thus, the parent–child interactive system can also be disrupted. Over time, as the transition to walking settles down, children's systems and environments will adapt and reach a new normal that supports the children's next developmental processes.

A number of developmentally salient transitions also emerge in adolescence and adulthood, including the transition from high school to a college or work setting, the transition from employment to retirement, and the transition from home to assisted living or nursing home care. Each of these transitions represents a significant strain on the motivational and adaptational resources of individuals. At each transitional phase, individuals are challenged by changes in the environment to call on personal and social resources (e.g., coping skills and emotional and instrumental support from others) in order to adjust to their new circumstances. Failure to successfully adapt to change has been associated with a number of poor developmental outcomes in adolescence and adulthood, including behavior problems, school dropout rates, anxiety, depression, and social isolation.

Life-Span Theory

In an effort to explain the positive behavioral adaptations that individuals evince in response to age-related losses, Baltes and colleagues introduced the selective optimization with compensation (SOC) model, which describes three factors critical to successful aging across the life span (Baltes et al., 1980; Freund & Baltes, 1998). These action-based processes include the selection of desired goals or strategies that one chooses to pursue, optimization of actions and abilities that can be used to achieve such goals and compensation, and adjustment of goals and strategies in response to losses in capacity (Baltes & Baltes, 1990). The main premise of this theory is that while there is marked variability in both intra- and interindividual developmental trajectories, the utilization of SOC helps to mitigate the effects of losses in functioning while also providing the basis for adaptive functioning and positive adjustment. Baltes's SOC model is a life-span developmental theory that describes the structure and direction of individual development over time. It is also a framework for understanding variations in the process of successful aging. Rather than viewing successful development as having a single path with a lone outcome for "typical" development, life-span developmental psychology posits that a wide range of developmental pathways can lead to numerous positive developmental outcomes (Baltes, 1987). The changes that occur over time as people age involve a wide range of domains (i.e., are multidimensional)—including social, emotional, and physical growth—that change over time to varying degrees, and are therefore multidirectional (Baltes, 1987). The SOC theory accounts for both age-graded changes (i.e., physical and cognitive transformations that occur in nearly all humans as they age) and nonnormative changes (i.e., those that happen to select individuals, such as disease or mental disorder) that characterize growth and decline over time. Although individuals are likely to experience age-related declines in motor and cognitive abilities, including difficulty walking and decrements in cognitive processing speed and working memory, there are nonetheless opportunities to compensate for these losses at each stage in life. For example, as they age into older adulthood, individuals increasingly rely on external aids such as reading glasses, note-taking, and mobility devices in order to maintain a stable level of everyday functioning and high vitality.

DOMAINS OF DEVELOPMENT

In this section, we review the three major domains of development: physical, cognitive, and social–emotional. While the borders between these developmental domains overlap, each encompasses unique aspects of development. Physical development includes genetic, neurocognitive, hormonal, motor, sensory and perceptual, and health and nutrition processes. Cognitive development includes processes related to sensation, perception, attention, memory, skills and achievements milestones, language, and theory of mind (ToM). Social–emotional development includes processes of self-concept, emotions and regulation, temperament, attachment, identity, and moral and prosocial behavior.

Before teasing apart physical, cognitive, and social–emotional development, we begin first with a section on prenatal development, for which domains of development are particularly intertwined.

Prenatal Development, Birth, and Neonatal Period
Meiosis and Mitosis
Reproductive cells, or gametes, reproduce by meiosis wherein cells containing only half of a set of chromosomes (i.e., half of the genetic material of the parent cell) are produced and commonly known as sperm or ova. During the first phase of meiosis, cells "cross over" one another. To accomplish this, each of the 23 pairs of chromosomes line up, wrap around each other, and exchange genetic material. During the second phase of meiosis, reshuffling takes place, in which some of the ova chromosomes align with the sperm chromosomes and vice versa. After reshuffling, the cell divides into two chromosomes with new, unique combinations of genetic material. These new cells then begin to produce duplicates of themselves. Notably, chromosomal abnormalities (e.g., Down syndrome) are often caused by mutations during meiosis.

At conception, the ovum and sperm unite to form a new cell called a zygote. During ordinary cell reproduction, or mitosis, a cell divides into a copy of itself. Each resulting cell receives a full copy of all 46 chromosomes. As the zygote travels toward the uterus, it begins to differentiate into cells with specialized roles, with the outer cells designated to become the placenta and the inner cells the embryo. Once the zygote reaches the uterus, implantation may occur. Sex differentiation begins at conception, with females having two X chromosomes and males having an X and a Y chromosome.

Periods of Prenatal Development
After implantation, the embryonic period begins. During the embryonic period, the basic structure of a human being appears and organs begin to function. For example, the ectoderm will become the skin, nerves, and sense organs. Further, the mesoderm will become the muscle, bones, circulatory system, and some organs, while the endoderm will become the digestive system, lungs, urinary tract, and glands. Neurogenesis also begins during the embryonic period, wherein neurons are produced in the embryo's primitive neural tube, migrate to form the major parts of the brain, and then differentiate to establish unique functions and synaptic connections (see "brain development" in the Physical and Motor Development section of this chapter for additional details). By the end of the embryonic period, all the major organ and body parts have been formed.

Once the embryonic period completes, the fetal period begins. During the fetal period, the primitive organ and body parts develop and grow. Neurogenesis is typically complete by the end of the sixth month, and the brain begins to organize itself, allowing some neurons to die off while others make new connections.

Environmental Impact During Prenatal Development
The impact of the environment on prenatal development can be significant. For example, the quality of maternal nutrition impacts the health of the embryo and fetus. Malnutrition in early pregnancy, particularly lack of folic acid, increases the risk for birth defects such as spina bifida

or anencelapathy. Evidence also suggests that prenatal folic acid deficiency is associated with increased risk for autism spectrum disorders (Hoxha et al., 2021). Malnutrition later in pregnancy is associated with lower birth weight, although the effects can be overcome by quality nutrition after birth in a stable, supportive environment. High stress in pregnancy increases the risk for premature birth, as well as poorer long-term physical, cognitive, and psychological health (Van den Bergh et al., 2020).

A teratogen is any substance that can have a negative impact on fetal development. An agent is teratogenic if it has the potential for increased risk of adverse pregnancy outcomes. The dosage, timing of exposure during pregnancy, and genetic factors of the pregnant person influence if something is identified to be teratogenic or not (Valladares & Rasmussen, 2020). Exposure during a sensitive period may alter anatomy or function irreversibly. Although some environmental factors have immediate effects, others have sleeper effects that do not emerge until later in development.

The placenta protects the fetus from many bacteria, but not viruses. For example, infectious diseases such as HIV contracted during the first 3 months of pregnancy can be devastating for the fetus. About one in four infants affected with HIV develops AIDS symptoms shortly after birth. An HIV-positive mother can protect her fetus by taking azidothymidine and other drugs that slow the HIV duplication.

Drugs with known teratogenic effects are also harmful to fetal development. These drugs and substances with teratogenic effects include corticosteroids, lithium therapy, retinoids, thalidomide, vitamin A in large doses, some antimicrobial medications, some antiepileptics, and some hormone therapies, as well as nicotine/smoking. Chemicals with known teratogenic effects include carbon monoxide, lead, mercury, polychlorinated biphenyls (PCBs), and the insecticide DDT (dichlorodiphenyltrichloroethane). Controlled substances with teratogenic potential include alcohol, cocaine, cannabis, methamphetamines, ecstasy, and heroin (National Institute on Drug Abuse, 2015).

Alcohol consumption during pregnancy is also known to negatively impact a developing fetus. Fetal alcohol syndrome (FAS) is a pattern of behavioral and cognitive disabilities and physical abnormalities found in infants whose mothers have alcohol use disorder. Babies with FAS typically have delays in cognitive development; attention and learning difficulties; worse motor-coordination; vision or hearing problems; and abnormalities of the heart, kidneys, bones, and facial features (Geier & Geier, 2022). Centers for Disease Control and Prevention (CDC) studies have shown that 1 case of FAS occurs for every 1,000 live births in certain areas of the United States. Other studies using different methods have estimated the rate of FAS to be higher, at six to nine cases per 1,000 school-age children (CDC, 2024). Rates of fetal alcohol spectrum disorders (FASDs), which are a group of conditions that can occur in a person who is exposed to alcohol prenatally, are even higher than that of FAS. In the United States and Western Europe, researchers estimate that FASD occurs in one to five out of 100 live births.

Birth Complications

Complications during labor and delivery can occur even in healthy pregnancies. There are several risks to the neonate, or newborn, which can have lasting effects, some of which can be ameliorated or prevented with assessment and treatment. Birth complications can also lead to traumatic childbirth experiences for the mother and family. Globally, 45% of new mothers report traumatic childbirths, and diagnosed posttraumatic stress disorder (PTSD) following childbirth happens in 1.5% to 9% of all births (Pop-Jordanova, 2022). Childbirth trauma can have immediate and lasting consequences such as difficulty with mother–child bonding, decreased confidence in parental decision-making, risk for heightened anxiety, and difficulty with the breastfeeding experience.

Some birth complications are positional. The vertex, head-down, back-facing position is ideal for childbirth; others, such as a breech or hammock position, may be problematic and warrant a cesarean section. The occiput posterior presentation is the most common abnormal position and happens when the fetus is head first but its head is facing up toward the mother's abdomen (Moldenhauer, 2022). Hypoxia, or in its most severe form, anoxia, is one of the most significant birth complications. It can be caused by the umbilical cord being pinched; maternal environmental factors, such as being exposed to high altitudes; or because of a placental abruption or placenta previa. Short-term anoxia is usually not a problem, but long-term oxygen loss can cause brain damage, as well as other conditions such as cerebral palsy. In the most extreme cases, anoxia can lead to fetal death.

Preterm birth is one of the highest risk factors for child development. Full-term pregnancies are normally between 38 and 40 weeks; newborns born before 37 weeks are considered premature and are at risk of complications, including immature lungs, respiratory distress, and digestive problems. There are subcategories of preterm babies, which are based on the gestational age. These include extremely preterm, less than 28 weeks, and very preterm, between 28 and 32 weeks.

Low birth weight is defined as less than 5.5 lbs and very low birth weight is below 2.5 lbs. The reasons for preterm birth are numerous, including structural abnormalities to the uterus, maternal age, lack of spacing between a previous pregnancy, and maternal or fetal distress. Preterm babies often suffer from respiratory distress syndrome (RDS), have difficulty with digestion, and are vulnerable to infection. The long-term impact of preterm birth includes increased risk of cerebral palsy, hearing and vision problems, learning disabilities, and poor growth. If preterm newborns are in a medical facility, they usually are fed intravenously or by feeding tube, and are at risk for brain hemorrhaging, necrotizing enterocolitis, sepsis, and heart problems (Cleveland Clinic, n.d.).

The Apgar assessment is given to newborns at 1 minute after birth and 5 minutes after birth by a trained health professional. The test scores the infant from 0 to 2 on color, heart rate, reflexes, muscle tone, and respiration. The score is then summed to get the total Apgar score. Scores above 7 indicate a healthy baby, and below 4 indicate a baby in critical condition. If an infant's Apgar score is 7 or less, the score will be taken again at continuing 5-minute intervals. The Neonatal Behavioral Assessment Scale (NBAS) uses reflexes and social interaction to assess the newborn's overall well-being, including motor capabilities, state changes, and central nervous system (CNS) stability (Brazelton & Nugent, 1995). The NBAS detects neonatal infants who might be at risk for later developmental problems by assessing competencies, strengths, difficulties, and deviations.

Failure to thrive (FTT) is a disorder of impaired growth (lack of height or weight gain). It can happen in older children who are seriously ill or undernourished, but it is most common and most dangerous during the earliest months and over the first 3 years. FTT can be caused by an organic underlying health problem that means the baby cannot obtain or make use of adequate nutrition, such as anemia, infections, or thyroid problems. Nonorganic FTT may be psychological or social and may be associated with the child or caregiver or the dyad. Examples include poverty, misperceptions about diet or feeding practices, inadequate breast milk production, behavioral feeding problems, child abuse, or neglect.

Physical and Motor Development

This section on physical and motor development includes the genetic, neurocognitive, hormonal, motor, sensory and perceptual, and health and nutrition aspects of development.

Genetics

Detailed explanation of genetics is beyond the scope of this chapter. However, a key concept of genetics in developmental science is epigenesis, or the gradual process of increasing differentiation and complexity in an individual due to an interaction between their heredity and the environment. A person's genotype, or genetic makeup, is set at conception and endures through life. Genes affect development through gene expression, or through the proteins they "instruct" the body to produce. Gene expression depends on both the genetic instruction code and on the context in which the genetic instructions occur. This happens through smaller molecules that work to activate and deactivate genes, making them harder or easier to be expressed. This process can be affected and changed throughout the life span by a person's environment, such as diet, chemical exposure, and medication. Probabilistic epigenesis is the probability that a trait, characteristic, or behavior will develop depending on certain conditions in the environment in a reciprocal process (Gottlieb, 2007).

Brain Development

Similar to details of genetics, the details of neurological and neurocognitive functions are beyond the scope of this chapter. The development of brain architecture prenatally through the early years establishes the foundation for all future learning, behavior, and health. Adverse experiences during early childhood can negatively affect brain architecture, such as gene/gene expression, brain structure/functions, the immune system, and the hypothalamic–pituitary–adrenal (HPA) axis. These neurobiological alterations may last through adulthood, particularly impacting higher-order functions (Hakamata et al., 2022). The development of the brain and CNS includes important processes of synaptogenesis, or the development of connections (synapses) between neurons through the growth of axons and dendrites, and synaptic pruning, or the process of elimination of unused and unnecessary synapses. Synapse formation begins at conception and rapidly develops during the first 2 years of life. Both the formation and pruning of synapses are fundamental to plasticity and the degree to which the developing brain and CNS are modifiable due to experience. Experience plays a central role in the selection, maintenance, and strengthening of connections among many neurons. If a neuron is used, it forms more synapses or connections with other cells and becomes functional. The more a neuron is used, the stronger the synaptic connection becomes (i.e., neurons that fire together will wire together). Without stimulation and the opportunity to function, neurons are unlikely to establish or maintain many connections with other neurons. Neurons that have previously formed synaptic connections without use become vulnerable to this pruning process. Thus, brain development is, in part, based on experience. Experience-expectant processes are one type of brain plasticity, whereby some neurons grow and differentiate rapidly at about the time they can be expected to receive relevant stimulation with overproduction of synapses in expectation that a particular sensory stimulus will occur (e.g., parts of the visual cortex involved in depth or pattern perception develop quite rapidly directly before and after birth). Another type of brain plasticity is experience-dependent processes, which involve the active formation of new synapses based on individual experience, thus allowing for unpredictable opportunities for learning (Greenough et al., 1987).

Hypothalamic–Pituitary–Adrenal Axis

The HPA axis is an important regulatory system that controls the levels of the stress hormone cortisol that are released in the body. The body's release of cortisol as a direct response to acute stress is an adaptive response that typically elevates the individual's ability to respond. However, sustained levels of cortisol are typically harmful, as the HPA axis may become dysregulated, particularly in the brain systems responsible for memory and emotion regulation. This biological dysregulation can lead to heightened stress and anxiety, as well as impaired cognitive, behavioral, and social functioning. The HPA axis is of particular importance in early childhood development, when individuals develop expectations of the levels of stress that they will encounter in their daily lives. The consistent presence of environmentally induced stressors during childhood, including neglectful and abusive parenting, can also lead to immune suppression and greater susceptibility to genetic predispositions to a range of developmental disorders. For instance, evidence in animal and human studies has revealed that sustained separation or abuse from one's primary caregiver can lead to hyperactivity in the HPA axis, resulting in elevated cortisol levels. Emotionally available parenting, on the other hand, can promote healthy HPA functioning and provide the individual with the ability to properly regulate their stress response systems. HPA functioning is adaptable, and although HPA dysregulation may have lifelong consequences, changes in an individual's lifestyle and environment—such as sleep, diet, and learning healthy stress management techniques—may help to reverse HPA dysfunction.

Malnutrition

According to the World Health Organization (2020), malnutrition is the underlying contributing factor in about 45% of deaths to children under age 5 worldwide. Malnourished children are not only at a higher risk of contracting diseases but also more likely to suffer from severe disease effects. Children afflicted by illness often experience diminished appetites and reduced nutrient absorption, perpetuating a detrimental cycle of sickness and delayed growth. Malnourishment and child mortality are linked to poverty, forming a destructive cycle. Poverty clearly contributes to malnourishment, but malnutrition and illness in turn exacerbate poverty through diminished cognitive development, lower school achievement, decreased earning potential and wages, and loss of income due to illness.

Motor Development

Motor development involves the development of the capacity for movement, action, and coordination of one's limbs, as well as the development of strength, posture control, balance, and perceptual skills, particularly those made possible by changes in the nervous system and muscles. Fine motor development includes the maturing of skills involving the smaller muscle groups, including the ability to manipulate small objects, transfer objects from hand to hand, and engage in various hand–eye coordination tasks. Gross motor development includes the maturing of skills related to simple, large muscle group actions, including lifting one's head, rolling over, sitting up, balancing, crawling, and walking.

Motor development is an important part of developmental science and understanding. First, behavior *is* movement, including visual exploration, manipulation of objects, and navigation of the environment. Movements are a medium for making inferences about thoughts, perceptions, and intentions that are not directly observable, especially in infants and nonverbal individuals. Second, movement perception, or the process of understanding your own and others' physical movements, provides new opportunities for learning (Cruz et al., 2020).

Motor skill development changes throughout the life span, with the most rapid changes occurring during the earliest months and years of life. Observations of infants and children show that motor development follows a fairly predictable pattern, denoted by parents and practitioners who have charted the norms of motor milestones including sitting, standing, and walking (see Table 6.1). In early development, norms represent the average outcomes, rather than being indicative of either actual or ideal results. Individual differences refer to variation among persons on a given characteristic. Individual differences take into account cultural and familial expectations and practices among other environmental and psychosocial factors. Although there are set "norms" in the timeline for achieving these motor milestones,

TABLE 6.1 Percentiles and Mean in Months for Six Gross Motor Milestones

Motor Milestone	Mean (SD)	5th Percentile	50th Percentile	95th percentile
Sitting without support	6.0 (1.1)	4.3	5.9	8.0
Standing with assistance	7.6 (1.4)	5.5	7.4	10.1
Hands-and-knees crawling	8.5 (1.7)	6.1	8.3	11.3
Walking with assistance	9.2 (1.5)	6.9	9.0	11.8
Standing alone	11.0 (1.9)	8.1	10.8	14.4
Walking alone	12.1 (1.8)	9.4	12.0	15.3

Source: Data from Martorell, R., de Onis, M., Martines, J., Black, M., Onyango, A., & Dewey, K. G. (2006). WHO Motor Development Study: Windows of achievement for six growth motor development milestones. *Acta Paediatrica Supplement, 450,* 86–95. https://cdn.who.int/media/docs/default-source/child-growth/child-growth-standards/indicators/motor-development-milestones/who-motor-development-study-windows-of-achievement-for-six-gross-motor-development-milestones.pdf

individual differences can influence these averages. However, for many years, it was assumed that these milestones unfolded universally along predictable timetables because of maturation, but the traditional maturational account could not explain how children move from one skill level to another. Recent research, adopting a dynamic approach, delves into the transformative processes behind acquiring new skills. Often, this is achieved through innovative experimental tasks that aim to uncover how children learn new skills and, consequently, the "universal" milestones, by engaging in exploration and selecting from a broader spectrum of potential behaviors and configurations to accomplish their objectives. Motivation to accomplish a task is thus assumed to be the driving force for change in this domain, rather than genetic instructions and biological maturation. Thus, motor development studies demonstrate that each component in the developing system is both cause and product in this dynamic process, even if on different levels and time scales: task motivates behavior, behavior enables new tasks, and biomechanical factors and changes both limit and facilitate movement (Fischer & Bidell, 2006).

Directionality refers to how body proportions change, and, to some extent, improvements in control and motor development. Change is generally *cephalocaudal* (from head to tail) and *proximodistal* (moves from the center of the body outward). The brain develops more rapidly, which regulates growth and development and influences basic drives (i.e., hunger and thirst). Gross motor development usually follows a universal pattern. Children typically gain control over their head, hands, and upper body before the lower body, and generally large muscles develop before smaller ones. Similarly, regions nearer the trunk tend to undergo growth and differentiation earlier than those more peripheral. For example, children typically gain control of their arms and legs much earlier than their fingers and toes. Gross motor development is the foundation for developing skills in other areas (such as fine motor skills).

Early motor behaviors are marked by "rhythmical stereotypies," or repeated sequences of motions performed with no apparent goal. As infants make gains in movement, they show progress in coordinating postural control (the ability to maintain an upright orientation to the environment), locomotion (the ability to maneuver through space), and manual control (the ability to manipulate objects), thus displaying more purposeful movements.

Milestones in postural control and locomotion are noted in Table 6.1. Notably, crawling is no longer regarded as a conventional "milestone" because various recognized crawling postures exist beyond the traditional hands-and-knees position. Furthermore, a child can skip crawling with no adverse effects on their motor development. In fact, rates of hands-and-knees crawling are dropping, which may be associated with the "Back-to-Sleep" public health campaign, which began in 1994 and recommends that infants be put on their back to sleep to reduce the occurrence of sudden infant death syndrome (SIDS). With an increasing number of parents and caregivers following this advice (resulting in a reduction of SIDS rates by more than 50%), infants spend less time on their fronts, reducing development of arm strength and limiting practice in that position.

The development of manual control encompasses reaching, grasping, and writing. The progression of reaching evolves from "prereaching," characterized by a lack of clear intent or coordination between reaching and grasping, to ballistic reaching, in which the trajectory remains unaltered once reaching commences until the hand makes contact with an object. This then advances to guided reaching, characterized by more coordination between visual cues and motor movements. Grasping progresses from an ulnar–palmar grasp technique, pressing objects against the palm, around 5 or 6 months, to the pincer grasp, where the thumb and index finger can work independently of the other fingers, giving infants the fine dexterity useful for eating, manipulating objects, and, eventually, writing.

Sensory and Perceptual Development
Preferential looking or sucking and habituation paradigms are used to study newborn and infant sensory and perceptual skills and development. In a preference paradigm, two stimuli are

presented side by side or alternating, and infant behavior is observed and measured to determine preference or interest. For example, a neonate's sucking amplitude, measured with a pacifier wired to a computer, changes when presented with the scent of her own mother's breast milk compared to that of another mother. Similarly, newborns look longer at high-contrast patterns than at indistinct patterns. In the case of two stimuli that may evoke no particular preference in an infant, in which looking time or other behaviors may be equal across two different stimuli, the habituation paradigm can be used. Habituation refers to the process of becoming accustomed to a repeated stimulus, providing insight into infants' ability to recognize and respond to changes in their environment (i.e., the assumption is that habituation is similar to boredom). Dishabituation occurs when the response to a stimulus increases with presentation of a novel change in the stimulus. The most frequently employed response is infant looking time, although sucking and other behaviors have been used as well. If an infant dishabituates to presentation of a new stimulus, such as a different face or a new color, it can be concluded that they perceive the difference.

From such studies, there is evidence that the five senses develop at different rates. Hearing, touch, taste, and smell are well developed at birth. Sight is the least developed sense in infants, with various aspects of vision gradually developing over the first few months of life. There is evidence suggesting limited color vision in infants until around 2 months of age, and limited depth perception until 4 months, when it begins to develop initially through sensitivity to kinetic cues, followed by binocular cues, and subsequently pictorial cues. Visual acuity reaches near-adult levels by about 6 months of age.

Sensation and perception are closely linked to the process of learning. When individuals perceive objects and events that engage multiple senses simultaneously, this is referred to as multimodal perception. Multimodal perception has been found to enhance the learning process. Cross-modal perception becomes evident when infants demonstrate recognition of an object with one sense, even if it was initially encountered with another; for example, recognizing a pacifier by sight, despite having previously experienced it through touch by sucking, or detecting discrepancies when visual and auditory stimuli do not align, as seen in the asynchronous sight and sound of a bouncing object. Early perception can aid with the beginnings of self-knowledge. For example, newborns may not show the rooting reflex if the stroke to their cheek comes from their own hand rather than another person or a pacifier. Although infants are born with some perceptual organization, additional improvements in perceptual abilities are associated with environmental stimuli and input. For example, infants naturally exhibit a preference for looking at faces; however, infants whose mothers frequently displayed smiles demonstrated heightened sensitivity to smiling faces in controlled laboratory environments.

Cognitive Development

Cognitive development encompasses various aspects including attention and memory, skill and knowledge milestones, language development, ToM, and more. In addition to the overall theoretical approaches to development described earlier, this section also explores additional relevant perspectives on cognitive development.

The information-processing approach draws a parallel between the brain and a computer, wherein cognitive development involves increasing capacity and efficiency of the brain's ability to continuously process information. Information is acquired (sensation and perception), selected (attention), stored (memory), and used to plan or solve problems.

Attention consists of focusing on some information and ignoring other information, and avoiding distraction to achieve a goal. It serves as a selective filter that enables individuals to concentrate on important details, maintain focus, and complete tasks effectively. This cognitive process is essential for efficient information processing and problem-solving and aids in the successful navigation of complex and dynamic tasks.

Memory is a complex cognitive process that encompasses numerous and diverse elements and types. Working memory pertains to conscious, short-term representations of what a person is actually thinking about at any given time. While working memory is brief and limited in capacity, long-term memory is potentially unlimited in capacity and duration. Long-term memory involves two primary components: recognition memory, which involves associating an event or object with one previously experienced, generating a sense of familiarity, and recall memory, which entails remembering a fact, event, or object not currently present, requiring retrieval of stored information from memory. Generic memory involves the development of scripts, or road maps, for familiar action sequences, which makes memory recall more efficient and reduces cognitive burden. Episodic memory involves recalling specific events that have occurred at particular times and places in an individual's life. It allows people to store, organize, and later retrieve information about past personal experiences. Autobiographical memory involves recall for events or episodes with personal meaning in one's life. These memories are the foundation for personal identity, self-concept, and narrative construction.

Children's early memory storage and recall are influenced by several factors. Notably, memories are more likely to endure if they involve unique events, if the child actively participated in the experience, and if the child talked about the event or experience with parents or others. Of note, interactions with parents influence the development of memory. Over the course of the life span, both semantic memory (recall of general facts and knowledge) and procedural memory (knowledge of how to perform routines and other organized actions) tends to remain relatively stable. Where there can be considerable variability in the rate and progression of memory decline as people age, it is generally observed that episodic memory experiences the greatest age-related declines in performance. Stress, anxiety, depression, substance abuse, and racial and ethnic disparities are all associated with declines in memory performance in adulthood (Hill et al., 2022; Sol et al., 2020).

Language and Communication

Language development begins in infancy with the development of communication skills. The most intensive period for the development of speech and language skills is the first 3 years of life, a period marked by rapid brain development and heightened plasticity. Infancy is a critical period for speech and language development, and there are essential developmental milestones that must be met during this time. The mastery of sound production and perception (phonology), the learning of word meanings (semantics), and the understanding of the shared set of grammatical rules (syntax) are critical skills that facilitate meaningful communication. During the earliest months and years, infants and young children who are not exposed to language nor have the opportunity for communicative interaction will find it more difficult to acquire language skills in later childhood.

Receptive communication and language, or comprehension, nearly always precedes expressive language, or production. Early on, most infants produce prelinguistic vocalizations of cooing and babbling; even deaf babies babble, suggesting that auditory input is not necessary for babbling. However, the optimal development of communication skills occurs in an environment rich in external input, with the most critical component being regular and interactive communication with others, particularly through speech and language interactions. These interactive communication experiences provide babies with opportunities to learn to differentiate others' speech and feedback and allows for prelinguistic vocalizations to begin. All newborns universally babble all consonants, but by about 6 months of age, infants begin to sort out the speech sounds of the native language most used in their environment, and infant babbles begin to favor the consonants found in that language, dropping those sounds and consonants not found in that language.

Children follow a natural progression for mastering the skills of language, but there is wide variation in the rate of language development. Individual differences are associated with many factors. Hearing loss can lead to language delays, while speech disorders such as apraxia may hinder the ability to make sounds and put syllables together in the correct order to form words. In the case of specific language impairments (SLI), some children may not begin to talk until their third or fourth year of life.

Individual differences in language development are also highly associated with a child's environment. The fact that all typically developing children in healthy environments learn to talk almost certainly reflects two critical ideas: Humans have biological capacities for language acquisition and human social environments support language acquisition (Lonyangapuo, 2021; Osher et al., 2020). One of the primary factors contributing to individual differences in language development is the variability in the support for language acquisition within the social environment. The socioeconomic status (SES) of a child's family is highly correlated with the quantity, variety, and quality of words children hear, as well as the amount of child-directed language. Children from high-SES families may hear three to four times as many words over the course of a week compared with children from families on public assistance (Hart & Risley, 1995), and parents with higher SES tend to expose their children to richer language-stimulating environments characterized by more talking, using a larger variety of words, engaging in educational programming related to language development, and asking more questions compared with lower SES parents. High-quality nonparental early care and education experiences are also associated with better child language outcomes; again, children from low-SES families are less likely to have such high-quality child-care experiences (Volodina et al., 2023). Early gaps in language proficiency can contribute to gaps in literacy, school readiness, and poorer health and behavioral outcomes that may persist into and throughout the school years and beyond (Becherer et al., 2021; Le et al., 2021).

Theory of Mind

ToM is an integrated, coherent understanding of what the mind is, how it works, and why it works that way. A child's awareness of their own and other people's thought processes and mental states must begin first with an understanding that others' thoughts are different from their own. Subsequently, it evolves to include an understanding that all individuals diverge in their thoughts, beliefs, desires, knowledge, and perspectives. This process unfolds over the course of an individual's life span, progressing through distinct developmental stages or periods marked by substantial advancements in the development of ToM. Like other cognitive processes, ToM development is associated with environmental factors, such as social interaction with adults and older children, and make-believe play. A related concept is metacognition, or "thinking about thinking"; this is an understanding or knowledge that people have about their own thought processes. Metacognition includes reflecting, monitoring, and regulating one's own thoughts, decisions, and problem-solving strategies. Metacognition, like ToM, begins to develop during early childhood but continues to develop throughout the life span.

Social–Emotional Development

Social–emotional development comprises five competencies: self-management, self-awareness, social awareness, relationship skills, and responsible decision-making. As in the section on cognitive development, additional theoretical approaches to social–emotional development are described in this section where relevant, in addition to the overall theoretical approaches to development described at the beginning of this chapter.

Emerging Self-Concept

A major developmental task of childhood is for the individual to establish an understanding of who they are, or a unified conception of the self. Throughout childhood, physical, cognitive, and social demands place increasing importance on the role of self in relation to others. Allport (1955) conceived of this process of self-realization as a crucial component of development in infancy, in which the child establishes a sense of their own body, a nascent self-identity, and self-esteem. The idea of self-concept can be further defined and understood when divided into knowledge and evaluative components. Knowledge components consist of a person's physical and cognitive characteristics, such as one's values or personal goals (Minarto et al., 2021). In contrast, evaluative components entail self-evaluation, including one's self-esteem and self-efficacy. As the individual develops from infancy through childhood and adolescence, they must continue to negotiate both individual and social demands on the self, and develop a self-concept across contexts (e.g., home, school, and peer settings). Once established, self-concept is a relatively stable characteristic in adolescence and adulthood. Discrepancies or conflicts in the conceptualization of self have been associated with poor outcomes, including depression, anxiety, and low self-esteem.

Gender Awareness, Identity, and Constancy

A person's sense of self in relation to gender, or gender identity, begins to develop very early, with the ability in toddlerhood to discriminate between males and females and then label the self and others by gender. However, children in the preoperational stage are only capable of understanding gender as a label or appearance, rather than an unwavering characteristic. Gender constancy, or the ability to comprehend gender as an immutable characteristic, does not fully develop in children until about age 6 or 7 (Unlüer & Öncü, 2022). In middle childhood, gender consciousness solidifies, functioning as an organizing framework for children's thoughts about themselves in relation to others, choices of friends and activities, and a guide for behavior. Gender plays a role in children's behavior and social interactions with adults and peers; similarities and differences in behaviors and interactions are discussed in the relevant topical sections. Importantly, what we know about gender and life-span development is mostly based in a gender dichotomy; recent work highlights the benefit of building toward more inclusive science (Hyde et al., 2019).

Emotional Development

Emotion can be defined as a subjective and conscious mental reaction, typically coinciding with physiological and behavioral changes in the body, as a result of an internal or external event. Emotions function to organize and regulate behavior; influence cognitive processes; and initiate, maintain, or terminate interactions with others. Emotional development encompasses emotional expression, understanding, and regulation. Some emotional expressions, like an infant crying, are adaptive as they encourage others to respond. Emotions are a regulator of social interactions. Interactions with caregivers that encourage emotional attunement and sensitivity to the caregivers' expressions allow the optimal environment for infants to develop emotional regulation (Bernardo et al., 2021).

Primary emotions are the first emotions that infants express and are immediate, intrinsic reactions in which one's thoughts or habits do not influence. Paul Eckman identified the six primary emotions as joy, sadness, surprise, disgust, anger, and fear. Secondary emotions, sometimes called self-conscious or other-conscious emotions, are habitual or learned responses that involve evaluation of oneself and increase as the infant becomes self-aware. They do not emerge until the second or third year of life and depend on higher mental capacities, including an objective sense of the self as distinct from others, awareness of standards for behavior, and a sense of responsibility for one's actions. Secondary emotions are associated with more negative emotions such as embarrassment, envy, guilt, or shame, but also positive emotions such as pride or excitement. Between 18 and 36 months of age, children begin to use language to describe feeling states and to label their own and others' emotions, which is associated with better social behaviors and more appropriate responses to emotions of friends.

Emotional understanding or comprehension begins with reading and recognizing emotional signals. Infants may imitate surprised, happy, and sad facial expressions when as young as 3 days old, although there is some controversy about how to interpret such findings. Infants show preferences for facial expressions, preferring to look less at sad faces and more at angry faces compared to happy faces. Infants exhibit resonating or matching of adult expressions. This phenomenon can be linked to mirror neurons, which are cells in the brain that are activated when one observes others' actions and when one imitates an action they have observed. Mirror neurons may play a role in empathy. Social referencing, or the use of others' emotional expressions to interpret ambiguous events, is another important part of social and emotional development.

There is evidence of cultural variation in the specifics of secondary emotions. Family norms, such as adult instruction and conversations about the appropriate time to feel and how to express secondary emotions, expectations, and understanding of emotional experiences, also affect an individual's secondary emotions. When family relations are less positive, lacking warmth, supportiveness, or negotiation and reasoning, children's emotional understanding may be impaired. Chronic or severe stress during childhood has persistent and pervasive effects on a child's development, leading to dysregulated and negative psychological outcomes (Smith & Pollak, 2020). Infants of mothers with depression may experience emotional or behavioral dysregulation such as increased negative affect, disturbances in attention, and less efficiency in processing contingent relationships (Flowers et al., 2018).

Emotional regulation refers to the process of evaluating, monitoring, and modifying emotional reactions to accomplish a goal by changing one's level of emotional arousal (Berzenski, 2019). Emotion regulation improves over early childhood, as the child interacts with peers and other individuals and is exposed to diverse situations. Effortful control, a particular aspect of emotion regulation and of temperament, can be described as the management of regulatory capacities, including the ability to inhibit a dominant response (Ferreira et al., 2021). Effortful control is negatively associated with social competence and behavior problems, including impulsive and aggressive actions when frustrated.

Temperament refers to an individual's characteristic and behavioral response to stimuli, particularly when encountering an unfamiliar environment or situation. There are both biological and environmental influences on temperament. However, research has demonstrated that the temperament infants are born with remains moderately stable throughout childhood. Children may inherit physiological characteristics such as heart rate, cortisol level, and right frontal lobe activity that may affect their temperament. Twin and adoption studies suggest heredity has a moderate influence on temperament. A child's gender and culture, as well as their personal experiences, may also play a role in modifying temperament. It is important to focus on the goodness of fit—the match between a child's temperament and environmental demands—rather than emphasize the temperament classification itself. An awareness of goodness of fit has implications for parenting, including ensuring parents are sensitive and flexible to an infant's signals and needs and that parents structure a child's environment to those needs. For example, implementing an awareness of goodness of fit might mean allowing a child who is classified as difficult or slow to warm up to have additional time to adjust to a crowded or noisy environment.

Through their research with the New York Longitudinal Study, Thomas and Chess (1977, 1991) defined nine temperament traits in young children: activity, regularity, initial reaction, adaptability, intensity, mood, distractibility, persistence and attention span, and sensitivity. Based on their findings, 65% of infants could be classified into three temperament categories, while 35% were unclassifiable. Children labeled easy (40%) are generally in a positive mood, are able to quickly establish regular routines, and easily adapt to new experiences. In contrast, 10% of children were labeled as "difficult," as they were found to frequently react negatively and cry, have irregular routines, and be slow to accept change. Lastly, 15% of children were considered slow-to-warm-up, with low activity levels, somewhat negative temperament, and low mood intensity.

Other researchers have further developed these temperament categories. For example, Kagan (2000, 2002, 2008, 2010) classified temperament into two categories: uninhibited and inhibited. Uninhibited children are outgoing, extroverted, sociable, and bold, and spontaneously approach unfamiliar situations and people. Inhibited children are timid, subdued, fearful, and shy in novel situations and around unfamiliar people. Around 7 to 9 months of age, inhibited children begin to approach new and unfamiliar situations with avoidance, distress, apprehension, and passive affect. An inhibited temperament has been found to be a relatively stable temperament style in early childhood. However, some research suggests that an inhibited temperament style can be influenced by physiological and environmental factors, such as early intervention (Bayer et al., 2019).

Rothbart and Bates (2006) proposed three broad dimensions of temperament: extroversion/surgency, negative affectivity, and effortful control (self-regulation). This extroversion/surgency dimension parallels Kagan's uninhibited category and includes "positive anticipation, impulsivity, activity level, and sensation seeking" (Rothbart, 2004, p. 495). Similar to Kagan's inhibited category, Rothbart and Bates' negative affectivity dimension includes "fear, frustration, sadness, and discomfort" (Rothbart, 2004, p. 495), and children who fit this temperament become easily distressed and often fuss and cry. Lastly, the effortful control (self-regulation) dimension includes "attentional focusing and shifting, inhibitory control, perceptual sensitivity, and low-intensity pleasure" (Rothbart, 2004, p. 495). These findings have been further supported in recent work (Andreadakis et al., 2020; Carrasco et al., 2020). Children with high effortful control can ensure that their arousal levels do not become too high and have developed self-soothing strategies. Children with low effortful control have difficulty regulating their arousal and become agitated and intensely emotional relatively quickly. Low effortful control in school-age children has been correlated with externalizing problems and reactive aggression. Research suggests that low effortful control in conjunction with high levels of general negative emotionality might lead to heightened risk for anxiety disorder, whereas low effortful control and high frustration could lead to heightened risk of conduct disorder (Halvorson et al., 2022).

In adulthood, lack of self-regulation is associated with overall difficulties in adaptation in various contexts, including interpersonal relationships and family and occupational settings. For example, a lack of self-control in adolescence contributes to an adolescent's violation of social norms and the personal liberties of others, which can lead to lack of self-regulation, a hallmark of antisocial behavior and psychiatric disorders, in adulthood. The dual-processing theory, also referred to as the dual systems model, describes the development of two neurological systems that compete when a child or adolescent makes a decision (Marquez-Ramons et al., 2023). This theory suggests that as adolescents experience a rapid transition in physical, biological, intellectual, and social changes, their risk behavior also increases. Risk behaviors refer to behaviors that are reinforced in the short term, but are damaging in the long term. The control of risky behavior can be attributed to the reward-seeking areas of the brain in the ventromedial prefrontal cortex. As adolescents transition into adulthood, an improvement in cognitive control and a decline in risky behavior is observed, which can be associated with a maturation in the prefrontal cortex (Marquez-Ramons et al., 2023).

Self-Regulation, Stress, and the Environment
A child's ability to regulate their stress response is heavily impacted by one's early environment. Over time, dysregulation of the HPA axis can result in difficulties responding to stressful situations in adolescence and adulthood, as a consequence of either heightened or stunted HPA secretion of cortisol. Two settings that have consistently been found to influence children's stress response systems are the home rearing and out-of-home child-care environments. In the home environment, abuse, maltreatment, and neglect from caregivers have all been shown to substantially impact children's cortisol levels. Chronic overactivation of the stress response system, such as that often experienced by children with inconsistent, abusive, or negligent caregivers, can significantly impact child functioning and has been linked to both major depression and recovery from disease in adults (Van Wert et al., 2019). Researchers have also shown that infants and toddlers placed in poor-quality child-care settings (i.e., unsafe environment, negative caregiving practices, and high child–staff ratios) display heightened levels of cortisol throughout the day (Burns et al., 2023).

Adverse childhood experiences (ACEs) typically include three categories of negative experiences: abuse (physical, emotional, and sexual), neglect (physical and emotional), and household challenges (substance abuse, mental illness, violent treatment of mother, parental separation/divorce, and incarcerated household member). ACEs disrupt brain development and have wide-ranging health, social, and behavioral consequences throughout the life span. ACEs have been linked to risky health behaviors, chronic health conditions, low life potential, and early death (Felitti et al., 1998). Physiological and biomolecular research suggests that ACEs and chronic stress contribute to changes in the nervous, endocrine, and immune systems, which lead to impaired cognitive, emotional, and social functioning (Karabatsiakis & Schönfeldt-Lecuona, 2020). The 2019 National Survey of Children's Health found that 33% of children in the United States reported experiencing at least one ACE, while 53% reported two or more ACEs (Walker et al., 2022).

An inability to regulate one's stress responses in adulthood is associated with two types of reactions. In the first, the stress response system is hyperactivated and individuals display more externalizing disorders and antisocial behavior. Hyperactive individuals show a propensity to "act out" aggressively in response to heightened emotions. The second involves stress responses that are hypoactivated or "stunted," and is associated with underdeveloped and passive responses to stress as well as social withdrawal.

Attachment

Attachment is an emotional bond between a child and his primary caregivers that endures over the lifetime (Bowlby, 1969). The creation and maintenance of a secure relationship with at least one primary caregiver, often the mother, promotes normal social and emotional development for a child. While children may form multiple secure attachments, such as with both caregivers, one is always primary. Secure attachment develops when caregivers are consistently sensitive and responsive to a child's expressed needs from ages 6 months to 2 years. Attachment-seeking behaviors include crying, smiling, babbling, sucking, grasping, and following. Each of these behaviors are intended to help the infant remain in close proximity to the caregiver. Early attachment relationships are critical in the later development of perceptions, emotions, and relational expectations over the life span; early attachment informs a child's later internal working models or expectations about others and social relationships. Thus, attachment is one of the most significant developmental tasks and serves as a protective factor for growth and development under adverse circumstances.

In an expansion of Bowlby's construct, Ainsworth (1979) developed the Strange Situation Procedure to help operationalize attachment. This procedure consists of a series of eight separations and reunions between 12- and 18-month-old children and their caregiver, during which the child's amount of exploration, behaviors, and reactions are observed, both during the independent play and subsequent reunion. The Strange Situation Procedure helped to explore individual differences in patterns of attachment behavior. Ainsworth identified three major attachment types (see Table 6.2): secure, avoidant, and ambivalent/resistant. A fourth attachment type, disorganized/disoriented, was added in 1996 by Main. Prevalence of attachment styles have remained fairly consistent over the last few decades. About 65% of children in the general population are securely attached and the remaining 35% are divided among the insecure attachment categories (avoidant, ambivalent, and disorganized). Table 6.2 provides typical child and caregiver behaviors displayed during the separations and reunions during the Strange Situation Procedure for each attachment classification (Bornstein, 2019; Bornstein & Lamb, 2002).

There have been several criticisms of attachment research, including the way it was conducted for many years, the Strange Situation Procedure, and the associated attachment classifications. Although some research has suggested that attachment styles are relatively universal, other research has found cultural variations among attachment styles. For example, infants in the United States are most frequently classified as securely attached. Compared to U.S. children, German infants are more likely to display avoidant attachment and Japanese infants are less likely to display avoidant attachment. However, attachment classifications and stigmas may be U.S.-centric. For example, German children's attachment behaviors may be categorized as avoidant because German caregivers encourage independence. Moreover, Japanese infants may demonstrate a resistant attachment because these children are normally cared for strictly by

TABLE 6.2 Attachment Classifications and Associated Child and Caregiver Behaviors

Attachment Type	Child Behavior	Caregiver Behavior
Secure	Uses caregiver as a secure base from which to explore. Protests caregiver's departure and seeks closeness and is comforted on return, resuming exploration. May be comforted by a stranger but shows clear preference for caregiver.	Responds appropriately, promptly, and consistently to child's needs.
Avoidant	Little affective sharing in play. Shows little or no distress after caregiver departure, and little or no visible response on return, turning away or ignoring with no effort to maintain contact if picked up. Interacts with stranger similarly to caregiver. Child feels there is no attachment and as a result is rebellious and develops a lower self-image and self-esteem.	Little or no response to distressed child; discourages crying and encourages independence.
Ambivalent/resistant	Unable to use caregiver as secure base, wanting closeness before separation occurs. Distressed on separation with ambivalence, anger, reluctance to be comforted by caregiver and resume play on return. Preoccupied with caregiver's availability, seeking contact but resisting angrily when it is offered. Not easily soothed by stranger. Child always feels anxious because caregiver's availability is inconsistent.	Inconsistent between appropriate and neglectful responses; in general, will only respond after child displays increased attachment behavior.
Disorganized	Exhibits atypical behavior on return such as rocking or freezing. Lack of a coherent attachment strategy demonstrated by contradictory, disoriented behaviors such as approaching but with back turned.	Frightened or frightening behavior, intrusiveness, withdrawal, negativity, role confusion, affective communication errors, and maltreatment; often associated with several forms of abuse toward the child.

their mothers and may become more stressed by a stranger than children who live in the United States and experience more liberal caregiving and socialization. The Strange Situation Procedure has been criticized because children's attachment behaviors are typically observed in an unfamiliar, laboratory setting instead of in a natural environment such as the home, potentially influencing the child's behaviors. Further, the procedure has received criticism for studying the infant–mother dyad more specifically than other caregiver relationships; however, the Strange Situation Procedure has now been used across a variety of caregivers, including fathers, adoptive parents, and foster caregivers (Madigan et al., 2023). Finally, by only coding the caregiver's behavior toward the child and not considering how the child's behavior may affect the caregiver, the Strange Situation Procedure approaches attachment from a unidirectional perspective rather than a bidirectional one. Nonetheless, much current child development research is rooted in aspects of attachment theory.

Moral Development

A dominant paradigm in moral development is Lawrence Kohlberg's stage theory (1976). Using the Moral Judgment Interview, Kohlberg was able to distinguish six stages of moral development by identifying qualitatively different forms of moral thinking by individuals in response to moral dilemma vignettes. The first two stages, termed "preconventional" thinking, involve the individual progressing from a focus on obedience to authority as well as from avoidance of punishment to prioritizing self-interest, in which moral behaviors are viewed as those representing the individual's best interest rather than simply avoiding perceived consequences. In stage 3, the first stage of "conventional" thinking, individuals abide by social norms and judge the morality of actions and the accompanying consequences by whether they encourage social approval. Stage 4 thinking is characterized by a desire to adhere to laws in order to maintain stability and harmony in society, while stage 5 represents "postconventional" thinking and emphasizes moral principles and values that should guide society through promoting democratic values. Stage 6 involves moral reasoning based on abstract, universal ethical principles that guide perceptions of actions as "right" or "wrong." Understanding how individuals progress through these stages is influential in developmentally informed research and applied work regarding empathy, prosocial and antisocial behavior, civic engagement, and so on.

Aggression and Prosocial Behavior

Research on aggression in youth has traditionally distinguished between two forms of aggression: overt and relational. Overt aggression seeks to inflict physical harm on others, often through using hostile and threatening language, pushing, and striking. Overt aggression is much more common in boys, and children engaging in overt aggression tend to use these behaviors to establish dominance over others or to obtain a desired outcome.

Relational aggression is more likely to emerge in girls, and tends to include behaviors focused on manipulation within and/or damage to existing social relationships. Research indicates that female peer-to-peer interactions are more likely to be affected by relational aggression and can include gossiping, encouraging social exclusion of a peer, or making threats toward others. Both overt and relational aggression are strong predictors of negative future social and behavioral outcomes. Persistently aggressive children are more prone to academic and peer difficulties as well as depressive symptoms (Evans et al., 2019).

In contrast to aggression, prosocial behavior in childhood is associated with more positive lifespan development. Prosocial behavior refers to the promotion of positive interactions with others, such as peers, siblings, and adults. Childrens' advances in social- and cognitive-developmental domains, such as sympathy, empathy, and moral reasoning, have been shown to predict increases in prosocial behavior, such as caring for and helping others, sharing, and perspective taking. Engaging in more prosocial behaviors and less aggressive behaviors is related to greater moral reasoning, self-regulation, and social competence (Ştefan & Avram, 2021). In addition, prosocial behavior has been linked with less aggressive behavior in youth, whereas antisocial behavior is associated with high levels of aggression.

Social Competence and Social Skills

An important theory in the social development of children is the role of an individual's social network in contributing to ontogenic growth. Social competence is a critical area of early development that is representative of social influences on individual development. Children first learn to socialize in their home with their caregivers and in early child-care or school settings with their peers. At home, children's interactions with their caregivers serve as the basis for the formation of internal working models. In the intimate setting of the home, children interact with parents and siblings on a daily basis and form cognitive schema about interpersonal relationships as well as social conventions. In contrast, youth have the opportunity to interact with peers and adults in the school setting, which is often less intimate, and are exposed to interactions that shape both their self-conception and their view of others. Importantly, individuals are not passive receptors of environmental input, but are active agents in their development. Sameroff's (Sameroff & Chandler, 1975; Sameroff & Fiese, 2003) Transactional Model understands development as a series of continuous reciprocal interactions between the individual and their context. The Transactional Model accounts for the myriad social influences that help to shape changes in the individual over time by placing equal emphasis on individual and environmental influences. For example, the development of social competence is affected in children with developmental delays (e.g., autism), which may inhibit individuals' ability to initiate *and* respond to social cues.

Identity

Identity is what characterizes an individual or group. Often made up of values, beliefs, and traits, in developmental science we understand identity to be developed in a variety of domains, such as in work, gender, racial/ethnic background, religiosity, and more. Erikson's (1968) stage theory, which described the process of identity as unfolding across the life span in a series of eight stages (see Table 6.3), is foundational in the understanding of identity development. Each of these stages is characterized by a conflict, wherein successful resolution of the conflict promotes the individual to the next stage. The early stages are characterized by establishing trust in one's caregivers to develop an understanding of the world as a safe space. A safe home rearing environment and responsive parenting style promotes a sense of trust in a child and ensures their basic needs for food and comfort are met. In early childhood, once basic needs are met, individuals begin to establish a sense of individualism and autonomy as they begin to explore the world on their own. Here, the individual comes to see themself as an individual entity, separate from a caregiver. As childhood progresses, individuals gain increasing ability to act on the world in more sophisticated ways, eventually mastering basic skills and integrating concepts. As adolescence is approached, an individual is met with an increased demand to establish a sense of self in relation to their peers. Failure to do so in multiple contexts (e.g., school, home, and work) can result in role confusion and a lack of a coherent self-concept. In adolescence, individuals are typically subject to increasing amounts of peer influence, particularly with respect to identity development. This is extended in early adulthood, as individuals strive to form a romantic connection or an intimate bond with a significant other, or risk experiencing feelings of loneliness and isolation. As adulthood progresses, identity development is more intrinsically linked to a sense of contributing to and nurturing others and, later, retrospective rumination on having accomplished one's life goals.

CONTEXTS OF DEVELOPMENT

Family

The family is a social system that consists of several subsystems that are defined in terms of generation, gender, role, and the division of labor and attachments. Each member of the family is a participant in several subsystems that can be dyadic (involving two people) or polyadic (involving more than two people). For example, the mother and child make up one dyadic subsystem, the mother and father another, whereas mother–father–child and mother and two siblings create polyadic subsystems. Family subsystems directly and indirectly influence each other through interactions within the marital relationship, parenting, and child behaviors. Family members are involved in reciprocal socialization, which refers to the process by which family members influence and learn from each other through social interactions. For instance, the marital relationship can affect child development, such that high-conflict households are associated with elevated risk for psychopathological developmental issues for children during their adolescent years (Harold & Sellers, 2018). Support of the marital relationship and promotion of marital satisfaction through marriage-enhancement programs and interventions that enhance parenting skills can increase affection, communication, and intimacy toward children. Family processes are also impacted by various sociocultural and historical influences.

TABLE 6.3 Erikson's Psychosocial Stages

Stage	Basic Conflict	Important Events	Outcome
Infancy (birth to 18 months)	Trust vs. mistrust	Feeding	Children develop a sense of trust when caregivers provide reliability, care, and affection. A lack of this will lead to mistrust.
Early childhood (2–3 years)	Autonomy vs. shame and doubt	Toilet training	Children need to develop a sense of personal control over physical skills and a sense of independence. Success leads to feelings of autonomy and failure results in feelings of shame and doubt.
Preschool (3–5 years)	Initiative vs. guilt	Exploration	Children need to begin asserting control and power over the environment. Success in this stage leads to a sense of purpose. Children who try to exert too much power experience disapproval, resulting in a sense of guilt.
School age (6–11 years)	Industry vs. inferiority	School	Children need to cope with new social and academic demands. Success leads to a sense of competence, whereas failure results in feelings of inferiority.
Adolescence (12–18 years)	Identity vs. role confusion	Social relationships	Teens need to develop a sense of self and personal identity. Success leads to an ability to stay true to oneself, whereas failure leads to role confusion and a weak sense of self.
Young adulthood (19–40 years)	Intimacy vs. isolation	Relationships	Young adults need to form intimate, loving relationships with other people. Success leads to strong relationships, whereas failure results in loneliness and isolation.
Middle adulthood (40–65 years)	Generativity vs. stagnation	Work and parenthood	Adults need to create or nurture things that will outlast them, often by having children or creating a positive change that benefits other people. Success leads to feelings of usefulness and accomplishment, whereas failure results in shallow involvement in the world.
Maturity (65 to death)	Ego integrity vs. despair	Reflection on life	Older adults need to look back on life and feel a sense of fulfillment. Success at this stage leads to feelings of wisdom, whereas failure results in regret, bitterness, and despair.

Gender

Gender is a complex construct and should be differentiated from biological sex. Biological sex is determined at birth based on genitalia and chromosomes, whereas gender is the cultural and social expectations about behavior, characteristics, and roles associated with one's sex. In early childhood, children begin to exhibit gender-based preferences for same-gendered playmates, a phenomenon known as gender segregation, which typically starts between ages 2 and 3 and becomes more prominent after age 3. As noted previously, it is important to recognize that our understanding of gender differences has been largely based on dichotomous groups, and work looking at more diverse gender identities is on the rise (Hyde et al., 2019). Once in gender-segregated peer groups, children tend to show some differences in play styles and activities, number of playmates, and levels of physical aggression. For example, girls tend to play in smaller groups, in closer proximity to adults, and with more cooperative group dynamics. Boys tend to play in larger groups, farther away from adults, and with more rough-and-tumble play and with more competition (Ruble et al., 2006). As adolescents, children move away from peer groups that are highly gender-segregated and increase their contact with opposite-gender friends, including nonromantic friendships. For most adolescents, friendships become more intimate. However, compared to adolescent boys, adolescent girls list more friends, are more likely to include intimacy as a defining aspect of close friendship, and show more complexity in their thinking about friendships.

Gender socialization involves the social norms conveyed to children concerning characteristics associated with being male or female, potentially contributing to observed gender differences in children's emotional and interactive styles. Adults may convey different messages to girls and boys about appropriate activities, interests, friends, skills, and achievements that are expected and valued. Children may form gender schemas about being male or female, and about perceived strengths of the differences between girls and boys. Research on gender differences does find some support for some differences in areas such as physical aggression, which is found to be higher in boys than in girls, and some aspects of cognitive abilities, with boys found to be stronger in special abilities and girls found to be stronger in verbal skills (Chaplin, 2015; Ruble et al., 2006). However, these differences may be exaggerated in common understanding as there is much more overlap between boys and girls in all areas than there are differences.

Divorce and Stepfamilies

The rates of divorce and remarriage are declining overall, although varying across groups in terms of consequences and likelihood. Factors including low educational attainment, low income levels, premarital pregnancy, divorced parents, and marriage at a young age are associated with higher rates of divorce (Raley & Sweeney, 2020). Consequences of divorce on adult well-being are complex, depending on individual and contextual factors as well as involving both short- and long-term effects on economic (e.g., decrease in household income, particularly for women and children) and mental health. Consequences of divorce on child well-being over time include increased likelihood for mental health issues (e.g., anxiety, depression, suicidality, distress) and substance use (e.g., alcohol, smoking, drugs; Auersperg et al., 2019). In the case of a remarriage, some difficulties that families experience include disciplining the child, navigating the relationship between the stepparent and child, expectations for the parental role, and relationship with nonresidential parents (Ganong & Coleman, 2018). Children in stepfamilies may also show more internalizing and externalizing behaviors; thus, communication and closeness among family members is important to buffer against negative child outcomes. The steprelationships are generally not as close as biological ones, and this may vary based on child age, gender, duration of relationship, and custody arrangements; however, many families adjust relatively well over time.

Same-Sex Families

Due to donor insemination, surrogates, and adoption, the number of same-sex families with children has increased in the last few decades. A meta-analysis examining the relationship between parents' sexual orientation and children's developmental outcomes found that child well-being was higher in same-sex family structures compared to different-sex parents (Suárez et al., 2023). Compared to children raised with different-sex parents, children raised with same-sex parents show no differences in positive parenting, cognitive and social development, mental health, academic performance, early sexual activity, and substance use (Golombok, 2017; Manning et al., 2014; Mazrekaj et al., 2020). Similar to different-sex parent families, differences in child well-being are largely due to family stability and socioeconomic circumstances.

Kinship Care

Kinship care is when children are raised by extended family members in parent-absent households, to which grandparents represent the most common caregiver. Grandparents play an important role in many families, including providing advice, support, and child care, and the extent of their role and function in the family is often culturally rooted and influenced by economical and situational differences. In the United States, kinship care may be due in part to parental substance abuse, incarcerations, and child maltreatment, and grandparents who take in grandchildren have experienced worse adverse mental health outcomes compared to noncustodial grandparents, although this may be offset when the grandparents are married with a middle-class background (Kelley et al., 2021).

Adolescent Pregnancy

In contrast to observed trends from 25 years ago, on a global, national, and subnational scale, current trends reveal that adolescent girls are inclined to marry at a later age, defer their initial sexual experiences, postpone their first childbirth, and use contraceptives (Liang et al., 2019). Teenage pregnancies are associated with risk factors such as poverty, low education, and inadequate family support. The repercussions of teenage pregnancy extend to the mother's educational opportunities, financial security, and overall health. Teenage women face higher odds of pregnancy compared to women aged 20 to 34, particularly if they are unmarried and/or have a basic or limited education. Teenage mothers are also more prone to smoking during pregnancy and experiencing preterm deliveries. Newborns born to teenage mothers are more likely to have lower birth weights (Diabelková et al., 2023). Children of adolescent mothers are more likely to become adolescent parents themselves, perpetuating this intergenerational cycle. Adolescent mothers who remain in school and who delay subsequent childbearing fare much better over time than do adolescent mothers who drop out of school or have additional children closely spaced together.

Transition to Parenthood

The average age at which women give birth for the first time has increased from 25.6 years in 2011 to 27.3 years in 2021 (Schaeffer & Aragão, 2023). Advantages of having children in the 20s include more physical energy, fewer medical problems during pregnancy and childbirth, and decreased likelihood of building up expectations for children. Advantages of childbearing in the 30s include parents who have more time to consider career and family goals, maturity, the benefit of their experiences to engage in more competent parenting, and more established careers and higher income for child-rearing expenses. In both planned and unplanned pregnancies, prospective parents experience mixed emotions and have romantic illusions about having and raising a child. Parents may find it difficult to manage the various aspects and roles in their lives, including developing a strong attachment with their infant; maintaining existing attachments to spouses, family, and friends; continuing their careers; and continuing to develop as an individual. The transition to parenthood can be challenging, and many couples report decreases in marital satisfaction within the first year after the birth of an infant (Bogdan et al., 2022).

Death in the Family

One in 12 children (8.3%) will experience the death of a parent or sibling before turning 18 (Judi's House/JAG Institute, 2024). Further, communities of color and areas affected by pandemics, natural disasters, or wars have even greater rates of familial death. Caregiving context, culture, and systems of oppression influence how children grieve, express, and manage their emotions and how families communicate and function after a death (Alvis et al., 2022). The death of a family member can compromise child development in profound ways, such as disrupting interpersonal relationships and skills, provoking challenges with academic learning, and contributing to the development of mental health problems. However, the ability to understand and process death evolves with age (Hoppe et al., 2024). While infants may experience familial death as a distressing disruption to routine or attachment, in early childhood death can be understood in more concrete terms. Still, young children often lack the ability to understand the more abstract components of death, such as its irreversibility. By middle childhood and adolescence, however, the development of abstract conceptualization contributes to the growing ability for children to process familial death in a more advanced way, largely through perceiving their own and others' emotions.

▶ REFERENCES

Full reference list available at http://examprepconnect.springerpub.com

KNOWLEDGE CHECK: CHAPTER 6

1. Which of the following best describes the concept of genotype?
   A. Observable characteristics influenced by the environment
   B. The dynamic process of development across the life span
   C. The physical and social contexts of the environment
   D. The set of genes inherited from one's parents

2. A child inherits genes associated with musical talent. How might the interactional model predict the child's musical development?
   A. It will be determined entirely by the child's environment, such as exposure to music education.
   B. It will be the result of the child's own motivation and exposure to music in their environment.
   C. It will follow a fixed trajectory regardless of the child's experiences.
   D. It will solely depend on the child's inherited genes.

3. How might the concept of plasticity influence the developmental trajectory of a child who has experienced early trauma?
   A. It implies that the child cannot recover from the trauma due to genetic predispositions.
   B. It indicates that environmental influences are insignificant in the face of genetic factors.
   C. It indicates that the child's development may still change in response to new, positive experiences.
   D. It suggests that the child's development is fixed and not subject to change.

4. What does the concept of a critical period in development suggest?
   A. An individual's development is flexible throughout life.
   B. Development is influenced only by genetic factors, not environmental experiences.
   C. Experiences have a uniform effect on development regardless of timing.
   D. There is a specific time when certain experiences must occur for development to proceed normally.

(See answers on the next page.)

1. **D) The set of genes inherited from one's parents**
   Genotype refers to the genetic makeup of an individual that is inherited from the parents at conception and remains consistent throughout life. It is essentially the blueprint of an individual's heredity. Observable characteristics influenced by the environment describe "phenotype," not genotype. The phenotype is the result of the interaction of the genotype with the environment. The dynamic process of development across the life span refers to the overall process of development influenced by both genetic and environmental factors, not the genotype specifically. The physical and social contexts of the environment describe the external factors that influence development and gene expression, but they do not define the genotype itself. The genotype is the internal genetic code, while the environment is external.

2. **B) It will be the result of the child's own motivation and exposure to music in their environment.**
   This answer aligns with the principles of the interactional model, which posits that development results from the constant interplay of biology (in this case, inherited genes) and the environment (like motivation and exposure to music). It acknowledges the role of both genetic predispositions and environmental influences. Suggesting that development is determined entirely by the child's environment negates the role of genetic factors and contradicts the interactional model's emphasis on the interplay between biology and environment. Implying a fixed trajectory for development does not consider the dynamic and reciprocal nature of development emphasized in the interactional approach. Suggesting that development depends solely on inherited genes is a trait model perspective and overlooks the significant impact of the environment and experiences as stipulated in the interactional model.

3. **C) It indicates that the child's development may still change in response to new, positive experiences.**
   Plasticity allows for a child's development to potentially change in response to new, positive experiences, even after early trauma. This concept indicates that while some aspects of development may be more resistant to change, others remain malleable and can be influenced by subsequent experiences. A deterministic view that negates the role of environmental experiences in light of genetic predispositions contradicts the concept of plasticity. A fixed developmental trajectory does not allow for the capacity for change and adaptation in response to experiences, whereas plasticity inherently does.

4. **D) There is a specific time when certain experiences must occur for development to proceed normally.**
   A critical period is described as an "all-or-nothing" period in the provided text, emphasizing that certain experiences must occur (or not occur) within this time frame for normal developmental progress. This period is characterized by its definitive start and end points, beyond which certain developmental processes cannot be initiated or altered. The statement that an individual's development is flexible throughout life contradicts the concept of critical periods, which suggests there are specific times when development is not flexible. The statement that development is influenced only by genetic factors, not environmental experiences, is incorrect as the concept of critical periods inherently involves the impact of environmental experiences on development. Experiences having a uniform effect on development regardless of timing is incorrect because the concept of a critical period implies that the timing of experiences is crucial and that the effect of experiences is not uniform across different developmental stages.

5. A child adopted from an environment where they experienced severe neglect and minimal language exposure is having difficulty with language development. How might this relate to the concept of sensitive or critical periods?

   A. The child may face challenges in language development due to missing experiences during a sensitive period.
   B. The child's current environment can completely compensate for the lack of early language exposure.
   C. The child's difficulties are unrelated to the timing of language exposure.
   D. The child will develop language skills normally as critical periods have little impact on development.

6. Considering the sensitive period for language development, how might interventions be designed for children who had limited verbal interactions in their early years?

   A. Interventions are not necessary as language development is not affected by environmental experiences.
   B. Interventions may need to be more intensive if the child is past the sensitive period for language acquisition.
   C. Interventions should focus on other areas of development, as language cannot be improved after a critical period.
   D. Interventions should focus solely on increasing the amount of language exposure, regardless of the child's age.

7. What is the key factor that Piaget's theory of cognitive development emphasizes about children?

   A. Children are active constructors of their cognitive worlds.
   B. Children are passive recipients of knowledge from adults.
   C. Children's cognitive development is solely based on internal maturation.
   D. Children's thinking is identical to adult thinking at all stages.

8. Considering Vygotsky's concept of the zone of proximal development (ZPD), how might a teacher's approach to instruction change as a student begins to master a new skill?

   A. The teacher would consistently maintain the same level of support throughout the learning process.
   B. The teacher would disregard the student's level of independence and continue direct instruction.
   C. The teacher would increase the complexity of tasks beyond the student's capabilities.
   D. The teacher would provide less scaffolding as the student's competence increases.

(See answers on the next page.)

5. **A) The child may face challenges in language development due to missing experiences during a sensitive period.**
Infancy is a critical period for speech and language development with essential milestones that must be met. Missing these experiences can make it more difficult to acquire language skills later on, which directly applies to the child's situation. Suggesting that the current environment can completely compensate for lack of early language exposure is incorrect because early interaction and exposure is important for language development. The early years are vital for language development and cannot be compensated for later in life. Critical periods are essential for normal language development and missing out on these experiences impacts development negatively.

6. **B) Interventions may need to be more intensive if the child is past the sensitive period for language acquisition.**
The first 3 years of life are a critical period for speech and language development. After this period, a lack of exposure to language and communicative interaction can make it more difficult to acquire language skills, thus requiring more intensive interventions. The text explicitly states that environmental experiences play a significant role in language development. The text does not mention an absolute critical period after which language cannot be improved; instead, it suggests that while there is a sensitive period, development can still occur afterwards, albeit with more effort. The text emphasizes the importance of interactive communication experiences, not just the quantity of language exposure; quality and interaction are also key factors in language development.

7. **A) Children are active constructors of their cognitive worlds.**
Piaget's theory emphasizes that children are not merely passive recipients of knowledge; instead, they actively construct their understanding through interaction with the world. This is illustrated by his description of children as "little scientists," exploring and trying to make sense of their environment. Suggesting children are passive recipients of knowledge contradicts Piaget's view of children as active learners. Piaget argued that cognitive development results from the interplay between internal maturation and environmental interaction, not from internal maturation alone. Piaget clearly outlined qualitative differences in the stages of cognitive development, indicating that children's thinking evolves and is not identical to adult thinking at any stage.

8. **D) The teacher would provide less scaffolding as the student's competence increases.**
Vygotsky's theory of cognitive development places significant emphasis on social interaction and cultural context, particularly through the ZPD. The ZPD is a range of tasks that a child cannot do alone but can achieve with guidance. Scaffolding is the method by which a teacher adjusts their level of support to match the child's current capabilities. As a child's competence increases, the amount of scaffolding provided by the teacher is reduced. This process reflects a dynamic approach to teaching, where the level of assistance is progressively withdrawn as the student becomes more skilled. The other options are incorrect because they do not account for the adaptive nature of scaffolding within the ZPD, which requires changing the level of support in response to the student's evolving abilities.

9. How might Baltes's selective optimization with compensation (SOC) model explain the adaptation strategies of an individual who experiences a decline in cognitive abilities with age?
   A. The individual would experience an inevitable decline without any potential for adaptation.
   B. The individual would ignore any declines and continue to set high, unachievable goals.
   C. The individual would rely solely on past experiences and refuse to adapt to new strategies.
   D. The individual would select new goals and optimize existing abilities to compensate for cognitive declines.

10. What is the significance of the Apgar score in assessing newborns?
    A. It determines genetic predispositions for diseases.
    B. It evaluates the newborn's immediate physical condition after birth.
    C. It is a diagnostic tool for long-term cognitive development.
    D. It is used to assess the physical characteristics of the newborn.

11. How might a healthcare provider use information from the Neonatal Behavioral Assessment Scale (NBAS) to support a newborn's development?
    A. By designing early intervention programs if the NBAS indicates developmental risks
    B. By determining the educational trajectory based on NBAS results
    C. By prescribing medications based on the NBAS scores
    D. By using the NBAS to predict future intelligence

(See answers on the next page.)

9. **D) The individual would select new goals and optimize existing abilities to compensate for cognitive declines.**
Baltes's SOC model posits that successful adaptation in the face of age-related cognitive decline involves actively choosing (selecting) new goals, making the most (optimizing) of remaining abilities, and compensating for lost capacities. An individual would adjust their goals and use their existing abilities to counterbalance cognitive declines. Implying that there is no potential for adaptation, a denial of decline, or a refusal to adapt and an overreliance on past experiences without accommodating new strategies are not compatible with the proactive and adaptive strategies endorsed by the SOC model. The model emphasizes positive adjustment through goal selection, optimizing abilities, and compensating for losses, which is a dynamic process of adapting to changes rather than succumbing to them or ignoring them.

10. **B) It evaluates the newborn's immediate physical condition after birth.**
The Apgar score is crucial for evaluating a newborn's immediate physical condition shortly after birth, focusing on five specific criteria: color, heart rate, reflexes, muscle tone, and respiration. The Apgar assessment is indeed administered to assess these vital signs at 1 and 5 minutes after birth. A score of above 7 suggests a healthy baby, while a score below 4 indicates a critical condition, requiring additional monitoring and potentially immediate medical intervention. The Apgar score does not determine genetic predispositions for diseases. The Apgar score is not a tool for diagnosing long-term cognitive development; it is solely focused on the newborn's initial physical state. While the Apgar score does assess physical characteristics, it does not provide a general physical assessment but rather a specific evaluation of vital functions critical at birth.

11. **A) By designing early intervention programs if the NBAS indicates developmental risks**
The NBAS assesses various aspects of a newborn's well-being, including motor capabilities, state changes, and central nervous system stability, as well as reflexes and social interaction. A healthcare provider might use information from the NBAS to design early intervention programs if the assessment indicates developmental risks. This is because the NBAS can detect neonatal infants who may be at risk for later developmental problems, thus allowing for timely interventions that could mitigate potential issues. The NBAS is not used to determine a child's educational trajectory. The NBAS focuses on immediate postnatal behavioral and neurological responses, not long-term educational outcomes. The NBAS is not typically used to prescribe medications; it's an assessment tool rather than a diagnostic one that would directly lead to medical treatment. The NBAS does not predict future intelligence. Its purpose is to evaluate the current state and immediate potential developmental risks, not to make long-term predictions about intellectual capabilities.

12. Considering the impact of environmental factors during prenatal development, analyze how prenatal exposure to a teratogen might influence developmental outcomes throughout the life span.

   A. Prenatal teratogen exposure determines the entire developmental trajectory, making later environmental factors irrelevant.

   B. Prenatal teratogen exposure has a uniform effect, causing irreversible damage regardless of later interventions.

   C. Teratogen exposure during prenatal development has no lasting effects beyond the neonatal period.

   D. The effects of prenatal teratogen exposure may vary, potentially being mitigated by postnatal environmental factors and interventions.

13. What is the primary difference between synaptogenesis and synaptic pruning in brain development?

   A. Synaptogenesis involves the reduction of neuronal connections, while synaptic pruning is the creation of new synapses.

   B. Synaptogenesis is related to the physical growth of the body, whereas synaptic pruning pertains to cognitive development.

   C. Synaptogenesis occurs only prenatally, while synaptic pruning happens during adolescence.

   D. Synaptogenesis refers to the development of connections between neurons, while synaptic pruning is the elimination of unused synapses.

14. How might a pediatrician apply the concept of probabilistic epigenesis when advising parents on the importance of a stimulating environment for their child?

   A. By advising that environmental influences are so powerful that they can change the child's genetic makeup

   B. By emphasizing that a stimulating environment has no impact on gene expression and subsequent development

   C. By explaining that the child's genetic makeup is the sole determinant of their development and environment plays no role

   D. By informing parents that a stimulating environment can interact with the child's genes to influence development positively

(See answers on the next page.)

12. **D) The effects of prenatal teratogen exposure may vary, potentially being mitigated by postnatal environmental factors and interventions.**
    While teratogens can have a significant negative impact on fetal development, the extent of this impact can be influenced by the dosage, timing, and genetic factors of the pregnant person, and not all effects are irreversible. The text indicates that some effects of malnutrition can be overcome with quality nutrition after birth and that an HIV-positive mother can protect her fetus by taking certain medications. This suggests that postnatal environments and interventions can indeed influence developmental outcomes that were affected by prenatal teratogen exposure. Prenatal teratogen exposure does not determine the entire developmental trajectory, making later environmental factors irrelevant; postnatal interventions can have a mitigating effect. Teratogen exposure does not have a uniform and irreversible effect; the text shows variability in effects and potential for mitigation. Teratogen exposure may have lasting effects beyond the neonatal period according to evidence of long-term effects such as those seen in fetal alcohol syndrome (FAS) and other developmental disorders. Teratogens can have long-term effects, but these can vary and may be influenced by later interventions.

13. **D) Synaptogenesis refers to the development of connections between neurons, while synaptic pruning is the elimination of unused synapses.**
    The primary difference between synaptogenesis and synaptic pruning lies in their respective roles in brain development. Synaptogenesis is the formation of synaptic connections between neurons, a process that initiates at conception and is especially rapid in the first 2 years of life, contributing to the brain's plasticity. It involves the growth of axons and dendrites to create these connections. Synaptic pruning, on the other hand, is the process of eliminating synapses that are not used, which is also crucial for the brain's development as it refines neural communication pathways. Contrary to incorrect options that suggest synaptogenesis reduces neuronal connections or is exclusively prenatal, and synaptic pruning is only about cognitive development or happens solely during adolescence, both processes are integral throughout early childhood and beyond. Synaptogenesis establishes neural connections, while synaptic pruning optimizes brain function by removing redundant synapses, thereby enhancing the efficiency of neuronal communication.

14. **D) By informing parents that a stimulating environment can interact with the child's genes to influence development positively**
    A pediatrician would advise parents that a stimulating environment can interact with a child's genes to positively influence development. This advice is based on the concept of probabilistic epigenesis, which suggests that development is a result of the interaction between genetics and environment. This concept acknowledges that while a child's genetic makeup is set at conception and endures through life, the expression of these genes is influenced by the environment through processes that can activate or deactivate genes. This interaction can shape traits, characteristics, or behaviors in a way that is not predetermined but is influenced by environmental conditions. Environmental influences do not change the child's genetic makeup; they can only affect gene expression. Negating the impact of the environment on gene expression contradicts the concept of epigenesis that emphasizes the interaction between genes and environment. Denying the role of the environment and suggesting that genetics alone determine development goes against the probabilistic nature of epigenesis that involves both genetic and environmental factors. The text clearly supports the idea that the environment plays a significant role in gene expression and development.

6. GROWTH AND LIFE-SPAN DEVELOPMENT   149

15. Considering the dynamic nature of motor development, how might researchers interpret individual differences in the age at which infants reach motor milestones?
    A. As an indication that any deviation from the average age of milestone achievement is a sign of developmental delay or disorder
    B. As an indication that while there are average ages for reaching milestones, individual differences can be influenced by a range of environmental and biological factors
    C. As a sign that motor development is rigidly fixed and not subject to variation
    D. As evidence that motor milestones are solely based on genetic maturation and not influenced by the environment

16. What are the two primary components of long-term memory, and what do they involve?
    A. Recall memory and autobiographical memory
    B. Recognition memory and procedural memory
    C. Semantic memory and generic memory
    D. Working memory and episodic memory

17. How might a child's exposure to language and communicative interactions during infancy impact their language development in later childhood?
    A. Adequate exposure to language and interactive communication in infancy is essential for healthy language development in later childhood.
    B. Exposure to language in infancy has no significant impact on later language development.
    C. Exposure to language in infancy primarily affects cognitive development, not language development.
    D. Limited exposure to language in infancy may lead to faster language development in later childhood.

18. How does socioeconomic status (SES) influence the quantity and quality of language exposure children receive, and what potential long-term consequences might it have on a child's development?
    A. SES has no significant influence on language development as it primarily depends on innate abilities.
    B. SES is correlated with quantity and quality of language exposure, with higher SES families providing richer language-stimulating environments.
    C. SES is unrelated to language development and has no long-term consequences on a child's development.
    D. SES only influences language development during early childhood but becomes less significant in later stages.

(See answers on the next page.)

15. **B) As an indication that while there are average ages for reaching milestones, individual differences can be influenced by a range of environmental and biological factors**
    While motor milestones have average ages, individual variations are influenced by a range of factors. Motor development follows a predictable pattern but also acknowledges that individual differences may be due to cultural and familial expectations and practices among other environmental and psychosocial factors. This indicates that while there are norms, individual differences are expected and are shaped by both environmental and biological factors. Any deviation from the average is not necessarily a developmental issue; individual differences are normal and expected. Implying motor development does not vary contradicts the assertion that individual differences are influenced by various factors. Motor milestones are not only based on genetics; environmental factors also play a role. Motivation and engagement in different behaviors and configurations are important, which implies that environment and experience, not just genetics, influence motor development.

16. **B) Recognition memory and procedural memory**
    Recognition memory allows individuals to identify previously encountered events or objects, giving a sense of familiarity, while procedural memory stores knowledge on how to perform various routines and actions. Recall memory and autobiographical memory are specific types of memory but not the primary components of long-term memory. Generic memory is not a recognized category for primary components of long-term memory. Working memory is a form of short-term memory and episodic memory, while a type of long-term memory, is not paired with procedural memory as a primary component.

17. **A) Adequate exposure to language and interactive communication in infancy is essential for healthy language development in later childhood.**
    The first 3 years of life are critical for speech and language development, with rapid brain development and plasticity allowing infants to learn phonology, semantics, and syntax through interactive communication. Language exposure and communicative interaction during this period can lead to difficulties in acquiring language skills later on. Early language exposure is crucial for later language development. Early language is also linked to exposure to language development, not just cognitive development. Limited early language exposure can hinder, not hasten, later language development. Early interaction and exposure to language set the foundation for later language abilities, underscoring the importance of a rich communicative environment during infancy.

18. **B) SES is correlated with quantity and quality of language exposure, with higher SES families providing richer language-stimulating environments.**
    Children from high-SES families are exposed to a larger quantity and variety of words and more child-directed language compared to children from lower SES families. This disparity in language exposure can lead to early gaps in language proficiency, which may affect literacy, school readiness, and even health and behavioral outcomes into the school years and beyond. SES is correlated with the quantity and quality of language exposure, which suggests that in addition to the child's abilities, the child's environment also plays a role in language development. There is a significant impact of SES on language exposure and the subsequent long-term consequences for a child's development. Early gaps in language proficiency have long-term consequences.

19. What are the two main components of self-concept mentioned in the text, and how do they differ?
    A. Gender awareness and identity; gender awareness involves labeling oneself by gender, and gender identity is the ability to understand gender as an immutable characteristic.
    B. Knowledge components and evaluative components; knowledge components involve self-evaluation, and evaluative components encompass physical and cognitive characteristics.
    C. Self-awareness and social awareness; self-awareness includes self-esteem, and social awareness involves understanding others' emotions.
    D. Self-regulation and effortful control; self-regulation refers to managing emotional reactions, and effortful control involves managing cognitive processes.

20. How might chronic or severe stress during childhood impact a child's emotional development and overall well-being?
    A. Chronic stress can lead to heightened emotional regulation and social competence.
    B. Chronic stress during childhood has no lasting effects on emotional development.
    C. Chronic stress may result in emotional dysregulation, behavioral problems, and long-term psychological consequences.
    D. Chronic stress primarily affects physical development, not emotional development.

21. How do overt and relational aggression differ, and what are their potential consequences for children's social development?
    A. Overt aggression and relational aggression are terms used interchangeably, and they both involve physical harm. These forms of aggression are not associated with social development.
    B. Overt aggression involves physical harm, while relational aggression involves manipulation within social relationships. Overt aggression is more common in girls, and relational aggression is more common in boys.
    C. Overt aggression is more common in boys and involves manipulation within social relationships, while relational aggression is more common in girls and focuses on physical harm. Both types of aggression predict positive social and behavioral outcomes.
    D. Overt aggression seeks to establish dominance over others through physical harm, while relational aggression damages existing social relationships through manipulation. Overt aggression is more common in boys, and relational aggression is more common in girls. Both types of aggression are associated with negative future outcomes.

22. What is a common consequence for children following their parents' divorce?
    A. Decreased risk of substance use
    B. Enhanced academic performance
    C. Improved mental health
    D. Increased likelihood for mental health issues

(*See answers on the next page.*)

19. **B) Knowledge components and evaluative components; knowledge components involve self-evaluation, and evaluative components encompass physical and cognitive characteristics.**
    The knowledge components of self-concept include an individual's physical and cognitive characteristics, like values and personal goals. In contrast, evaluative components are about self-evaluation, which encompasses self-esteem and self-efficacy. Although gender awareness and identity are an extension of a person's sense of self, they are not what defines self-concept. Self-concept is not defined as comprising self-awareness and social awareness; rather, it distinguishes between knowledge and evaluative components. Self-regulation and effortful control are components of emotional development.

20. **C) Chronic stress may result in emotional dysregulation, behavioral problems, and long-term psychological consequences.**
    Chronic stress can have a negative impact on a child's ability to regulate stress responses, resulting in difficulties in adolescence and adulthood. Chronic overactivation of the stress response system is also linked to major depression and other health issues in adults. Additionally, there are wide-ranging consequences of adverse childhood experiences (ACEs), including impaired cognitive, emotional, and social functioning. An inability to regulate stress can lead to hyperactivated stress responses with externalizing disorders or hypoactivated stress responses with social withdrawal. Chronic stress leads to dysregulation of the stress response, not heightened emotional regulation and social competence. Chronic stress and ACEs have significant long-term effects on emotional development and well-being. Chronic stress affects emotional and social functioning, not just physical development.

21. **D) Overt aggression seeks to establish dominance over others through physical harm, while relational aggression damages existing social relationships through manipulation. Overt aggression is more common in boys, and relational aggression is more common in girls. Both types of aggression are associated with negative future outcomes.**
    Overt aggression is more common in boys, and relational aggression is more common in girls. Both types of aggression are associated with negative future outcomes. Overt and relational aggression are not used interchangeably, and they are indeed associated with social development. Overt aggression is more common in boys and relational aggression is more common in girls. There are no positive outcomes related to aggression.

22. **D) Increased likelihood for mental health issues**
    The consequences of divorce on child well-being include an increased likelihood for mental health issues such as anxiety, depression, and suicidality. Divorce is associated with an increased likelihood of substance use, not a decreased risk. Divorce is not associated with enhanced academic performance. Divorce is typically associated with negative impacts on mental health rather than improvements.

23. What factors primarily influence child well-being in same-sex family structures?
    A. Family stability and socioeconomic circumstances
    B. Societal acceptance and legal rights
    C. The gender of the parents
    D. The sexual orientation of the parents

24. In what ways might societal expectations and norms influence the experiences of new parents during their transition to parenthood?
    A. May create unrealistic expectations and pressures
    B. No significant influence
    C. May create realistic expectations and preparation
    D. Solely impacts financial aspects of parenting

25. What is the most common form of kinship care in the United States?
    A. Aunts and uncles caring for nieces and nephews
    B. Grandparents raising grandchildren
    C. Older cousins raising younger cousins
    D. Siblings caring for each other

26. How might remaining in school affect the long-term outcomes for adolescent mothers?
    A. Contributes to higher rates of mental health issues
    B. Has no impact on long-term outcomes
    C. Leads to increased financial security and educational opportunities
    D. Increases the likelihood of additional closely spaced pregnancies

27. Considering cultural and societal factors, what approaches might be beneficial in supporting a child who has experienced the death of a family member?
    A. A one-size-fits-all approach to grief counseling
    B. Avoiding discussions about death to prevent trauma
    C. Focusing only on the immediate emotional responses
    D. Tailored support acknowledging the child's cultural background and age

(See answers on the next page.)

23. **A) Family stability and socioeconomic circumstances**
    Like different-sex parent families, differences in child well-being in same-sex family structures are largely attributable to family stability and socioeconomic circumstances. Research does not show significant differences in developmental outcomes for children raised by same-sex parents compared to those raised by different-sex parents. The gender of the parents and the sexual orientation of the parents are not primary influencing factors of child well-being. Societal acceptance and legal rights, while potentially important, were not discussed as primary factors influencing child well-being in same-sex family structures.

24. **A) May create unrealistic expectations and pressures**
    Prospective parents may have "romantic illusions" about having and raising a child. These illusions are likely influenced by societal expectations and norms about parenthood. There are various challenges new parents face, such as managing different roles and maintaining relationships, which can be exacerbated by societal pressures to perform these roles perfectly. There is a significant influence by mentioning the difficulties parents face, which can stem from societal norms. Societal expectations and norms typically create unrealistic expectations and pressures. The impact of societal expectations is not limited to financial aspects, as there are emotional and relationship challenges as well.

25. **B) Grandparents raising grandchildren**
    Grandparents represent the most common caregiver in kinship care situations in the United States. Grandparents play a vital role in many families, particularly in parent-absent households. Although aunts and uncles, older children, and siblings are excellent examples of kinship care, they are not the most common.

26. **C) Leads to increased financial security and educational opportunities**
    Adolescent mothers who remain in school and delay subsequent childbearing fare much better, implying improved long-term outcomes in terms of education and financial stability. This suggests that staying in school provides adolescent mothers with a more stable educational path, which can lead to better job prospects and financial security. Staying in school is associated with better outcomes, not negative ones like mental health issues. Remaining in school and delaying childbearing results in better outcomes for adolescent mothers. Remaining in school and delaying subsequent pregnancies is beneficial and does not increase the likelihood of having additional closely spaced pregnancies.

27. **D) Tailored support acknowledging the child's cultural background and age**
    Children's understanding and processing of death evolve with age and are influenced by their cultural environment, implying that support should be developmentally appropriate and culturally sensitive. The other options are incorrect for the following reasons: A one-size-fits-all approach to grief counseling is incorrect because individual factors such as age, cultural background, and the nature of the familial death significantly influence the grieving process, which means a singular approach would not be suitable for every child. Avoiding discussions about death to prevent trauma is incorrect because avoidance is not beneficial. On the contrary, understanding and processing the concept of death is part of how children manage grief, so discussions about death are likely necessary for healthy emotional management. Focusing only on the immediate emotional responses is incorrect because it fails to consider the long-term developmental impact of a family member's death on a child. The death of a family member can profoundly affect various aspects of a child's development, not just their immediate emotional responses.

Assessment and Diagnosis

Megan N. Scott, Lauren Bush, and Scott J. Hunter

> **BROAD CONTENT AREAS**
> - Psychometrics
> - Assessment models and instruments
> - Assessment methods for initial status of and change by individuals, couples, families, groups, and organizations/systems

▶ INTRODUCTION

Psychological assessment is a process of gaining information about and an understanding of an individual to facilitate informed decision-making. The goals of psychological assessment are varied and include screening; measurement of specific characteristics or traits; determination of risk; diagnosis; vocational planning; evaluation of the impact of intervention; and intervention planning. Testing comprises numerous assessment methods, including interview, direct observation, informal assessment procedures, and norm-referenced (standardized) assessment.

▶ ASSESSMENT THEORIES AND MODELS

Broadly, *psychometrics* refers to the study of psychological measurement and includes the development of measures for the assessment of intelligence, specific abilities, knowledge in a given area, personality traits, behavior, attitudes, symptoms, and educational or vocational progress. The field of psychometrics focuses primarily on the creation and validation of measurement instruments that are employed primarily (but not only) in psychological professional practice, for both research and clinical use. Among the first psychometric measures were those developed in the early 20th century for the purpose of intelligence testing. One of the earliest tests was the Binet–Simon Scale, developed by Alfred Binet and Theodore Simon in 1905 to identify children with what we now call intellectual disability who were enrolled in French schools (Binet & Simon, 1905; Sattler, 2018). This was the first standardized intelligence test and was administered in a fairly consistent way across test takers. It consisted of 30 items with increasing levels of difficulty. Binet and Simon used this scale to provide what they characterized as an objective diagnosis of the presence and severity of intellectual disability in test takers, and with an implied understanding of age-based development when providing diagnosis; we do know now that these scales were not fully "objective" in their assessment of development and capacity, and instead were biased in regard to the conceptualization of both assessment approach and interpretation in line with pernicious models of racial and cultural superiority prevalent at the time of their authorship (C. R. Reynolds et al., 2021; Rosales & Walker, 2021).

Since the introduction of intelligence testing with the creation of the Binet–Simon Scale, two primary competing theories of intelligence have developed and supported the growth and structure of batteries created and put in use to date: a *general-factor* (g) *theory of intelligence* and a *multiple-factor theory of intelligence* (Sattler, 2018). Current hierarchical models underlying testing view intelligence as consisting of a general intelligence factor that is situated at the top of a pyramid of skills, with broad abilities comprising the middle and specific factors or abilities situated at the base. Additionally, more recent views of intelligence highlight the roles of underlying biology and unfolding cognitive and adaptive development as significant influences on intelligence and its representation (Sattler, 2018; Sternberg & Kaufman, 1998). As will be discussed in the Psychometric Theory section in greater detail, these models of how intelligence is best understood and assessed are accompanied by two principal theories underlying the development of measurement tools used in psychological assessment, including intelligence testing. These are classical test theory (CTT) and item response theory (IRT).

▶ ASSESSMENT IN PRACTICE

Assessment is a core component of psychological practice and research. Many different specialties within the field of psychology use tests and measures to capture and define domains of interest. As such, the development and use of psychological measures is an important skill that remains pertinent to the identity of a psychologist. Within professional psychology, clinical, counseling, school, developmental, industrial–organizational, vocational, rehabilitation, and social psychologists all commonly use tests and measures. Tests for the characterization and classification of select groups of individuals are used particularly by applied psychologists. A discussion of domains of practice that commonly require the use of standardized measures follows.

Clinical and counseling psychologists typically make use of tests that define and characterize patterns of adaptation and functioning, either to classify an individual and/or to provide diagnosis. Personality assessment; measurement of basic cognition, mood, and behavioral functioning; and assessment of current performance and adaptive capacity are commonly considered. Measures used are typically referenced to a range of functioning, spanning typical developmental presentation to dysfunction, and capture the degree to which symptoms and traits are present and either influence or interfere with functioning.

School psychologists most typically employ measures that characterize and define how an individual is able to learn. Functioning within the school setting is the primary focus of the school psychologist; measures tapping intelligence, academic skill, language, visual and motor processing, and behavior are among the tools most used. Monitoring of the impact of intervention is also an important component of school psychology practice.

Neuropsychology is a specialty within clinical psychology that incorporates knowledge of brain functioning and the relationship between the brain and cognition and behavior (Boake, 2008). It makes use of standardized testing approaches to elucidate and describe these relationships. Neuropsychologists apply this knowledge to understand and characterize an individual's profile of neurocognitive strengths and weaknesses in relation to expected patterns of brain development and abnormal brain functioning. Neuropsychological assessment can provide information to help determine whether dysfunctional behavior is primarily due to a neurological or other organic cause, or whether the behavior is more functional in nature. By comparing the pattern of strengths and weaknesses to known neurocognitive profiles of specific disorders, neuropsychological evaluations help to clarify the nature and severity of neurological injury or insult and are used to clarify both medical and psychological diagnoses. Neuropsychological evaluations are also frequently used to assess learning disabilities, as well as complex behavioral and emotional conditions.

Vocational and rehabilitation psychologists frequently emphasize how well an individual can meet demands for independence across development, with a goal of increasing success at work and learning as a primary focus. Measures used by these professionals typically address such areas as functional skill for meeting specific vocational and educational goals, monitoring of skill development, and adaptations that are required to facilitate adaptive and behavioral functioning. Assessment of underlying capacity and how this may be broadened and refined, as possible, is also considered an important element of practice.

▶ APPROACHES TO ASSESSMENT

Behavioral assessment has been defined as "an exploratory hypothesis-testing process in which a range [of] specific procedures are used . . . to understand a given child, group, or social ecology, and to formulate and evaluate specific intervention strategies" (Ollendick & Hersen, 1984, p. 6). The basis of behavioral assessment lies in the assumption that behavior is the product of an interaction between an individual and their environment. Typically, behavioral assessment is used to describe a particular behavior or pattern of behavior and to understand what leads to and maintains it across time. This information is important in determining a treatment or intervention to address a problematic behavior and then to evaluate the efficacy of the intervention used to alter or change that given behavior.

Functional behavioral assessment (FBA) is a specific method of behavioral assessment that operationalizes and then characterizes the presence and impact of a select behavior or group of behaviors. It additionally defines the parameters that influence and underscore the display of the behavior, and guides how to best intervene by developing and evaluating the effectiveness of a behavioral intervention plan (Miller et al., 1998). The key components of an FBA are to define a problem behavior, determine the antecedents or the events that precede the problem behavior, and outline the consequence or function of the behavior. This information allows the clinician to develop a hypothesis about why a given behavior is occurring, and supports the systematic assessment of that hypothesis.

Ecological assessment uses primarily observational methods to examine and understand the physical and psychological variables that impact behavior in a given environment or setting (Sattler, 2018). Psychological variables include an individual's relationships with peers, teachers, parents, spouses, coworkers, or other individuals in a given setting, whereas physical variables include such specific physical aspects of the environment as lighting, noise, spatial arrangement of furniture, or seating. Hiltonsmith and Keller (1983) have described a framework for organizing data collected in ecological (person setting) assessment. Their model consists of three components: "setting appearance and contents," which are observable physical aspects of the setting; "setting operation," or the interaction and communication patterns within an environment and how the setting is being used; and "setting opportunities," which are opportunities contained within the environment that support the development of cognition and language, as well as social–emotional growth.

▶ ASSESSMENT METHODS

There are a number of different assessment methods used by psychologists. These include standardized administration, self-report, informant report, structured and semistructured interviews, direct observation, and psychophysiological assessment. In industrial–organizational psychology, important assessment methods include direct observation, assessment centers, and work samples.

Standardized administration in assessment refers to giving a test or measure under consistent, or standard, conditions. This includes the use of the same administration, item content, and scoring criteria across all individuals who are presented with the measure. In test development, *standardization* refers to the process through which a measure is first administered to a representative sample of a given group under consideration for the test—for example, children in the United

States who are between 6 and 17 years of age—in order to develop scoring norms. These norms represent the range of performance that can be expected across the measure and serve to define the typical pattern of response the test elicits.

Norm-referenced tests are standardized tests or measures that compare an examinee's performance to the performance of a specified group of participants. The reference population, or the population of participants represented by the measurement norms, is most commonly defined by age, as seen with the previous example. Other characteristics, including grade, clinical presentation, diagnostic group status, gender, and racial or cultural group status, may also be used. The use of norms allows the psychologist to determine a score for the person being tested that is compared to the distribution of scores attained on the measure by the normative sample. This quantifies the examinee's performance on the given measure relative to the reference group. Norm-referenced testing can also allow for evaluation of changes in an individual's performance over time.

A criterion-referenced test is used to assess where an examinee stands on a particular criterion, or domain of skill, status, or functioning. Criterion-referenced tests tend to be used to assess an individual's knowledge or skill in a hierarchical fashion, as would be consistent with expectations for learning. These types of tests are most often used in educational and vocational settings to assess progress or mastery of a given skill or subject matter. Examples of criterion-referenced tests include driving tests, licensing exams, or high school graduation examinations.

Self-report measures are typically symptom-based questionnaires and surveys, or semistructured and structured interviews (discussed further in the following section). These include both broad-based measures of a range of symptoms across a number of diagnostic categories (e.g., symptom checklists or broad personality inventories, like the *Personality Assessment Inventory* [PAI]), and narrow measures of symptoms seen with specific disorders (e.g., the *Beck Anxiety Inventory* [BAI] or the *Children's Depression Inventory–Second Edition*). When working with children and adolescents, informant reports are particularly important. An informant report is a questionnaire, rating, or checklist measure that is most typically completed by a parent or teacher, but, depending on the measure, may be used with a caretaker or spouse. As with self-report measures, informant-report measures may be broad in nature (e.g., *Behavioral Assessment System for Children/Adolescents–Third Edition*) or specific to the symptoms of a given disorder (e.g., *Conners Third Edition*, which is used to assess attention deficit hyperactivity disorder [ADHD]-related concerns). With the use of self- and informant-report measures, it is important to consider that different informants completing these measures may view an individual quite differently based on the context of the interaction with the person being evaluated and the opportunities the informant may have for comparison. Therefore, it is quite helpful to seek information regarding a particular individual being assessed from multiple informants whenever possible. In addition, it is important to remember that informant ratings are never without some degree of bias and can be impacted by a range of variables, including the severity of the individual's symptoms; the child's ethnicity, gender, and socioeconomic status; the informant's familiarity with the individual; or their tolerance for problematic behavior (Sattler, 2018).

Clinicians gain critical assessment information through interviews with clients, parents, spouses, teachers, and other informants. Unstructured and semistructured interviews are less formal opportunities to gain information, providing an examinee with the opportunity to provide information about themselves outside of a standardized assessment format. Unstructured interviews are typically open-ended interactions with an examiner or clinician, frequently conducted without a standard format or structure, aside from some initial questions of interest. Unstructured interviews allow for flexibility, rapport building, and the ability to further examine information that arises in the context of the interview. However, due to their lack of standardization, there is some concern when unstructured interviews are used as the sole source of information when developing a diagnosis, given the limited reliability and validity inherent in the nonstructured approach. Semistructured and structured interviews, in contrast, have been developed to be administered in a standardized manner and, as a result, reduce problems with reliability and validity found in unstructured interviews. There are a number of commonly used semistructured and structured interviews that have good psychometric properties; these include the Schedule for Affective Disorders and Schizophrenia (SADS), the Diagnostic Interview Schedule (DIS), and the Structured Clinical Interview for the *DSM-5* (SCID-5). These tools are most used within research settings but are not uncommon in clinical settings where focused diagnostic procedures are required.

Together, the use of direct observation and behavioral assessment provide useful sources of information about an examinee of interest. By observing an individual in their natural environment, such as the school setting for children, the psychologist can gain an understanding of antecedent and consequent responses that may influence learning and behavior. Additionally, direct observation methods provide a snapshot of an individual's behavior within and across a variety of settings outside of the testing environment. As such, they can be useful when assessing interpersonal and social behavior, contextual learning, and how behavior may differ across environments. The accuracy of informant-report of behavior or functioning in a given environment can be evaluated with direct observation. Systematic observations and FBAs further allow the examiner to identify and describe target behaviors, as well as understand the antecedents and consequences of behavior to inform behavioral interventions. These methods can be further used to examine the effectiveness of behavioral and psychological interventions. When conducting systematic or structured observations, individuals are typically observed in a naturalistic environment, such as home, work, or school, and the examiner records objective data about behaviors observed. In FBA, counts of behavior and descriptions of controls and guides are also made.

There are several observational assessments that can be employed by a psychologist. These range from global descriptions of behavior to targeted ratings of the frequency and intensity of specific behaviors. Narrative recording assessments provide a running record of an individual's behavior throughout the observation period, with the examiner noting behaviors of interest. Interval recording methods, also known as time-sampling methods, require target behaviors to be operationally defined in objective, clear, and specific terms for the examiner to effectively identify and monitor the behavior during observation. Observation is divided into brief time intervals and the examiner records whether a specific behavior occurs during each interval recorded. The occurrence or absence of the behavior during each interval is then tallied across the entire observation. This type of observational assessment is appropriate when a given behavior occurs frequently or does not have a clear beginning or ending. With event sampling, the psychologist records the frequency of a target behavior during the observation. With this method, it can be quite challenging to assess behaviors that occur frequently or take place over a long duration; hence, it is more common to use time-sampling methods when addressing a frequent problematic behavior.

Rating recordings allow the examiner to rate a given behavior, in regard to its intensity or duration. These types of ratings are typically made using a 5-point Likert scale (e.g., from not present to present). As just mentioned, these ratings typically assess intensity or severity of a behavior; they are also used to gain broad impressions of behavior. Although this approach allows for the collection of qualitative data about the behavior, the reliability of this approach across raters or examiners varies significantly, due to the difficulty found in objectively and consistently rating target behaviors.

Direct observation, assessment centers, and work samples are methods of assessment in work settings and are common methods in industrial and organizational psychology. Assessment centers are defined as a setting where "a standardized evaluation of behavior based on multiple inputs" can occur (Rupp et al., 2015, p. 1248). An assessment center "consists of multiple components, which include behavioral simulation exercises, within which multiple trained assessors observe and record behaviors, classify them according to the behavioral constructs of interest, and (either individually or collectively) rate (either individual or pooled) behaviors" (Rupp et al., 2015, p. 1248). The raters or observers meet to discuss the results of the behavior observed during the assessment and generate an assessment score based on consensus or data aggregation.

There are 10 key components needed for an evaluation process to be considered an assessment measure: systematic analysis to determine job-relevant behavioral constructs, behavioral classification, multiple assessment center components, linkages between behavioral constructs and assessment center components, simulations, assessors, assessor training, recording behavior and scoring, data integration, and standardization (Rupp et al., 2015).

Assessment centers typically evaluate behaviors and skills that are specific to a job's content, as well as evaluate the types of problems that typically arise on the job. The purpose is to "(1) to predict future behavior for decision making, (2) to diagnose developmental needs, and (3) to develop assessees on behavioral constructs of interest" (Rupp et al., 2015, p. 1253). They may include norm-referenced testing to assess cognitive abilities or personality and criterion-based tests that assess job knowledge. During the assessment process, raters observe and evaluate an individual's performance on the simulation activities. An overall rating is provided at the end of the assessment that integrates the information from the assessment activities. Work samples are most often used to assess job potential and are constructed activities or exercises meant to simulate on-the-job situations, specifically ones that are important to a given job. These may include giving a presentation, role-playing an interaction with a customer or coworker, or completing a series of in-basket exercises that test the individual's ability to handle administrative tasks required by a position.

▶ PSYCHOMETRIC THEORY

CLASSICAL TEST THEORY, ITEM RESPONSE THEORY, AND GENERALIZABILITY THEORY

CTT and IRT are the two primary theories that underlie the development of measurement tools used in psychological assessment. CTT is based on the work of Charles Spearman and was first presented in 1904. It is defined as "a psychometric theory based on the view that an individual's observed score on a test is the sum of a true score component for the test taker, plus an independent measurement error component" (American Educational Research Association [AERA], American Psychological Association [APA], & National Council Measurement in Education [NCME], 1999, p. 172; AERA, APA, & NCME, 2021, p. 169). In other words, an individual's score on any given instrument (i.e., the observed score) is composed of that individual's true score and error, neither of which is individually observable. According to CTT, the true score is conceptualized as the average score an individual would achieve on a specific test, given an infinite number of administrations of that test (Alagumalai & Curtis, 2005; DeVellis, 2006).

The equation for CTT is $S_i = t_i + e_i$, where S_i is the raw score on the test, t_i is the true score, and e_i is the error term. The error term in CTT is assumed to be random error and should not be correlated with either the raw score or the true score according to the assumptions of CTT. As a result, error sources cannot be distinguished or identified.

Generalizability theory (G theory) is an extension of CTT. It conceptualizes error in a way that allows for the evaluation of both error and the reliability of measurement procedures (AERA, APA, & NCME, 2021; Gao & Harris, 2012). G theory identifies sources of measurement error, separates the influence of each source, and then estimates the individual sources of measurement error. In G theory, an individual's score on a test or measure is conceptualized as a sample from among an infinite number of administrations or possible observations on that measure. Potential sources of error are all of the characteristics of the assessment measure, including test forms, test items, circumstances under which the test is administered, the rater, and other related sources. Reliability of measurement is evaluated by conducting a generalizability study (G study), the purpose of which is to quantify individual sources of measurement error (AERA, APA, & NCME, 2021; Gao & Harris, 2012; Webb et al., 2006).

IRT focuses on the examination of individual items in test development. In IRT, the relationships between the construct being measured and the individual test responses are examined across multiple levels. Test developers rely on three parameters when examining test item relationships: item difficulty (the percentage of test takers who get a specific item correct), item discrimination (how that item discriminates between those who do well versus those who do poorly on the test as a whole), and the probability that a question is answered correctly by guessing. The item characteristic curve (ICC) or item response function is then calculated; the ICC is a mathematical function that is used to illustrate the increasing proportion of correct answers for an item, at higher levels of the ability or trait being measured by a given assessment.

ITEM AND TEST CHARACTERISTICS

When developing an assessment battery or choosing which individual tests to administer, the psychometric properties of the measure under consideration must be considered. For a measure to have adequate psychometric properties, it must be both reliable and valid.

Reliability refers to the degree to which test scores are consistent. When referring to G theory, reliability will include the degree to which testing is free from measurement error (Gao & Harris, 2012). In CTT, a score on a test is thought to reflect an individual's true score on the ability or trait being assessed as well as error. Therefore, the reliability coefficient is an indicator that reflects the degree of consistency or the degree to which scores are free from error. Reliability coefficients are denoted with the letter *r* and range from 1.00 (indicating perfect reliability) to 0.00 (indicating the absence of reliability).

There are different types of reliability estimates to consider in test development and selection. *Test–retest reliability* refers to the stability of scores over time. The test–retest reliability correlation is obtained by administering a specific test to the same group at two different points in time. The pair of scores for the same people across the two administrations is then correlated. Generally, a closer test–retest interval leads to a higher reliability coefficient. The use of test–retest to assess reliability is appropriate when the trait or ability being measured is thought to be relatively stable over time.

The alternate form reliability coefficient (also known as equivalent or parallel form reliability) is generated by administering two or more interchangeable forms of a given test to the same group and correlating the results across test forms. An example of this is the *Woodcock–Johnson IV Tests of Achievement* (WJ-IV Ach; Schrank et al., 2014), which has two comparable forms, A and B. These alternate test forms measure the same constructs, have similar content, and use the same directions. A key factor in the reliability between alternate forms is that the items included with both have the same level of difficulty. An advantage of using parallel or alternate forms of a test is that the practice effect, or memory for content of a previously administered test or measure, is minimized.

Internal consistency reliability is based on the scores obtained by an individual during one administration of a test. It is calculated to determine the consistency of the items within the measure. The internal consistency reliability coefficient allows test developers and users to assess the reliability of a measure without requiring a second administration of the same measure or a parallel form of the measure. There are two types of internal consistency reliability. In split-half reliability, the test is divided into two equivalent halves and correlated. According to Cohen and Swerdlik (2002), there are three steps to computing a split-half reliability coefficient: dividing the test into two halves (typically odd and even items), calculating the correlation between the two halves, and then adjusting the split-half reliability score using the Spearman–Brown formula. The Spearman–Brown formula is used to estimate the internal consistency of an entire test from the reliability of one half of a test. It is derived from the formula that is used to estimate the reliability of a test that has been shortened or lengthened by several test items. The Spearman–Brown formula is:

$$r_{SB} = \frac{nr_{xy}}{1+(n-1)r_{xy}}$$

where r_{SB} is the Spearman–Brown adjusted reliability coefficient, r_{xy} is the Pearson r in the original length test, and n is the number of items in the revised version of the test divided by the number of items in the original version of the test.

An internal consistency reliability coefficient can also be estimated by examining inter-item consistency, the correlation among all items on a scale. The inter-item consistency coefficient is only useful when test items are homogeneous, and therefore meant to measure a single trait or factor. The Kuder–Richardson formula 20 (KR-20) can be used as an alternative approach for calculating split-half reliability when examining internal consistency of a homogeneous test.

Finally, *interrater* or *interscorer reliability* refers to the consistency of the performance or behaviors of a test taker. A high interrater reliability coefficient indicates that scores on a test are calculated or derived in a consistent and systematic manner across examiners. It is evaluated using percentage agreement, kappa, the interclass correlation coefficient, or the product-moment correlation coefficient.

Once reliability of a measure is established, validity can be examined. A measure must be reliable to be considered valid. *Validity* refers to the extent to which a given test accurately and precisely measures what it is meant to measure. The validity coefficients represent the strength of the relationship between a predictor and a criterion or outcome measure. As with reliability, there are several different types of validity to consider when examining the psychometric properties of a test.

Face validity has to do with the examinee's perception of the validity of a test while taking it. Face validity is different than actual validity, as a test may seem valid even when it is not. However, face validity is important because it can impact how an examinee approaches a test and a lack of face validity may lead to a lack of confidence in the effectiveness of the test.

Early on, four types of validity were described: content validity, construct validity, concurrent validity, and predictive validity (AERA, APA, & NCME, 1954). Concurrent and predictive validity were later combined into criterion validity. Together criterion, content, and construct validity became referred to as the "holy trinity," "the trinitarian," or the "three-in-one model of validity." There has been ongoing debate over this model of validity since its identification. According to the APA's Standards for Educational and Psychological Testing (AERA, APA, & NCME, 2014), evidence for validity is to be considered in test construction and selection, including evidence based on test content, response processes, internal structure, and relations to other variables.

Content validity describes how well a test includes the range of information that is needed, across items, to test the construct that is being measured. Content validity is often assessed by independent evaluators or experts in the field and is usually addressed during test development. As noted earlier, criterion validity is composed of both concurrent validity and predictive validity. It provides a judgment about the adequacy with which a test score can estimate an individual's performance on a criterion of interest. For example, the criterion validity of the *Beck Depression Inventory–Second Edition* (BDI-II; A. T. Beck et al., 1996) refers to the extent to which the test's score estimates an individual's level of depressive symptoms within a 2-week period. Concurrent validity is calculated by examining the correlation between a new measure and an established measure that is administered at the same time to assess the criterion of interest. Using the same example, if a new measure of depression being developed is well correlated with the BDI-II when administered to the same sample, that measure is considered to have good concurrent validity. Predictive validity is the extent to which scores on the test predict a specified criterion score established to address the presence or absence of a particular criterion. Therefore, the predictive validity coefficient represents the correlation between obtained test scores and the criterion of interest.

When a test or measure is used to predict classification within a group or to assign a diagnosis, such as using a test to accurately diagnose a disorder like posttraumatic stress disorder (PTSD), sensitivity and specificity are important statistical concepts to consider, particularly when interpreting the results of the test. *Sensitivity* refers to the proportion of people who are accurately identified as possessing a certain trait, attribute, or behavior that is being measured;

in our example, that would be the number of people with PTSD who are accurately diagnosed. In turn, *specificity* refers to the proportion of people who are accurately classified as not having the condition or trait, attribute, or behavior being measured, for example, the number of people who do not have PTSD and who are appropriately not given a diagnosis. Sensitivity and specificity are often considered in relationship to Type I and Type II errors.

Construct validity refers to the extent to which a test is correlated (or associated) with the trait or ability it claims to assess. While criterion-related validity assesses the relationship between a new measure and established measures that assess the same criterion, construct validity refers to the relationship between the new test and the construct itself. This is much harder to measure, but one method for establishing construct validity is the use of a multitrait–multimethod matrix. The multitrait–multimethod matrix (D. T. Campbell & Fiske, 1959) compares a new measure with another measure that examines the same trait or condition in a different way, as well as with measures that use the same method for measuring different traits or conditions. This results in a matrix of correlations that determine both convergent validity (the extent to which a measure correlates with other measures designed to assess the same trait or condition) and divergent validity (the extent to which a measure does not correlate with ones with which it should not theoretically correlate). Factor analysis is another means of demonstrating convergent and divergent validity. In test development and psychometric research, factor analysis is typically used to examine the factor or factors being assessed by the items on a given test, and how well the items comprising the measure combine into selected, appropriate domains that are relevant to the condition or trait's identification.

Finally, test bias and fairness are important considerations when discussing the validity of a test or selecting tests for use in clinical practice. Test bias refers to the presence of a factor or element within a test that causes systematic variation or error leading to impartial measurement across groups. An example of test bias is when a test is found to systematically underpredict the performance or ability of members of a specific group; for example, changes in how school-age youth are identified as eligible for special education placement in California were instituted when test bias was suspected because many youth from lower socioeconomic backgrounds were found to consistently underperform on a standardized test of knowledge acquisition in comparison with same-age, middle-class peers (*Larry P. v. Riles*, 1979). Test bias can be assessed by examining the regression lines derived from a measure used to predict performance on a criterion, specifically through examination of the slope, intercept, and the error estimate of the regression lines for different groups completing the test.

In contrast to test bias, test fairness refers to the extent to which a test is used fairly to classify and categorize a specific criterion. According to the Standards for Educational and Psychological Testing there are four primary ways to consider fairness in relation to psychological testing: "fairness as a lack of bias," "fairness as equitable treatment in the testing process," "fairness as equality in outcomes of testing," and "fairness as opportunity to learn" (AERA, APA, & NCME, 2021, p. 22). Each of these is assessed and interpreted through a process of review, typically by a group of experts evaluating the success by which a measure or set of measures supports these standards. Ultimately, fairness is an aspirational goal of testing, which is achieved through rigorous attention to both reliability and validity.

▶ TESTS FOR THE MEASUREMENT OF CHARACTERISTICS AND BEHAVIORS OF INDIVIDUALS

SOCIAL, RELATIONAL, EMOTIONAL, AND BEHAVIORAL FUNCTIONING IN CHILDREN/ADOLESCENTS

A number of measures are available to assess social–emotional, behavioral, and relational functioning across the life span. These can be either broad-based measures of assessment, meaning they assess a number of internalizing and externalizing problems within one behavior rating or checklist, or more circumscribed measures of a particular mood or behavioral pattern. For children and adolescents, self-report, parent-report, and teacher-report questionnaires are typically used to assess functioning across environments. It is important to seek information from multiple informants because each individual will have a different frame of reference, or may interpret an individual's behavior in different ways, based on the demands of the setting in which they observe the child. In addition, demands can vary substantially across environments, so it is important to assess an individual's behavior and social–emotional functioning across the range of environments they participate in in order to fully appreciate and conceptualize their social, emotional, and behavioral functioning.

The Achenbach System of Empirically Based Assessment (Child Behavior Checklist: Achenbach & Rescorla, 2001; Teacher Report Form: Achenbach & Rescorla, 2001; Youth Self-Report: Achenbach & Rescorla, 2001) generates three primary index scores: total problems, internalizing problems, and externalizing problems. Scores are represented as T scores and compared with a mean of 50 and an SD of 10. Although the reliability of the attained dimensional scores is adequate, the psychometric properties of some of the syndrome scales are low and should not be used independently for determining diagnosis. The Achenbach System is particularly used in clinical research.

The Behavior Assessment System for Children–Third Edition (BASC-3; C. R. Reynolds & Kamphaus, 2015) measures adaptive skills, behavioral symptoms, internalizing problems, externalizing problems, and school problems. There are Parent and Teacher Rating scales available for individuals ages 2 to 21 and Self-Report of Personality forms for individuals ages 8 to 25, as well as a Self-Report of Personality Interview Form that can be administered to children 6 to 7. It has reasonable reliability and validity (Altmann et al., 2018). In addition, the BASC-3 has a Structured Developmental History form and Student Observation System form that can be used. The BASC-2 was principally developed to coordinate with the *Diagnostic and Statistical Manual of Mental Disorders* (4th ed., text rev.; *DSM-IV-TR*; American Psychiatric Association, 2000) diagnostic categories, with the update to the BASC-3 continuing to relate specifically to behavioral and neurodevelopmental disorders found in the fifth edition of the *DSM* (*DSM-5*; American Psychiatric Association, 2013). As such, the BASC-3 holds greater reliability and validity with regard to the characterization of psychopathology seen in youth.

For the assessment of autism spectrum disorder (ASD), measures such as the *Gilliam Asperger Disorder Scale* (GADS; Gilliam, 2001), the *Gilliam Autism Rating Scale–Third Edition* (GARS-3; Gilliam, 2014), the Social Communication Questionnaire (SCQ; Rutter et al., 2003), and the *Social Responsiveness Scale–Second Edition* (Constantino, 2012) are all regularly used with parents and caregivers. These measures assess symptom domains pertinent to diagnosis, including communication, social interaction, repetitive and stereotyped behaviors, and restricted areas of interest. While these measures are important tools in screening for ASD symptomatology, like any clinical tools, they should not be used in isolation for diagnosis and should be included as part of a broader assessment, as scores may increase in the context of other behavioral concerns that can impact social functioning (e.g., ADHD; mood/anxiety disorders; Pine et al., 2008; Reiersen et al., 2007). Family demographic factors, such as maternal education and socioeconomic status, may also influence scores on such screening instruments (e.g., Moody et al., 2017). When available, the use of gold-standard instruments (i.e., Autism Diagnostic Observation Schedule–Second Edition [ADOS-2; Lord, Luyster, et al., 2012; Lord, Rutter, et al., 2012]; Autism Diagnostic Interview, Revised [ADI-R; Rutter et al., 2003/2008]), alongside in-depth clinical interview, are recommended in making a diagnosis of ASD. However, this is not always feasible in many settings given that a high-level of ASD-specific training is required to administer such instruments.

Mood Assessment in Children

To assess specific concerns regarding mood in children, such as anxiety, measures like the *Multidimensional Anxiety Scale for Children–Second Edition* (Marsh, 2013) and the *Revised Children's*

Manifest Anxiety Scale–Second Edition (C. R. Reynolds & Richmond, 2008) can be administered. The *Child Depression Inventory–Second Edition* (CDI-II) and the *Beck Youth Inventories–Second Edition* (J. S. Beck et al., 2005) can both be administered to assess symptoms of depression, with critical items looking at suicidal ideation.

Assessment of Mood in Adults

With regard to the assessment of mood concerns in adults, the Beck scales are commonly administered by brief self-report measures of a client's symptoms of anxiety or depression. The BDI was originally developed in 1961 and was copyrighted in 1978 (A. T. Beck et al., 1961, 1979; A. T. Beck & Steer, 1993). It emphasized assessing both cognitive and behavioral symptoms of depression and is consistent with the etiological model of depression developed by A. T. Beck et al. (1979). The current version, the BDI-II (A. T. Beck et al., 1996), is widely used for the assessment of depression in individuals aged 18 and above and is commonly used with both psychiatric populations as well as to assess levels of depression in nonpsychiatric patients. It has high test–retest (0.93 over a 1-week interval) and internal consistency reliability (0.89 to 0.94), as well as good content and divergent validity (A. T. Beck et al., 1996; Dozois et al., 1998; Groth-Marnat, 2003). The BDI-II has reasonable concurrent validity with other commonly used measures of depression, including the Hamilton Rating Scale for Depression (HRSD), the Beck Hopelessness Scale (BHI), and the Depression Anxiety Stress Scale (Groth-Marnat, 2003). The BDI-II has a two-factor structure, addressing somatic–affective and cognitive symptoms (A. T. Beck et al., 1996). This structure has been replicated in other studies (Dozois et al., 1998).

Several other Beck scales are also commonly used with adults, including the BAI (A. T. Beck, 1993a) and the BHI (A. T. Beck, 1993b). The BAI can be administered to individuals between 17 and 80 years of age to assess the presence of and interference from anxiety symptoms over a period of 1 month. Like the BDI-II, the BAI also has a two-factor structure, addressing both cognitive and somatic symptoms, and it is consistent with Beck's cognitive model of anxiety (A. T. Beck, 1993a).

The State-Trait Anxiety Inventory (STAI) is one of the older and more commonly researched measures of anxiety (Spielberger et al., 1983). It has three separate test forms. The purpose of the STAI is to assess current state-associated symptoms of anxiety, including temporary experiences of worry and fear, and what has been termed *trait anxiety*, otherwise known as longstanding personality traits that are consistent with anxiety.

Finally, commonly used clinician ratings of mood include the HRSD (Hamilton, 1967) and Hamilton Rating Scale of Anxiety (HRSA; Hamilton, 1959). Both of these scales are publicly available; they offer brief ratings of observed symptoms of depression and anxiety and are most commonly used in clinical research. Because both the Beck and Hamilton scales are meant to assess current symptoms of depression and anxiety, they can be used to monitor not only present mood status, but also treatment progress.

COGNITIVE FUNCTIONING

Both psychoeducational and neuropsychological assessment involve systematic, standardized testing across multiple domains of cognitive functioning, including general intellectual ability, attention, verbal and language skills, visual perceptual and motor capacities, memory, and executive functioning skills (Sparrow & Davis, 2000). Assessment of general cognitive capability typically involves the use of an intelligence test battery, like the Wechsler scales, whose construction is primarily based on psychological theories of skill and capacity. Many of the most commonly used intellectual batteries are based on or incorporate aspects of the Cattell–Horn–Carroll (CHC) theory of intelligence in their development.

CHC theory refers to the combination of two prominent models of intelligence: the Cattell–Horn model and Carroll's three stratum model (1993). The Cattell–Horn model (Horn & Cattell, 1967) postulates two types of intelligence: fluid and crystallized. *Fluid intelligence* refers to nonverbal and primarily nonculturally biased abilities, such as new learning and efficiency on novel tasks (Sattler, 2018). *Crystallized intelligence* refers to an individual's knowledge base or range of acquired skills, which are dependent on exposure to both culture and the specific general information that is valued by a given culture. Carroll's three stratum model, also known as Carroll's three stratum factor analytic theory of cognitive abilities, was developed following a review of research studies that emphasized the presence of individual differences in cognitive abilities and suggested that the relationship among these individual differences can be captured across three categories: a set of narrow cognitive abilities, such as reading comprehension (narrow); a set of eight broad factors that include fluid intelligence, crystallized intelligence, general memory and learning, visual perception, auditory perception, retrieval capacity, cognitive speediness, and processing speed (broad); and a general intelligence factor (commonly referred to as g; general; Carroll, 1993). Because there was significant overlap among these theories, the CHC integrated model was proposed.

Historically, the CHC has included nine broad stratum abilities: crystallized intelligence (*Gc*), fluid intelligence (*Gf*), quantitative reasoning (*Gq*), reading and writing ability (*Grw*), short-term memory (*Gsm*), long-term storage and retrieval (*Glr*), visual processing (*Gv*), auditory processing (*Ga*), and processing speed (*Gs*; Sattler, 2018). In a review of the factor analysis research on CHC, McGrew (2005) proposed that six additional domains should be added to this structure to improve its capacity for fully representing the range of abilities that ultimately comprise g.

COMMON INTELLECTUAL BATTERIES

The first version of the Stanford–Binet Intelligence Test was published in 1905 and was based on an adaptation of the Binet–Simon Scale. It is currently in its fifth version. The *Stanford–Binet Intelligence Scales–Fifth Edition* (SB-5) is appropriate for individuals age 2 to 85 years. It generates a Full Scale IQ score, which is a measure of general cognitive abilities, and nonverbal and verbal domain scores. Cognitive factor scores across verbal and nonverbal demands for information processing include fluid reasoning, knowledge, quantitative reasoning, visual–spatial processing, and working memory. The psychometric properties of the SB-5 are quite good, with internal consistency reliability scores between the full scale and domain scores falling above 0.90 and the subtest coefficients ranging from 0.84 to 0.89 (Roid, 2003). The SB-5 also offers an extended IQ scale that supports scores at the low and high extremes.

The current Wechsler intelligence scales include the *Wechsler Adult Intelligence Scale–Fourth Edition* (WAIS-IV), *Wechsler Intelligence Scale for Children–Fifth Edition* (WISC-5), and *Wechsler Preschool and Primary Scale of Intelligence–Fourth Edition* (WPPSI-IV). The first version of the Wechsler–Bellevue Intelligence Scale was published for use with adults in 1939 and the Wechsler Intelligence Scale for Children was published in 1949. Wechsler defined intelligence as "the capacity to act purposely, think rationally, and to deal effectively with [the] environment" (Wechsler, 1949, p. 3). Each edition of the Wechsler scales is designed to provide an understanding of capability across domains that support this overall model of intellectual functioning. Notably, the Wechsler scales have been adapted for use in other languages and countries and, in this regard, have made important contributions to the cultural contexts for which the measures can be applied. While this has very importantly increased accessibility, there are also some limitations related to the adaptation and validation processes that should be noted (McGill et al., 2020). As an example, the WISC-V Spanish sample, which is routinely administered in clinics throughout the United States, was collected in the United States and is primarily designed to assess abilities among bilingual Spanish-speaking students in the United States (McGill et al., 2020). For six subtests (Block Design, Visual Puzzles, Matrix Reasoning, Figure Weights, Coding, and Symbol Search), the instructions were directly translated from the corresponding English subtests, but no other changes were required (e.g., stimuli, administration rules, scoring). The remaining subtests (Similarities, Vocabulary, Information, Comprehension, Arithmetic, Digit

Span, Picture Span, Letter-Number Sequencing) necessitated a higher level of change, including modified instructions, scoring rules, and/or content changes (Wechsler et al., 2017). The Spanish version, alongside many of the other international forms, is thus quite similar to the original versions developed for English speakers living in the United States.

The WAIS-IV is appropriate for use with individuals age 16 to 89 (Wechsler, 2008). It generates a Full Scale IQ score, consistent with the standing model of a general intellectual factor, as well as factor analytically derived subscales that reflect separable domains of skill. These four factors are verbal comprehension, perceptual reasoning, working memory, and processing speed, and each is represented as a primary index score. The reliability coefficients for the subtests, the index scores, and the Full Scale IQ scores range from 0.88 to 0.98. With the most recent iteration, the WAIS-IV, several new subtests were introduced, based on a move to a more neuropsychologically informed structure for the battery. These include visual puzzles, finger weights, and cancellation. Several subtests were no longer found to aggregate within the principal factor structure and were made optional. With this version, updated norms were developed that relate well with previous versions of the battery.

The WISC-5 (Wechsler, 2014a) is appropriate for use with children age 6 to 16. This measure generates a Full Scale IQ score as well as verbal comprehension, visual spatial, fluid reasoning, working memory, and processing speed index scores. Ancillary index scales include quantitative reasoning, auditory working memory, nonverbal, general ability, and cognitive proficiency scales. The internal consistency coefficients among the index scores and the Full Scale IQ score range from 0.88 to 0.93 (Wechsler, 2014b).

For children aged 2 years and 6 months to 7 years and 7 months, the WPPSI-IV (Wechsler, 2012a, 2012b) can be administered to assess intellectual functioning. The WPPSI-IV is structured quite differently from the WPPSI-III, following the broad neuropsychological model developed with the WISC-V and WAIS-IV. It provides for a Full Scale IQ score, and then five subfactors: a Verbal Comprehension Index (VCI), Visual Spatial Index (VSI), Working Memory Index (WMI), Fluid Reasoning Index (FRI), and Processing Speed Index (PSI). Ancillary measures and indices are also incorporated to support improved clinical utility. It should be noted that in the 2:6 to 3:11 age range, the primary index scales include only verbal comprehension, visual spatial, and working memory scales. The internal consistency scores for the scales ranged from 0.86 to 0.94 and it is reasonably well correlated with other measures assessing similar constructs (Syeda & Climie, 2014).

The *Differential Ability Scales–Second Edition* (DAS-II; Elliott, 2007) can also be used with children as young as 2:6 through adolescents age 17:11 and consists of an Early Years Battery and a School-Age Battery. The DAS-II follows the CHC theory of cognitive development and yields an overall composite called the General Conceptual Ability (GCA), as well as a Special Nonverbal Composite (SNC). The GCA is comprised of verbal ability, nonverbal reasoning, and spatial ability (for ages 3:6 to 17:11). The Early Years Battery has been translated into Spanish and can be used with Spanish-speaking children. Similarly, the School Years Battery offers Spanish and American Sign Language Instruction for the nonverbal subtests that make up the SNC.

The *Woodcock–Johnson IV Tests of Cognitive Abilities* (WJ-IV Cog; Schrank et al., 2014) is a test of cognitive abilities that is predominantly based on the CHC theory of cognitive abilities. The WJ-IV Cog is administered to individuals from the age of 2 to older than 90. It is commonly used in educational settings, often in tandem with its partner battery, the WJ-IV Ach. It has been found to have solid psychometric properties and is considered both reliable and valid (Schrank et al., 2014). Both the WJ-IV Cog and the WJ-IV Ach have been translated or adapted for use with Spanish-speaking individuals, with the parallel measure *Batería IV Woodcock-Muñoz* (Woodcock et al., 2019). The *Woodcock-Muñoz Language Survey* (WMLS III; Woodcock et al., 2017) can also be administered to determine academic language proficiency in English and Spanish and can be used as a guide to help determine which language to subsequently structure course material/complete neuropsychological testing in for a given individual.

There are also several nonverbal measures of intelligence that can be administered to individuals who are either unable to effectively use language, do not speak English as a primary language, or who are lower functioning, and hence less linguistically skilled. The *Leiter International Performance Scale–Third Edition* (Leiter-3; Roid et al., 2013) and the *Universal Nonverbal Intelligence Test* (UNIT-2; Bracken & McCallum, 2016) were both developed to be used in situations in which language is an issue. The Leiter-3 is meant to be a nonverbal, nonculturally biased test of cognitive abilities. It is administered to individuals aged 3 to 75 and up. It does not require verbal comprehension skill, as instructions are provided primarily through pantomime and gestures. The UNIT-2 is another nonverbal measure of intelligence assessing memory, reasoning, and quantitative reasoning that is appropriate for use in individuals between the ages of 5 to 21 years, 11 months. It, as well, requires no language for administration and is considered a useful nonculturally biased measure of cognitive functioning. As previously noted, both nonverbal intelligence measures are reliable and appropriate for use with individuals who are non-English speakers, come from different cultural backgrounds, or have language impairment, hearing impairment, or known cognitive delays.

Developmental measures are also routinely used in the assessment of younger children (i.e., from infancy through age 5). This includes measures such as the *Bayley Scales of Infant and Toddler Development–Fourth Edition* (Bayley-4; Bayley & Aylward, 2019), which can be administered to newborn babies as young as 16 days old through 42 months, and the *Mullen Scales of Early Learning* (Mullen, 1995), which can be used from birth through 68 months of age. These measures are used to assess a child's developmental functioning in the domains of emerging cognition, expressive and receptive language, and fine and gross motor skills. In addition to assessing young children, there are times in which developmental assessment may be used for individuals with intellectual impairment above the age of 5, although notably these measures are not normed for individuals above age 5 and thus are used to provide more descriptive information on an individual's strengths and weaknesses. Age equivalence scores can also be obtained, but these are associated with poor psychometrics that limit reliability (Bracken, 1988). Clinicians assessing individuals with intellectual disability may also incorporate measures with growth scale values (GSVs) or change sensitive scores (CSSs) into their assessment. GSVs are equal interval scales that allow a clinician to track even small changes within an individual over time. CSSs (which are available on measures such as the SB-5) are based on IRT and convert raw scores to criterion-referenced scores, with excellent measurement properties reported (Roid & Pomplun, 2012)

NEUROPSYCHOLOGICAL FUNCTIONING

Neuropsychological evaluations typically assess a number of domains of cognitive functioning, including attention and orientation, executive functioning, perceptual abilities, language and verbal abilities, memory, motor function, visual construction, and visual motor integration skills. There is an extensive list of neuropsychological assessment tools that are used during these evaluations; as a result, the most common batteries developed for neuropsychological assessment are discussed here from a broad standpoint and without a focus on any one specific assessment tool. For more extensive information on the variety of specific tests that are available for use by the neuropsychologist, the reader is directed to other references, including detailed texts by Baron (2004), Lezak et al. (2012), and Strauss et al. (2006).

Among the most commonly used fixed-battery approaches to neuropsychology, the Halstead–Reitan Neuropsychological Test Battery was most recently revised in 1993 (Reitan & Wolfson, 1993). In its current version, the Halstead–Reitan is composed of a number of individual measures that, when used together, allow the clinician to distinguish patients with neurological insult from those who are healthy. Each of the tests that make up the Halstead–Reitan Neuropsychological Test Battery can also be administered individually as a measure of a particular domain of functioning, and separate tests from the battery are commonly used as parts of more flexible assessment approaches to cognitive and neuropsychological functioning. The core tests include the Category test, Tactual Performance test, Speech–Sounds Perception test, Seashore Rhythm test, the Finger Tapping test, and the Trail Making test. There are also tests of aphasia, lateral dominance, and sensory–perceptual abilities. The core tests are typically administered along with the Wechsler intelligence scales and, often, measures of personality. The Halstead Impairment Index provides cutoff scores to help determine whether the examinee's performance is consistent with neurological insult.

The *Neuropsychological Assessment Battery* (NAB; Stern & White, 2003) consists of 36 subtests that examine five areas of neuropsychological functioning: attention, language, memory, spatial, and executive functioning. It is appropriate for use with individuals between the ages of 18 and 97. A screening module is available for use. The assessment can be used in its entirety as a full battery, or individual subtests can be administered for screening or to address specific questions. There are descriptive statistics for the raw scores available for several specific populations, including individuals with ADHD, dementia, traumatic brain injury, multiple sclerosis, aphasia, and/or HIV/AIDS, as well as those in a rehab setting.

For children and adolescents, there are very few neuropsychological assessment batteries available. There are children's versions of the Halstead–Reitan Neuropsychological Test Battery, which includes downward extensions to some of the subtests. However, norms for these measures are both significantly out of date and comprise very small, nondiverse samples. Additionally, norms for mid-adolescent ages are unavailable. The NEPSY-II (A Developmental NEuroPSYchological Assessment; Korkman et al., 2007) is a battery designed to evaluate multiple domains of neuropsychological development from preschool through adolescence. The NEPSY-II has two forms available: one for children aged 3 to 4 and the other for children aged 5 through 16. It yields six domain scores across 32 subtests. The domains assessed are attention/executive functioning, language, memory and learning, sensorimotor functioning, visual-spatial processing, and social perception. Like the NAB, the NEPSY-II can be administered in its entirety, or specific subtests can be administered individually to address targeted questions. The NEPSY-II has been conormed with the WPPSI-3, WPPSI-4, and the WISC-4.

ABILITY, APTITUDE, AND ACHIEVEMENT

The term *ability* has been used to describe an individual's capacity to perform a specific skill or task and is thought to encompass both aptitude and achievement. Achievement typically refers to measures of knowledge acquired in specific settings like a classroom. Aptitude is thought to represent an individual's potential to learn a given task.

The *Wechsler Individual Achievement Test–Fourth Edition* (WIAT-IV; Wechsler, 2020) is used to assess academic achievement in individuals aged 4 through 50. It has been conormed with all other Wechsler intelligence scales and the DAS-II. Like each of the following measures discussed, the WIAT-IV focuses principally on reading, including decoding and comprehension; mathematical operations and problem-solving; and written expression. Listening comprehension and oral sharing of knowledge are also assessed.

The *Kaufman Test of Educational Achievement–Third Edition* (KTEA-3; Kaufman & Kaufman, 2014) can be administered to individuals aged 4 through 25 years, 11 months. The KTEA-3 has two parallel and nonoverlapping forms. It emphasizes core academic skill development.

The WJ-IV Ach (Schrank et al., 2014a) assesses academic achievement in reading, mathematics, and written language as well as academic knowledge. It was conormed with the WJ-IV Cog and the Woodcock–Johnson Tests of Oral Language (WJ-IV OL; Schrank et al., 2014b). The WJ-IV has three parallel forms of the standard battery, and also includes one version of the extended battery. The WJ-IV Ach is appropriate for use with individuals aged 2 through 90 years and older.

There are several assessments that focus on specific areas of academic achievement, such as reading (e.g., the *Gray Oral Reading Test–Fifth Edition*, the Gray Silent Reading Test, and the Nelson–Denny Reading Test), writing (*Test of Written Language Fourth Edition*), and mathematics (Key Math-3). Each of these tests taps essential elements of academic skill development and supports data attained from the broader academic batteries.

Curriculum-based measurement is the regular assessment of children with short standardized and validated measures for the purpose of monitoring the development and mastery of academic skills. Performance-based measurement involves the evaluation of an individual's ability to perform a specific skill or produce a specific item or skill. These assessments can be completed through observation and/or ratings, or through use of a psychometric test of performance addressing the specific skill of interest.

Aptitude tests typically include a number of subtests that assess an individual's aptitude or potential to learn and master different skills and are often used for job placement programs or educational and vocational counseling. There are few tests that assess aptitude purely; instead, most assess both achievement and aptitude. An example is the Armed Services Vocational Aptitude Battery, which is used to determine both whether an individual is qualified to enroll in the Armed Forces and to address aptitude for specific jobs or careers within the military.

The General Aptitude Test Battery (Form C & D, [GATB]; Hunter, 1983) was developed by the U.S. Employment Service to assess general intelligence, verbal aptitude, numerical aptitude, spatial aptitude, form perception, clerical perception, motor coordination, finger dexterity, and manual dexterity. The GATB is used for job placement and vocational counseling with high school students and adults. Many of the tasks on the GATB are timed, so individuals with slow processing speed or fine motor impairment may earn scores that are impacted. There has been some concern raised regarding differential validity and prediction across groups by race with this battery (Hartigan & Wigdor, 1989).

The *Differential Aptitude Test–Fifth Edition* (Bennett & Seashore, 1990) is an aptitude test developed for use with students in grades 7 to 12, as well as into adulthood. It assesses general cognitive abilities, perceptual abilities, and clerical and language skills.

In addition to these aptitude test batteries, there are specific aptitude tests that examine focused domains of potential job performance. Psychomotor ability tests assess fine motor speed, coordination, and dexterity as related to job performance; examples include the Purdue Pegboard Test and the Minnesota Rate of Manipulation Tests. Another form of special aptitude measures is mechanical aptitude tests, which assess an examinee's performance on motor dexterity, spatial and perceptual reasoning, mechanical reasoning, and mechanical comprehension. Examples include the Bennett Mechanical Comprehension Test and a mechanical reasoning test.

PERSONALITY

Structured personality assessment typically involves the use of self-administered, multiple-choice, objective tests of personality and psychopathology. The PAI (Morey, 1991) consists of 344 items, all written at a fourth-grade reading level. The PAI is appropriate for use with adults aged 18 to 89 years. It was developed using a construct validation approach, in which subscales were first created during the initial design of the test, and the content and discriminant validity of the items included in the test were then examined to determine whether they were appropriate to the domains being measured. Items found nondiscriminant were removed from the test (Morey, 2003). The PAI consists of 22 scales, including four validity scales, 11 clinical scales tied to the *DSM-IV-TR* (American Psychiatric Association, 2000) diagnostic criteria, five scales that examine variables related to treatment, and two interpersonal functioning scales. Validity is assessed using the inconsistency, infrequency, negative impression, and positive impression scales. A malingering index has been published that provides guidelines for integrating information across a number of scales of the PAI to assess the likelihood of malingering (Morey, 1996). The clinical scales include somatic complaints, anxiety, anxiety-related disorders, depression, mania, paranoia, schizophrenia, borderline features, alcohol problems, and drug problems. The treatment scales include aggression, suicidal ideation, nonsupport, and treatment rejection. The dominance and warmth scales comprise the interpersonal domain. An adolescent version of the PAI is available as well, for administration to individuals aged 12 through 18 years. The PAI also exists for Spanish-speaking adults in the United States (PAI

Spanish: Revised Translation; Morey & PAR Staff, 2022), as well as clients speaking European Spanish (PAI: European Spanish with Norms) between the ages of 18 and 99, with normative data collected primarily in Spain and some Latin American countries.

The Minnesota Multiphasic Personality Inventory (MMPI) was originally developed by Hathaway and McKinley in 1940 as a method for identifying psychiatric diagnoses. An empirical criterion keying strategy was used as the framework for its development. Empirical criterion keying refers to a process of test development in which test items are selected for inclusion and then scored within a scale, based on whether a target clinical population has responded differently from a comparison group. For the MMPI, items that differentiated between a control group and a clinical group comprising patients at the University of Minnesota Hospital who had major psychiatric diagnoses were ultimately included. The second edition of the MMPI (MMPI-2) was published in 1989 and included several important changes, including the addition of new scales, replacement of out-of-date test items, and updated norms (Butcher et al., 1989). During the revision process, the content scales were redeveloped using a content analysis approach as opposed to the empirical criterion keying approach. There were 10 clinical scales on the MMPI-2: hypochondriasis, depression, hysteria, psychopathic deviation, masculinity–femininity, paranoia, psychasthenia, schizophrenia, hypomania, and social introversion. It yielded validity scales, including the Lie scale, F (Frequency scale), K (Correction scale), ? scale (Cannot Say), VRIN scale (Variable Response Inconsistency scale), TRIN scale (True Response Inconsistency), and S scale (Superlative Self-Presentation). The MMPI-2 Restructured Form (MMPI-2-RF) was subsequently published in 2008 and improved efficiency, enhanced construct validity, and restructured the clinical scales. The MMPI-2-RF is a shorter version of the MMPI-2 that shares the MMPI-2 normative sample (Ben-Porath & Tellegen, 2008). Most recently, the MMPI-3 was developed in 2020 and can be used with adults aged 18 and older. The MMPI-3 builds on the MMPI-2-RF foundations and introduces new scales, including Combined Response Inconsistency (CRIN), Eating Concerns (EAT), Compulsivity (CMP), Impulsivity (IMP), and Self-Importance (SFI). Other scales were significantly changed or dropped. There are now a total of 52 scales consisting of 10 validity scales, three higher-order scales, eight restructured clinical scales, 26 specific problem scales, and the personality psychopathology five (PSY-5) scales (Ben-Porath & Tellegen, 2020).

Across versions of the MMPI, raw scores are converted to T scores, with a T score of 65 (94th percentile) or above considered clinically significant. There is a Spanish version of the MMPI-3, which includes norms derived from a sample of Spanish speakers in the United States. An adolescent version, the MMPI-A, which can be administered to individuals between 14 and 18 years of age, also exists (Butcher et al., 1992). Results obtained from the MMPI-3 are typically used to describe patterns of personality and behavioral difficulty. Review involves profile analysis as opposed to diagnostic assignment, as research has consistently indicated that the MMPI is not effective in facilitating specific diagnoses.

The *Millon Clinical Multiaxial Inventory–Fourth Edition* (MCMI-IV) is a self-report questionnaire developed to assess personality (Millon et al., 2015). It was originally introduced in 1977 to support diagnosis of Axis II personality disorders. In its original development, both a rational-theory–based method and empirical criterion keying were used. In rational-theory–based methodology, specific items are selected to assess a construct that is determined a priori; in the case of the MCMI, content items were determined based on an overarching theory of personality and then validated to ensure that they in fact fit with the given theory being used. The MCMI-IV can be administered to individuals 18 years and older. It views personality patterns on a spectrum ranging from adaptive to maladaptive. It yields the following scales: three "modifying indices" (disclosure, desirability, and debasement); two "random response indicators" (invalidity and inconsistency); 12 personality profiles (schizoid, avoidant, melancholic, dependent, histrionic, turbulent, narcissistic, antisocial, sadistic, compulsive, negativistic, and masochistic); three severe forms of personality pathology (schizotypal, borderline, and paranoid); seven clinical syndromes (generalized anxiety, somatic symptom, bipolar spectrum, persistent depression, alcohol use, drug use, and posttraumatic stress); and three severe syndromes (schizophrenic spectrum, major depression, and delusional disorder).

The use of unstructured personality assessments, also known as projective testing, is based on the assumption that determining how an individual responds to ambiguous stimuli can yield useful clinical information and diagnostic clarification. The Rorschach Inkblot Test (or Technique) is one of the most well-known projective assessments. With this procedure, Rorschach developed one of the first empirically based scoring systems to support the clinical interpretation of an examinee's responses to inkblot stimuli. The Rorschach, as it is commonly referred, consists of 10 cards containing bilaterally symmetrical inkblots on a white background. Although half of the inkblots are black and grey, three contain pastel colors and two have portions that are red. The administration of the procedure involves two parts: the initial association phase, during which the examinee is presented with the cards in a predetermined order and is asked to freely describe what is seen; and the inquiry phase, which involves the examiner collecting additional information from the examinee about the initial responses made through structured questioning.

While there are several different scoring systems available for the Rorschach, Exner's (2003; Exner & Erdberg, 2005) scoring system remains the most widely used at this time. With the Exner system, the examiner scores each of the individual's responses based on a set of criteria, including location (where on the inkblot the examinee is focused when giving a response), determinants (the style or characteristics of the blot that led to an examinee's response), content (either the category under which the examinee's response and description falls, or the quantity perceived in the response), and whether the response offered is popular (frequently observed in the sample population) or not. A series of special scores based on 15 categories that can be used to take into account rare or unusual aspects of responses have been developed. It is noteworthy that significant controversy surrounding the use of the Rorschach continues, due mostly to concerns regarding the psychometric properties of the measure and the scoring systems utilized. Research has yielded inconsistent findings in terms of validity and reliability; for example, research regarding the sensitivity of the Rorschach to discriminate psychopaths from nonpsychopaths has been quite inconsistent (Gacono & Meloy, 2009; Wood et al., 2010). Presently, many programs in professional psychology provide limited instruction in the Rorschach, given this ongoing uncertainty about its validity and usefulness apart from other means of clinical information gathering.

VOCATIONAL INTEREST

Assessments of vocational interest have been used in the field of psychology for almost a century. Many of the commonly used vocational interest assessments have been developed from Strong's early work in the empirical construction of occupation scales and John Holland's theory of vocational interest (D. P. Campbell & Borgen, 1999). Holland posits that there are six dimensions of vocational interest, which he conceptualized in terms of a hexagon (Holland, 1997). Each dimension is arranged around the hexagon in a clockwise direction starting with what he termed "Realistic." The interest domains identified are denoted as R-I-A-S-E-C: Realistic, Investigative, Artistic, Social, Enterprising, and Conventional.

Based on Holland's work, the Self-Directed Search (SDS) was originally published in 1979. The now-named Standard SDS was most recently revised in 2013 (Holland & Messer, 2013). It is a self-report questionnaire that can be both scored and interpreted by the individual taking the test. Scoring allows the examinee to identify a score profile (the top three domain scores from the R-I-A-S-E-C hexagon) and compare it to an assortment of profiles for different occupations and fields of study.

Strong first published the Strong Vocational Interest Inventory in 1927. To generate scoring scales and develop norms for this measure, he asked participants from several occupational backgrounds what they were interested in and then compared the results obtained across a diverse group of individuals both employed in and apart from the occupations that were of interest (D. P. Campbell & Borgen, 1999). The Strong Vocational Interest Inventory has been revised several times to support its continued use, given occupational changes over time. The most recent version of the *Strong Interest Inventory* (Herk & Thompson, 2012) yields scores across four scales: General Occupational Themes scale, Basic Interest scale, Personal Style scale, and Occupational scale. The General Occupational Themes scale measures the six R-I-A-S-E-C categories of occupational interest developed by Holland's work. The Basic Interest scale assesses areas of vocational interest, whereas the Personal Style scale assesses work style, learning environment, leadership style, risk-taking, and team orientation. Finally, the Occupational scale assesses the fit between an individual's interests and the interests of people of the same gender in a given occupation or career.

The Kuder Occupational Interest Survey is a self-report measure of vocational interest that was developed by measuring the similarity between an individual's responses and the average interests of people employed in a given occupation. It yields scores across four domains: Occupational scales, College Major scales, Vocational Interest Estimates, and Dependability Indices.

The Campbell Interest and Skill Survey (D. P. Campbell, 1992) is the most recent addition to the vocational interest inventories. It was published in 1992 and yields scores related to occupational orientation (Orientation scales), which are similar to the range of interests described by Holland's theory. It also includes Basic and Occupational scales, making it similar to other surveys mentioned previously.

Information from vocational interest assessments along with information regarding abilities and personality are used in career assessments, specifically interdomain career assessments. Abilities "refer to what one is able, or potentially able, to do rather than what one has an interest in doing" (Lowman, 2022, p. 16). This may refer to intellectual abilities or, more specifically, career-related abilities.

Finally, in terms of the personality domain of career assessment, much of the literature continues to focus on the five factor model of personality (Lowman, 2022). The five factors are neuroticism (N), extroversion (E), openness to experience (O), agreeableness (A), and conscientiousness (C). "N refers to the chronic level of emotional adjustment and instability . . . E refers to the quantity and intensity of preferred interactions, activity level, need for stimulation, and capacity for joy" (Widiger & Costa Jr., 2013, p. 4). Openness to experience is less clearly defined, but is described as the ability to seek out and appreciate experiences. Agreeableness "refers to the kinds of interactions a person prefers along a continuum from compassion to antagonism" and "C assesses the degree of organization, persistence, control, and motivation in goal-directed behavior" (Lowman, 2022, p. 4).

HEALTH BEHAVIOR

A growing number of measures have been developed over the latter half of the 20th century and into the 21st century to assist in understanding emotional and behavioral status in individuals with medical and health concerns, particularly as psychology has intersected more directly with primary care medicine. Many of these measures have been developed for use in ongoing research looking at the interface between health and behavior (e.g., health-related quality-of-life inventories, such as the EQ-5D [cf., www.euroqol.org] or the PedsQL [Pediatric Quality of Life Inventory; cf., www.pedsql.org]). A small number of measures have been introduced into the clinical realm, given their usefulness in helping characterize specific concerns, such as difficulties with treatment adherence and mood secondary to illness.

Most of these measures are devoted to a particular domain or focus of interest, such as physical activity; risky behaviors, such as drinking or cigarette smoking; or eating patterns. The Youth Risk Behavior Surveillance System (YRBSS; www.cdc.gov/healthyyouth/data/yrbs/index.htm) is a self-report measure comprising questions addressing activity level (e.g., television watching) and engagement in risky behaviors (e.g., drinking, substance use, and sexual behaviors) that can be administered to adolescents and early adults. An adult version, the Behavioral Risk Factor Surveillance System (BRFSS; cf., www.cdc.gov/brfss/index.html), covers similar domains of functioning. An additional set of measures, the MacArthur Health and Behavior Questionnaire (MacArthur HBQ; cf., www.macarthurhbq.wordpress.com), has been developed by a team of developmental scientists for research regarding children's and adolescents' health-related functioning. The first edition, the HBQ-1, allows collection of information about children between 4 and 8 years of age from parents and teachers. The HBQ-2 focuses on children and adolescents between 9 and 18 years of age, with multiinformant formats (self, parent, and teacher). It has been utilized in multiple studies across the world and has demonstrated significant validity and reliability.

Broad assessments of health behaviors are less available for general clinical use. One example of a broad health measure is the *Battery for Health Improvement–Second Edition* (BHI-2; Bruns & Disorbio, 2003), which was developed to assess psychological issues that impact evaluation and treatment of medical patients. The results of the BHI-2 can be used to facilitate the development of a treatment plan to address ongoing concerns, improve quality of life, and potentially improve treatment adherence. The BHI-2 can be administered to individuals 18 through 65 years of age. It generates validity scales, physical symptom scales, affective scales, character scales, and psychosocial scales.

VALIDITY TESTING

The question of the validity of testing has received a significant amount of focus in recent years and there have been many terms used to describe this, including *malingering, symptom validity, performance validity,* and *effort*. This focus has arisen both due to concerns regarding secondary gain and its impact on assessment as well as the impact of noncredible or poor effort on assessment. Noncredible effort results from a number of different factors and, different from malingering, is not always intentional. As psychologists have become increasingly involved in forensic consultations, questions regarding motivation and investment have become more common. Validity testing refers to the development and use of measures and assessment procedures to try to assess an examinee's level of effort and investment during psychological testing. Symptom validity tests are used to identify when a reporter is providing noncredible responses on symptom/behavior questionnaires and structured interviews (Kirkwood, 2015; Larrabee, 2012).

Personality assessment instruments, including the PAI, PAI-A, MMPI-2, MMPI-A, MMPI-2-RF, and MCMI-III, all include validity scales, which should be examined first in order to determine whether an examinee's approach to the completion of the measure was reliable and consistent. The validity scales specifically support the examiner's ability to interpret the results of these assessment measures and to evaluate response biases that may impact profiles obtained. Similarly, many of the self-report and informant-report questionnaires assessing behavior and social–emotional functioning include symptom validity indices. Objective measures of validity are now included in neuropsychological assessments. Performance validity tests (PVTs) are assessment stand-alone measures that appear to assess an ability, but actually require little skill, and are used to identify noncredible performance during ability- or performance-based testing (Kirkwood, 2015). PVTs commonly used by neuropsychologists include the Test of Memory Malingering, Medical Symptom Validity Test, Nonverbal Medical Symptom Validity Test, Word Memory Test, and Rey 15-Item Test (Emhoff et al., 2018). There are also embedded PVTs.

ASSESSMENT OF COMPETENCE AND CRIMINAL RESPONSIBILITY

Competency to stand trial refers to a defendant's ability to understand and participate in legal proceedings. This law comes from the ruling set forth in *Dusky v. United States* (1960), in which the U.S. Supreme Court provided that a defendant must have "sufficient present ability to consult with his lawyer with a reasonable degree of rational understanding . . . [and have a] rational as well as factual understanding of the proceedings against him" (Otto, 2006, p. 83). The role of psychologists in competency evaluations is to assess and describe an individual's ability to both understand and participate in legal proceedings, and identify and describe any psychological disorders, cognitive impairment, or neurological insult that may impact capacity. It is most common at this time that the approach to answering a question of competency to stand trial involves the use of an evidence-based tool (Rogers & Johansson-Love, 2009), including empirically developed structured interviews such as the MacArthur Competence Assessment Tool-Criminal Adjudication (MacCAT-CA; Poythress et al., 1999).

Separate from competency to stand trial is the question of whether a "not guilty by reason of insanity" defense is appropriate for use with a specific trial involving a person claiming mental illness as a reason behind their crime. Although this plea is rarely used in court, forensic psychologists are frequently called on to evaluate criminal responsibility (Stafford & Ben-Porath, 2002). The majority of jurisdictions in the United States have adopted the American Law Institute Test (1962) as a standard for determining criminal responsibility. The first paragraphs read:

(1) A person is not responsible for criminal conduct if at the time of such conduct as a result of mental disease or defect he lacks substantial capacity either to appreciate the criminality [wrongfulness] of his conduct or to conform his conduct to the requirements of law.
(2) As noted in this Article, the terms "mental disease or defect" do not include an abnormality manifested only by repeated criminal or otherwise anti-social conduct.

Furthermore, in 1984, Congress passed the Insanity Defense Reform Act, which now stands in all federal jurisdictions. This Act adopts the M'Naghten Rule (Stafford & Ben-Porath, 2002), a standard of criminal responsibility, which must prove that, at the time of committing a criminal act, the accused did not know what they were doing because of a "severe mental disease or defect," putting the burden of proof on the accused. There are other legal definitions that psychologists should be aware of that apply to the idea of criminal responsibility, specifically the "guilty but mentally ill" plea and a finding of "diminished capacity." Similar to the previous discussion regarding the insanity defense, "guilty but mentally ill" is a plea that acknowledges the contribution of a mental illness and its impact on functioning when addressing the defendant's guilt and advises the approach to sentencing as a result. Diminished capacity is a legal doctrine that allows psychologists to testify as to whether or not a defendant had mental capacity to intend to commit a crime (in legal terms, *mens rea*; Stafford & Ben-Porath, 2002). A number of structured instruments, including the Rogers Criminal Responsibility Assessment Scales (Rogers, 1984) and the Criminal Responsibility Scale (Meyer et al., 2020), have been developed to facilitate this type of evaluation (Parmigiani et al., 2023). Guidelines are also available in several texts to assist in this area of practice (Rogers & Shuman, 2000; Stafford & Ben-Porath, 2002).

RISK OF FUTURE VIOLENCE

There are two types of assessments of aggression that psychologists are commonly asked to undertake: retrospective and prospective assessment of aggression risk. Retrospective assessments involve an attempt to assess or evaluate aggression that has happened in the past in order to explain the ongoing propensity toward such behavior moving forward. This type of assessment is important in treatment planning because past aggressive acts can inform ongoing understanding of risk for poor behavior and, as a result, help to guide the identification and implementation of appropriate treatment interventions aimed at preventing future aggression (Douglas et al., 1999/2007; Megargee, 2002).

Prospective evaluations of aggression are risk assessments used to examine "dangerousness." This is a legal term used to describe "an individual's propensity to commit dangerous acts" (Scott & Resnick, 2006, p. 599). With this type of assessment, a psychologist is asked to determine whether aggression will occur in the future, committed either by a person or group, and if it is believed likely to occur, what the aggressive behavior will ultimately look like (Douglass et al., 1999/2007).

Individual risk assessments attempt to determine whether there is a threat, currently or in the immediate future, that a specific individual will engage in aggressive behavior. Unfortunately, there are no structured psychological measures or interviews currently in use that have demonstrated strong predictive validity for assessing future aggression (DeMatteo et al., 2020; Megargee, 2002; Mills, 2017; Scott & Resnick, 2006).

With regard to risk for violence and aggression, available assessment approaches that are typically used include collecting information about an individual's past from case history; conducting a clinical interview with the individual suspected to be at risk for such behavior; and conducting interviews with that individual's family members, friends, coworkers, and acquaintances. When reviewing the patient's history, attention should be paid to known factors that increase risk for violence, including a history of aggressive behavior and violent acts (Klassen & O'Connor, 1988; Mills, 2017 University of Virginia, n.d.); a history of substance abuse; a history of psychosis, specifically prior to hospitalization or treatment; and a history of psychiatric and personality disorders that have been associated with an increased risk of violence, such as antisocial personality disorder, borderline personality disorder, and personality disorder not otherwise specified (Scott & Resnick, 2006). During an interview with the examinee, a clinician should attend to the individual's affective state and interpersonal style with regard to emotion; it has been found that individuals who are angry or are unable to show empathy for others are at a higher risk for committing a violent act (Menzies et al., 1985; Mills, 2017). Clinicians should assess for and about the experience of emotions that often lead to aggression, such as anger, hostility, rage, and hatred (Megargee, 2002). These can be assessed through direct interview and the use of psychological measures such as the MMPI-2 or MMPI-A, the MCMI-IV, the PAI, or the State-Trait Anger Expression Inventory-2 (DeMatteo et al., 2020; Spielberger, 1999).

There are several risk assessment instruments that have been developed to be used directly in this context, including the Hare Psychopathy Checklist–Revised (PCL-R; Hare, 1991), the Violence Risk Appraisal Guide (Webster et al., 1994), and the Historical, Clinical, Risk Management-20 (HCR-20; Webster et al., 1997). It is important to note that none of these measures should be used in isolation when determining risk; however, each can be useful in conjunction with other clinical data when gathering information regarding risk. Finally, clinicians must also be attentive to and aware of the role secondary gain and extrinsic motivation can play with regard to the risk for and display of aggressive behavior (DeMatteo et al., 2020; Megargee, 2002; Mills, 2017).

SUICIDE EVALUATION

Assessment of suicide risk should be part of any evaluation conducted with a client, either as part of the initial diagnostic evaluation, as part of a neuropsychological or psychological evaluation, or integrated into ongoing treatment (D'Anci et al., 2019; Pistorello et al., 2021; Sommers-Flanagan & Shaw, 2017). Clinicians need to ask patients about the presence of current and/or past suicidal ideation and behaviors. If past ideation and behaviors are endorsed, detailed information about when these past thoughts and behaviors occurred, the content of the ideation, whether a plan was developed, and the details of the behaviors should be openly discussed, including assessing whether the patient exhibited active or passive suicidal behaviors. When assessing current risk, information should be gathered, through an interview with the patient that is either structured or unstructured, about their current thoughts and plans. Additionally, a set of psychological measures that address risk of suicide can be administered; see a list of assessment measures later in this section. Information can also be gathered from other informants such as spouses, family members, and friends.

Assessment of suicide risk requires the clinician to examine the seriousness of the threat, the ideation associated with the threat, the motivating factors related to the threat, the presence and viability of the plan, and access to means to complete the suicide plan (Pistorello et al., 2021;

Sattler, 2018; Sommers-Flanagan & Shaw, 2017). When conducting an interview, the clinician is advised to keep in mind seven risk factors for suicide that have been identified by Joiner et al. (1999): previous suicidal behavior, types of current suicidal ideation and symptoms, precipitant stressors, overall symptom presentation, self-control and impulsivity, predispositions, and protective factors. Furthermore, Bryan (2021) has discussed that there are different trajectories involved when considering suicide risk, with progression to suicidal behavior ranging from a more rapid pace to others showing ideation solely. As noted earlier, there are specific assessment tools that are available to help assess suicide risk; these include the BDI-II (A. T. Beck et al., 1996), BHI (A. T. Beck, 1993b), Beck Scale for Suicidal Ideation (A. T. Beck, 1991), Suicidal Ideation Questionnaire (W. M. Reynolds, 1987, 1988), and the Suicidal Behavior History Form (W. M. Reynolds & Mazza, 1992). More commonly used as well is the Columbia-Suicide Severity Rating Scale (C-SSRS; Posner et al., 2011), which addresses suicide risk within a semistructured interview format. Clinicians are required to obtain formal web-based training to administer this scale. For additional information regarding measures of suicide risk, and the emerging trends in advanced digital and teletherapy models for addressing suicide assessment and management, the reader is referred to suicide assessment measures available on the National Institute of Mental Health (NIMH) website such as the Brief Suicide Assessment Measure (www.nimh.nih.gov /sites/default/files/documents/research/research-conducted-at-nimh/asq-toolkit-materials /adult-outpatient/bssa_outpatient_adult_asq_nimh_toolkit.pdf). The results of a systematic review conducted by the U.S. Department of Veterans Affairs (Haney et al., 2012), the more recent synopsis of the same department's clinical practice guidelines regarding suicide risk (Sall et al., 2019) as well as Jobes's (2023) third edition of *Managing Suicide Risk: A Collaborative Approach*.

▶ ISSUES ASSOCIATED WITH DIFFERENTIAL DIAGNOSIS

Differential diagnosis refers to the process by which a clinician considers the possible multiple sources behind a patient's symptoms, cognitive deficits, or behavioral difficulties, by assessing which of several possible diagnostic categories, together or independently, best explain or describe a given pattern of concerns. The process of making a differential diagnosis involves generating multiple hypotheses that are based on the presenting patient's current problems, their history of difficulty, the information obtained from informants, and the clinical impression that develops, based on interviews with the individual (Lezak et al., 2012). These hypotheses regarding possible diagnoses are evaluated systematically by comparing the symptom profile, performance on assessment measures (if administered), and the degree of current impairment in tandem with knowledge about base rates of the disorder. Ultimately, the clinician comes to a decision regarding a likely given diagnosis or diagnoses, in the case of multiple concerns. For example, in clinical neuropsychology, this process references a profile of strengths and weaknesses across neuropsychological testing data, and a resulting comparison of this data with profiles that are empirically developed and described in the literature regarding individuals with neurological, medical, developmental, and/or psychiatric disorders. As data are collected, hypotheses regarding diagnosis are revised and adapted in order to match and fit with criteria consistent with a given psychiatric, medical, or neuropsychological diagnosis (Lezak et al., 2012).

▶ CRITERIA FOR SELECTION AND ADAPTATION OF ASSESSMENT METHODS

One of the primary considerations when selecting an assessment method or tool is the extent to which the measure can be used to answer the referral question. In addressing this decision, the clinician considers their own training, familiarity with a given measure, and the experience and knowledge required to appropriately interpret the data generated by a given assessment. The time and expense required to administer one assessment compared to another are also considered. To support the choice, the psychometric properties of the measure under consideration are reviewed to assist in ensuring that the measure(s) to be administered within an assessment battery are valid and reliable for the questions being asked (Groth-Marnat & Wright, 2016). Furthermore, it is imperative that psychologists also consider the appropriateness of the scale under consideration with regard to its capacity to assess ethnically, culturally, and socioeconomically diverse populations reliably and validly. Review of the psychometric history of the measure being selected requires that the psychologist understand the potential biases and lack of available normative data that may complicate the scale's use, and that limits its acceptability (APA, 2017; Laher & Cockcroft, 2017; Suzuki & Ponterotto, 2007).

Special considerations are required when selecting and administering assessment measures with specific populations (APA, 2017, 2022; Thompson et al., 2018). For patients with sensory (e.g., vision or hearing) or motor impairment, consideration is given to the disability status of the examinee to ensure that measures used are least likely to be impacted by a given impairment. Additional attention is paid to how test administration materials may be adapted for use with individuals with impairment (e.g., enlarging text for patients with vision impairment or ensuring that test materials are in the appropriate visual field for those patients with a visual field cut). Lezak et al. (2012) and a growing set of other excellent references (e.g., APA, 2021; Davis, 2010) discuss how to best accommodate when assessing individuals with sensory, motor, or severe cognitive impairment.

When working with patients from culturally and linguistically diverse backgrounds, clinicians must be aware of issues related to racial and ethnic identity, acculturation, language, and cultural norms in terms of how they impact and influence behavior (APA, 2017; Suzuki & Ponterotto, 2007). Additionally, expectations about gender roles and family dynamics, religion, socioeconomic status, understanding and acceptance of the field of psychology, and cultural patterns for handling stress or crisis, among other issues, are important factors to consider and address (APA, 2017; Clauss-Ehlers et al., 2023). When conducting standardized assessments with individuals who are from diverse backgrounds, clinicians need to be very cognizant of concerns regarding evaluation bias in assessment; this is specifically the case with regard to intellectual testing (Laher & Cockcroft, 2017). It is best when the examiner can choose a test that has been found to have more limited differences across cultural groups in its understanding and completion; this, however, is not the norm (Suzuki & Ponterotto, 2007). For example, Levav et al. (1998) found that reaction-time measures embedded in tests of sustained attention were less impacted by culture or education level, whereas other aspects of attention assessed were significantly different based on both country of origin and education level. For individuals for whom English is not the primary language, there are a select number of assessment measures available that require a nonverbal response or that are standardized for use with other languages that can be considered. Additionally, use of a translator may be warranted, although there are several risks involved in taking that approach that do require both considerations regarding test validity and interpretation, and the implementation of guidelines regarding how to effectively engage and make use of the translator during the assessment (Fujii, 2016; Fujii et al., 2022). Measures of cognitive abilities that are theoretically culture-free and are less likely to be impacted by language difference (e.g., the Leiter-3 or UNIT-2, both discussed previously) are considered among acceptable options. For additional information on this topic, the reader is referred to the *Handbook of Multicultural Assessment Third Edition* (Suzuki & Ponterotto, 2007).

▶ DIAGNOSTIC CLASSIFICATION SYSTEMS

INTERNATIONAL CLASSIFICATION OF DISEASES

The International Classification of Diseases (ICD) is recognized as the universally accepted classification system used by the medical community. Described by the World Health Organization (WHO) as "the standard diagnostic tool for epidemiology, health management, and clinical purposes" (WHO, 2012, p. 85), the *ICD* is used for disease classification and is the core system used in the coding of claims for the purpose of health insurance reimbursement. *ICD* classifications also enable the collection and storage of diagnostic data for such purposes as determining incidence and prevalence, as well as mortality and morbidity. The *ICD* has its roots in a diagnostic coding system initiated in Great Britain in 1839. Known as the London Bills of Mortality and later as the International List of Causes of Death, the formal classification of disease came under the direction of the WHO in 1948 in an effort to track trends in disease and international health (Grider, 2012). Interest in using the *ICD* clinically resulted in a revision of the *ICD-9* known as the *International Classification of Diseases, Ninth Revision, Clinical Modification (ICD-9-CM)*. In the United States, the final transition from *ICD-9-CM* to *ICD-10-CM* was implemented on October 1, 2015. Over time, the use of the *ICD* has been broadened to include billing and reimbursement, healthcare quality and safety research, and monitoring. While the *ICD-11* (WHO, 2022) became available for international use as of January 1, 2022, it has not yet been implemented in the U.S. healthcare system. The *ICD-10* classifies disorders by specifically identifying the area or system of the body that is affected and the nature of the injury or condition. Modifications presented with the *ICD-10* allow for greater specificity. The *ICD-10* allows for codes of three to seven characters in length, providing more detail in terms of anatomy, injury or condition, and type of intervention.

DIAGNOSTIC AND STATISTICAL MANUAL OF MENTAL DISORDERS

The *DSM-5*, published by the American Psychiatric Association in 2013, provides the criteria required to diagnose mental health disorders in both children and adults. This formal classification of mental disorders was first developed in response to the need for collecting statistical information. The initial documentation of mental illness fell under one category, "idiocy/insanity," in the U.S. 1840 census. Disorders were further broken down into seven categories for the 1880 census. In 1917, a formal committee was convened, consisting of the Committee on Statistics of the American Psychiatric Association and the National Commission on Mental Hygiene, to gather statistics across mental health institutions. The U.S. Army later formed its own system of categorization to address disorders that presented in outpatient settings that were treating veterans and servicemen during World War II. The *ICD-6* was released following the war, largely in collaboration with the Veterans Administration, and for the first time included a section addressing mental disorders. The first edition of the *DSM* was published in 1952 (American Psychiatric Association, 1952). As with each subsequent revision, the *DSM-I* was developed in coordination with the *ICD*. With an emphasis on clinical utility, the *DSM-I* contained descriptions of diagnostic categories. The *DSM-II* was published in 1968 and included a greater number of disorders as well as changes in terminology. The seventh printing of the *DSM-II*, published in 1974, removed homosexuality as a diagnostic category (American Psychiatric Association, 1974). The *DSM-III*, published in 1980, introduced significant changes such as the multiaxial system and explicit diagnostic criteria (American Psychiatric Association, 1980). Several inconsistencies were found within this new system, as well as unclear criteria for several categories. As such, revisions and corrections were made in the publication of the *DSM-III-R*, which was released in 1987 (American Psychiatric Association, 1987).

The *DSM-IV*, published in 1994, was developed using a three-stage empirical process: comprehensive and systematic literature review, reanalysis of data, and field trials comparing *DSM-III*, *DSM-III-R*, *ICD-10*, and proposed *DSM-IV* criterion sets across several sites (American Psychiatric Association, 1994, 2000). A text revision of the *DSM-IV* was published in 2000. The *DSM-IV-TR* sought to bridge the gap between the *DSM-IV* and the *DSM-5*, which was released in 2013. Although no new categories, disorders, or subtypes were introduced in the *DSM-IV-TR*, revisions and additions were included in the text sections to reflect updated empirical findings. This elaboration and clarification, in such areas as diagnostic features, associated features and disorders, specific culture and gender features, and prevalence, served to enhance the clinical value of the *DSM-IV*.

The *DSM-5* involved a thorough reorganization of the diagnostic classification system, although it maintains consistency with the *DSM-IV-TR*. A number of significant changes to the classification system included a reconceptualization of the *Autism Spectrum Disorders*, including removal of *Asperger Disorder* and *Pervasive Developmental Disorder* as separate diagnoses; the movement of childhood-onset disruptive behavior disorders into a category specific to disruptive and impulse-control disorders across the life span; the elimination of subtypes of *Schizophrenia*; removal of the bereavement exclusion for *depressive disorders*; the introduction of *Gender Dysphoria* instead of *Gender Identity Disorder* and changes to its conceptualization; the addition of *Binge Eating Disorder* as a discrete eating disorder; and a recharacterization in identification of *paraphilic disorders*. Personality disorders are maintained as previously classified, but an alternative, dimensional-categorical model has also been provided. Most significant was the removal of the five-axis system that had defined earlier *DSM* classifications. Lastly, *DSM-5* removed the category of "disorders not otherwise specified," and began using "other specified disorders" and "unspecified disorder" categories.

DSM-5 considers 19 diagnostic classes: *neurodevelopmental disorders; schizophrenia spectrum and other psychotic disorders; bipolar and related disorders; depressive disorders; anxiety disorders; obsessive-compulsive and related disorders; trauma- and stressor-related disorders; dissociative disorders; somatic symptom and related disorders; feeding and eating disorders; elimination disorders; sleep–wake disorders; sexual dysfunctions; gender dysphoria; disruptive, impulse-control and conduct disorders; substance-related and addictive disorders; neurocognitive disorders; personality disorders;* and *paraphilic disorders*. Eight disorder categories still under research consideration are presented including Caffeine Use Disorder, Internet Gaming Disorder, and Neurobehavior Disorder Associated With Prenatal Alcohol Exposure. The most significant change to the classification system is the removal of the multiaxial system; instead, diagnoses are now conceptualized simultaneously, including personality and neurodevelopmental diagnoses (which were previously classified on Axis II) and medical diagnoses (which were previously classified on Axis III). Cultural considerations are now more prominent, including conceptualization of cultural factors that may impact symptom presentation; this is characterized through three specific concepts, *cultural syndrome*, *cultural idiom of distress*, and *cultural explanation or perceived cause*, allowing for a more coherent causal description of symptoms within a cultural context when formulating a diagnosis. Axes IV and V of the former classification system have been superseded by use of *ICD-10-CM* codes and extenders that capture psychosocial and contextual considerations in diagnosis. The WHO Disability Assessment Schedule has been proposed as a means for characterizing global functioning. Of note, the *DSM-5* was updated in 2022 with a text revision (*DSM-5-TR*; American Psychiatric Association, 2022). While there were no major changes to any of the existing diagnostic criteria, a number of text revisions were made primarily for the purposes of clarification. A new diagnosis, Prolonged Grief Disorder, was added, as was Unspecified Mood Disorder. Additionally, a number of updates were made related to race and culture and the impact of race, ethnicity, nationality, and related concepts on diagnosis. For a more detailed overview of the changes in the *DSM-5-TR*, readers are directed to the American Psychiatric Association website.

While the *DSM-5* continues utilizing a categorical approach for diagnosis, it remains an important consideration that each category of mental disorder does not exist as a discrete entity, mutually exclusive of other diagnostic categories. Additionally, because individuals must meet only subsets of items from a longer list in a polythetic criterion set, there remains no singular presentation of diagnosis. Individuals may meet criteria for the same disorder, but presentation of symptoms may not be homogeneous. Although this categorical approach presents limitations in terms of boundaries between diagnoses and heterogeneity between cases within classes, it is a stronger choice than a dimensional approach. Although the dimensional approach has the benefit of classifying disorders based on quantification of characteristics, thus allowing for more reliable diagnosis of boundary cases and the reporting of subthreshold cases, dimensional approaches continue to show only variable success as descriptors of the clinical picture of disorders (American Psychiatric Association, 2013). Additionally, they are incompatible with settings requiring discrete labeling of disorders, such as is required for insurance billing coding. As with the *DSM-IV-TR*, with the *DSM-5* cases where full criteria are not met for a diagnosis, but clinical presentation is positive for significant symptomology, diagnosticians can utilize classifiers to indicate diagnostic uncertainty, including *Other Specified Disorders* and *Unspecified Disorder* classifiers. A provisional diagnosis may be made when information is lacking to make a firm diagnosis, but there is ample evidence that full criteria for the disorder will be met once this information is obtained. This may occur when additional history must be gathered, or the information provided is incomplete or lacking in detail. A provisional diagnosis is also warranted when symptoms are present and do not appear to be remitting imminently but have not met the minimum time requirement for a specific disorder. Diagnosis is deferred when inadequate information is provided for diagnostic judgment.

▶ FACTORS INFLUENCING INTERPRETATION OF DATA AND DECISION-MAKING

Once data are collected, whether through interview, observation, assessment, or collateral report, interpretations are made. Psychologists ideally follow an evidence-based approach to diagnosis. Evidence-based decisions are made by integrating empirical research, clinician training, and comprehensive data collection, typically garnered through the use of standardized, norm-referenced measures; however, as has been previously discussed, considerations are required regarding the reliability and validity of the measures selected for multiculturally diverse groups being evaluated (APA, 2017; Fujii, 2016; Suzuki & Ponterotto, 2007). This model limits the use of the clinician's intuitive judgment and does not allow for heuristics such as trial and error, rules of thumb, or educated guesses, all of which may contribute to error or bias. Clinicians and researchers such as Paul Meehl and Sir Karl Popper supported the use of algorithmic analysis of data as opposed to subjective inference in interpreting and predicting behavior. Meehl's research supported the use of "mechanical data" over clinical prediction (Meehl, 1978).

Cultural and other group differences exist (APA, 2017; Clauss-Ehlers et al., 2023), and these are necessary to acknowledge and address. Furthermore, examination of base rates provides a context for the interpretation of information. Rather than focusing solely on observable qualities, base rates provide important statistical information that guides diagnostic judgments by addressing directly the quantity of a population that will likely meet specific criteria, thus providing a perspective in terms of population characteristics and expectations.

METHODS FOR THE MEASUREMENT OF INDIVIDUAL, COUPLES, FAMILY, GROUP, AND ORGANIZATIONAL CHANGE

Once an intervention has been put in place, adherence to that intervention is critical in the evaluation of the efficacy of that treatment. Additionally, in cases of empirically proven interventions, adherence to a treatment plan is of the utmost importance for positive outcomes. Participants must comply with treatment plans in order to fully benefit from the intervention. There are several methods of monitoring treatment compliance and efficacy. Continuous monitoring of behavior can be accomplished through continuous observation. This may be conducted by an outside observer or the subject and recorded in writing, through video recording, or via computerized documentation. Examiners focus on the count or number of occurrences of the behavior, the rate or frequency of the behavior per unit of time, how that rate changes over time, and the duration of the behavior.

Behavioral analysis refers to the observation and measurement of a specific behavior. The target behavior should be measured prior to intervention and then continually monitored throughout the course of intervention to observe change. Ideally, the behavior is observed across environments. Examiners note antecedents to the behavior as well as consequences of the behavior. Observers may also note the subject's responses to the behavioral consequences. Knowledge on the part of the participant that the behavior is being observed may actually serve to impact the target behavior. This is known as the *observer effect*.

Organizations monitor behavior to promote best practices. This process, known as benchmarking, follows the same general methodology of identifying a target behavior, observing and recording the frequency of the behavior, and developing an intervention to alter, eliminate, or replace the behavior. Organizations encourage behaviors that fit into their model of best practice and focus on behaviors that interfere with efficiency, productivity, and growth within the organization.

Response to intervention (RTI) uses frequent progress measurement to determine the efficacy of treatment planning and services. RTI employs short-term, as well as long-term, discrete measurable goals that can be assessed at predetermined points in time. RTI is most frequently used in schools to address learning and behavior difficulties. As with other forms of intervention monitoring, RTI serves to encourage accountability, both on the part of the student participating in the intervention and for those providing services.

In the case of treatment, and in RTI, relapse or failure to meet goals is defined by the continuation or return to the maladaptive behavior or unsatisfactory level of performance. Once relapse has been determined, care providers must then reassess the original treatment plan, revise interventions, and resume the monitoring of patient adherence. Several factors will affect treatment compliance. These include the patient's readiness and willingness to change, feasibility of intervention, and external support.

▶ USE OF COMPUTERS, THE INTERNET, AND RELATED TECHNOLOGY IN ASSESSMENT AND EVALUATION

As technology has progressed over the last several decades, and particularly more rapidly following the recent COVID-19 epidemic, the field of psychology has sought to adjust to and benefit from these advances. The use of computers, the internet, and related technologies has had an increasingly significant impact on how assessments and diagnostic evaluations are conducted and scored, how therapeutic needs are met, and how issues of confidentiality are addressed. There have been many advantages resulting from the use of technological strides, including broader access to assessment and intervention for communities in less-resourced areas, greater ease of record-keeping and data management, better coordination of care, quick and accurate computer scoring programs and statistical programs, and research accessibility (Strecher, 2007; Wright et al., 2020).

Of particular consideration regarding assessment has been the development and implementation of specific approaches to psychological, educational, and neuropsychological test administration and completion. Working in tandem with test publishers and professional associations, psychologists have worked to develop accommodations to standardized assessment protocols, as well as methods for test administration that allow for greater flexibility in how technologies can be engaged more effectively with individuals and groups requiring assessment (Hewitt et al., 2020).

Although there appear to be many benefits inherent in these innovations, technological approaches to assessment continue to present with questions related to such issues as validity, efficiency, ethics, and confidentiality. Examples of current research into these areas include the potential for compromised validity in computer-administered measures, patient resistance to computerized interfaces, threats to protected health information, and misuse of the internet in terms of self-diagnosis and information gathering. Early findings suggest positive responses to such innovations as computer-based intervention (Marks & Cavanagh, 2009) and assessment; for example, this has been further supported, post-COVID-19, through a series of meta-analyses addressing efficacy and reliability (Snoswell et al., 2023).

▶ REFERENCES

Full reference list available at http://examprepconnect.springerpub.com

KNOWLEDGE CHECK: CHAPTER 7

1. Which domain of practice is typically focused on understanding the relationship between brain and behavior through assessment?
   A. Clinical psychology
   B. Industrial–organizational psychology
   C. Neuropsychology
   D. School psychology

2. Hiltonsmith and Keller's (1983) framework for organizing data from an ecological assessment includes all of the following EXCEPT:
   A. Setting appearance and contents
   B. Setting foundation
   C. Setting operation
   D. Setting opportunities

3. Which of the following is an example of a criterion-referenced test?
   A. Driving exam
   B. Graduate Record Examinations (GRE)
   C. Minnesota Multiphasic Personality Inventory-2 (MMPI-2)
   D. Wechsler Adult Intelligence Scale–Fourth Edition (WAIS-IV)

4. The process of defining a target behavior, determining the antecedents of the behavior, and describing the consequence or function of the target behavior is referred to as:
   A. Direct observation
   B. Event sampling
   C. Functional behavioral assessment (FBA)
   D. Narrative recording

5. A psychologist is attempting to gather more information regarding the severity and frequency of a patient's target behavior problems of hitting peers through a school observation. The student typically engages in this activity when returning to the classroom after lunch. What is the most appropriate observation method to use?
   A. Event sampling
   B. Direct observation
   C. Interval recording
   D. Narrative recording

(See answers on the next page.)

1. **C) Neuropsychology**
Neuropsychology is the study of the relationship between the brain and behavior. Clinically, neuropsychologists use standardized assessments to examine an individual's profile of neurocognitive strengths and weaknesses. This profile is then compared to known profiles of specific disorders to help clarify the nature and severity of neurological insult. While school psychology has a focus on assessment, the goal of the assessment is to evaluate and address educational and developmental issues that impact learning and education. Industrial-organizational psychology may also include some assessment though the goal is focused on understanding and optimizing human behavior within organizations and work systems. Neuropsychology is a subspecialty within clinical psychology, which is an umbrella term that also encompasses other types of assessment and clinical service provision within the field of psychology.

2. **B) Setting foundation**
The three components of the model are setting appearance and contents, setting operation, and setting opportunities.

3. **A) Driving exam**
A criterion-referenced test is used to assess where an examinee stands on a particular criterion, or domain of skill, status, or functioning. A driving exam assesses a specific acquired or learned skill. The GRE, MMPI-2, and WAIS-IV assess a broader range of abilities and/or characteristics and thus are not criterion-referenced tests.

4. **C) Functional behavioral assessment (FBA)**
FBA is a method of behavioral assessment in which observation is used to determine the antecedent and consequence or function of a target behavior. The data collected through the FBA are then used to develop and implement a behavioral intervention. Direct observation, narrative recording, and event sampling may be included within an FBA as a means to understand the frequency and intensity of a behavior as well as information about the broader context in which they occur and to characterize the behaviors, but are not sufficient to constitute an FBA, which encompasses multiple types of data collection to fully understand the behavior.

5. **A) Event sampling**
Event sampling is appropriate when the target behavior has a clear beginning and ending and does not occur at a very high frequency. With event sampling, the observer rates the frequency of the behavior during a set period of time. Given that this behavior occurs consistently during a specific period of the day, event sampling is a good way to capture data regarding the behavior. Narrative recording provides a running record of the behavior within an observation period though this does not necessarily focus on frequency data. Interval recording methods, also known as time-sampling methods, require target behaviors to be operationally defined in objective, clear, and specific terms for the examiner to effectively identify and monitor the behavior during observation. Observation is divided into brief time intervals and the examiner records whether a specific behavior occurs during each interval recorded. In this case, the behavior may not be captured if each time interval is brief. All of these observations are direct observation and thus this is not a specific enough observation method.

6. It is helpful to gain information from multiple informants regarding an examinee because informant ratings may be influenced by:
    A. Ethnicity
    B. Familiarity with the individual
    C. Socioeconomic status
    D. All of the above

7. Which of the following is NOT a key component of an assessment center?
    A. Assessor training
    B. Job analysis
    C. Simulations
    D. Single assessor evaluation

8. In item response theory, item discrimination refers to:
    A. How well the item distinguishes who scores high versus low on a test
    B. Probability of getting an item correct by chance
    C. The percentage of test takers who get the answer correct
    D. The proportion of test takers who fail the item

9. According to generalizability theory, which of the following constitutes potential sources of error in test measurement?
    A. Rater/examiner
    B. Test items
    C. Time of day test was administered
    D. All of the above

10. Which of the following is NOT true about reliability and validity?
    A. In order for a measure to be reliable it must be valid.
    B. In order for a measure to be valid it must be reliable.
    C. The reliability coefficient reflects the degree of consistency of a measure.
    D. Validity of a measure indicates the extent to which it measures what it is supposed to measure.

11. Which of the following is NOT true about test–retest reliability?
    A. It is appropriate to use when the trait or ability is thought to be variable across time.
    B. It is assessed by administering the measure to the same group at two time points.
    C. It refers to the stability of a test over time.
    D. The interval between test and retest can impact the reliability coefficient.

(See answers on the next page.)

6. **D) All of the above**
   Informant ratings can be impacted by a range of variables, including the severity of the individual's symptoms; the child's ethnicity, gender, and socioeconomic status; the informant's familiarity with the individual; and the informant's tolerance for problematic behavior.

7. **D) Single assessor evaluation**
   By definition, for a process to be considered an assessment center it requires that multiple assessors observe and rate each examinee's performance. Because the process relies on ratings from multiple assessors, it is important for assessors to have appropriate training. A job analysis is used to determine the skills or competencies vital to success in a given job. The assessment includes job-simulation activities to observe the examinee's performance on these tasks.

8. **A) How well the item distinguishes who scores high versus low on a test**
   There are three key parameters when examining test-item relationships: item difficulty (the percentage of test takers who get a specific item correct), item discrimination (how that item discriminates between those who do well versus those who do poorly on the test as a whole), and the probability that a question is answered correctly by guessing.

9. **D) All of the above**
   In generalizability theory, sources of measurement error can include aspects of the measurement itself as well as the circumstances under which a test was administered.

10. **A) In order for a measure to be reliable it must be valid.**
    A test can be reliable and not valid. It can consistently measure the same construct even if it is not measuring the construct it is supposed to measure. The reliability coefficient reflects the degree of consistency of the measure.

11. **A) It is appropriate to use when the trait or ability is thought to be variable across time.**
    The use of test–retest reliability is appropriate when the trait or ability being measured is thought to be relatively stable over time.

12. The Kuder–Richardson formula is used to measure:
    A. Internal consistency reliability
    B. Interrater reliability
    C. Parallel form reliability
    D. Test–retest reliability

13. As part of a research study, psychologists are rating caregiver responsiveness to children during a play-based assessment. The team has trained 10 research assistants in the use of this tool. In order to make sure that all researchers are rating responsiveness in the same way, the principal investigator has calculated _____ on this new tool.
    A. Content validity
    B. Criterion validity
    C. Interrater reliability
    D. Test–retest reliability

14. The trinitarian model of validity includes all of the following EXCEPT:
    A. Concurrent validity
    B. Construct validity
    C. Content validity
    D. Criterion validity

15. Which type of validity refers to the extent to which a measure or test is associated with the trait or ability it is intended to measure?
    A. Concurrent validity
    B. Construct validity
    C. Content validity
    D. Criterion validity

16. A decrease in Type II error leads to:
    A. A decrease in Type I error
    B. An increase in sensitivity
    C. An increase in specificity
    D. None of the above

17. Which of the following would be appropriate to use as a broad-based measure of social–emotional and behavioral functioning in an assessment with a 10-year-old?
    A. Beck Anxiety Inventory (BAI)
    B. Behavior Assessment System for Children–Third Edition (BASC-3)
    C. Child Depression Inventory–Second Edition (CDI-II)
    D. Social Responsiveness Scale–Second Edition (SRS-2)

(See answers on the next page.)

12. **A) Internal consistency reliability**
    The Kuder–Richardson formula (20; KR-20) is used to calculate split-half reliability, which is one of several approaches to assessing internal consistency reliability. This is used when the measurement has dichotomous choices. Interrater reliability is analyzed statistically using Cronbach's alpha. Interrater reliability can be calculated by calculating percent agreement among raters, using interclass correlation, Cohen's Kappa, or several other methods. Parallel form reliability is obtained by administering different versions of a tool to the same group and correlating scores across the measures to evaluate reliability. Test–retest reliability is estimated by calculating the correlation coefficient of the scores on a measure across two time points.

13. **C) Interrater reliability**
    Interrater reliability refers to the consistency of the performance or behaviors of a test taker. A high interrater reliability coefficient indicates that scores on a test are calculated or derived in a consistent and systematic manner across examiners. Kappa is a measure of interrater reliability, which estimates the reliability between two raters. Kappa takes the interrater agreement that occurs by chance into account when estimating reliability. While content validity, criterion validity, and test–retest reliability are important in the development of assessment and research tools, they are not measures of reliability between raters.

14. **A) Concurrent validity**
    The trinitarian model of validity posits that there are three primary components of validity that should be considered: construct validity, content validity, and criterion validity. Concurrent validity is not included in this model because criterion validity (which is included in the model) consists of both concurrent and predictive validity, so this is not the best response.

15. **B) Construct validity**
    Content validity describes how well a test includes the range of information that is needed to test the construct being assessed. Concurrent validity examines the correlation between a new measure and other measures known to assess the construct of interest. Finally, criterion validity refers to the adequacy with which a test or measure estimates an individual's performance on a construct of interest. Thus, construct validity is the correct response.

16. **B) An increase in sensitivity**
    A decrease in Type II error would lead to a decrease in the false negative rate, which would improve sensitivity or the proportion of people who are accurately identified as possessing a certain trait, attribute, or behavior that is being measured.

17. **B) Behavior Assessment System for Children–Third Edition (BASC-3)**
    The BASC-3 is a broad measure of social–emotional and behavioral functioning. There are parent, teacher, and self-report forms of the BASC-3. The BAI and CDI-II are specific measures of anxiety and mood symptoms. The SRS-2 is used to assess social skills and social responsiveness when considering a diagnosis of an autism spectrum disorder.

18. The Cattell–Horn–Carroll (CHC) theory of intelligence has historically included nine broad stratum abilities, including all of the following EXCEPT:
    A. Fine motor ability
    B. Long-term storage and retrieval
    C. Quantitative reasoning
    D. Writing ability

19. According to the Cattell–Horn model, what were the two types of intelligence?
    A. Crystallized intelligence and perceptual reasoning
    B. Fluid intelligence and crystallized intelligence
    C. Perceptual reasoning and emotional intelligence
    D. Quantitative reasoning and perceptual reasoning

20. Which of the following is considered an unstructured personality assessment?
    A. Millon Clinical Multiaxial Inventory–Fourth Edition (MCMI–IV)
    B. Minnesota Multiphasic Personality Inventory–3 (MMPI–3)
    C. Personality Assessment Inventory–Adolescent (PAI–A)
    D. Rorschach Inkblot Test

21. In Holland's theory of vocational interest, which of the following dimensions are listed in the order expected on the hexagon?
    A. Conventional, Realistic
    B. Investigative, Enterprising
    C. Realistic, Artistic
    D. Social, Conventional

22. Which of the following is NOT true of symptom validity testing (SVT)?
    A. It assesses the number and severity of symptoms a patient presents with.
    B. It is a necessary component of forensic work.
    C. It should be used when there is a question of secondary gain.
    D. SVT can include use of the Rey 15-Item Test and the Recognition Memory Test.

23. Which of the following is appropriate for a defense when a trial involves a patient who claims mental illness as a reason behind the crime?
    A. Diminished capacity
    B. Guilty but mentally ill
    C. Mens rea
    D. Not guilty by reason of insanity

(See answers on the next page.)

18. **A) Fine motor ability**
    The CHC has included nine broad stratum abilities: crystallized intelligence (*Gc*), fluid intelligence (*Gf*), quantitative reasoning (*Gq*), reading and writing ability (*Grw*), short-term memory (*Gsm*), long-term storage and retrieval (*Glr*), visual processing (*Gv*), auditory processing (*Ga*), and processing speed (*Gs*).

19. **B) Fluid intelligence and crystallized intelligence**
    The Cattell–Horn model postulates two types of intelligence: fluid and crystallized.

20. **D) Rorschach Inkblot Test**
    The MMPI-3, PAI-A, and MCMI–IV are considered structured personality assessment measures. In contrast, the Rorschach Inkblot Test is a projective test, which is often considered to be an unstructured measure of personality.

21. **A) Conventional, Realistic**
    In Holland's theory of vocational interest, each dimension is arranged around the hexagon in a clockwise direction starting with what he termed "Realistic." The interest domains identified are denoted as R-I-A-S-E-C: Realistic, Investigative, Artistic, Social, Enterprising, and Conventional. While the other responses are part of the theory dimensions, they are not provided in the order expected on the hexagon.

22. **A) It assesses the number and severity of symptoms a patient presents with.**
    SVT refers to the development and use of measures and assessment procedures to try to assess an examinee's level of effort and investment during psychological testing; measures used for this purpose are referred to as SVTs. Assessments of examinee effort should always be included in forensic testing. SVTs or performance validity tests (PVTs) do not assess symptoms.

23. **D) Not guilty by reason of insanity**
    "Not guilty by reason of insanity" is the defense used in cases in which mental illness is examined as a factor being considered when evaluating criminal responsibility. In contrast, guilty but mentally ill indicates criminal responsibility while taking mental illness into account when addressing the individual's guilt and advising sentencing. Diminished capacity refers to whether the individual had the capacity to form the intention to commit a crime or mens rea.

24. In evaluating risk for future violence, which of the following historical factors should be considered in terms of their likelihood of increasing the risk for future violence?
    A. History of aggressive behavior
    B. History of school failure
    C. History of substance abuse
    D. A and C

25. A psychologist asks a parent to complete the Social Responsiveness Scale–Second Edition (SRS-2) because the client is experiencing difficulties getting along with peers. The scores came back elevated, but the psychologist completed the Autism Diagnostic Observation Schedule–Second Edition (ADOS-2) and the Autism Diagnostic Interview, Revised (ADI-R) and does not believe that autism spectrum disorder (ASD) is an accurate diagnosis. Which of the following options could be the best alternative explanation for the elevated SRS2 scores?
    A. The child has average cognitive skills.
    B. The child has poor impulse control, is hyperactive, and is inattentive.
    C. The parent does not see the child interact often enough with others to provide a reliable report.
    D. The SRS-2 should be weighed more heavily than the ADOS-2, ADI-R, and clinician's judgment, as it is a standardized parent-report measure.

26. The clinician is working with a 14-year-old who moved to the United States from Mexico 5 years ago. They speak Spanish with their family at home, but for the last 1.5 years they have completed schooling in English. Prior to that time (but since living in the United States), they have attended a dual language (Spanish-English) program, and prior to that had only had schooling in Spanish. The student is now receiving primarily Cs in school but had previously been a straight A student. The school would like to complete an evaluation to determine the underlying cause(s) of the student's decline in grades. Which of the following measures would be helpful for them to consider using?
    A. Woodcock-Muñoz Language Survey (WMLS)
    B. Wechsler Intelligence Scale for Children–Fifth Edition (WISC-V) Spanish
    C. Batería IV Woodcock-Muñoz
    D. All of the above

27. A 2-year-old presents to the clinic due to a history of developmental delay. They currently use about 25 words and do not yet have phrased speech. They did not begin to use any words until 3 months ago. In addition to delayed language, there are also concerns about motor delays, as the child only recently started to walk independently. Which of the following options would be the best measure to use to more comprehensively assess this individual's developmental skillset?
    A. The Leiter International Performance Scale–Third Edition (Leiter-3)
    B. The Mullen Scales of Early Learning (Mullen)
    C. The Universal Nonverbal Intelligence Test–Second Edition (UNIT-2)
    D. None of these

(See answers on the next page.)

24. **D) A and C**
Attention should be paid to known factors that increase risk for violence, including a history of aggressive behavior and violent acts; a history of substance abuse; a history of psychosis, specifically prior to hospitalization or treatment; and a history of psychiatric and personality disorders that have been associated with an increased risk of violence, such as antisocial personality disorder, borderline personality disorder, and personality disorder not otherwise specified.

25. **B) The child has poor impulse control, is hyperactive, and is inattentive.**
Scores on measures such as the SRS-2 may be elevated because of overlapping behavioral concerns that can also have an impact on social functioning. For example, children with poor impulse control, hyperactivity, and inattention, which may reach the threshold for an attention deficit hyperactivity disorder (ADHD) diagnosis, are at a higher risk of social difficulties because of these concerns. This does not mean that they also have autism, although ADHD and autism can co-occur at high rates. This is why diagnosis must occur as part of in-depth clinical evaluation and cannot be limited to a single questionnaire measure, though evaluation for ASD should always include report from a parent/caregiver or other informant. While parents may not always have an opportunity to directly observe their child interacting with peers, this is not the best explanation for elevated scores. The parents also brought the child in for the evaluation because of their concerns in this area. Finally, average cognitive skills would not explain elevated SRS-2 scores.

26. **D) All of the above**
This individual was primarily exposed to Spanish up until they were about 9 years old. While more information may be needed, it seems quite likely that their dominant language is Spanish. The WMLS should be administered to help determine their academic language proficiency. If this identifies Spanish, a strong hypothesis for this individual's recent decline in grades would be that they are not understanding the material because it is being presented in English. Cognitive and academic testing (in their assumed dominant language) should also be included to rule out any underlying cognitive or learning disability, which could also explain a decline in grades, particularly as an individual transitions from the elementary/middle school level to high school.

27. **B) The Mullen Scales of Early Learning (Mullen)**
The Mullen is commonly used for children ages 5 and under and is able to assess a child's developmental functioning across emerging cognition, language, and motor skills. This would be the most appropriate measure to use of the choices given the child's age and presenting concerns, as this will be able to evaluate for developmental delay and provide information regarding the child's developmental strengths and weaknesses, which can be used to guide treatment and intervention plans and track developmental progress. While the Leiter-3 and UNIT-2 are good choices for assessing intellectual abilities in populations with language difficulties, these measures (a) do not assess *developmental* functioning and (b) are not normed for 2-year-olds.

28. A 10-year-old client is presenting with concerns for an intellectual disability, and their mental age is reportedly much lower than their chronological age. The child's school and family would like a better understanding of the child's intellectual abilities, and they would like to be able to track the child's progress as the child gets older and continues to engage in different therapies. Which of the following test measures would be most appropriate to use in an evaluation with this young child?

   A. Minnesota Multiphasic Personality Inventory–Adolescent Version (MMPI-A)
   B. Stanford-Binet Intelligence Scales–Fifth Edition (SB-5)
   C. The Neuropsychological Assessment Battery (NAB)
   D. The Wechsler Adult Intelligence Scale–Fourth Edition (WAIS-IV)

29. According to Joiner et al. (1999), which of the following risk factors should be assessed when evaluating suicide risk?

   A. Precipitant stressors
   B. Predispositions
   C. Protective factors
   D. All of the above

30. When preparing to conduct a neuropsychological evaluation of an immigrant Latinx middle school student who is showing issues with academic skill development, the psychologist is advised to consider which of the following regarding the appropriateness of measures for the testing?

   A. Consider the cultural and linguistic acceptability of the scales with regard to the examinee.
   B. Review the reliability and validity of the measures with regard to their normative standardization, and the ability of the test to be used with this examinee.
   C. B solely
   D. A and B

31. Assessment of a defendant's capacity to stand trial by a forensic psychologist requires meeting criterion that are set through the ruling made in *Dusky v. United States* in 1960, stipulating that:

   A. Defendants demonstrate both the ability to understand rationally and factually the legal proceedings held against them.
   B. Defendants must be shown to possess sufficient ability to consult with their attorney with a reasonable level of understanding and comprehension.
   C. Defendants show on a structured assessment tool examining their competency that they are able to demonstrate intellectual skills consistent with adult functioning.
   D. A and B

(See answers on the next page.)

28. **B) Stanford-Binet Intelligence Scales–Fifth Edition (SB-5)**
The SB-5 is an intelligence measure appropriate for children as young as age 2. The SB-5 also provides extended IQ norms, meaning that it can support calculations of scores at extreme ends, which could be appropriate given concerns for a possible intellectual disability and the reported discrepancy between the client's mental age and chronological age. Change sensitive scores (CSS) are also available on the SB-5, which can be useful when assessing individuals with intellectual disability, particularly given that this family would like to track their child's progress over time. Nonverbal measures and developmental assessment could also be appropriate. The other choices (MMPI-A, NAB, and WAIS-IV) are all out of age range for a 10-year-old. In addition, the NAB is used to assess attention, language, memory, spatial, and executive functioning in adults, so it would not be able to provide an estimate of IQ. The WAIS is for adults and would be harder to track change over time in a way that would be sensitive to even minor progress or decline. The MMPI-A assesses personality traits.

29. **D) All of the above**
The seven identified risk factors for suicide are previous suicidal behavior, types of current suicidal ideation and symptoms, precipitant stressors, overall symptom presentation, self-control and impulsivity, predispositions, and protective factors.

30. **D) A and B**
The most appropriate approach is one that considers the totality of the examinee's background, culturally and linguistically, and to simultaneously ensure that the reliability and validity of the scales available can meet these considerations. It is more clearly shown through research regarding the intersection between multicultural considerations and both intellectual and academic assessment that common tests used for assessing capability and capacity in youth in the United States remain vulnerable to some bias in terms of both reliability and validity for diverse populations. This is most clearly seen with recent immigrant families, given the constraints on how test standardization samples are identified and included. See C. R. Reynolds et al. (2021) regarding the underlying biases that remain challenging to address in test development and standardization. But this alone is not the only factor at hand with this question. Similarly, it is key to consider both the questions being posed with the test and the ability for that test to be appropriately used with someone who may not be facile with the language level and vocabulary being used, given their primary and secondary language status. Recognizing that someone who has recently immigrated to the United States from a primarily Spanish-speaking country may have limited language skill, it is important for the psychologist to recognize that either use of an interpreter or a Spanish-language measure would be the more appropriate approach to assessment of this student; this, however, is not a sole consideration.

31. **D) A and B**
The *Dusky* standard specifies two important prongs that must be met to support a defendant's capacity to stand trial, both being able to understand the legal proceedings and collaborate with their attorney in their defense. Structured assessment tools, like the MacArthur Competence Assessment Tool (MacCAT), can be valid approaches to ascertaining capacity for standing trial when used in the context of a full evaluation by the psychologist. They do not, however, focus solely on intellectual capacity, or intellectual functioning. Additionally, adult level functioning is not a prerequisite for competency to stand trial. The defendant's ability to show on a structured assessment tool that they are able to demonstrate intellectual skills consistent with adult functioning is an element of the *Dusky* standard, but it requires the defendants to possess sufficient ability to consult with their attorney with a reasonable level of understanding and comprehension.

32. One of the more frequent measures used to assess suicide risk, particularly in clinical research and randomized controlled clinical trials, is the Columbia-Suicide Severity Rating Scale (C-SSRS), developed by Posner and colleagues. Its efficacy studies have indicated:
    A. Poor predictability of actual suicide outcome
    B. Reasonable internal and external sources of reliability and validity, adequate specificity, and above adequate sensitivity, but a necessity for a broader interview to determine fully the level of suicide risk
    C. Strong sensitivity for classification of suicidal risk, moderate specificity regarding suicidal risk
    D. Sufficient reliability and predictability allowing sole use as a diagnostic tool

33. Multicultural considerations regarding assessment have become an important focus for ongoing research regarding test construction. In line with suggestions made by both the APA Multicultural Guidelines (APA, 2017) and researchers like Suzuki and Ponterotto (e.g., 2007), determining that a measure meets appropriateness for use across populations relies on what factors during standardization?
    A. Breadth in the standardization and normative validation, cultural sensitivity, and linguistic validity
    B. Internal and external reliability, cultural validity, and local standardization
    C. Internal consistency, linguistic validity, and breadth in the standardization and normative validation
    D. Intersectional consideration, cultural sensitivity, and normative breadth

34. An 8-year-old child has a diagnosis of attention deficit hyperactivity disorder and autism spectrum disorder. They have been demonstrating significant behavioral dysregulation and aggression in the classroom when challenged by academic tasks or sensory triggers, though there are times staff are unsure of what is triggering the behavior. The child's teacher and paraprofessional have tried multiple strategies without much progress. What would be an appropriate next step?
    A. Conduct a diagnostic assessment.
    B. Conduct a functional behavioral assessment (FBA).
    C. Implement a behavior intervention plan.
    D. Implement a daily report card for behavior.

35. The clinician is doing a diagnostic evaluation of a 6-year-old client who presents with a history of language delays, hand flapping, sensory sensitivities, delayed response to name and inconsistent eye contact, and persistent social communication difficulties. As you consider a diagnosis of autism, which of the following tools should be administered in order to meet the standards for a multidisciplinary evaluation as recommended by the American Academy of Pediatrics and American Academy of Child and Adolescent Psychiatry?
    A. An adaptive functioning measure
    B. A measure of intellectual functioning
    C. The Autism Diagnostic Observation Schedule-2 (ADOS-2)
    D. All of the above

(See answers on the next page.)

32. **C) Strong sensitivity for classification of suicidal risk, moderate specificity regarding suicidal risk**
    No scale developed and used for assessing suicide risk is able to be considered a sole diagnostic tool. Assessment of suicidal risk is a multicomponential process, looking at current thoughts, behaviors, and plan, in the context of collateral information and a comprehensive interview with the person considered at risk. The C-SSRS is considered a reliable and valid instrument for assessing suicide risk within the context of a multicomponential assessment, with a reasonable role in predicting that risk.

33. **A) Breadth in the standardization and normative validation, cultural sensitivity, and linguistic validity**
    Internal consistency of the scale is a strong component of a measure's reliability, but it does not address cultural and linguistic considerations necessary for a test's ability to be used more broadly. Both linguistic validation and breadth in the standardization and normative validation processes do support cultural considerations with a new measure. The addition of cultural sensitivity to the construction of a test, coupled with strong approaches to both linguistic validation and standardization and normative validation breadth foster a more sensitive and successful scale for use across multicultural populations.

34. **B) Conduct a functional behavioral assessment (FBA).**
    Although the implementation of a behavior intervention plan or daily report card to address behavioral challenges is a reasonable next step, staff still do not have a clear understanding of the function of the behaviors being described in the question. An FBA will help to determine the function the behavior serves, and then this data can be used to develop a behavior intervention plan in the school setting. The FBA should be conducted prior to the development of the behavioral intervention plan. Finally, a diagnostic assessment is an important component in understanding a child's behavioral presentation, but in this case, diagnoses have already been provided.

35. **D) All of the above**
    The recommendation across a number of publications and white papers published by professional organizations is that autism assessment be multidisciplinary in nature. This does not require assessment by multiple providers but assessment across multiple domains including intellectual functioning, adaptive functioning, and language functioning in conjunction with direct assessment of social communication and interaction such as an ADOS-2 or CARS-2 (Childhood Autism Rating Scale-2), along with a thorough diagnostic interview.

36. As an applicant for a competitive position as a computer programmer, an individual was asked to complete a Minnesota Multiphasic Personality Inventory-2, solve a mock computer programming program and talk through their strategy from an architecture and coding perspective, and role-play how they would manage an interaction with someone they would manage in this position. This is an example of:

A. A personality assessment
B. A direct observation
C. An assessment center
D. A work sample

(See answers on the next page.)

36. **C) An assessment center**
    While a work sample, direct observation, and personality assessment can be a part of an assessment center, the assessment center typically includes an evaluation of multiple skills or behaviors that directly relate to the job description. The goal of the assessment center is to "(1) to predict future behavior for decision making, (2) to diagnose developmental needs, and (3) to develop assessees on behavioral constructs of interest" (Rupp et al., 2015, p. 1253).

Treatment, Intervention, Prevention, and Supervision

Ashley B. Batastini and Ashley C. T. Jones

> **BROAD CONTENT AREAS**
> - Contemporary Theories of Treatment, Supervision, and Consultation
> - Intervention Decision-Making
> - Adaptation for Special Populations, Communities, and Settings

▶ INTRODUCTION

Content areas of treatment, intervention, prevention, and supervision make up a significant proportion (about 14%) of the EPPP questions. More specifically, this domain addresses the foundational concepts in commonly used theories of psychotherapy and interventions for engendering positive change among individuals, couples and families, organizations, and the larger community—the latter typically includes mental health prevention and advocacy. To best understand how to choose and implement treatments and interventions, it is also important to be familiar with best practices for specific problem areas or disorders, as well as research addressing treatment considerations for diverse populations. Related to treatment planning and delivery are theories of clinical supervision and consultation, both of which involve the sharing of specialized expertise in psychotherapy practice with a less-expert individual, group, or agency. This section may feel overwhelming because of the breadth of material it includes; however, keep in mind the EPPP is focused on general theoretical models and their empirical support (if any), rather than highly detailed and nuanced information.

▶ CONTEMPORARY THEORIES OF TREATMENT AND THEIR EVIDENCE BASE

PSYCHODYNAMIC THEORIES

Freud's Psychoanalysis
Sigmund Freud (1905; Freud & Brill, 1913) and images reflective of traditional psychoanalysis have become the stereotypical representation of psychotherapy. The association of Freud with contemporary therapy is not without merit—his work helped lay the foundation for modern therapeutic practices; however, practitioners of traditional psychoanalysis and related interventions (like free association and dream analysis) are less frequently used today. Freud conceptualized the human mind, or psyche, in three main parts: the id, the superego, and the ego. The *id* includes primal, instinctual drives such as the libido (sexual energy) and aggressive impulses. The *id* operates on the *pleasure principle*, meaning the *id* is driven by immediate

gratification and the satisfying of primal needs (like hunger, the drive to reproduce). *The superego* operates as an opposing force to the id, retraining sexual or aggressive impulses by imposing rules and moral codes—often informed by the rules learned from caregivers or larger society. To exemplify this, consider the women with whom Freud first worked when developing psychoanalytic theory: Women in Freud's time were said to have wild, unacceptable sexual impulses (driven by the *id*) which were being repressed by the strict, modest, sexist norms of the time (via the *superego*). The neurosis was said to be the product of this conflict. The *ego* works to reconcile or balance these opposing forces. The ego attempts to satisfy the impulses of the id while simultaneously adhering to the restraints of the superego (a principle called the *reality principle*).

Freud proposed the psychosexual theory of development, which posits individual personality is developed through the progression of one's libido through five stages: (1) *oral stage* (birth to 1 year), (2) *anal stage* (1–3 years), (3) *phallic stage* (3–6 years), (4) *latency stage* (6 years to puberty), and (5) *genital stage* (puberty to death). At each stage in the theory, different areas of the body are developing or changing, and an individual's libido is implicated in that particular area of development. The stages also include important tasks or processes for managing one's sexual or aggressive drives to progress to later psychosexual stages. Freud hypothesized that if a child failed to effectively satisfy the libidinal drive within each stage, they would become fixated on that task associated with that stage, and neuroses develop—continuing into adulthood if not treated. For example, if an infant failed to appropriately gratify her desires to feed at her mother's breast, then she would become orally fixated, which may manifest in adulthood as a personality characterized by passivity or immaturity. Nail-biting is a more benign potential outcome.

Perhaps most notorious is Freud's identification of the *Oedipus complex* as a crucial task in the phallic stage. During this stage, the child competes with his father for the attention of his mother. Male children develop *castration anxiety*, or a fear they will not be able to compete with their fathers. Female children instead develop *penis envy* based on the belief they cannot possess their mother without male genitalia. The jealousy of children from either biological sex and their desires to remove the father is driven by the id. The ego, then, is responsible for accepting that the father is destined to remain in the family and finding a more socially acceptable outlet for these frustrations. For example, when a man eventually marries a woman with similar qualities to his own mother Freud believed that, to satisfy the impulses of the id within the bounds set by the superego, the ego unconsciously develops *defense mechanisms,* or specific behaviors meant to cope with or eliminate the inappropriate underlying desires (or latent content) of the id. These defense mechanisms become a target of intervention in psychoanalysis: by acknowledging the unhealthy coping skills in defense mechanisms, latent content is uncovered and ultimately resolved. The following are some examples of defense mechanisms:

- *Repression* is the unconscious rejection of the content of the id. Example: A victim of childhood sexual abuse has no memory of the specific event.
- *Projection* involves misattributing one's own unconscious motives and desires to another person. Example: A woman unhappy in her marriage suspects her partner is cheating.
- *Reaction formation* is the replacing of one unacceptable motive or desire with its opposite. Example: A man who is insecure about his attraction to men engages in advocacy toward promoting traditional values.
- *Displacement* involves shifting energy from some unacceptable desire to a separate, potentially unrelated object. Example: A woman who is frustrated in her job goes home and yells at her wife.
- *Sublimation* involves converting libidinal drives arising from the id into healthy and socially acceptable outlets. Freud considered this defense mechanism to be reflective of greater maturity and appropriate functioning. Example: An artist who experienced psychological trauma is able to express his inner conflict through painting.

Given that the content of the id is largely unconscious, and therefore not readily accessible, Freud believed this content could only be accessed indirectly through specialized techniques, which he referred to as psychoanalysis. *Free association* involves the patient expressing whatever thoughts or ideas enter their mind, without any attempt to alter its content. Freud was also interested in exploring patients' dreams, which he believed possessed symbolic or latent content representing the impulses of the id. An exploration of *transference* was also an important part of Freud's psychoanalysis. Freud believed patients were prone to projecting their positive or negative thoughts, emotions, and drives onto the therapist. For example, a patient's anger toward her father may manifest as anger toward the male therapist, and it is the job of the therapist to identify this transference and process its content. During each intervention, Freud emphasized the potential for *resistance* on the part of the client, who may be reluctant or psychologically unable to access the content of their unconscious. However, if the therapist can confront, interpret, and process the patient's unconscious content, *catharsis* (i.e., an emotional release of previously repressed content) may occur, leaving the patient with greater insight and a new ability to function in a healthy, effective manner.

Freud's approach to psychoanalysis, while groundbreaking at the time, has been widely critiqued by a number of researchers and theorists over the years, who have commented on the lack of research support (Fonagy et al., 2005), its fixation on sex and dichotomous cisgenderism (Erikson, 1950; Horney, 1939), and its view of humanity as inherently flawed and deterministic (Rogers, 1961).

Jung's Analytical Psychology

Carl Jung was a contemporary of Freud who eventually parted ways to form his own theory of psychodynamic psychology, known as "analytical psychology" (Jung & Long, 1916). Unlike Freud, Jung conceptualized the unconscious as consisting of two levels. The first is the *individual/personal* unconscious, which exists uniquely within each individual. The second is the *collective unconscious*, which exists across all of humanity. The collective unconscious is less intuitive than the part of our unconscious that lives inside our own heads. For Jung, the collective unconscious consists of *archetypes*, or universally known and understood prototypical representations of various ideas (e.g., "the hero"). Jung also developed the idea of the *Electra complex*, which is the female equivalent of Freud's Oedipus complex, whereby young girls express an attraction toward their fathers. Jung is also responsible for the development of the personality constructs of *introversion* and *extroversion*, which refer to the preference for seeking pleasure inside or outside oneself, respectively.

Adler's Individual Psychology

Adler's theory is based on the idea that people strive to proactively create and construct their own *style of life* to best meet their goals and overcome life's challenges (Watts, 2000). This *creative self* is influenced by individuals' social world, most notably their *family constellation*, which includes children's birth order and inherited cultural values. Our style of life evolves over time, and healthy styles of life are reflected by a greater degree of *social interest* (i.e., healthy and useful social functioning). Adler's theory in many ways can be seen as an integration of a variety of different theories, and his technical approach to therapy is considered eclectic. However, some unique techniques developed by Adlerian theorists (Watts, 2000) include Acting "As If" (e.g., someone who experiences social anxiety may be told to act *as if* they were confident), Paradoxical Intention or "prescribing the symptom" (e.g., a client is told to purposefully display a specific emotional symptom, with the goal of understanding and replacing it), and the Magic Wand Technique (e.g., asking a client, "If you could wave a magic wand and change anything in your life, what would be different?"). Adler also emphasized the importance of encouragement, particularly in the therapy relationship itself. While research examining Adlerian therapy specifically is somewhat sparse, the integrative and eclectic nature of Adler's theory works well with many evidence-based approaches (Watts, 2000).

Neo-Freudian Theorists

The Neo-Freudians departed from Freud in focusing more so on social-cultural factors in the development of personality, as opposed to viewing instinctual drives as the determinants of personality. We briefly discuss four notable Neo-Freudians.

Regarded as a pioneer of feminist psychology, **Karen Horney** (1939) is perhaps most widely known for countering Freud's concept of "penis envy" among girls with her theory of "womb envy" among boys. More broadly, Horney theorized that children's maladaptive personality development was due to the experience of *basic anxiety*, resulting from poor interpersonal relationships, and especially a poor relationship between parent and child. For Horney, children attempt to alleviate this basic anxiety by either moving toward, moving against, or moving away from others. Failed attempts to alleviate basic anxiety, which typically rely on only one such strategy, were considered responsible for unhealthy interpersonal functioning. Conversely, healthy functioning is characterized by a flexible integration of these movements in relation to others.

Harry Stack Sullivan (1953) highlighted the importance of cognitive development in forming one's personality and identified three "modes" of cognition. The most basic mode is *protaxic*, which involves treating cognitions as separate, isolated events without clear connection. For Sullivan, the protaxic mode occurs during infancy, but can also be applied to understand symptoms of serious mental illness such as the often-concrete cognitive perceptions associated with schizophrenia. The *paratexic mode* involves making an inference about causal relationships where causality does not actually exist; for example, believing someone's glance on the train is evidence they find you attractive. The paratexic mode can also help explain the development of mental disorders. In fact, Sullivan believed neuroses were based on *paratexic distortions;* that is, anxieties can form when we assume the people with whom we previously encountered will be representative of any future interactions. Finally, Sullivan identified the *syntaxic mode* as consisting of logical, rational, and symbolic cognition, which would ultimately serve as the basis of healthy psychological functioning.

Erik Erikson (1950) developed a theory of *psychosocial development*, which is characterized by different challenges throughout the life span (as opposed to Freud's emphasis on childhood alone). Erikson's stages of psychosocial development are: (1) trust versus mistrust (0–18 months), (2) autonomy versus shame (1–3 years), (3) initiative versus guilt (3–6 years), (4) industry versus inferiority (6–11 years), (5) identity versus role confusion (12–18 years), (6) intimacy versus isolation (18–35 years), (7) generativity versus stagnation (35–64 years), (8) ego integrity versus despair (65+ years). These stages are discussed in more detail in Chapter 6, "Growth and Life-Span Development," focused on developmental psychology.

Finally, **Erich Fromm** (1947) is noted for his contributions to further understanding the role of society in the development of personality. Fromm identified five character orientations, or personality "types": productive, receptive, exploitative, hoarding, and marketing. Productive character orientations are reasonable, follow rules, value freedom, and are considered to be a sign of a healthy childhood and adaptive coping. Fromm believed the latter four orientations were maladaptive and developed in response to the constraints imposed from society, but people innately possessed the potential to develop a productive character orientation. A receptive orientation includes passivity and relying upon other people to make decisions. Individuals with an exploitative character orientation will do anything within their power to get what they want, including taking advantage of or manipulating others. Hoarding and marketing character orientations are self-explanatory: They describe individuals who find freedom in collecting material positions and selling their own abilities, respectively.

Object-Relations Theory

While individual *object-relations* theorists vary in their specific understanding and explanations, object-relations theory broadly focuses on individuals' mental representations of either themselves (i.e., "self-representation") or others (i.e., "object-representation"). The nature of these mental representations is thought to have its origin in childhood, with these representations carrying over into adulthood and forming the basis by which adults understand and relate to themselves or others. For example, a child raised with an intrusive and overinvolved parent may grow into an adult who relies on others for their sense of self and self-worth (Kohut, 1977). Notable object-relations theorists include Melanie Klein, Heinz Kohut, Otto Kernberg, Donald Winnicott, Ronald Fairbairn, and Margaret Mahler.

COGNITIVE BEHAVIORAL THERAPIES

Beck's Cognitive Therapy

Aaron Beck's (1976) development of cognitive therapy (CT) formed the backbone of contemporary understandings of cognitive behavioral therapy (CBT). The underlying assumption of Beck's CT is that thoughts/cognitions reciprocally affect both emotions and behaviors. For Beck, the goal of psychological intervention is to address, refute, and replace maladaptive, unhelpful, and inaccurate cognitions.

Beck defined *automatic thoughts* as those that arise automatically and often without conscious awareness in response to specific stimuli. For example, a socially anxious person may see someone nearby laughing and experience the automatic thought of "they're laughing at me." Automatic thoughts often include *cognitive distortions*, which are logical errors in thinking. In one such distortion, personalization, the individual assumes events or stimuli pertain to them personally without sufficient evidence. The automatic thought of "they're laughing at me" is personalization. Beck identified a number of other cognitive distortions, including dichotomous "all-or-nothing" thinking (assuming there are only two polarized outcomes), magnification ("catastrophizing") or minimization (dismissing the implications of some event), selective abstraction (using a "mental filter" to focus on one particular detail while neglecting other details or the broader context), overgeneralization (making an assumption based on one or a few experiences), and emotional reasoning (assuming one's subjective feelings are an objective reflection of reality; e.g., "I feel bad; therefore, I must be bad"). The content of an individual's automatic thoughts serves to reinforce broader, more implicit beliefs. Beck labeled these beliefs as *schemas*, which may include intermediate beliefs and core beliefs. Intermediate beliefs are assumptions individuals hold about themselves or others (e.g., "I will likely make a fool of myself"), while core beliefs are general, often unconscious beliefs, which form the foundation of individuals' cognitions (e.g., "I am inadequate").

In CT, Beck sought to intervene primarily at the level of automatic thoughts with the purpose of eventually revealing and adjusting deeper schemas. To identify automatic thoughts and cognitive distortions, clients are often asked to trace their thought processes and content in session, or complete thought logs as homework, which are then reviewed in session. Once clients can identify and recognize their distorted thinking patterns, they are overtly challenged (e.g., "What's the evidence the person was laughing at you specifically?") and replaced with more accurate, helpful, and adaptive thinking patterns (e.g., "that person may have been laughing at me, but they could have just as easily been laughing at someone else, or perhaps no one at all"). Over time, and especially through the completion of thought logs, clients gain mastery of *cognitive restructuring*, and can identify and alter their maladaptive cognitions within their day-to-day lives. CT interventions, which tend to be manualized, have been shown to be efficacious in the treatment of depression (Hollon, 2003), anxiety disorders (Dobson, 2010), and a variety of other psychiatric disorders, such as bulimia nervosa (Shapiro et al., 2007). CT approaches extend beyond the treatment of mental health symptoms; for example, interventions in correctional settings that aim to reduce thought patterns that lead to criminal behavior have become standard (e.g., *Thinking for a Change*; Bush et al., 1997). Elements of CT also underlie a number of new wave approaches such as acceptance and commitment therapy (ACT) and dialectical behavior therapy (DBT), which are discussed in some detail in the text that follows.

Ellis' Rational Emotive Behavioral Therapy

Similar to Beck's CT, Albert Ellis' *rational emotive behavioral therapy* (REBT; Ellis, 1993) focuses therapy on altering individuals' patterns of thinking, deciding, and doing. Relatedly, it is assumed individuals' emotions stem from their *beliefs* about specific situations, and not the specific situations themselves. Ellis also emphasized the need to correct beliefs that were *irrational*, rather than simply unhelpful (as was often the case with Beck). To do this, Ellis' REBT approach uses a more straightforward and didactic approach than Beck's CT, and involves directly confronting and challenging individuals' irrational beliefs and dysfunctional attitudes. Ellis also considered the manner in which fixed and rigid thinking patterns play into irrational beliefs. For example, Ellis stipulated that clients' use of "must" and "should" language (what Ellis termed "musturbatory thinking") was directly responsible for the development of irrational beliefs. In further diverging from Beck, Ellis' REBT approach is more amenable to incorporating behavioral interventions because it encourages clients to choose a course of action that is more consistent with their core values and one that will lead to more desirable outcomes (Ellis, 1995). REBT has been shown to be efficacious for a variety of clinical concerns, such as depression, anxiety, anger management, and health-related behaviors (David et al., 2017).

Acceptance and Commitment Therapy

Relatively speaking, ACT is a more recent psychotherapeutic approach pioneered by Steven Hayes (Hayes et al., 1999) that uses a mindfulness-based approach to enhance clients' *psychological flexibility* (i.e., "be present, open up, and do what matters"; Harris, 2009, p. 12), and subsequently help them lead a more effective and value-consistent life. Although specific protocols vary, ACT generally contains six modules, with the first four grounded in mindfulness: (a) *cognitive defusion*, or separating oneself from and "giving space" to thoughts, emotions, and feelings; (b) *acceptance*, or allowing thoughts, emotions, and feelings to exist as they are without struggling; (c) *contacting the present moment*, rather than dwelling on the past or worry about the future; (d) *observing the self*, which requires a more transcendent and higher form of mindfulness reflective of one's place in the world. These initial four modules enhance clients' psychological flexibility, and decrease *experiential avoidance* (i.e., "trying to avoid, get rid of, suppress, or escape from unwanted 'private experiences'"; Harris, 2009, p. 23), which empowers healthy living. Once clients have gained psychological flexibility and are thus effectively "in touch" with themselves and their lived experiences, ACT interventions progress to the remaining modules, (e) discovering client *values* and (f) enacting *committed action* consistent with those values. Meta-analyses have shown ACT to be efficacious in the treatment of depression and anxiety, among other disorders (Hacker et al., 2016). Furthermore, studies have revealed similar improvement in symptom reduction for ACT compared to more traditional CBT for anxiety-related disorders (Arch et al., 2012) and depression (Ruiz, 2012).

Dialectical Behavior Therapy

DBT was developed by Marsha Linehan (2015) for the primary purpose of treating clients with borderline personality disorder (BPD). However, DBT-related skills may be used for other purposes. DBT is grounded in the biosocial theory of BPD, which stipulates that a consistent pattern of invalidation in the environment, coupled with a biological predisposition toward emotion dysregulation, leads to pervasive difficulties in managing or regulating emotions for individuals with BPD (Crowell et al., 2009). Thus, DBT strives to help clients relearn responses to emotionally charged situations by embracing dialectics (i.e., holding two seemingly contradictory ideas simultaneously) as a worldview. For example, clients experiencing emotional volatility may begin to understand they can experience feelings of both love and hatred at the same moment. This dialectical approach to therapy is fully incorporated into the DBT protocol, which also includes skill-building modules related to mindfulness, interpersonal functioning, emotion regulation, and distress tolerance. A DBT protocol typically includes regular individual therapy, group therapy for skills training, and telephone coaching for real-world problems. Research has shown DBT-related interventions to be efficacious for the treatment of BPD (Kliem et al., 2010) and suicidal behavior (Panos et al., 2014). Recent reviews have also found some evidence for the use of DBT to treat bipolar disorders (B. D. M. Jones et al., 2023).

Trauma-Focused Therapies Grounded in Cognitive Behavioral Therapy

A number of CBT-related interventions have been developed specifically for treating symptoms related to posttraumatic stress. In prepping for the exam, three of the more prevalent approaches are discussed in the text that follows.

Prolonged exposure (PE) therapy is a primarily behavioral intervention designed to alleviate posttraumatic stress disorder (PTSD) symptoms by exposing clients to progressively more upsetting thoughts, memories, flashbacks, and other trauma triggers (Foa et al., 2007). PE is based on the principles of systematic desensitization (Wolpe, 1961), where clients construct a *fear hierarchy* outlining the progression of distressing stimuli and fears specific to the individual, before being counterconditioned to an incompatible response (e.g., relaxation). PE usually offers a manualized application of these principles. Following the construction of a fear hierarchy, the PE therapist guides clients through both *imaginal exposure* (i.e., thoughts, memories, or mentally reexperiencing events) and, whenever feasible, *in vivo exposure* (i.e., exposure to real-life situations and physical stimuli which may potentially trigger symptoms), ultimately working all the way through the fear hierarchy. Throughout the protocol, clients are instructed to complete exposures as homework, as well as engage in healthy self-care activities. Through this approach, clients are counterconditioned to learn that previously triggering stimuli are not, in fact, dangerous. Or, triggering stimuli at least have a low probability of being dangerous again (for example, understanding that most car rides will not result in a serious accident). Skills related to relaxation inducement are also often taught in PE to help moderate stressful reactions in clients (see section on Relaxation Training). Research has supported the effectiveness of PE in the alleviating of PTSD symptoms (Powers et al., 2010), although attrition is relatively common with this approach. Good PE therapy should also include adequate preparation in which the therapist thoroughly explains the process, lays out a plan for dealing with immediate stress or more serious symptoms (e.g., feeling suicidal), and ensures client understanding.

Cognitive processing therapy is a manualized intervention developed for the treatment of PTSD that has a stronger emphasis on cognitions compared to PE. In this approach, PTSD-related trauma is thought to produce strong, maladaptive changes in clients' emotions and cognitions. In response, clients tend to avoid these thoughts and emotions, which prevents them from effectively processing the traumatic event. Clients are first introduced to this model of PTSD, as well as the general cognitive model in the form of psychoeducation, and are then given opportunities to understand their own thinking and potential cognitive distortions. Written narratives are used to help clients process their trauma and related event(s). Upon having clients read these narratives out loud, therapists assist clients to identify the *stuck points* (i.e., cognitive distortions) that are preventing them from adaptively processing their traumatic event. Clients also write *impact statements* to explore ways in which their trauma may have impacted their broader beliefs related to safety, trust, power and control, esteem, and intimacy. These impact statements are similarly processed and stuck points are modified where appropriate to enable clients' healthy processing of their traumatic experience.

Lastly, *trauma-focused cognitive behavioral therapy* (TF-CBT) is a treatment approach that was originally designed to address trauma-related symptoms (specifically about sexual abuse) among children, adolescents, and their nonoffending parents and caregivers (Cohen et al., 2006). By using individual and joint sessions for both the child and caregiver, clients are led through the components of TF-CBT, which follow the acronym PRACTICE: **P**sychoeducation and **P**arenting skills, **R**elaxation, **A**ffective expression and regulation, **C**ognitive Coping, **T**rauma narrative development and processing, **I**n vivo exposure, **C**onjoint parent–child sessions, and **E**nhancing future safety and development (Cohen et al., 2006). These components may be highly tailored and individualized to meet the specific needs of both the children and their caregivers.

Importantly, specific interventions designed to process and overcome the impacts of trauma are not the same as trauma-informed care (TIC). TIC is a set of principles that help trauma survivors feel safer in a space and reduce the risk of retraumatization. TIC can be applied in almost any context and is not specific to a brand of therapy. In fact, a client does not need to be involved in a trauma-focused therapy protocol to benefit from TIC. TIC also does not require specialized training to implement, as would be required for the interventions we discussed so far. TIC may include asking clients about lighting preferences, not touching clients without asking permission, or calmly informing clients if you are walking behind or past them. While evidence regarding the direct impacts of TIC on psychologic outcomes is promising, rigorous research is currently lacking (Fernández et al., 2023; Han et al., 2021).

Other Interventions Based on Cognitive Behavioral Therapy

More behaviorally based principles of learning may also be included with CBT interventions. *Behavioral activation* (BA), developed primarily for the treatment of depression, views depression as resulting from a lack of positive reinforcement, and therefore aims to increase clients' opportunities for reinforcement within their environment (Jacobson et al., 2001). BA typically involves the self-monitoring of moods, identification of avoidance tendencies, and a commitment to engaging in alternative actions aimed at enhancing positive emotional experiences. The subsequent positive changes in mood are recorded by the client, who can then appreciate the utility of engaging in certain actions, even (and especially) when feeling depressed. BA has been shown to be similarly efficacious in alleviating depressive symptoms compared to both CT and medication (Dimidjian et al., 2006; Richards et al., 2016).

Based on classical conditioning theory, *stimulus control* refers to interventions that alter a pattern of behavior by adjusting the stimulus–response relationship. This may take on many forms. For example, a person addicted to alcohol who craves a drink when he drives past a liquor store on his way home from work may be instructed to take a different route home. In this way, he may avoid the stimulus associated with craving alcohol, and therefore be less likely to drink. Similarly, someone with insomnia may be instructed to keep time spent in her bedroom reserved only for sleep and not any other activity. Strengthening the association between her bedroom and sleep (and breaking the ones between all other activities like scrolling through social media) will increase her ability to fall asleep more quickly. In fact, this approach has demonstrated evidence of efficacy in treating sleep disorders (Morin et al., 2006).

Found to be efficacious for the treatment of anxiety and panic-related symptoms (Bernstein et al., 2000), *relaxation training*, which is based on *progressive muscle relaxation*, involves teaching skills to reduce tension and thereby induce feelings of relaxation. While encouraging *diaphragmatic breathing* (i.e., deep breathing involving the expansion of the diaphragm, rather than the chest), individuals are instructed to alternate between tensing and relaxing different muscles and muscle groups, and to concentrate on the differing physical sensations between these two states. Over time, alternating between the tensing and relaxing of specific muscles is consolidated into fewer and fewer muscle groups, until clients can broadly induce feelings of relaxation on their own, which can be utilized in response to stress-inducing stimuli.

Although CBT has been a dominating force in psychotherapy that has transcended clinical presentations and care settings, it is worth recognizing that most research on CBT effectiveness has included White participants (see Horrell, 2008). More recently, researchers and clinicians are exploring cultural adaptations of CBT to better treat clients from historically marginalized identities (Naeem, 2019). For example, attempting to restructure someone's thoughts related to experiences of racism or sexism is likely to be invalidating and reinforce feelings of oppression. CBT approaches have also been criticized for being too manualized and prescriptive (Gaudiano, 2008); however, they are not incompatible with other styles of therapy, such as the humanistic theories we discuss next.

HUMANISTIC AND EXISTENTIAL THEORIES

Considered the "third wave" of psychotherapy, existential and humanistic therapies initially emerged as a response to the deterministic approaches of psychoanalysis and behaviorism, which saw humans as having little control over their fate. These forms of therapy share a more optimistic view of human behavior and intentions, and focus on the here-and-now, rather than one's childhood or other past events.

Maslow's Theory of Self-Actualization

Abraham Maslow (1954) is best known for his *hierarchy of needs*, which are essentially the steps necessary for progressing toward self-actualization. For Maslow, *physiologic needs* (e.g., food, water) are the most fundamental, followed by *safety needs* (e.g., security, stability), needs of *love and belonging* (e.g., friendship, intimacy), needs of *esteem* (e.g., success, recognition), and finally *self-actualization*, where individuals realize their full potential. Additionally, Maslow believed lower needs must be fully satisfied before moving on to higher needs. Therapy that incorporates Maslow's theory focuses on progressing clients through the hierarchy to achieve and maintain a state of actualization.

Rogers' Person-Centered Therapy

Carl Rogers (1961), the founder of psychotherapy research and of *person-centered therapy* (PCT), saw human beings as having the inherent capacity to grow and be happy if the appropriate needs and conditions were met. According to PCT, psychopathology develops when clients have only been accepted by others in certain, specific circumstances (i.e., *conditions of worth*). The therapist in PCT strives to provide the client with *unconditional positive regard* (i.e., absolute acceptance of the client, regardless of what they say or do) and *accurate empathy* (i.e., genuine recognition and understanding of the client's lived experience), by reflecting clients' feelings, thoughts, and understandings of their own experiences. Ultimately, the goal of PCT is to provide the client with a *corrective emotional experience*, by altering previously held conditions of worth. In this manner, clients in PCT grow toward greater *congruence*, meaning their self-concept is compatible with their personal experience, and healthy self-directed growth is made possible. Many of Rogers' principles, such as his emphasis on the working alliance and openness between client and therapist, are considered to be necessary basic elements of successful therapy, regardless of the specific brand of treatment used.

Existential Therapy

Emphasizing a philosophical rather than a technical approach to therapy, *existential therapy* strives to increase clients' awareness by moving toward authenticity, confronting normal "existential anxiety" (i.e., worry about one's purpose or meaning in life), and increasing clients' understanding of the freedom and responsibility to live their lives (G. Corey, 2009). Existential therapy emphasizes larger concerns (e.g., meaning of life and existence), as opposed to short-term, immediate problems. Key figures in existential therapy include Viktor Frankl, Rollo May, James Bugental, and Irvin Yalom.

Gestalt Therapy

Gestalt therapy (GT), developed by Fritz Perls, is a phenomenological approach that views clients holistically by attending to clients' in-the-moment thoughts, feelings, behaviors, and environment. More specifically, GT is based on field theory, which stipulates that an individual should be viewed as a part of their specific yet constantly changing environment. For Gestaltists, a client cannot be understood apart from their given context(s). The goal is for clients to become aware of who they are; only when clients are truly themselves can they effect change (this phenomenon is known as the *paradoxical theory of change*). Thus, Gestalt therapists help clients live authentically, in the present, to enact a healthy and natural process of psychological growth and maturation.

Rather than helping clients reach their full potential in life, like the humanists, both existentialists and Gestaltists focus on helping clients find meaning in life. While both existential therapy and GT share other key similarities (e.g., present focus, emphasis on authentic living), GT is differentiated by its emphasis on specific techniques associated with the theory. For example, in the *empty chair technique*, clients will speak to an empty chair that they imagine is occupied by a specific person to effectively process their thoughts and emotions surrounding their relationship to that person. Conversely, existential therapy is better conceptualized as a general approach to therapy, rather than consisting of any specific techniques, like those found in GT.

Feminist Therapy

Inspired by second-wave feminist social activism in the 1960s and 1970s, *feminist therapy* (Conlin, 2017) seeks to apply principles from this movement to counseling and therapy. Feminist therapy posits that "the personal is political," as problems are viewed within a sociopolitical and cultural context. Clients' intersecting identities (e.g., gender, race, class, sexual orientation, etc.) are seen through a lens of privilege and oppression; therefore, feminist therapy emphasizes the importance of social activism, both on the part of the therapist and the client, who becomes empowered through the process of therapy. To facilitate this empowerment, the therapeutic relationship within feminist therapy is characterized by egalitarianism, with the goal of minimizing power imbalances that may easily occur in a therapist–client relationship. Adaptations of feminist therapy have also been applied to specific subgroups or women, usually focusing on racial or ethnic factors (e.g., L. V. Jones & Guy-Sheftall, 2017; Malone, 2000).

Reality Therapy

Grounded in choice theory, which posits all behavior is chosen (i.e., Total Behavior), *reality therapy* emphasizes clients' own role and responsibility in shaping their lives. Rejecting the notion of traditional mental illness, William Glasser (2011) believed all "symptoms" of mental illness were essentially misguided attempts at meeting clients' needs, especially their goals centering on personal relationships. For example, rather than acknowledging "depression," a client would be conceptualized as "choosing to depress." Glasser identified five basic needs (i.e., survival, love and belonging, power/achievement, freedom/independence, and fun) that each exist to a certain degree for all individuals, and an ideal arrangement of these needs would make up an individual's *quality world*, or their ideal life. In therapy, clients evaluate what they want in their reality and whether or not their current actions are bringing them closer to or further away from their goals. Reality therapy is really more of a crossover between humanistic theories and CBT, as it also requires clients to identify and take control over their thoughts, feelings, and behaviors.

Motivational Interviewing

A more recent addition to the humanistic school of psychotherapy is *Motivational Interviewing* (MI), which is a style of counseling developed by Bill Miller and Steve Rollnick (2013) aimed at *eliciting* clients' own internal motivation to change. Acknowledging Carl Rogers' values of empathy, warmth, compassion, and congruence, MI attempts a more directive approach than Rogers' PCT by reinforcing clients' *change talk*, and guiding clients toward developing discrepancy between their personal values and actions. In this way, MI also incorporates elements of CBT. MI further attempts to reinforce clients' autonomy, while maintaining a collaborative partnership in therapy. The therapist's approach in MI is largely dependent on which stage of change a client happens to inhabit: precontemplation, contemplation, preparation, action, or maintenance (Prochaska & DiClemente, 1982). Overall, the spirit of MI is characterized by the four principles of compassion, collaboration, evocation (i.e., eliciting clients' own motivations for change), and acceptance. The latter component of acceptance can be further broken down into acknowledging clients' *absolute worth*, respecting their *autonomy*, *affirming* clients' strengths and efforts, and using *accurate empathy*. MI has been found to be efficacious for problems related to substance use, gambling, and encouragement of healthy behaviors, as well as addressing issues related to a lack of treatment adherence and motivation (Lundahl et al., 2010).

FAMILY AND SYSTEMS THERAPIES

Many psychologists work with couples and families, and therefore a basic understanding of family systems therapy and processes is expected for the EPPP. In this section, two foundational theories, as well as three common approaches to therapy, are discussed. It should also be noted that, in practice, these therapies and approaches are often blended in the delivery of therapy, rather than used separately. For the purposes of this review, however, these approaches will be discussed distinctly.

Systems Theory

Systems theory views the family as consisting of a dynamic pattern of interpersonal relationships and inter-related interactions (Carr, 2016; Hecker et al., 2015). In this manner, the family is viewed as greater and more complex than any one person (i.e., the family is "greater than the sum of its parts"). Furthermore, the family tends to maintain *homeostasis* or keep things the way they are. This tendency is greater in families that emphasize negative feedback (e.g., punishment, discipline) as opposed to positive feedback (e.g., encouragement in new endeavors).

A family may be viewed as an *open system* when the tendency toward homeostasis is low and it is able to adaptively interact with its environment. An open family system can evolve and reenergize based on interactions with others who exist outside of the family system. Conversely, a *closed system* is characterized by boundaries, rules, and norms which are inflexible and rigid. A closed family system typically leads to maladaptive functioning and disordered interactions (both within and outside of the family) and is generally resistant to growth and change.

Communication Theory

Originally derived from the field of mathematics, *communication theory* examines the manner in which information is transmitted and processed through human communication (Anderson, 1972). According to communication theory, all behaviors within a family are regarded as some form of communication, however subtle the messages given and received may be.

Communication theory emphasizes the importance of understanding power imbalances between the communicator and receiver. A greater imbalance of power is often seen in parent–child relationships; however, even narrower imbalances of power may be associated with power struggles, such as those observed between spouses. Other concepts associated with communication theory include *double-bind communication*, or when aspects of a particular message contradict. For example, a family member's words (e.g., "I love you") may not match their actions (e.g., neglect of family members). *Metacommunication* is the idea that messages contain both explicit and implicit content, the latter of which may match or contradict the former. For example, the explicit content of a message may be belied by an inference of sarcasm or irony in the tone of the speaker.

Murray Bowen's Extended Family Systems Therapy

Regarded as the founder of family systems therapy, Murray Bowen emphasized the importance of assessing relationships between members of the extended family. By constructing a *genogram*, or a structural diagram outlining an individual's extended family and the relative quality of those familial relationships, Bowen sought to identify intergenerational patterns of familial dynamics (passed down through the *multigenerational transmission process*), which could then be addressed directly in the context of therapy. Bowenian therapy is encapsulated by the following interrelated constructs:

- *Differentiation of self* refers to an individual's ability to distinguish between their feelings and thoughts. In the context of family therapy, this concept refers especially to the importance of separating oneself from unhealthy family values and dynamics, while maintaining an appropriate emotional bond.
- *Triangulation* occurs when two individuals show a propensity to involve a third person in managing conflict, which often takes the form of two parents using their child to navigate disputes and occurs more frequently when there is less differentiation of self among family members. Bowen believed the therapist should use triangulation (by using the therapist as the third party) to manage conflict between family members.
- *Nuclear family emotional patterns* are emotional styles that are passed down through generations and are observed directly at the level of the nuclear family.
- The *family projection process* is the tendency for family members to "project" dysfunctional emotional or cognitive patterns on a third party within the family, who may in turn experience greater difficulty in differentiating themselves from this dysfunction.
- *Emotional cutoff* is the response of a family member who attempts to separate entirely from certain other members of the family because of the family projection process. Despite this attempt to separate emotionally, this individual is in fact *more* likely to replicate dysfunctional familial patterns.
- *Sibling position,* or birth order, often leads to projections from other family members based on birth order-related stereotypical assumptions (e.g., the youngest may be assumed to be reckless and irresponsible).
- Bowen understood *societal emotional processes* as society's expectations and prejudices which impact the family itself. For example, families from certain racial or socioeconomic groups may experience unique stressors not found among other families.

Research examining the outcomes of family systems therapy suffers from several methodological and practical constraints (Pote et al., 2003), yet outcome studies are generally supportive of the efficacy of this approach, including in the treatment of substance abuse and conduct-related disorders (Cottrell & Boston, 2002; see also Carr, 2020 for a review).

Salvador Minuchin's Structural Family Therapy

In *structural family therapy* (Minuchin & Fishman, 1981), the therapist seeks to adjust and alter dysfunctional family patterns and dynamics by "joining" the family system as a member. By incorporating both systems theory and communication theory into the therapeutic framework, Minuchin believed that the therapist should learn the rules, messages, and relational dynamics occurring between family members—known as the *family map*—and even adopt these norms as their own to alter the functioning of the family as a system.

Structural family therapy also differentiates *subsystems* within the family, such as the relationships existing between two spouses, the parent and a child, or a child and their sibling. The *family structure*, or manner in which family members interact, tends to be implicit and unspoken. This structure includes rules regarding *boundaries*, which may range from enmeshed to disengaged, which tend to create dependence or isolation, respectively. Issues with boundaries often occur when a subsystem attempts to use a third party to manage conflict (Minuchin, 1974). This may take a variety of forms, such as *triangulation* (e.g., parent attempts to draw child to their "side" during a divorce proceeding, which may be observed as the child rejecting the other parent) or *detouring* (e.g., parents who are unable to navigate their differences focus instead on the deficiencies of the child).

Once a family map has been established, the therapist attempts to restructure maladaptive transactional patterns through various interventions, such as *enactment* (i.e., highlighting interaction patterns through role-play), *blocking* (i.e., forcing a new pattern of behavior by preventing old behavior), and *reframing* (i.e., reinterpreting the meaning of a behavior).

Critics of structural family therapy argue this approach does not adequately account for more nontraditional family structures, or other issues related to gender differences (Vetere, 1992). While key concepts associated with Minuchin's theory have been incorporated into other family therapy approaches, it is less often used as a stand-alone approach (Cottrell & Boston, 2002; Simon, 1995).

Strategic Family Therapy

Jay Haley's *strategic family therapy* (Haley, 1976) approach emphasizes addressing a specific, current problem within the family, which in turn serves to improve the greater functioning of the broader family system. Haley relied on a number of specific interventions, including therapist *directives* (i.e., commands) to members of the family, *reframing* of specific behaviors which may be presently viewed as unacceptable, and *circular questioning*. Circular questioning involves the therapist asking each member of the family the same question about a particular issue, and then comparing responses. This intervention has the effect of allowing family members to broaden their own perspectives of certain issues. Haley's (1976) work also helped form the basis of brief strategic family therapy (BSFT; Szapocznik & Williams, 2000), which further incorporates elements of structural family therapy with a strong cultural emphasis. Research has shown BSFT to be efficacious for the treatment of substance abuse and other behavioral disorders among adolescents (Horigian et al., 2015; Szapocznik et al., 2016).

PSYCHOTHERAPY WITH GROUPS

Given the ability to treat multiple people at once and the benefit of interacting with others who have similar experiences, the practice of group therapy has become increasingly common in the field of psychotherapy. Several key concepts that differentiate group from individual therapy should be understood for the EPPP.

The composition of *psychotherapy groups* may differ based on a number of factors (e.g., age, intelligence, gender, presenting concerns), with the objective of the group ultimately determining the optimal composition. Typically, some degree of homogeneity should be balanced with diversity to ensure group members feel both comfortable in the setting and challenged to handle conflicts. Additionally, groups may be either "open" or "closed," depending on whether new members are accepted (i.e., rolling admission) or membership remains fixed, respectively. The optimal size of groups is typically considered to be between 5 and 10 members, with 7 to 8 being ideal (Yalom & Leszcz, 2008). Because of this, psychotherapy groups are often considered to be a cost-effective, economical form of therapy; yet, others maintain that group therapy offers unique benefits above and beyond savings that are not found elsewhere, including the ability for group members to examine and adjust their interpersonal style in relating to and working with other group members (M. S. Corey et al., 2014).

Theorists have identified several forms of groups (M. S. Corey et al., 2014; Yalom & Leszcz, 2008). *Process groups* are more likely to be open-ended and involve here-and-now processing of issues that group members share on a volunteer basis. *Task groups* are more structured and pertain to the accomplishment of specific tasks (e.g., study groups). Similarly, *psychoeducational groups* involve the specific teaching of psychological skills and information (e.g., parenting, learning about mental illness) and are typically reserved for higher functioning groups. *Group psychotherapy* aims to alleviate current psychological distress and is most similar to therapy in the traditional sense. Within group psychotherapy is *brief group therapy* (BGT), a structured form of therapy typically lasting 8 to 12 months, which aims to address specific problems, or provide interventions with a specific type of client. BGT has the advantage of cost-effectiveness and is therefore well suited for managed care.

A discussion of group psychotherapy would be incomplete without mentioning the contributions of Irvin Yalom. According to Yalom and Leszcz (2008), effective group leaders can handle conflict and other group dynamics between members, as well as address issues of transference and countertransference. These functions may be managed more effectively when groups include cotherapists, who may offer complementary perspectives and reactions to group dynamics and transferential content. The use of cotherapists may be particularly useful when cotherapists are of different genders, as this dynamic may enrich clients' transferential reactions to separate therapists, as well as provide healthy modeling of opposite-gender interactions. However, cotherapists should be mindful of how to navigate disagreements between cotherapists, especially in earlier group stages, when cohesion has yet to fully develop (Yalom & Leszcz, 2008). Group therapists should also encourage group members to maintain confidentiality of fellow members, both during and after the completion of the group. However, limitations of confidentiality should be noted, as group members are not bound ethically or legally to maintain the confidentiality of other members.

Yalom and Leszcz (2008) identified 11 *therapeutic factors*, or benefits, to group therapy: an installation of hope, universality (recognizing that others experience similar struggles), learning and conveying information, altruism, corrective recapitulation of one's family of origin, development of social skills (e.g., by experimenting with different ways of interacting with others), the opportunity to imitate behavior, processing existential-related concerns (e.g., search for higher purpose), cohesiveness within the group, catharsis, and interpersonal learning (e.g., how to build stronger relationships). Yalom considered these last three factors as most important to group success.

Group therapy also has benefits when used in conjunction with individual therapy, as it provides substantive interpersonal-related content which may be further explored in individual therapy. Concurrent group and individual therapy is standard in DBT protocols for the treatment for BPD. Group therapy without accompanying individual therapy may even present risks. For example, individuals within groups may not experience the same degree of benefits as they would in individual therapy, due to the broader scope of the group format, and less one-on-one attention. Relatedly, social loafing may be more problematic in groups, thus enabling individual group members to avoid interpersonal engagement that would otherwise be beneficial (M. S. Corey et al., 2014).

UNIVERSALLY APPLIED THEORIES OF CLIENT CHANGE

The following sections should be considered within a broader approach to psychotherapy and may (or even should) be applied to a range of treatment modalities.

The Transtheoretical Model

The *transtheoretical model* (TTM), developed by Prochaska and Norcross (2010), is a conceptual model of psychotherapy that attempts to unify seemingly diverging theories of psychotherapy under one universal conceptualization. The TTM recognizes two main *processes of change*: (a) experiential processes, which include the systems of *catharsis* (e.g., corrective emotional experiences) and *consciousness raising* (e.g., psychoeducation, interpersonal feedback); and (b) behavioral processes, which include systems of *conditional stimuli* (e.g., counterconditioning), *contingency control* or contingency management, and *choosing* (e.g., liberation).

The psychotherapeutic interventions contained within these systems also vary by the *stages of change* identified by Prochaska and DiClemente (1982). These stages were discussed earlier in the context of MI and include

1. *Precontemplation*, which is characterized by clients who are defensive, resistant to therapy, and may lack insight into any need for change. Interventions in this stage are less behavioral and may focus more on increasing the client's awareness and motivation for change (e.g., MI).

2. Following the Precontemplation stage is *Contemplation*. Contemplative clients appear ambivalent about change and are actively weighing the pros and cons to enacting changes within their lives. Effective interventions in this stage may include consciousness raising, psychoeducation, and MI.
3. Once clients feel confident and prepared to enact changes, they move on to *Preparation*, where they intend to change their behavior and may actively plan ways in which to act.
4. Clients who are fully prepared to change, and have developed a working plan to do so, progress to *Action*. The Action stage involves more overtly behavioral interventions aimed at enacting changes. Clients in this stage appear motivated and committed to the therapy process.
5. The final stage of change is *Maintenance*, where clients work to sustain the changes made within the Action phase. This stage can be thought of as relapse prevention. Interventions in this phase may appear more consultative with therapy sessions occurring less frequently.

It should also be noted that the stages of change do not always happen linearly; clients often cycle forward and backward across these stages. The TTM emphasizes the need for therapists to tailor their style and interventions to fit the needs of the client based on the client's stage of change.

According to the TTM, the stages of change and the interventions included therein can further be conceptualized across *levels of change*. These levels of change are ordered hierarchically, with higher levels generally requiring longer and more intensive psychotherapeutic interventions. The five levels of change are (a) symptom and situational problems, (b) distorted/maladaptive cognitions, (c) interpersonal conflicts, (d) conflicts within families/systems, and (e) intrapersonal conflicts.

Common Therapeutic Factors

The *common factors approach* to therapy (see Laska et al., 2014) emphasizes the existence of several nonspecific variables, which are pervasive (in differing degrees) across all theories of psychotherapy and are ultimately responsible for the positive changes that occur in psychotherapy. The common factors approach emerged from research suggesting that various diverging forms of therapy ultimately appeared to produce similar outcomes as long as certain elements were present (this finding is known as "The Dodo Bird Effect"; Rosenzweig, 1936). The following are typically regarded as important common factors regardless of therapeutic orientation:

1. Positive expectations, which refer to the therapeutic benefits of clients believing therapy will be effective. This factor highlights the importance of implementing interventions and approaches for specific individuals, who must buy in to the selected approach.
2. The importance of the therapeutic relationship varies across theories. For example, radical behaviorists place relatively little emphasis on the therapeutic relationship, while Carl Rogers' PCT views the relationship itself as the catalyst of therapy. Regardless, at least a positive dynamic between client and therapist is considered necessary for effecting client change.
3. The working (or therapeutic) alliance refers to the quality of the therapist–client relationship. Attempting to match therapist and client characteristics, therefore, may be a useful way to improve the therapy outcomes. This factor also highlights the importance of attending to cultural considerations in therapy. Interestingly, however, while many clients express a preference for therapists who share characteristics such as race and ethnicity, gender, or sexual orientation, there is little substantial evidence demonstrating therapist–client match is associated with the efficacy of psychotherapy. Nevertheless, consideration of matching therapists and clients (based on clients' preferences) may still be clinically appropriate (Bhati, 2014; Cabral & Smith, 2011).

CULTURE-SPECIFIC THEORIES FOR CLIENTS FROM HISTORICALLY MINORITIZED GROUPS

While there are a variety of theories and research on treatment with culturally diverse clients, two main theories are likely to appear on the EPPP. Practitioners may use these models as a way to help conceptualize clients who are experiencing distress related to their identity in a minoritized and/or marginalized group. These models should not, however, be used to stereotype or make assumptions of individual clients and their differing needs.

Ethnic and Racial Identity Development

A common model for explaining ethnic and racial identity development is Atkinson et al.'s (1979, 1989) *minority identity development model* (MID). MID attempts to encapsulate the internal struggle that oppressed groups experience in developing a strong sense of self; it is based on a North American experience. Atkinson and colleagues saw this model as continuous, with its five stages blending or even overlapping. Features of each stage are noted in the list that follows:

1. Individuals in the *conformity* stage perceive the dominant group as more positive. They share the main culture's values and belief system.

2. The *dissonance* stage is a time in which members of a minoritized group alternate between feelings of shame and pride for their cultural identity. Later in this stage, individuals begin to question their conformity to the dominant culture and lifestyle.

3. During the *resistance and immersion* stage, the person rejects the dominant culture in favor of their own culture. People in this stage acknowledge being a victim of racism or xenophobia and take an interest in learning about the history of oppression toward their respective culture; they may also demonstrate a strong dislike for members of the dominate group.

4. In the *introspection* stage, individuals transition from an "all good–all bad" orientation toward understanding cultural differences. Here, they begin to see dominant and minoritized cultures as similarly flawed and are uncomfortable with absolutist viewpoints (e.g., all White people are racist).

5. Finally, in the *synergistic* stage, individuals reach a point of self-fulfillment; they are not only comfortable with who they are, but they are also comfortable with who others are. This stage involves a greater appreciation and respect for multiple cultural groups.

A similar theory that may appear on the EPPP is the **integrated model** proposed by John and Joy Hoffman. This model is unique in that it describes two developmental trajectories for people of color and White people. In the first stage (*conformity*), both groups strive to emulate "Whiteness" because it is perceived to be the preferred culture. However, stages 2 through 5 show diverging patterns. These are briefly outlined in Table 8.1.

The sixth and final stage, *Integrative* awareness, is the same for both groups and is similar to Atkinson et al.'s MID stage 5. The integrated model has also been applied to women's experiences with sexism. Various other stage-based theories have been proposed for Black (e.g., Cross & Fhagen-Smith, 2001) and White people (updated model in Helms, 2014), as well as other specific ethnic groups, including Hispanic people (e.g., Ferdman & Gallegos, 1996), Asian-American (Kim, 1981), Indigenous American (Horse, 2005), and biracial identities (Poston, 1990).

Sexual Minority Identity Development

The first dominant theory to examine sexual minority status was Cass's (1979) *model of homosexual identity formation*. Cass identified six stages by which she believed gay people achieve a sense of pride and commitment to their identity as a sexual minority: (1) identity confusion, (2) identity comparison, (3) identity tolerance, (4) identity acceptance, (5) identity pride, and

TABLE 8.1 Integrated Model of Identity Development

	People of Color	People of White-European Descent
Stage 2	**Dissonance:** discover their minority status is a barrier and White people benefit from privilege	**Acceptance:** dismiss oppression of people from minoritized groups as unique, suggesting that everyone has struggles
Stage 3	**Immersion:** feel angry about racism and see most of dominant group as racist	**Resistance:** insist racism is not problematic and may ascribe to idea of "reverse racism"
Stage 4	**Emersion:** feel they can only belong with people of the same race; avoid contact with White people	**Retreat:** begin to feel shame for not acknowledging privilege and become frustrated with other White people
Stage 5	**Internalization:** realize negative qualities of own racial group; understand White people are not the enemy and racism can be fought against together	**Emergence:** start to understand the benefits of privilege and work to become more self-aware

(6) identity synthesis. Later in the 1980s, Troiden presented a similar, but more condensed, four-stage sociodevelopmental *model of homosexual identity development* (Troiden, 1989). In Trioden's model, homosexual identity formation begins earlier in the life span. The four stages of this model are summarized in the list that follows:

1. *Sensitization* typically occurs prior to puberty and involves the feeling of being different from other same-age peers. At this stage, this difference may not be labeled as sexual in nature or identified specifically as "homosexual."
2. *Identity confusion* is most common during puberty when individuals begin to experience arousal for people of the same sex and may question their sexual orientation. At this stage, there may be feelings of anxiety, guilt, social isolation, and the need for secrecy. This is similar to Cass's stage 1.
3. *Identity assumption* occurs when individuals establish they are, in fact, attracted to the opposite sex. At this stage, people begin to associate more with other people, accept themselves as being queer, engage in sexual experimentation, and may disclose their orientation to significant others. Identity assumption essentially encompasses Cass's stages 3 and 4.
4. *Commitment* represents an integration of one's sexual identity into everyday life. People at this stage openly engage in same-sex or same-gender romantic relationships, more freely disclose their identity to heterosexual others, and participate in advocacy and efforts to reduce stigma. In this final stage, gay people consider their sexual orientation to be a valid and satisfying lifestyle. This stage generally maps onto Cass's fifth and sixth stages; however, "identity pride" (stage 5) encompasses more of a divided worldview into "gay" versus "not gay," where individuals may assume a confrontational or oppositional position with heterosexual culture.

While potentially useful in understanding sexual identity development and the coming out transition, these theories have been criticized for failing to acknowledge the continuum of sexual orientation (i.e., they still ascribe to a binary classification of gender); the potential differences across, and even within, subgroups of minoritized sexual orientations; and the role other aspects of a person's identity (e.g., racial, ethnic, socioeconomic class) may play in this process (e.g., Kenneady & Oswalt, 2014). Some newer theories have also been posited to help explain and understand transgender identity development (Devor, 2004; Doyle, 2022).

ADJUNCTIVE AND SELF-DIRECTED INTERVENTIONS

In addition to various traditional psychotherapeutic approaches, clinicians are also encouraged (when clinically indicated) to incorporate various adjunctive interventions with clients. These interventions may be sought in addition to more formal psychotherapy, after formal psychotherapy (as a measure to maintain successful outcomes), or to address a separate issue altogether.

The nature of these interventions may vary widely. As a well-known example, Alcoholics Anonymous (AA; and other such groups like Narcotics Anonymous [NA]) offers individuals the opportunity to meet regularly and discreetly with others who experience similar alcohol-related issues. Research appears to support regular attendance of AA meetings as efficacious in preventing relapse (Humphreys et al., 2014). However, some clients may feel uncomfortable with the spiritual/religious components of AA/NA membership. More broadly, support groups in general may offer clients opportunities to gain therapeutic benefits from supportive peer relationships. Support groups exist for a wide range of concerns, including problematic eating behaviors (e.g., Weight Watchers), caregiver stress (e.g., for older adult family members, or relatives with dementia), and parent stress (e.g., raising a child with a clinical diagnosis). These interventions offer clients an opportunity to increase appropriate social support, which may be helpful in achieving benefits to overall mental health.

Adjunctive interventions may also have a strong cultural component. For example, clients with differing cultural beliefs and backgrounds may benefit from the therapist explicitly viewing their culture as a strength. This may take the form of using a client's own religion and spirituality as a means of achieving therapeutic gains (Asnaani & Hofmann, 2012). Psychoeducation, either delivered through the therapist or through self-help resources, may also provide an important component to achieving therapeutic gains. Psychoeducation can be used to educate family members about specific issues involving clients, as well as for educating clients themselves regarding the nature of their presenting concerns. Psychoeducation may also empower clients to be active in their own therapy.

STRENGTHS- AND PERFORMANCE-FOCUSED THEORIES

There are a number of intervention models grounded in psychological principles and theories that do not exclusively target individuals with mental health problems. Instead, these interventions focus on existing strengths and abilities to enhance the performance of individuals, groups, and organizations. Three main areas will be covered in this next section: (a) positive psychology, (b) industrial and organizational psychology, and (c) sport and exercise psychology.

POSITIVE PSYCHOLOGY

The positive psychology movement gained attention in the early 2000s through the work of Martin Seligman. Seligman believed clinical psychology had become overly committed to the disease model of psychopathology, where treatment was largely designed to remedy some problem area (Seligman & Csikszentmihalyi, 2000). Disturbed by the "you're broken, let's fix you" mentality, Seligman sought to promote a strengths-based approach to psychotherapy. According to the webpage of the Positive Psychology Center at the University of Pennsylvania, where Dr. Seligman is the director, positive psychology "is the scientific study of the factors that enable individuals and communities to thrive. The field is founded on the belief that people want to lead meaningful and fulfilling lives, to cultivate what is best within themselves, and to enhance their experiences of love, work, and play" (n.d., "Welcome"). Positive psychologists understand that the way in which people define their best selves and their happiness is subjective. However, positive psychology does not mean pathology, distress, and human suffering are not relevant; rather, proponents of positive psychology advocate for a more balanced viewpoint when conceptualizing clients and developing a course of action. Primary goals of positive psychology are to relieve pain while increasing happiness (Seligman et al., 2005) and build resilience (Gable & Haidt, 2005).

To guide assessment and intervention based on positive psychology theory, Seligman and colleagues empirically identified six relatively culture-free strengths with 24 corresponding virtues that enable a person to thrive in their respective environments (Peterson & Seligman, 2004). These are:

- wisdom and knowledge (creativity, curiosity, open-mindedness, love of learning, and perspective);
- courage (authenticity, bravery, persistence, and zest);
- humanity (kindness, love, and social intelligence);
- justice (fairness, leadership, and teamwork);
- temperance (forgiveness, modesty, prudence, and self-regulation); and
- transcendence (appreciation of beauty, gratitude, hope, humor, and religiousness).

The virtue of religiousness deserves some further clarification, as it does not imply people who follow formal religious practices are necessarily happier or better adjusted than those who do not. In this context, religiousness may be defined as having a clear set of beliefs about the purpose and meaning of life. Detailed explanations of each strength and its virtues can be found in *Character Strengths and Virtues: A Handbook and Classification* (Peterson & Seligman, 2004). For the exam, it may be helpful to be able to recognize these traits as belonging to the positive psychology literature base.

Based on the assumptions that happiness is correlated with other positive outcomes (e.g., reduced depression, better social adjustment), and that psychotherapy can be a mechanism for engendering client happiness, several intervention strategies have been developed to be consistent with positive psychology theory. So-called positive psychology interventions (PPIs) have shown promise. One study that examined client acceptability of a 10-session PPI program compared to a CBT-based intervention for depression found that both treatment groups were highly attended, but that the PPI participants rated their satisfaction with treatment significantly higher than the CBT group (Lopez-Gomez et al., 2017). Another randomized-controlled study among cardiac patients showed that, while posttreatment effects did not differ, those who were exposed to PPIs had greater long-term improvements on measures of happiness, hope, and depressive symptoms (Nikrahan et al., 2016). PPI has even been successfully applied in reentry programs for people in prison (Huynh et al., 2015). PPI often includes exercises in self-acceptance, assertive communication, gratitude, and mindfulness with continued positive reinforcement of practiced skills. For example, clients may be asked to complete an autobiographical story or self-addressed letter outlining personal strengths, journal daily positive affirmations, or role-play effective communication of complaints and desires. PPI may also incorporate elements of CBT such as cognitive restructuring to overcome perfectionistic self-ideals or other maladaptive thought patterns.

INDUSTRIAL AND ORGANIZATIONAL PSYCHOLOGY

Though industrial and organizational psychology has been jointly dubbed "I-O" psychology for their overlapping emphases, each side refers to a slightly different way in which psychology is applied to work and the workplace. I/O psychology is a recognized specialty within the American Psychological Association (Division 14).

Industrial Psychology

Industrial psychology is like human resources (it is sometimes referred to as human resources psychology)—it focuses on how to increase an industry's efficiency and effectiveness through its employees. There are four primary focal points in industrial psychology, and it is very common for a question about them to appear on the exam. *Job or work analysis* is essentially the process of creating a good job description to guide the hiring process (i.e., personnel selection) and subsequent evaluation of the employee. Sanchez and Levine (2013) offer a more comprehensive definition: "Job analysis is made up of a set of systematic methods aimed at explaining what people do at work and the context in which they do it, understanding the essential nature and meaning of their role in an organization, and elucidating the human attributes needed to carry out their role" (p. 711). Job analyses can either be job-oriented, such that it focuses on which duties are intrinsic to the job (i.e., what is the employee expected to do?) and/or person-oriented, such that it focuses on what personal traits, skills, or abilities are best suited for the job (this may be abbreviated as KSAO—**k**nowledge, **s**kills, **a**bilities, **o**ther characteristics—or simply KSA; King, 2014). As alluded to in Sanchez and Levine's definition, this process is more complex than it may initially seem. Employers should not simply list the responsibilities and job qualities based on instinct or what they think sounds right; rather, job analyses require formal information gathering from multiple data sources including, but not limited to, people who supervise that position, people who have held that position, specialized job analysts, or other third parties. In addition, there may be ethical or legal considerations when formulating a job analysis. For instance, jobs that require heavy lifting may inherently exclude more women from consideration, while jobs that require a good fashion sense may exclude many men (obviously, these examples are highly gender stereotyped, but they are only to illustrate the point). The American Disabilities Act (ADA) of 1990 also restricts employers' ability to refuse work to someone with a physical or mental disability. Importantly, those who are covered by the ADA cannot be denied employment or promotion if they are able to perform essential functions of the job, even if other less essential functions cannot be performed. Further, employers are required to provide reasonable accommodations (e.g., policy changes, workspace modifications) whenever possible.

Based on a thorough job analysis, employers can then search for the best person to fit the position; this is known as *employee or personnel selection*. Again, this process is likely more complicated than might be imagined. Industrial psychologists have examined several strategies that are often used to select the most effective employee from the applicant pool. These include testing, interviews, and work samples. *Testing*, of course, involves more formal evaluation of a candidate's KSAOs. Some employers conduct cognitive ability and/or standardized psychologic testing to assess intelligence, personality traits, or screen for other job-related factors such as motivation, temperament, or interests. The military and police departments commonly use these types of tests to determine fitness for duty. Other types of job selection tests include integrity tests, where applicants are asked questions to determine how likely they are to be honest in the workplace, and situational judgment tests, where applicants are asked to describe how they would handle a hypothetical scenario (King, 2014). As an example of the latter, because all staff are considered correctional officers first, predoctoral internship sites within the Federal Bureau of Prisons require applicants to answer situational judgment questions. These can range from how to properly search a room for contraband to appropriately resolving an incarcerated person's attack on a fellow staff member.

Work samples or exercises are similar to situational judgment tests in that they assess a person's problem-solving or decision-making abilities. However, instead of asking a candidate to simply describe what they would do in each situation, work samples require the candidate to show off actual work products (e.g., a photographer's portfolio) or perform a mock job task. Drawing again from the authors' experience, the prison internship interview also included a work exercise in which applicants watched a prerecorded video of two adults in custody engaging in a conflict and were instructed to complete a mock incident report. Other examples include the "in the basket" test (candidates organize and prioritize potential job tasks), the "business game" (candidates navigate a simulated business transaction), and leaderless group exercises (candidates are observed in a peer decision-making task).

Interviews are the most common method of evaluating a potential job candidate. Anyone reading this chapter has likely been through the process of a job interview. Many job interviews are structured in nature, meaning the questions are specific and asked in a systematic manner with the goal of honing the person's abilities and qualities that are directly related to job performance (King, 2014). As King notes, structured interviews (as opposed to unstructured or informal interviews) have the benefit of placing all applicants on equal grounding, as each person is exposed to a standardized set of questions.

The process of selecting the most optimal person for the job often involves some combination of interviewing, testing, and work samples or exercises. In fact, applicants may be asked to go through a particular sequence or set of tasks during the hiring process. The following selection models may be applied when multiple tasks or criterion measures are used to evaluate job candidates: (a) multiple cutoff, (b) multiple hurdle, and (c) multiple regression. When multiple cutoff is used, applicants must obtain at least a minimum score across all designated criterion measures; that is, an applicant will only be considered for the job if all the minimum qualifications are met. Multiple hurdle is similar to multiple cutoff except the minimum criteria for employability are established in stages rather than simultaneously—applicants must pass one "hurdle" to make it to the next. For example, an applicant may need to demonstrate basic interpersonal skills via a phone interview before being invited to interview on-site. Multiple hurdle can be a more efficient and perhaps less costly process, as it weeds out unqualified or subpar candidates earlier in the process. Ultimately, in both multiple cutoff and multiple hurdle, the potential employee must show proficiency across all criterion measures. In multiple regression, on the other hand, an employee's deficits in one domain can be compensated for by high performance on another; thus, it is considered a compensatory model. Like the statistical analysis of the same name, the multiple regression selection model involves assessing applicant qualifications according to known predictors of work performance and then using the applicant's aggregate score across all criteria to determine their probability of job success (Krumm, 2001). The applicant with the highest probability of success should get the job. The obvious downside to this approach is that serious weaknesses could be masked. A clinical psychologist with impeccable organizational skills and intellect likely would not make for a good hire if her ethical decision-making is poor.

Industrial psychology also focuses on *training*. Regardless of how skilled a new employee is, there is likely to be a period of acclimation and on-the-job learning. Typically, this involves orientation to the new workplace, additional formal training, and mentoring. It is important to recognize that employee training is not just for new hires; training for experienced employees and management should be viewed as a continued process. Some research has shown that even more senior level employees can benefit from further education and training (Brown & Sitzmann, 2010). I/O psychologists are often retained as consultants for the development of these programs.

Lastly, industrial psychology is concerned with *performance appraisal*, or the evaluation of an employee's success in performing their job duties consistent with the organization's goals. Performance appraisals not only provide an opportunity to give feedback to employees, but they also assist management in making decisions about promotion or termination. Measures of job performance can be objective (e.g., how many cars were sold in a month) or subjective (e.g., a supervisor's rating of time management). Researchers in industrial psychology often focus on predictors of job success. For the EPPP, a key finding to remember from this literature is that *general cognitive ability* has consistently been found to be the strongest predictor of successful work performance (Ones et al., 2005), even above other psychologic factors such as self-efficacy, optimism, and resilience.

Performance appraisal, especially those based on subjective ratings, are of course prone to bias. One example is the *halo effect* in which a supervisor may judge all aspects of an employee's performance in a similar manner, even though the employee exhibits greater variation across assessment domains. That is, the supervisor's general impressions (good or bad) of the employee color the whole of the assessment. Research has also explored other sources of bias, such as employee-supervisor gender, in rating job performance. Interestingly, one meta-analysis showed little evidence for overall gender biases in performance appraisals (Bowen et al., 2000). One method to mitigate the effect of personal biases is to gather data from multiple sources, often referred to as the 360-Degree Feedback approach. Here, the employee's performance is rated not only by the direct supervisor, but also by other people who are impacted by or familiar with the employee's work (King, 2014). Performance evaluations may be solicited from the employee (self-report rating), peers, subordinates, or customers. In determining academic tenure, for example, other professionals within the field who have no personal or professional relationship with the candidate are typically asked to review the application and provide feedback. However, while one study showed greater discrepancy between raters on work performance (i.e., peer and supervisor ratings were more consistent than self-appraisals), there was little variability within individual ratings across the specific factors assessed (Beerh et al., 2001). Thus, these authors suggest that the 360-Degree Feedback method may not be entirely free of the halo effect.

Organizational Psychology

Organizational psychology, as the name implies, focuses on the organization as a whole, particularly factors affecting the relationships among people within the workplace. Organizational psychologists place less emphasis on the final economic output of the organization and more on the human factors, such as job satisfaction and commitment, that facilitate productivity. One area of interest for organizational psychologists is approaches to *management and leadership*. The EPPP has been known to include questions on various management styles, the most common styles being (a) Theory X, (b), Theory Y, and (c) Theory Z. Theories X and Y were first proposed by Douglas McGregor (1960). Theory X-oriented managers are more pessimistic and view employees as inherently lazy; they typically employ greater external controls over subordinates to motivate productivity. On the other hand, Theory Y-oriented managers work from the assumption that people are generally hard-working; they believe employees can positively contribute to the workplace and encourage employee autonomy and input. One way to remember the difference between these two theories is to picture Theory X bosses with their arms crossed and closed off (in the shape of an "X") and Theory Y bosses with their arms up and open (in the shape of a "Y"). However, little empirical research has been done to substantiate the relationship between these theories of management and job performance. More than 50 years after McGregor's discussion on Theory X and Y, one recent study did show support that managerial attitudes and behaviors more consistent with Theory Y were significantly positively predictive of subordinate and work-group performance (Lawter et al., 2015).

Another well-known model of employee management is William Ouchi's Theory (or Type) Z, which is based on collectivist Japanese ideals; it contrasts with Theory (or Type) A, which is based on individualist American ideals. Specifically, Theory Z involves consensual decision-making, holistic concern, only moderate task specialization, and more informal oversight. Ouchi believed a Theory Z approach would foster employee well-being and thus long-term employment and economic productivity. Conversely, he theorized that Theory A was associated with higher job turnover due to the lack of loyalty and commitment to the organization (Ouchi & Price, 1978). In one of his pivotal texts, Ouchi (1981) discussed how Theory Z could be applied to American companies who, at the time, had drastically fallen behind in global productivity compared to Japanese companies.

A newer model of management was proposed by former CEO of Gallop polling, Donald Clifton (King, 2014), which emphasizes employees' existing strengths. Similar to Theory Y, this management approach is more optimistic in nature. Instead of punishing or firing employees for below-expected performance, supervisors are encouraged to appreciate the unique talents each employee brings to the table and reevaluate the match between the employee's strengths and a given task. One study by Clifton and Harter (2003) surveyed 65 organizations and found only four endorsed a strengths-based approach to management; however, those four showed increases in productivity compared to the other 61 at a rate of about $1,000 per employee. Thus, the take-home message regarding managerial styles seems to be: If employees are given the room to grow and thrive, they will.

Leadership is not necessarily the same as management. That is, workers can assume leadership roles, regardless of where they are in the managerial hierarchy. Take a class project, for example: All students working together are being equally evaluated by the teacher—no one person is considered more senior than the others—yet someone is likely to emerge as the group leader to delegate tasks and oversee their completion. Leaderless groups risk disorganization and poor productivity. In addition, some managers may not be good leaders. Even a well-intentioned Theory Y manager could prove ineffective if they cannot lead their employees through critical incidents such as internal changes (e.g., company mergers), employee conflict, or economic crises. Leadership styles can be categorized in one of two ways: transactional or transformational. In simplest terms, transactional leaders see themselves as the "man in charge"—they give the orders and their employees carry them out. The exchange of ideas is mostly one-way. These leaders closely follow standard operating procedures, rarely challenging the existing paradigm. They tend to lead by enforcing set rules and giving firm directives to subordinates. Transactional leaders are like Theory X managers in that they believe the opportunity for rewards (and threat of punishment) motivates worker performance (King, 2014).

Transformational leaders, on the other hand, are more dynamic and charismatic; rather than sticking with the norm, they aim to make positive changes within an organization. Transformational leaders strive to inspire motivation and good work ethic through modeling, build employee trust in the organization, and encourage innovation and collaboration. These leaders view employees as individuals, not just work horses for the company, and are concerned for their well-being. In fact, a systematic review conducted in 2017 concluded that transformational leadership is positively associated with measures of employee well-being (e.g., feelings of personal accomplishment); however, the author suggested that the strength of this relationship may be conditional (Arnold, 2017), possibly depending on such factors as trust in the leader, leader intelligence, finding meaning from work, sense of belongingness in the workplace, and feelings of burnout or work–life stress. As King (2014) points out, the success of transformational leadership is also dependent on the behaviors of followers. Transformational leaders need employees to buy in to their vision for change. Some research has also examined personality traits that make for a good leader. According to a large meta-analysis of 94 articles, *conscientiousness, extroversion, and openness to experience* were among the strongest predictors of effective leadership (Judge et al., 2002). Not surprisingly, these traits are consistent with the conceptualization of transformational leaders. Neuroticism, however, has been shown to negatively affect leadership (Cavazotte et al., 2012).

Factors that impact *job satisfaction* are another main focal point for organizational psychologists. Job satisfaction has been defined as: "a pleasurable or positive emotional state resulting from the appraisal of one's job or job experiences" (Locke, 1976, p. 1300). Of course, management and leadership styles may relate to job satisfaction. However, the extent to which an employee enjoys their job likely depends on any number of other variables. Some important findings in the literature to remember for the exam are that job satisfaction is related to job turnover, absenteeism, work performance, and organizational citizenship behavior (i.e., employee actions that contribute to the effectiveness of an organization but are not part of formal job responsibilities; Crampton & Wagner, 1994; Judge et al., 2001; Organ & Ryan, 1995). Interestingly, income does not appear to be as important to ratings of job satisfaction as one might think (Dalal, 2013). One meta-analysis showed only a small, but positive relationship between pay and job satisfaction (Judge et al., 2010). This finding was confirmed in a later study examining this relationship (Parker & Brummel, 2016). Rather, it seems that an employee's *perception* of fair pay (i.e., pay satisfaction) may matter more (Cohen-Charash & Spector, 2001).

Organizational psychologists have also examined the role of *commitment to work* in predicting job-related outcomes. Work commitment has been classified into three types: (a) affective/attitudinal, (b) continuance, and (c) normative (Meyer et al., 2004). Affective commitment relates to a worker's emotional attachment to the job. These individuals have a passion for their work and are loyal to the organization because they want to be. Many psychologists feel this type of commitment to their work because of a strong desire to help and advocate for others. While affective commitment is thought to influence a number of positive organizational behaviors (e.g., attendance, longevity), some research suggests affective commitment is only moderately (and nonsignificantly) related to job performance (Riketta, 2002). Employees who are committed to work due to continuance remain with an organization for economic or social reasons—they perceive leaving as too costly (e.g., effort in searching for a new job, relocating, additional training) and thus stay out of need. Lastly, normative commitment refers to a sense of loyalty based on investments the company has already made in the employee. In other words, the employee stays out of obligation. An example would be if an employer agreed to pay for an employee's education or paid off some portion of their student loans.

Other variables of interest to organizational psychologists that will not be covered here include meaning of work, organizational culture (e.g., the impact of aggression and violence in the workplace), role conflict (e.g., work–life balance), job stress and burnout, customer preferences and behaviors, workplace legislation (e.g., sexual harassment laws), and motivation and reward systems (King, 2014). Since the COVID-19 pandemic, a surge of literature has also emerged on the impact of the pandemic on work-related outcomes, particularly in the context of work-from-home and return-to-office policies. One study, for example, found that job satisfaction for those working from home was largely dependent on the availability of a suitable home workspace (Yu & Wu, 2021). Other studies found women experienced significant decreases in work productivity and satisfaction postpandemic onset relative to men (Z. Feng & Savani, 2020).

SPORT AND EXERCISE PSYCHOLOGY

Sport and exercise psychology does not commonly appear on the EPPP; however, it is another recognized specialty area by the APA (see Division 47, The Society for Sport, Exercise, and Performance Psychology). So, while it would be a good idea to have some knowledge about what sport psychologists do, this may be a topic to skim if you are pressed for study time. APA defines sport psychology as: "a proficiency that uses psychologic knowledge and skills to address optimal performance and well-being of athletes, developmental and social aspects of sports participation, and systemic issues associated with sports settings and organizations" (www.apa.org/ed/graduate/specialize/sports.aspx). Sport and exercise psychology may be a concentration within a broader area of psychology, such as clinical or counseling (e.g., University of North Texas, Department of Psychology), or a degree program all on its own (e.g., Florida State University, College of Education). Sports psychologists are also required to pass the EPPP if they want to practice.

In further describing sports and exercise psychology, APA outlines three overlapping principle strategies used within the speciality to address problems faced by athletes, teams, and other sport participants (e.g., coaches, administrators, parents, fans). First, sport psychologists often use basic *cognitive and behavioral skills* training to enhance athletic performance. Examples include helping teams or individuals set performance goals, developing concentration and attention control techniques, or teaching emotional management strategies, sportsmanship behavior, and leadership skills. Second, sport psychologists may rely on *clinical or counseling interventions* to, among other things, enhance athletic motivation, address weight management problems, combat substance use, or help athletes cope with psychologic distress resulting from burnout, injury and rehabilitation, or career transitions (e.g., retirement from sport). Finally, sport psychologists may assist with *consultation and training*. For instance, psychologic approaches may be used to develop team-building exercises, or educate coaches about increasing motivation, fostering interpersonal skills and inclusion among players, or preventing and detecting signs of psychologic strain. Having a foundational knowledge of other disciplines, such as kinesiology and sports medicine, is also relevant to the work of sport and exercise psychologists. Sport psychologists may be hired by individual athletes, teams, schools, or sport organizations (e.g., NCAA, NFL). Applications of sport psychology have also grown to include businesses, where an understanding of group dynamics, leadership, and motivational strategies is useful, as well as other performance-related activities and professions such as dance, music, and even emergency first-responders (Blann et al., 2011).

CAREER COUNSELING THEORIES, ASSESSMENT, AND INTERVENTION

Psychologists are often able to assist clients with concerns related to career decision-making and occupational functioning. Theories and techniques in career counseling frequently appear on the EPPP. For the purposes of this review, seven dominant theories and approaches to career counseling are summarized here.

The *cognitive information processing* (CIP; Sampson et al., 2004) approach conceptualizes career decision-making as a pyramid comprised of three levels. The bottom level addresses "Self Knowledge" (a client's knowledge of their skills, values, and interests) and "Occupational Knowledge" (a client's knowledge of their career-related options). The gap between these two domains is addressed through the *CASVE cycle*, which represents the middle level. The CASVE cycle is a decision-making model involving Communication (i.e., identifying a "gap" between self and occupational knowledge), Analysis (i.e., exploring career options and alternatives; clarifying self-knowledge), Synthesis (i.e., generating options and alternatives, then narrowing down), Valuing (i.e., prioritizing alternatives through cost/benefit analysis), and finally Execution (i.e., creating and committing to a plan for implementing choice). The CASVE cycle loops back to the Communication phase, where the "gap" and the plan to assess the "gap" are reviewed and readdressed. The top level of the CIP pyramid addresses metacognitions and executive processing. This level involves assessing a client's maladaptive cognitions (e.g., self-defeating cognitions; commitment anxiety), which may be impeding their effective career decision-making.

John Holland's Personality and Environmental Typology (1997) proposes a classification system of six types of vocational interests (i.e., R-I-A-S-E-C), which are often represented in a hexagon. These Holland Occupational Themes (or Holland codes) are assessed with clients, typically using measures such as the Self-Directed Search or the Strong Interest Inventory. A Holland code comprised of the three most prominent interests (e.g., S-A-I) is then generated. This code refers to the client's most prominent career-related interests that can be matched to careers that tap into interests and abilities related to the individual's code. It should be noted that interests and abilities represented by these codes may be dissimilar; therefore, a discussion of potential discrepancies between interests and abilities is crucial when applying this approach.

The first R-I-A-S-E-C Holland type is *Realistic*, which refers to work that is mechanical, physical, and "hands-on." *Investigative* pertains to intellectual and scientific pursuits and characterizes individuals who are curious and inquisitive. The *Artistic* code describes individuals who are creative and imaginative and includes work that is more abstract in nature. *Social* is related to many "helping" professions and captures individuals who are more caring and empathetic. The *Enterprising* code describes individuals who are charismatic, ambitious, and entrepreneurial, and includes careers such as business and politics. The sixth Holland code is *Conventional*, which refers to careers that emphasize organization and rule-based work. Related careers include many professions in a structured and/or office setting. Additionally, Holland types which are adjacent to each other on the R-I-A-S-E-C hexagon are more closely related, which is thought to offer a greater consistency of vocational work.

Super's career and life development theory (Super, 1985) emphasizes a more developmental perspective, and acknowledges shifting social roles and situations, which lead to multiple and oftentimes co-occurring self-concepts or *life spaces* (e.g., parent, accountant). These life spaces evolve over the course of the life span. Super identified five main stages of the average life span: *growth* (ages 4–13 years), which involves the accumulation of knowledge related to the self and the possibilities of work; *exploration* (14–24 years), where individuals explore options, weigh alternatives, and implement a career trajectory; *establishment* (25–44 years), where individuals stabilize and advance in their career trajectory; *maintenance* (45–65 years), which is characterized by individuals maintaining their work, and adapting where necessary; and *disengagement* (over 65 years), where individuals slow their work pace until retiring.

Gottfredson's theory of circumscription and compromise (Gottfredson, 2005) emphasizes how individuals manage career options available to them within society, while accounting for their social status and personality variables. Gottfredson identified four developmental processes: (1) cognitive growth, (2) self-creation, (3) circumscription (i.e., elimination of alternatives which conflict with one's self-concept), and (4) compromise. She further described four stages of circumscription: *Orientation to Size and Power* (ages 3–5 years), *Orientation to Sex Roles* (6–8 years), *Orientation to Social Valuation* (9–13 years), and *Orientation to Internal, Unique Self* (14+; may include recognition of R-I-A-S-E-C codes during this stage). In this manner, individuals will narrow down potential career options based on the gradual eliminating of occupational alternatives. Gottfredson also identified three factors in the compromise process: (1) *Truncated Search/Limited Knowledge* is the potential for individuals to limit their options based on which ones are more convenient, less costly, and less time-consuming; (2) *Bigger Investment/Better Accessibility* describes individuals who are more proactive in seeking occupational information, and more likely to take initiative in pursuing their options; and (3) *The Good Enough or Not Too Bad* includes individuals with a tendency to settle for alternatives they deem "good enough." Additionally, according to Gottfredson, individuals are more likely to compromise their interests first, and roles related to sex-type last, when settling for certain alternatives. For example, a woman interested in being a hairstylist is more likely to compromise her interest in hair for, say, a job as a manicurist (both of which are at least in the beauty industry) than to compromise for a job as a hardware salesperson. This is another theory heavily grounded in gender-based stereotypes. Nonetheless, Gottfredson's theory can be credited for considering the development of individuals' interests and preferences, while also recognizing the constraints imposed on them through society.

Krumboltz's two-part learning theory (Krumboltz et al., 1976) first includes the social learning theory of career decision making (SLTCDM), which attempts to account for individuals' decisions to explore certain career paths. Founded on learning more broadly, Krumboltz identified four factors that influence individuals' decisions to pursue certain career paths: (a) genetic endowment/special abilities, (b) environmental conditions/events, (c) learning experiences, and (d) task approach skills (i.e., how different individuals approach certain tasks; e.g., proactive vs. looking for others to lead). It is through the interaction of these four factors that people ultimately decide which career opportunities to pursue. The second aspect of Krumboltz's theory is his learning theory of career counseling (LTCC), which strives to facilitate practitioners' career counseling approach. More specifically, Krumboltz's LTCC encourages practitioners to (a) widen individuals' career-related interests and capabilities, (b) prepare individuals for future changes in their careers and in the workforce, (c) empower individuals to be proactive in their career decision-making, and (d) manage career-related issues more broadly (i.e., beyond merely the selection of an occupation). More recently, Krumboltz (2009) has updated his theory to include the concept of "Planned Happenstance," which places greater emphasis on the inherent unpredictability of career decision-making.

Lent's social-cognitive career theory (SCCT; Lent, 2005) is composed of four models: interest model, choice model, performance model, and satisfaction model. This theory emphasizes the interaction between the environment and individuals' cognitions (e.g., beliefs, expectations, goals, preferences). SCCT aims to explain how individuals develop career-related interests (interest model), make career-related decisions (choice model), and achieve career-related success (performance model) and satisfaction (satisfaction model).

Grounded in postmodern philosophy, *career construction theory* (CCT; Savickas, 2005) advances the theories of Super and Holland by emphasizing how individuals construct their own interpretations of the world and adapt to their specific environments, rather than "discovering" their own career-related values and preferences. Essentially, CCT applies principles of postmodernism to the field of career counseling by highlighting how individuals create meaning and representations of the world, and how this "meaning making" is reflected in individuals' decisions to pursue specific career paths. In this manner, CCT attempts to meet the demands of functioning within a diverse society and a global economy. CCT includes 16 propositions, and is composed of three main tenets (i.e., vocational personality type, career adaptability, and life theme). These tenets enable CCT to create a more nuanced and comprehensive understanding of what, how, and why individuals construct their own unique career-related narratives.

▶ INTERVENTIONS IN HEALTH PROMOTION AND PREVENTION PSYCHOLOGY

Health psychology is an increasingly popular subfield of clinical and counseling psychology that focuses on health promotion and wellness to adaptively manage life stressors and prevent or manage disease and illness. This section will address issues of health promotion, resilience, and risk reduction to improve general wellness. Models of mental health and disease prevention will also be discussed.

HEALTH PROMOTION

As wellness is a primary outcome of interest in this section, it seems necessary to first define it. Cohen (1991) conceptualized wellness as comprising of four components: (a) competence, (b) resilience, (c) social system modification, and (d) empowerment. Competency suggests an individual is doing well considering their current phase of life; this may include good interpersonal skills and problem-solving abilities. Resilience is the ability to maintain healthy mental states or bounce back from stressors. Social system modification is the ability to increase one's social support network (e.g., church, school, work; Cowen, 1991). Finally, empowerment enables people to gain control in their lives to increase wellness (Cowen, 1991).

Because poor physical health has been shown to impact psychological health (McBride et al., 2000), health promotion programs focused on building resilience, reducing risk, and enhancing overall wellness enhancement can help prevent or manage disease or even prolong life (Wu et al., 2012). Health promotion programs may be effective for a variety of populations, such as individuals diagnosed with cancer or experiencing chronic pain. These programs aim to reduce distress and promote healthier lifestyles by allowing patients to receive support from others experiencing similar health concerns (McBride et al., 2000). As an example, Wu et al. (2012) developed a health promotion program for hypertension and high cholesterol that included information on hypertension and high cholesterol (a brochure), information on motivation and importance of self-regulation (DVD), group counseling sessions, exercise support sessions, and a telephone follow up. Those who completed the program had more positive efficacy expectations, outcome expectations, and self-care behaviors (Wu et al., 2012).

Resilience

Resilience refers to an individual's adaptability to adversity, such as trauma and other significant life stressors (Newman, 2005). Resilience acts as a protective factor against stress and helps to increase general wellness. Because resilience is a multidimensional concept and is different from one individual to another, building it can be a complex process (Newman, 2005). Recognizing this challenge, APA initiated a campaign aimed at helping the public learn methods of building resilience (e.g., creating and maintaining healthy relationships, setting goals and working toward them) through workshops, pamphlets, and forums (Newman, 2005). Increasing resilience can be done through community-based interventions such as youth mentorship programs and other community outreach campaigns (Fletcher & Sarkar, 2013). In Bensimon (2012), for example, trait resilience was found to impact the association between trauma, PTSD, and posttraumatic growth. Specifically, while trauma was positively associated with PTSD and posttraumatic growth, higher levels of resilience were negatively associated with PTSD; that is, individuals with higher resilience were less likely to develop PTSD following trauma.

Risk Reduction

Health promotion programs also typically incorporate risk prevention strategies (Cowen, 2000). For example, McBride et al. (2000) showed that individuals diagnosed with cancer experienced less psychological stress when engaging in risk-reducing behaviors such as exercise, maintaining a healthy diet, not smoking, and obtaining sufficient sleep. Byrne et al. (2016) also concluded that the factors most associated with healthy outcomes were eating a low-fat diet, engaging in aerobic exercise, maintaining a nonsmoking status, and obtaining adequate sleep. X. Feng and Astell-Burt (2016) found that risk for psychological distress was decreased when social interactions were increased; however, the types of social interactions that were beneficial differed across men and women. Interactions included increasing telephone calls (more beneficial for men), spending more time with friends and family (more beneficial for women), and living within an hour of people an individual feels they can depend on (X. Feng & Astell-Burt, 2016). Thus, it appears that increasing healthy behaviors and avoiding risky behaviors typically leads to an increase in overall wellness and health.

STAGES OF MENTAL HEALTH PREVENTION

Mental health prevention is a key concept in the subfield of community psychology. Rather than focusing on an individual after the onset of a problem, prevention strategies focus on educating the community-at-large with the goal of reducing the likelihood of a problem developing in the first place. The EPPP has been known to have a question or two on prevention (in fact, such a question appeared on the first author's exam). Thus, for the exam, it will be helpful to understand the difference between primary, secondary, and tertiary prevention stages (Figure 8.1). The

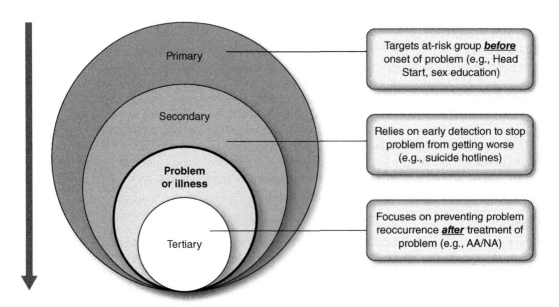

Figure 8.1
AA, Alcoholics Anonymous; NA, Narcotics Anonymous.

distinction between these three can be confusing to remember because primary prevention is actually the furthest away from the onset of the illness or problem, while tertiary is the closest. Think of primary as the *first* and *most preventative* phase in attempting to stop the onset of an undesired outcome. For ease of memory, Figure 8.1 summarizes each of the prevention stages with respective examples.

▶ TECHNOLOGY-ASSISTED PSYCHOLOGICAL SERVICES

Telepsychology, or the use of telecommunication systems (e.g., videoconferencing, mobile apps) to provide psychological services, has become a more normative practice in the field of psychology. Initially, the expansion of telepsychology was largely due to the need to reach more geographically remote clients and help alleviate other barriers to service access (Frueh, 2015). In fact, in a 2013 survey of psychologists, the integration of technology into mental health was predicted to be one of the most expansive advancements in the field by 2022 (Norcross et al., 2013). While telepsychology had already been on the rise, the COVID-19 pandemic, which hit most parts of the world by March 2020, propelled remote psychological services to the forefront as a way to continue providing needed clinical care while preventing the spread of disease (Sammons et al., 2020). Today, telepsychology is a routine method of service delivery for most practitioners (Montoya et al., 2022). Telepsychology has a number of advantages, as well as potential limitations and risks, when compared to traditional in-person provision of psychological services. The practice of telepsychology also poses important ethical and professional considerations for psychologists (see APA, 2013b).

One major benefit of telepsychology is the ability to remotely access psychological services, which in turn increases access of mental health services for individuals who may otherwise have limited or no access. Access to needed services may be limited due to transportation difficulties, certain psychological or medical conditions that reduce mobility, or geographical constraints (Bouchard et al., 2004). Of course, during the pandemic, service access was further limited by the need to adhere to public health safety measures and regulations. Other benefits include increased convenience, cost effectiveness, reduced wait-times for service, and potential improvement to quality of life (McCord et al., 2015). In institutional settings such as prisons or inpatient psychiatric facilities, treatment delivered via telepsychology may reduce issues of safety and security. Alternately, concerns related to telepsychology include technology failures, potential breaches of confidentiality, and challenges related to the therapeutic process itself (e.g., difficulty establishing rapport; APA, 2013b; Baker & Bufka, 2011). However, many of the concerns previously expressed by practitioners have decreased post-COVID onset, although some research suggests attitudes toward telepsychology may depend on practitioners' level of training (Montoya et al., 2022). However, overall, it appears the use of telepsychology for treatment purposes is feasible, acceptable, and can produce outcomes similar to in-person approaches for a variety of client populations (Buckley & Weisser, 2012; Germain et al., 2009; Ruskin et al., 2004). Cullum and Grosch (2013) also argue that psychological assessment is generally reliable when videoconferencing is used. In a recent set of meta-analyses examining treatment and assessment outcomes, Batastini et al. (2021) further established that being in the same physical space as a client seems to make little difference. Similar conclusions have also been found in forensic settings, such as evaluations of competency to stand trial (e.g., Manguno-Mire et al., 2007).

APA (2013b), in collaboration with the Association of State and Provincial Psychology Boards (ASPPB) and the APA Insurance Trust (APAIT), developed the *Guidelines for the Practice of Telepsychology*. These guidelines offer specific suggestions for psychologists who provide telepsychological services above and beyond the general professional ethics code of conduct. Consistent with the general code, psychological providers have an ethical responsibility to only provide services for which they have the appropriate training, education, or experience. In the context of telepsychology, training may include how to determine appropriateness of services to maintain standard care, addressing technical issues, and dealing with crises and emergencies that occur remotely (APA, 2013b).

Informed consent raises some unique challenges when using telepsychology, as logistical barriers may impede the exchange of information, including properly explaining the nature and purpose of the interaction, documenting consent, communicating risks related to confidentiality and security of data and information (which can be heightened with electronic communication), and assessing client understanding (APA, 2013b). Protecting clients' data and information is another core ethical responsibility of mental healthcare providers, and psychologists are expected to minimize the risk of security breaches to the extent possible; for example, by using protected software programs, limiting transmission of confidential data, and implementing procedures to maintain and destroy this data securely (APA, 2013b).

Testing and assessment guidelines further encourage psychologists to evaluate the risks and benefits of providing psychological assessments over telecommunication technologies. Providers must not only determine the appropriateness of the test or assessment to the referral question, but they must also consider the feasibility of administration over remote channels, and the degree to which the integrity of the testing environment and the test itself can be maintained (APA, 2013b). Lastly, because of the potential for services to be provided outside of a provider's jurisdiction (e.g., across state lines), it is important for licensed psychologists to be aware of, and practice in accordance with, the laws and regulations of the state where they are licensed and the state in which the telepsychological service is being rendered (APA, 2013b). Licensed psychologists can apply for an Interjurisdictional Practice Certificate (IPC) through the ASPPB Mobility Program, which grants short-term ability (e.g., 30 days) to provide psychological services without having to obtain full licensure in that jurisdiction (ASPPB, 2020). While these guidelines are not rules, they aim to provide telepsychological service providers with some foundational principles to inform client care and ethical practice. It should also be noted that, at the time of this writing, the current 2013 guidelines were undergoing the process of revision (APA guidelines expire every 10 years to ensure they are consistent with the most recent research and practice standards). Readers should consult the updated version of the guidelines and/or review any amendments, as applicable.

▶ HEALTHCARE CONSIDERATIONS FOR THE PROVISION OF PSYCHOLOGICAL SERVICES

The next section discusses funding and resource allocation, cost–benefit considerations, and patient outcomes within healthcare systems and structures that are important to providing psychological services. The APA's *Guidelines for Psychological Practice in Health Care Delivery Systems* (2013a) provides an overview of considerations for psychologists practicing within healthcare systems.

FUNDING SOURCES

Given the costs associated with psychological practice, healthcare systems and overarching funding sources and resource allocation play a major role in the availability and feasibility of mental health services, especially to already underserved populations, and what type of service providers choose to perform. The United States healthcare system typically involves a balance between patient care needs and available insurance coverage. Funding for healthcare services may be provided through several sources including government funded programs (e.g., Medicare, Medicaid, Children's Health Insurance Program [CHIP], Veterans Health Administration), public health insurance companies, and private health insurance companies. For low-income clients, coverage typically comes from Medicaid and CHIP, whereas those who have median to high incomes typically receive coverage through their employer (Pauly, 2009). Golberstein and Gonzales (2015) evaluated the effects of Medicaid eligibility on mental health services and found that, while it does not impact the use of services, eligibility does decrease the cost of mental health services for the consumer.

COST–BENEFITS TO CLIENTS

Cost effective analysis (CEA) involves comparing "the costs of alternative ways of achieving an objective measured along a single dimension, traditionally measured in 'natural' units (such as life-years saved or cancer cases detected)" (Brazier et al., 2009, p. 706). CEA is a systemwide approach to determining cost-effective policies related to treatment provision (Brazier et al., 2009). For example, Revicki et al. (2005) evaluated the cost-effectiveness of interventions on depression for low-income women from minoritized communities. Although outpatient costs for combined pharmacotherapy and CBT were higher than those associated with a community referral group, pharmacotherapy and CBT were considered a more reasonable investment for the healthcare system because they resulted in decreased depressive symptoms and a more desirable cost-effectiveness ratio per quality-adjusted life year (QALY). Clients also appear to engage in their own cost–benefit analysis process. According to Singer et al. (2014), patients' confidence in medical decisions made by professionals is significantly related to their perceptions of the costs and benefits of that decision. Singer et al. (2014) further explained that patients' decisions are not always grounded in accurate information and knowledge; therefore, healthcare professionals should work to ensure the costs and benefits of treatment are adequately reviewed with and understood by clients. Doing so is a crucial responsibility of a competent psychologist.

FACTORS AFFECTING CLIENT OUTCOMES

Client-centered care is the general model of most healthcare systems and is critical for positive therapeutic outcomes. Frosch (2015) emphasized both the quality of care provided to patients and the quality of life for patients. Similar to Rogers' person-centered approach, health psychologists advocate for a collaborative relationship between the practitioner and the client and empathic bedside manner. Many medical settings are increasingly employing psychologists or other mental health professionals for this purpose (Koocher et al., 2020; Robiner et al., 2014), particularly following diagnosis or other life-altering news. The evaluation of therapies often incorporates patient-reported outcome measures or "measures that capture patients' subjective experience of illness, impairment and disability" (Frosch, 2015, p. 1383). The use of interdisciplinary healthcare teams also has benefits for patient health and well-being, as they allow for better continuity of care and more effective communication between healthcare providers (Brummel-Smith et al., 2016; Robiner & Petrik, 2017). Particularly for disadvantaged populations, who experience a high prevalence of chronic disease comorbidities and health disparities (Vanderbilt et al., 2013), interprofessional collaborations create an opportunity to provide comprehensive patient care to those who may not otherwise receive it (Vanderbilt et al., 2013). Using tools, such as patient-reported outcome measures and working on interdisciplinary healthcare teams, can help the healthcare system to provide better patient-centered care (Frosch, 2015; Vanderbilt et al., 2013), which in turn helps improve quality of care (Brummel-Smith et al., 2016).

▶ THEORIES OF CLINICAL SUPERVISION AND PROFESSIONAL CONSULTATION

Clinical supervision and consultation are overlapping concepts but differ in a number of significant ways. According to Bernard and Goodyear (2019), the single most important distinction is whether the evaluation of someone else's clinical work is necessary. Evaluation is a primary feature in supervision, but not in consultation. Other key distinguishing factors include (a) professional membership of involved parties, (b) relationship dynamics, (c) temporal expectations of the relationship, and (d) ethical responsibilities of the supervisor/consultant. Yet, the general goal of clinical supervision and consultation is the same: to enhance another person's professional effectiveness by sharing expert knowledge and experience.

CLINICAL SUPERVISION

According to Bernard and Goodyear (2019), clinical supervision involves a more senior member of a profession providing intervention and oversight to a more junior member or members of that same profession. Inherent in this definition is the hierarchical nature of this relationship, such that the supervisor and supervisee are not professional equals. Also included in this definition is the fact that both members of the supervisory relationship are from the same profession. In applied health service psychology disciplines, this means that clinical psychologists should supervise clinical psychology trainees, school psychologists should supervise school psychology trainees, and so on. Bernard and Goodyear go on to describe the supervisory relationship as evaluative in nature and continuing over time (that is, supervision is typically more than a one-time event). Furthermore, supervisors have simultaneous ethical responsibilities to advance the professional efficacy of the junior person, monitor the quality of services rendered to clients, and serve as a gatekeeper for the profession at large.

Section 7 (Education and Training) of the APA *Ethical Principles of Psychologists and Code of Conduct* (2016) also contains information related to clinical supervision. Of particular relevance is Subsection 7.06: Assessing Student and Supervisee Performance. This part of the guidelines encourages supervisors to "establish a timely and specific process for providing feedback" and that this process be determined at the start of the working relationship. This subsection also reminds supervisors to objectively evaluate their supervisees on the basis of their performance on program- and profession-specific requirements. Whether or not a supervisee brings you a pumpkin spice latte before your meetings should never factor into your evaluation of their work with clients! And, of course, always avoid sexual interactions with your supervisees (see 7.07: Sexual Relationships With Students and Supervisees); not only is this exploitative given the power differential in the supervisory relationship, but it is sure to lead to a biased evaluation.

Fundamental Components of Supervision

Table 8.2 shows the conceptual model of supervision, which includes three basic components that are fundamental to the supervision process: (a) supervision parameters, (b) supervisee developmental level, and (c) supervisor tasks. First, supervision parameters are aspects of supervision that are constant no matter what developmental stage the supervisee is in or what supervisory tasks are being performed. That is, whether the supervisee is a new or advanced therapist, supervision will always involve evaluation of professional skills, consideration of ethical and legal obligations, discussion of individual differences (between clients and therapists, and supervisee and supervisors), and processing through interpersonal conflict, all of which are guided by a specific supervisory model or structure (discussed in the next section).

TABLE 8.2 Conceptual Model of Supervision

Supervision Parameters	Supervisee Developmental Level	Supervisor Tasks
Evaluation	Novice supervisee	Organizing supervision
Ethical and legal considerations	⬇	Individual supervision
Supervision models		Group supervision
Individual differences	Expert practitioner (supervision becoming more like consultation)	Live supervision
Relationship processes		Documentation

Source: Adapted from Bent, R., Carlson, C., Eisman, E., Hammeke, T., James, L., King, C., Kloffer, S., Matthews, J., Nelson, P., Ritchie, P., Rodolfa, E., & Yeates, K. (2002, November 9). *Specialties and proficiencies of professional psychology* [Conference presentation]. Association of Psychology Postdoctoral and Internship Centers 2002 Competencies Conference, Scottsdale, AZ.

Second, a supervisee's developmental level is assessed on a continuum from beginner or novice trainee to independent clinician. Where a supervisee is along this continuum determines how frequently and intensely a supervisor will need to intervene and monitor client care. Newer therapists will require more supervision while more advanced therapists will require less. Lastly, supervisor tasks are what the supervisor does to educate and train the supervisee. Supervision may involve any number of tasks beyond those that were previously listed (Bernard & Goodyear, 2019).

Models and Theories of Supervision

Next, we broadly discuss several theoretical models that have been applied to the supervisory relationship. These theories mirror many of those discussed previously. Here, we outline how the basic principles of these psychological theories can also provide a logical framework for engendering a productive training experience. Empirical support for these theories will also be discussed where applicable. However, despite the varying models and theories of supervision that have been proposed (some of which are not discussed in this chapter), very little empirical evidence exists regarding the effectiveness of one approach over another (Simpson-Southward et al., 2017). In fact, many theories have no known empirical evidence to support their effectiveness on clinical practice or client outcomes (Simpson-Southward et al., 2017).

Psychotherapy Theories. Theories of supervision grounded in psychotherapy theories generally include the following:

1. Psychodynamic
2. Person-centered
3. Cognitive behavioral
4. Systemic
5. Constructivist (narrative, solution-focused)

According to Bernard and Goodyear (2019), concepts originating from *psychoanalysis* have affected supervision theory and practice more than any other. In fact, Freud has been credited as the first supervisor of therapeutic practice. In particular, psychodynamic approaches focus on the *working alliance* and *parallel process*. The importance of the working alliance has been well-documented in both client–therapist and supervisor–supervisee relationship dyads. Supervisory working alliance has been associated with positive outcomes, such as reduced counselor stress and multiple coping resources (Gnilka et al., 2012). In a classic analysis, Holloway (1987) concluded that the quality of the relationship between a supervisor and trainee is the primary mechanism by which professional growth takes place, even above developmental processes. Largely in response to this finding, the Supervisory Working Alliance Inventory (SWAI) was developed as a tool to measure this dimension (Efstation et al., 1990).

Parallel process is a psychodynamic concept in which a therapist-in-training mirrors, or parallels, their client's problems or mannerisms when relating to their supervisor. An example of this is a supervisee who expresses frustration because their client cannot seem to stop talking in session about the role other people play in their current problems, only to have trouble themselves engaging in self-reflection. Parallel process may also occur in the opposite direction: A supervisor imposes values or behaviors onto the supervisee, who then imposes them onto their clients. Parallel process is similar to transference and countertransference in the therapy room (Sumerel, 1994). However, there appears to be little empirical evidence on the frequency or importance of parallel process to the training experience, with most accounts of parallel processing being anecdotal. One of the few empirically rigorous attempts to study this phenomenon concluded that parallel process does in fact occur in a bidirectional manner, and that behavioral similarities between the therapist and supervisor can lead to positive outcomes for clients (Tracey et al., 2012).

Person-centered supervision models stem primarily from the work of Carl Rogers. For Rogers, supervision also relied on the main tenets of his humanistic approach to therapy: (a) genuineness,

(b) empathy, (c) warmth, and (d) unconditional positive regard. The first three are consistent with the notion that working alliance is of utmost importance. Supervisors who follow a person-centered model also believe their trainees are highly motivated toward growth and possess the ability to move toward self-actualization as a competent and independent practitioner. The trainee and supervisor must also accept, value, and trust each other (as well as the client) to facilitate a successful transition from novice to expert. While helpful in conceptualizing supervision, the Rogerian perspective seems to have reached a plateau regarding what guidance it can give to practitioners (Bernard & Goodyear, 2019).

As in CBT, supervisors who operate under a *cognitive behavioral* model of supervision believe that adaptive and maladaptive behaviors are learned based on their consequences. Most CBT models conceptualize the purpose of supervision as teaching appropriate therapist behaviors and eliminating inappropriate ones. These behaviors are seen as definable and can be altered through classical learning theories (e.g., positively reinforcing effective interventions). CBT-oriented supervisors tend to be more structured in their discussion of supervisory goals and assessment of those goals across the supervision process than other types of supervisors (Bernard & Goodyear, 2019). CBT supervisors also frequently employ Socratic questioning (e.g., "Why do you say that?"; Rosenbaum & Ronen, 1998) and statements meant to challenge supervisee cognitions and misperceptions ("What is an alternative way of seeing this?"; Liese & Beck, 1997). In a national survey of psychology interns, CBT supervisors were seen as being more consultative in their style and focused more on skill-building and teaching intervention strategies (Putney et al., 1992).

Systemic supervision maps closely onto family systems therapy, and supervisors who ascribe to this approach focus on ways the supervisory relationship replicates family dynamics (Bernard & Goodyear, 2019). This mirroring of supervision with the family structure has been termed *isomorphism*. Not surprisingly, systemic supervision is used most often in the supervision of couples and family counseling where systems therapy is the primary treatment modality. Common models of systemic supervision include the structural model, the Mental Research Institute brief model, strategic models, the solution-focused model, and the Milan approach (Todd, 2014). The difference between these models is minimal, and a question related to their differences is unlikely to appear on the EPPP. Of them, however, strategic supervision has been met with the most criticism because some techniques, such as paradoxical directives (i.e., doing the opposite of what common sense might dictate to demonstrate the absurdity of the originally intended behavior), used to disrupt a supervisee's problematic behavior can create a nonegalitarian relationship that may border on being manipulative (Bernard & Goodyear, 2019). Systemic supervision approaches in general have had a broader impact on the supervision process by emphasizing the use of live observation (via two-way mirror) and/or review of taped sessions to produce raw data on the trainee's progress with clients (Todd, 2014).

Constructivist supervisors assume the position that truth and reality are in the eye of the beholder. That is, someone's truth about the world is constructed by their own experiences of it. Supervision is seen as more of a collaboration between supervisor and trainee to construct meaning in a given context. Similar to humanistic approaches in general, constructivist supervisors attempt to maintain a largely egalitarian relationship, preferring to act more like a consultant than a superior, and focus on strengths of the supervisee to promote further growth. Constructivist models can be subdivided into *narrative* and *solution-focused* approaches. From the perspective of narrative therapy, clients present to therapy with a story about themselves, and the therapist's role is to help them edit or modify that story in a way that is more meaningful and adaptive. In narrative supervision, the supervisor's role is to assist the therapist-in-training to edit the client's story without projecting a particular point of view onto the client. In addition, supervisors assist supervisees in developing their own professional storyline. Narrative supervision usually involves the use of questions (or implied questions; e.g., "I am wondering what you were feeling in the moment when the client said that") rather than absolute statements when discussing client interventions (Bernard & Goodyear, 2019). Solution-focused supervision is similar to narrative supervision in its emphasis on collaboration. Supervisors who practice from this orientation also deemphasize the trainee's deficits or faults, and instead focus more on achievements and acquired competence. In fact, small, achievable gains are preferred over large, dramatic changes. Solution-focused supervisors, for example, may use questions such as "Tell me the best thing you did with your client this week" to refocus supervisees on their growth as a therapist (Presbury et al., 1999).

Table 8.3 summarizes key concepts of these theories as they relate to the supervision process.

TABLE 8.3 Theories of Supervision

Theoretical Orientation	Key Concepts
Psychodynamic	Working alliance Parallel process
Person-Centered	Supervisor empathy, warmth, genuineness, unconditional positive regard Therapist self-actualization Trust in therapist and supervisor
Cognitive-Behavioral	Reinforcement of therapist skills Structured, mutually agreed up goals Socratic questioning
Systemic	Isomorphism Live supervision
Constructivist (narrative and solution-focused)	Supervisee strengths Supervisor as consultant

Developmental theories of supervision assume (a) supervisees develop competency by moving through a series of distinct stages or phases, and (b) that each stage involves differing levels of supervisory intervention to foster growth and advancement to the next (Chagnon & Russell, 1995). According to Bernard and Goodyear (2019), a booming interest in developmental supervision models began in the 1980s, even though such models had been introduced as early as the 1950s. The following approaches are discussed next:

1. The Loganbill, Hardy, Delworth model
2. The integrated developmental model (IDM; Stoltenberg, 1981)
3. The Rønnestad and Skovholt model

The *Loganbill, Hardy, Delworth model* was arguably the first published model of counselor development (Holloway, 1987). This model is characterized by three developmental stages and eight supervisory issues that may be at play during these stages. The Loganbill, Hardy, Delworth model is unique from the others in this section due to its focus on a cyclical (or repeating) pattern of development. In the Stagnation stage, trainees lack awareness about their areas of growth or needs, and may experience therapy as dull. In the Confusion stage, trainees become aware of problems, but are unsure how to solve them. They may see supervisors as incompetent or purposefully withholding information when a concrete answer is not provided. In the final stage, Integration, supervisees assume greater responsibility for what occurs in supervision, make efforts to get the most out of supervision time, and set more realistic expectations for the supervisor. Throughout these stages, supervisors may need to address issues related to the supervisory relationship, supervisee competence, emotional awareness, purpose and direction in therapy, autonomy, personal issues that interfere with client work, respect for individual differences, professional ethics, motivation, and therapist identity.

The *IDM* includes four levels of therapist development. Within each level, counselor progress is assessed across the same three domains: self–other awareness, motivation, and autonomy. In Level 1, trainees have limited experience, are dependent on the supervisor (low autonomy), and are self-focused (low self–other awareness), but are highly motivated to learn the "correct" approach with clients. Level 2 therapists have typically completed between two and three semesters of practicum. This stage is rather turbulent and is marked by ambivalence regarding competency and autonomy. Much like an adolescent, trainees in this stage may show greater resistance to supervision as they test the waters of their own abilities. In addition, while there is an improved capacity for client empathy, supervisees in Level 2 may overcompensate and become enmeshed with clients. Level 3 supervisees begin to take a more personalized approach to treatment implementation. Supervisees at this level are relatively confident in their skills, although some self-doubt is likely to occur, and their motivation for learning is consistent. Because greater autonomy is afforded at Level 3, the environment of supervision becomes more collegial. Furthermore, a Level 3 therapist can focus on their clients while separately attending to their own personal reactions. Personal reactions are then used to inform therapeutic decisions. It is relevant to note that a trainee may be at one developmental level for one skill domain but remain on another level for other skill domains (e.g., Level 3 motivation, but Level 2 autonomy). The last stage in IDM is Level 3i (integrated). Here, the trainee reaches Level 3 across all three measured domains.

Unlike IDM, the *Rønnestad and Skovholt model* focuses on counselor development across the life span, rather than the narrow period between graduate matriculation and graduation. The original eight-phase model was derived from a qualitative survey of counselors with varying levels of training; however, a more refined model of six phases has since been proposed (Rønnestad & Skovholt, 2003), consisting of the lay helper phase, the beginning student phase, the advanced student phase, the novice professional phase, the experienced professional phase, and the senior professional phase. In an oversimplification of this model, individuals move from a casual, emotional support role with no formal training (think of the doctoral applicant who became interested in psychology because her friends always ask for advice anyway) to a seasoned, often modest and skeptical professional, looking forward to retirement.

Overall, there appears to be little empirical evidence to support one developmental theory over another, yet it is generally accepted that counselor training involves at least a general developmental process whereby trainees advance in terms of both confidence and competence, with accompanying modifications in how supervisors relate to their supervisees and the extent to which they directly intervene on behalf of client care.

Social role model theories focus on the various roles supervisors play in the training experience of their supervisees. Although the EPPP will almost certainly not require you to memorize the details of these models, it may be worthwhile for you to understand the basic structure of common social role models. Three of these are summarized briefly in the text that follows.

The *discrimination model* (Bernard, 1979) outlines three areas of supervisory focus and three distinct supervisor roles. Specifically, a supervisor is likely to address a trainee's intervention skills (ability to implement techniques in-session), conceptualization skills (ability to make sound clinical decisions regarding client goals and care), and personalization skills (ability to take a personalized approach to treatment without interjecting bias). In addressing these issues, supervisors may take on a teacher, counselor, or consultant role—with each role along this continuum requiring less direct instruction than the previous. This model assumes supervisors will need to tailor their approach based on the situation at hand and the supervisee's level of experience with similar situations. For example, the teacher role would be appropriate for a supervisee who has never worked with a client of a particular cultural background and requires more didactic education about multicultural awareness.

The *Hawkins and Shohet model* (2000) is based on the idea that supervision encompasses two overlapping systems: (a) the therapy system (between trainee and client) and (b) the supervisory system (between trainee and supervisor). These systems are joined, of course, because the supervisory system requires oversight of the therapy system. Like the discrimination model, this model also describes several modes of focus (e.g., content of therapy, the therapist's process, the supervisory relationship) that may take place within and across the two systems. The *Holloway systems approach model* (Holloway, 1995) is a similar model in which supervision is broken down into the *what* (i.e., tasks) and *how* (i.e., function) of supervision (Bernard & Goodyear, 2019). While this model is a bit more complex than what is presented here, Holloway has identified the following five tasks: monitoring-evaluating, instructing-advising, modeling, consulting, and support-sharing. These five tasks are then used to build and refine a trainee's counseling skills, case conceptualization, professional role/identity, emotional awareness, and self-evaluation. Thus, there are 25 possible task-function combinations.

Multicultural Considerations in Supervision

As in therapy, supervision requires competence in multicultural awareness. Most research in this area has focused on the impact of gender and race and ethnicity differences in the supervisor–supervisee relationship. For purposes of the EPPP, it is relevant to know that the literature on the benefits (or not) of gender matching has been mixed. Regardless, many researchers have shown there are some normative differences between supervisors and supervisees who identify as women versus men, and supervisors should be mindful of these differences to mitigate bias. In a systematic review of studies published from 1996 to 2010, Hindes and Andrews (2011) concluded that gender may affect how supervisees and supervisors view the quality of their relationships. Women supervisors tended to place greater emphasis on the supervisory relationship itself and were more conservative with boundaries than men supervisors. This review also highlighted that men supervisors may be more likely to view women supervisees negatively compared to same-gender supervisees. In terms of matching on race and ethnicity, the available research suggests that supervisor–supervisee differences on these variables can influence the supervision process; however, other supervisor attributes (e.g., willingness to discuss racial differences) are at least equally important. As a general rule, it appears most advantageous for trainees to work with supervisors who have varying degrees of shared demographics and cultural experiences (Bernard & Goodyear, 2019). However, research also shows that when clinical supervisors are perceived to have higher levels of cultural humility by supervisees, there is a positive impact on the relationship (Zhang et al., 2021).

PROFESSIONAL CONSULTATION

Unlike clinical supervision, the interpersonal dynamics of consultation involve two or more people of relatively equal standing. That is, while supervision occurs between a trainee and an expert within the same field, consultation occurs between two parties who are often from differing fields. In consultation, one party freely seeks expertise from a profession in which they lack needed expertise. Consultation can take place at the individual, community, or organizational level. The temporal nature of consultation is also more variant than in supervision, and generally occurs on an as-needed basis rather than a recurrent schedule. An expert may be consulted frequently and routinely or for a specific, one-time purpose. And, as previously noted, consultants are free of any evaluative role and do not have the same ethical obligations to serve as a professional gatekeeper. However, relevant to this discussion is Section 2 (Competence) of APA's ethics code that highlights the need for all psychologists to function within the boundaries of their training and professional experience. Thus, consultants must be aware of and acknowledge areas in which they are not competent to offer guidance. To maintain competence (see Subsection 2.03), it is expected that consultants stay current with the literature and best practices within their respective field of expertise.

Forms of Consultation

Like the previously discussed models of supervision, there are several forms of consultation in which psychologists may engage to enhance social justice and change. These include mental health consultation, behavioral or educational consultation, systems or organizational development consultation, and advocacy consultation.

In the 1960s, increasing attention was given to community mental health as more people were being released from psychiatric institutions. The area of *mental health consultation*, which is widely credited to the work of Gerald Caplan (Erchul, 2009), emerged as a means for preventing the onset of psychopathology. Caplan came from a psychoanalytic background and promoted a nondirective, noncoercive, and nonhierarchical relationship between consultant and consultee. For the EPPP, it is relevant to know that Caplan classified mental health consultation in four ways (Caplan, 1963). In *client-centered case consultation*, the consultant is asked to help the consultee develop an effective plan to work with a specific client. In other words, the client's presenting issue(s) is the main reason for seeking consultation. As an example, a therapist may reach out to a colleague for additional ideas on how to engage with a resistant client. *Consultee-centered case consultation*, as might be expected, focuses on issues with the consultee such as lack of knowledge or ability. For example, a licensed psychologist who has limited experience working with Indigenous clients in general may contact another licensed psychologist who does for guidance on rapport-building, constructing an assessment battery, treatment planning, resources to improve cultural competence, and so on. This type of consultation may also occur during situations in which the consultee has become too emotionally involved with a client, is having difficulty restraining biases, or is experiencing countertransference. Consultants who perform *program-centered administrative consultation* provide feedback and recommendations to consultees that are aimed at improving their effectiveness at the program or organizational level. This might involve a new director of clinical training consulting with a more senior training director on how best to structure clinic policy. *Consultee-centered administrative consultation* is like consultee-centered case consultation in that the consultee is the primary focus of intervention. Here, however, the goal is to effect changes in the consultee's ability to administer or modify a program, rather than address issues related to an individual client.

Behavioral or educational consultation is relatively straightforward—it focuses on helping a consultee make changes by implementing classical behavioral techniques, such as direct instruction and feedback, modeling, shaping, and homework. It is common for this type of consultation to take place in an educational setting. For example, a special education teacher might approach a school psychologist for assistance in developing and implementing a behavioral modification program for a student with autism.

Unlike the forms of consultation discussed thus far, which generally involve an individual consultee, *systems or organizational development consultation* views an entire organization as the consultee and change agent. The primary goal of this type of consultation is to increase the overall efficiency and success of the organization. Although most consultation services are initiated because of a perceived problem in the organization's productivity, much of systems consultation focuses on improving interpersonal skills and relationships within the organization that are thought to be at the root cause of the issue. Core concepts of Industrial and Organizational Psychology are often applied in systems consultation. Systems consultation may take place in schools or universities, government agencies, nonprofit organizations, corporate businesses, or sports teams.

Lastly, as with systems consultation, *advocacy consultation* also targets bigger picture change beyond the individual. However, rather than focus on one particular organization and its development, advocacy consultants seek to enhance the well-being and goals of an underserved or disadvantaged group, such as historically marginalized ethnic or racial groups, women, people with intellectual disabilities, prisoners, at-risk youth, members of the LGBTQ community, or abuse survivors. Consultants who do advocacy work are interested in bringing about broader policy or political change through education. Advocacy consultants may also assist social change groups in achieving a desired goal (e.g., initiate legislative change, organize a protest, perform fundraising, negotiate with opponents).

▶ REFERENCES

Full reference list available at http://examprepconnect.springerpub.com

KNOWLEDGE CHECK: CHAPTER 8

1. According to Freud, the defense mechanism most representative of mature and healthy adjustment is:
   A. Projection
   B. Reaction formation
   C. Repression
   D. Sublimation

2. In Gottfredson's theory of circumscription and compromise, the final stage of circumscription includes which task?
   A. Completing a personality inventory
   B. Learning what careers may be available or promoted based on gender
   C. Narrowing occupations based on a sophisticated understanding of their unique personality and strengths
   D. Seeking out job information to make an informed decision

3. In acceptance and commitment therapy (ACT), what foundational concept drives four of the six tasks of *psychological flexibility*?
   A. Mindfulness
   B. Unconditional positive regard
   C. Use of metaphors
   D. Validation

4. A client who rates high on the Holland code of Artistic may find which career fields least appealing?
   A. An office assistant at a dental office
   B. A privately hired wedding planner
   C. A set painter at a local theater
   D. A teacher at a dance studio

5. Irvin Yalom considered three of the 11 therapeutic factors in group therapy to be most important for the group to be successful. One of them is:
   A. Accountability
   B. Catharsis
   C. Modeling
   D. Universality

(See answers on the next page.)

1. **D) Sublimation**
   For Freud, sublimation involves converting psychic energy toward a healthy outlet (e.g., art). In his theory, using sublimation as a defense mechanism showed increased maturity. He also believed that reaction formation involved replacing an unconscious desire with its opposite (e.g., a man who experiences insecurities about his sexual orientation advocating for traditional values). Projection involves attributing one's own desires to be the desires of others. Finally, repression includes pushing down the angry or sexual impulses of the id past the point of consciousness, so they are not salient.

2. **C) Narrowing occupations based on a sophisticated understanding of their unique personality and strengths**
   Gottfredson's theory of circumscription and compromise included four developmental processes, one of which was circumscription. Circumscription includes four stages: Orientation to Size and Power, Orientation to Sex Roles, Orientation to Social Valuation, and Orientation to Internal, Unique Self. The final stage, Orientation to Internal, Unique Self, involves narrowing down potential career options based on an understanding of one's own constellation of character traits and abilities. Completing a personality inventory can assist in learning what one's traits and strengths are but is not all that's required to complete the final stage of circumscription. Individuals in other stages of circumscription may complete other activities like seeking out job information to make an informed decision or learning what careers may be available or promoted based on gender.

3. **A) Mindfulness**
   ACT teaches six skills related to psychological flexibility. Four of the six tasks (cognitive defusion, acceptance, contacting the present moment, and observing the self) are explicitly grounded in mindfulness techniques. Use of metaphors is a hallmark of ACT but is not the building block of flexibility skills; it is a modality used to teach the skills in treatment. Validation and unconditional positive regard are key interventions to other orientations, namely dialectical behavioral therapy and person-centered therapy, respectively.

4. **A) An office assistant at a dental office**
   Holland's *Personality and Environmental Typology* classifies jobs into six different categories. Individuals scoring high in the Artistic category are creative and imaginative, and likely enjoy work that is abstract or creative. Thus, it is reasonable to conclude that they might enjoy a job that allows for creative liberty, abstract tasks, or creating; it is also reasonable to conclude they likely will enjoy an office assistant job less, as it by nature discourages creativity.

5. **B) Catharsis**
   Yalom considered certain therapeutic factors to be more important than the rest. Specifically, he felt that cohesiveness within a group, catharsis, and interpersonal learning are most important in successful group therapy. Universality, while one of the 11 therapeutic factors of group therapy, is not one of the most important key factors. Accountability and modeling are not included in the therapeutic factors identified by Yalom.

6. Gestaltists would most likely hold what worldview regarding patients and their problems?
   A. Individuals are products of their specific, frequently changing environment.
   B. Individuals create their own suffering through their use of language to give meaning to events.
   C. Individuals' current problems should be considered separate from societal views and roles.
   D. Individuals' current relationships are influenced by past relationships.

7. Carl Rogers believed healing in therapy was achieved through:
   A. Exposing oneself to the situations and behaviors that induce the most distress
   B. Improving boundaries with family members
   C. Increasing congruence between values and behaviors
   D. Restructuring current, cynical, or critical thoughts into more accurate, empathetic versions

8. The automatic thought of "If I don't get this job, I'll have to move back in with my parents" is an example of which cognitive distortion?
   A. Dichotomous thinking
   B. Minimization
   C. Personalization
   D. Sublimation

9. Which of the following would be seen by a family systems therapist as a healthy family system?
   A. A family capable of adapting when members go through behavioral changes
   B. A new family that is amenable to new family members contributing to the system
   C. A family that is susceptible to the negative influence of authority figures
   D. A family that is so adaptable to change, it becomes flexible and permissive

10. Which of the following is NOT a benefit of supplementing group therapy with individual therapy?
    A. Addressing individual needs so members can focus on interpersonal content
    B. Increasing profits for the practice
    C. Increasing benefits from group therapy
    D. Reinforcing skills and interventions learned in individual therapy

(See answers on the next page.)

6. **A) Individuals are products of their specific, frequently changing environment.**
   Gestalt therapy is based upon the field theory, which stipulates that an individual should be viewed as a part of their specific, yet constantly changing environment. While part of GT is creating meaning in one's life, it does not directly relate to meaning through suffering or the use of language—this is better attributed to the relational frame theory of Acceptance and Commitment Therapy. The concept that individuals' current relationships are influenced by past relationships is the basis for psychodynamic theory. No theory explicitly indicates that current problems should be separated from contextual views of society and social roles.

7. **C) Increasing congruence between values and behaviors**
   Rogers believed congruence was the goal of person-centered therapy, in that clients' perceptions of themselves and their beliefs should be compatible with the manner in which they live their lives. Other options describe the goals of other modalities of therapy, like family systems therapy, cognitive behavioral therapy, and behavioral therapy.

8. **A) Dichotomous thinking**
   Aaron Beck identified a number of cognitive distortions, or logical errors in thinking, which he believed were responsible for individuals' depressive or anxiety-related symptoms. These include personalization, magnification/minimization, selective abstraction, dichotomous thinking, and overgeneralization, among others. Dichotomous thinking specifically describes "black-or-white" thinking in which there are no alternative options other than best- and worst-case scenarios. Sublimation is a defense mechanism as part of psychoanalytic theory. Minimization is not an automatic thought described by Beck.

9. **A) A family capable of adapting when members go through behavioral changes**
   A component of family systems therapy is systems theory, which describes two types of families: open system families and closed system families. Open systems specifically are described as easily adapting to the environment and can effectively cope with changes. Closed systems, on the other hand, attempt to stay as close to homeostasis as they can. Closed systems are characterized by boundaries, rules, and norms that are rigid and difficult to change. Within family systems therapy, the goal is for a family unit to be more open in that they can adapt to changes while maintaining some structure and rules for the family unit. So, in choosing the best description of a healthy family system according to a family systems therapist, the best answer would be a family capable of adapting when members go through behavioral changes. A new family that is amenable to new family members contributing to the system describes a closed system, which would be antithetical to the goal of family systems therapy. A family that is susceptible to the negative influence of authority figures and a family that is so adaptable to change, it becomes flexible and permissive describe other characteristics of a family system that are not germane to the goals of family systems therapy.

10. **B) Increasing profits for the practice**
    Yalom indicated that pairing group therapy with individual therapy has many benefits. For example, individuals can use individual therapy to address matters like emotion regulation on a more personal level to allow for group sessions to focus on the interpersonal process. Individual therapy can also be used to conduct deeper explorations of interpersonal dynamics uncovered in group therapy to enhance insights gained in group settings. Conversely, group therapy can be used to supplement primary individual therapy to either practice skills gained in individual therapy or to reinforce skills practiced, similar to the joint group and individual therapy model utilized in dialectical behavioral therapy. Decisions about which therapeutic services clients receive should never be made with the potential profits for the therapist in mind.

11. Which of the following describes an individual in the *Preparation* stage within the transtheoretical model (TTM)?
    A. A client who discusses ways she could tell her partner she is quitting alcohol
    B. A client whose homework for last session was to create a pros and cons list for leaving his abusive partner
    C. A client whose therapy schedule was just reduced to monthly appointments after being symptom-free for 4 months
    D. A client who showed up 15 minutes late for her first appointment, stating "I wasn't sure if I was going to come at all."

12. Neo-Freudian schools of thought include which of the following theorists?
    A. Aaron Beck
    B. Andrew Hayes
    C. Erik Erikson
    D. Murray Bowen

13. According to Alfred Adler, one's *style of life* is influenced by:
    A. Biological systems like the central nervous system
    B. Birth order
    C. Preferences for career and work
    D. The creative self

14. What does the S in CASVE stand for?
    A. Social
    B. Sorting
    C. Synthesis
    D. Systemic

15. The concept of *triangulation* in family systems therapies involves:
    A. Enmeshed or dysfunctional relationships between the child and both parents
    B. The employment of a therapist to resolve a child custody matter
    C. The influence of past relationships onto an individual's current relationship
    D. Visualizing relationships between multiple generations of a genogram

(See answers on the next page.)

11. **A) A client who discusses ways she could tell her partner she is quitting alcohol**
    According to the TTM, an individual in the Preparation stage feels confident in their ability to change their behavior. They begin making plans on how exactly they intend to change their behavior, an example of which may include discussing potential strategies for changing behavior with their therapist. Communicating one's intention and planning to stop using substances could be a step in a client's plan for behavior change about which they may strategize with their therapist while in the Preparation stage, prior to making any behavioral changes. This would help the client to be more successful in implementing change by anticipating difficulties and resolving them before making concrete changes. Decisional balance activities, such as creating a pros and cons list, are common exercises used in the Contemplation stage of change, when they are open to the idea of changing a behavior and the therapist desires to elicit reasons they may want to engage in behavioral change. Reductions in treatment dosage and extended periods of time without substance use or target behaviors are typical signs that a client is in the Maintenance stage of change and has successfully changed the target behavior. Late appointments, no-shows, and ambivalence toward engaging in treatment are common signs that a client is in the Precontemplation stage of change, where they are not yet open to the idea of changing their behavior.

12. **C) Erik Erikson**
    Erik Erikson is considered a Neo-Freudian theorist, as well as others like Karen Horney and Alfred Adler. They each modified psychoanalytic theory and practice to emphasize (or deemphasize) particular elements in traditional psychoanalytic theory. Murray Bowen was integral in developing family systems therapy; Steven Hayes was one of the developers of acceptance and commitment therapy; and Aaron Beck is considered the father of cognitive behavioral therapy.

13. **D) The creative self**
    Alfred Adler theorized that people construct a style of life to meet their own goals and help to overcome challenges. This style of life is comprised of one's creative self. Although the creative self is influenced by factors like birth order, this is not the driving factor to one's style of life. Biological systems are considered in some theories of behavior, such as dialectical behavioral therapy, but is not relevant to Adlerian therapy. And while a client's preferences for career and work may be related to their style of life, remember that Adlerian therapy is not a vocational theory. We would therefore expect them to have little impact on one's behavior.

14. **C) Synthesis**
    In the cognitive information processing approach, the CASVE decision-making cycle is utilized to decrease the gap between self and occupational knowledge. The acronym stands for: Communication, Analysis, Synthesis, Valuing, and Execution.

15. **A) Enmeshed or dysfunctional relationships between the child and both parents**
    Family systems therapy focuses on relationships within the family, both including and excluding the client, to make inferences about the client's interpersonal functioning within that same system. Family systems therapy describes triangulation as dysfunctional relationships between the child and both parents; different subtheories of family systems approaches have slightly different ideas as to why triangulation occurs, but all agree that triangulated relationships occur in parent–child relationships and result from poor boundaries or decreased differentiation between the parties. Triangles of relationships are a component of psychodynamic therapy, but do not address the specific interpersonal dynamics occurring, nor do they exclusively occur between parents and children. A therapist may use triangulation as a strategy to manage conflict between family members, but simply employing a therapist is not sufficient to achieve that as it is a formal intervention technique to be used during therapy.

16. The *paradoxical theory of change* states what about clients achieving behavior change?
    A. Changing cognitions can result in changes in behavior and emotions.
    B. Clients change when they become their true selves.
    C. Even small behavioral changes are meaningful in achieving complete change.
    D. Therapeutic relationship and working alliance are most conducive to achieving change.

17. Which of the following is one of the four components of wellness according to Cowen?
    A. Emotion regulation
    B. Insight
    C. Interest
    D. Resilience

18. Which scenario would benefit the most from the use of telepsychologic services?
    A. The psychologist who has been working for 3 years without a break and is experiencing symptoms of burnout
    B. The therapist who experiences social anxiety and wants to improve therapeutic relationships
    C. The patient who lives 45 minutes outside of town and has unreliable transportation
    D. The practice which cannot afford overhead costs and is at risk of closing down

19. What sort of responsibilities do health service psychologists have when providing services?
    A. Consider therapist's personal expenses when setting fees for services
    B. Ensure the costs of treatment outweigh the benefits
    C. Ensure they review and understand the costs and benefits of treatment
    D. Put health and well-being secondary to other therapeutic concerns

20. The main stages of the average life span according to Super are:
    A. Exploration, growth, establishment, disengagement, maintenance
    B. Growth, exploration, disengagement, establishment, maintenance
    C. Growth, exploration, establishment, maintenance, disengagement
    D. Growth, maintenance, exploration, establishment, disengagement

(See answers on the next page.)

16. **B) Clients change when they become their true selves.**
    The paradoxical theory of change states that clients achieve true change when they accept and become their true selves. It is paradoxical in the sense that, according to the theory, when one accepts who they are at that time, it becomes easier to make movement toward change. Ideas that even small behavioral changes are meaningful in achieving complete change stem from Motivational Interviewing. The transtheoretical model posits the therapeutic relationship and working alliance are most conducive to achieving change, whereas cognitive behavioral therapy suggests that changing cognitions can result in changes in behavior and emotions.

17. **D) Resilience**
    According to Cowen, wellness is comprised of four different components: competence, resilience, social system modification, and empowerment. Insight, emotion regulation, and interest may be important to symptom reduction or changing behaviors according to other theories, but not within Cowen's conceptualization of health and wellness.

18. **C) The patient who lives 45 minutes outside of town and has unreliable transportation**
    Telepsychological services have many potential benefits; one benefit that many sources agree upon is the increase in provision of mental health services to individuals who may not otherwise have access for one reason or another. Examples of this are seen in the utilization of telepsychological services in rural areas with individuals who would otherwise drive long periods of time to access a clinic, or the provision of telehealth services in jails and prisons where mental health providers are important, but secondary to other services like correctional safety and medical services. The choice to implement telepsychological services should be made with the client's needs and best interests as the primary deciding factor. For patients who have difficulty accessing mental healthcare because of their location and transportation needs, they would directly benefit from the implementation of telepsychological services as it would offer them healthcare they may not otherwise have. Other options describe reasoning that, while helpful to the clinician or their practice, are secondary to the most important factors for using telepsychological services.

19. **C) Ensure they review and understand the costs and benefits of treatment**
    Health service psychologists are obligated to walk through cost–benefit analyses both individually about the services they provide and with the client in regard to their own unique services; consider seeking external funds to offset costs of mental health services for their clients; and ensure that the services they provide include research-supported elements of change to maximize effectiveness. While it is tempting to prioritize a psychologist's needs, like how much money they want to make, this is not a responsibility they have when providing services and should be considered secondary to the responsibilities one has to the client. Other options, like ensuring the cost of treatment outweighs benefits and putting health and well-being secondary, are directly counter to the responsibilities psychologists hold in the provision of services.

20. **C) Growth, exploration, establishment, maintenance, disengagement**
    Super's career and life development theory offers five stages in the average lifespan, each with its own career-related tasks/conflicts to be resolved. The stages are as follows: growth, exploration, establishment, maintenance, and disengagement. Given that the stages are based in part on developmental age, they are expected to occur in sequential order.

21. An individual in the resistance and immersion stage of the minority identity development model (MID) is described as:
    A. Favoring one's own culture and learning the history of oppression
    B. Feeling both shame and pride toward one's cultural identity
    C. Perceiving the dominant group as more positive
    D. Seeing all cultures as equally flawed

22. Which theory involves two separate development trajectories for majority and nonmajority individuals?
    A. The integrated model
    B. The minority identity development model (MID)
    C. The psychosocial stages of development
    D. The transtheoretical model (TTM)

23. According to Trioden's model of homosexual identity development, sexual identity begins forming in which developmental period?
    A. After their first sexual experience
    B. At birth
    C. During puberty
    D. Prior to puberty

24. According to Seligman, which of the following individual strengths is needed to thrive?
    A. Courage
    B. Humility
    C. Obedience
    D. Perseverence

25. Organizational psychology focuses primarily on:
    A. Ergonomic workspaces
    B. Factors that influence relationships within the workplace
    C. Industry efficiency through employees
    D. The organizational structure of businesses

(See answers on the next page.)

21. **A) Favoring one's own culture and learning the history of oppression**
    The resistance and immersion stage of the MID describes a stage when minority individuals begin identifying weaknesses or faults in the majority culture or way of living and reject the majority culture. They then begin learning about and embracing their minority culture, including the historical context for the relationship between the majority and minority cultures. Other stages include the Conformity stage in which individuals perceive the dominant culture as more positive, the Dissonance stage in which individuals alternate between feelings of shame and pride for their cultural identity, and the Synergistic stage in which individuals see all cultures as equally beneficial and valuable, with their own unique flaws.

22. **A) The integrated model**
    The integrated model describes identity development for both majority and minority individuals; both groups proceed through the first stage, conformity. However, their subsequent stages differ in that minority individuals begin identifying flaws within the majority culture then lean into their minority culture, and eventually embrace a balanced view of the majority culture. Majority individuals, on the other hand, progress through stages in which they grapple with the idea of racism, feeling shame, and commitment to self-awareness and cultural humility. The MID only describes the development trajectory of minority individuals. The psychosocial stages of development describes a development trajectory, but for early human development rather than identity development. The TTM is not a development model, but a model of therapeutic intervention.

23. **D) Prior to puberty**
    Trioden's model of homosexual identity development posits that there are four stages of development for gay individuals when exploring their identity. According to Trioden, sexual identity begins before puberty when individuals realize they are "different" from their peers, but the differences or feelings are not necessarily sexual in nature. While it is considerably young in the life span, it occurs after the early childhood years and, according to this model, is not biologically predetermined in any way. They also occur irrespective of any sexual experiences, regardless of if they were with a same-sex or opposite-sex individual.

24. **A) Courage**
    Martin Seligman, in founding positive psychology, identified six different strengths that are shown through research to be required in thriving: wisdom/knowledge, courage, humanity, justice, temperance, and transcendence. Humility, obedience, and perseverance are not individual strengths that are considered essential to thriving according to Seligman.

25. **B) Factors that influence relationships within the workplace**
    Organizational psychology focuses on the organization as a whole, particularly factors affecting the relationships among people within the workplace. Organizational psychologists emphasize human factors that facilitate productivity, like job satisfaction and commitment. Industrial psychology, however, focuses on examining the efficiency or efficacy of an industry through the functioning of its employees. The organizational structure of businesses and ergonomic workspaces are not primary considerations of these areas of psychology.

8. TREATMENT, INTERVENTION, PREVENTION, AND SUPERVISION   247

26. Which of the following is NOT one of the four focal points in industrial psychology?
    A. Efficiency
    B. Employee selection
    C. Performance appraisal
    D. Work analysis

27. Job satisfaction is related to which of the following outcomes at work?
    A. Citizenship behavior
    B. Efficiency
    C. Salary increase requests
    D. Work commitment

28. Which of the following is an example of the *halo effect*?
    A. An employee disclosing knowledge of moral/ethical problems to inflate perceptions of himself
    B. A job candidate being hired after performing well in multiple interviews
    C. A supervisor rating a historically moderately performing employee as performing well in all areas of their work
    D. A White employee being rated more favorably on a performance review compared to their Hispanic counterpart despite their equal success in their roles

29. According to Douglas McGregor, managers who view employees as generally hard workers who can offer benefits to the workplace are following which theory of management and leadership?
    A. Theory X
    B. Theory Y
    C. Type A
    D. Type Z

(See answers on the next page.)

26. **D) Work analysis**
There are four primary focal points in industrial psychology: job or work analysis, employee or personnel selection, training, and performance appraisal. While industrial psychology is focused on increasing efficiency and efficacy through their employee management, there are four different points that are used to achieve efficiency. Efficiency is not itself one of these four areas of focus.

27. **A) Citizenship behavior**
Research has demonstrated that job satisfaction is related to job turnover, absenteeism, work performance, and organizational citizenship behavior. One meta-analysis found a small positive relationship between pay and job satisfaction, but the relationship is driven more by employees' perception of fair pay and has little to do with salary increases. Work commitment has been associated with several positive organizational behaviors, like work attendance, but is not directly connected to job satisfaction. Efficiency has not been connected to job satisfaction—it could be a factor related to job performance, but there are many components of job performance other than efficiency, so this would be an insufficient answer to the question.

28. **C) A supervisor rating a historically moderately performing employee as performing well in all areas of their work**
The "halo effect" is described as a type of bias in which a supervisor may judge all aspects of an employee's performance in a similar manner, even though the employee exhibits greater variation across assessment domains. Their general impressions of the employee color their entire assessment of the employee's performance. With that in mind, when a supervisor rates an employee highly in all areas of an evaluation because they historically performed moderately well, this would be the closest example to the halo effect. A job candidate being hired after performing well in multiple interviews is less likely a bias and more of an example of thorough employee selection processes. A White employee being rated more favorably than their Hispanic counterpart despite equal success is an example of racism in the workplace (another form of bias or prejudice). There is no research to suggest that employees who report problems in the workplace, or discredit their coworkers for personal gain, are viewed more favorably by management.

29. **B) Theory Y**
Douglas McGregor proposed a theory of employee management including Theories X and Y. Managers with a Theory Y style assume that their employees are generally hard workers and believe they can make positive contributions to the workplace. These supervisors encourage input from their employees and support their autonomy. Theory X managers, on the other hand, view their employees as naturally lazy and attempt to assert control over their employees to increase productivity. Types A and Z are grounded in William Ouchi's model of employee management and describe management from the perspective of collectivistic Japanese ideals (Type Z) versus individualistic American ideals (Type A).

30. Which of the following scenarios does NOT describe a scenario of high commitment to work?
    A. Georgia has worked at the same veterinarian's office for 10 years and loves working with animals.
    B. Jaime has only managed the food processing plant for 2 years, but the salary covers all of his expenses for his family.
    C. Mona enjoys her job as a laboratory technician less now than she did 20 years ago—but her company continues to pay for her certifications, and has generously funded her retirement account. She chooses to stay until she reaches retirement age.
    D. Roderick's supervisor for his position as a deckhand on a commercial fishing line has requested he work each fishing season for the last 4 years. The boat dock from which they depart is only 15 minutes away from his in-laws' home.

31. Which of the following is an example of a tertiary prevention strategy?
    A. Autism screenings at first- and second-year pediatrician appointments
    B. Crisis hotlines
    C. Follow-up appointments after cancer enters remission
    D. Inpatient mental health treatment

32. What aspect of the supervisory relationship best distinguishes it from a consultative relationship?
    A. The regular evaluation of assessment reports and session tapes
    B. The expectations the supervisor and supervisee have of one another
    C. The supervisor teaching the supervisee about conducting a new therapy with their current population
    D. The difference in power between supervisor and supervisee

33. APA Ethics Code 7.06 addresses which of the following training issues?
    A. Assessing trainee performance
    B. Consultation guidelines
    C. Mandatory group or individual therapy for trainees
    D. Sexual relationships with supervisees

(See answers on the next page.)

30. **D) Roderick's supervisor for his position as a deckhand on a commercial fishing line has requested he work each fishing season for the last 4 years. The boat dock from which they depart is only 15 minutes away from his in-laws' home.**
Work commitment is classified in three different categories: affective or attitudinal, continuance, and normative. The time that a person has spent with a company has less weight on their commitment to the work than these other factors, such as positive emotions associated with the work and the amount of investment the company has made into the employee. Georgia loves her job at the veterinarian's office, so regardless of how long she has worked for them she is likely committed to the job (affective commitment). Jaime's job is financially secure and has significant socioeconomic benefits for him and his family, so even though he has only been in the position for a short time, he is likely to remain in his position longer (continuance commitment). Although Mona's job does not offer the affective component of work commitment, the company has invested in her career development and her future for many years, which increases her commitment to the position (normative commitment). Research has not demonstrated that components like an employer's desire for employees to continue their positions or a position's geographic location compared to family supports an increase in one's long-term commitment to a position. Therefore, Roderick's situation is not conducive to work commitment.

31. **C) Follow-up appointments after cancer enters remission**
A crisis hotline is considered a secondary prevention effort because it is a method of resolving a problem, which has been detected at an early stage, or preventing it from becoming worse. People who call suicide hotlines are already experiencing some level of distress and the hotline representative is responsible for mitigating that distress. Primary prevention targets an at-risk group whose members have not yet experienced a problem and can include screening or preventive care like autism screenings at the pediatrician's office. Tertiary prevention focuses on preventing the reoccurrence (or relapse) of a problem after it's been addressed, like continuing to attend Alcoholics Anonymous meetings or attending regular follow-up appointments with an oncologist after cancer enters remission. Inpatient mental health treatment is a form of intervention or remedy when a problem has developed and is not considered a preventive measure.

32. **A) The regular evaluation of assessment reports and session tapes**
According to Bernard and Goodyear (2019), the single most important distinction between supervision and consultation is whether the evaluation of someone else's clinical work is necessary. This is a primary feature in supervision, but not consultation. While each activity may have different expectations within the relationship, this is considered a less important difference between the two professional activities. Sharing of expert knowledge could happen in either interaction and is not exclusive to either supervision or consultation. Lastly, there is certainly a power differential in a supervisory relationship, and while it is not inherent in a consultative relationship, one may still be present depending on the individuals participating in consultation and the reason for the consultative relationship.

33. **A) Assessing trainee performance**
APA Ethics Code 7.06 is titled "Assessing Student and Supervisee Performance." This statute outlines expectations and guidelines for the supervisor to ensure ethical supervision practices. Consultation guidelines are not addressed in the APA Ethics Code outside of addressing the role of confidentiality in consultative roles. Guidelines around requiring therapy for trainees are addressed in Code 7.05. APA Ethics Code 7.07 addresses sexual relationships with students and supervisees.

34. An experienced deaf psychologist offers a regular consultation meeting to other psychologists who want to gain competencies in working with clients in the deaf and hard of hearing community. This is an example of which kind of mental health consultation?

    A. Client-centered administrative consultation
    B. Client-centered case consultation
    C. Consultee-centered administrative consultation
    D. Consultee-centered case consultation

(See answers on the next page.)

34. **D) Consultee-centered case consultation**

In consultee-centered case consultation, consultees attending the consultation group need to increase broader cultural awareness and expertise in working with deaf clients generally. In client-centered consultation, the focus is more on the client with whom the consultee is working. There is something particular about their presenting problem or clinical presentation that the consultee needs assistance with from someone more experienced. Administrative consultation takes place at the agency or organization level and may involve a new manager learning how to carry out program-level job responsibilities (program-centered) or to effect change on an existing program or policy (consultee-centered).

Research Methods and Statistics

Amy E. Ellis, Nicole Mantella, Brianna Domaceti, and Luca Hartman

> **BROAD CONTENT AREAS**
> - Research design, methodology, and program evaluation
> - Instrument selection and validation
> - Statistical models, assumptions, and procedures
> - Dissemination methods

▶ INTRODUCTION

This chapter focuses on four broad content areas: (a) research design, methodology, and program evaluation (PE); (b) instrument selection and validation (topics covered under the more general topic of measurement); (c) statistical models, assumptions, and procedures; and (d) dissemination methods.

▶ RESEARCH METHODOLOGY

Science can be described as a systematic approach to knowledge acquisition. This continuum of knowledge acquisition is vast and ranges from simple observation/description to more sophisticated causal investigations. Research methods are the tools scientists use to describe, predict, determine the causes of and from, and understand/explain clinical phenomena such as behavior, experiences, cognitions, and emotions. Research endeavors in psychology generally involve hypothesis generation, operationalizing variables, data collection, and analyses, producing formal hypothesis tests and revision of initial hypotheses/theories.

THEORY AND HYPOTHESES

A theory is an organized set of beliefs about a phenomenon. For example, a theory of alcohol-use disorder etiology might posit several interrelated yet distinct developmental pathways to problematic alcohol use involving a broad spectrum of genetic, family environment, and broader social influences. According to Popper (1959), scientific theories must result in a set of propositions, or hypotheses, that can be refuted or disconfirmed. Hypotheses are predictions about associations between/among variables that often derive from a larger theoretical framework. Examples of hypotheses include (a) inconsistent discipline is associated with behavior problems in children, (b) cigarette smoking causes lung cancer, and (c) there are underlying barriers to advocacy in the field of psychology.

Simply stated, independent variables are often regarded as causes, whereas dependent variables are regarded as the effect, or change. Independent variables can be "manipulated." In social sciences, this may be less due to the researcher doing something overt and more so related to normal changes. For example, in studying whether age is associated with impostor syndrome, age would be the independent variable. Although a researcher cannot change age, this is subject to change depending on the individual. Also, we would expect that the older someone is, the less impostor syndrome they endorse (the dependent variable).

▶ STUDY DESIGN

In the ideal scenario, the primary research question proactively drives all decisions regarding participant sampling, study design, measurement of key study constructs, and analyses. In the next section, several study designs are described.

GROUP-BASED RANDOMIZED EXPERIMENTS

Randomized experiments are considered the gold standard for assessing causality (i.e., increasing internal validity). In a randomized experiment, participants might be randomly assigned to either brief dynamic psychotherapy for depression or a no-treatment control condition. In a basic two time-point (pretest–posttest) design, individuals who meet eligibility criteria are typically assessed at baseline, randomly assigned to a condition, exposed to treatment (or not, depending on condition), and then assessed at posttest. In this hypothetical study, the hypothesis is whether exposure to brief dynamic treatment (independent variable) *causes* a reduction in depression (dependent variable).

Random assignment of participants to treatments uses a chance process (similar to a lottery drawing) to determine which participants are exposed to treatment and which are not. The use of random assignment precludes systematic pretest group differences because the groups are probabilistically equated on all measured and unmeasured characteristics. Consequently, the randomized control condition generates an important hypothetical counterfactual scenario regarding what would have happened to individuals had they not been exposed to brief dynamic treatment. Note that the benefits of random assignment can be undone once the study commences should groups become unequivalent. For example, when studying differences between randomly assigned individuals with a history of trauma undergoing formal trauma exposure therapy as compared to person-centered therapy, those in the trauma-processing condition may have more attrition (i.e., drop-out) due to the nature and intensity of treatment, thereby making group comparisons unequivalent.

Efficacy Trials
In efficacy trials, an intervention's effects are examined under ideal circumstances, particularly with respect to treatment implementation. Efficacy trials often feature substantial clinician training and supervision and close monitoring of treatment adherence (often to a manual).

Effectiveness Trials
In effectiveness trials, an intervention's effects are examined under real-world conditions. Such trials often take place outside of academic settings (e.g., community mental health centers). Training and supervision will be less intensive relative to what is typically observed in efficacy trials and clients will often be less homogeneous diagnostically (e.g., more severe cases or comorbid cases may be included).

Intent-to-Treat Analyses
Intent-to-treat analyses were designed to analyze outcome data from randomized experiments involving participant attrition. In intent-to-treat analyses, researchers analyze outcome data from participants as a function of their original group assignment, regardless of their level of exposure to treatment. The analysis is intended to provide a conservative (and real-world) estimate

of the treatment effect because it is based on cases exposed to varying levels of treatment. Unfortunately, when individuals drop out of treatment, they usually fail to provide additional outcome data, creating *missing data* problems in the analysis. Analyses are complicated greatly by the presence of missing data; in such instances, researchers have to impute, or use alternative values for, the missing data or base analyses on individuals without complete data. Although "mean-substitution" and "last observation carried forward" are common methods of imputation, more sophisticated approaches (e.g., multiple imputation) are recommended by statisticians.

QUASI-EXPERIMENTAL STUDIES

Quasi-experimental studies are experiments that lack random assignment of participants to conditions. Similar to randomized experiments, a subset of participants is typically exposed to an intervention. Two common quasi-experiments in clinical psychology are when participants self-select into treatment conditions (e.g., participants can choose whether they want medication or not) and when groups are differentially exposed to treatment conditions (e.g., clients at one mental health clinic receive adjunctive pharmacotherapy and clients at a different clinic receive therapy only). When assignment is nonrandom, the burden is on the researcher to identify and render implausible alternative explanations for an apparent intervention effect (i.e., the researcher must rule out various threats to internal validity). Quasi-experiments can sometimes produce causal inferences that rival those from randomized trials. Two quasi-experimental designs known to produce stronger causal inferences are the interrupted time series design and the regression discontinuity design. For additional discussion of causal inferences in different types of designs, the reader is referred to West et al. (2000).

CORRELATIONAL STUDIES

Correlational studies (also called passive observational studies) are conducted when the researcher is not actively manipulating anything. These studies are often used to gain insight into the emergence of a relevant phenomenon. An example includes examining the correlation between personality traits of openness and agreeableness and psychological well-being.

Case–Control Designs

Case–control designs compare a group of participants who possess a certain characteristic (e.g., diagnosis of attention deficit hyperactivity disorder [ADHD]) with a group of participants who do not possess the characteristic. The former group comprises the *case* group, and the latter group, the *control* group. For example, a researcher might be interested in examining whether children with ADHD (case) differ from children without ADHD (control) on peer relations.

Cohort Designs

In cohort designs, an intact group (i.e., cohort) is followed over time to examine the emergence of and/or change in some outcome of interest. These designs are classified as longitudinal (also known as prospective) because individuals are assessed on at least two occasions. In some instances, a single cohort of individuals is followed. For example, researchers interested in the possible effects of neighborhood-level variables on substance use might follow a cohort of preschoolers in a given neighborhood for several years to examine associations among variables of interest. Multiple cohorts might also be followed. For example, one might be interested in following adolescents at high risk versus low risk for eventual alcohol-use disorders (AUDs). Multiple cohort studies are distinguished from case–control studies because in case–control studies, the groups differ on a central characteristic (e.g., diagnosis of ADHD), whereas in multiple cohort studies, the groups differ on exposure to some factor (e.g., poverty). If the multiple cohorts also differ in their age or some other salient developmental marker at the study's inception, the study is called a cross-sequential design. Such designs allow for the study of a longer developmental period over fewer years of data collection because several developmental cohorts (e.g., toddlers, preschoolers, and school-age children) are embedded in the study. Prospective studies that include age heterogeneity at the baseline assessment (e.g., 13-, 14-, and 15-year-olds) are also referred to as accelerated longitudinal designs or cross-sequential designs because researchers can observe phenomena over a longer developmental time frame using fewer waves of data collection.

SINGLE-CASE EXPERIMENTS

As with group-based experiments, single-case experiments are often designed to increase internal validity, that is, assess the causal influence of an intervention on an outcome. (Discussion of single-case experiments follows that presented by Kazdin [2003].) Common features of single-case experiments include intensive assessment before, during, and after intervention. Prolonged baseline assessment provides information about the pattern of changes in the outcome in the absence of the intervention.

ABAB Designs

The ABAB design is a single-case design that alternates the baseline A phase (intervention absent) with an intervention B phase (intervention present). The outcome of interest is assessed on multiple occasions within each phase. For example, in studying a child with frequent tantrums, a clinician might collect baseline tantrum data during days 1 to 4 (i.e., the first A phase) and tantrum data during days 5 to 8, in which parents are implementing time-out in response to all tantrums (i.e., the first B phase). This 8-day sequence would then be repeated one more time to observe the outcome under the second A and B phases. The idea is that the frequency of tantrums will be higher in the absence of the intervention (during the A phases; see Figure 9.1 for a hypothetical outcome plot).

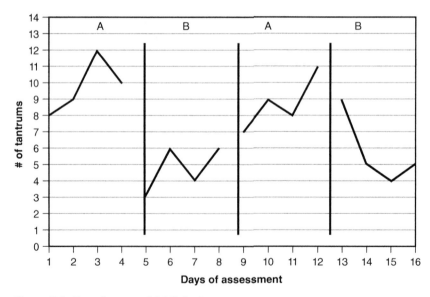

Figure 9.1 Data from an ABAB design.

Multiple Baseline Designs

In multiple baseline designs, replication of an effect is sought over multiple baselines, which can reflect different behaviors, settings, and/or groups (just to name a few). In continuing with the tantrum example, Figure 9.2 outlines results from a hypothetical multiple baseline design for measurements of tantrums, aggressive acts toward siblings, and foul language (for a single child). Solid lines represent the frequency of the relevant behavior in the absence of the intervention (i.e., during a baseline phase). Dashed lines represent the frequency of the relevant behavior once the intervention is implemented for the given behavior (e.g., time-out implemented following each

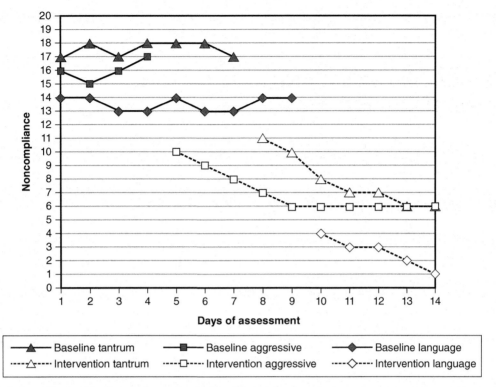

Figure 9.2 Results from a hypothetical multiple baseline design.

aggressive act directed toward a sibling). Figure 9.2 shows that the baseline for aggressive acts toward siblings lasted 4 days (i.e., measurement was conducted and no intervention applied), the baseline for tantrums lasted 7 days, and the baseline for foul language lasted 9 days. The results suggest that each behavior occurred less often once the intervention was introduced for that particular behavior—consistent with an intervention effect.

Evaluating Results in Single-Case Experiments

Although inferential statistical procedures can be used to analyze data from single-case experiments, it is more common for clinicians to rely on visual inspection of the data. Visual inspection is often supplemented with descriptive statistics. For example, clinicians can examine *mean changes* by comparing the average frequency of the outcome across different phases of the experiment (e.g., during the A vs. B phases). Clinicians can also examine *level shifts,* in which they compare the last data point in an immediately prior phase to the first data point in an immediately subsequent phase. If the latency of response is hypothesized to be immediate (e.g., the behavior will reduce dramatically as soon as the intervention is implemented), one might predict dramatic level changes between adjacent (baseline–intervention) phases. Clinicians can also examine *slope* (or functional form) *changes* by examining the rate of behavior change in different phases. For example, the behavior might increase in a fairly linear (i.e., constant) manner during the initial A phase and become fairly stable during the initial B phase. Such a change can be described as a change in slope—with the slope being positive in the A phase and flat (i.e., near zero) in the B phase.

Uncontrolled Case Studies

Case studies—in which one or a few cases are studied intensively—can also be subsumed under correlational research (if the researcher's status is passive, as described earlier). The prototypical uncontrolled case study is a retrospective examination of a single individual over time in the hope of understanding the case in a more comprehensive and nuanced manner without any researcher manipulation (hence, uncontrolled). Some famous case studies have been described in the literature (e.g., the case of Phineas Gage, who suffered personality changes after suffering an accident in which a railroad spline went through his frontal lobe).

▶ CRITICAL APPRAISAL AND APPLICATION OF RESEARCH FINDINGS

Campbell outlines four types of validity typology that can be used to describe and appraise research studies: internal, external, statistical conclusion, and construct. Note, no one type of validity is better than another, and often there are competing relationships among the types. For example, controlling for internal validity threats may render the experiment lacking in generalizability (external validity) and vice versa.

INTERNAL VALIDITY

Internal validity is the extent to which the association between x and y is *causal* in nature. For example, one might examine whether psychotherapy is causally related to a reduction in depression. A valid causal inference requires satisfaction of three criteria: (a) statistical association, (b) temporal precedence, and (c) nonspuriousness. Statistical association occurs when the hypothesized cause and its effect covary (e.g., exposure to psychotherapy is associated with lower levels of depression, relative to no treatment). Temporal precedence occurs when the cause precedes the effect (e.g., decreases in depression must come after exposure to therapy if we are to assume that psychotherapy is the cause).

Nonspuriousness occurs when the hypothesized cause—and not some other factor—is responsible for the effect (e.g., psychotherapy is responsible for decreased depression symptoms as opposed to the natural progression of symptoms which may remit or decrease in severity over time independent of any treatment). In the previous example, natural symptom remission is regarded as maturation and may be the "true" cause of symptoms decreasing and not the result of psychotherapy exposure. Spurious causes, or threats to internal validity, are described in the section titled Threats to Internal Validity. For a complete listing and definitions, refer to Shadish et al. (2002).

EXTERNAL VALIDITY

External validity is the extent to which the causal association can be *generalized to* or *across* variations in study instances (e.g., individuals, treatments, outcomes, settings, and times). An example of external validity is as follows. In a randomized controlled trial in which trans individuals are assigned to a peer-led 6-week affirmative care group as compared to a peer-led 6-week psychoeducational group, individuals in the affirmative care group were found to show greater reductions in minority stress as compared to the psychoeducation group. While this treatment may show benefit for trans folks, it may lack generalizability to other minoritized identities such as gay, bisexual, and lesbian individuals. Furthermore, it may lack generalizability when led by therapists.

STATISTICAL CONCLUSION VALIDITY

Statistical conclusion validity examines whether there is a statistical association between x and y, and the magnitude of this association. Many statistical conclusion validity issues—including statistical significance, effect size estimation, and statistical power—are discussed in the Statistical Methods section of this chapter.

CONSTRUCT VALIDITY

Construct validity is the extent to which inferences can be made from particular study instances (e.g., individuals) to the higher-order constructs from which they presumably derive. For example, researchers sometimes use inadequate labels to describe study instances (e.g., label a treatment "progressive relaxation" when the treatment has many additional therapeutic components). Not all studies are created equal. Moreover, the conclusions reached by authors are not always consistent with the contents of their research reports. Consequently, readers must play active roles in critically appraising research. Next, we present results from three hypothetical studies designed to examine the effects of brief dynamic psychotherapy on depression.

The data in Figure 9.3 derive from a design in which a single group of individuals was assessed at pretest, exposed to brief dynamic psychotherapy, and then assessed at posttest and two subsequent follow-ups. In such plots, average symptom levels (in this case, depression) are plotted as a function of treatment group and time point. Assuming the change depicted in Figure 9.3 is clinically meaningful, these data are *consistent* with an intervention effect. Although heartening, these data raise the question: "Did the treatment, and not some other variable, cause the observed reductions in depression?" Unfortunately, given the study's design in its absence of a control group, it is difficult to answer this causal question unambiguously, suggesting a possible internal validity threat.

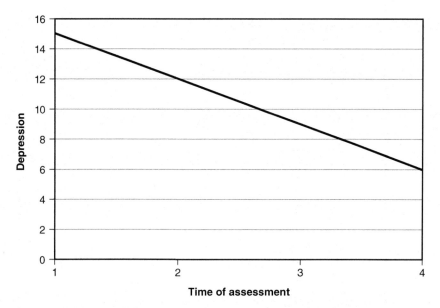

Figure 9.3 Hypothetical outcome plot from a single-group design. The bold line represents treated participants.

The data in Figure 9.4 derives from a randomized controlled trial in which brief dynamic psychotherapy was compared to a no-treatment control condition. The results are *not consistent* with an intervention effect because the reductions in depression exhibited by individuals exposed to brief dynamic treatment are identical to reductions exhibited by no-treatment control participants. Both groups improved at the same rate over time.

The results in Figure 9.5 are *consistent* with an intervention effect because individuals exposed to brief dynamic treatment reported greater reductions in depression relative to no-treatment control participants. Given the presence of a randomized no-treatment control group and the presumed absence of plausible alternative explanations, we assume a true treatment effect.

In all three plots, the average change in depression among treated participants is identical. As such, the proper interpretations of the trends for treated participants (i.e., the bold lines) are embedded within broader contexts—involving a mixture of logical and statistical inferences,

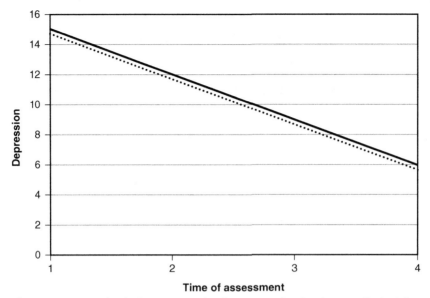

Figure 9.4 Hypothetical outcome plot from a randomized controlled trial not consistent with an intervention effect. The bold line represents treated participants and the dotted line, controls.

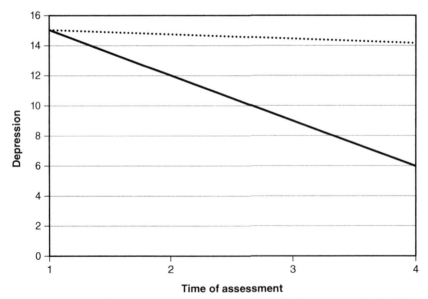

Figure 9.5 Hypothetical outcome plot from a randomized controlled trial consistent with an intervention effect. The bold line represents treated participants and the dotted line, controls.

often linked to design features. In the following section, several common threats to internal validity that can be particularly salient in studies that resemble the one-group pretest–posttest design are discussed. These threats—if deemed plausible in a given study—can help explain how results like those in Figure 9.3 could be mistaken for an intervention effect.

THREATS TO INTERNAL VALIDITY

Maturation
Maturation occurs when naturally occurring changes are mistaken for an intervention effect (e.g., when symptoms remit because of the passage of time rather than the effects of an intervention). For example, symptoms of posttraumatic stress disorder are known to decrease over time, even without intervention or treatment.

History
History occurs when some event (or constellation of events) takes place during the study and impacts the results in a manner mistaken for an intervention effect. For example, in a study in which students at School A are exposed to a peer support group for anxiety (intervention) and students at School B receive psychoeducation materials on anxiety (control), the authors concluded that because School A students fared better on anxiety and test scores, the peer intervention was effective. However, a history threat, such as the students at School B being exposed to a school shooting threat a week prior to the posttest assessment, would likely impact scores. Thus, such a historical influence—and not the intervention—might be responsible for relative lower levels of anxiety in School A students and maintained levels of anxiety in School B.

Statistical Regression
Statistical regression—also known as regression to the mean—occurs when extreme scores tend to revert to the mean on a subsequent evaluation. Statistical regression is more plausible in single-group studies in which *extreme performers* (e.g., severely depressed individuals) comprise the study sample.

Attrition
Attrition occurs when the pattern of participant drop-out impacts the way one might interpret the results as an intervention effect. In a single cohort study, if individuals who either remained stable in their symptoms or worsened dropped out of the study, it would leave mostly participants who improved. An outcome analysis based solely on the improvers might be mistaken for an intervention effect.

Testing
Testing occurs when exposing individuals to the pretest changes them in ways that might be mistaken for an intervention effect. For example, a pretest that asks detailed questions about the personal and social consequences of one's alcohol use might inspire individuals to lower their consumption.

Instrumentation
Instrumentation occurs when the measurement tool changes during the course of the study and impacts the results in a manner mistaken for an intervention effect. For example, if a more restrictive operationalization of "alcohol-related ED visits" was used following a media campaign designed to reduce alcohol-related injuries, an ostensible reduction in such visits might be mistaken for an effect of the media campaign. Additionally, context changes (such as changes in instructions by the experimenter) and response shifts (such as changes in the meaning of one's self-evaluation of a target) can also occur.

Selection and Interactions With Selection
Selection occurs in multiple-group studies when systematic differences among intervention groups can be mistaken for an intervention effect. In multiple-group studies, selection will typically combine with another threat (e.g., maturation) to produce the pattern of results. An example is provided in the following section.

Evaluating the Potential Impact of Internal Validity Threats

In single-group studies, a threat has to be *capable* of producing the pattern of results that were observed (e.g., in one group receiving a treatment for depression, other behaviors, like reading self-help books, could account for improved outcomes following treatment). In multiple-group studies, a threat has to be both *capable* of producing the pattern of observed results *and* it has to *vary systematically by group*. In other words, the threat has to be more prevalent in one of the groups. For example, in a two-group study, if the intervention group is more likely to naturally experience symptom remission relative to the control group, this differential maturation pattern could be mistaken for an intervention effect. This threat would be labeled a selection by maturation threat because the two groups are systematically different (i.e., selection) in their maturation. In multiple-group studies, all internal validity threats are considered interactions with selection because any threat (e.g., statistical regression) must vary systematically by group.

EXTERNAL VALIDITY ISSUES

Thus far, our discussion of critical appraisal has focused on internal validity issues. Clinicians and researchers are also interested in the generalizability of causal inferences to different populations, contexts, settings, and time periods. The following questions are relevant to external validity: Would the intervention be effective for men and women? Would the intervention be effective if delivered by paraprofessionals rather than clinical psychologists? Would the effects of the intervention persist over a longer follow-up? Would the intervention—developed with White families of European descent—produce similar results in Latine families of Cuban descent? Would the intervention produce similar results across university-based and community clinics? To test such questions empirically, one must test statistical interactions between the primary predictor (e.g., intervention) and the external validity characteristic of interest (e.g., participant gender). Consequently, threats to external validity are often framed as "interactions of the causal effect with. . . ." Answers to these questions help establish possible boundaries of an intervention's effects and are often quite useful to researchers and clinicians.

CONSTRUCT VALIDITY ISSUES RELATED TO CLINICAL INTERVENTIONS

Internal validity asks, "Does the intervention work?", whereas external validity asks, "Under what conditions does it work?" Another valuable question is, "How does the intervention work?" This last question involves establishing the construct validity of a given intervention in which the primary mechanisms of change are elucidated (e.g., Are decreases in social isolation and increases in positive cognitions leading to improvements in depressive symptoms following treatment?). Given the comprehensive nature of many psychological interventions, it is rare that participants are randomly assigned to interventions targeting a single mechanism. As such, attempts to elucidate mechanisms often involve statistical mediation analyses in which hypotheses about putative mechanisms are tested explicitly. An example of mediation is provided in the statistics section.

Therapeutic attention (i.e., "common factors" that span across all treatment regardless of specific intervention or modality) is a classic construct validity threat in randomized controlled trials in which an active intervention is compared to a no-treatment control. Intervention effects might result from *therapeutic attention* rather than from the mechanisms targeted by the intervention (e.g., reduced depressive cognitions). Measuring client change on the mechanisms (i.e., mediators) and conducting mediation analyses can help clarify issues of construct validity. Confounding clinicians with treatments is another possible threat to construct validity. That is, if two interventions are compared and each is delivered by a different clinician, the apparent superiority of one treatment over the other might actually result from the superiority of one clinician over the other. Finally, when interventions are delivered in groups, group cohesion—and not the proposed mechanisms of the therapeutic intervention—might be responsible for positive gains observed (another threat to construct validity).

LEVELS OF EVIDENCE

The current discussion of levels of evidence is modeled after Mudford et al. (2012). As knowledge in an area accumulates, discussions of ordering *evidence sources* along a continuum from low to high become more prominent. Often, for example, results from studies that tend to produce stronger internal validity inferences (e.g., well-conducted randomized controlled trials) are categorized as providing higher levels of evidence. Results from studies that tend to produce weaker internal validity inferences (e.g., single-group pretest–posttest designs) are categorized as providing lower levels of evidence. In addition to considering internal validity, external validity might be considered in levels of evidence. For example, replication of findings across multiple research groups and/or client populations would further strengthen a relatively higher level of evidence. Results from smaller-scale uncontrolled studies (e.g., case study) would be rated the lowest level of evidence among empirical studies. Expert opinions that are not data-based are considered the lowest level of evidence overall.

Researchers use various forms of research synthesis to integrate several studies on a related topic. Historically, these syntheses were narrative reviews of the literature in which researchers organized "box counts" of significant, nonsignificant, and counter findings. In the more recent past, researchers have relied on meta-analytic techniques to conduct formal quantitative syntheses of the literature. Systematic reviews involve curating an entire foundation of knowledge based on particular inclusion criteria (publication period, populations studied, design used, and independent and dependent variables assessed) and synthesizing primary findings across various studies. A systematic review is far more rigorous than a literature review, as it includes inclusion and exclusion criteria for studies. Where empirical studies set inclusion and exclusion criteria for participants, a systematic review/meta-analysis allows for articles to be aggregated and synthesized and follows a priori inclusion and exclusion criteria. In meta-analysis, researchers seek to explain variability in study effect sizes (e.g., the magnitude of the treatment–outcome association) as a function of study characteristics (e.g., methodological features and types of interventions). As such, meta-analysis can be a powerful tool in the accumulation of knowledge.

ETHICS AND RESEARCH

Much of research in clinical psychology involves human participants. To ensure that such research is conducted in an ethical manner and human participants are afforded necessary protections, it is common for researchers to request oversight from institutional review boards (IRBs). Such an oversight might be required (e.g., if the study is conducted using federal funds from certain agencies). Research is defined statutorily as systematic investigation designed to develop or contribute to generalizable knowledge. The Belmont Report (U.S. Department of Health, Education, and Welfare, 1979) details three basic principles that investigators must follow in conducting research with human participants: beneficence (not causing harm to individuals), respect for individuals' autonomy, and justice (equitable distribution of the potential risks/benefits). Researchers will communicate about the purposes of the research and the prospective participant's role so that the individual can make an informed decision about participation. This process of disclosure and discussion typically occurs collaboratively in the context of informed consent. Finally, participants are made aware that their participation is voluntary and that they may withdraw their participation at any time during the study. Vulnerable populations are defined as those individuals who may not have full autonomy due to situational power imbalances (i.e., prisoners, employees, pregnant individuals, or students), or limited capacity to make decisions (e.g., individuals with cognitive impairment, infants, or minors). Additional protections are typically undertaken when research is conducted with vulnerable groups. Research with animals is also held to ethical standards. Animal research must be justified and investigators should not only have IRB approval but also conform to the Animal Welfare Act, among other legal protections.

▶ MEASUREMENT

The next section covers topics related to how psychologists measure constructs. This section was informed primarily by the following sources: Clark and Watson (1995), West and Finch (1997), John and Benet-Martinez (2000), and Messick (1995).

LATENT CONSTRUCTS AND OBSERVABLE MEASURES

Observable study measures (i.e., tests) are considered fallible representations of latent (unobserved) constructs of interest (e.g., depression). For example, a measure of depression might capture several sources of variance—including systematic variance related to depression (e.g., depressive symptoms vary across individuals), systematic variance related to other constructs (e.g., overlap of symptoms with anxiety), systematic method variance related to its measurement format (e.g., self-report of depression may vary as opposed to clinician observation), and random error. Psychologists study these and other related issues by theorizing about a nomological network (Cronbach & Meehl, 1955)—the relations among observed measures, relations between observed measures and latent constructs, and relations among latent constructs. Looking at a measure's reliability and validity can facilitate understanding of the nomological network.

CLASSICAL TEST THEORY AND RELIABILITY

Classical test theory assumes that the variance of an observed measure comprises true score variance and random error variance. *True score variance* reflects the construct of interest (e.g., depression). *Random error variance* reflects all other factors that vary randomly over testing occasions to impact an individual's score (e.g., test fatigue). As such, the reliability of a measure is viewed as the ratio of true score variance to total variance. (True score variance is consistent with *consistency* or *dependability*, concepts that are often present in discussions of reliability.) Because it is impossible to know an individual's true score on a psychological attribute, in order to estimate reliability, classical test theorists assume that two psychological tests can be constructed in a parallel manner. Tests are considered parallel if (a) the tests measure the same psychological construct (also known as "tau equivalence") and (b) the tests have the same level of error variance. These assumptions allow researchers to estimate reliability using respondents' observed scores through various methods—including internal consistency, test–retest, alternate or parallel forms, and interrater or interobserver.

Internal Consistency

Internal consistency is used to measure reliability on a single testing occasion by examining the degree of inter-item correlation in multiple-item tests. The Cronbach alpha is a common index of internal consistency and is a function of the number of test items and the degree of inter-item correlation. Other measures of internal consistency reliability include: (a) Kuder–Richardson Formula 20—often abbreviated KR-20—which can be used when the items are dichotomous (e.g., true/false), and (b) split-half reliability—based on sorting the items on a psychological test into two parallel subtests of equal size. Note that measures of internal consistency are often erroneously interpreted as evidence of a scale's unidimensionality—suggesting that the multiple items reflect a single construct.

Test–Retest

Test–retest reliability is used to measure the reliability of a measure over time in repeated administrations. The test–retest approach is heavily dependent on the assumption that true scores remain stable across the test–retest interval. Consequently, test–retest reliability coefficients are often referred to as stability coefficients. The Pearson correlation and the intraclass correlation coefficient are common indices of test–retest reliability. One example of where test–retest reliability would be beneficial is in measuring attachment style as it is presumed to be stable over time.

Alternate or Parallel Forms
Alternate-forms reliability is assessed by correlating two tests meant to measure the same construct. The tests are of alternate or parallel forms because the items on each test—although distinct—are thought to represent the same underlying construct. The Pearson correlation and the intraclass correlation coefficient are common indices of alternate-forms reliability. One such example of this is looking at the alternate-forms reliability between the Beck Depression Inventory and the Patient Health Questionnaire as both are thought to measure depression as a latent construct.

Interrater Reliability
Sometimes, raters or coders are used to code observational data. Interrater reliability is the extent to which coding is consistent or stable among raters. An example might involve asking a parent–child dyad to participate in a puzzle-completion task that is videotaped. The tape can later be coded for various constructs (e.g., cooperation). If at least two raters are used, interrater reliability can be computed by one of several indices (e.g., the Cohen kappa and the intraclass correlation).

VALIDITY
Historically, validity has been framed with the following question: "Does the test measure what it purports to measure?" In the past two decades, this fairly simple question has been expanded. In a recent publication of measurement standards in psychology and education, the American Educational Research Association, the American Psychological Association, and the National Council on Measurement in Education (1999) agreed that construct validity is an organizing framework that should include evidence from five primary domains: (a) test content, (b) response processes, (c) internal structure, (d) relations with other variables, and (e) consequences of use. In the following section, we describe several of these elements and how they relate to the forms of validity commonly discussed in textbooks (e.g., content validity).

Face Validity
Face validity is the extent to which items appear to measure the construct of interest. Face validity has implications for how individuals respond to items; as such, it can be conceptualized as an element of response processes. An example is a measure of anxiety that directly asks about symptoms of nervousness and agitation.

Content Validity
Content validity examines whether test items adequately represent the content domains for the relevant construct. In measurement design, content validity is often examined empirically by asking experts to rate the adequacy of items in relation to the relevant content domains. For example, when examining the construct of depression, experts might require the inclusion of items rating hopelessness, anhedonic symptoms, and suicidal ideation.

Structural Validity
Structural validity—also known as internal structure—is the extent to which the structure of the *measure* is consistent with the theorized factor structure of the *construct*. Structural validity questions can be assessed empirically using exploratory and/or confirmatory factor-analytic procedures (see the following section). For example, the Big Five Inventory is a measure theorized to capture five broad personality factors—extraversion, agreeableness, conscientiousness, neuroticism, and openness—and its factor structure is consistent with these five factors (John, 1990).

Criterion and Concurrent Criterion Validity

The measure should correlate with other measures (i.e., criterion variables) in a manner consistent with a priori hypotheses. For example, a measure of deviance proneness should correlate with measures believed to reflect deviance (e.g., early onset of illicit drug use). When these associations are contemporaneous, concurrent criterion validity is examined. When the criterion is measured at a subsequent time point, predictive criterion validity is examined. Criterion validity can also be evaluated by examining whether relevant groups vary on the characteristic of interest (e.g., youth with juvenile justice involvement should be higher on deviance proneness relative to youth without juvenile justice involvement).

Convergent and Discriminant Validity

Theory regarding associations among constructs—that is, a piece of the nomological network described earlier—can be used to predict how measures of constructs *converge* with either measures of similar constructs or different measures of the same construct and *diverge* from measures of dissimilar constructs. A multitrait–multimethod matrix can be used to evaluate convergent and discriminant validity. For example, a measure of psychological well-being and a measure of self-esteem would correlate with one another (individuals who report more psychological well-being will also report higher levels of self-esteem), suggesting convergent validity. In the case of discriminant validity, a measure of psychological well-being should not correlate highly with a measure of impostor syndrome. If it does correlate highly, this suggests that our measure of psychological well-being does not measure a separate construct.

EXTENSIONS OF CLASSICAL TEST THEORY AND STATISTICAL TOOLS USED IN MEASUREMENT

Generalizability Theory

Generalizability theory assumes that in addition to true score variance, there are additional possible sources of *systematic* variance (i.e., facets) that contribute to an individual's score on a test. Researchers can vary these facets and see whether they account for significant variance in an individual's score. For example, a researcher could examine whether person (e.g., gender and age) or setting (e.g., classroom, playground, and home) variables impact observer agreement on aggression ratings.

Item Response Theory

Item response theory (IRT) extends classical test theory by taking into account that an individual's response is influenced by qualities of both the individual and the test item. In the classic single-parameter (Rasch) model for dichotomous items, the probability of a correct response is viewed as a function of (a) item difficulty and (b) the respondent's level on the trait. For example, the vast majority of respondents with an average level of a trait (e.g., intelligence) might respond correctly to an easy item but incorrectly to a hard item. Furthermore, in a two-parameter model, items also vary in their level of *discrimination*. Items that are high on discrimination are better able to differentiate individuals on the trait of interest (e.g., can distinguish those with low vs. high intelligence).

Exploratory and Confirmatory Factor Analysis

Exploratory factor analysis (EFA) and confirmatory factor analysis (CFA) are statistical procedures used to examine factor structure. Underlying both approaches is the notion that the latent (i.e., unobserved) constructs account for common variance in the observed items. EFA is used when developing/refining a measure or when researchers are less certain about the measure/construct's factor structure. CFA is used when existing theory makes specific predictions about a measure/construct's factor structure. Both procedures quantify factor loadings (i.e., the association between an item and its factor) and correlations among factors. Also, both procedures require the researcher to make many analytical decisions. In EFA, three primary decisions are (1) choosing a method of factor extraction, (2) choosing a method of factor rotation, and (3) deciding on the number of factors to retain. Factor rotation methods—which impact factor loadings and correlations among factors—are either orthogonal or oblique. In orthogonal rotations, the factors are assumed to be uncorrelated. In oblique rotations, the factors are assumed to be correlated—often the case in psychology. In practice, determining the number of factors to retain is frequently accomplished by visual inspection of the screen plot and by the "eigenvalues greater than 1" criterion. Both approaches attempt to differentiate between factors that account for meaningful variance and those that do not. A more sophisticated approach to determining the number of factors is based on parallel analysis in which factors are retained when their eigenvalues are greater than *parallel* eigenvalues based on randomly generated data.

In CFA, the researcher chooses an estimation routine and typically chooses a means of comparing competing models for relative fit (e.g., comparing a three-factor solution with a two-factor solution). Several fit indices can help with this last decision—including the chi-square test, root mean square error of approximation (RMSEA), and standardized root mean square residual (SRMR). All fit indices quantify (albeit in slightly different ways) how well the model-implied covariance matrix reproduces the estimated population covariance matrix of the analysis variables, based on the particular parameterizations of the specified models.

Measurement Error

For a set of depression measures, one can capture the shared depression-related variance across the measures in the form of a latent variable by using CFA. This latent variable is theoretically free from measurement error because the nondepression-related variance has been removed. One of the advantages of conducting statistical analyses on latent variables (as in the case of structural equation modeling, described in the following section) is the gain in statistical power that results when measurement error is removed from the constructs of interest.

MEASURE DEVELOPMENT, SELECTION, AND USE WITH HETEROGENEOUS PARTICIPANT POPULATIONS

The topics discussed earlier are also relevant for measure development and selection. The nomological network surrounding a particular construct and its dimensions (i.e., factors) can be used to develop a measure. Researchers often begin this process by reading the relevant literature to refine understanding of the construct, its potential factors, and its possible boundaries (how it is different from other related constructs). From there, the researcher can begin to develop a broad item pool covering the content dimensions (i.e., factors) that map their current theoretical understanding. Items should be well-written and easily understood by the target population. Items that are hard to understand (e.g., use double negatives) and items that create possible response conflicts (e.g., use of a compound question) should be avoided. Experts in the area can help the scale developer assess whether the construct content is adequately captured by the item pool. Once the initial item pool is finalized, different samples of respondents are typically asked to complete the measure. Early in the process, respondents might be asked to give qualitative feedback (e.g., feedback on item readability, understandability, and language usage). Later, statistical analyses (e.g., EFA, CFA, and IRT) may be used to make decisions about final items to retain. The initial process concludes when the desired psychometric properties (e.g., reliability) have been achieved and preliminary construct validation efforts suggest the measure is operating in a way consistent with theory. The process of construct validation, however, is iterative and subject to revision as the relevant nomological network is augmented by additional research.

In selecting a measure, the type of data of primary interest should be considered. John and Benet-Martinez (2000) categorize data sources into four categories: LOTS. The L is for life events data; O, for observational data; T, for testing (including standardized measures of performance, motivation, and/or achievement); and S, for self-report data. Researchers will often collect data from at least two data sources for a more comprehensive view of a construct. For example, clinicians who work with parents of children with disruptive behaviors might ask parents to report on parenting practices. Researchers might also videotape parent–child interactions and ask independent judges to objectively rate parenting practices. In this case, parents' self-report of parenting practices (S) can be corroborated by observational ratings of parenting practices (O). At the minimum, measures should (a) fit the researcher's conceptualization of the construct and (b) be psychometrically reliable and valid.

These criteria are more easily satisfied when the researcher is studying individuals similar to those on whom the original measure was developed. If the researcher is studying individuals who have not been represented in existing theory and research, the researcher should examine whether the measure "behaves the same way" in the novel sample. This issue is often examined in the context of *measurement invariance*. As in this instance, researchers might examine if the measure remains invariant over different groups of individuals (e.g., licensed clinical social workers and licensed clinical psychologists), or over different developmental periods (e.g., adolescence and emerging adulthood). Empirical examination of measurement invariance typically involves estimating a series of statistical models to test more basic assumptions (e.g., the construct involves the same number of factors) to more advanced assumptions (e.g., factor loadings are equal across groups of participants). Also, various forms of criterion validity can be examined. For example, researchers can examine whether the construct predicts subsequent outcomes in a similar manner in the novel sample. These strategies are based on the assumption that the construct's nomological network is similar for the original and novel samples. If the nomological network is different in the novel sample (e.g., because the construct has a different factor structure and/or the construct has a different pattern of criterion validity), results obtained in that sample can be misleading. In such a situation, researchers should work to develop a measure that captures the richness of the construct in the novel sample. This would require following the steps noted earlier regarding measure development/validation.

▶ STATISTICAL METHODS

Statistical methods are organized around two broad categories—descriptive (description of existing sample data) and inferential (predictions about populations from sample data). Inferential statistics are often further divided into parametric and nonparametric methods. Prior to discussing these various classes of statistics, levels of measurement are discussed.

LEVELS OF MEASUREMENT

Characteristics of interest to psychologists (e.g., depression, IQ, and extraversion) are measured using many different response scales. There are four common levels of measurement: nominal, ordinal, interval, and ratio.

Nominal
A nominal scale is used to categorize qualitative variables that cannot be ordered quantitatively (e.g., political party affiliation). Nominal scales specify differences in *kind*, but not differences in amount.

Ordinal
An ordinal scale allows researchers to arrange responses according to order or relative rank. Although response options can be judged *greater than* or *less than* one another, the magnitude of such differences is unknown (e.g., high confidence, average confidence, and low confidence where there is a clear order but the quantitative difference between categories is unknown). Many variables in psychology are measured by a Likert response scale, such as 1 (strongly disagree) to 5 (strongly agree).

Interval

An interval scale of measurement allows for the ordered examination of the magnitude of differences among responses. Magnitude differences can be examined because every unit of measurement is equal to every other unit along the entire range of responses. An interval scale lacks a true zero point (suggesting the complete absence of the characteristic). The Fahrenheit temperature scale is an example of interval data (although a temperature of 0 degrees exists, this does not represent a true absence of temperature).

Ratio

Variables measured on a ratio scale have both equal intervals and a true zero point. Although it is hard to imagine psychological variables with a true zero point (e.g., someone with no extraversion), many physical variables are measured on ratio scales (e.g., height, weight, distance).

DESCRIPTIVE STATISTICS

Descriptive statistics (descriptives) are used to organize, describe, and simplify data. Descriptives include measures of central tendency and variability. Researchers often use tabular and/or graphical displays like the histogram in Figure 9.6, which plots responses (aggregated into columns or pillars) along the *x*-axis (i.e., the horizontal axis) and the frequency of occurrence along the *y*-axis (i.e., the vertical axis).

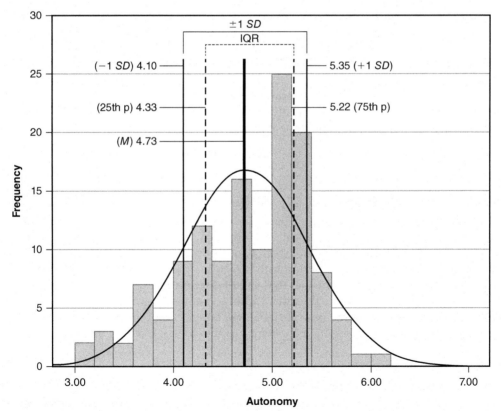

Figure 9.6 Histogram of autonomy subscale of Ryff's measure of psychological well-being.

IQR, interquartile range; M, sample mean.

Central Tendency

Measures of central tendency are used to identify the center of a distribution of scores. The mean is the arithmetic average and is computed by adding up the scores and dividing by the number of scores. The mean is used for interval or ratio scales when the distributions are not highly skewed. The median is the score that corresponds to the 50th percentile; it cuts the distribution of scores in half. The median is used when (a) data are ordinal or (b) when data are interval or ratio, but the distribution is highly skewed (the median is less affected by skewness). The mode is the most commonly occurring score. The mode is used when data are nominal.

In symmetrical distributions with a single mode, the mean, median, and mode are identical. In real-world data, in which some departure from symmetry is typical, these values will vary somewhat. Adding/subtracting constants (e.g., subtracting the number 10) from all scores will have the same impact on the mean (e.g., the new mean equals the original mean minus 10). The same is true for multiplying or dividing all scores by a constant.

The data presented in Figure 9.6 are based on a measure of autonomy (Ryff, 1989) assessed by nine items on a six-point Likert response scale ranging from 1 (*strongly disagree*) to 6 (*strongly agree*). In this case, each individual's score ($n = 133$) is based on a mean of the nine items. The overall sample mean (*M*), represented by the thicker solid black line, is 4.73. Although not presented in the histogram, the median and mode are 4.89 and 5.00, respectively.

Variability

Measures of variability describe the scatter or dispersion of scores in a distribution. The range is computed by subtracting the minimum from the maximum observed value. The interquartile range (IQR) captures the middle 50% of the distribution and is computed by subtracting the 25th percentile (first quartile) from the 75th percentile (third quartile). The SD captures the average distance of scores from the mean; its computation involves a series of steps (see the following section). The variance is the square of the SD. In Figure 9.6, two dashed vertical lines denote the 25th (4.33) and 75th percentiles (5.22). Consequently, the IQR is 0.89. The SD for this subscale is 0.62. The thinner solid vertical lines denote −1 SD (4.10) and +1 SD (5.35).

In general, the variance and SD are preferred measures of variability, given that they are derived from all scores and are involved in the computation of many parametric statistics. The definitional formula for the sample SD is as follows:

$$SD = \sqrt{\frac{\sum(x-M)^2}{N-1}}$$

If the square root symbol was removed, the resulting quantity would be the variance. The numerator of the fraction is commonly called the sum of squares (SS) and is short for sum of squared deviations (i.e., the mean is subtracted from each score, squared, and the resulting numbers are added). The denominator of the fraction, sometimes called the finite sample correction, is equal to degrees of freedom (*df*). Dividing the SS by a smaller number ($N - 1$, rather than N) makes the SD larger to correct for the fact that samples tend to be less variable than the populations from which they derive. Unlike the mean, adding/subtracting constants from a set of scores does not alter the SD (the SD of the new variable will equal that of the original variable). Similar to the mean, multiplying/dividing by a constant has the same impact on the SD.

The Normal Distribution and z-Scores

Figure 9.6 suggests that the shape of the distribution of autonomy responses is *approximately* normal. Many physical and psychological characteristics follow a normal distribution, but are measured by different scales (e.g., inches for height and pounds for weight) with different means and SDs. It is sometimes helpful to place these characteristics on a common scale such as *z*-scores; the *z*-distribution is often referred to as the standard normal distribution. Because the standard

z-Score Conversion

Values for any variable believed to follow a normal distribution can be converted to z-scores with the following formula:

$$z = \sqrt{\frac{x - M}{SD}}$$

(These are sample statistics, quantities based on samples of observations. If one had all scores from the entire population, they would report population parameters instead of statistics. Population parameters are represented by Greek symbols: M would be replaced by μ and SD would be replaced by σ.)

Properties of the Normal z-Distribution

When a z-score conversion is used, the resulting z-distribution has the following properties: (a) the mean is 0, (b) the SD is 1, and (c) each z-score represents the position of the score in relation to the mean, in SD units. In other words, an z-score of −1.27 denotes a score exactly 1.27 SDs *below* the mean.

Probability and the Normal z-Distribution

Figure 9.7 contains the standard normal distribution for IQ. The x-axis displays values of original scores, z-scores, and T-scores. Vertical lines denote the mean and ± 1, 2, and 3 SDs. A percentile suggests that a certain proportion of scores fall at or below the score in question. For example, the percentile associated with a z-score of 1.96 is 0.975 (suggesting that 97.5% of scores are less than or equal to a z-score of 1.96). This also suggests that the proportion of z-scores falling above 1.96 is 0.025 (or 2.5%), because these two proportions have to sum to 1.0. The percentages of scores in each area of the standard normal distribution are also displayed.

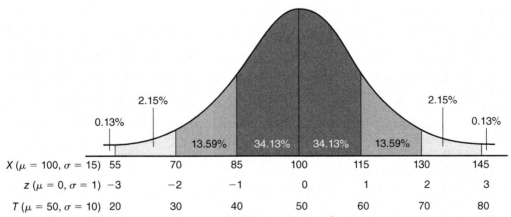

Figure 9.7 The standard normal z-distribution based on IQ (with raw scores, z-scores, and T-scores depicted on x-axis).

Note that in addition to using a z-score standardization, researchers sometimes use a T-score standardization (e.g., the Minnesota Multiphasic Personality Inventory–3). The T-score standardization sets the new mean at 50 and the new SD at 10. As such, a score of 60 falls 1 SD above the mean and a score of 40 falls 1 SD below the mean. Relevant percentiles can be computed by conversion of T to z: $(T − 50)/10$.

Distribution Shape and Departures From Normality

Figure 9.6, which is based on real-world data for the autonomy subscale of psychological well-being, and the depiction of the standard normal (z) distribution in Figure 9.7 are different. While Figure 9.7 is perfectly symmetrical, Figure 9.6 is skewed. Skewness measures departures from symmetry in which there is a piling of cases on the lower (positive skew) or higher end (negative skew) of the x-axis. Figure 9.6 data are negatively skewed (skewness = −0.57). When variables are negatively skewed, the mean, median, and mode are typically ordered from lowest to highest (the opposite is true of positively skewed data). Kurtosis measures the relative peakedness of the distribution. Leptokurtic distributions (positive kurtosis values) are more peaked than the normal curve, whereas platykurtic distributions (negative kurtosis values) are flatter. Kurtosis for Figure 9.6 is −0.24. Note that if a distribution is skewed, converting the original scores to z-scores will not alter the shape of the distribution (skew and kurtosis values will remain unchanged). Statisticians will sometimes use "normalizing" transformations to reduce skewness prior to analyses (e.g., natural log transformations).

INFERENTIAL STATISTICS

Parametric and Nonparametric Approaches

Inferential statistics are often divided into two broad classes—parametric and nonparametric. Compared to nonparametric statistics, parametric statistics (a) make more distributional assumptions (e.g., that the distribution is normal), (b) assume data are measured on an interval or ratio scale, (c) are conducted on actual data (as opposed to on ranks derived from data), and (d) allow researchers to test more specific hypotheses about the populations from which observations are drawn. Nonparametric statistics are typically used when assumptions of parametric approaches are (seriously) violated and/or when the data cannot be used to compute necessary quantities for parametric statistics. If the assumptions of parametric statistics are met, they result in more powerful statistical tests.

Given that parametric statistics are more commonly used in psychology, this general analytical approach is described extensively, and examples are provided.

Null Hypothesis Significance Testing

Inferential statistical procedures use sample data to test hypotheses about presumed population parameters. Because samples are fallible representations of the populations from which they derive, probability theory is used to quantify the likelihood of the data (e.g., the sample mean), given the presumed population parameter (in this case, the population mean). If the sample data would occur relatively infrequently (<5% of the time), the data suggest that the assumption made about the original population parameter should be rejected. Null hypothesis significance testing (NHST) is the most commonly encountered hypothesis testing method in psychology. As such, NHST forms the backdrop of inferential statistics in psychology. In NHST, the researcher specifies two mutually exclusive hypotheses (null and alternative) regarding the population parameter of interest. The typical null hypothesis posits no effect in the population. On the other hand, the alternative hypothesis (or the researcher hypothesis) subsumes all other possible outcomes. For example, in a study examining the effects of psychotherapy on depression in a group that received treatment and a control group, the null hypothesis specifies that the two population means are equal ($\mu_t = \mu_c$) and the alternate hypothesis specifies that the group that receives treatment will show lower scores on depression than the control group. Remember that because inferential statistics involve testing hypotheses about population parameters based on sample data, the null and alternative hypotheses are specified in terms of population parameters.

Statistical Significance and Probability

Once sample data are collected and analyzed using an appropriate test statistic, the researcher makes a decision to declare results as statistically significant (i.e., rejecting the null hypothesis) or nonsignificant (i.e., failing to reject the null hypothesis). When the sample data would occur relatively infrequently assuming the null hypothesis (e.g., the data would occur less than 5% of the time if the null hypothesis were true—$p < .05$), the results are considered statistically significant and the null hypothesis is rejected.

Correct and Incorrect Researcher Decisions

As NHST operates with two hypotheses on which to base scientific judgment, it follows that two types of errors can occur. Type I errors occur when a *true* null hypothesis *is* incorrectly rejected (i.e., results are declared statistically significant even though the null hypothesis is true). The probability of Type I errors is equal to the alpha (α) or the a priori criterion set for statistical significance (usually 0.05 or 5%). Type II errors occur when a *false* null hypothesis *is not* rejected (i.e., results are not declared statistically significant even though the null hypothesis is false). The long-range probability of Type II errors is beta (β). Understanding the differences between null and alternative hypotheses is easier when you make the assumption that the truth in reality is known (which is rarely the case in psychological research). For example, if we assume that in the population $\mu_T = \mu_C$ (e.g., we know a treatment will have no effect on those exposed to it and the population means in both treated and control participants would be identical), then researchers who rejected this true null hypothesis based on their sample data would be committing a Type I error (identifying an effect of treatment that does not exist in the population). If 100 independent investigation teams conducted studies to test this treatment effect (using alpha = 0.05 as the criterion for statistical significance), we would expect five teams to commit Type I errors. Conversely, if we assume that in the population a treatment has an effect (e.g., null: $\mu_T = \mu_C$; alternative: $\mu_T \neq \mu_C$) and researchers failed to reject the null, in this instance, researchers would be committing a Type II error (failing to identify an effect that *exists* in the population). If 100 independent investigation teams conducted this study under circumstances in which statistical power was equal to 0.90, we would expect 10 teams to commit Type II errors (i.e., fail to detect an effect that exists in the population).

Statistical Power

Statistical power is the probability of correctly rejecting a false null hypothesis (i.e., finding an effect when one exists in the population), and it is calculated as $1 - \beta$. If the probability of a Type II error (β) in a given study was 0.20, then statistical power would be equal to 0.80 (i.e., $1 - \beta = 1 - 0.20 = 0.80$). Several factors can influence power, including sample size (as N increases, power increases), alpha (as alpha increases, power increases), directional versus nondirectional hypothesis tests (directional tests are more powerful; see the following section), the magnitude of the effect (larger effects result in more power), and the reliability of the measures used (more reliable measures result in more power).

Supplementing Information Regarding Statistical Significance

Statistical significance is influenced by sample size (e.g., larger, meaningful effects might not reach statistical significance in smaller samples, but smaller, less meaningful effects might reach statistical significance in larger samples). Therefore, statistical significance information should be supplemented with effect size estimates that describe the magnitude or strength of the effect under consideration. For example, a common effect size estimate used in treatment outcome research is the Cohen *d*, which reflects the standardized mean difference between two groups (e.g., treatment and control). The Cohen *d* is computed as the mean difference between two groups divided by the pooled SD. Cohen's interpretational guidelines indicated that |*ds*| of 0.2, 0.5, and 0.8 are suggestive of small, moderate, and large effects, respectively. CIs construct an interval around a given population parameter (e.g., a correlation coefficient). These intervals provide information regarding statistical significance and provide lower- and upper-bound estimates of the parameter—based on a certain level of confidence (e.g., 95%). For example, a correlation of 0.47 with a 95% CI ranging from 0.20 to 0.69 suggests that one can be 95% confident that this specific interval contains the population parameter. In this example, because the interval does not contain zero (the typical population parameter assumed under the null), the results will be regarded as statistically significant (at $\alpha = 0.05$). CIs are helpful in conceptualizing the notion of uncertainty, which is useful to keep in mind as one is making statistical inferences.

Clinical significance, like effect size, goes beyond statistical significance to describe the clinical importance of an effect. Clinical significance can be quantified in several ways. For example, in a study examining the effects of cognitive-behavioral treatment on women with body dysmorphic disorder, Rosen et al. (1995) showed that following treatment, 81.5% of treated participants were classified as clinically improved versus 7.4% in the control group. Clinically significant improvement was operationalized as (a) no longer meeting diagnostic criteria and (b) scoring two standard errors (SEs) below a pretest score on one of the primary study outcomes. Based on these data, the odds of reaching this threshold of clinically significant improvement were 55 times higher in the treated group relative to the control group! An additional measure of clinical significance that has been reported in the literature more recently is the number needed to treat (NNT). For a binary (success/failure) outcome, NNT = $1/(S_t - S_c)$, where S_t and S_c reflect rates of success in the treatment and control groups, respectively. The NNT quantifies the number of additional patients in the treatment and control conditions needed to generate one additional positive outcome in the treatment group relative to the control group. As such, when NNT is larger, the effect is smaller (because many additional patients would need to be treated to generate an additional positive outcome in the treatment group). The NNT for the data presented earlier in this paragraph would be 1.35 or $1/(0.815 - 0.074)$, suggesting a clinically meaningful effect. For additional discussion of NNT and other measures of clinical significance, see Kraemer and Kupfer (2006).

The One-Sample z-Test

The one-sample z-test can be used to compare a single sample mean to a population mean, when the population SD is known. Assume that a researcher was interested in testing whether a sample of college students ($N = 20$) scored significantly different than average (100) on a standard intelligence (i.e., IQ) test. We will also assume a population SD of 15. The null hypothesis in this situation would be $\mu = 100$ and the alternative hypothesis would be $\mu \neq 100$. Assume that the average IQ in the sample is 110. On its face, this sample statistic appears different than the population parameter under the null hypothesis (100). Remember that hypothesis testing examines the probability of the data, given the null. In this instance, it would be important to know the probability of obtaining a sample mean of 110, given a population mean of 100. If it is determined that this sample mean would occur relatively infrequently (less than 5% of the time) under the null, the null hypothesis would be rejected. Probability theory helps inform this decision.

The Sampling Distribution of the Mean

If data are collected from all possible random samples of size 20 (the current sample size) from a population with a mean IQ of 100 (the value assumed under our null hypothesis), many of these sample means will be close to the population mean (e.g., 99, 98, 101, 102) and fewer sample means will be farther away (e.g., 80, 81, 120, 121). If a histogram is used to plot all of these sample means (i.e., create a sampling distribution of the mean), three important facts are observed: (a) the mean of all sample means will equal the population mean, (b) the SD of the sampling distribution (also called the SE of the mean) will equal the population SD divided by the square root of the sample size (in this case, $15/\sqrt{20} = 3.35$), and (c) the sampling distribution will be normal. The SE of the mean and other SEs quantify the average distance of sample statistics from relevant population parameters. With these pieces of information, the probability of observing the particular the sample statistic ($M = 110$) based on a population parameter of 100 can be quantified. This is where the one-sample z-test becomes relevant.

Computations for the One-Sample z-Test
The formula for the one-sample z-test is as follows:

$$z = \frac{M - \mu}{\sigma_M}$$

The numerator is the difference between the sample mean ($M = 110$) and the population mean ($\mu = 100$). The denominator is the SE of the mean (3.35, computed earlier). If z is solved, the answer is 2.98. Although not stated explicitly earlier, the hypothesis test in this instance is two-tailed or nondirectional (leaving open the possibility that the sample mean will be greater than or *less* than the population mean of 100). This lack of specificity (regarding the difference between the sample statistic and the population parameter) results in a two-tailed or nondirectional hypothesis test. Because it is known that the sampling distribution of the mean follows a normal distribution, the standard normal table can be used to quantify the probability of our sample data—given the population mean assumed under the null.

Determining Statistical Significance
We mentioned earlier that results are deemed statistically significant if the data would occur relatively infrequently under the null hypothesis. In this specific instance, the question revolves around the probability associated with our one-sample z statistic. Critical z values of ±1.96 separate the middle 95% of z-test statistics from the extreme 5% (2.5% of z values greater than 1.96 and 2.5% of z values less than –1.96). Consequently, our z value of 2.98 would satisfy the 5% criterion for statistical significance under a two-tailed (nondirectional) hypothesis test (because it exceeds the critical value of 1.96). Critical z values of ±1.65 separate the extreme 5% of z statistics in one distribution tail only (5% of z values are less than –1.65 on the left side of the distribution and 5% of z statistics are greater than 1.65 on the right side of the distribution). Although not obvious, comparing these two critical z values helps demonstrate why directional hypothesis tests are more powerful than nondirectional tests. All of the z-test statistics between 1.65 and 1.95 would satisfy the criterion for statistical significance under a one-tailed (directional) test but would fail to satisfy the criterion under a two-tailed test (resulting in a power deficit associated with the two-tailed test).

The One-Sample *t*-Test
One sample *t*-tests are used to test the difference between a single sample mean and a hypothesized population mean. The one-sample *t*-test is used instead of the one-sample z-test if the population SD is unknown (a more typical scenario). The sample SD would be used in the formula (mentioned earlier) in lieu of the population SD and the *t*-test would be assessed for statistical significance by computing the probability of the observed *t* statistic based on a *t*-distribution on $N - 1$ *df*.

The Independent Samples *t*-Test
Uses
The independent samples *t*-test (i.e., student's *t*-test) is used to test mean differences between two populations when the population distributions are normal. For example, one might want to test whether older adults and younger adults differ significantly in their average level of need for emotional support.

Assumptions and Technical Information
Assumptions include (a) an interval- or ratio-level dependent variable (e.g., emotional support), (b) the observations in each sample are independent of one another (i.e., the independence assumption), (c) the dependent variable is normally distributed in each population (i.e., the normality assumption), and (d) the population variances of the dependent variables

are equal (i.e., homogeneity of variance assumption). The test statistic forms a ratio of the mean difference between the two samples to its SE. The $df = N - 2$ (where N is the total sample size). A relevant effect size is the Cohen d (see earlier section for computation and interpretational guidelines).

Hypothetical Example

The results of an independent samples *t*-test revealed that on average younger adults reported a significantly higher need for emotional support than did older adults, $t(98) = 2.50$, $p = .014$, $d = 0.50$. The technical statistical information is as follows: (a) *t* is the name of the test statistic used, (b) $98 = df$, (c) 2.50 is the independent samples *t*-value, (d) $p = .014$ is the exact probability value from a two-tailed hypothesis test, and (e) $d = 0.50$ is the effect size estimate based on the Cohen *d*, which denotes a moderate effect size.

The Paired Samples or Related Samples *t*-Test

In the independent samples *t*-test, each participant contributes a single data point to the analysis (e.g., a single score on depression). These data are assumed to be independent across the various individuals in the study. In the paired samples *t*-test, each "participant" contributes a pair of data points to the analysis, which are assumed to be dependent (i.e., correlated). The pair of data points can include one's report of the same construct (e.g., pretest and posttest depression), one's report of two constructs (e.g., anxiety and depression), or two judges of the same construct (e.g., mother and father report of a child's anxiety). The paired samples *t*-test examines mean differences across the observation pairs.

The Analysis of Variance and Related Models

General Structure

Where the independent samples *t*-test is used to compare two sample means, the analysis of variance (ANOVA) model is used to compare multiple sample means. It is often used when predictor variables can be coded as finite categorical variables (e.g., with two, three, or more categories) and the outcome is at the interval or ratio level. Predictor variables are referred to as independent variables or factors. Factor categories are referred to as levels and the outcome is referred to as the dependent variable. One-way ANOVA models include one factor, whereas factorial ANOVAs include two or more factors. ANOVAs can also be categorized as (a) between-subjects (in which all groups comprising the various factor levels are independent), (b) within-subjects (in which the same individuals are exposed to all levels of all factors), and (c) mixed (in which at least one between- and one within-subjects factor is included).

General Assumptions and Technical Information

Assumptions include (a) an interval- or ratio-level dependent variable, (b) the independence assumption, (c) the normality assumption, and (d) homogeneity of variance. As the name ANOVA implies, the ultimate analysis focuses on ratios of variance estimates. Note that a variance is an "SS" quantity divided by a relevant *df* quantity. (The variance estimates are typically referred to as mean squares.) The test statistic is the *F* test, named after Fisher, who invented ANOVA.

In a simple one-way between-subjects ANOVA, the *F* test is computed as follows:

$$F = \frac{SS_b / df_b}{SS_w / df_w}$$

The numerator quantities are often referred to as *between-group* quantities ($_b$) and capture variability due to treatment and error. The denominator quantities are *within-group* quantities ($_w$) and capture variability only due to error. Numerator degrees of freedom (df_b) are equal to G – 1 (where G is the number of factor levels). Denominator degrees of freedom (df_w) are equal to N – G (where N is the overall sample size). A number of effect sizes could be used with ANOVA models. The various indices—like omega squared, ω^2—reflect the proportion of variance in the outcome that is explained by the factors. Interpretive guidelines for ω^2 are small = 0.01, medium = 0.06, and large = 0.15.

Note that a one-way between-group ANOVA with two factor levels has the same structure as the independent samples t-test. In such instances, the test statistics are related as follows: $t^2 = F$.

Main Effects and Interactions

In a two-way ANOVA examining the effects of stress (high and low levels) and support (high and low levels) on test performance, the full-factorial design (i.e., a design in which all possible main and interaction effects are estimated) yields a main effect of stress, a main effect of support, and a stress-by-support interaction. In general, main effects examine the unique effect of an independent variable on an outcome. In the present example, a main effect of stress might suggest that test performance is significantly lower in the high-stress condition relative to the low-stress condition. In general, interactions examine whether the effects of one predictor on an outcome vary significantly as a function of another predictor. In the present example, a stress-by-support interaction might indicate that the effects of stress depend on the level of support. For example, the difference in test performance in the low- and high-stress conditions might be attenuated in the high-support condition and exacerbated in the low-support condition—suggesting that the effects of stress on performance vary significantly by support. (When interactions are significant, main effects are usually not interpreted.) Additional discussion of interactions can be found in the section discussing mediators and moderators.

Omnibus Tests of Significance and Post Hoc Contrasts

In models for which there are three or more levels of a factor (e.g., low, medium, and high levels of stress), the test of the factor's main effect is an omnibus statistical test. When significant, the researcher can reject the null that all population means are equal. Differences between two specific groups (e.g., low and high stress levels) are not revealed by this omnibus statistical test. Instead, omnibus tests are typically followed by a series of additional tests (e.g., comparing each pair of means). These more focused contrasts are often referred to as post hoc tests. Conducting multiple statistical tests raises the familywise Type I error rate associated with the full set of analyses (beyond the desired 0.05 level). Consequently, researchers typically use an alpha adjustment procedure to limit the familywise error rate. Perhaps the simplest of these methods is the Bonferroni correction, which takes the original alpha level (say 0.05) and divides it by the number of post hoc tests performed. The resulting quantity becomes the criterion for statistical significance for all post hoc tests. If there are G factor levels and the post hoc comparisons compare every factor level to every other factor level, there are $(G \times [G-1])/2$ unique pairwise contrasts. If there are three factor levels (i.e., G = 3), there are three unique pairwise contrasts, $(3 \times [3-1])/2$. The Bonferroni-adjusted alpha level for the set of post hoc tests would be 0.05/3 or 0.017.

One-Way Between-Subjects

A one-way between-subjects ANOVA can be used to contrast two or more treatment groups on a dependent variable (e.g., contrasting the effects of cognitive behavioral therapy [CBT], interpersonal therapy, or no-treatment on mild depression).

One-Way Within-Subjects

A one-way within-subjects ANOVA can be used to examine a single cohort's symptom levels over two or more assessments (e.g., pretest, posttest, and follow-up measures for individuals exposed to a single intervention). In within-subjects designs that include three or more levels of a (quantitative) factor, researchers can examine trend analyses to see whether the average trend is linear (the means can be plotted along a straight line), quadratic (the shape of the plot of means has one distinct bend), or some other higher order form. An additional assumption of these kinds of repeated-measures designs is the sphericity or circularity assumption, which assumes that the *variances of the differences* of the various factor levels are equal. (The sphericity assumption extends the typical homogeneity of variance assumption to these difference scores.) If the sphericity assumption is violated, researchers might report ANOVA results based on adjusted *df*. Two prominent adjustments are the Greenhouse–Geisser and Huynh–Feldt adjustments. If the same individuals are exposed to different interventions (e.g., three interventions to improve basic math skills), the order of exposure might have an impact on the outcome. In such instances, researchers might incorporate counterbalancing as a design feature (e.g., through the use of a Latin square design). Such design features allow researchers to examine the possible effects of treatment ordering on the outcome.

Two-Way Between-Subjects

A two-way between-subjects ANOVA evaluates the effect of two independent variables on a dependent variable. For example, one might be interested in examining whether ADHD diagnosis (present or absent) and testing environment (quiet or noisy room) have an impact on performance. The full-factorial two-by-two design yields (a) a main effect of ADHD diagnosis, (b) a main effect of testing environment, and (c) the diagnosis-by-testing environment interaction.

Two-Way Within-Subjects

A two-way within-subjects ANOVA could be built by exposing a group of children with ADHD to two levels of a psychostimulant drug-dose factor (e.g., 5 mg and 10 mg) crossed with two levels of a testing-environment factor (e.g., quiet and noisy rooms). In other words, all children would be observed under all four study conditions (e.g., 10 mg, quiet room) and performance would be the dependent variable. This design yields (a) a main effect of psychostimulant dose, (b) a main effect of testing environment, and (c) the psychostimulant dose-by-testing environment interaction.

Two-Way Mixed Design (One Between-Subjects Factor and One Within-Subjects Factor)

The two-group, pretest–posttest treatment outcome study is an example of a two-way mixed design. The between-subjects factor is the treatment group (e.g., treatment vs. control) and the within-subjects factor can be labeled time of assessment (e.g., pretest vs. posttest). Similar to other designs, this design yields (a) a main effect of treatment, (b) a main effect of time of assessment, and (c) a treatment-by-time-of-assessment interaction. In this type of design, the interaction is typically the effect of primary interest because it suggests that the pretest to posttest change varies significantly as a function of the treatment group (e.g., the treatment group declines in symptoms, whereas the control group remains stable).

Higher-Order Designs

All of the designs discussed earlier can be extended to include additional factors—for example, a two (treatment vs. control) by two (male vs. female) by two (pretest vs. posttest) design. Although ANOVA designs can include many factors, it is worth noting that psychologists rarely predict and/or probe interactions involving more than three factors.

Analysis of Covariance

Any of the designs described earlier can be changed from an ANOVA model to an analysis of covariance (ANCOVA) model by adding one or more covariates. A covariate is a variable whose influence the researcher hopes to *control* while examining the effect of the variable of primary theoretical interest. ANCOVAs are used in two primary manners: (a) to increase statistical power in randomized experiments (when the covariate is uncorrelated with intervention conditions, but highly correlated with the dependent variable), and (b) to *control* for possible confounding influences (i.e., controlling for variables associated with both intervention conditions and the dependent variable) in nonrandomized designs.

When researchers use ANCOVA, they often present group comparisons of adjusted means (i.e., means adjusted for the effects of the covariates) on the dependent variable of interest. Assumptions of the ANCOVA model include (a) the covariates are measured without error, and (b) the effects of the covariates on the outcome are constant over levels of the independent variable (although not necessarily intuitive, this last assumption precludes the presence of covariate–independent variable interactions and is also known as the homogeneity of regression lines assumption). If important covariates are omitted, statistical control will not be optimal. It is worth noting that a design that occurs commonly in treatment outcome research in clinical psychology is the two-group pretest–posttest design (e.g., in which treatment and control groups are measured at pretest and posttest). The two most common ways to analyze data from this kind of design are by estimating a mixed-model ANOVA (see the two-way mixed design mentioned earlier) or by estimating an ANCOVA (with the pretest serving as the covariate). If the ANCOVA assumptions are met, the ANCOVA provides a more powerful test of the effect of treatment and this power differential might be particularly salient in studies with smaller sample sizes.

Multivariate Analysis of Variance

Many of the ANOVA models described earlier are referred to as univariate ANOVA models because the analysis focuses on a single dependent variable. In contrast, the multivariate ANOVA model (MANOVA) allows for multiple dependent variables to be analyzed in a single model. In MANOVA, the actual analysis is performed on an optimized linear combination of the multiple dependent variables (one that maximizes between-group differences while minimizing within-group differences). A number of test statistics are generated by MANOVA (the Pillais trace, Wilk lambda, Hotelling trace, and Roy largest root).

In the discussion of inferential statistics thus far, the focus has mostly been on comparisons among means. In the following section, statistical associations typically described in the context of correlation and regression are explored.

The Pearson Product-Moment Correlation (*r*)
Uses

Assume that a researcher was interested in examining the relationship between achievement motivation and grade point average in a sample of college students. The association between these two variables could be quantified by the Pearson product–moment correlation (r), which measures linear associations between two continuous variables. The null hypothesis in this situation is typically $\rho = 0$ and the alternative hypothesis would be $\rho \neq 0$ (where ρ is the symbol for the population correlation).

Assumptions and Technical Information

Assumptions include (a) both variables are interval or ratio level, (b) bivariate normality (i.e., the joint distribution is normal), and (c) the variability in one of the variables is relatively constant across values of the other variable (i.e., homoscedasticity). Proper interpretation requires a linear association between the two variables. Correlations range from −1 to +1, with larger absolute values suggesting stronger associations. Positive correlations result when cases above the mean on one variable tend to be above the mean on the other variable (e.g., study time and academic performance). Negative correlations result when cases above the mean on one variable tend to be below the mean on the other variable (e.g., illicit drug use and academic performance in high school). Correlations near zero result when an individual's score on one variable conveys little information about their score on the other variable (e.g., number of siblings and academic performance). Effect size is estimated by computing the square of the correlation (i.e., the coefficient of determination), which is the proportion of shared variance between the two variables. Common interpretative guidelines for r^2 are as follows: small = 0.01, medium = 0.09, and large = 0.25. Several factors can influence the magnitude of a correlation, including the shape of the two distributions (as distributions diverge, the correlation diminishes), the reliability of measures (less reliable measures limit the maximum possible correlation), and restricted range (homogeneous responses on one or both variables diminish the correlation).

Other Correlations

Although less widely used in psychology, alternatives to the Pearson r exist and are generally used with ordinal data or when the assumptions of the Pearson r are not satisfied. The point–biserial correlation is used when one variable is dichotomous (i.e., yes/no) and the other is continuous. The tetrachoric correlation is used when both variables are dichotomous. The polychoric correlation, which is a generalization of the tetrachoric correlation, is used when both variables are ordinal and comprise a relatively finite number of categories (say, 3–5). The Spearman rank correlation coefficient and the Kendall tau coefficient are both nonparametric tests that are used when responses on the two variables are rank ordered.

Ordinary Least Squares Regression

Uses

Ordinary least squares (OLS) regression allows for the prediction of a single continuous outcome (often referred to as the criterion) from one or more predictor variables (which can be nominal, ordinal, interval, or ratio). The multiple regression model (i.e., a model with multiple predictors) can be specified as follows: $Y_i = a + b_1(x_{1i}) + b_2(x_{2i}) + \ldots + b_k(x_{ki}) + e_i$. Terms that carry the subscript i are free to vary by individual. As such, Y_i is individual i's value on the outcome. The a is the y-intercept (i.e., the predicted value of Y when all predictors are equal to zero). The bs represent the unstandardized linear regression coefficients. Each quantifies the linear association between the relevant predictor and the outcome and has the following interpretation: for every one-unit increase in x, Y changes by b units. There are k predictors in all (i.e., in a three-predictor model, $k = 3$). The e_i (i.e., the residual) is the error in prediction associated with the model for each individual: $e_i = Y_i - \hat{Y}_i$ (where $\hat{Y}_i$ is the predicted value of the outcome for the individual in question). The regression constants (as and bs) are determined by minimizing the error in prediction associated with the model.

Assumptions and Technical Information

Assumptions include that (a) the predictors are fixed variables (suggesting that the same values are sampled over studies), (b) the predictors are measured without error, (c) the predictor–outcome associations are linear, (d) the means of the errors "balance out" (i.e., are assumed to be zero over many replications), (e) errors are independent of one another, (f) the residuals have constant variance for all predictor values (homoscedasticity; heteroscedasticity results if this assumption is violated), and (g) the residual is uncorrelated with the predictor variables (can be ensured through randomization of treatments in experiments). Multicollinearity results when predictors are redundant (i.e., highly correlated in a pairwise or generalized manner). Regression diagnostics can be used to assess for violations of these various assumptions.

In practice, significance tests are examined for the full model (which tests whether the full set of predictors accounts for significant variance in the outcome) and for the individual predictors. ANOVA models are used to test the significance of overall regression models and R^2 multiples can be used to quantify the overall effect of the predictors. The test of an individual predictor examines whether the predictor in question accounts for significant incremental variance in the outcome, above all other predictors in the model. Significance tests for individual predictors are t-tests (derived by dividing the unstandardized regression coefficient by its SE) on $N - k - 1$ df (where N is overall sample size and k is the number of predictors in the model). Effect size estimates for individual predictors are the Cohen f^2, which is derived by dividing the incremental variance associated with the predictor in question (also known as the semipartial correlation between the predictor and outcome) by $1 - R^2$. It is often desirable to examine the incremental variance associated with various subsets of predictors. This last approach is referred to as hierarchical regression analysis, which results when the full model is built by adding predictors to the model sequentially.

In hierarchical regression models, the incremental variance associated with the predictor block is tested for significance using *F change* tests and the relevant effect size is R^2 *change*. (Hierarchical regression analysis is sometimes confused with stepwise regression analysis, which is an atheoretical approach to predictor entry used more often in exploratory analyses.)

Example

Table 9.1 presents output from a hierarchical regression model in which the criterion—positive relations with others (a facet of Ryff's [1989] conceptualization of psychological well-being)—was predicted from six predictors organized into three subsets or blocks: demographics, other covariates, and recovery-related predictors (as mentioned earlier, these data were part of a larger study examining recovery-related correlates of psychological well-being in Narcotics Anonymous members; DeLucia et al., 2012). The full model was statistically significant, $F(6, 126) = 14.66$, $p < .001$, $R^2 = 0.41$, suggesting that the complete set of six predictors accounted for significant variance in the outcome.

TABLE 9.1 A Hierarchical Regression Model Predicting Positive Relations With Others From Demographics, Other Covariates, and Recovery-Related Practices

	B	SE	p	F^2
Block 1: Demographics:				
$F(2, 130) = 3.90, p = .023, R^2 = 0.057$				
Age	0.001	0.006	.863	<.001
Sex (0 = female, 1 = male)	−0.157	0.109	.150	0.012
Block 2: Other covariates:				
$\Delta F(2, 128) = 26.44, p < .001, \Delta R^2 = 0.276$				
Substance-use severity	−0.161	0.071	.024	0.041
Neuroticism	−0.304	0.056	<.001	0.235
Block 3: Recovery-related predictors:				
$\Delta F(2, 126) = 8.42, p < .001, \Delta R^2 = 0.079$				
Home group comfort	0.197	0.053	<.001	0.110
Abstinence duration	0.015	0.008	.056	0.029

Note: Full model was statistically significant, $F(6, 126) = 14.66, p < .001, R^2 = 0.41$. All coefficients are from final model.

The incremental variance associated with the addition of each predictor block was as follows: (a) The demographic predictors accounted for significant variance in positive relations with others, $F(2, 130) = 3.90, p = .023, R^2 = 0.057$; (b) when entered second, the other covariates accounted for significant incremental variance in positive relations with others (over the demographic predictors), $\Delta F(2, 128) = 26.44, p < .001, \Delta R^2 = 0.276$; and (c) when entered last, the recovery-related predictors accounted for significant incremental variance in the outcome (over the demographics and person-level covariates), $\Delta F(2, 126) = 8.42, p < .001, \Delta R^2 = 0.079$. (The delta symbols, Δ, are used in place of the words "change in.")

The entries in the *b* column of Table 9.1 are the unstandardized partial regression coefficients for all six predictors from the final model (when all predictors are included). In the example, the regression coefficient for neuroticism is statistically significant, $b = -0.304$, SE $= 0.056$, $p < .001$, which suggests that a one-unit gain in neuroticism is associated with a 0.304 unit *decrease* in positive relations with others (i.e., the outcome or criterion variable). The f^2 values provide an effect size estimate for the individual predictors. Interpretive guidelines are as follows: small = 0.02, medium = 0.15, and large = 0.35. Standardized regression coefficients can also be used to quantify the effect of a single predictor. Although not presented in the table, the standardized regression coefficient for neuroticism is −0.41, suggesting that a one (SD) unit increase in neuroticism is associated with a 0.41 (SD unit) *decrease* in positive relations with others. It is worth noting that in single predictor regression models, the significance of the overall model and the significance of the individual predictor are redundant and the standardized regression coefficient will equal the (zero-order) correlation between the predictor and outcome.

Testing Interactions
In the previously described six-predictor regression model, no interactions between or among predictor variables were estimated. Models that do not include interaction effects are referred to as additive effects models. In regression, an interaction between two predictors can be included in the analysis by creating a cross-product of the two predictors (by multiplying them together) and entering this additional variable in the analysis. The significance test for the cross-product predictor is the test of the interaction.

Testing Nonlinear Effects
In the same way that trend analyses are conducted in ANOVA models, tests of nonlinear effects of various predictors can be estimated in regression models. In practice, testing nonlinear effects is accomplished by raising the predictor in question to various powers—where 1 = linear, 2 = quadratic, 3 = cubic, and so on. If a researcher was interested in testing the possible quadratic effect of abstinence duration in the model described earlier, the researcher would square the predictor in question and add the new predictor to the model. The test of its coefficient would be the test of the quadratic effect.

Extensions of the Ordinary Least Squares Regression Model
Logistic Regression
Logistic regression is used when the outcome variable comprises ordered (e.g., symptom severity: low, medium, or high) or unordered (e.g., political affiliation: Democrat, independent, or Republican) categories. Substantive interpretations of the effects of predictors in logistic regression models often involve discussion of relevant odds ratios. For example, a researcher might be interested in predicting AUDs in young adulthood (0 = no disorder, 1 = disorder) from two predictors (parent diagnosis of an AUD: 0 = no parent, 1 = at least one parent; and sex assigned at birth: 0 = female, 1 = male). Assume that both predictors are associated with significantly higher rates of diagnoses and the odds ratios are as follows: parent AUD, 4.22; and sex assigned at birth, 2.48. These data suggest that the odds of diagnosis are 4.22 times higher for young adults with parents who have an AUD relative to young adults without parents who have an AUD. The combined odds of diagnosis for having a parent with an AUD and being assigned male at birth would be 4.22 × 2.48 or 10.46 times higher relative to females assigned at birth without parents with AUDs.

Path Analysis
Although the OLS regression model is extremely flexible in that the predictors can take on myriad forms, it is limited in that the effects of the predictors do not reflect a strong causal ordering. In path analysis, models can be structured to reflect a stronger *causal ordering*. (This class of models is sometimes referred to as causal models.) In Figure 9.8, a path diagram modeled after an analysis conducted by Newcomb and Bentler is presented (1988, p. 80). The authors were interested in examining the possible prospective associations between adolescent drug use and social conformity, and both constructs were assessed in adolescence and young adulthood. Such an analysis provides several useful pieces of information—including (a) the cross-sectional association between the constructs during each developmental period (see "a" and "f" in figure); (b) the degree of stability in each of the constructs across the developmental periods (see "b" and

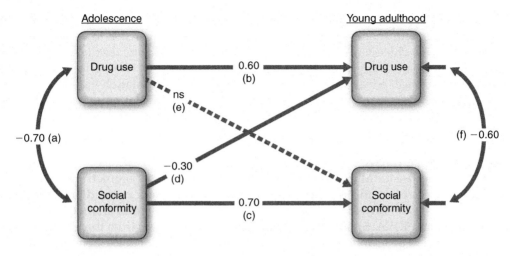

Figure 9.8 A path diagram examining prospective cross-lagged associations between drug use and social conformity.

"c" in figure); and (c) the prospective (cross-lagged) associations between the constructs (see "d" and "e" in figure). In the figure, these prospective paths indicate that social conformity in adolescence is a significant prospective predictor of changes in drug use from adolescence to young adulthood. Drug use in adolescence is not a significant prospective predictor of changes in social conformity from adolescence to young adulthood. Consequently, these data suggest a stronger causal ordering from social conformity to drug use, not the other way around.

Structural Equation Modeling

Structural equation modeling further extends path analysis to include path analysis with latent variables. Latent variables were described earlier in the context of measurement theory. The classic structural equation model is often discussed as comprising two interrelated parts—the measurement model (in which relations between latent variables and their observed indicators are modeled) and the structural model (in which relations between/among latent variables are modeled). In the Newcomb and Bentler (1988) example discussed earlier, the constructs were actually latent variables (although the figure did not depict them as such). For example, the latent construct of drug use had three observed indicators: (a) alcohol frequency, (b) cannabis frequency, and (c) hard-drug frequency. Similarly, the latent construct of social conformity had three observed indicators: (a) law abidance, (b) liberalism, and (c) religious commitment. The primary advantage of structural equation modeling over path analysis involves gains in statistical power that result when measurement error associated with predictors and outcomes is reduced.

Nonparametric Statistical Tests

As discussed previously, nonparametric statistical tests often make few if any assumptions about the underlying relevant population distributions—that is, they do not assume that data is distributed normally. As such, they are sometimes referred to as distribution-free methods. In the following, the chi-square test, which is a nonparametric statistical test commonly used in psychology, is discussed. In addition, nonparametric alternatives to some of the more commonly used parametric tests described earlier are covered.

Chi-Square Test

Chi-square tests are used in two primary manners in psychology. *Chi-square tests of independence* are commonly used to test whether two categorical variables are associated. For example, if a researcher were interested in examining whether men had higher rates of AUDs than did women, a chi-square test of independence could be computed. If sex and alcoholism status were not associated, the researcher would expect the rate of AUDs to be similar for men and women (and the chi-square test to be nonsignificant). *Chi-square tests of goodness of fit* are commonly used in path analysis, CFA, and structural equation modeling to test whether the model-implied variance/covariance matrix fits the estimated population variance/covariance matrix. In these instances, researchers are hoping for nonsignificant chi-squares, which suggest little discrepancy between the two matrices (suggesting that the specified model fits the data well).

Nonparametric Alternatives to Commonly Used Parametric Tests

The Mann–Whitney Test (or Mann–Whitney–Wilcoxon Test) is a nonparametric alternative to the independent samples *t*-test and is used when data that can be rank ordered are collected from two different samples of individuals. The Kruskal–Wallis Test is a nonparametric alternative to the between-group ANOVA. Similar to the Mann–Whitney Test, data from three or more samples can be rank ordered to determine whether the samples are similar, or at least one sample is different from the remaining samples. The Wilcoxon Signed Ranks Test is a nonparametric alternative to the paired samples *t*-test. This test statistic is used when a sample of individuals contributes a pair of data points to the analysis (and the paired differences can be rank ordered in absolute value). The Friedman Test can be used as a nonparametric alternative to the within-subjects ANOVA with three or more levels. In this analysis, the repeated observations for the various participants are rank ordered within participants and then summed within factor levels. These sums are analyzed to see whether rankings appear similar or different.

▶ OTHER TOPICS IN STATISTICS

SENSITIVITY AND SPECIFICITY

Sensitivity, specificity, and related topics are often discussed in the context of screening tests. Assume a clinician is using a screening test to differentiate individuals with psychosis from individuals without psychosis. If the clinician examines the test's performance in a sample of individuals who have been evaluated for psychosis by a panel of expert psychologists, the test's sensitivity and specificity can be computed. In this example, the consensus diagnosis conferred is used to reflect the *true state of affairs* (e.g., if the expert panel diagnosed as psychotic, the individuals are categorized as psychotic individuals).

Figure 9.9 presents the number of cases in each of the four table cells that result when crossing the two possible outcomes from the screener (not psychotic, psychotic) with the two possible outcomes from the panel's consensus diagnosis (not psychotic, psychotic). The cell labeled "A" includes the number of true positives (i.e., psychotic individuals the test *correctly* classified as psychotic). The cell labeled "B" includes the number of false positives (i.e., nonpsychotic individuals the test *incorrectly* classified as psychotic). The cell labeled "C" includes the false negatives (i.e., psychotic individuals the test *incorrectly* classified as nonpsychotic). The cell labeled "D" includes the true negatives (i.e., nonpsychotic individuals the test *correctly* classified as nonpsychotic). In the present example, sensitivity is the proportion of psychotic individuals correctly classified as psychotic by the test. It can be computed as $A/(A + C) = 19/(19 + 1) = 0.95$. In general, sensitivity is the conditional probability of a positive test result, given the presence of the condition. In the present example, specificity is the proportion of nonpsychotic individuals the test correctly classified as nonpsychotic. It can be computed as $D/(B + D) = 475/(5 + 475) = 0.99$. In general, specificity is the conditional probability of a negative test result, given the absence of the condition. In this example, the test does a very good job of correctly classifying individuals with the condition (sensitivity) and individuals without the condition (specificity). Another quantity that is of more use clinically provides information about the conditional probability of having the disorder, given a positive test result. The quantity is sometimes referred to as positive predictive

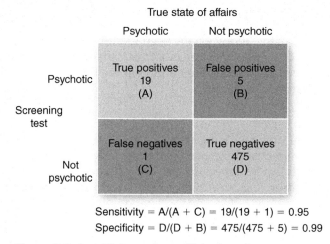

Figure 9.9 Sensitivity and specificity based on hypothetical data for a screening test for psychosis.

value, and for the data in the following section is defined as $A/(A + B) = 19/(19 + 5) = 0.792$. The negative predictive value (NPV) is the conditional probability of not having the disorder, given a negative test result. For the data in the following, the NPV is $D/(D + C) = 475/(475 + 1) = 0.998$. Finally, the hit rate (HR) is the proportion of all diagnoses that are accurate. For the data in the following section, the $HR = (A + D)/(A + B + C + D) = (19 + 475)/(19 + 5 + 1 + 475) = 0.988$.

MODERATION AND MEDIATION

Moderators are variables that alter the association between another variable and an outcome. Testing for moderation is the same as testing for a statistical interaction between a predictor and a moderator. For example, a researcher might test whether an intervention effect is moderated by participant gender to see whether the effects of the intervention on the outcome are stronger for one gender as compared to others. A mediator is the mechanism through which a distal predictor operates in influencing an outcome. For example, the impact of a cognitive behavioral treatment for depression might result in lower levels of depression by reducing patients' cognitive distortions. In this scenario, the distal predictor is treatment, the mediator is cognitive distortion, and the outcome is depression. Mediated effects can be tested in many different ways—all of which center on examining whether the indirect effect (of the distal predictor on the outcome through the mediator) is significant.

▶ QUALITATIVE RESEARCH

Where quantitative research follows a deductive process (testing theory with observation), qualitative research can use inductive (moving from specific observations to broader existing generalizations) and abductive (finding specific observations that necessitate a new theory or generalization) processes. Qualitative research seeks to describe and understand problems using methods that enable a pattern to be identified, analyzed, and interpreted from data that are more abstract in nature, such as interviews, focus groups, observations, review of naturalistic documents, and other nonnumerical data. Theoretical and purposeful sampling (aimed at selecting the data that will most serve the researcher's purpose, such as specifically selecting extreme cases) is often used in qualitative research (in contrast with representative sampling). Although quantitative research methods typically involve theory testing, qualitative methods are often used to generate hypotheses, theory, or a rich understanding of a group's experiences, perspectives, and context.

TYPES OF QUALITATIVE INQUIRY

Over 25 approaches to qualitative inquiry have been identified. Approaches vary in terms of the epistemology (philosophy of science) they are most associated with, the disciplines they are associated with, and how systematically they are defined in the literature. Two common approaches are phenomenology and grounded theory.

Phenomenology

Phenomenology centers on understanding participants' lived experiences and emphasizes subjective experience (e.g., understanding personal knowledge, motivations, and perspectives). Phenomenological research can be especially helpful when a phenomenon of interest has been poorly defined in the literature (e.g., seeking to understand in rich detail how adults experience and value social relationships after the COVID-19 pandemic).

Grounded Theory

The ultimate goal of grounded theory is to develop a theory ("grounded" in data) about a concept of interest. This approach is used when current theory is lacking, nonexistent, or incomplete. An iterative process of collecting and coding data about a phenomenon of interest occurs until a theoretical understanding of the phenomenon and its processes and relationships to other concepts emerges.

EXAMPLES OF QUALITATIVE METHODOLOGY

There are various methods for collecting rich, nonnumerical data. Some of the most common include focus groups, interviews, and case studies, which are described in the following section.

Focus groups are of interest when researchers want to know about groups' perceptions, feelings, and experiences on a defined area of interest (Krueger & Casey, 2014). They consist of a small group of individuals (typically six to eight) who are asked questions, primarily open-ended questions, from an interview guide by a moderator. The moderator is often recording the group for transcription and later analysis, as well as taking notes about their observations of the group (e.g., nonverbal behaviors that might be important to consider). An example might be inviting men with histories of trauma to answer questions about barriers to seeking help and facilitators of treatment engagement.

In-depth interviews are often used to elicit rich data regarding an individual's perspective on particular ideas, programs, or phenomena. Interviews can be used to generate hypotheses, develop theories, or provide context for other data. They are often used when the goal is to understand concepts at an individual level (e.g., individual decision-making) or when sensitive topics are of interest that may make participants uncomfortable in a group setting (e.g., sexual behavior). Findings from in-depth interviews of individuals with HIV, for example, helped develop theories about the mechanisms through which HIV stigma may impact health (e.g., by reducing social support and contributing to other health risks; Jeffries et al., 2015). Interviews, like focus groups, are often recorded and transcribed for analysis.

Uncontrolled case studies, described in the earlier section on research design, can be quantitative or qualitative in nature. The definition of a single case in case study research is left to the researcher but is typically an individual patient or client. It may also be a system such as a clinical practice. As with other kinds of qualitative research, case study research uses "in-depth data collection involving multiple sources of information" (Creswell, 2013, p. 97) and cases are chosen for a particular reason (e.g., they are representative of or have specific characteristics). An example of a famous qualitative case study was that of Little Hans, on whom Freud collected detailed data from observation and interviews with the patient's father. The case study was helpful to Freud in developing his theory of psychosexual development.

ANALYSIS IN QUALITATIVE RESEARCH

Across the multiple approaches to qualitative research, data are often analyzed using thematic analysis, a process of identifying and analyzing patterns or themes within data. This can occur either deductively (i.e., starting from a particular theory or hypothesis) or inductively (i.e., as in grounded theory, discussed earlier). Braun and Clarke (2006) outline six phases: transcribing and reading through data, generating initial codes or points of interest in the data, searching for themes where codes may be combined, creating a "thematic map" that indicates how themes are interconnected, defining and naming the themes, and producing a report that relates the thematic map to the original research question and reviews the literature.

RELIABILITY/VALIDITY ISSUES IN QUALITATIVE RESEARCH

Some qualitative paradigms use parallel criteria to those used in quantitative research to examine validity (i.e., credibility, transferability, dependability, and confirmability). These criteria differ from those used in quantitative research because qualitative research focuses on idiographic and emic knowledge claims (finding meaning from individuals studied) as opposed to nomothetic or etic knowledge claims like those made in quantitative research (obtaining knowledge from standardized methods in large samples; Morrow, 2005). The term *trustworthiness* is often preferred to *validity*, and there are different means of increasing trustworthiness in qualitative research. For example, data collection in qualitative research often occurs until saturation (point at which data are consistently redundant and provide no new information). In addition, the following techniques are used: triangulation (the use of multiple, varied sources of data, methods, and researchers in order to corroborate results), audits (the use of an external consultant to complete an independent analysis), and member checking (having participants in the study review and provide feedback on the credibility of findings). Of note, the validity of qualitative research findings is sometimes criticized by standards applied to quantitative research (e.g., generalizability).

▶ PROGRAM EVALUATION STRATEGIES AND TECHNIQUES

Researchers and clinicians in psychology often work together to use data to make determinations about the value of interventions and programs that exist in the community. Program evaluation (PE) examines how an intervention or service works, for whom, and under what conditions. In both standard research and PE, the design is intended to be rigorous, systematic, and may even use some of the same methods (e.g., surveys and focus groups). However, there are key differences between the two: PE is often applied to specific programs (traditional research focuses on generalization of knowledge and theory), PE often aims to facilitate decision-making and improve programs (as opposed to testing theories/hypotheses), PE questions are often derived from stakeholders and program staff (not researchers), and PE almost always occurs in natural settings (as opposed to controlled settings).

The first step in PE is to identify and engage stakeholders (e.g., administrators, staff, and clients). Next, a needs assessment of existing data, or collection of new data, might be conducted to assess the relative priority of the needs, or "problems," of a specific population to determine where resources should be allocated. Evaluators often assess the extent to which services are already available to meet the identified needs, usage rates for existing services, and the potential for needs to be in conflict with one another (e.g., situations where addressing one need might create/exacerbate another need). Needs assessment is one type of formative evaluation, designed to provide information that will result in changes that can improve the effectiveness of that program.

Several evaluation strategies may be used later on in the program's implementation. Process or implementation evaluation strategies are used to determine how program activities are delivered and whether the program is being implemented as planned. Summative evaluations are used to determine whether or not programs have been effective at reaching desired outcomes. They can include a comparison with alternative programs. Formative and summative evaluations may use the same measures and methods, but with *different goals*. Formative evaluations provide information to make needed changes early on, whereas summative evaluations determine a program's success once delivered.

In addition to summative evaluation, cost–benefit analysis (CBA) can also be used to measure the impact of a program. CBA answers the question, "Have resources been well spent on this program?" This results in a benefit/cost ratio, the worth of a program's outcomes divided by the program's costs, which can then be compared to alternative programs. CBA is controversial in part because it assigns monetary values to the benefits arising from a program.

▶ PARTICIPANT SAMPLING AND RECRUITMENT

Early on in the research process, researchers must define the population of interest and consider sampling and recruitment strategies. Two primary goals in the recruitment of research participants are to achieve adequate representation of a target population and obtain a sufficient sample size to achieve adequate levels of statistical power for planned analyses. Representativeness is important because a primary research goal is to generalize findings to a target population. This may warrant specialized consultation to ensure inclusion of multicultural variables.

SAMPLE SELECTION

Samples can be categorized into representative samples (probability sampling) and nonrepresentative samples (nonprobability sampling). In probability sampling, researchers ensure that all individuals in the population of interest have an opportunity to be selected. There are two main kinds of representative samples. In simple random samples, all individuals in the population have an equal likelihood of being selected. In stratified random samples, the researcher creates classes or strata, and then a percentage of the overall sample is selected randomly from each stratum. Note that the terms *random selection* and *random assignment* are often confused. Random selection is how individuals from the population are *selected* for the study. Random assignment, which necessarily occurs after random selection, is how individuals already in the study are *assigned* to various study conditions.

Given the resource requirements of probability sampling, the use of nonprobability sampling is more common. A convenience sample, one kind of nonprobability sample, is collected when participants are recruited because of the researcher's ease of access (e.g., students are asked to volunteer for a study). Purposive sampling is when researchers collect data from individuals with specific characteristics. Snowball sampling, a type of purposive sampling, involves participants inviting others to participate in the study. Respondent-driven sampling uses incentives to overcome possible biases that result from snowball and other chain-referral sampling methods.

The law of large numbers suggests that larger samples tend to be more representative of their populations. Consequently, sampling error (i.e., the difference between the sample and population) is inversely related to sample size (i.e., error increases as sample size decreases). The sampling error that results from probability sampling is random or free from systematic bias. In nonprobability samples, sampling error can reflect systematic bias (e.g., individuals with particular characteristics are systematically under- or overrepresented). Nonparticipation can create a biased sample (regardless of sampling strategy) because individuals who refuse participation are often different from those who consent to participate. Therefore, it is very important to understand barriers to recruitment.

BARRIERS TO RECRUITMENT

Several barriers exist in the recruitment of a representative sample. Participant barriers can include language barriers, transportation barriers, interference with work and family responsibilities, fear/distrust of research, aversion to treatment assignment, and stigma associated with study concepts (e.g., stigma associated with mental health). Investigator barriers may include a lack of knowledge about the target population, limited cultural competence, and research staff members who are not representative of the diversity in the community of interest. Both barriers disproportionately affect racial/ethnic minority individuals and may lead to an underrepresentation of these minorities in research, requiring additional outreach efforts to recruit and retain such individuals. The National Institutes of Health has mandated inclusion of women and racial/ethnic minorities in its sponsored clinical research since 1993.

OUTREACH STRATEGIES

Several strategies are used by researchers in trying to engage potential research participants. These are often tested in pilot studies examining the feasibility of the research, especially the researcher's recruitment plan. Recruitment outreach can take the form of advertising or communicating with potential participants about the study through the mail, phone, internet, or in person. Maximizing the representativeness of a sample often involves building trust and relationships with community members of interest, aligning the research question and design with the goals and needs of the community, addressing barriers to participation, ensuring that materials are designed with community members in mind (e.g., literacy level, language preference, and relatable images), and recruiting a diverse research staff.

▶ COMMUNITY PARTNERSHIPS

Community-based participatory research (CBPR) is a collaborative approach that emphasizes the engagement of community members in research endeavors. CBPR has three objectives: (a) equitable involvement of researchers and community members, (b) incorporation of the unique strengths of both community members (e.g., lived experiences, values, and attitudes) and researchers (e.g., technical knowledge) in research, and (c) outcomes that include new knowledge and direct benefits to the community.

In order to achieve these objectives, CBPR researchers establish close partnerships with community stakeholders. Stakeholders are individuals or agencies in the community who are directly involved or affected by the work of interest to the researcher. Community representatives (e.g., parents, community clinicians, and criminal justice officials) are particularly important partners when working with vulnerable populations because they may serve a "gatekeeping" role, mediating researchers' access to these communities. Partnerships between key community stakeholders and researchers may be formalized through an organizational structure called a community advisory board (CAB), which facilitates ongoing communication between researchers and community members. CABs can have a number of roles and responsibilities, including providing guidance to the researcher on community perspectives and participating in important decisions about sampling, study design, survey wording, interpretation of findings, and how best to use the results for community benefit.

CBPR, which aims for equal participation of community members with researchers in various aspects of the research endeavor (including formulating the research question of interest, determining the methodology, and implementing the findings), is considered at one end of a spectrum of possible community engagement in research. On the other end of this spectrum is "traditional research," in which the only community engagement may be participation as a research subject or receipt of information regarding the findings from research.

Developing partnerships with community members can require substantial time and resources (e.g., formative work often needs to be done in order to increase community readiness to participate and to build trust in the researcher/research institution). However, partnerships such as these may have several important benefits for both researchers and community members, such as recruitment of a broader population, culturally sensitive research methods, and development of more sustainable and effective intervention efforts.

▶ DISSEMINATION AND PRESENTATION OF RESEARCH FINDINGS

One of the final phases of the research cycle is the dissemination of research findings. Traditional dissemination to the academic community occurs in peer-reviewed formats (e.g., journal publications and conference presentations) and includes a clear description of the relevant literature, the significance of the research, and its aims (introduction); description of the study design, procedures, and analysis (method); a report of the findings (results); and a discussion of the major findings, limitations of the research, and implications (discussion).

Less traditional research dissemination efforts (i.e., outside of academia) can also be considered in order to increase the likelihood that communities can access research and that research findings have the potential to result in community benefit. In developing a nontraditional dissemination plan, it is important to consider the source of the message (what is the perceived credibility of the researcher for the stakeholders?), the message content (how useful and relevant is the research to the stakeholders?), the dissemination method (how can the benefits of the intervention be clearly communicated to the stakeholders?), and the intended user of the information (do stakeholders have the resources, skills, and support to benefit from the research?). Nontraditional dissemination efforts can include communication of research findings through local community meetings, media outlets, and policy reports.

▶ REFERENCES

Full reference list available at http://examprepconnect.springerpub.com

KNOWLEDGE CHECK: CHAPTER 9

1. _____ trials, or explanatory trials, are used when researchers want to determine if an intervention creates the expected changes in participants under the most ideal circumstances, whereas _____, or pragmatic trials, are used when researchers want to determine if the intervention creates the expected changes in participants in a real-world setting.
   A. Effectiveness; efficacy
   B. Effectiveness; quasi-experimental
   C. Efficacy; effectiveness
   D. Quasi-experimental; efficacy

2. Which of the following hypotheses is the best example of a simple correlational study design?
   A. Strong identification with being a therapist at pretest predicts lower outcome monitoring scores in clients at posttest.
   B. Strong identification with being a therapist is associated with lower outcome monitoring scores in clients.
   C. Strong identification with being a therapist is related to latent constructs of therapist self-confidence, self-esteem, and adherence to a theoretical orientation.
   D. Strong identification with being a therapist predicts client outcome monitoring scores over and above demographic factors of the therapist and treatment length.

3. Which of the following best explains the similarities and/or difference(s) between a case study and a single-case experiment?
   A. Case studies and single-case experiments both involve active manipulation of the intervention on the part of the researcher.
   B. Case studies do not involve active manipulation of an intervention, but single-case experiments do.
   C. Neither case studies nor single-case experiments involve active manipulation of the intervention on the part of the researcher.
   D. Single-case experiments do not involve active manipulation of an intervention, but case studies do.

4. A team of researchers is interested in whether exercise is associated with improved mood. A total of 168 individuals who are already enrolled with an exercise program app are studied over the course of 2 weeks to determine participants' rated mood. Participants are asked about their exercise and mood preintervention daily through the app, and monthly for the next 3 months. The authors find that mood scores improved with increased activity. Given this design, which of the following threats to internal validity are plausible?
   A. Attrition—participants drop-out due to the expectations of engagement with the app.
   B. History—participants are exposed to a brand new commercial on TV about U.S. Food and Drug Administration-approval for a weight loss drug.
   C. Selection—participants are motivated to exercise and thus may be more likely to follow through with the app's recommendations.
   D. Testing—after being asked about their preintervention exercise routine, participants are primed to start exercising.

(See answers on the next page.)

1. **C) Efficacy; effectiveness**
   Efficacy trials evaluate treatment effects under ideal circumstances and implementation is closely monitored and controlled. Effectiveness trials are less controlled and designed to study an intervention's effect in real-world settings. Quasi-experimental studies, on the other hand, lack random assignment; both efficacy and effectiveness trials require this key feature.

2. **B) Strong identification with being a therapist is associated with lower outcome monitoring scores in clients.**
   Several keywords can aid in determining which is the best answer choice (as well as ruling out others). In correlational studies, we look for the word *association* to imply that there is a relationship, but no true cause and effect, making "Strong identification with being a therapist is associated with lower outcome monitoring scores in clients" the best answer choice. The keyword *prediction* implies cause and effect (therapist identity is the causal effect on monitoring scores). In "Strong identification with being a therapist predicts client outcome monitoring scores over and above demographic factors of the therapist and treatment length," the phrase *over and above* hints at regression analyses, in which the researcher can control for some variables and look at the association with the dependent variable. Technically, a regression analysis is a type of correlational study, but goes above and beyond to control for the variance in the outcome by looking at each variable separately. In the case of this question, it was looking for a simple correlational design. Lastly, "Strong identification with being a therapist is related to latent constructs of therapist self-confidence, self-esteem, and adherence to a theoretical orientation" uses measurement theory language, such as latent constructs that underlie the premise of therapist identity.

3. **B) Case studies do not involve active manipulation of an intervention, but single-case experiments do.**
   Case studies are typically written during or after treatment to highlight what has happened naturally during the course of a treatment. A single-case experiment involves active manipulation of an intervention by introducing and removing it to see the effects on a particular target behavior.

4. **C) Selection—participants are motivated to exercise and thus may be more likely to follow through with the app's recommendations.**
   In a one-group design, there are many limitations because there is no control group to examine systematic differences between intervention and no intervention. Therefore, we are looking for anything that is capable of causing a spurious effect. The answer is selection because participants are not randomly assigned (there are not two conditions) and because participants can self-select into the study, meaning that they may possess a particular quality that makes them more likely to follow through with the app's recommendation. It would not be a testing threat because participants have already been primed to exercise as they self-enrolled in the app. It would not be a history threat, as we would not expect this news to impact their scores on mood (remember, in order for it to be spurious it must be that the threat is related to the variable of interest). It would not be an attrition threat because there is not differential attrition between groups. Although participants may drop out due to the intervention's lack of effectiveness, we do not know that this is the reason for significant/nonsignificant findings.

5. In developing a new measure of depression, researchers find a correlation coefficient of 0.82 with an existing measure of depression (i.e., Beck Depression Inventory [BDI]). What does this represent?

   A. Convergent validity
   B. Discriminant validity
   C. Face validity
   D. Structural validity

6. Researchers are interested in whether recess during the school day has an impact on academic performance and whether this corresponds to U.S. test scores. The researchers find that the mean academic performance is 54 (SD = 10). To aid in their interpretations, researchers use z-scores. What would the z-score be of a student who obtained a score of 74?

   A. 1
   B. 2
   C. –1
   D. –2

7. Which of the following is an example of an alternative and null hypothesis?

   A. Alternative: Trauma survivors who report abuse by a family member will report higher degrees of attachment insecurity as compared to those who report abuse by a nonfamily perpetrator. Null: There will be no differences on attachment insecurity between trauma survivors.
   B. Alternative: Trauma survivors who report abuse by a family member will report higher degrees of attachment insecurity as compared to those who report abuse by a nonfamily member. Null: Trauma survivors who report abuse by a family member will report lower degrees of attachment insecurity as compared to those who report abuse by a nonfamily member.
   C. Alternative: Trauma survivors who report abuse by a family member will report the same degree of attachment insecurity as compared to those who report abuse by a nonfamily member. Null: There will be no differences on attachment insecurity between trauma survivors.
   D. Alternative: Trauma survivors who report abuse by a nonfamily member will report higher degrees of attachment security as compared to those who report abuse by a family member. Null: Trauma survivors who report abuse by a family member will report higher degrees of attachment insecurity as compared to those who report abuse by a nonfamily member.

8. If you determine statistical power to be 0.93, what is the probability of making a Type II error?

   A. 0.05
   B. 0.07
   C. 0.50
   D. 0.70

(See answers on the next page.)

5. **A) Convergent validity**
Convergent validity refers to how two measures on a similar construct converge, often depicted as a positive correlation coefficient, with higher correlation coefficients indicating higher convergent validity. The high correlation coefficient between the new measure of depression and the BDI (a popular measure of depressive symptomatology) is indicative of convergent validity. It would not be discriminant validity, as this refers to how two measures on nonrelated constructs differ from each other, often depicted by a negative correlation coefficient. It is not structural validity, as this refers to the internal structure of the new measure of depression, or how the parts of the new measure of depression are related to each other, yet seemingly unrelated to the BDI. Face validity is incorrect, as this refers to how respondents, or nonexperts, view the items of the measure as relevant to the construct measured.

6. **B) 2**
A z-distribution assumes that the mean is 0 and the SD is 10. As such, we need to use this formula: $z = \frac{x - M}{SD}$. This becomes 74 (student score) − 54 (sample mean), divided by 10 (sample SD). This results in the z-score = 2.

7. **A) Alternative: Trauma survivors who report abuse by a family member will report higher degrees of attachment insecurity as compared to those who report abuse by a nonfamily perpetrator. Null: There will be no differences on attachment insecurity between trauma survivors.**
A null hypothesis states that there will be no effect in the population; in other words, there will be no difference between those abused by a family member compared to those abused by a nonfamily member on attachment insecurity. When the null hypothesis is not true, or rejected, the alternative hypothesis is true. The alternative hypothesis assumes that there will be an effect in the population studied, such as differences on attachment insecurity when comparing trauma survivors abused by family members to nonfamily members. "Alternative: Trauma survivors who report abuse by a family member will report higher degrees of attachment insecurity as compared to those who report abuse by a nonfamily member. Null: Trauma survivors who report abuse by a family member will report lower degrees of attachment insecurity as compared to those who report abuse by a nonfamily member" provides two alternative hypotheses, as both statements indicate a difference on attachment insecurity between two groups of trauma survivors. "Alternative: Trauma survivors who report abuse by a family member will report the same degree of attachment insecurity as compared to those who report abuse by a nonfamily member. Null: There will be no differences on attachment insecurity between trauma survivors" provides two null hypotheses, as both statements indicate no difference between trauma survivors. "Alternative: Trauma survivors who report abuse by a nonfamily member will report higher degrees of attachment security as compared to those who report abuse by a family member. Null: Trauma survivors who report abuse by a family member will report higher degrees of attachment insecurity as compared to those who report abuse by a nonfamily member" provides two alternative hypotheses because a difference between the two groups of trauma survivors is indicated.

8. **B) 0.07**
The formula for computing statistical power is as follows: $1 - \beta$. Therefore, to compute β, 0.93 would be deducted from 1.

9. What level of measurement is used when data points can be ordered by relative rank and the magnitude of differences between data points can be determined?
   A. Interval
   B. Nominal
   C. Ordinal
   D. Ratio

10. A multisite study sought to examine the superiority of posttraumatic stress disorder treatment among individuals enrolled in a course of prolonged exposure compared to those enrolled in cognitive processing therapy (CPT). The study was designed such that individuals at Site 1 were enrolled in prolonged exposure with Clinician A, and individuals at Site 2 were enrolled in CPT with Clinician B. This is an example of which type of threat to construct validity?
   A. Maturation
   B. Multiple interventions and multiple clinicians
   C. The modality with which the intervention was applied (i.e., individual versus group format)
   D. Therapeutic attention

11. Adverse childhood experiences (ACEs) often lead to numerous negative outcomes, including a high risk of developing mental illness in adulthood. Research shows that minoritized populations in the United States are disproportionately affected by ACEs, and often less likely to seek mental health services or participate in research studies due to language barriers, stigmatization of mental illness, and more. In a study examining the effects of ACEs on a minoritized community in the United States, how can researchers facilitate participant recruitment and increase study participation?
   A. Employ a community-based participatory research (CBPR) study design.
   B. Work with probability sampling or representative sampling strategies.
   C. Use random selection.
   D. Use a qualitative analysis such as grounded theory.

12. In a study examining barriers to psychologists' engagement in advocacy behaviors, clinical psychologists were interviewed and asked about potential barriers to their advocacy. The principal investigator and a graduate student then each rated the qualitative interviews, searching for indications that a particular barrier had been endorsed. The extent to which the ratings were similar between the principal investigator and graduate student is an example of:
   A. Alternate-forms reliability
   B. Internal consistency
   C. Interrater reliability
   D. Test–retest reliability

(See answers on the next page.)

9. **A) Interval**
   Interval scales are used when data points can be ordered by relative rank and the magnitude of the differences between the data points can be determined. Nominal scales are only used for data points that can be categorized by qualitative qualities, such as hair color. Ordinal scales are used when data points can only be ordered by relative rank, but the magnitude of the differences between the data points cannot be ascertained. The question prompt does not specify that there is an absolute zero—ratio scales would involve an ordered ranking, with intervals and an absolute zero.

10. **B) Multiple interventions and multiple clinicians**
    If two interventions are compared and each is delivered by a different clinician, the apparent superiority of one treatment over the other might actually result from the superiority of one clinician over the other. Thus, the outcome of the study outlined may be a more accurate reflection of the therapeutic skills of Clinician A compared to Clinician B, and not the interventions themselves. Modality is inaccurate, as there is no mention of variable treatment type in the study design. Therapeutic attention is not correct, because the study is looking at differences between interventions (i.e., prolonged exposure and CPT), and not the efficacy of the treatment itself. Finally, maturation (i.e., when naturally occurring changes are mistaken for an intervention effect) is incorrect because it is associated with internal validity, and not construct validity, as the question asks.

11. **A) Employ a community-based participatory research (CBPR) study design.**
    CBPR studies aim to increase community participation through establishing close partnerships with community stakeholders, which refer to those who will be directly affected by the work done by the researchers. Probability sampling refers to recruiting a representative sample but does not directly increase study participation in minoritized populations. Random selection of research participants refers to a method of recruiting participants at random but does not directly contribute to increasing actual study participation nor would it help with barriers to engagement. Although qualitative analysis can be useful in hard-to-study populations, this is not a method of participant recruitment, but rather a form of data analysis.

12. **C) Interrater reliability**
    This is an example of interrater reliability, or the extent to which coding remains stable and consistent across various types of raters. Test–retest reliability is incorrect as this relates to a temporal construct. The question is not aimed at the reliability of a measure over time in repeated administrations, as test–retest reliability implies. Internal consistency is incorrect, as internal consistency is associated with the degree to which the items on a measure are measuring the same thing. Alternate-forms reliability is incorrect because alternate-forms reliability relates to the degree to which multiple tests measure the same construct, and only one form is highlighted in this example.

13. Researchers are interested in studying the mechanisms through which cognitive behavioral therapy (CBT) reduces social anxiety. Researchers predict that CBT will have an indirect effect on social anxiety by changing negative self-talk. Which of the following statistical analyses would be most appropriate to test their hypothesis?

    A. Analysis of covariance (ANCOVA)
    B. Chi-square test of independence
    C. Mediation analysis
    D. Multivariate analysis of variance (MANOVA)

14. Program evaluation (PE) strategies are often used to examine how an intervention or service works, what populations it works for, and under what circumstances it works. Which of the following steps are recommended in conducting a PE?

    A. Conduct a needs assessment with data to determine the relative priority of needs within the population; select an appropriate evaluation strategy after program implementation; identify and engage stakeholders.
    B. Identify and engage stakeholders; conduct a needs assessment with data to determine the relative priority of needs within the population; conduct a cost-benefit analysis (CBA).
    C. Identify and engage stakeholders; conduct a needs assessment with data to determine the relative priority of needs within the population; select an appropriate evaluation strategy after program implementation.
    D. Identify and engage stakeholders; select an appropriate evaluation strategy after program implementation; conduct a needs assessment with data to determine the relative priority of needs within the population.

15. Due to a lack of financial resources, researchers decide to use a convenience sample of graduate students to examine the association between gender and psychological well-being. Only participants who have experienced discrimination based on their gender are allowed to participate. Due to the sampling method used, this study is at greater risk for which of the following?

    A. Sampling error due to systematic bias
    B. Sampling error free from systematic bias
    C. Nonparticipation
    D. Underpowered study

(See answers on the next page.)

13. **C) Mediation analysis**
    In this study, researchers are predicting that changing negative self-talk is a mediator or mechanism through which CBT decreases social anxiety. In this study, CBT is the distal predictor, and social anxiety is the dependent variable or outcome variable. The researchers are interested in the indirect effects between CBT and negative self-talk, and negative self-talk on the outcome. MANOVA is incorrect, as MANOVAs are used to compare the means of different groups on more than one outcome variable and do not allow researchers to examine the indirect effects of a predictor variable on an outcome variable. ANCOVA is incorrect, as an analysis of covariance is used when a researcher wants to compare the means of different groups on an outcome variable while controlling for the effects of another variable (covariate). Chi-square test of independence is incorrect, as it is used when researchers want to determine whether there is a significant association between two categorical variables.

14. **C) Identify and engage stakeholders; conduct a needs assessment with data to determine the relative priority of needs within the population; select an appropriate evaluation strategy after program implementation.**
    "Identify and engage stakeholders; conduct a needs assessment with data to determine the relative priority of needs within the population; select an appropriate evaluation strategy after program implementation" is the only correct option. Stakeholders (such as community members, administrative staff, clients) need to be identified prior to conducting a needs assessment or evaluating the effectiveness of the implemented program. Selecting an appropriate evaluation strategy (such as a process evaluation strategy) is excluded from the steps listed for PE, and a CBA is not a mandatory step in PE. The needs assessment needs to occur prior to program implementation, which occurs prior to the selection of an evaluation strategy of program effectiveness.

15. **A) Sampling error due to systematic bias**
    In this study, researchers only used graduate students enrolled in one college. All members of the population of interest (i.e., all individuals who have ever experienced gender-based discrimination) did not have an equal opportunity to participate in the study. The sampling method used in this study, therefore, is nonprobability sampling, which is at greater risk for sampling error due to systematic bias when compared to probability sampling. Systematic bias refers to when individuals with specific characteristics are systematically under or overrepresented in the sample. In this study, individuals with undergraduate education only will be underrepresented in the study. Sampling error free from systematic bias occurs in probability sampling and as nonparticipation occurs regardless of the sampling method used. Statistical power is related to sample size, not sampling method.

16. A research lab studying the impact of childhood abuse on risky behaviors in adulthood sought to create a self-report measure aimed at correlating specific experiences of abuse with specific behaviors. In doing so, the researchers were hoping to identify particular areas in which victims of childhood abuse may benefit from early intervention. They created a pilot version of the assessment which was then administered to a sample of 25 clients actively enrolled in treatment. Based on the information provided, which of the following would accurately assess the new measure developed by this research team for internal consistency?

   A. The researchers compared the results of each participant on their first administration to the results of a second administration.

   B. The researchers compared the results of their instrument against a similar, already established, shorter screening tool.

   C. The researchers looked to the Cronbach alpha to determine how closely related the items on their measure were to one another.

   D. The researchers videotaped the administration and independently coded the responses of the participants.

(See answers on the next page.)

16. **C) The researchers looked to the Cronbach alpha to determine how closely related the items on their measure were to one another.**
    The researchers looking to the Cronbach alpha to determine how closely related the items on their measure were to one another identifies an example of internal consistency, or the extent to which items within an instrument measure various aspects of the same characteristic or construct. The researchers comparing the results of each participant on their first administration to the results of a second administration is incorrect, as this relates to test–retest reliability, or the reliability of a measure over time in repeated administrations. It is not the researchers comparing the results of their instrument against a similar, already established, shorter screening tool, as this is assessing for alternate-forms reliability, or the correlation between two different tests meant to measure the same construct. The researchers videotaping the administration and independently coding the responses of the participants is incorrect, as this demonstrates interrater reliability, or the extent to which coding is consistent or stable among raters.

Ethical, Legal, and Professional Issues

Rodney L. Lowman and Linda M. Richardson

> **BROAD CONTENT AREAS**
> - Codes of ethics
> - Professional standards for practice
> - Legal mandates and restrictions
> - Guidelines for ethical decision-making
> - Professional training and supervision

▶ INTRODUCTION

The ethical, legal, and professional issues portion of the EPPP addresses an area of psychology that is fundamental to all areas of psychology: ethics. Additionally, it considers areas related to ethics including professional standards and guidelines, legal issues, ethical decision-making, and professional training and supervision. This section will help readers understand broad and general principles and standards and also to apply that knowledge to specific situations. Because the EPPP covers a broad range of areas of professional practice, questions will likely be encountered that are not in the applicant's specific area of practice. The expectation, however, is that licensed psychologists will understand in at least general terms how the ethical principles and standards apply not just in their area of specialization, but all areas. Because the material available on ethics, guidelines, standards, and professional practice is continuously changing, readers need to know about current versions of the ethics code, standards, and applications. To better prepare for the EPPP, therefore, it is important to develop a thorough understanding of the principles and standards of the ethics codes and to have a working knowledge of how they apply to situations that may be encountered in practice.

The information contained in this chapter should not be considered exhaustive (and does not cover material in preparation for the EPPP2). Since the same ethics codes apply to a wide range of practice areas, there is an extensive literature on a number of different ethical applications. However, the information provided here is intended to raise awareness of some common ethical issues that can then be applied to a variety of specific applications.

▶ STRUCTURE OF THE ETHICS CODES

The section of the EPPP pertaining to ethical principles and codes of psychologists typically consists of items requiring application of the American Psychological Association's (APA) *Ethical Principles of Psychologists and Code of Conduct* (APA, 2017a) or the Canadian Psychological Association's (CPA) *Canadian Code of Ethics for Psychologists* (CPA, 2017) to real-life scenarios and dilemmas. Test items regarding ethics are written and selected on the basis of whether or not they can be answered correctly by studying *either* the APA or CPA codes of ethics, so there is no specific requirement to study both the APA and CPA codes. That said, reading both of these ethics codes may help you understand the principles and standards better by seeing two different approaches to the same, or highly similar, ethical concepts. (The Association of State and Provincial Psychology Boards [2018] has also published a Code of Conduct which could be consulted for a third perspective.)

Note that in this chapter, unless otherwise identified, we use the term *Ethics Codes* when referring collectively to both the APA and the CPA codes. When referring specifically to one or the other of the two codes we use the terms *APA Code* and *CPA Code*. Unless for specific quotes, the year of publication will not be included.

The APA Code includes four sections: an Introduction and Applicability section (which is important to read), a Preamble, a section on General Principles, and one containing the Ethical Standards. The five general principles are aspirational and not intended to be enforceable but identify the Code's aspirations and values. The 10 standards of the APA Code and their subparts are intended to be enforceable.

The CPA Code consists of a preamble including definitions, code applicability, and an ethical decision-making guide, and four sections for each of the ethical principles and the associated ethical standards. Each of the four sections begins with a narrative values statement followed by the standards related to that principle.

▶ ETHICAL PRINCIPLES

Here, each of the five APA Code's ethical principles (and the analogous principles in the CPA Code) will be introduced and briefly discussed.

A. BENEFICENCE AND NONMALEFICENCE (SEE ALSO CPA II. RESPONSIBLE CARING)

This classic ethical principle has been part of professional ethics requirements since long before the first psychology ethics codes were created. Today, the term *beneficence* refers to the expectation of promoting the well-being of those with whom the professional works. As stated in the CPA Code's Principle II: Responsible Caring, "A basic ethical expectation of any discipline is that its activities will benefit members of society" (2017, p. 18). The APA Code's Principle A: Beneficence and Nonmaleficence principle similarly states: "Psychologists strive to benefit those with whom they work" (2017a, p. 3).

In addition to beneficence (doing good), psychologists are expected to avoid, or to minimize, doing harm. This is called *nonmaleficence*. The APA Code refers to this as "[taking] care to do no harm" (2017a, p. 3) and the CPA Code as "or, at least, do no harm" (2017, p. 18). Although popular accounts sometimes frame the nonmaleficence principle as "doing no harm," it is not always possible to avoid harm altogether. For example, if a psychological treatment causes adverse reactions or pain, which the client views as being harmful, but the net effect is improvement and relief of the condition for which help was sought, there may be a positive overall effect. Additionally, even when harm is unavoidable, such as in an otherwise effective intervention, clients would still need to be informed in advance of the possibilities of harm so they can decide whether or not to participate.

However, psychologists should avoid activities that have been demonstrated to be ineffective or unnecessarily harmful. An example is the use of conversion therapy for gay, lesbian, bisexual, or transgender clients.

In the next two sections of this chapter, we discuss the APA Code's Principle B: Fidelity and Responsibility and Principle C: Integrity. We first note that the APA Code has two separate principles in this area, whereas the CPA Code discusses most of these areas in one section, Principle III: Integrity in Relationships.

B. FIDELITY AND RESPONSIBILITY (SEE ALSO CPA PRINCIPLE III: INTEGRITY IN RELATIONSHIPS)

This principle addresses establishing relationships of trust with others, accepting responsibility for one's actions, upholding professional standards of conduct, and avoiding conflicts of interest. Psychologists recognize their responsibilities to their clients and peers, to the profession, and to society. They are expected to take responsibility for their own behavior and also to take appropriate actions when they are aware that other psychologists may not be behaving in an ethical manner. For example, suppose a psychologist observed another psychologist passing out copies of a copyrighted psychological test to members of a class of psychology graduate students and asking them to complete the tests. The behavior was ethically problematic because the psychologist did not obtain permission from the copyright holder to reproduce the measures, and it was not clear whether standardized procedures were used in administering the measures. If the professor observing the behavior did not discuss the seemingly unethical behavior with the colleague, that too might be an ethical violation, since psychologists have the obligation to address (informally or formally) the unethical behavior of other psychologists.

C. INTEGRITY (SEE ALSO CPA PRINCIPLE III: INTEGRITY IN RELATIONSHIPS)

Concerning integrity, psychologists are expected to be accurate and honest in their dealings with others. They are committed to objectivity, minimizing bias, and keeping the commitments they have made. They do not steal, cheat, or exploit others. They take care when entering into dual or multiple relationships (which are inevitable in some applications of psychology or in some cultural contexts) to assure that all parties understand, and agree to, the terms. Psychologists are clear with their research participants about parameters of studies; when there are compelling reasons for ethically using deceit in research, they are careful to minimize harm, especially that associated with mistrust that research participants may feel after learning of the deception.

Suppose, for example, that a psychologist underestimated the likely positive outcomes of a new intervention method and minimized the potential negative outcomes associated with it. This suggests a likely violation of the Integrity principle in that the psychologist misrepresented the likelihood of causing harm and of receiving positive outcomes. If the psychologist further had a personal stake in the outcome, such as standing to gain financially from the recommendation, the possibility of unethical conflict of interests would also arise.

D. JUSTICE (SEE ALSO CPA PRINCIPLE I: RESPECT FOR THE DIGNITY OF PERSONS AND PEOPLES)

This principle has to do with treating people fairly, with dignity, avoiding bias, providing high-quality treatment to all of those with whom one works, and offering at least some psychological services at low or no cost to those with limited resources. The APA Code states that "Psychologists recognize that fairness and justice entitle all persons to access to and benefit from the contributions of psychology and to equal quality in the processes, procedures, and services being conducted by psychologists" (2017a, p. 4), whereas the CPA Code speaks of the "inherent worth [of persons and peoples and the need for] non-discrimination, moral rights, distributive, social and natural justice" (CPA, 2017, p. 4).

An example of this principle follows. A psychologist completed a study of the academic performance of students in a graduate program in psychology. Their findings included that the dropout rate for graduate students in the department was highest among persons who had a lower-than-average grade point average (the average among the students was 3.9 on a 4-point scale). In presenting the results of the study to the faculty, several faculty members argued that the students dropping out were poor quality students and that the admission standards should not be lowered to enhance diversity. The psychologist presenting the report argued that the objecting faculty members needed to better understand the challenges that disadvantaged students experience and that the department needed to address these issues in constructive ways, trying to identify solutions that would be effective. They provided multiple alternative factors that characterized the drop-out group including inadequate financial resources, having to work multiple jobs to cover the costs of education and living, and perceptions that the department was not welcoming to students of color and that they had experienced what they considered to be disrespect from both their fellow students and from faculty.

E. RESPECT FOR PEOPLE'S RIGHTS AND DIGNITY (SEE ALSO CPA PRINCIPLE I: RESPECT FOR THE DIGNITY OF PERSONS AND PEOPLES AND PRINCIPLE 4: RESPONSIBILITY TO SOCIETY)

Both the APA and CPA codes identify the need to treat those with whom they work with dignity and respect. As the CPA Code puts it, "Respect for the dignity of persons is the most fundamental and universally found ethical principle across disciplines, and includes the concepts of equal inherent worth" (2017 p. 11). Psychologists are also expected to respect peoples' rights to self-determination and privacy and to be aware of and respect cultural and other differences (e.g., those based on sex, race, sexual orientation, disability status, and age). The APA Code further states, "Psychologists try to eliminate the effect on their work of biases based on those factors, and they do not knowingly participate in or condone activities of others based upon such prejudices" (2017a, p. 4).

Everyone has biases, including those of which they may not be aware. The principle of treating people equally requires that psychologists strive to be aware of and understand their own biases, that they minimize or correct the effects of their biases, and that, in their own work, they work to make their services accessible to a broad range of people.

Psychologists have the ethical obligation to develop and maintain cultural competence as a way of respecting people's dignity. Suppose a psychologist started working with a client from a different race and socioeconomic status than themselves. To the psychologist's surprise, the client terminated the therapy after two sessions. This occurred after the psychologist made a racially insensitive remark often associated with bias. The psychologist was unaware that their comments had been considered racist. The psychologist had done no work to prepare for work with individuals not of their own racial group.

▶ ETHICAL STANDARDS

In contrast to the General Principles section, the Ethical Standards section includes specific, enforceable rules. For example, Standard I.4 of the CPA Code states that psychologists "[a]bstain from all forms of harassment, including sexual harassment" (2017, p. 13), and the APA Code's Standard 3.01 Unfair Discrimination states, "In their work-related activities, psychologists do not engage in unfair discrimination based on age, gender, gender identity, race, ethnicity, culture, national origin, religion, sexual orientation, disability, socioeconomic status, or any basis proscribed by law" (2017a, p. 6).

Thus, ethics standards are generally prescriptive or proscriptive. They tell psychologists what they must do or what they must not do, whereas the ethical principles are foundational and aspirational. If psychologists are brought up on charges by Ethics Code enforcement tribunals, licensing boards, or committees, specific standards are usually identified that were allegedly violated.

Here are the names of the 10 Standards of the APA Code and of the specific standards that are included with each. This provides an overview of the contents of the APA standards. As you read through the rest of the chapter, you can return to this list to see how specific standards fit into the overall APA Code. You may want to also compare this list with the standards in the CPA Code.

Standard 1: Resolving Ethical Issues
1.01   Misuse of Psychologists' Work
1.02   Conflicts Between Ethics and Law, Regulations, or Other Governing Legal Authority

1.03 Conflicts Between Ethics and Organizational Demands
1.04 Informal Resolution of Ethical Violations
1.05 Reporting Ethical Violations
1.06 Cooperating with Ethics Committees
1.07 Improper Complaints
1.08 Unfair Discrimination Against Complainants and Respondents

Standard 2: Competence
2.01 Boundaries of Competence
2.02 Providing Services in Emergencies
2.03 Maintaining Competence
2.04 Bases for Scientific and Professional Judgments
2.05 Delegation of Work to Others
2.06 Personal Problems and Conflicts

Standard 3: Human Relations
3.01 Unfair Discrimination
3.02 Sexual Harassment
3.03 Other Harassment
3.04 Avoiding Harm
3.05 Multiple Relationships
3.06 Conflict of Interest
3.07 Third-Party Requests for Services
3.08 Exploitative Relationships
3.09 Cooperation with Other Professionals
3.10 Informed Consent
3.11 Psychological Services Delivered to or Through Organizations
3.12 Interruption of Psychological Services

Standard 4: Privacy and Confidentiality
4.01 Maintaining Confidentiality
4.02 Discussing the Limits of Confidentiality
4.03 Recording
4.04 Minimizing Intrusions on Privacy
4.05 Disclosures
4.06 Consultations
4.07 Use of Confidential Information for Didactic or Other Purposes

Standard 5: Advertising and Other Public Statements
5.01 Avoidance of False or Deceptive Statements
5.02 Statements by Others
5.03 Descriptions of Workshops and Non-Degree-Granting Educational Programs
5.04 Media Presentations

5.05 Testimonials
5.06 In-Person Solicitation

Standard 6: Record Keeping and Fees
6.01 Documentation of Professional and Scientific Work and Maintenance of Records
6.02 Maintenance, Dissemination, and Disposal of Confidential Records of Professional and Scientific Work
6.03 Withholding Records for Nonpayment
6.04 Fees and Financial Arrangements
6.05 Barter with Clients/Patients
6.06 Accuracy in Reports to Payors and Funding Sources
6.07 Referrals and Fees

Standard 7: Education and Training
7.01 Design of Education and Training Programs
7.02 Descriptions of Education and Training Programs
7.03 Accuracy in Teaching
7.04 Student Disclosure of Personal Information
7.05 Mandatory Individual or Group Therapy
7.06 Assessing Student and Supervisee Performance
7.07 Sexual Relationships with Students and Supervisees

Standard 8: Research and Publication
8.01 Institutional Approval
8.02 Informed Consent to Research
8.03 Informed Consent for Recording Voices and Images in Research
8.04 Client/Patient, Student, and Subordinate Research Participants
8.05 Dispensing with Informed Consent for Research
8.06 Offering Inducements for Research Participation
8.07 Deception in Research
8.08 Debriefing
8.09 Humane Care and Use of Animals in Research
8.10 Reporting Research Results
8.11 Plagiarism
8.12 Publication Credit
8.13 Duplicate Publication of Data
8.14 Sharing Research Data for Verification
8.15 Reviewers

Standard 9: Assessment
9.01 Bases for Assessments
9.02 Use of Assessments
9.03 Informed Consent in Assessments

9.04 Release of Test Data
9.05 Test Construction
9.06 Interpreting Assessment Results
9.07 Assessment by Unqualified Persons
9.08 Obsolete Tests and Outdated Test Results
9.09 Test Scoring and Interpretation Services
9.10 Explaining Assessment Results
9.11 Maintaining Test Security

Standard 10: Therapy
10.01 Informed Consent to Therapy
10.02 Therapy Involving Couples or Families
10.03 Group Therapy
10.04 Providing Therapy to Those Served by Others
10.05 Sexual Intimacies with Current Therapy Clients/Patients
10.06 Sexual Intimacies with Relatives or Significant Others of Current Therapy Clients/Patients
10.07 Therapy with Former Sexual Partners
10.08 Sexual Intimacies with Former Therapy Clients/Patients
10.09 Interruption of Therapy
10.10 Terminating Therapy

▶ SOME MAJOR THEMES IN THE ETHICS CODES STANDARDS

Readers may be a little intimidated by the sheer number of ethical standards in the APA and CPA Codes. In all, the APA Code includes 89 standards organized around 10 categories. The CPA Code contains 170 standards organized around 30 categories.

We do recommend that, in preparation for the EPPP, students read the APA and/or the CPA standards carefully and in their entirety several times. The large number of standards also makes it impossible in a chapter of this length to discuss each standard in the two Ethics Codes in detail. Fortunately, there is substantial overlap between the APA and the CPA standards both in terms of what is covered and what the respective standards require to be done or not to be done.

In this chapter, we use an integrative approach. Specifically, we identify major content areas and themes that are important in both Ethics Codes, discuss some of the major and illustrative standards, give examples, and focus in more detail on some of the standards that can be a little tricky to understand and apply. For example, a standard prohibiting sexual relationships with current clients does not require much elaboration; one concerning multiple relationships does.

This is not to suggest that areas singled out here for discussion constitute the full list of what is important in the Ethics Codes. But while needing to read and understand all the standards, we also encourage readers to pay attention to general trends. What are the Ethics Codes' principles trying to achieve in the standards? What are the specific standards that are derived from them? How would the standards be applied to real-life situations?

In this chapter, we use the following notation method. Standards from the APA Code will be referred to as APA with the number of the standard cited immediately following (e.g., APA 1.0). Similarly, standards from the CPA Code will be referred to by the abbreviation CPA followed by the standard number being cited (e.g., CPA I.1). When quotes from the Ethics Codes are included, they are referenced in the standard way by listing a page number from the print version of the code from which the quotation was taken.

HARM AVOIDANCE, MINIMIZATION, AND CORRECTION

Psychologists have fundamental ethical obligations to use their knowledge for good and to avoid or minimize harm (see, e.g., APA 3.04, 3.05, 3.06, 8.03, 8.05, 10.10). In all, there are 26 references in the APA Code to "harm," "harming," or "harmed."

The CPA Code likewise has "harm standards" throughout the document (e.g., CPA II.2, II.4, III.31), and the words "harm" or "harmed" are used 56 times. Of interest in the CPA Code is the section on "Offset/correct harm"), which contains eight standards (II.40–II.47) such as the following: "II.40 Terminate an activity when it is clear that the activity carries more than minimal risk of harm and is found to be more harmful than beneficial, or when the activity is no longer needed" (2017, p. 23). Harm avoidance is also discussed in the CPA Code's Values Statement for Principle 2.

Clearly, there are many specific areas in the Ethics Codes that concern themselves with avoiding, minimizing, or correcting harm associated with the actions of psychologists. Harm can arise in emerging areas of the field (APA 2.01[e]), in research (APA 8.08[b], 8.08[c]), in assessment (APA 9.04[a]), and in therapy (APA 10.10[a]), to name just a few areas. Additionally, potential harm may need to be avoided by making exceptions to confidentiality as when harm to self or others is threatened (APA 4.05[b]). Collectively, these standards require psychologists to continuously be alert to potential harm that can arise in their work.

For example, a school psychologist who worked in an elementary school was asked to conduct an evaluation of his sister's child, who attended the psychologist's school and who was in the same classroom as his own stepchild. The psychologist declined to do the assessment, stating that it would create an unethical situation for him since he had a conflict of roles and relationship with the child, the child's mother, and, through his stepson, with others in the child's class. The school principal indicated that because he was the only school psychologist in the school, he would have to do the assessment anyway and if he did not do it, there would be "consequences." The psychologist cited the APA Code 3.05, indicating that this would constitute an unethical multiple relationship in which his objectivity could be impaired. He also cited APA 1.03, Conflicts Between Ethics and Organizational Demands, that required psychologists to "make known their commitment to the Ethics Code, and take reasonable steps to resolve the conflict consistent with the General Principles and Ethical Standards of the Ethics Code" (2017a, p. 4). The principal continued to insist, even after the psychologist noted that a psychologist at another school in the district could do the assessment. Ultimately, the psychologist's sister declined to sign the consent form for the testing to be done and pursued the testing elsewhere. This vignette raises several different ethical concerns, but the psychologist was persistent in trying to avoid any potential harm that might otherwise have come from the assessment.

INTEGRITY

Psychologists have a positive ethical obligation to behave with integrity and to avoid behavior that may compromise their integrity. This is a fundamental premise of ethical behavior and essential for the trust that integrity engenders among others, including trust for the profession. This concern is articulated in APA Principles B and C and finds its way into a number of standards.

A broad category of integrity that cuts across multiple areas is the need to avoid exploitative relationships. APA 3.08 states, "Psychologists do not exploit persons over whom they have supervisory, evaluative or other authority such as clients/patients, students, supervisees, research participants, and employees" (2017a, p. 6). The standard is elaborated in its applications to a number of other areas including multiple relationships (APA 3.05), fees and financial arrangements (APA 6.04), bartering (APA 6.05), and sexual relationships and intimacies (APA 10.05, 10.05, 10.07, and 10.08).

Elaborating, the Ethics Code prohibits unfair discrimination (APA 3.01, CPA I.9), sexual harassment (APA 3.02, CPA I.4), other harassment APA 3.03, CPA I.4), or exploitative relationships (APA 3.08). Psychologists are not to make false or deceptive statements in their marketing or public statements (APA 5.01, CPA III.2, III.5), and they do not engage in plagiarism (APA 8.11, CPA III.7), fabricate data in their research (APA 8.10[a]), or take inappropriate credit for research done by others (APA 8.12, CPA III.7). They correct their mistakes in research (APA 8.10[b]) and take reasonable steps to correct misrepresentation of their work by others (APA 1.01, CPA III.12). They are honest in their teaching (APA 7.03) and in advising people with whom they will be working about assessment and intervention techniques that they may undertake. Should they become aware of ethical problems by other psychologists, they address the concerns either directly (APA 1.04) or by reporting the behavior or taking other appropriate action (APA 1.05). Psychologists avoid conflicts of interest that may impair their objectivity or cause harm or exploitation to others (APA 3.06). Similarly, they avoid inappropriate sexual relationships with students over whom they have or may have evaluative roles (APA 7.07, CPA II.29) or current therapy clients (APA 10.05, CPA II.28) or, generally, past therapy clients (APA 10.08, CPA II.28), or past clients (APA 10.08). They also avoid sexual relations with close relations of therapy clients (APA 10.06) and do not accept as therapy clients those with whom they have had past sexual relations (APA 10.07).

Here is a situation related to personal integrity. Suppose a psychologist developed a new test to measure situational depression with the goal of not having to pay for use of similar, well-validated, and widely used measures. The instrument was markedly similar to an existing, copyrighted measure. However, the new test was validated only with the psychologist's clients using their personal judgment of the degree of depression as the criterion. The psychologist also charged the clients for use of the measure, even for those who were taking the measure as part of the validation effort.

There are a number of integrity concerns here. First, there is the question of possible plagiarism (APA 8.11, CPA III.7) in that the copyright of the other measure may have been violated in the creation of the new one. There is also a conflict-of-interest concern (APA 3.06) in that the psychologist was potentially using an inferior measure based on the desire to save money rather than on the validity of the measure used for the intended purposes. Finally, the fact that the psychologist charged the clients (or perhaps a third-party payer) for an unproved assessment measure suggests a possible concern of exploitation (APA 3.08). (Other issues also arise including the psychologist's competencies in test development and assessment; see the next section.)

COMPETENCE

Psychologists have an ethical obligation throughout their career to work only within their areas of competence. This does not mean they cannot become qualified in new techniques and methods or even new areas of specializations, but to do so they need to obtain appropriate training and experiences to be able to demonstrate competence in the new areas.

During psychology training programs, students are usually monitored and evaluated as to whether they have mastered the required competencies for the area of psychology in which they are training. A similar process is expected at the internship level, as well as during any postgraduate level training. Evaluation for licensure such as with the EPPP is also means for assessing competency at the entry level to the field. Other credentials may later be added such as board certification in a specialty area of practice such as in clinical psychology or assessment psychology. Demonstration of competency does not end there, however.

The APA and CPA codes mandate competence in one's professional areas of work (APA 2.0, CPA II.6) throughout one's career (APA 2.03, CPA II.9). The specific competencies are tied to scientific and professional knowledge of the discipline (APA 2.04).

The use of the term *boundaries of competence* (APA 2.01[a], CPA II.6) implies that in a field as vast as psychology, psychologists need to stay within the areas in which they are demonstrably competent to work. When a psychologist needs to expand competencies to areas new to them (APA 2.01[c]) or in emerging areas (APA 2.01[e]), they take appropriate steps to ensure they have demonstrable expertise and are not putting others at risk of harm.

The APA Code also recognizes that personal problems can potentially impair psychologists' competencies and identifies ethical mandates (APA 2.06) including refraining from work when competence is impaired (APA 2.06[a], CPA II.11) and seeking out appropriate help or consultation when that is needed (2.06[b], CPA II.11).

Note that when psychologists delegate work or supervise other professionals or students, the Ethics Code identifies specific ethical obligations (see APA 2.05, CPA II.7). Proficiency in cultural competencies, as relevant to the particular area of professional work, must also be acquired (2.01[b]; see section that follows). Specific areas of competence, for example, for forensic work (2.01[f]) and in providing emergency mental health services (APA 2.02), are also articulated in the APA Code.

Consider the following example. Would it be appropriate for a clinical or counseling psychologist who had no or minimal training in industrial-organizational or consulting psychology to start working as a coaching psychologist? In this case, APA Standard 2.01(c) would apply, "Psychologists planning to provide services, teach, or conduct research involving populations, areas, techniques, or technologies new to them undertake relevant education, training, supervised experience, consultation, or study" (2017a, p. 5). The burden of proof would fall on the psychologist to demonstrate they had acquired the appropriate competencies to practice in this new area.

INFORMED CONSENT

The APA and CPA codes are based on the ethical construct that the people with whom psychologists work are autonomous agents and should be provided sufficient information about potential engagements with psychologists so that they can independently decide whether to take part in psychological activities or services (APA 3.10, CPA I.19). Of course, not all individuals are able to make informed choices, such as underage children, those with cognitive impairments, or those who have certain physical or psychological disorders. There are also those who may not be able to legally consent because of external circumstances such as being ordered by a court to complete a psychological evaluation or because they are incarcerated. Even then, psychologists try to explain the services that are to be provided and obtain assent to proceed with them.

The term *informed consent* is also based on the idea that psychologists need to present objective information to prospective participants in psychological activities so that they can make appropriate decisions on whether to participate. People need to know up front what information will be collected, what will happen to it, how long it will be retained, the risk of harm, confidentiality of data provided, and any exceptions to confidentiality (APA 3.11, 8.02, 9.03; CPA I.23). They need to know at the outset if there are third parties involved, if the psychologist(s) have any potential conflicts of interest (such as benefiting financially from a recommendation), the circumstances under which they can withdraw from the activities, and, if they do withdraw, with what consequences (APA 8.02; CPA I.23, I.26).

As an example, imagine that a sports psychologist is asked to evaluate an athlete concerning their psychological fitness to play in an important upcoming game. The evaluation request was made by the student athlete's coach who wanted the psychologist's "confidential" evaluation of the student, who was of legal age. In this case, there are two parties involved, a coach, who is requesting a "confidential" evaluation, and the athlete who would be evaluated. Given that this assessment would take place in a university, there might also be institutional rules and other parameters that need to be considered. The psychologist would need to explain to the coach that the evaluation could not be conducted without the athlete's voluntary consent to the evaluation, its purposes, what uses would be made of the information obtained and recommendations made, and who would have access to the information. The psychologist would need to be sensitive to any implied pressure on the student that would make the student's consent less than voluntary.

MULTIPLE RELATIONSHIPS

Multiple relationships are not uncommon, but they are often complicated. The APA Code defines multiple relationships as follows:

> A multiple relationship occurs when a psychologist is in a professional role with a person and (1) at the same time is in another role with the same person, (2) at the same time is in a relationship with a person closely associated with or related to the person with whom the psychologist has the professional relationship, or (3) promises to enter into another

relationship in the future with the person or a person closely associated with or related to the person. (2017a, p. 6)

The CPA Code states the following:

III.30 Avoid dual or multiple relationships (e.g., with primary clients, contract examinees, research participants, employees, supervisees, students, trainees) that are not justified by the nature of the activity, by cultural or geographic factors, or where there is a lack of reasonably accessible alternatives.

III.31 Manage dual or multiple relationships or any other conflict-of-interest situation entered into in such a way that bias, lack of objectivity, and risk of exploitation or harm are minimized. This might include involving the affected party(ies) in clarification of boundaries and expectations, limiting the duration of the relationship, obtaining ongoing supervision or consultation for the duration of the dual or multiple relationship, or involving a third party in obtaining consent (e.g., approaching a primary client or employee about becoming a research participant). (2017, pp. 29–30)

Multiple relationships often have a bad reputation because of blatantly unethical dual or multiple personal and professional relationships such as those involving sexual relationships between psychologists and current or past clients. Similarly, it is ethically inappropriate to terminate a psychotherapist–client relationship solely for the purpose of initiating a sexual relationship (see APA 10.08). But both APA and CPA codes indicate that multiple relationships are not per se unethical. There are many circumstances in which multiple relationships are likely. Examples of situations in which multiple relationships are common include psychological consulting work with organizations in which there are simultaneous relationships between managers or employees as clients and the organization itself (see APA 3.11); working with families and at the same time with individual members of the family; and serving as a forensic psychologist in contexts where the psychologist has simultaneous duties both to a court, to the person being assessed, and to attorneys who contracted the psychologist's services. These types of multiple relationships should raise concerns, among others, at the outset of the need to clarify roles, duties, confidentiality, and informed consent among the various parties involved. It is very important to establish the nature of the relationships with each party, reporting responsibilities, confidentiality rules and exceptions, and financial information as part of the contracting process.

CULTURAL AND MULTICULTURAL ISSUES

In recent decades, multicultural issues have assumed ever-broadening importance in a range of areas of psychologic practice and research. This trend reflects society's increased interest in addressing issues of discrimination, economic inequities, and long-simmering social problems. Fortunately, a large and growing literature addresses these topics including the APA's Multicultural Guidelines (APA, 2017b). CPA IV.16 states: "In their scientific and professional activities, convey respect for and abide by prevailing mores, social customs, and cultural expectations of organizations, communities, and peoples, provided that this does not contravene any of the ethical principles of this *Code*" (2017, p. 33). Similarly, APA 9.02(c) states, "Psychologists use assessment methods that are appropriate to an individual's language preference and competence, unless the use of an alternative language is relevant to the assessment issues" (2017a, p. 13).

Note that multicultural issues are not just about not discriminating against people based on their personal characteristics. They involve the positive obligation to take into account such factors as they relate to the particular psychological activities. When psychologists engage in activities with members of particular cultural or identity groups with which they are unfamiliar, it is the responsibility of the psychologists to become competent to work with them. APA 2.01(b) states:

> Where scientific or professional knowledge in the discipline of psychology establishes that an understanding of factors associated with age, gender, gender identity, race, ethnicity, culture, national origin, religion, sexual orientation, disability, language, or socioeconomic status is essential for effective implementation of their services or research, psychologists have or obtain the training, experience, consultation, or supervision necessary to ensure the competence of their services, or they make appropriate referrals, except as provided in Standard 2.02, Providing Services in Emergencies. (2017a, p. 5)

A psychology researcher examined the effectiveness of an intervention and came up with promising initial outcomes. The product was marketed as being one "helpful for all" application to relieve everyday stress and "developed by psychologists." There were almost no persons from historically underrepresented groups in the validation samples and complaints were received from users of the application that all of the graphics in the application were of the majority race, young, and were more male than female. Although there are several ethical concerns here, the most relevant to this section is the blatant disregard for diversity in the creation and marketing of the psychological app. The normative data should have included diverse categories, and no marketing claims should have been made that the product is widely usable if that contention was not supported by appropriate evidence.

ASSESSMENT

The competent administration and interpretation of educational, psychological, and neuropsychological instruments is a core competency for many psychologists. Some of the major ethical points about the appropriate use of assessment measures include ensuring that the instruments being used have sufficient evidence of reliability and validity for the intended inferences the test is designed to make. Second, there is the question of whether the test is properly normed and appropriate for the particular individuals or groups being assessed. For example, the required reading level and language fluency and suitability for people with disabilities are all factors, among many others, that psychologists need to consider. Additionally, the recency of the test's development, whether there is a test manual and evidence from the literature supporting the use of the test, and the degree to which the test has excess adverse effects are factors to consider. Efficiency and expense also need to be considered. What happens to the data from the assessment's use, who gets access to the data, and whether the person taking the measure will receive feedback on it are just some of the ethical and professional practice issues that need to be addressed at the outset of the assessment. Relevance of the test for particular groups and other multicultural factors must also be taken into account both in the decision to administer a particular test and in interpreting the obtained results (APA 9.03, CPA I.13). In some forensic or other testing contexts, there may also be questions about whether translators or observers can be present during the testing. Careful consideration in such cases would need to be given to the potential impact on test results from having such individuals present.

THERAPY AND OTHER INTERVENTIONS

There are many ways that psychologists can be involved in interventions with clients. These can include interventions at the individual, group, organizational, or systemic levels. Because some interventions, such as those involving psychotherapy, have extensive literature regarding ethical issues that may arise (e.g., concerning sexual or other relationships with current or past clients), the Ethics Codes single these out for special discussion.

But whether interventions involve mental health, health, career, organizational, or any other psychological interventions, the Ethics Codes require that psychologists work within the parameters of their expertise, use interventions that are based on evidence as to their effectiveness, work with the consent of the client, avoid exploitative relationships, avoid potential or actual conflicts of interest, and maintain confidentiality as stipulated in the informed consent (e.g., APA Preamble, 8.02[b], 9.08[b]; CPA II.16, II.18, III.8).

A psychologist conducting therapy was seeing a couple both together and individually. In one joint session the psychologist let slip something that one of the partners wanted to remain confidential. The consent forms each individual signed were focused on working with the couple, not on the individual sessions that were later added. When the psychologist offered the separate sessions and essentially created a multiple relationship with the two partners individually and together, there should have been a new consent form signed and the terms of engagement agreed upon if that possibility had not been addressed at the outset of the treatment.

ETHICS IN RESEARCH

Research activities raise a host of ethical issues but especially involve protection of participants. For any type of research, there are essential safeguards that need to be followed before any work can be initiated.

In most situations, a designated body from the institution at which the research will be conducted (typically called an institutional review board [IRB]) will need to approve the research in advance of the study starting. This process is designed to assure that the rights and well-being of participants are safeguarded, and that participants (or those with legal authority to make choices on their behalf) will give proper consent to being part of the study.

The APA *Ethical Principles of Psychologists and Code of Conduct*, Section 8 deals with many essential requirements of research, whereas in the CPA Code research ethics are spread throughout the text (e.g., I.20, I.32, I.39, II.16, II.20). These address most of the same themes already covered (e.g., avoiding harm, maximizing benefit, obtaining informed consent, avoiding dual or multiple relationships), but the standards elaborate the specific issues, including use of deception in research (APA 8.07; CPA III.23–III.27) and when consent can be dispensed with (APA 8.05).

Here is an example of an ethical issue in research. Several research participants complained to the researcher and IRB that they felt stress when they were told about the deception used in the study. The researcher had indicated in the IRB application that the research involved minor use of deception that was necessary for the particular research questions addressed in the study. However, no arrangements had been made to help those experiencing stress as the result of the study and the psychologist sent a palliative email to those complaining about stress. When the IRB was informed about this, they revoked the IRB approval and insisted that the research refer participants experiencing stress to an appropriate referral source.

PATIENT/CLIENT AND OTHER RIGHTS

Although the Ethics Codes are clear about the need to protect the rights of those with whom they work (see, e.g., CPA I.5–I.8), some psychological activities require elaboration. In the case of health and mental healthcare, certain laws provide extensive protection for the confidentiality of medical records including those created by psychologists. In the United States, for example, the Health Insurance Portability and Accountability Act of 1996 (HIPAA) requires strict protection for the confidentiality of records and information. Other groups whose rights must be carefully protected include those with diminished capacities or those not legally able to give consent (e.g., APA 3.10[b]) and what the CPA terms *vulnerable individuals* (e.g., CPA I.31–I.36).

▶ PROFESSIONAL STANDARDS FOR THE PRACTICE OF PSYCHOLOGY

There are more things than ethics to be kept in mind. Increasingly there are also guidelines and standards which provide detailed guidance for practicing in a particular area or with a particular population.

The APA differentiates between guidelines and standards. It states that standards "include any criteria, protocols, or specifications for conduct, performance, services, or products in psychology or related areas . . . . [They] are considered to be mandatory and may be accompanied by an enforcement mechanism" (APA, n.d., "Standards"). In contrast, guidelines include "pronouncements, statements, or declarations that suggest or recommend specific professional behavior, endeavor, or conduct for psychologists or for individuals or organizations that work with psychologists. [Unlike] standards, guidelines are aspirational in intent" (APA, n.d., "Guidelines").

An example of standards are the *Standards for Educational and Psychological Testing* jointly issued by the American Educational Research Association (AERA), APA, and National Council on Measurement in Education (NCME; 2014). They provide a comprehensive overview of standards related to the use of psychological tests. Not only are they illustrative of parameters governing assessment practice, but they also delve into many topics important for technical knowledge related to scientific and methodological principles in testing such as the chapters on Validity (Chapter 1); Reliability/Precision and Errors of Measurement (Chapter 2); and Fairness in Testing (Chapter 3). Several chapters cover applications of measurement in specific content areas including educational and personnel selection uses.

The APA has also published a number of guidelines in specific areas. Examples of these include Guidelines for the Practice of Telepsychology (www.apa.org/practice/guidelines/telepsychology) and Guidelines for Child Custody Evaluations in Family Law Proceedings (www.apa.org/about/policy/child-custody-evaluations.pdf). At the time of this writing, APA has approved and published 22 guidelines covering a wide range of topics. In addition to those already mentioned, there are guidelines on people with low income and economic marginalization, and on assessment and intervention with persons with disabilities. The APA has also published sets of treatment guidelines for a few disorders, such as, depression and posttraumatic stress disorder, and more are being developed. See, for example, www.apa.org/depression-guideline.

You may not be expected to know about each of these guidelines in detail for the EPPP, but you do need to know that they exist and where you would go to find out if relevant guidelines have been issued in an area of practice. These guidelines are defined as being aspirational and not per se enforceable; however, to the extent they represent professional consensus of the field in a particular area, it behooves you to be familiar with them. Imagine being in a court case and an opposing attorney asks you about a set of guidelines in the area of the case that you did not know existed.

▶ LAWS, STATUTES, AND JUDICIAL DECISIONS THAT AFFECT PSYCHOLOGICAL PRACTICE

Laws affecting the practice of psychology can be found at the state, national, and even local level. Psychology licensing laws for the jurisdiction in which practice will occur are a good place to begin. In some states, licensed psychologists may have protected confidentiality in their conversations, which is often called privilege. But privilege may only apply to certain kinds of psychologists (e.g., mental health and health psychologists), not others such as industrial-organizational (I-O) or applied social psychologists. The law in your jurisdiction may also specify whether you have reporting obligations in the case of allegations of child abuse or neglect or older adult abuse. Or such reporting requirements may be found in other laws. The important point is that you need to know what legal parameters govern the practice of the kind of psychology you are performing in a particular jurisdiction.

The section of the EPPP pertaining to federal, state, and provincial laws/statutes and/or jurisdiction decisions that affect practice does not usually require detailed knowledge of specific laws, statutes, or decisions. Indeed, it would be impossible to have specific knowledge of each state's or province's regulations related to psychology. (Candidates for licensure in some jurisdictions have a separate examination on state or provincial laws affecting the practice of psychology in the jurisdiction where they will be licensed.) Here is a relevant standard from the CPA Code (see also APA 1.02):

> IV.17 [Psychologists] Familiarize themselves with the laws and regulations of the societies in which they work, especially those that are related to their activities as psychologists (e.g., mandatory reporting, research regulations, jurisdictional licensing or certification requirements), and abide by them. If those laws or regulations seriously conflict with the ethical principles contained herein, psychologists would do whatever they could to uphold the ethical principles. If upholding the ethical principles could result in serious personal consequences (e.g., jail, physical harm), decision for final action would be considered a matter of personal conscience. (2017, p. 33)

Psychologists should, however, be able to consider how laws or statutes may apply in real-life clinical and professional situations, and how they may be consistent with or in conflict with ethical codes. For example, if a psychologist is working with a client under terms of confidentiality but the individual then threatens suicide, APA 4.01 and CPA I.43 on maintaining confidentiality may conflict with the need to release confidential information to law enforcement, medical personnel, and/or family members in order to help prevent the suicide.

▶ ETHICAL DECISION-MAKING

Given the diversity and complexities of the practice of psychology, it is not possible to develop prescriptive policies or guidelines to address all potential situations that arise in practice. This is recognized by the APA Code, which in its Introduction and Applicability section states:

> The modifiers used in some of the standards of this Ethics Code (*e.g., reasonably, appropriate, potentially*) are included in the standards when they would (1) allow professional judgment on the part of psychologists, (2) eliminate injustice or inequality that would occur without the modifier, (3) ensure applicability across the broad range of activities conducted by psychologists, or (4) guard against a set of rigid rules that might be quickly outdated. As used in this Ethics Code, the term *reasonable* means the prevailing professional judgment of psychologists engaged in similar activities in similar circumstances, given the knowledge the psychologist had or should have had at the time. (2017a, p. 3)

The APA Code also makes clear that in making a professional decision, a number of sources of considerations must be taken into account. It states the following:

> In the process of making decisions regarding their professional behavior, psychologists must consider this Ethics Code in addition to applicable laws and psychology board regulations. In applying the Ethics Code to their professional work, psychologists may consider other materials and guidelines that have been adopted or endorsed by scientific and professional psychological organizations and the dictates of their own conscience, as well as consult with others within the field. If this Ethics Code establishes a higher standard of conduct than is required by law, psychologists must meet the higher ethical standard. If psychologists' ethical responsibilities conflict with law, regulations, or other governing legal authority, psychologists make known their commitment to this Ethics Code and take steps to resolve the conflict in a responsible manner in keeping with basic principles of human rights. (2017a, p. 3)

Not all ethical situations are clear cut as to the appropriate course of action. An ethical dilemma occurs when two competing courses of action are both problematic. For example, a psychologist might be court ordered to submit to opposing counsel the actual items on a copyrighted instrument (rather than the client's answers on the test) to a nonpsychologist attorney or face contempt of court with possible fines or incarceration. Or, a military psychologist might be required to report certain information disclosed in a psychotherapy session that will likely result in a soldier being removed from the military.

When such situations arise, psychologists need to consider information about legal parameters affecting the ethical decision to be made, consider all available options from the perspective of which would cause the least harm, and be clear on an informed consent process that includes information on consequences if certain information is disclosed during sessions.

Fortunately, psychologists are rarely without sources of help in difficult ethical situations. Contacting the Ethics Office of the APA or one's professional liability insurer may be useful, as can be discussing the situation with trusted colleagues and professionals working in the same area. In such cases, it is important to keep a record of the steps taken to get help with the decision-making, the options considered, and why the one chosen was the best alternative among several problematic choices.

In other situations, psychologists must consider conflicting guidelines of behavior, principles, or standards that are in conflict. The CPA Code provides explicit guidance for ordering ethical principles in decision-making when they are in conflict, indicating the following order of importance: Principle I: Respect for the Dignity of Persons and Peoples; Principle II: Responsible Caring; Principle III: Integrity in Relationships; and Principle IV: Responsibility to Society.

Although the APA Code does not provide any such prioritization, it does provide guidance when there are conflicts between "organizational demands" and the Code. It states:

> **1.03, Conflicts Between Ethics and Organizational Demands**
> If the demands of an organization with which psychologists are affiliated or for whom they are working are in conflict with this Ethics Code, psychologists clarify the nature of the conflict, make known their commitment to the Ethics Code, and take reasonable steps to resolve the conflict consistent with the General Principles and Ethical Standards of the Ethics Code. Under no circumstances may this standard be used to justify or defend violating human rights. (2017a, p. 4)

As a general approach, ethical decision-making starts with an understanding of the ethical principles and standards that apply to the situation. Then, the applicable guidelines and standards are considered. Relevant laws and statutes also need to be carefully reviewed and potential ethical conflicts and dilemmas need to be considered. Psychologists can consider all available options from the perspective of which would cause the least harm, be clear to affected parties using an informed consent process that includes information on possible adverse outcomes, and take a reasonable course of action. As the APA Code puts it, "As used in this Ethics Code, the term *reasonable* means the prevailing professional judgment of psychologists engaged in similar activities in similar circumstances, given the knowledge the psychologist had or should have had at the time" (2017a, p. 3).

▶ PROFESSIONAL DEVELOPMENT

During professional training programs a great deal of attention is directed to a student's or trainee's professional development. But, what happens after training is complete and the psychologist is licensed to maintain professional development over the course of a career?

Although APA 2.03 clearly states, "Psychologists undertake ongoing efforts to develop and maintain their competence" (2017a, p. 5) and licensure jurisdictions will require ongoing continuing education credit, most psychologists work in fields where the knowledge base is rapidly escalating. New skills will need to be developed, literature will need to be read, and engagement with professional colleagues is essential. Keeping one's knowledge and skills up to date is a professional responsibility. There are many ways to stay current in one's area of practice including reading journal articles and textbooks; attending seminars, workshops, and conferences; and consulting with colleagues.

▶ ETHICS IN SUPERVISION

Clinical supervision is a specialized area of psychological practice that has its own foundation of knowledge and skills as well as potential ethical issues. The supervisory relationship is highly interactive, and both the supervisor and supervisee are responsible for adhering to ethical guidelines in their relationships to ensure a positive learning and training environment. However, the supervisor, because of the higher status, power, and knowledge base, has the greater responsibility (CPA, 2017).

Supervisors need to have specific competence in supervision in addition to being competent in the services being supervised (e.g., intervention, assessment, or consultation). This not only protects the supervisee from harm, but also the clients whom they see.

The Ethics Codes do address supervision. APA Code Section 7.06[a] Assessing Student and Supervisee Performance states "In academic and supervisory relationships, psychologists establish a timely and specific process for providing feedback to students and supervisees. Information regarding the process is provided to the student at the beginning of supervision" (2017, p. 10). The CPA Code discusses ethics of supervision in several places (e.g., CPA III.9, III.31).

Note also that the consent of the supervisee's client is required for supervision. The confidentiality issues are particularly important to address since the client's personal information will be discussed in supervision sessions. Supervisors also need to ensure that the clients of supervisees are not being harmed by inappropriate or poorly delivered services. In addition, they need to ensure that supervisees themselves are not being harmed in the context of the supervisory relationship. It should be noted that sexual relationships with supervisees are prohibited. Section 7.07, Sexual Relationships with Students and Supervisees, of the APA Code states "Psychologists do not engage in sexual relationships with students or supervisees who are in their department, agency, or training center or over whom psychologists have or are likely to have evaluative authority" (2017a, p. 10; see also CPA II.29).

Clinical and other supervision often raises issues of multiple relationships and professional boundaries. Consistent with APA Code 3.08, Exploitative Relationships, supervisors should not benefit from the supervisee relationship at the expense of the supervisee. It states: "Psychologists do not exploit persons over whom they have supervisory, evaluative, or other authority such as clients/patients, students, supervisees, research participants, and employees" (APA, 2017, p. 6). For example, an internship supervisor asks an intern to teach section(s) of a class being taught at a local college. If this is a paid faculty position, the supervisor may be exploiting the intern for financial gain if the intern is not paid. In such situations, it would be very difficult for the intern to decline the request given the power differential.

Some multiple relationships are inherent in supervisor–supervisee relationships. Supervision in practicum, internship, and postdoctoral settings not only involves guiding skill acquisition and fostering competency but also addressing professional development, which can sometimes blur professional and personal boundaries. Similarly, in such settings, supervisors may also hold management or leadership roles that may conflict with the supervisor role.

▶ TECHNOLOGY, SOCIAL MEDIA, AND EMERGING ISSUES

The speed of change in technology has surpassed the efforts of ethical standards and guidelines to address them. The APA Code currently addresses very little on technology or social media except for competencies. APA 2.01(c) states "Psychologists planning to provide services, teach, or conduct research involving populations, areas, techniques, or technologies new to them undertake relevant education, training, supervised experience, consultation, or study" (2017a, p. 5). The CPA Code similarly states that psychologists "[k]eep themselves up to date with a broad range of relevant knowledge, research methods, techniques, and technologies, and their impact on individuals and groups (e.g., couples, families, organizations, communities, and peoples), through the reading of relevant literature, peer consultation, and continuing education activities, in order that their practice, teaching, supervision, and research activities will benefit and not harm others" (2017, p. 20). Neither is sufficient ethical guidance for a rapidly changing world of technology.

We already mentioned APA's Telepsychology Guidelines, which provide very useful guidance when conducting assessment or intervention services virtually. But, increasingly, we are dealing with confidentiality compromises from technology or social media posts, and discussions of the psychological behavior of leaders in public contexts that may breach ethical codes. The important thing to remember is that all these technological changes do not change the ethical requirements of psychologists. Confidentiality must be kept whatever the modality being used, public statements must still be accurate and reliable, and corrective action taken when there are data breaches and the like. Psychologists must be aware of and keep up with laws, statutes, and guidelines relating to technology.

As an example, psychologists may practice in states where data security laws require particular approaches to maintain the integrity of data. But, psychologists still have to anticipate that despite their best efforts, a data breach can occur anyway. It is therefore important to alert those clients and others whose data the psychologist has about how data is protected, how breaches might still occur, and what would be done in such contingencies.

In the case of social media, psychologists need to be very careful in what they post online and in their public statements to ensure they are not disclosing sensitive or confidential information. The ethical obligations of the psychologist after the breach is an issue better considered in advance of, rather than after, such a breach would occur.

Finally, as of this writing, it is important to mention the growing reliance of many, including psychologists, on artificial intelligence (AI). AI is already providing assessments, coaching, and even therapy. The ethical responsibility for psychologists regarding the use of such technology is exactly the same as for those not using it. They, not the AI, will be the ones responsible for its use in their practices that may entail misinformation, copyright violations, and mistaken assessments and interventions. This is not to say that AI cannot be of value in some applications, but it is the psychologist who is responsible for the ethicality and legality of what is done when they make use of it.

▶ CONCLUSION

Psychologists' ethics are one of the defining characteristics of their profession. We have identified a number of (but by no means all) important ethical principles and standards in this chapter. Other topics discussed included guidelines and standards, law and statutes, ethical decision-making, and supervision. The chapter has also included a number of examples to illustrate how this material can apply to real-life cases. The review questions that follow provide the opportunity to practice answering questions similar to those that might be encountered on the EPPP.

▶ REFERENCES

Full reference list available at http://examprepconnect.springerpub.com

KNOWLEDGE CHECK: CHAPTER 10

1. According to the Ethics Codes, pro bono services provided by a psychologist are:
   A. Forbidden
   B. Not addressed
   C. Recommended
   D. Required

2. Which of the following would most likely be cited if a psychologist was accused of an ethical violation?
   A. Both principles and standards would be cited.
   B. Neither principles nor standards would be cited.
   C. One or more ethical principles would be cited.
   D. One or more ethical standards would be cited.

3. A psychologist confides in a colleague that they are experiencing symptoms of long COVID and are increasingly having difficulty getting their work done. The most appropriate response of the psychologist is to:
   A. Contact the licensing board to report them as an impaired psychologist.
   B. Empathize with their situation and offer support as needed.
   C. Express concern about the colleague to the academic department head.
   D. Talk with the colleague about their diminished competence in their work.

4. A sports psychologist with a small solo practice agrees to conduct an assessment using a battery of psychological tests. The psychologist is not able to afford to purchase the most recent versions of psychological tests due to their high cost. For this assessment, the best option for the psychologist is to:
   A. Borrow the tests needed from a colleague.
   B. Conduct a brief assessment without using tests.
   C. Copy the newer tests from the nearby counseling center.
   D. Use outdated, low-cost versions of well-regarded tests.

5. When conducting research, potential participants should complete a consent form that includes the:
   A. Driver's license number of every participant
   B. Penalties for not participating
   C. Purpose of the research study
   D. Reasons for requiring participation

(See answers on the next page.)

1. **C) Recommended**
   Both Ethics Codes recommend that psychologists offer some services pro bono. Pro bono services provide persons with limited financial means access to care. The Ethics Codes do not require or forbid the provision of pro bono services, and the issue is addressed in the Ethics Codes.

2. **D) One or more ethical standards would be cited.**
   Ethical principles are aspirational goals that guide psychologists while ethical standards are enforceable rules. In the case of an alleged ethical violation, the ethical standards, not the principles, would therefore be cited.

3. **D) Talk with the colleague about their diminished competence in their work.**
   It is the ethical obligation of psychologists to ensure their own competence and to address the problematic behavior of their colleagues. When psychologists become aware that a colleague's competence may be compromised, there is an ethical obligation to bring this to the attention of the colleague and to encourage the colleague to take corrective action. This might include the colleague seeking help or suspending practice until competence is restored. If the colleague does not take action in response to the psychologist's concerns, or it is otherwise inappropriate to deal directly with the colleague, the psychologist may need to take further action which might include talking with the supervisor or contacting the licensing board. While the psychologist may empathize with their colleague, empathy alone is generally insufficient.

4. **A) Borrow the tests needed from a colleague.**
   A psychologist has an ethical obligation to employ psychological tests that are up-to-date and well validated for their intended purpose. It is unethical to make unauthorized copies of copyrighted tests. Although the psychologist might conduct a brief assessment without using any tests, the more appropriate choice is to use the tests that were judged to be needed and borrow them from a colleague if the psychologist is going to conduct the assessment.

5. **C) Purpose of the research study**
   A participant consent form for a study should include the purpose of the study. It is ethically problematic to require participation without the consent of the research participant. It is also not appropriate to require the inclusion of information (e.g., driver's license number) that might compromise participants' privacy. There is no obligation to indicate the possible risks of nonparticipation and there may be no risks related to nonparticipation.

6. Once psychologists are licensed, they should:
    A. Have sufficient skills so they only need to read new research.
    B. Only take state required continuing education classes.
    C. Take trainings to enhance their knowledge and skills.
    D. Take only those trainings which their employer pays for.

7. When attempting to resolve a complicated ethical dilemma, the most appropriate action is to:
    A. Confer with an attorney friend.
    B. Consult a friend from graduate school.
    C. Discuss the situation with the affected client.
    D. Talk with a respected senior colleague.

8. A psychologist is a manager in a health services organization. A former outpatient client of the manager applies for a job in the department that they supervise. The candidate is interviewed and is independently found by the search committee to be the most qualified person for the position. The most appropriate response of the psychologist-manager would be to:
    A. Hire and supervise the former client since they know each other well.
    B. Hire the candidate but assign the candidate's supervision to a colleague.
    C. Not hire the candidate because of the potentially problematic dual relationship.
    D. Refer the candidate to a similar job opening at another agency.

9. Which of the following principles does a psychologist most clearly fail to uphold when referring a gay client for conversion therapy?
    A. Beneficence and Nonmaleficence
    B. Fidelity and Responsibility
    C. Integrity
    D. Justice

10. A psychologist's client is receiving an advanced degree and asks the psychologist to attend the graduation ceremony. Which of the following is the best response?
    A. Accept the invitation if the psychologist can bring their spouse.
    B. Attend the graduation to avoid hurting the client's feelings.
    C. Decline the invitation due to the discomfort about attending.
    D. Discuss with the client the risks and benefits of attending.

(See answers on the next page.)

6. **C) Take trainings to enhance their knowledge and skills.**
   According to both Ethics Codes, it is the responsibility of a psychologist to maintain competence by keeping up-to-date with their areas of knowledge and practice. This can be accomplished in a variety of ways including attending training, conferences and seminars, taking courses, attending conventions, and reading the literature. Limiting attendance to those trainings required for continuing education by a licensing board or trainings paid for by employers and limiting reading to new research restricts access to current or past knowledge needed to maintain competence.

7. **D) Talk with a respected senior colleague.**
   There are many possible sources of support when dealing with an ethical dilemma including consulting senior colleagues, licensing boards, malpractice insurance companies, and ethics committees. Consulting friends including those whose professions are law or psychology is not recommended unless these individuals have expertise in the domain of the ethical dilemma. Likewise, discussing the dilemma with the affected client is not sufficient to resolve a complicated ethical dilemma requiring professional expertise, and, in some cases, may be inappropriate.

8. **B) Hire the candidate but assign the candidate's supervision to a colleague.**
   A psychologist should avoid dual/multiple relationships that have potential conflicts. Although a highly qualified candidate should not be rejected solely on the basis of the past status as a client, the manager who was once the client's therapist should not be the individual's supervisor in order to avoid potentially conflictual dual relationships. Not hiring the job candidate and referring them to another agency may not be in the best interest of either the candidate or the organization.

9. **A) Beneficence and Nonmaleficence**
   The psychologist must follow the principle of do no harm. Referring a client to a treatment that is known to be harmful is unethical. This is the principle of Beneficence (the expectation of promoting well-being of those with whom the professional works) and Nonmaleficence (minimizing harm). The principle of Fidelity and Responsibility addresses establishing relationships of trust with others, accepting responsibility for one's actions, upholding professional standards of conduct, and avoiding conflicts of interest. The principle of Integrity expects psychologists to be committed to objectivity, minimize bias, and keep their commitments. The principle of Justice focuses on treating people fairly and with dignity, while avoiding bias. While the decision to refer for conversion therapy may also reflect personal bias, the established harms associated with the treatment prove that the decision most clearly fails to uphold the ethical responsibility to do no harm.

10. **D) Discuss with the client the risks and benefits of attending.**
    If the psychologist accepts the invitation to attend the client's graduation, there is a possibility that the confidentiality of the client may be breached. The psychologist is best advised to discuss the risks and benefits of attending the graduation with the client and let the client decide whether the psychologist attends rather than declining the invitation or attending the graduation without having discussed the risks and benefits of attending with the client. Because of the additional role of conflicts or potential confidentiality breaches, it would not be appropriate for the psychologist to attend only if they could bring a guest.

11. A psychologist in a consulting practice is having difficulty paying the office bills due to an economic downturn. Without consulting the client, the psychologist bills the organizational client for services to be provided the following month. Which ethical principle is this behavior most consistent with?

    A. Fidelity and Responsibility
    B. Integrity
    C. Justice
    D. Respect for People's Rights and Dignity

12. A psychologist in a community mental health center is referred a new client who is an immigrant from a cultural background unfamiliar to the psychologist. How should the psychologist best handle the situation?

    A. Accept the referral and practice as usual with a new client.
    B. Ask the client if they prefer a therapist from their own cultural background.
    C. Refuse the referral but seek training on the client's particular cultural background.
    D. Use the therapy experience to learn about the client's cultural background.

13. An experienced psychologist is establishing a private practice and wants to appeal to a wide range of clients. The therapist has recently read a book on narrative therapy and attended a short course online and is eager to make use of it. In the advertisements of the practice, the psychologist lists narrative therapy as one of their specialty areas. This is a violation of the:

    A. Principle of Justice
    B. Principle of Respect for People's Rights and Dignity
    C. Standard of Advertising
    D. Standard of Human Relations

14. A psychologist who is supervising a postdoc asks the postdoc to lead a therapy group in the psychologist's private practice. The supervisor declines to pay the postdoc. This is an example of:

    A. Bartering
    B. Exploitation
    C. Pro bono work
    D. Training

15. A psychologist working in an outpatient clinic is seeing a 14-year-old who discloses self-harming behavior. The client asks the psychologist not to tell their parents because the parents would be upset. The most appropriate response of the psychologist is to:

    A. Encourage the client to discuss the matter with their parents.
    B. Report the client's behavior to a clinic administrator.
    C. Respect the client's wishes and not tell the parents.
    D. Tell the parents because they are paying for the client's therapy.

(See answers on the next page.)

11. **A) Fidelity and Responsibility**
    It is the ethical responsibility of the psychologist not to engage in fraudulent billing. Since the client was not asked if the psychologist could bill for their services in advance, this is an example of fraudulent billing. This best falls under the principle of Fidelity and Responsibility, which addresses establishing relationships of trust with others, accepting responsibility for one's actions, upholding professional standards of conduct, and avoiding conflicts of interest. The principle of Beneficence and Nonmaleficence is the expectation of promoting well-being of those with whom the professional works and minimizing harm. The principle of Integrity expects psychologists to be committed to objectivity, minimize bias, and keep their commitments. The principle of Justice focuses on treating people fairly and with dignity, while avoiding bias.

12. **B) Ask the client if they prefer a therapist from their own cultural background.**
    Clients deserve culturally competent services. Each client has their unique needs and preferences. The psychologist should disclose to the prospective client that they are not familiar with the client's culture and ask them if they want to have services with the psychologist or to be referred to another provider who is more knowledgeable about their culture. The cultural issues may or may not be important to the prospective client, which is why the issues need to be discussed. If the client decides to undertake the treatment, the psychologist may still need to learn more about the client's culture during treatment, but the focus needs to be the client's needs, not the needs of the psychologist to learn about the culture.

13. **C) Standard of Advertising**
    The psychologist is misrepresenting their competence in narrative therapy by claiming to be an expert when they are not. According to APA Ethical Standard 5.01, psychologists do not make false, deceptive, or fraudulent statements concerning their training, experience, or competence. The principle of Justice focuses on treating people fairly and with dignity, while avoiding bias. The principle of Respect for People's Rights and Dignity has to do with treating people fairly and providing high-quality treatment to everyone with whom one works and offering at least some psychological services at low or no cost to those with limited resources. The Standard of Human Relations guides psychologists on how to avoid things such as unfair discrimination, harassment, harm, exploitative relationships, and conflicts of interest when treating patients.

14. **B) Exploitation**
    A supervisor is prohibited from exploiting their supervisees. Not paying the postdoc when the supervisor is being paid is exploitative. Psychologists typically refrain from bartering, but it is permissible to accept nonmonetary remuneration in exchange for services if it does not adversely affect the patient and it is agreed upon. Both Ethics Codes recommend that psychologists offer some services pro bono. Pro bono services provide persons with limited financial means access to care. Training was not the primary purpose of hiring the postdoc.

15. **A) Encourage the client to discuss the matter with their parents.**
    It is the responsibility of the psychologist to maintain client privacy and confidentiality. One exception, however, is when the client is reporting behaviors of harm to self or others. Since the client's behavior is not life threatening, the best response of the psychologist is to discuss the situation with the client and encourage the client to discuss it with their parents. If the client is not willing to do so, the psychologist may break confidentiality and tell the client of their obligation to inform the parents. The decision to share the 14-year-old's behavior with parents is unrelated to the fact that they are paying for treatment. The psychologist is not obligated to share the information with the clinic administrator.

16. A psychologist is conducting an intake with a new client in a prison. The client does not have the legal capacity to consent to treatment. The most appropriate response of the psychologist is:

   A. Ask a friend or family member of the client for consent.
   B. Provide treatment to the client without obtaining consent.
   C. Seek assent from the client instead of written consent.
   D. To not provide treatment to the client since they cannot consent.

17. A psychologist is supervising a graduate student who reveals that they have been feeling very depressed since the recent death of their father. The most appropriate response of the psychologist is to:

   A. Empathize with the student and offer them coffee.
   B. Ignore the student's depression and focus on supervision.
   C. Offer to refer the student to a clinician in the community.
   D. Report concern about the student to the department chair.

18. An academic psychologist is having a casual dating relationship with one of his students. The student is more than 10 years older than the other students and is of similar age to the psychologist. The behavior of the psychologist is:

   A. Ethical because the relationship is not serious
   B. Ethical because the student is a consenting adult
   C. Unethical due to the nature of the multiple relationship
   D. Unethical only if they are having sexual relations

19. When a psychologist is meeting with a new client for the first time, they should discuss a number of issues including limits of confidentiality, scope of practice, fees, and responding to emergencies. This best exemplifies:

   A. Documenting care of the client
   B. Practicing in their areas of competence
   C. Protecting confidentiality of the client
   D. Respecting people's right to autonomy

20. A psychologist researcher is planning to conduct a study involving students in their class. The university institutional review board (IRB)/research ethics board (REB) meets monthly and has not yet acted on their application. The psychologist wants to start the study right away due to the term's ending soon. The psychologist should:

   A. Ask a peer to review the study proposal instead of the IRB/REB.
   B. Not wait for IRB/REB approval because the participants are students.
   C. Start the study and obtain approval from the IRB/REB the next month.
   D. Wait until IRB/REB approval is received before starting the study.

(See answers on the next page.)

16. **C) Seek assent from the client instead of written consent.**
    When a client is unable to give written informed consent due to age, diminished capacity, legal limitations, or other reasons, the psychologist is still obligated to seek their assent (agreement) for services (APA 3.10). If the client has a legal guardian, informed consent may be obtained from this individual. Obtaining consent from a family member or friend of the client, if neither is the legal guardian, is not appropriate since the person has no legal authority to provide consent. It is unethical to provide care without consent if the client can provide the consent orally.

17. **C) Offer to refer the student to a clinician in the community.**
    Psychologist supervisors have a duty to their supervisees to help them address personal situations that are potentially interfering with their work. However, it would be a conflict of interest and a dual relationship if the supervisor were to become the student's therapist. A referral to a qualified professional is an example of one way the student's need for assistance might be supported by the supervisor. Empathizing with the student and offering coffee, while kind, would not assist the student in addressing their distress. Reporting concern about the student to the department chair would not respect the student's privacy and would potentially break the confidentiality of the relationship.

18. **C) Unethical due to the nature of the multiple relationship**
    It is unethical for a psychologist to be dating a current student because of the power differential and the likelihood of a problematic dual relationship. The nature of the relationship, the age and maturity of the student, the student's consent, and other factors are irrelevant to the requirements of the Ethics Code.

19. **D) Respecting people's right to autonomy**
    Respecting the client's autonomous decision-making is an important part of psychologists' ethical responsibilities. By providing clients with detailed information about their services at the outset, they can help clients make an informed decision regarding engaging with the services. According to the Ethics Codes, psychologists are expected to practice in their areas of competence, to protect the client's confidentiality, and to document the care provided, but they do not relate to the primary focus of this item.

20. **D) Wait until IRB/REB approval is received before starting the study.**
    University IRBs exist, among other reasons, to protect students; they are not exempted from IRB approval. When a psychologist is conducting research in a university class, obtaining IRB/REB approval is necessary before (not after) proceeding with the study, even if the review process delays the start of the study. The review of a peer is not a substitute for an IRB review.

21. Informed consent is required when a person:
    A. Cooperates with an annual program evaluation
    B. Is ordered by the court to be evaluated
    C. Participates in any online study anonymously
    D. Takes part in a study required for course credit

22. A psychologist is conducting an intake on a new client, during which the client reveals that they ended treatment with the prior therapist because the therapist had made sexual advances. The most appropriate response for the psychologist is to:
    A. Ask the client for the therapist's name and file a licensing board complaint.
    B. Obtain the therapist's name and confront the therapist in person about the behavior.
    C. Take no action since they did not witness the behavior the client is describing.
    D. Tell the client that such behavior was likely unethical and discuss possible actions.

23. A psychologist providing telehealth services wants to conduct a psychological evaluation of a client using paper-and-pencil measures that were validated for in-person administration. The client is unable to come into the office for the evaluation due to lack of transportation. The psychologist should:
    A. Choose measures which were validated for online administration.
    B. Go to the home of the client and conduct the planned evaluation.
    C. Insist the client find a means of transportation to the office.
    D. Make unvalidated changes to a measure standardized for in-person administration.

24. A psychologist was interviewed by a local reporter who reported that the psychologist's treatment had a 100% success rate, a statement that had not been made by the psychologist. What is the best response by the psychologist?
    A. Ask the newspaper to retract the statement about success rate.
    B. Do nothing since the article is already in print and circulated.
    C. File a complaint with the newspaper's human resources department.
    D. Provide the reporter names of satisfied current clients to interview.

25. A psychologist is treating a client for substance abuse. The client was referred by their employer who is funding the services. The employer's human resources department asks the psychologist for all the client's treatment records. What is the most appropriate response of the psychologist?
    A. Give the employer all the client's records since the employer is paying for the services.
    B. Refuse to give the employer any of the client's records due to client confidentiality.
    C. Only provide the employer drug testing results.
    D. Send the client's records if the client signs a release of information for them.

(See answers on the next page.)

21. **D) Takes part in a study required for course credit**
    Informed consent is generally required when a person participates in a study, but there are some exceptions, such as when no harm is likely and online results are collected anonymously (see APA 8.05). Although psychologists should attempt to obtain informed consent in most circumstances, it is also not required when an evaluation is court ordered or for participation in a program evaluation, which is a routine activity in an organization. However, when students are required to participate in a research study and earn course credit for doing so, informed consent is required since there is the potential for exploitation.

22. **D) Tell the client that such behavior was likely unethical and discuss possible actions.**
    The client is reporting behavior on the part of the prior therapist that appears to have been sexual harassment. The psychologist has an ethical obligation to discuss the situation with the client, including possible actions the client might take. The client is in the best position to decide whether or not to file a report, since the client experienced the behavior, though, for a variety of reasons, the client may not wish to file a complaint. However, the psychologist may not just ignore the described behavior, nor would confronting the prior therapist be the place to begin, particularly if that was not the client's preference. If jurisdictional laws mandate psychologists reporting such alleged behavior, that information should be part of the informed consent process.

23. **A) Choose measures which were validated for online administration.**
    The psychologist must follow the ethical guidelines for psychological testing, which include using tools that were validated under conditions that match the conditions for their proposed use, in this case, virtual administration. Modifying the tools without validation is ethically problematic if the original instrument was standardized for in-person administration and the changes for online administration have not been validated. It is not ethically required for psychologists to conduct evaluations in clients' homes and there may be a number of reasons not to do so. The client has already made clear that they have no transportation to the therapist's office so "demanding they do so" is problematic.

24. **A) Ask the newspaper to retract the statement about success rate.**
    The psychologist has an ethical obligation to correct any misinformation or misrepresentation of themselves in the media once the psychologist becomes aware of the errors. Doing nothing does not meet the psychologist's ethical obligation to correct misinformation. Interviewing current clients is generally not allowed because of the potential for conflicts of interest or exploitation. Filing a complaint with the human resources department is not likely to result in a correction of the error.

25. **D) Send the client's records if the client signs a release of information for them.**
    While it is understandable that an employer might request treatment records for an employee when the employer is paying for the services, the psychologist is ethically obligated to maintain client confidentiality, and the terms of disclosure should be established prior to the beginning of the services. Psychologists can release client records if the client signs a release specifying the records the client is willing to have released (e.g., dates of service, drug testing data, treatment notes) and so long as there is no likelihood that the records will be misused. If the client refuses to sign a release of information, the psychologist may decline to share any client information with the employer unless an alternative policy had been established at the outset of services.

26. A psychologist is starting a therapy group for individuals who have experienced domestic violence. What should the psychologist tell the group members about confidentiality?
    A. They are legally obligated to maintain confidentiality related to the group.
    B. They can share confidential information, but only with their family members.
    C. They have no obligation to keep confidential information shared in group.
    D. They must provide formal consent which includes confidentiality terms before joining the group.

27. A psychologist offers low-cost smoking cessation services. Many people applied for the services, but only 20 people could be accepted. The psychologist felt more comfortable working with individuals of Middle Eastern background than those of African background and did not accept anyone of African background for treatment. Which ethics principle most applies?
    A. Beneficence and Nonmaleficence
    B. Fidelity and Responsibility
    C. Integrity
    D. Justice

28. A master's thesis supervised by a psychologist generated some promising findings that might be publishable. The psychologist should:
    A. Claim first authorship and give the student second authorship.
    B. Give the student first authorship of the paper.
    C. Prepare a paper on the research as the sole author.
    D. Revise the paper and claim first authorship.

29. A newly licensed psychologist wants to learn more about conducting child custody evaluations. Which of the following would be the best source of information?
    A. American Psychological Association's (APA) practice guidelines on child custody evaluations
    B. Classic textbooks on conducting child custody evaluations
    C. Consultations with recently trained child custody evaluators
    D. Reputable newspaper articles on child custody evaluations

30. A psychologist is seeing a client for counseling services using telehealth. Which of the following issues is of greatest concern for the psychologist?
    A. The availability of headphones
    B. The light in the client's room
    C. The privacy of the client's room
    D. The size of the client's room

(*See answers on the next page.*)

26. **D) They must provide formal consent which includes confidentiality terms before joining the group.**
In any treatment setting, psychologists have an ethical obligation to honor and protect client confidentiality. When conducting a therapy group, where there is a known risk of possible disclosure of information by group members, the psychologist must provide the confidentiality rules, review them with the group members, and obtain their consent prior to the start of the group or at the first group meeting. Any breaches of confidentiality should also be addressed both in the consent process and if any breaches should occur. Sharing confidential information with the family members of group participants does not respect client confidentially. The obligation by group members to maintain client confidentiality may be an ethical obligation, but it is generally not a legal obligation.

27. **D) Justice**
The principle of Justice focuses on treating people fairly and with dignity, while avoiding bias. The psychologist providing the smoking cessation services has an ethical responsibility to serve anyone in need of service regardless of their racial and ethnic background. If the psychologist does not feel competent in serving persons from certain groups, the psychologist should refer those persons to a provider who is competent and comfortable in serving them. The principle of Beneficence and Nonmaleficence reflects the expectation of promoting well-being of those with whom the professional works and avoiding or minimizing harm. The principle of Fidelity and Responsibility addresses establishing relationships of trust with others, accepting responsibility for one's actions, upholding professional standards of conduct, and avoiding conflicts of interest. The principle of Integrity expects psychologists to be committed to objectivity, minimize bias, and keep their commitments.

28. **B) Give the student first authorship of the paper.**
When a psychologist is supervising a student's research, publication credit should be decided at the outset. If the paper concerns a student's research and the student has primary responsibility for the research and the paper, the student should be the first author. The psychologist supervisor has an ethical obligation not to take primary credit for the work of others. It is unethical for the psychologist supervisor to use the student's research for a paper and claim sole authorship or, without the student's permission, to revise the paper and then claim first authorship (see APA 8.12[b], 8.12[c]).

29. **A) American Psychological Association's (APA) practice guidelines on child custody evaluations**
Professional practice guidelines provide guidance in a particular area of practice. Practice guidelines such as those provided by the APA (apa.org) are a key resource for areas of practice. "Classic textbooks" and consultations with child custody evaluators can also provide useful information but may be dated or, in the case of consultations, may not consistently reflect the consensus of the discipline at present. Newspaper articles are not a primary source to guide professional practice.

30. **C) The privacy of the client's room**
When providing services by telehealth, the psychologist must ensure that their environment and their client's environment are private and free of noise. Size of room, lighting, and availability of headphones are also factors to consider, but privacy takes priority since, if confidentiality is compromised, it can affect trust and willingness to continue with the services. In the case of assessments, lack of a protected space can also compromise the validity of the results.

31. There are many laws and statutes that may pertain to the practice of psychology. The psychologist must be knowledgeable about:
    A. The local and federal laws related to psychology
    B. The local and state/provincial laws related to psychology
    C. The local, state/provincial, and federal laws related to psychology
    D. The state/provincial and federal laws related to psychology

32. A psychologist initiates a sexual relationship with the mother of the psychologist's 6-year-old client whom they had met during the child's services. This is an example of:
    A. A multiple relationship
    B. An adult relationship
    C. An appropriate relationship
    D. An immature relationship

33. Which of the following would likely be an ethical method of recruiting new therapy clients?
    A. Ask current clients to refer their friends and family.
    B. Offer a financial incentive to persons on Facebook.
    C. Post an ad in a store promising treatment success.
    D. Solicit clients as part of a disaster relief effort.

34. A psychology graduate student believes their research study may be causing harm to some participants. The student's supervisor says there is no reason for concern because their study was approved by the university's institutional review board (IRB). Who is responsible for addressing the apparent harm?
    A. The staff at the research site
    B. The supervisor of the study
    C. The student conducting the study
    D. Both the supervisor and the student

35. When considering ethics and clinical supervision, which of the following statements is true?
    A. A seasoned psychologist with no supervisory experience can be a supervisor.
    B. Multiple relationships are uncommon in clinical supervision.
    C. The client's welfare is more important than the trainee's welfare.
    D. The higher power and status of the supervisor can create challenges.

36. Which of the following should be a priority when using technology-assisted psychological services?
    A. Nonencrpyted email and text can be used in telepsychology.
    B. Few legal concerns exist since laws regarding telehealth are limited.
    C. Steps need to be taken to protect the client's privacy and confidentiality.
    D. The psychologist does not need prior experience with technology.

(See answers on the next page.)

31. **C) The local, state/provincial. and federal laws related to psychology**
    A licensed psychologist has an ethical obligation to follow the laws at every level—local, state and federal—that pertain to the practice of psychology where they reside.

32. **A) A multiple relationship**
    The Ethics Code prohibits a psychologist from engaging in a sexual relationship with relatives of their clients. The appropriateness, maturity, and adult nature of the relationship are irrelevant in this circumstance.

33. **D) Solicit clients as part of a disaster relief effort.**
    The Ethics Code states that a psychologist can solicit clients in a disaster relief effort to make services available quickly to those in need. The Ethics Code prohibits a psychologist from asking current clients for referrals, offering financial incentives for referrals, and posting advertisements that promise treatment success.

34. **D) Both the supervisor and the student**
    When a student is conducting research under the supervision of a psychologist, both the student and the supervisor are responsible for avoiding and minimizing harm. Neither the student alone nor the supervisor alone are solely responsible. Although the staff at the research facility have a responsibility to report possible harm, it is the supervisor and student who need to address the implications for the research.

35. **D) The higher power and status of the supervisor can create challenges.**
    The power and status differential can create challenges in the relationship between supervisor and supervisee. Multiple relationships are common in supervisory relationships due in part to the multiple roles supervisors may fill. Both the welfare of the client and the trainee are important. An experienced psychologist is not necessarily a competent supervisor unless the psychologist has training and experience as a supervisor.

36. **C) Steps need to be taken to protect the client's privacy and confidentiality.**
    It is always important to take steps to protect the privacy and confidentiality of the client when providing services using telepsychology. Providing telepsychology services requires some technical competence and experience as standards related to competence include providing services new to psychologists. Although unencrypted email and text might at times be used if the psychologist and client agree to use them, the risks of hacking and compromise to intended-confidential information are greater. Written consent from the client would need to specify what kind of information can be transmitted in this manner. There are a number of laws and regulations that relate to telehealth, and psychologists need to be familiar with the ones that apply to their particular situation.

Practice Test

1. The concept of archetypes, or universally known and understood prototypical representations of various ideas, is a hallmark of which theorist?

    A. Adler

    B. Jung

    C. Sullivan

    D. Fromm

2. A client and Gestalt psychologist mutually agree to terminate care after reaching all treatment goals. The client is now engaged in meaningful relationships and progressing toward vocational success. How would the psychologist describe the client's status?

    A. Introjects are regular aspects of this client's life.

    B. The client's self-image is strong.

    C. The client's self is strong.

    D. The client's interactions with the environment no longer affect their well-being.

3. A small minority of citizens in a town would like to raise taxes to repair an aging and outdated community center as their neighboring towns recently built new community centers. Most citizens are opposed to higher taxes. What would most likely aid the small group of citizens in changing the minds of those opposed to their plan?

    A. Remain steadfast and unyielding in their plans for the community center.

    B. Engage in the social punishment of those who oppose their plan.

    C. Gain the support of the most respected citizens of the community.

    D. Emphasize the poor state of the current community center (i.e., emphasize the problem).

4. A client begins wearing clothes that are deemed fashionable by their peers and listening to music that other students enjoy. According to Kohlberg, at which stage of moral judgment does this person find themselves?

    A. Stage 1

    B. Stage 2

    C. Stage 3

    D. Stage 4

5. A mental strategy a person utilizes to save time and more efficiently make conclusions is known as what?

   A. Schema
   B. Attribution of cause
   C. Heuristic
   D. Cognition structure

6. A psychologist completed an intake with a 47-year-old client who had recently begun experiencing impairment with reading following a stroke in the posterior region of the left hemisphere. The client denies difficulty with writing. Which term describes this disorder?

   A. Dyslexia
   B. Alexia
   C. Agraphia
   D. Apraxia

7. Which of the following intelligence tests is most likely to be biased against minority test takers?

   A. Leiter International Performance Scale, Revised
   B. Raven Progressive Matrices
   C. Project Rainbow practical and creativity measures
   D. Wechsler Adult Intelligence Scales–Fourth Edition (WAIS-IV)

8. According to object relations theory, how old would a child be when fused with their mother and cannot differentiate between "I" and "not-I"?

   A. Birth to 1 month
   B. 2 to 3 months
   C. 4 months to 3 years
   D. 3 years and beyond

9. A child at the park is approached by a growling dog. The child processes the visual image of the dog's menacing teeth and the sound of the growls. The child becomes fearful. The child experiences muscle tension, breathes heavily, and wants to run away. This is an example of which theory?

   A. James–Lange theory
   B. Cannon–Bard theory
   C. Basic emotion theory
   D. Drive theory

10. Two children are adopted by same-sex parents. What is the most likely impact of being children of same-sex parents when they begin elementary school when compared to classmates with heterosexual parents?

    A. They will be comparably popular with peers.
    B. Their academic performance will be marginally lower than that of their peers.
    C. Their academic performance will be marginally higher than that of their peers.
    D. They may be ostracized from their peers.

11. A client with generalized anxiety disorder was referred to a psychoanalyst for treatment. The psychoanalyst develops a case conceptualization. What is this case conceptualization most likely to state?

    A. The client has an overdeveloped superego.
    B. The client continues to overindulge the id.
    C. This client's ego has difficulty inhibiting the id.
    D. The id is overdeveloped.

12. Which neurotransmitter is also an amino acid that primarily serves an excitatory function?

    A. Serotonin
    B. Acetylcholine
    C. Glutamate
    D. Gamma-aminobutyric

13. A supervisor and supervisee concur on the egalitarian approach they will take during supervision sessions with the supervisor functioning as a consultant and emphasizing the supervisee's strengths. Given this, what would be the most likely goal for the supervisee?

    A. Develop a deep understanding of two new therapeutic modalities.
    B. Improve the presentation of informed consent during intakes.
    C. Improve responses to Socratic questions during supervision sessions.
    D. Understand how the supervisory relationship mirrors the relationships with the client.

14. Which theory of employee management emphasizes consensual decision-making, moderate task specialization, and informal oversight?

    A. Theory X
    B. Theory Y
    C. Theory Z
    D. Theory A

15. A working person has financial disagreements with their spouse, who focuses on raising their child and does not have an income. The working person repeatedly emphasizes to their spouse that they earn the income, so their opinion should have greater weight. This emphasis on power differential would lend itself most closely to which family and systems theory/therapy?

    A. Communication theory
    B. Systems theory
    C. Structural family therapy
    D. Extended family systems therapy

16. A client was recently prescribed clozapine to address their diagnosis of schizophrenia. Which potential side effect would be most concerning to this client?

    A. Hyperprolactinemia
    B. Hypertensive crisis
    C. Serotonin syndrome
    D. Agranulocytosis

17. Which of the following types of brain imaging techniques is widely utilized to detect acute hemorrhage in an ED?

    A. EEG
    B. MRI
    C. CT
    D. PET

18. Cognitive behavioral therapy (CBT) has been utilized for a client diagnosed with major depressive disorder (MDD). The client has actively participated in all sessions and completed their homework. They continue to struggle with challenging unhelpful thoughts and "trying not to feel depressed." The psychologist is considering a different treatment protocol. Which therapy would be most appropriate?

    A. Acceptance and commitment therapy (ACT)
    B. Rational emotive-behavioral therapy (REBT)
    C. Cognitive therapy (CT)
    D. Dialectical behavior therapy (DBT)

19. Which mood stabilizer has a narrow therapeutic window and may lead to renal (kidney) toxicity?

    A. Lithium
    B. Aripiprazole
    C. Lamotrigine
    D. Olanzapine

20. A client presents to a clinic with the goals of reducing their symptoms of depression and smoking cessation. Which of the following types of antidepressants would be most appropriate?

    A. NE–DA reuptake inhibitor (NDRI)
    B. Selective serotonin reuptake inhibitor (SSRI)
    C. Monoamine oxidase inhibitor (MAOI)
    D. Serotonin–norepinephrine reuptake inhibitor (SNRI)

21. What type of seizure is characterized by usually experiencing loss of consciousness or altered consciousness, and experiencing muscle spasms?

    A. Generalized
    B. Simple partial
    C. Absence
    D. Nonepileptic

22. Which psychotropic medication is a nonstimulant medication that may be used to treat attention deficit hyperactivity disorder (ADHD)?

    A. Lisdexamfetamine
    B. Atomoxetine
    C. Methylphenidate
    D. Paroxetine

23. An individual presents to an ED at the local hospital due to experiencing alcohol withdrawal. Which class of psychotropic medications will likely be prescribed to assist this person?

    A. Selective serotonin reuptake inhibitors (SSRIs)
    B. Serotonin–norepinephrine reuptake inhibitors (SNRIs)
    C. Anxiolytics
    D. Atypical antipsychotics

24. A psychologist conducting a forensic evaluation notes atypical validity scales on the Minnesota Multiphasic Personality Inventory–3 (MMPI-3). To further assess the client's potential goal of secondary gain, which assessment should the psychologist administer?

    A. Millon Clinical Multiaxial Inventory–IV (MCMI-IV)
    B. Rey 15-item test
    C. Personality Assessment Inventory (PAI)
    D. Weschler Adult Intelligence Scale–Fourth Edition (WAIS-IV)

25. During which stage of Atkinson, Morten, and Sue's minority identity development model do individuals transition from an "all good-all-bad" orientation?

    A. Dissonance
    B. Resistance and immersion
    C. Introspection
    D. Synergistic

26. A 78-year-old male was hospitalized with a sudden, significant alteration in consciousness. While hospitalized, he was also treated for a serious infection. After a 1-week stay in the hospital, his infection and cognitive symptoms ameliorated, and he was released. What is the most likely explanation for his change in consciousness?

   A. Concussion from a fall
   B. Absence seizure
   C. Mild cognitive impairment
   D. Delirium

27. An employee at a major company informs a colleague she is unsure of the quality of her performance and standing at the company due to not yet receiving a performance review from her supervisor. According to the need for achievement theory, this employee is describing a lack of what consideration?

   A. Achievement
   B. Authority
   C. Competence
   D. Affiliation

28. What is the term for the fatty, insulating layer that aids transmission in neurons?

   A. Cerebellar peduncles
   B. Myelin sheath
   C. Dendrite
   D. Synapse

29. A psychologist is treating an 87-year-old woman who was recently diagnosed with dementia. At the end of the last appointment, the patient's daughter informed the psychologist that the patient engages in inappropriate behavior in public, having recently yelled at people in church for their poor singing. Which type of dementia is most likely present, given the symptoms reported?

   A. Alzheimer disease
   B. Vascular dementia
   C. Pick disease
   D. Dementia due to HIV

30. A psychologist works with a client who is strongly motivated to complete her bachelor's degree with honors. Maslow would describe this client as being at what level of the hierarchy?

   A. Safety
   B. Self-actualization
   C. Esteem
   D. Love/belonging

31. A client was recently diagnosed with schizophreniform disorder. Overactivity of which catecholamine likely resulted in this diagnosis?
    A. Acetylcholine
    B. Norepinephrine
    C. Dopamine
    D. Serotonin

32. A psychologist is referred a client who was recently placed on probation following a conviction for manslaughter while driving under the influence of illicit drugs. Though this client has a difficult background, the psychologist decides to work with him. What General Principle did the psychologist exemplify in this scenario?
    A. Beneficence and Nonmaleficence
    B. Fidelity and Responsibility
    C. Integrity
    D. Respect for People's Rights and Dignity

33. A psychologist who provides conversion therapy to a lesbian client is violating which General Principle?
    A. Beneficence and Nonmaleficence
    B. Fidelity and Responsibility
    C. Integrity
    D. Respect for People's Rights and Dignity

34. Which antidepressant is used to treat insomnia more often than depression?
    A. Venlafaxine
    B. Tranylcypromine
    C. Bupropion
    D. Trazodone

35. Which three therapeutic factors does Yalom consider to be the most important in ensuring group success?
    A. Installation of hope, universality, learning and conveying information
    B. Cohesiveness within the group, catharsis, interpersonal learning
    C. Interpersonal learning, development of social skills, cohesiveness within the group
    D. Altruism, catharsis, development of social skills

36. Which theory is an extension of classical test theory and allows for error and the reliability of measurement procedures to be evaluated?
    A. Item response theory (IRT)
    B. Generalizability theory
    C. Psychometrics
    D. Item characteristic curve

37. Which type of seizure most likely results in changes to olfactory or auditory experiences?
    A. Simple partial
    B. Febrile
    C. Generalized
    D. Tonic–clonic generalized

38. An individual planning to enter the military completes an assessment that assists in determining if someone is qualified for the military and which career within the military would be most appropriate. This is an example of what type of test?
    A. Achievement
    B. Aptitude
    C. Intelligence
    D. Curriculum-based

39. A client who is at risk for dementia had routine tests completed. Results from one test show a CD4+ count of 195, indicating the client's dementia risk has increased. What type of dementia is likely, given this test result?
    A. Parkinson dementia
    B. Alzheimer disease
    C. Chronic traumatic encephalopathy
    D. Dementia due to HIV

40. Two people are passengers in a vehicle when they hear a nearby car screech to a halt. Person A fears there may be an impending accident, while Person B views the screech as typical noise experienced while riding in a car. What could be said about these individuals' response biases?
    A. Person A has a more liberal response bias than Person B.
    B. Person A has a neutral response bias, while Person B has a liberal response bias.
    C. Person A has a more conservative response bias than Person B.
    D. Person A and Person B have a comparable response bias to the stimulus.

41. A psychologist meets with a new client who presents with concerns of depression. After completing their evaluation, the psychologist diagnoses the client with major depressive disorder, severe, without psychotic features. Which treatment recommendation is most appropriate for this client?
    A. Light therapy, dietary changes, and exercise
    B. Initiate cognitive behavioral therapy (CBT)
    C. A referral to a psychiatrist for medication
    D. A referral for medication and initiation of CBT

42. A patient being treated for depression reported to a psychologist that they are positive a new neighbor perceives them as unintelligent because they were unable to provide directions to a local shopping center. This patient's belief is an example of what concept?
    A. Self-defeating thought
    B. Cognitive distortion
    C. Learned helplessness
    D. Cognitive dissonance

43. A psychologist is asked to assess an individual's dangerousness. Which of the following assessments would be most appropriate to aid in discerning the individual's dangerousness?
    A. Personality Assessment Inventory (PAI)
    B. Minnesota Multiphasic Personality Inventory–3 (MMPI-3)
    C. Hare Psychopathy Checklist–Revised (PCL-R)
    D. Suicidal Ideation Questionnaire (SIQ)

44. What is the appropriate term for frequently utilized interpretations of situations that are viewed as accurate despite potentially being positively or negatively biased?
    A. Stroop effect
    B. Automatic thought
    C. Expectancy
    D. Affiliation

45. A 57-year-old client presents to a psychologist's office with extrapyramidal symptoms. The client denies using any illicit substances, which is confirmed by laboratory results ordered by their primary care provider. What is the most likely diagnosis to explain these symptoms?
    A. Alexia
    B. Parkinson disease
    C. Wernicke aphasia
    D. Klüver–Busy syndrome

46. A college student taking a psychology final fixates on their poor performance on the midterm earlier in the semester, telling themselves, "Don't screw it up again." This focus on their midterm performance exemplifies what concept?
    A. Learned helplessness
    B. Zeigarnik effect
    C. Nondeclarative memories
    D. Cognitive interference theory

47. A psychologist is attempting to aid a client in discerning which college majors may be most appropriate for them through formalized assessment. What is the most appropriate assessment instrument to utilize?
    A. Self-Directed Search (SDS)
    B. Strong Vocational Interest Inventory
    C. Kuder Occupational Interest Survey
    D. Campbell Interest and Skill Survey

48. Damasio, Everitt, and Bishop emphasized the role of somatic and emotional responses in decision-making. This theory of emotion is known as what?
    A. Expectancy
    B. Dimensional
    C. Basic emotion
    D. Somatic marker

49. A psychologist seeks to develop appropriate peer interactions for a student with an individualized education plan who has a well-documented history of becoming aggressive with peers. Which means would be most appropriate for discerning the appropriate social interactions with peers?
    A. A comprehensive assessment battery of the Beck Youth Inventories and Social Responsiveness Scale
    B. Systematic observations in the school
    C. Semistructured clinical interview and parent interviews
    D. Teacher report scales

50. Providing services, teaching, and conducting research with populations and in areas within a psychologist's knowledge base is the definition of what key ethical term?
    A. Competence
    B. Impairment
    C. Disclosure
    D. Confidentiality

51. A patient recently returned from a deployment where they experienced a head injury. Since their return, fellow servicemembers noted the patient having difficulty with executive functioning tasks. What other component of executive functioning might the psychologist wish to assess?
    A. General intelligence
    B. Behavioral coherence
    C. Multisensory processing
    D. Working memory

52. The utilization of a frequently occurring behavior, such as playing a favorite video game, as a reward for completing an infrequent behavior, such as completing one's chores, is an example of what?

    A. Fixed ratio scheduling
    B. Mediated generalization
    C. Premack principle
    D. Yerkes–Dodson law

53. A child will likely start representing objects that aren't present via language use during which stage of the Piaget model?

    A. Sensorimotor
    B. Symbolic function
    C. Intuitive thought
    D. Concrete operational

54. An expectant mother regularly smokes cigarettes throughout the duration of her pregnancy. As a result, the baby is born with a cleft palate. Cigarette smoke is best described as what to the developing fetus?

    A. Toxic inhibitor
    B. Teratogen
    C. Poison
    D. Birth defect

55. An elementary school student's self-concept has been influenced by their family members' actions toward the student and their reactions to the student's behaviors. Additionally, their self-concept has been impacted by how they play and work with classmates and their classmates' interactions and behaviors toward them. This is best described as:

    A. Prosocial normative development
    B. Transactional model of development
    C. Postconventional thinking
    D. Initiative versus guilt stage of development

56. The reinforcement of behaviors that are close to the target behavior is known as:

    A. Shaping
    B. Stimulus-response paradigm
    C. Mediated generalization
    D. Attentional load

57. A psychologist works with couples and families due to being able to charge higher hourly rates than when working with individuals. This psychologist has no formal training in marriage and family therapy. What factors should a fellow psychologist consider in determining if it is appropriate to report this to the state ethics committee?

    A. The efficacy of previous attempts at informal resolutions
    B. How the psychologist markets the services provided and level of expertise with couples and families
    C. The amount of experience the psychologist in question has working with individuals
    D. Patient satisfaction with the services provided

58. A Medicare client is apprehensive about initiating care with a psychologist and the recommendation for cognitive behavioral therapy (CBT) and medication to treat their depression. The client prefers a different treatment plan. What would be the most appropriate next step in addressing the client's apprehension?

    A. Ensure the client has an appropriate understanding of the costs and benefits of treatment.
    B. Defer to the client and initiate their preferred course of treatment.
    C. Refer to a psychologist who is willing to utilize a different treatment plan.
    D. Acknowledge the client's preference and proceed with CBT and medication.

59. An experimental psychologist would like to assess the potential impact of military deployment on cognitive functioning. To accomplish this, they have recruited a number of service members who have deployed to participate in their study. The psychologist wishes they had the opportunity to gather premorbid data on intellectual functioning. Which would be the best method for gathering such information?

    A. Ask the service members about their functioning before deployment.
    B. Administer a standardized intelligence test, such as the Wechsler Adult Intelligence Scale–Fourth Edition (WAIS-IV), before deployment.
    C. Review the relevant medical records before deployment.
    D. Have a service member's spouse complete a questionnaire.

60. A graduate student raised concerns to their professor regarding potential harm to study participants. The professor notes the institutional review board (IRB) has approved the study, and the research team has made efforts to ensure participant safety and well-being. Therefore, the student's concerns are unfounded. Who bears responsibility for this ethical violation?

    A. The IRB for approving a harmful study
    B. The professor
    C. The professor and the student
    D. The student

61. At what ages would a person's crystallized and fluid intelligence peak?

    A. Crystallized: 62; Fluid: 33
    B. Crystallized: 17; Fluid: 45
    C. Crystallized: 45; Fluid: 17
    D. Crystallized: 33; Fluid: 62

62. A client was referred to a psychologist by their primary care provider for concerns of a thought disorder. Following an initial diagnosis, the client is diagnosed with schizophrenia. Which would be the appropriate treatment recommendation?

    A. Psychoactive medications
    B. Family therapy and skills training
    C. Primarily psychoactive medications with family therapy and skills training as adjuncts
    D. Family therapy and skills training with medication as an adjunct

63. A large corporation's president meets with an industrial organizational psychologist in an effort to improve retention issues at the company. The president believes that fully remote positions may help with the issue. The psychologist, who operates from a self-determination theory, would provide what feedback?

    A. This plan will likely help employees feel a greater sense of achievement in their work.
    B. Working remotely may prove difficult for those with minimal intrinsic motivation.
    C. Remote work places a greater emphasis on extrinsic rewards as a behavioral motivator.
    D. Developing a sense of relatedness may prove difficult with fully remote work.

64. A manager operates from a Theory X orientation. The manager informs employees of an upcoming merger with a corporate competitor and that layoffs may be necessary. What is the most likely method this manager will use to protect the employees' jobs after the merger?

    A. Work to improve employee trust in the newly merged company.
    B. Model characteristics of a quality employee based on the new company's goals.
    C. Ensure opportunities for time off and healthcare benefits are available to employees.
    D. Encourage collaboration with new coworkers coming from their former competitor.

65. What is the best definition of the Lazarus sophisticated appraisal model of emotion?

    A. Emotional experiences stem from appraisals of ongoing environmental interactions.
    B. Emotions are derived from primarily noncognitive functions.
    C. Physiological responses in the body are critical to understanding emotion and motivation.
    D. All emotions may be described by a small set of specific emotions.

66. Which definition best matches Vroom's definition of valence as it relates to expectancy theory?

    A. The value someone places on a particular consequence
    B. The view that a person possesses the resources to achieve a specific goal
    C. The belief that completing a behavior will lead to a certain outcome
    D. Changing one's beliefs to manage psychological tension

67. A client presents to a neuropsychologist due to a loss of spontaneous speech, disinhibited behaviors, and reduced divergent thinking. Which of the following is the most likely genesis for these symptoms?

    A. Damage to the amygdala
    B. Frontal lobe lesion
    C. Hippocampal damage
    D. Basal ganglia injury

68. If a person who uses recreational drugs consumes a drug in the same context each day, such as the same time, room, similar background noise, and so on, what changes would likely occur?

    A. The individual would eventually require increased doses to achieve the desired high.
    B. The person would eventually require a lower dose to achieve the same high as the context aids in becoming high.
    C. The individual's antagonistic response to the drug would take longer.
    D. No changes would occur for the person.

69. A first-semester practicum graduate student seeks supervision for a new client diagnosed with bipolar II mood disorder. What would the discrimination model-oriented supervisor most likely do during this supervision session?

    A. Serve as a consultant to the student regarding proper assessment.
    B. Teach how to treat this client, given the nascent stage of the student's training.
    C. Ensure the two overlapping systems in supervision are adequately addressed.
    D. Emphasize the counseling role due to the stress the supervisee may experience.

70. An intern works under the direct supervision of the internship training director. The intern applies for a postdoctoral position, where the internship training director serves as the chair of the postdoctoral selection committee. The intern received regular feedback from this psychologist before applying for the postdoctoral position and while waiting for results from the postdoctoral selection committee. What ethical problem may this represent?

    A. This supervisor and supervisee should sign a memorandum stating there could be a conflict of interest.
    B. The applicant may present personal information in the application that a supervisor is not allowed to require of the supervisees.
    C. The psychologist's standing as the internship training director and postdoctoral selection committee chair represents a multiple relationship in supervision.
    D. It does not represent an ethical problem if the supervisor and supervisee are aware.

71. Utilizing Locke's goal-setting theory, how might a psychologist assist a client who is finding it difficult to complete their coursework in the evenings after working at a full-time job?

   A. Aid the client in developing specific study strategies to complete coursework.

   B. Assist the client in viewing "healthy" amounts of anxiety as beneficial to coursework completion.

   C. Explore the "all or nothing thinking" the client may have about their ability to accomplish coursework and a full-time job.

   D. Work toward improving the client's expectancy, or the belief that a person has the resources to achieve a specific goal.

72. What two sources combine to create the variance of a specific measure according to classical test theory (CTT)?

   A. Error and variance

   B. Consistency and dependability

   C. True score variance and random error variance

   D. Random score variance and true error variance

73. Legal mandates regarding the storage and dissemination of client records are, in part, laid out in what?

   A. Health Insurance Portability and Accountability Act (HIPAA)

   B. Belmont Report

   C. General Principles

   D. Association of State and Provincial Psychology Boards (ASPPB) Code of Conduct

74. What organization is most widely accepted as offering board certification to psychologists in a number of specialty areas, including neuropsychology, forensic psychology, and behavioral and cognitive psychology?

   A. Each state or provincial licensing board

   B. The American Board of Professional Psychology (ABPP)

   C. The American Psychological Association (APA)

   D. The Association of State and Provincial Psychology Boards (ASPPB)

75. A psychologist hopes to discern if a new behavioral intervention reduces irritability in clients with dementia. The psychologist has baseline information on irritability from psychologists treating the clients. Each client then receives the behavioral intervention for 2 weeks before stopping the intervention for 2 weeks, measuring irritability throughout this time. The psychologist applies the behavioral intervention a second time before withdrawing again. This study is best described as what?

   A. Multiple baseline design

   B. ABAB design

   C. Efficacy trial

   D. Single-case design

76. When is the most appropriate time to discuss authorship credit for a publication?
    A. At the beginning of the research study
    B. At the conclusion of the research study, so that each contributor's work may be assessed
    C. After data has been gathered and analyzed, but before the results are written
    D. After final edits have been made at the request of the publisher

77. On the Minnesota Multiphasic Personality Inventory–3 (MMPI-3), what standard score indicates clinical significance?
    A. z-score of 75
    B. z-score of 85
    C. t-score of 50
    D. t-score of 65

78. A client with whom a psychologist has worked for approximately 1 year asks the psychologist to attend their retirement ceremony from the military. What would be the psychologist's most appropriate course of action?
    A. Discuss the potential pros and cons of attendance with the client.
    B. Attend the ceremony to ensure that no harm to the therapeutic relationship occurs.
    C. Do not attend the ceremony as this would violate professional boundaries.
    D. Attend the ceremony but sit in the back and leave as soon as the event concludes.

79. A new patient presents to a clinic for treatment. During the intake, the client reports they terminated care with their previous psychologist due to being friends and having a falling out at a party. What would be the most appropriate step for the new psychologist to take?
    A. Inform the client their previous psychologist acted unethically by seeking a friendship and discuss steps they may take to address such behavior.
    B. Confront the previous psychologist via phone or in person.
    C. Immediately contact the state licensure board regarding this unethical behavior.
    D. Do nothing, as the client may not have an accurate recollection of events.

80. A psychologist is interested in if college students are diagnosed with a mental health disorder (yes or no) from the predictor variable of the number of credits taken (1 = 0 to 5, 2 = 5 to 10, or 3 = 10 to 15 credits, respectively). The researcher has also discerned the appropriate odds ratios. Based on this research study, which ordinary least squares test would be most appropriate for the psychologist to utilize?
    A. Path analysis
    B. Structural equation model
    C. Chi-square
    D. Logistic regression

81. A client schedules an intake appointment with a psychologist due to a strained relationship with their spouse. Incorporating social exchange theory, what might the psychologist most likely attempt to accomplish with the client?
   A. Assist the client in defining themselves to reduce anxiety.
   B. Assess the client's perceptions of equity in the relationship.
   C. Understand if the client's evaluation of their spouse began in a negative or positive fashion.
   D. Develop an understanding of the costs and benefits of the relationship.

82. When conducting telepsychology services, psychologists should disclose which of the following to their clients?
   A. Improved access to care is available for therapy services via telepsychology.
   B. Treatment outcomes are generally not as strong as outcomes for in-person services.
   C. Guidelines have yet to be developed for telepsychology, which may bring added risk.
   D. Confidentiality is harder to ensure with telepsychology versus in-person treatment.

83. An adolescent sees themselves as bright and competent regarding academics and managing responsibilities at home. Concurrently, they are quite self-conscious and have low self-esteem overall due to viewing themselves as not well-liked by several peers. What is the most accurate description of this adolescent's self-concept?
   A. They have positive knowledge components and negative evaluative components.
   B. They have negative knowledge components and positive evaluative components.
   C. Their overall self-concept is positive now, but risks worsening should they not become more social.
   D. Their overall self-concept is negative now and risks worsening should they not become more social.

84. A psychologist has 125 study participants who are categorized as: slightly depressed, moderately depressed, or severely depressed. This is an example of what level of measurement?
   A. Nominal
   B. Ordinal
   C. Interval
   D. Ratio

85. A client who cannot afford therapy with a psychologist due to financial hardship is happy to barter to continue services. The psychologist agrees and suggests that since the client has found benefits with therapy, the client should write up a brief testimonial the psychologist can use online to expand their therapy practice. The client agrees to this arrangement. Which of the following statements is true?
   A. There is no ethical dilemma as both parties agree to this arrangement to continue services.
   B. This is an ethical arrangement as both parties agree to the arrangement, and it prevents the psychologist from abandoning the client.
   C. This is an unethical arrangement, as bartering is forbidden by the ethics code, and the psychologist should not solicit testimonials.
   D. This is an unethical arrangement as the psychologist should not solicit testimonials.

86. A client with whom a psychologist has been completing a course of cognitive processing therapy (CPT) recently lost their job. They have offered to pay for treatment with produce that they and their spouse grow in their garden. What is the most appropriate response to offer?
    A. Refer the client to a different psychologist who is willing to barter for services.
    B. Decline the offer as the American Psychological Association Code of Conduct disallows bartering for services.
    C. Agree to the bartering arrangement out of a desire not to abandon a client.
    D. Decline the offer due to the likelihood that such an arrangement may become exploitative.

87. A study of prosocial behaviors in new parents is conducted. The study's researchers want to determine the potential correlation with academic performance during high school. Which type of validity does this potential correlation represent?
    A. Face validity
    B. Content validity
    C. Structural validity
    D. Criterion validity

88. A client was referred by a primary care provider for neuropsychological testing due to a recent loss of spontaneous speech. Which of the following assessments would best assess this presenting concern?
    A. Wisconsin Card Sort Test
    B. Multilingual Aphasia Examination
    C. Stroop Color Word Test
    D. Weschler Adult Intelligence Scale (WAIS)

89. The Piaget cognitive developmental theory is best described as which of the following terms?
    A. Continuity
    B. Discontinuity
    C. Prosocial
    D. Sensitive

90. When reviewing the results of a Minnesota Multiphasic Personality Inventory–3 (MMPI-3), the Combined Response Inconsistency (CRIN) scale is significantly elevated. What would be the most likely inference to make from this scale elevation?
    A. The client is likely experiencing a unipolar mood episode.
    B. Further assessment should occur to confirm there is a cluster C personality disorder.
    C. Concentration deficits are prominent, and further neuropsychological assessments should occur to rule out attention deficit hyperactivity disorder (ADHD).
    D. Additional validity indices from other assessments should be reviewed.

91. A psychologist would like to find out if the amount of light and the amount of noise impact employees' moods during the workday. Which analysis of variance (ANOVA) would be utilized to evaluate the possible role light and noise play on mood?

A. One-way between-subjects

B. One-way within-subjects

C. Two-way between-subjects

D. Multivariate ANOVA (MANOVA)

92. A team aims to research the impact of educational programs on mental health outcomes for those diagnosed with posttraumatic stress disorder (PTSD). What would be most applicable for this research team when conducting this study?

A. Ensure the study occurs in a quiet room.

B. Take additional steps to ensure consent is freely given.

C. Ensure that materials for study participants are at the appropriate reading level.

D. Make sure the potential benefits outweigh the potential costs of conducting the study.

93. A psychologist providing telepsychology services would like to utilize the Minnesota Multiphasic Personality Inventory–3 (MMPI-3) to clarify diagnostic questions. What should the psychologist do in order to adjust the MMPI-3 for telepsychology services?

A. The psychologist should modify the administration of the assessment to use via telehealth platforms.

B. The psychologist should mail the MMPI-3 to the client who will then return it to the psychologist after completion.

C. The psychologist should travel to the client and complete the MMPI-3 in person.

D. The psychologist should choose an assessment similar to the MMPI-3 that can be administered via telepsychology.

94. A one-sample z-test would be most appropriate in which circumstance?

A. Comparing a single sample mean to a population mean with a known population SD.

B. Assessing the difference between a single sample mean and a hypothesized population mean.

C. Comparing a single sample mean to a population mean with an unknown population SD.

D. Assessing the mean differences between two populations with normal population distributions.

95. A positive psychologist begins working with a client. The client is engaged in therapy out of a desire to further their spiritual development, as meditation has become a key part of their life. Which strength is most likely to be the focus of this therapeutic relationship?

A. Courage

B. Wisdom and knowledge

C. Temperance

D. Transcendence

96. A psychologist is developing a new instrument for symptoms of bipolar disorder. The psychologist wants to ensure the new instrument appropriately assesses depression symptoms. What would be the most appropriate means for the psychologist to ensure the new instrument assesses what it purports to assess?

    A. Ensure the instrument has a high interrater reliability coefficient.
    B. Utilize a multitrait–multimethod matrix.
    C. Confirm the examinees can clearly infer the symptoms the items are assessing.
    D. Ensure the instrument isn't biased against historically marginalized populations.

97. A psychologist plans to utilize an analysis of covariance (ANCOVA) to discern if an intervention effect (cognitive behavioral therapy [CBT] vs. acceptance and commitment therapy [ACT]) on posttest depression symptoms occurs while controlling for pretest depression symptoms. Should the homogeneity of regression lines assumption be satisfied, what conclusions could be drawn?

    A. A logistic regression would be preferred to an ANCOVA.
    B. A mixed-model analysis of variance (ANOVA) would be preferable.
    C. An omnibus statistical test should be run first.
    D. The association between pretest and posttest depression symptoms is comparable in the CBT and ACT groups.

98. A psychologist is referred a client to address their longstanding insomnia. The client informs you that they are already working with a colleague to treat their diagnosis of generalized anxiety disorder. As a result, the psychologist is concerned about the client's potential confusion. What is the most appropriate course of action?

    A. Inform the client you cannot treat them, given they are already working with a psychologist.
    B. Treat the client for their insomnia as the other psychologist focuses on a different diagnosis.
    C. Assume care for both the anxiety disorder and the insomnia diagnosis.
    D. Speak with the client about potential confusion.

99. The classification system of the *Diagnostic and Statistical Manual of Mental Disorders*, Fifth Edition, Text Revision (*DSM-5-TR*) is best described as which of the following?

    A. Transdiagnostic
    B. Integrative
    C. Categorical
    D. Empirical

100. A psychologist wants to discern if average symptom screening inventory scores decrease after a group of 30 patients were treated for posttraumatic stress disorder. The psychologist gives a screener before the first session of treatment and after the last session of treatment. What test could the psychologist run to determine if scores improved from the first session to the last session?
    A. Paired samples *t*-test
    B. One sample *z*-test
    C. Independent samples *t*-test
    D. One-way between-subjects analysis of variance (ANOVA)

101. A psychologist who has worked with a child for approximately 1 year is asked by the mother to conduct a custody evaluation for a pending divorce. What should the psychologist do in order to ensure the evaluation meets ethical standards?
    A. Ensure the child's other parent consents to the psychologist conducting the evaluation.
    B. Utilize objective assessment measures to remain unbiased when providing an opinion.
    C. Refer the mother to a different psychologist to avoid multiple relationships.
    D. Have a peer who is an expert in child custody review the final assessment report to ensure impartiality and objectivity.

102. An older adult woman struggles to remember where she went last night and the names of her new neighbors. Which part of the brain is most likely having difficulty encoding these memories?
    A. Amygdala
    B. Prefrontal cortex
    C. Hippocampus
    D. Nucleus accumbens

103. It is potentially acceptable to provide therapy services to a former sexual partner after how many years?
    A. One year
    B. Two years
    C. Never
    D. Never, unless in the most unusual of circumstances where the psychologist must demonstrate there is no coercion

104. A psychologist deciding to retire must do what with each remaining client?
    A. Discontinue care with all clients.
    B. Transition clients to a different psychologist.
    C. Terminate care or transition to other services based on each client's needs.
    D. Inform each client of the final date of seeing clients.

105. At a minimum, how much time must have elapsed following therapy to have sexual intimacy with former clients?

    A. It is never acceptable to engage in sexual intimacy with a former client
    B. One year
    C. Two years
    D. Seven years

106. What is the most appropriate definition of specificity?

    A. The proportion of people accurately identified as possessing a certain trait
    B. The proportion of people accurately identified as not having a trait
    C. How far each test score is from the mean
    D. The extent to which a score shows the relationship between the obtained test score and the criterion

107. A researcher seeks to address issues of attrition and the accompanying missing data. To accomplish this, which analysis would be most appropriate?

    A. Efficacy trial
    B. Observed cases
    C. Intent-to-treat
    D. Relative risk ratio

108. A psychologist meets with a client who was diagnosed with an alcohol use disorder and generalized anxiety disorder. This client has remained sober for 6 months; however, anxiety symptoms remain generally unchanged. As a result, the client wants to begin medication to address anxiety and asks for your thoughts on what medication might help prior to meeting with their new psychiatrist the next morning for a medical intake. Which response is most appropriate?

    A. Medication should not be considered at this time due to the client's substance use disorder.
    B. Consider discussing benzodiazepines as they demonstrate good efficacy for anxiety disorders.
    C. Selective serotonin reuptake inhibitors (SSRIs) and serotonin–norepinephrine reuptake inhibitors (SNRIs) are good options to discuss in part due to their relative safety.
    D. Mood stabilizers may assist in reducing anxiety symptoms.

109. Which of the following is a critique of qualitative research?

    A. Inductive thematic analysis often proves to be inferior to deductive analysis.
    B. In-depth interviews often provide unhelpful information on individual perceptions of the phenomena being studied.
    C. It is difficult to develop generalizable outcomes.
    D. Phenomenological research only works well for clearly defined phenomena of interest.

110. Which of the following theories is the basis for many commonly used intellectual batteries?
    A. Cattell–Horn–Carroll (CHC)
    B. Generalizability theory (G theory)
    C. Classical test theory (CTT)
    D. Item response theory (IRT)

111. A psychologist working as a mental health prevention specialist is assisting a community with increasing rates of suicide attempts. What would be an appropriate tertiary stage intervention?
    A. Suicide attempt survivors' support group
    B. Suicide crisis hotline
    C. Psychoeducational group about suicide warning signs
    D. Making gun locks available for free to community members

112. A psychologist in the United States attempts to diagnose a new client accurately. The client recently emigrated from a central Asian country and presents with unipolar mood and anxiety concerns. When formulating the diagnosis, which factor(s) should be most important for the psychologist?
    A. Developing a nuanced understanding of the client's culture of origin via the ADDRESSING model
    B. Base rates and algorithmic analysis
    C. Depth and breadth of experience with clients like this one
    D. Objective screening measures

113. What is the best definition of respondent-driven sampling?
    A. Participants in this type of sampling invite others to join the study.
    B. Participants are utilized because of their ease of access to the researcher.
    C. Participants are selected due to having specific characteristics.
    D. Incentives are utilized to overcome potential sampling biases.

114. Which of the following represents the three levels of the "modal model" memory of information processing, in order?
    A. Sensory memory, short-term memory, long-term memory
    B. Sensory memory, encoding, long-term memory
    C. Encoding, sensory memory, long-term memory
    D. Short-term memory, encoding, long-term memory

115. Which factor would influence the magnitude of a correlation?
    A. Homogeneous responses on one variable
    B. Both variables are ratio level
    C. Bivariate normality
    D. Population correlation equals zero

116. Which assessment yields scores across four scales: General Occupational Themes, Basic Interest Scales, Personal Style Scales, and Occupational Scales?

    A. Strong Vocational Interest Inventory
    B. Self-Directed Search (SDS)
    C. Campbell Interest and Skill Survey
    D. General Occupational Themes Scale

117. At their first supervision session, a supervisor first goes over recordings of sessions, providing feedback on the care provided. Over the next several months, this process continues during supervision. At the end of the semester, the supervisor recommends that the student not move on to the next phase of their training based on program requirements. The student filed a complaint with the supervisor, noting regular feedback was written down and provided to the student. Where did the supervisor make an error(s) in their feedback?

    A. The supervisor should not make the decision about the student's standing.
    B. The supervisor did not review the supervisory process at the beginning of supervision.
    C. The program requirements were not appropriately tailored to the student but were uniform for all students.
    D. The supervisor did not make errors. Regular feedback was provided and documented at each supervision session.

118. A psychologist receives threatening emails and voice messages from the spouse of a client who believes the psychologist is damaging the client's marriage. Identify which factor should take precedence when determining an appropriate course of action.

    A. The client's right not to be abandoned by the provider during a course of treatment.
    B. The client's potential risk from a volatile spouse
    C. The need of the spouse to get their own mental health treatment
    D. The psychologist's safety

119. An undergraduate abnormal psychology professor offers their students the opportunity to earn extra credit by completing a brief survey for a research study. Several students elect not to participate in the extra credit opportunity. The best course of action for this professor is:

    A. Speak with the students and explain the potential risks and benefits of participating to ease their concerns.
    B. Accept the students' decision and do not discuss it with them.
    C. Encourage the students to participate, emphasizing the benefit to their course grade.
    D. Offer the students an alternative means of earning extra credit.

120. A psychologist hopes to conduct research in a highly secluded community in the Yukon territory. How can the psychologist best ensure equitable involvement in the study?

    A. Ensure the study has statistical power to aid in generalizability for the community.
    B. Meet with the community's leader to understand cultural nuances and mores.
    C. Meet with the community advisory board at regular intervals.
    D. Provide culturally relevant recommendations after gathering and analyzing data.

121. While concluding work with a career counseling client, a psychologist focuses on self-defeating cognitions and anxiety about committing to a career trajectory. What career counseling theory is this psychologist likely utilizing to support this client?

   A. Cognitive information processing (CIP)
   B. The Super career and life development theory
   C. The Gottfredson theory of circumscription and compromise
   D. Career construction theory (CCT)

122. A team of psychologists works to develop a new anxiety screening measure to assist mental health clinicians in assessing for an anxiety diagnosis. What would be the most effective means of determining the concurrent validity of this new anxiety measure?

   A. Determine the proportion of people accurately diagnosed with an anxiety disorder.
   B. Determine the correlation between the new assessment and anxiety.
   C. Give the Beck Anxiety Inventory at the same time and determine the correlation.
   D. Ensure the test includes the range of information to assess anxiety appropriately.

123. A client diagnosed with chronic pain is referred to a psychologist to treat co-occurring depressive symptoms. The client reports a direct relationship between increasing pain and depressed mood. Which approach is most appropriate in treatment planning to address the pain and depressive symptoms?

   A. Thoroughly review the electronic health record and referral.
   B. Begin cognitive behavioral therapy for chronic pain (CBT-CP) to address both issues.
   C. Discuss the case with the referring physician and complete a health-related quality-of-life inventory.
   D. Focus on progressive muscle relaxation and diaphragmatic breathing to reduce physical arousal for the client.

124. The Halstead–Reitan Neuropsychological Test Battery is often administered in conjunction with which assessment?

   A. Nelson–Denny Reading Test
   B. Weschler Intelligence Scales
   C. Developmental Neuropsychological Assessment
   D. Woodcock–Johnson IV Tests of Cognitive Abilities

125. A father and mother talk to their daughter about poor grade performance. Her older sister interjects and offers to help with homework. This is an example of what type of interaction?

   A. Dyadic
   B. Polyadic
   C. Disciplinary
   D. Prosocial

126. A child observes a new student in their class sit quietly and not speak to classmates. The child deduces the new student must be "shy" and "not that friendly." The child's deduction is an example of what?

   A. Situational causal attribution

   B. Dispositional causal attribution

   C. Social categorization

   D. Prototypical social behavior

127. On a website where clients may find a psychologist to meet their needs, a psychologist notices a fellow psychologist from the community who presents themselves as an expert in working with children. The psychologist knows this person has no formal training in working with children outside of one course in graduate school. What would be the appropriate way to resolve this concern?

   A. Report the psychologist to the state licensure board.

   B. Report the psychologist to the American Psychological Association (APA).

   C. Speak with the clinic director at the psychologist's group practice.

   D. Attempt to resolve the concern via informal action with the psychologist.

128. A person was mugged several years ago outside of a gas station in their local community. Since the robbery, their friends have avoided that gas station as they view it as dangerous. What best describes the person's friends' avoidance of that gas station?

   A. Exemplar model of attribution

   B. Representative heuristic

   C. Availability heuristic

   D. Correspondent inference

129. Every month, an elementary school teacher has their students complete a standardized 5-minute math quiz to assess their mastery of class material. This is an example of what type of assessment?

   A. Curriculum-based measurement

   B. Aptitude testing

   C. Achievement testing

   D. Intelligence testing

130. A client is referred to a psychologist to assess for the neurodevelopmental disorder attention deficit hyperactivity disorder (ADHD). The psychologist has an interpreter to assist with the assessment process. Which of the following tests would be most appropriate for this assessment?

   A. Conners Continuous Performance Test–3

   B. Wisconsin Card Sorting Test

   C. Wechsler Adult Intelligence Scale–Fourth Edition (WAIS-IV)

   D. Personality Assessment Inventory (PAI)

131. Prior to meeting his coworkers, a new employee practices his introduction and carefully lays out his clothes for the first day of work. This employee's behavior is most representative of:
    A. Self-promotion
    B. Self-handicapping
    C. Impression management
    D. Self-monitoring

132. What level of influence does heredity have on a child's developing temperament?
    A. None
    B. Low
    C. Moderate
    D. High

133. A psychologist is hired by a court to assess a defendant accused of murder. The question to answer surrounds whether the defendant had the cognitive skillset to intend to murder the victim. The psychologist is being asked by the court to answer a question related to which term?
    A. M'Naghten Rule
    B. Insanity Defense Reform Act criteria
    C. Guilty but mentally ill
    D. Mens rea

134. A car thief breaks into a luxury vehicle in a parking lot and begins removing the stereo and several items belonging to the owner. No one in the parking lot calls the police or attempts to inhibit the thief in any way. What best explains the lack of action on the part of the bystanders?
    A. There were only two bystanders who witnessed the break-in.
    B. The bystanders fear social disapproval if their behavior is inappropriate.
    C. The bystanders had a high level of egoism regarding altruistic motivation.
    D. The bystanders had low motivation for prosocial behavior.

135. Though performing well in their engineering program, a 20-year-old college sophomore finds it difficult to speak with anyone other than their roommate and professors when they have academic concerns. What is the most likely Eriksonian explanation for the student's social concerns?
    A. The student's academic success has not resulted in the wisdom or knowledge about social relationships one would expect from this student.
    B. This student had difficulty developing a sense of self and personal identity.
    C. This student may have struggled to advance through the industry versus inferiority stage.
    D. The student may not have developed a sense of personal control.

136. A new achievement test developed for elementary-aged children is reviewed by psychologists to ensure the assessment supports a lack of bias, equitable treatment in the testing process, and opportunity to learn. What are these psychologists attempting to discern?

    A. Test bias
    B. Test fairness
    C. Reliability
    D. Validity

137. Which factor is most likely to decrease a bully's aggressive behavior toward peers in the classroom?

    A. Threat of retaliation
    B. Deindividuation
    C. Observation of other bullies in the school
    D. Stable levels of aggression over time

138. A young client known to have gone through multiple adverse childhood experiences (ACEs) presents to a clinic for therapy after the display of socially inappropriate externalizing behaviors. Which of the following would most likely be true for this client?

    A. Drastically reduced hypothalamic–pituitary–adrenal (HPA) axis activity during the day
    B. Reduced recovery time from physical health concerns
    C. Atypically low cortisol levels
    D. Average academic performance

139. A woman who is an atheist spends time volunteering at a homeless shelter in her community on Saturday mornings. While there, the woman shares her atheism with a peer. The peer comments, "It's really impressive to see someone who is an atheist being so generous with her time." What best describes this comment?

    A. Prejudice
    B. Bias
    C. Microaggression
    D. Discrimination

140. A psychologist is treating a 22-year-old client who presents with symptoms of anxiety. During the initial appointment, the client discloses recently having thoughts of suicide. The client adds these thoughts have increased in frequency in the past 2 weeks. What factors should the psychologist consider when developing a plan to ensure the client's safety?

    A. Systems of support for the client, such as friends and family
    B. The client's motivation to engage in therapy and address the presenting concerns
    C. The client's possible history of a suicide attempt
    D. The utility of an objective suicide assessment

141. A paramedic who witnessed several traumatic deaths is concerned they may develop posttraumatic stress disorder (PTSD) or another trauma and stressor-related disorder. Enhancement of which of the following would most decrease the likelihood of a diagnosis of a trauma and stressor-related disorder for the paramedic?
    A. Prolonged exposure (PE)
    B. Resilience
    C. Tertiary prevention efforts
    D. Health promotion

142. A child pushes a fellow child on the playground, causing them to fall. This action is an example of which of the following?
    A. Relational aggression
    B. Overt aggression
    C. Conventional moral behavior
    D. Typical childhood behavior

143. A patient who wants to improve their overall health has not engaged in daily runs around the track as recommended by their physician. When they feel down about their lack of running, they remind themselves that prolonged running may eventually lead to joint damage. This makes the patient feel better about not following the physician's recommendations. This is an example of:
    A. Social proof
    B. Communicator credibility
    C. Cognitive dissonance
    D. Obedience

144. An infant becomes less interested in their favorite toy over time. The infant's parents paint the toy a different color, which rekindles the infant's interest in the toy. Their interest in the newly painted toy is an example of what?
    A. Habituation
    B. Dishabituation
    C. Ulnar–palmar grasping
    D. Improving visual acuity

145. A psychologist lives in a coastal community that experienced a hurricane and severe flooding. The local school district asks them to work with several students in a shelter whose homes have been destroyed. Mental health resources are limited due to the flooding, and the psychologist has minimal experience working with children. What would be the most appropriate response from the psychologist when asked to assist the students?
    A. Temporarily assist the students and refer them to child psychologists as soon as feasible.
    B. Regretfully decline to provide care due to a lack of competence in child psychology.
    C. Enroll in a child intervention course to receive adequate training.
    D. Provide care to several students as long as the students and their guardians request it.

146. A psychologist has a longstanding advertisement in a local newspaper. Out of appreciation for the longstanding advertisement, the newspaper's editor offers to write an article on the psychologist to publicize further the quality services the psychologist provides to the community. What would be the most appropriate response to this offer?

    A. Accept the offer as the psychologist did not request the publicity.
    B. Ensure the article is marked as an advertisement in the newspaper.
    C. Decline the offer to avoid a multiple relationship with the editor.
    D. Offer to pay the rate given for the regular advertisement so as not to obtain free advertising.

147. A final exam in an undergraduate psychology course has historically proven difficult for most students. A professor is attempting to persuade their students to take the exam seriously and dedicate significant time studying by emphasizing how difficult the exam will be and the exam's impact on students' final grade. What would most likely ensure students realize the difficulty of the exam?

    A. Review the steps students may take to perform well on the exam.
    B. Inform the students that the professor is going to attempt to motivate them to study.
    C. Emphasize to students that the professor is personally invested as their performance reflects upon the professor.
    D. Encourage the students by reminding them they have done well in the course so far.

148. Dr. Jackson receives a records request from a former client who established care with a new psychologist. The client's new psychologist hopes to review the record. The former client did not pay for the final three sessions before terminating care with Dr. Jackson. Dr. Jackson refuses to release the records due to the client's lack of payment. Which of the following best describes Dr. Jackson's decision?

    A. This is an ethical decision as Dr. Jackson can deny records requests for financially delinquent clients.
    B. This is unethical as clients' health and well-being override Dr. Jackson's lack of compensation.
    C. Dr. Jackson acted ethically as long as the former client was not experiencing a mental health emergency.
    D. This is an ethical decision only if Dr. Jackson has given fair notice that medical records may be withheld.

149. What document highlights three ethical principles for conducting research: respect for persons, beneficence, and justice?

    A. General Principles
    B. Ethical standards
    C. Belmont Report
    D. Association of State and Provincial Psychology Boards (ASPPB) Code of Conduct

150. Which stage of the "White racial identity development model" can be defined as an individual attempting to resolve moral difficulties through, in part, idealizing White society?
    A. Contact status
    B. Disintegration status
    C. Pseudoindependence status
    D. Reintegration status

151. An infant expresses a desire for their bottle upon seeing it next to them. Previously, they only expressed interest in the bottle when it was placed in their mouth. This change is an example of:
    A. Cross-modal perception
    B. Proprioception
    C. Improved visual perception
    D. Sensory development

152. Which of the following is the best definition of fluid intelligence?
    A. Nonverbal and primarily nonculturally biased abilities, such as efficiency on novel tasks and new learning
    B. An individual's knowledge base or range of acquired skills, which are dependent on exposure to both culture and the specific information value by a given culture
    C. Construction that is primarily based on the psychological theories of skill and capacity
    D. An individual's potential to learn and master different skills

153. Which of the following childhood events is most likely to be remembered?
    A. A long event
    B. An event the child observes from beginning to end
    C. An event the child discusses with their parents
    D. A common occurrence

154. A Black man experienced low racial salience prior to the Black Lives Matter movement and multiple instances of other Black men being killed by law enforcement. These events partly facilitated his interest in further defining his Black identity. What may indicate this man's movement to the next state of the Black racial identity development model?
    A. A lowering of his self-esteem
    B. His identity aligning with Afrocentrism
    C. An increase in his interest in racial/cultural awareness
    D. Experiencing anger and resentment of White culture

155. A school psychologist working with an 11-year-old student hopes to primarily assess the student's reading and other important academic functions. Which assessment would best meet the school psychologist's needs?

   A. Weschler Individual Achievement Test–Third Edition (WIAT-III)
   B. Woodcock–Johnson IV Tests of Achievement (WJ-IV)
   C. Test of Written Language–Fourth Edition
   D. Gray Oral Reading Test–Fifth Edition

156. Which stage of change comprises specific behavioral interventions and clients who are committed to the therapeutic process?

   A. Contemplation
   B. Preparation
   C. Action
   D. Maintenance

157. A young person raised in a conservative, religious household decides to leave the cultural environment where they grew up. After 2 years away from this community, they no longer feel a sense of identity with their community of origin or a sense of identity with mainstream culture. This individual's acculturation status is best defined as:

   A. Integration
   B. Assimilation
   C. Separation
   D. Marginalization

158. Which assessment consists of 36 subtests examining five neuropsychological functioning areas?

   A. Halstead–Reitan Neuropsychological Test Battery (Halstead–Reitan)
   B. Neuropsychological Assessment Battery (NAB)
   C. Leiter International Performance Scale–Third Edition (Leiter-III)
   D. Weschler Preschool and Primary Scale of Intelligence–Fourth Edition (WPPSI-IV)

159. What needs to be included in the informed consent for those agreeing to participate in a research study?

   A. The potential risks and benefits of the therapeutic relationship
   B. Limits of confidentiality
   C. Fees for each appointment with the psychologist
   D. Informing participants of the requirements to complete all aspects of the study

160. An employer recently hired a new employee who qualifies for accommodations under the Americans With Disabilities Act. The new employee described their disability using a social model. How should the employer conceptualize the employee's physical disability?

   A. "Our new employee experienced a significant medical concern that resulted in a disability. We are creating accommodations for him in the office."

   B. "In his past job, our new employee was not allowed to participate in workplace functions due to an outdated office layout. We will modify the office to facilitate that."

   C. "Our new employee's ongoing healthcare concerns will not prevent him from being a valued team member. He is integral to our future success."

   D. "The new employee's previous healthcare issues will not impact his ability to make meaningful contributions."

161. Which cognitive behavioral therapy posits that human behavior is purposeful and originates from within the individual rather than external forces?

   A. Reality
   B. Social cognitive
   C. Radical behaviorism
   D. Systematic

162. An outpatient mental health clinic asks clients who complete a treatment protocol for posttraumatic stress disorder to answer a brief questionnaire regarding their care. This ensures clinicians appropriately implement treatments in the clinical practice guidelines. This practice is an example of which of the following?

   A. Patient satisfaction
   B. Benchmarking
   C. Behavioral analysis
   D. Accountability

163. A psychologist receives a subpoena to testify against their client. What is the appropriate response from the psychologist?

   A. Given a subpoena is a legal order, the psychologist should testify while only providing brief, direct answers during testimony.
   B. Decline to testify, citing client confidentiality.
   C. Work with their legal counsel to take appropriate steps to resolve the conflict surrounding the subpoena.
   D. Only provide written statements to the court.

164. The Social Responsiveness Scale is utilized to assess for what diagnoses?

   A. Cluster B personality disorders
   B. Trauma and stressor-related disorders
   C. Autism spectrum disorder (ASD)
   D. Bipolar depressive disorders

165. A child who has only played with their siblings and neighbors goes to preschool for the first time, meeting new children. Their new social interactions motivate them to play new games at recess and try new foods when visiting their new friends' homes. New cognitions about relationships develop. After 7 to 8 months a new routine forms for the child. This is an example of what development model?

   A. Dynamic systems theory
   B. Ecological systems theory
   C. Cognitive-developmental theory
   D. Sociocultural cognitive theory

166. Officials of a large school district are making a concerted effort to bus students to schools that may not be closest to their homes to ensure diverse student bodies at each respective school. The aim is to mitigate the risks of prejudicial views within the district. This example is the best example of what?

   A. Implicit bias mitigation
   B. Contact hypothesis
   C. Microaggression reduction
   D. Social exchange theory

167. A client is administered two assessments on a computer in their psychologist's office to assist with differential diagnosis. Which of the following should the psychologist be mindful of when interpreting the results?

   A. Potential for compromised validity of the assessment results
   B. Accuracy of the assessments' software in scoring
   C. Ease of record keeping of raw testing data
   D. Administration time

168. A practicum student practices under the license of their supervisor. Before beginning an intake appointment, the student should take additional care to:

   A. Receive consent for treatment from the client.
   B. Discuss payment policies.
   C. Receive assent for treatment from the client.
   D. Ensure the client is aware of the student's training status.

169. To create a cost-effective option for clients, a psychologist is forming a group focused on treating generalized anxiety disorder. What type of group would this be considered?

   A. Psychoeducational
   B. Process
   C. Brief
   D. Task

170. A person finds themselves angry and frustrated by recent work and family stressors and joins a gym to "take out their frustrations" through weightlifting. According to Freud, this would be an example of what?

   A. Reaction formation
   B. Projection
   C. Sublimation
   D. Displacement

171. A researcher wants to streamline data collection and will petition the institutional review board (IRB) to waive informed consent for participants. Which of the following statements is true?

   A. This is not possible; all potential research participants must complete informed written consent to participate in research.
   B. If granted, the researchers do not need to inform the participants about any study aspects.
   C. Written consent may be waived if the potential participant is given all the necessary information, including risks and benefits, prior to their participation.
   D. This is possible, but only when using archival data for research purposes.

172. Students in an orchestra class attempt to learn a new piece of music. Though talented, the students are struggling to learn the new music. The teacher provides guidance on the new challenging piece of music. According to Vygotsky, what would the provided support be called?

   A. Zone of proximal development (ZPD)
   B. Educational support
   C. Scaffolding
   D. Shaping

173. A psychologist developed a new scale for symptoms of mania. The psychologist is concerned about the homogeneity of the items on the scale. What would be the most appropriate means of assessing the new scale's homogeneity?

   A. Discern the split-half reliability via the Spearman–Brown formula.
   B. Adjust scale items to lower the overall reliability coefficient.
   C. Examine inter-item consistency via the Kuder–Richardson formula.
   D. Compare the ability to assess the construct of mania with a well-validated mania scale.

174. A child wakes up and returns to the living room in order to find the toy they played with the previous evening. Which of the following terms does this exemplify?

   A. Object permanence
   B. Primary circular reactions
   C. Secondary circular reactions
   D. Simple reflexes

175. A psychoanalytic psychologist works with a client who was referred for dissatisfaction with his career and relationship with his romantic partner. When attempting to engage in a free association exercise, the client becomes noticeably frustrated with the psychoanalyst. How would the psychologist conceptualize this frustration?

   A. The client is engaging in the repression of certain thoughts about their work.

   B. The frustration is an example of the client's resistance to free association.

   C. The client's ego is impeding the id's ability to function.

   D. The frustration is the transference of frustration with their partner to the psychologist.

176. Which subcortical brain region performs critical relay functions between the brainstem and the cortex?

   A. Basal ganglia

   B. Thalamus

   C. Cerebellum

   D. Hippocampus

177. A client and psychologist identify the automatic thought of "I'll never find true love," after the client's recent breakup. Operating within this framework, what should the psychologist do to address the thought?

   A. Ask the client to describe what feelings are associated with this thought.

   B. Consider a trauma-focused cognitive-behavioral intervention to address this pattern of thinking.

   C. Review the cognitive distortion of dichotomous thinking and examine the evidence for the automatic thought.

   D. Discuss the lack of benefit from the emotional reasoning the client used to develop this thought.

178. A psychologist works with a client who reports being depressed "for years." When the client first became depressed, they reported making an effort to take antidepressants as prescribed, attend group therapy appointments, and continue their exercise routine. As the depression remained, they began reducing efforts to ameliorate their symptoms. The client's reduced efforts over time are an example of what?

   A. Negative thinking

   B. Learned helplessness

   C. Self-defeating thinking

   D. Attributional theory

179. What factor is most predictive of success for academic achievement in young children?

   A. Linguistic maturity

   B. Gender

   C. Religiosity

   D. Cultural traditions

180. Psychologists who conduct research in which experimental treatments are given to participants must provide which of the following to participants who elect to withdraw from the study?
    A. Treatment alternatives
    B. Potential risks and benefits of participating in the study
    C. Information on incentives for completing the entirety of the study
    D. Limits of confidentiality

181. A client diagnosed with posttraumatic stress disorder (PTSD) was referred to a psychologist. The psychologist plans to utilize prolonged exposure (PE) to treat this diagnosis. What would make the client a poor candidate for PE?
    A. The concern that retelling the trauma story may retraumatize the client.
    B. The client struggled with cognitive restructuring while working with their last psychologist.
    C. The client has difficulty recalling the trauma due to being intoxicated at the time.
    D. A worry that a manualized treatment protocol would be unwelcome by the client.

182. After completing an assessment battery, a patient is diagnosed with schizoid personality disorder. Results from which assessment were likely the most useful in making this diagnosis?
    A. Minnesota Multiphasic Personality Inventory–3 (MMPI-3)
    B. Personality Assessment Inventory (PAI)
    C. Millon Clinical Multiaxial Inventory–IV (MCMI-IV)
    D. MacArthur Health and Behavior Questionnaire (HBQ)

183. A 93-year-old client whose intelligence is declining is referred by their primary care provider for an intellectual assessment. Which intellectual battery would be most appropriate?
    A. Woodcock–Johnson IV Tests of Cognitive Abilities (WJ-IV)
    B. Stanford-Binet Intelligence Scales–Fifth Edition (SB-5)
    C. Wechsler Adult Intelligence Scale–Fourth Edition (WAIS-IV)
    D. Universal Nonverbal Intelligence Test (UNIT-2)

184. On the weekends, a father is quite responsive to his child's needs and desires for interaction. During the week, the father is far less available and attentive due to focusing on vocational demands. Which attachment type is this father's behavior most likely to result in?
    A. Secure
    B. Avoidant
    C. Ambivalent/resistant
    D. Disorganized

185. A client is referred to a psychologist to address excessive gambling. The client does not view their regular gambling as problematic despite interpersonal and financial problems. What would be the best approach to assisting this client?

   A. Have a frank discussion about the financial and relational costs with the client.
   B. Provide psychoeducation around the cognitive distortions the client has about gambling.
   C. Aid the client in confronting normal existential anxiety about their gambling.
   D. Work to elicit the client's own internal motivation to address their gambling.

186. A school psychologist developed a treatment plan to address learning difficulties in a particular class. Which of the following would be the most effective method to assess the plan's efficacy?

   A. Response to intervention (RTI)
   B. Behavioral analysis
   C. Standardized assessment
   D. Relapse prevention

187. A young child learns that their mother and father each drive a car. The child begins referring to fire trucks and semi-trucks as cars. Which of the following best describes this behavior?

   A. Assimilation of new information
   B. Demonstration of formal operational activity
   C. Accommodation of new information
   D. Critical period of development

188. A psychologist working with a family focuses on the concept of nuclear family emotional patterns with their clients. To garner a better understanding of the origins of these emotional patterns, the psychologist should do which of the following?

   A. Engage in the family projection process.
   B. Complete a genogram.
   C. Identify family subsystems.
   D. Discern the amount of emotional cutoff in the family.

189. The stability of assessment scores over time is known as what?

   A. Reliability
   B. Internal consistency reliability
   C. Test–retest reliability
   D. Interrater reliability

190. An ophthalmologist encourages parents of a child with strabismus (lazy eye) to wear a patch over the dominant eye as early as possible in an effort to improve the functioning of the weaker eye. This is an example of which concept?
    A. Preoperational stage
    B. Plasticity
    C. Selective optimization with compensation (SOC)
    D. Discontinuity

191. What has been found to be the strongest predictor of successful work performance?
    A. Resilience
    B. Self-efficacy
    C. General cognitive ability
    D. Motivation

192. A psychologist represents themselves as an expert in neuropsychological assessment despite only taking an introductory course in neuropsychological assessment in graduate school. Which General Principle does this psychologist's misrepresentation go against?
    A. Fidelity and Responsibility
    B. Beneficence and Nonmaleficence
    C. Justice
    D. Integrity

193. A mother with a young child reports to her new psychologist that she has low mood, anhedonia, amotivation, and lethargy throughout the day. She reports she and her spouse love each other greatly but states there isn't much warmth between them. She stated her spouse is generally in a good mood. Which of the following is most likely true?
    A. The child will become an adult with significant mental health concerns.
    B. The child may experience additional guilt.
    C. The child will show a greater desire for the mother than if she was not depressed.
    D. There will be little to no impact as long as one parent is in good mental health.

194. A supervisor begins the session with the supervisee by ensuring they agree on the agenda and goals for their time together. In session, the supervisor helps the supervisee improve their suicide assessment skillset. What model of supervision does this supervisor utilize?
    A. Constructivist
    B. Systemic
    C. Parallel process
    D. Cognitive behavioral

195. A 4-month-old infant has failed to thrive. It has been determined the parents are taking adequate care of the child and no neglect is taking place in the home. What is the best approach to discern the genesis of the lack of weight gain?

   A. Complete an Apgar assessment to get an overview of the child's health.
   B. Discern if the baby is anemic or if a referral to an endocrinologist is appropriate.
   C. Test for various teratogens in the child.
   D. Complete a Neonatal Behavioral Assessment Scale.

196. Two psychologists assume leadership positions in a clinic following the previous directors' respective retirements. For the last 12 months, the clinic's schizophrenia treatment initiative has experienced decreasing client satisfaction. What could the new psychologists do to address this issue?

   A. Engage in program-centered administrative consultation.
   B. Engage in consultee-centered administrative consultation.
   C. Engage in advocacy consultation.
   D. Engage in client-centered case consultation.

197. A high school baseball player works tirelessly toward playing professional baseball. Following graduation, they worked part-time to focus most of their efforts on the sport. They eventually suffered a career-ending injury and adjusted their goal toward coaching and helping other baseball players develop their skills. What best describes this individual's developmental experience?

   A. Their theory of mind was forced to adapt based on changes in their professional goals.
   B. The player worked within the zone of proximal development (ZPD) to change goals.
   C. They adjusted to undesired changes in the mesosystem and exosystem.
   D. They selectively optimized their behaviors in an effort to optimize.

198. Which of the following best describes the mesoderm layer that is formed during the embryonic period?

   A. This layer becomes the skin, nerves, and sense organs.
   B. It forms the muscles, bones, circulatory system, and some organs.
   C. The layer becomes the digestive system, lungs, urinary tract, and glands.
   D. This layer is primarily responsible for brain and neural development.

199. A researcher has a form signed by a 12-year-old study participant's mother agreeing to her child's participation. Prior to beginning the study, the researcher receives confirmation from the 12-year-old that they would like to participate. What is the 12-year-old's statement known as?

   A. Consent
   B. Assent
   C. Debriefing
   D. Inducement

200. Which of the following is recognized as the universally accepted classification system used by the medical community?
   A. *Diagnostic and Statistical Manual of Mental Disorders* (*DSM*)
   B. World Health Organization (WHO)
   C. Structured Clinical Interview for *DSM* Disorders (SCID)
   D. *International Classification of Diseases* (ICD)

201. A child survivor of sexual abuse seeks care from a psychologist for a diagnosis of posttraumatic stress disorder (PTSD). Which treatment modality would be most appropriate?
   A. Cognitive processing therapy (CPT)
   B. Prolonged exposure (PE)
   C. Trauma-focused cognitive behavioral therapy (TF-CBT)
   D. Dialectical behavior therapy (DBT)

202. A psychologist decides to see several clients who are indigent pro bono or for reduced rates. Which General Principle does this psychologist's decision exemplify?
   A. Beneficence and Nonmaleficence
   B. Fidelity and Responsibility
   C. Integrity
   D. Justice

203. Which assessment is completed in the association and inquiry phases?
   A. Millon Clinical Multiaxial Inventory–Fourth Edition (MCMI-IV)
   B. Rorschach Inkblot Test
   C. Exner Assessment
   D. Minnesota Multiphasic Personality Inventory–3 (MMPI-3)

204. A client in psychotherapy identifies as lesbian and would like to disclose her sexual orientation to a close friend and, perhaps, go on a date with a woman for the first time. According to Troiden, at what stage would this client be?
   A. Sensitization
   B. Identity confusion
   C. Identity assumption
   D. Commitment

205. An individual recently completed a training course to become a paramedic. The individual now must pass an exam to earn a paramedic's license. Which of the following best describes this type of exam?
   A. Criterion-referenced
   B. Norm-referenced
   C. Standardized
   D. Self-report

206. A supervisee completes thought records with a client diagnosed with depression during their sessions. On a survey, the client notes, "I don't really feel heard in the session." As the supervisor, what would be the most appropriate way to address this with the supervisee?

    A. Discontinue utilizing thought records with this client.
    B. Discuss the criticality of common factors in ensuring therapeutic success.
    C. Work with the supervisee to find a different treatment modality.
    D. Wait for two to three additional sessions to be completed to see if the relationship improves organically.

207. Which theorist would posit that individuals should strive toward achieving "perfect completion" and follow a "style of life" that unifies their personality?

    A. Jung
    B. Adler
    C. Rogers
    D. Klein

208. In 2015, the United States Supreme Court legalized same-sex marriage throughout the United States. For the LGBTQIA+ community, this represented a substantive change in which system of the Bronfenbrenner biological model of human development?

    A. Microsystem
    B. Mesosystem
    C. Exosystem
    D. Macrosystem

209. Which career counseling theory is comprised of these four models: Interest, Choice, Performance, and Satisfaction?

    A. Lent's social-cognitive career theory (SCCT)
    B. Career construction theory (CCT)
    C. Cognitive information processing (CIP)
    D. Gottfredson theory of circumscription and compromise

210. A client presents to their psychiatrist for an initial appointment following a diagnosis of narcolepsy by their psychologist. Which medication might the psychiatrist consider prescribing for this diagnosis?

    A. Modafinil
    B. Diazepam
    C. Methylphenidate
    D. Sertraline

211. A teacher seeks to ensure that her class takes the fire alarm at school seriously and evacuates the building in under 60 seconds. She considers rewarding the class with extra time at recess to motivate the students to evacuate quickly. What would most likely result in the students evacuating in under 60 seconds for the remainder of the school year?

   A. Provide the students with extra recess each time they evacuate in under 60 seconds.
   B. Do not let the students know when they will or will not receive extra recess.
   C. Let students know beforehand if additional recess will be awarded.
   D. Rewarding recess likely won't impact students' behavior.

212. A talented pianist recently mastered a difficult piece of music for an audition. At a competition, they struggled to play the piece well, informing a friend, "I was so nervous with the judges there." What best describes the pianist's poor performance at the competition?

   A. Conscious processing hypothesis
   B. Negative thinking
   C. Expectancy theory
   D. Prospective memory

213. A researcher at a major university hopes to garner a sample of undocumented immigrants to develop a novel depression protocol. What potential barriers to recruitment would prove most problematic?

   A. Participants may not understand the function and purpose of a psychological study.
   B. Investigators may have limited cultural competence or not represent the target population.
   C. Potential participants may not find value in the potential compensation for their time.
   D. Investigators may not make strong enough efforts to recruit a representative sample.

214. A recent high school graduate begins their first semester of community college. They feel a sense of excitement and worry about their ability to do well in their chosen degree program. What type of conflict is exemplified by this example?

   A. Approach–approach conflict
   B. Avoidance–avoidance conflict
   C. Approach–avoidance conflict
   D. Double approach–avoidance conflict

215. A major company asks for the assistance of an industrial and organizational psychologist to assist in hiring their next president. What would the psychologist initially focus on while assisting the company in the hiring process?

   A. Develop work samples or exercises.
   B. Conduct a work analysis.
   C. Select employees.
   D. Conduct interviews with applicants.

216. A high school student purchases new clothes and listens to music that his favorite celebrity enjoys to emulate them. This example describes what concept?
    A. Identification
    B. Compliance
    C. Internalization
    D. Social influence

217. Which of the following is the best definition of gender?
    A. A person's sense of self as male, female, or other
    B. How an individual presents as male, female, or other given the culture through physical expression
    C. A person's biological status, which is assigned before or at the time of birth based on visible characteristics
    D. Culturally prescribed norms, mores, and behaviors associated with biological sex

218. Working with a client to aid them in understanding that they can be angry with their ex-husband while still loving him is a concept that would most likely be utilized in what modality?
    A. Cognitive processing therapy (CPT)
    B. Rational emotive-behavioral therapy (REBT)
    C. Dialectical behavior therapy (DBT)
    D. Cognitive behavioral therapy (CBT)

219. Two friends are sitting in a noisy café. One friend pauses the conversation to get her coffee after hearing her name called. The friend's ability to hear their name called amid the noise is an example of:
    A. Hierarchical processing
    B. Attention
    C. Signal detection theory
    D. Structural interference

220. A client's motivation to make appreciable improvements to their physical health, earn a promotion at work, and complete their associate's degree at a local community college is based in their desire for self-improvement and to better support their parents and church community. Which resource-focused theory is best exemplified by this client?
    A. Goal-setting
    B. Conscious processing
    C. Conservation of resources
    D. Processing efficiency

221. A feminist psychologist works with an adult male regarding a history of difficult platonic and romantic relationships. During care, the psychologist and client concur that his personality has been a common factor in his problematic interpersonal functioning. How would this psychologist conceptualize the client's personality and interpersonal functioning?
   A. The client has a history of poor relationships with his parents, resulting in basic anxiety.
   B. Parataxic distortions contribute to his personality and interpersonal difficulties.
   C. During childhood, the client was unable to differentiate between intimacy and isolation appropriately.
   D. The client has a low degree of social interest.

222. What is the best definition of a Type I error in significance testing?
   A. A failure to retain the null hypothesis
   B. A failure to retain the alternative hypothesis
   C. A failure to reject the null hypothesis
   D. A failure to reject the alternative hypothesis

223. A client has only found work in a factory completing a repetitive task. They complete the task well and receive positive feedback from their supervisor. Their motivation to continue in their job has diminished greatly. Utilizing the framework of drive theory, what could a psychologist consider in addressing worsening motivation?
   A. Assist the client in developing both intrinsic and extrinsic motivations for employment.
   B. Help the client find sources of frustration, such as the number of task completions impacting his pay.
   C. Explore the client's inherent growth tendencies and how this job stifles these tendencies.
   D. Provide psychoeducation on valence and arousal as a first step toward creating change.

224. A researcher in a city notes a significant and pervasive fear of dying from home break-ins in the sample he studied. What additional information would most clearly lead the researcher to determine this is an example of the illusory correlation?
   A. Overvaluing dispositional traits of fellow citizens as dangerous
   B. The strength of the relationship between variables
   C. Participants attributing their own safety to being vigilant
   D. Frequency of errors and biases in social thinking

225. A vocational psychologist works with a 27-year-old client to assist them in garnering a promotion. According to Super, at which stage does this client currently find themselves?
   A. Establishment
   B. Maintenance
   C. Growth
   D. Exploration

Practice Test: Answers

1. **B) Jung**
Jung's archetypes are a part of what he termed the "collective unconscious." Adler is known for his individual psychology, focusing on the family constellation. Sullivan highlighted three "modes" of cognition." Fromm is most known for his understanding of the role society has in personality development.

2. **C) The client's self is strong.**
Self is the creative aspect of personality that promotes an inherent tendency for self-actualization. Introjects create conflict with personality and would not be prominent for a client who met all treatment goals. Self-image is known as the "darker side" of personality and would not have an outsized role for this client. Environmental interactions just require balance rather than elimination.

3. **C) Gain the support of the most respected citizens of the community.**
Influence is far more likely to occur when the minority or majority is a part of the "in-group," such as the respected citizenry. Minority influence is likely to occur when a point of view is flexible. The majority, not the minority, complies for normative reasons such as avoiding punishment. Emphasizing the state of the current community center may help but it does not specifically relate to minority influence.

4. **C) Stage 3**
Stage 3 is the first stage of "conventional" thinking, where concern with conforming to social norms and social approval is key. Stages 1 and 2 are "conventional," which involve the pressure from obedience to authority and avoiding punishment to self-interest. Stage 4 is driven by a desire to adhere to laws and a desire for stability.

5. **C) Heuristic**
Heuristics are strategies or shortcuts utilized to make deductions quickly. A schema is a pattern of thought that aids in determining how we absorb new information. Attribution of cause specifically references deducing the causes for people's behaviors. Cognition structure is a broad term for concepts such as schemas and heuristics.

6. **B) Alexia**
Alexia is the acquired inability to read. Dyslexia is a developmental reading disorder that begins in childhood. Agraphia is an acquired disorder of writing. Apraxia is an acquired disorder of purposeful movement.

7. **D) Weschler Adult Intelligence Scales–Fourth Edition (WAIS-IV)**
The WAIS-IV was normed in a grossly Caucasian, North American population. The Raven Progressive Matrices and the Leiter International Performance Scale, Revised were both created to alleviate cultural biases in intelligence testing. Project Rainbow practical and creativity measures demonstrate reduced ethnic difference gaps.

8. **B) 2 to 3 months**
The lack of differentiation between "I" and "not-I" is typical symbiosis. From birth to 1 month, a child is oblivious and experiences normal autism. From 4 months to 3 years, a child takes steps toward separation and sensory exploration. From 3 years and beyond, the child develops object constancy and sees others as separate and related.

9. **B) Cannon–Bard theory**
The Cannon–Bard theory postulates that physiological responses stemming from emotions result from an emotional experience. In contrast, the James–Lange theory argues that emotions occur after physiological responses. Basic emotion theory posits that humans have six basic emotions. Drive theory is a motivation theory focusing on the return to homeostasis.

10. **A) They will be comparably popular with peers.**
Research demonstrates that children raised in gay or lesbian families are just as popular with peers and have no differences in mental health or cognitive and social–emotional development when compared to peers raised in heterosexual households.

11. **A) The client has an overdeveloped superego.**
The client's overdeveloped superego, which includes a sense of right and wrong, may result in anxiety, guilt, and eating disorders. Overindulgence of the id is more likely to result in addiction and anger. The superego inhibits the id rather than the ego. In this example, the id is unlikely to be overdeveloped as the inhibitory function of the superego is most prominent.

12. **C) Glutamate**
Glutamate is the primary excitatory neurotransmitter for the brain. Excessive glutamatergic excitation may lead to cell death. Serotonin is a biogenic amine and is primarily inhibitory. Acetylcholine is a biogenic amine and is primarily associated with movement. Gamma-aminobutyric is an amino acid but is primarily inhibitory.

13. **B) Improve the presentation of informed consent during intakes.**
This is an example of a constructivist supervisor. Constructivist supervisors emphasize small, achievable gains such as improving informed consent presentations. Developing a deep understanding of two new therapeutic modalities would be considered a large, significant change. Socratic questioning is a hallmark of cognitive behavioral supervision. The supervisory relationship mirroring the clinical relationship is emblematic of parallel-process supervision.

14. **C) Theory Z**
Theory Z is based on collectivist Japanese ideals with the goal of fostering employee well-being. Theory X has more pessimistic management and views employees as inherently lazy. Theory Y-oriented managers believe people are generally hard workers and encourage autonomy. Theory A-oriented managers are based on individualist American ideals.

15. **A) Communication theory**
Communication theory emphasizes the importance of understanding power imbalances between the communicator and receiver. Systems theory's emphasis is on the maintenance of homeostasis. Structural family therapy focuses on family mapping and potential subsystems that may exist. Extended family systems therapy emphasizes extended family rather than a spousal relationship.

12. PRACTICE TEST: ANSWERS 381

16. **D) Agranulocytosis**
Agranulocytosis is a potentially fatal lowering of one's white blood cell count, which can limit the body's ability to fight infectious diseases. Clozapine is one of the most effective antipsychotics; however, it is considered a last resort due to the risk of agranulocytosis. Hyperprolactinemia is most associated with risperidone. A hypertensive crisis may occur with clozapine; however, the concern is far lower than agranulocytosis. Serotonin syndrome may occur but is not the most significant risk associated with clozapine.

17. **C) CT**
CT is used to detect acute hemorrhage or skull fractures immediately after trauma. MRI is used to detect small lesions or plaques. EEG measures brain activity. PET, like EEG, is used to assess brain activity or provide functional neuroimaging.

18. **A) Acceptance and commitment therapy (ACT)**
The client has difficulty with cognitive disputations and trying not to feel depressed. ACT emphasizes acceptance or allowing thoughts and emotions to exist as they are without trying to stop them. ACT also emphasizes decreasing experiential avoidance or eliminating private thoughts or emotions. These are the opposite of CBT's emphasis, making it the best option for this client. REBT involves directly confronting irrational beliefs, which is like CBT. CBT was born from Beck's CT; therefore, it would likely be too similar to the current treatment. DBT was developed for borderline personality disorder. Therefore, it wouldn't be a relevant treatment for MDD.

19. **A) Lithium**
Lithium's narrow therapeutic window may lead to toxicity. It is also one of the few psychiatric medications metabolized by the kidneys. Aripiprazole is metabolized by the liver. The primary side effect of concern for lamotrigine is a rash that may lead to Stevens–Johnson syndrome. The most common side effect of olanzapine is weight gain.

20. **A) NE–DA reuptake inhibitor (NDRI)**
NDRIs (Wellbutrin) work by inhibiting the reuptake of norepinephrine and dopamine. This class of antidepressants may be used for both depression and smoking cessation. SSRIs may be helpful for depression but not beneficial for smoking cessation. MAOIs may address depression but not smoking cessation. They also have more side effects associated. SNRIs may prove beneficial for depression but not smoking cessation.

21. **A) Generalized**
Tonic–clonic generalized seizures are defined by lost or altered consciousness, rigidity, and repetitive jerking. Simple partial seizures do not result in loss of consciousness. A person experiencing an absence seizure would likely appear to have a blank stare. Someone experiencing a nonepileptic seizure may have no observable symptoms.

22. **B) Atomoxetine**
Atomoxetine is a nonstimulant norepinephrine reuptake inhibitor that does not act on dopamine that may be prescribed for ADHD. Lisdexamfetamine and methylphenidate are both stimulants used for ADHD. Paroxetine is an SSRI that, while a nonstimulant, is not used for ADHD treatment.

23. C) Anxiolytics
Anxiolytics, specifically benzodiazepines, are used to assist with alcohol withdrawal in a medical setting due to acting on gamma-aminobutyric acid (GABA). SSRIs and SNRIs are often used for unipolar mood and anxiety disorders and do not assist with alcohol withdrawal. Atypical antipsychotics are prescribed for multiple diagnoses but not acute alcohol withdrawal.

24. B) Rey 15-item test
The Rey 15-item test overtly assesses an examinee's malingering or feigning of symptoms. It is one of numerous symptom validity tests (SVT). The MCMI-IV and PAI, like the MMPI-3, have validity scales but are not specifically designed to assess malingering. The WAIS-IV does not have specific scales to assess malingering.

25. C) Introspection
The introspection stage sees individuals view dominant and minority cultures as equally flawed and are uncomfortable with absolutist viewpoints. The dissonance stage sees members of a minority group vacillate between feelings of shame and pride toward their identity. The resistance and immersion stage sees an individual reject the dominant culture in favor of their culture. The synergistic stage sees individuals find self-fulfillment and comfort with who they are and others.

26. D) Delirium
Delirium is an abrupt change of consciousness that is more prevalent in older adults and may occur following a serious infection. It is often reversible. Concussions often result from head trauma, and a known infection makes this a less plausible option. Absence seizures usually result in a person staring into space. Mild cognitive impairment is a transitional time between typical aging and dementia. It is not acute.

27. A) Achievement
Achievement describes the need for a sense of accomplishment through advancement and feedback. Authority is the need to make an impact and lead others. Competence is a concept in self-determination theory describing the need for mastery. Affiliation is the need to have positive social interactions in the workplace.

28. B) Myelin sheath
The myelin sheath insulates axons and speeds up transmission. The cerebellar peduncles are parts of the cerebellum and assist with muscle movement. A dendrite is an extension of a nerve cell which receives impulses. A synapse is the place where neurons connect and communicate.

29. C) Pick disease
Pick disease is characterized by personality changes and behavioral inhibition. Alzheimer disease's primary symptom is memory loss. Vascular dementia tends to begin earlier in life and is more common in men. Social disinhibition is not a common symptom of dementia due to HIV.

30. C) Esteem
Esteem incorporates self-esteem and achievement. Safety includes shelter, employment, and health. Self-actualization includes morality and creativity. Love/belonging incorporates relationships.

31. **C) Dopamine**
Excessive dopamine in the pathway to the frontal lobes strongly contributes to schizophreniform disorder. Excessive acetylcholine likely impacts movement. Excessive norepinephrine may lead to anxiety. Overactivity of serotonin may lead to sexual side effects and gastrointestinal issues.

32. **D) Respect for People's Rights and Dignity**
The psychotherapist recognizes that this client, like all potential clients, has basic human rights and is entitled to appropriate healthcare. The psychologist would still incorporate the other General Principles of Beneficence and Nonmaleficence, Fidelity and Responsibility, and Integrity while providing care, but the specific decision to assume care for this client reflects the client's right to care.

33. **A) Beneficence and Nonmaleficence**
Beneficence and Nonmaleficence means to do good and avoid harm. Conversion therapy is well-documented to be ineffective and harmful to clients. Therefore, it violates the first General Principle.

34. **D) Trazodone**
Trazodone is an atypical antidepressant commonly prescribed for insomnia as the antidepressant effect requires a very high dose. Venlafaxine does not promote sleepiness. Tranylcypromine is an monoamine oxidase inhibitor that is rarely used due to its side effect profile. Bupropion is an antidepressant that is sometimes used to promote attention and concentration.

35. **B) Cohesiveness within the group, catharsis, interpersonal learning**
These three therapeutic factors are three of the 11 factors impacting group success. Interpersonal learning focuses on how one builds strong relationships.

36. **B) Generalizability theory**
Generalizability theory identifies sources of measurement error, separates the influence of each source, and estimates the individual sources of measurement error. IRT focuses on examining individual items in test development. Psychometrics is the broad study of psychological measurement. The item characteristic curve is a mathematical function that is used to illustrate the increasing proportion of correct answers for an item.

37. **A) Simple partial**
Simple partial seizures may result in olfactory and auditory changes. Febrile seizures often result from high fevers and occur in children. Sensory experiences are not impacted. Generalized seizures often lead to loss of consciousness, falls, or muscle spasms. Tonic–clonic generalized seizures lead to loss of consciousness, stiffening of the body, and jerking of limbs.

38. **B) Aptitude**
Aptitude tests include subtests that assess one's potential to learn and master different skills and are often used in vocational counseling and job placement. Achievement tests assess knowledge acquired in a specific setting. Intelligence tests may assess either fluid intelligence or crystallized intelligence. Curriculum-based testing is the regular assessment of children for the purpose of monitoring the development of academic skills.

39. **D) Dementia due to HIV**
CD4+ levels below 200 are a hallmark of dementia due to HIV. Parkinson dementia is associated with tremors. Alzheimer disease is often associated with atrophy in the cerebral cortex. Chronic traumatic encephalopathy stems from a history of repeated head trauma.

40. **A) Person A has a more liberal response bias than Person B.**
Person A's response bias is deemed to be far more liberal than Person B's because Person A perceived the screeching car as a potential threat (liberal) while Person B viewed the screeching car as "noise." The more liberal the response bias is, the more likely a person is to view stimuli as a threat.

41. **D) A referral for medication and initiation of CBT**
Research demonstrates that for severe depression, a combination of medication and CBT is most effective. Light therapy, dietary changes, and exercise, while beneficial, are not the primary intervention. CBT or medication on their own or a combination are equally effective for only mild depression.

42. **B) Cognitive distortion**
The patient's view of the new neighbor is an example of "magical thinking," which is a type of cognitive distortion. Self-defeating thought was coined by Ellis as leading to maladaptive behavior. Learned helplessness describes a person's sense of being unable to escape pain. Cognitive dissonance is the changing of beliefs about behavior to manage psychological tension.

43. **C) Hare Psychopathy Checklist–Revised (PCL-R)**
The PCL-R is utilized to assess dangerousness and the potential for violence directed toward others. The PAI and MMPI-3 both have questions regarding violence toward others; however, that is not the purpose of these assessments. The SIQ assesses the risk of harming oneself, not others.

44. **B) Automatic thought**
An automatic thought is a quickly utilized interpretation that contributes to depression. The Stroop effect is a delay between congruent and incongruent stimuli. Expectancy is a belief that one has the resources to achieve a goal. Affiliation is a need to be liked and develop a social network.

45. **B) Parkinson disease**
Extrapyramidal symptoms, or motor abnormalities, are common in diagnoses affecting the basal ganglia. Parkinson disease results from atypical activity in this subcortical structure. Alexia is an inability to read that is acquired over time. Wernicke aphasia, or receptive aphasia, disrupts one's ability to comprehend and express language. Klüver–Busy syndrome causes people to put objects in their mouths.

46. **D) Cognitive interference theory**
Cognitive interference theory notes negative self-talk unrelated to the task inhibits the quality of performance on the current task. Learned helplessness describes a person's sense of being unable to escape pain. The Zeigarnik effect states people remember interrupted tasks better than those they completed. Nondeclarative memories are unconscious and unintentional.

47. **C) Kuder Occupational Interest Survey**
The Kuder Occupational Interest Survey yields scores in four domains: occupational scales, college major scales, vocational interest estimates, and dependability indices, making it the most appropriate assessment tool for this client deciding on a college major. The SDS is a self-score measure allowing the examinee to compare occupations. The Strong Vocational Interest Inventory yields scores across four scales. The Campbell Interest and Skill Survey yields scores related to occupational orientation.

48. D) Somatic marker
The somatic marker hypothesis is a recent addition to the theories of emotion. It emphasizes that physiological responses or somatic markers are regulated in the ventromedial prefrontal cortex. Expectancy theory is related to motivation. The dimensional theory focuses on broader descriptions of emotion. Basic emotion theory postulates that humans only experience six emotions.

49. B) Systematic observations in the school
Systematic observations allow an examiner to identify and describe target behaviors and understand antecedents and consequences. Improved peer interactions would qualify as target behaviors. A comprehensive assessment battery may aid. However, the Beck Youth Inventories assess personality symptoms, and the Social Responsiveness Scale assesses autism. A semistructured clinical interview and parent interviews would be helpful but would not specifically assess behavioral response chains. Likewise, teacher report scales would be a part of an assessment but would not aid in developing target behaviors.

50. A) Competence
American Psychological Association Code Standard 2.01 obligates psychologists to practice within their scope of competence, which includes working with areas and populations within their knowledge base. It additionally lays out guidelines to obtain competence and when those without competence may, in limited cases, provide services outside their scope of knowledge and competence.

51. D) Working memory
Working memory is a core component of executive functioning and has a strong correlation with executive attention. Executive functioning is an aspect of general intelligence. Behavioral coherence is an attentional term relating to the unity of actions limiting attentional resources. Multisensory processing relates to interpreting data from multiple senses (i.e., smell, sight, sound).

52. C) Premack principle
The Premack principle or "Grandma's principle" notes that reliably occurring behaviors can reinforce irregular behaviors, such as using play time as a reward for completing homework. Mediated generalization is the response to a stimulus that is dissimilar to the conditioned stimulus. Fixed ratio scheduling is a reinforcement schedule that varies in proportion and leads to steady response rates. Yerkes–Dodson law indicates that the optimal level of anxiety leads to good performance.

53. B) Symbolic function
Symbolic function is a substage of the preoperational stage. It includes mental representation and pretend play. Children learn about themselves and the environment in the sensorimotor stage by coordinating senses with physical actions. Intuitive thought is when a child uses simple reasoning and asks "why" questions. The concrete operational stage is exemplified by a child beginning to reason.

54. B) Teratogen
Teratogens are any substances that have a negative impact on a developing fetus. Cigarette smoke is toxic and does inhibit healthy fetal growth, though it is not a specific term for developing fetuses. Cigarette smoke is a poison, but this is a less descriptive term than teratogen. The cleft palate would be considered the birth defect, not the cigarette smoke.

55. **B) Transactional model of development**
    The transactional model of development posits a series of reciprocal interactions between the individual and their context, leading to social competence and self-conception. Prosocial normative development is not clear in this example as no specifically positive behaviors are cited. Postconventional thinking is emblematic of Kohlberg's fifth stage of moral development, which emphasizes moral principles and values. Initiative versus guilt occurs in preschool and describes a child's need to develop a sense of control and independence.

56. **A) Shaping**
    Shaping, sometimes called successive approximation, is a type of operant reinforcement of behaviors that are successively closer to the desired behavior. Stimulus-response paradigm is a Pavlovian term to describe the relationship between conditioned and unconditioned stimuli. Mediated generalization is the response to a stimulus that is dissimilar to the conditioned stimulus. Attentional load theory is a theory of attention that explains the push–pull relationship of facilitative and inhibitory mechanisms.

57. **A) The efficacy of previous attempts at informal resolutions**
    American Psychological Association (APA) Code 1.04 encourages psychologists to resolve ethical concerns in an informal fashion with the psychologist for whom they have concerns. This vignette also speaks to APA Code 1.05, which notes that formal reporting of ethical violations should occur if the issue is not resolved via informal means or there is risk to clients or the issue isn't appropriate for informal resolution. How the psychologist markets the services, the level of experience and expertise, and patient satisfaction with the service are irrelevant if the psychologist does not have the appropriate training.

58. **A) Ensure the client has an appropriate understanding of the costs and benefits of treatment.**
    Ensuring a client has accurate information about costs and benefits is crucial to clients' developing confidence in medical decisions. While a psychologist may ultimately utilize the client's preferred treatment plan or refer to a different psychologist, this should be done after ensuring the client understands the costs and benefits. Acknowledging the client's preference and proceeding regardless may be dismissive of the client and does not provide the client with accurate information about the recommendation.

59. **B) Administer a standardized intelligence test, such as the Wechsler Adult Intelligence Scale–Fourth Edition (WAIS-IV), before deployment.**
    A standardized intelligence test, such as the WAIS-IV, serves as an objective, gross estimate of cognitive functioning at a certain point in time, such as before a military deployment. Asking the service members about their functioning and having their spouse complete a questionnaire are subjective reports from biased parties. A review of the relevant medical records would provide valuable data but would not provide a comprehensive overview of cognitive functioning.

60. **C) The professor and the student**
    Both are charged with ensuring the safety and well-being of participants. This aligns with American Psychological Association Code 3.04, which describes the need for psychologists to avoid harming clients, students, research participants, and so on.

61. **A) Crystallized: 62: Fluid: 33**
    Developmental research on models of intelligence indicates that a person's crystallized intelligence improves until one's 60s and 70s. Meanwhile, fluid intelligence, such as executive functioning, working memory, and processing speed, peaks in the 30s and worsens with age.

62. **C) Primarily psychoactive medications with family therapy and skills training as adjuncts**
Medication and complementary psychotherapy modalities are most appropriate for schizophrenia. Psychoactive medications on their own will not assist the client with integration into society and completing activities of daily living. Family therapy and skills training, while helpful, will not address the primary symptoms of schizophrenia.

63. **D) Developing a sense of relatedness may prove difficult with fully remote work.**
The statement that developing a sense of relatedness may prove difficult with fully remote work references self-determination theory's basic need for relatedness, which is the need to develop relationships with others. Stating that this plan will help employees feel a greater sense of achievement references achievement, which is closely related to the need for achievement theory. Stating that remote work may prove difficult for those with minimal intrinsic motivation may prove accurate; however, it does not relate to self-determination but rather the two-factor theory. Stating that remote work places emphasis on extrinsic rewards as a behavioral motivator may also be true but is closely tied to a Skinnerian view of conditioning in the context of motivation.

64. **C) Ensure opportunities for time off and healthcare benefits are available to employees.**
Theory X-oriented managers are quite similar to transactional leaders in believing reward opportunities motivate performance. Improving organizational trust, modeling good employee characteristics, and encouraging collaboration are all qualities of transformational leaders, which are often contrary to Type X managers.

65. **A) Emotional experiences stem from appraisals of ongoing environmental interactions.**
Lazarus developed a two-stage appraisal model incorporating the valence and threat of a stimulus and means of coping with the stimulus. The theory that emotions are derived from primarily noncognitive functions is closely aligned with Zajonc, which goes away from Lazarus's cognitive work. The theory that physiological responses in the body are critical to understanding emotion and motivation defines the somatic marker hypothesis. The belief that all emotions may be described by a small set of specific emotions is the definition of the basic emotion model.

66. **A) The value someone places on a particular consequence**
The value someone places on a particular consequence best describes valence. The view that a person possesses the resources to achieve a specific goal is the definition of expectancy. The belief that completing a behavior will lead to a certain outcome is the definition of instrumentality. Changing one's beliefs to manage psychological tension is, in part, the definition of expectancy theory.

67. **B) Frontal lobe lesion**
The frontal lobe is most responsible for executive functioning, which includes spontaneous speech, inhibition, and divergent thinking. The amygdala is responsible for stress responses via the autonomic and endocrine systems. An injury to the hippocampus would impact spatial relations and encoding of declarative memory. Damage to the basal ganglia would likely involve atypical movements.

68. **A) The individual would eventually require increased doses to achieve the desired high.**
The individual would begin an antagonistic response to the drug as soon as they entered the context, therefore decreasing the drug's effect. A lower dose for the same high would be more likely in a different context. The individual's antagonistic response would take less time.

69. **B) Teach how to treat this client, given the nascent stage of the student's training.**
Teaching is the first role on the continuum in this model. Given this is a first-semester student and a new client, this would be appropriate. The consultant role is the last role on the continuum of the discrimination model and would not be appropriate for a first-semester student. Two overlapping systems are a core component of a Hawkins and Shoeht-oriented supervisory relationship. A counseling role for the supervisor is the intermediate role on the continuum for discrimination-oriented supervision.

70. **D) It does not represent an ethical problem if the supervisor and supervisee are aware.**
This vignette relates to the American Psychological Association Code Standard 3.08, which discusses potentially exploitative relationships. There may also be concerns regarding multiple roles, so as long as both parties are aware of the overlap in faculty, no multiple relationship would exist inherently. There is also a potential for any supervisory relationship to become a conflict of interest, but it is not immediately so in this scenario.

71. **A) Aid the client in developing specific study strategies to complete coursework.**
Goal-setting theory postulates the importance of facilitating strategies to complete the goal, such as specific study strategies. While assisting the client in viewing "healthy" amounts of anxiety as beneficial may help, it aligns with the Yerkes–Dodson law. Exploring the "all or nothing thinking" more closely aligns with Beck's work on cognitive distortions. Expectancy stems from Vroom's work on expectancy theory.

72. **C) True score variance and random error variance**
True score variance and random error variance are the two additive sources for variance in a measure. Error and variance are not specific enough to account for variance of a specific measure. While important terms in CTT, consistency and dependability are closely related to reliability. Random score variance and true error variance are the opposite types of variances necessary to create variance for a specific measure.

73. **A) Health Insurance Portability and Accountability Act (HIPAA)**
HIPAA governs how client records are maintained and the rules that facilitate their release to clients, third-party payers, and other healthcare providers. The Belmont Report guides IRBs in the conduct of ethical research. General Principles are broad and aspirational in nature. The ASPPB Code of Conduct represents the profession's own standards to protect welfare and integrity.

74. **B) The American Board of Professional Psychology (ABPP)**
ABPP offers certification and credentialing of advanced training in many specialty areas, with each specialty area having its own requirements for certification. State licensing boards strictly cover licensing, and the APA does not license or certify psychologists. It does provide oversight of graduate and internship programs. ASPPB emphasizes protecting the public and ensuring the competent practice of psychology. This occurs, in part, by overseeing the EPPP.

75. **B) ABAB design**
ABAB design involves assessing a baseline and then adding an intervention followed by a withdrawal. The process is then repeated, with assessment occurring throughout. Multiple baseline design involves assessing multiple baselines, such as assessing a baseline for irritability and depression. An efficacy trial occurs when an intervention is assessed under ideal circumstances. A single-case design occurs when only a single participant is studied.

76. **A) At the beginning of the research study**
   This vignette is based on American Psychological Association Code 8.12, which reviews publication credit. Authorship order should be based on contributions to the study. This level of contribution should be discussed at the outset of the study, not at the conclusion, after data gathering, or after final edits have been made.

77. **D) *t*-score of 65**
   On the MMPI-3, raw scores are converted to *t*-scores. A *t*-score of 65 (94th percentile) or above is deemed to be clinically significant.

78. **A) Discuss the potential pros and cons of your attendance with the client.**
   American Psychological Association Code 4.01 discusses the obligation to maintain a client's confidentiality. Attending such a ceremony risks breaking that confidentiality. However, there is no specific permission or prohibition against attending such an event. Attending the ceremony would not be appropriate for this reason. Attending does not violate professional boundaries inherently, but confidentiality may be breached as a result.

79. **A) Inform the client their previous psychologist acted unethically by seeking a friendship and discuss steps they may take to address such behavior.**
   This conduct is a violation of American Psychological Association Code 1.04. Discussing the previous psychologist's behavior and its impacts, along with potential avenues of remedy, is appropriate. Confronting the psychologist or state licensure board is not appropriate. The conduct should be addressed with the client.

80. **D) Logistic regression**
   A logistic regression is utilized when the outcome includes ordered or unordered variables. Relevant odds ratios are usually included in logistic regressions. A path analysis would be used to ensure a stronger causal ordering. Structural equation modeling is used when you hope to use a path analysis but require the inclusion of latent variables. Chi-square is a non-parametric statistical test rather than ordinary least squares.

81. **D) Develop an understanding of the costs and benefits of the relationship.**
   According to social exchange theory, attraction will occur when the benefits outweigh the costs. Assisting the client in defining themselves, while potentially beneficial, is accomplished more directly with affiliation rather than attraction. Assessing the perceptions of equity in the relationship is a core component of equity theory, though it may also prove beneficial. Understanding the initial evaluation as positive or negative is a core component of gain–loss theory.

82. **D) Confidentiality is harder to ensure with telepsychology versus in-person treatment.**
   As with in-person care, confidentiality should be protected. However, it is more difficult via telepsychology. Improved access to services is true; however, it is not necessary to share this with clients. Treatment outcomes with telepsychology are generally comparable to in-person care. Treatment guidelines have, in fact, been published to ensure a high standard of care for telepsychology services.

83. **A) They have positive knowledge components and negative evaluative components.**
   They are said to have positive knowledge components as knowledge components speak to one's physical and cognitive abilities while evaluative components speak primarily to self-esteem and self-assessment. It is difficult to summarize their overall self-concept with limited information, but the vignette is clear about views of cognitive abilities and self-esteem.

84. **B) Ordinal**
Ordinal scales arrange participants or responses according to relevant rank, such as in this example or in a Likert scale. Nominal scales categorize qualitative variables, such as religion. Interval scales focus more on magnitude differences as each unit of measurement is an equal unit along the range. Ratios are rare in psychology as they have a true zero point and equal variables.

85. **D) This is an unethical arrangement as the psychologist should not solicit testimonials.**
American Psychological Association (APA) Code 5.05 forbids the solicitation of testimonials from current therapy clients due to being vulnerable. This vignette also speaks to APA Code 6.05, which notes that psychologists may barter if it is not clinically contraindicated or exploitative; for instance, trading services for a testimonial from a current client.

86. **C) Agree to the bartering arrangement out of a desire not to abandon a client.**
This situation speaks to Standard 6.05 of the American Psychological Association (APA) ethics code on bartering. It additionally speaks to Standard 3.12, the interruption of psychological services. CPT is a structured treatment for posttraumatic stress disorder. Discontinuing services could cause harm to the client and be contraindicated in treatment. Following the completion of the course of treatment, a referral to a psychologist who is more comfortable with bartering may be appropriate. It would be appropriate to monitor potential exploitation in nontraditional payment agreements, but it is not evident in this situation.

87. **D) Criterion validity**
In criterion validity, the measure should correlate with other variables consistent with the a priori hypothesis. Face validity is the extent to which items seem to measure the construct of interest. Content validity discerns whether test items represent the content domains for the construct. Structural validity is the extent to which the structure of the measure aligns with the factor structure of the construct.

88. **B) Multilingual Aphasia Examination**
The Multilingual Aphasia Examination includes a controlled oral word association test that assesses spontaneous speech. The Wisconsin Card Sort Test assesses executive functioning. The Stroop Color Word Test assesses attention control. The WAIS assesses overall intelligence.

89. **B) Discontinuity**
Developmental theories of discontinuity involve the belief that development has discreet periods of rapid change and the sudden emergence of new forms of thought and behavior. Continuity theories emphasize development as gradual and continuous. Prosocial are types of behavior that are deemed socially acceptable and are reinforced. Sensitive periods encompass the idea that periods can lead to a multitude of outcomes or trajectories given the impact of the environment on a person during these periods.

90. **D) Additional validity indices from other assessments should be reviewed.**
Elevations on the CRIN scale indicate that results from the assessment may not be valid. Assessing the validity of other assessments given during the battery will aid in determining the overall utility of the battery results. A unipolar mood episode, a personality disorder, or ADHD are diagnostic considerations rather than validity considerations.

91. C) Two-way between-subjects
Two-way between-subjects are utilized to evaluate the effects of two independent variables on a dependent variable. One-way between-subjects are used to contrast multiple treatment groups on a dependent variable. One-way within-subjects are used to examine a single cohort's symptom levels over two or more assessments. MANOVAs have two dependent variables.

92. B) Take additional steps to ensure consent is freely given.
Persons diagnosed with PTSD are vulnerable to coercion, and therefore, additional steps must be taken to ensure their participation is voluntary. A quiet room may be beneficial for those with PTSD, but it may not be necessary. Materials for any study should be at the appropriate reading level. Similarly, potential benefits should outweigh risks when conducting research.

93. D) The psychologist should choose an assessment similar to the MMPI-3 that can be administered via telepsychology.
American Psychological Association (APA) Code 9.02 emphasizes that psychologists should only use assessment instruments that are valid and reliable for the population being tested. Additionally, the APA Guidelines for the Practice of Telepsychology discusses using assessments via telepsychology.

94. A) Comparing a single sample mean to a population mean with a known population SDs.
One-sample z-tests compare a single sample to a population mean with defined SDs. Assessing the difference between a single sample mean and a hypothesized population mean is an example of a one sample t-test. Comparing a single sample mean to a population mean with an unknown population SD is close to when you would utilize a one-sample z-test. However, you need to have a known SD, not an unknown SD. Assessing the mean differences between two populations with normal population distributions describes an independent samples t-test.

95. D) Transcendence
Transcendence incorporates the virtues of appreciation of beauty, gratitude, hope, humor, and religiousness. Courage incorporates authenticity, bravery, and persistence. Wisdom and knowledge include creativity, curiosity, open-mindedness, love of learning, and perspective. Temperance includes forgiveness, modesty, prudence, and self-regulation.

96. B) Utilize a multitrait–multimethod matrix.
This question asks about construct validity, the extent to which a test correlates with the trait it purports to assess. One method of assessing construct validity is through a multitrait–multimethod matrix. A high interrater reliability demonstrates scores are calculated in a consistent manner across examiners. Confirming the examinees can clearly infer the symptoms being assessed ensures face validity. Ensuring instruments are unbiased is important; however, this does not speak to the issue of construct validity.

97. D) The association between pretest and posttest depression symptoms is comparable in the CBT and ACT groups.
"The association between pretest and posttest depression symptoms is comparable in the CBT and ACT groups" is one way of describing the lack of interaction between the covariate and the primary independent variable. A logistic regression looks at outcome variables comprising ordered or unordered categories. It is an ordinary least squares regression model. An ANOVA may be appropriate; however, the question seeks an answer to an ANCOVA-related question.

98. **D) Speak with the client about potential confusion.**
American Psychological Association Code Standard 10.04 discusses the potential confusion and impact to clients' welfare when being treated by multiple psychologists. The first course of action is to discuss the issue with the client directly and then potentially discuss the potential confusion with the other service provider.

99. **C) Categorical**
The *DSM-5-TR* is best described as categorical, treating each diagnosis as a discreet entity. There is growing research for transdiagnostic approaches, which may prove more prominent in future iterations. The *DSM-5-TR* is based on empirical data; however, that is a vague term.

100. **A) Paired samples *t*-test**
A paired samples *t*-test is appropriate due to a single group of participants who provide a single data point to the analysis. Each data point is independently compared to the other participants. A one-sample *z*-test compares a single mean to a population mean and a known population mean which is unknown. An independent samples *t*-test treats the mean between two populations. There are not two populations in this example. Like an independent samples *t*-test, a one-way between-subjects ANOVA implies two populations.

101. **C) Refer the mother to a different psychologist to avoid multiple relationships.**
American Psychological Association Code 3.05 states that psychologists should refrain from entering into multiple relationships, such as holding two roles with a client (therapist and custody assessor), if objectivity could reasonably be impaired. Given the nearly year-long relationship with the client, the psychologist has already formed opinions. The most appropriate decision would be to have another psychologist conduct the custody evaluation.

102. **C) Hippocampus**
The hippocampus is located within the medial aspect of the temporal lobe. In addition to encoding declarative memories, it assists in the understanding of spatial relations. The amygdala is primarily involved in coordination of behavioral and autonomic responses to emotionally laden stimuli. The prefrontal cortex is involved in inhibitory influence on impulsive emotional responses and executive functioning. The nucleus accumbens is sometimes referred to as the brain's "pleasure center" and is involved in positive reinforcement.

103. **C) Never**
This vignette relates to American Psychological Association Code Standard 10.08, which states that psychologists are never allowed to treat former sexual partners. Psychologists do not engage in sexual intimacies with former clients even after 2 years, except in the most unusual of circumstances. Even then, psychologists have a high bar to prove there has been no exploitation.

104. **C) Terminate care or transition to other services based on each client's needs.**
American Psychological Association (APA) Code Standard 10.10 provides an overview of when it is appropriate to terminate therapy. Additionally, APA Code Standard 10.09 discusses that when therapy must end, psychologists must make efforts to provide appropriate resolution of responsibility to clients. The other responses do not provide a complete explanation of the retiring psychologist's responsibilities.

105. **C) Two years**
American Psychological Association Code Standard 10.08 addresses sexual intimacies with former clients. At a minimum, two years must have elapsed since the termination of therapy. Even then, it must only occur "only under the most unusual circumstances."

12. PRACTICE TEST: ANSWERS 393

106. **B) The proportion of people accurately identified as not having a trait**
The proportion of people accurately identified as possessing a certain trait identifies sensitivity, while the proportion of people accurately identified as not having a trait identifies specificity. How far each test score is from the mean describes variance. The extent to which a score shows the relationship between the obtained test score and the criterion is the definition of predictive validity.

107. **C) Intent-to-treat**
Intent-to-treat aims to provide a conservative estimate of treatment effects. Efficacy trials do not address attrition and instead examine the effects of an intervention. Observed cases ignore attrition or those who have dropped out. The relative risk ratio compares the proportion of those patients improving with an intervention versus those improving with a placebo or treatment as normal.

108. **C) Selective serotonin reuptake inhibitors (SSRIs) and serotonin–norepinephrine reuptake inhibitors (SNRIs) are good options to discuss in part due to their relative safety.**
SSRIs and SNRIs are widely utilized for anxiety and are relatively safe. Additionally, they have low addiction potential. Medication is a common tool in addressing comorbid substance use and anxiety disorders; thus, the patient's substance use disorder should not be a reason to rule out medication. Benzodiazepines, while helpful for acute withdrawal, may be addictive. Mood stabilizers are not recommended for anxiety as an initial treatment.

109. **C) It is difficult to develop generalizable outcomes.**
Due to the number of individuals participating in focus groups or in-depth interviews, it may prove difficult to generalize results to a broader population, as is the case in quantitative research. Inductive and deductive thematic analyses are not superior or inferior to each other but rather appropriate in different contexts. In-depth interviews often provide a deeper understanding of an individual's perception of the topic at hand. Phenomenological research is appropriate when the phenomena is poorly defined.

110. **A) Cattell–Horn–Carroll (CHC)**
CHC combines two models of intelligence: the Cattell–Horn model and Carroll's three stratum model. G theory is a psychometric theory conceptualizing error. It is an extension of CTT, a theory in which an observed score comprises the true score plus error. IRT is a psychometric theory examining test items' relationships between the measured construct and individual test responses on multiple levels.

111. **A) Suicide attempt survivors' support group**
According to the stages in the prevention of mental health problems, tertiary stage interventions focus on preventing problem reoccurrence, which is the aim of a suicide attempt survivors' group. A suicide crisis hotline would be considered a secondary-stage intervention. A psychoeducational group would be primary as it is preventative in nature. Making gun locks available would also be preventative and, therefore, a primary stage intervention.

112. **B) Base rates and algorithmic analysis**
Base rates and algorithmic analysis are most critical as they are based on objective, statistical data. Understanding the client's culture is key; however, it does not outweigh the importance of algorithmic analysis and base rates. Depth and breadth of experience may be helpful, but this lends itself to the clinician's intuitive judgment, which may contribute to error and bias. Objective screening measures may prove a useful tool in diagnostic clarification.

113. **D) Incentives are utilized to overcome potential sampling biases.**
Incentives are utilized to overcome biases from snowball and other chain-referral sampling methods in respondent-driven sampling. Snowball sampling is a type of sampling where participants invite others to join the study. Convenience sampling is when participants are utilized because of their ease of access to the researcher. Purposive sampling is when participants are selected due to having specific characteristics.

114. **A) Sensory memory, short-term memory, long-term memory**
Initially presented by Waugh and Norman with revisions by Atkinson and Shiffrin, sensory memory, short-term memory, and long-term memory represent the three levels, in order, of the modal model of information processing.

115. **A) Homogeneous responses on one variable**
Homogeneous responses on one or both variables may diminish correlation. Both variables being ratio levels and bivariate normality are assumptions. The population correlation equaling zero is the null hypothesis for the Pearson Product-Moment Correlation.

116. **A) Strong Vocational Interest Inventory**
The Strong Vocational Interest Inventory scores across General Occupational Themes, Basic Interest Scales, Personal Style Scales, and Occupational Scales. The SDS provides the top three domain scores as interpretable. The Campbell Interest and Skill Survey is based on basic and occupational scales. The General Occupational Themes Scale measures Holland's six R-I-A-S-E-C categories.

117. **B) The supervisor did not review the supervisory process at the beginning of supervision.**
This vignette relates to American Psychological Association Code Standard 7.06, which notes information regarding the supervision process is provided to the student at the beginning of supervision. The supervisor may make recommendations regarding a student moving forward in a program. A program is allowed to have uniform standards for its students.

118. **D) The psychologist's safety**
American Psychological Association Code 10.10(c) allows psychologists to terminate therapy when threatened by a client or another person with whom the client has a relationship, such as a spouse. The psychologist's safety takes precedence over the client's or spouse's rights or safety given the overt threats made by the spouse. Other services may be provided to the client to receive care elsewhere.

119. **D) Offer the students an alternative means of earning extra credit.**
This vignette relates to American Psychological Association Code Standard 8.04, which discusses students and subordinates serving as research participants. While discussing concerns may be appropriate, the standard is overt that alternative means to study participation must be offered. Encouraging the students to participate despite their dissent is not appropriate.

120. **C) Meet with the community advisory board at regular intervals.**
Meeting with the community advisory board can ensure equitable involvement and is crucial for historically marginalized populations. While statistical power is important and may suggest equitable involvement, it does not ensure it. A community leader could be a valuable resource; however, that person may not represent the wider community. Culturally relevant recommendations are an important part of community-based participatory research, but such recommendations would occur after study participants were garnered.

121. A) Cognitive information processing (CIP)
The top level of CIP addresses metacognitions and executive processing, which may include commitment anxiety and self-defeating cognitions. Super's work emphasizes a developmental lens guided by one's age. Gottfredson's approach focuses on career options within society while accounting for social status and personality. CCT expands upon Holland's and Super's work, focusing on environmental adaptations versus finding career values and preferences.

122. C) Give the Beck Anxiety Inventory at the same time and determine the correlation.
Concurrent validity is determined by examining the correlation between an established measure and the new measure that is administered at the same time to assess the criterion of interest. Determining the proportion of people accurately diagnosed with an anxiety disorder would determine specificity. Determining the correlation between the new assessment and anxiety defines construct validity. Ensuring the test includes the range of information to assess anxiety appropriately defines content validity.

123. C) Discuss the case with the referring physician and complete a health-related quality-of-life inventory.
Discussing the case with the referring physician and completing a health-related quality-of-life inventory speaks to the growing role psychologists have in health behavior and the specialty of clinical health psychology. Specific health-related assessment and collaboration with medical staff are integral to client success. Reviewing the electronic health record should be done when seeing any new client and is not specific to this case. CBT-CP would be an appropriate intervention for this client, but it should only occur after assessment and collaboration with the referring physician. Relaxation techniques are an integral part of treating pain; however, it is not sufficient to utilize relaxation only.

124. B) Weschler Intelligence Scales
Typically, the Weschler Intelligence Scales and a measure of personality are administered alongside the Halstead–Reitan. The other three options listed may be administered depending on the question that is being answered through assessment.

125. B) Polyadic
Polyadic subsystems involve more than two people, while dyadic involves two family members. Given concerns are being expressed and no punishment is occurring, it is not considered a disciplinary interaction. Prosocial actions speak to a person's behaviors that are deemed socially desirable.

126. B) Dispositional causal attribution
Dispositional attribution refers to a personality trait. An assumption is being made about this student being shy and quiet instead of situational causal attribution, which would mean the new student is just nervous about their new school. Social categorization is a broad term for information processing. Prototypical social behavior is a model of social categorization.

127. D) Attempt to resolve the concern via informal action with the psychologist.
APA Code 1.04 encourages informal means of resolving the issue by bringing it to the individual's attention before bringing it to the attention of a third party. This vignette also speaks to APA Code 1.05, Reporting Ethical Violations, which states that psychologists should take appropriate action when they learn of a colleague who has engaged in behavior that has resulted, or is likely to result, in substantial harm. This code would become relevant if the psychologist's actions may cause harm to a person or informal means are unsuccessful.

128. C) Availability heuristic

The availability heuristic is a shortcut that comes to mind when someone evaluates a concept (gas station). The friends now overestimate the likelihood of the gas station being dangerous based on one event that occurred years ago. The exemplar model of attribution represents specific and concrete categorical information. The representative heuristic emphasizes a judgment based on memories of stereotypes. Correspondent inference describes the process of inferring rationale for others' behavior.

129. A) Curriculum-based measurement

Curriculum-based measurement is the regular assessment of children with standardized measures for monitoring skill progression. Aptitude testing assesses the potential to learn different skills. Achievement testing assesses knowledge acquired; however, it is often individualized. Intelligence testing will assess a broad range of abilities rather than a specific subject, such as math.

130. A) Conners Continuous Performance Test–3

Assessments of reaction time and sustained attention are not significantly impacted by cultural and linguistic differences. The Wisconsin Card Sorting Test and the WAIS-IV, while potentially appropriate to incorporate into an ADHD battery, may be culturally biased for this individual even with an interpreter. Some psychologists may include the PAI but given its focus on personality and its possible cultural bias issues, it would not be appropriate for this client.

131. D) Self-monitoring

Self-monitoring regulates behavior for situational appropriateness via self-presentation, behavior, or nonverbal affective displays. Self-promotion occurs when a person emphasizes their abilities or success to others. Self-handicapping is the creation of obstacles due to the belief that failure will occur. Impression management is a broad term that encompasses the other three options.

132. C) Moderate

Heredity has a moderate level of impact. Other factors, such as parenting and the environment, also impact a child's temperament. The "goodness of fit," which matches a child's temperament and environmental demands, is also critical.

133. D) Mens rea

Mens rea, also known as diminished capacity, is a legal doctrine that allows psychologists to discern if a defendant has the mental capacity to intend to commit a crime. The M'Naghten rule is a standard of criminal responsibility, which must prove that the accused did not understand what they were doing due to a "severe mental disease or defect." Insanity Defense Reform Act criteria is a broad law that applies to mental capacity in all federal jurisdictions. It incorporates the M'Naghten Rule. Guilty but mentally ill is a plea acknowledging the contribution of a mental illness and its role on functioning when assessing guilt and advises approaches to sentencing.

134. B) The bystanders fear social disapproval if their behavior is inappropriate.

Fear of social disapproval is a known inhibitor of intervention regarding the bystander effect. This is known as evaluation apprehension. The fact there were only two witnesses goes against the concept of responsibility diffusion, which states that the probability of help is inversely related to the number of bystanders. Egoism as a motivator to altruism may impact one's behavior, but it does not mean one would not have a collectivist or principalist approach. While low motivation for prosocial behavior is possible, it does not specifically relate to the bystander effect.

12. PRACTICE TEST: ANSWERS 397

135. **B) This student had difficulty developing a sense of self and personal identity.**
Developing a sense of self and personal identity is a common outcome of adolescence, according to Erickson, which emphasizes social relationships. Concepts of garnering wisdom are not something expected until Erickson's final stage of development. A hallmark of the industry versus inferiority stage is coping with academic demands, which this student does well. Personal control is an important aspect of early adulthood, but personal skills are often examined in the context of physical skills and independence. By all accounts, the student is doing well outside of the social setting.

136. **B) Test fairness**
Test fairness is aspirational in nature and is discerned through four primary considerations, specifically a lack of bias, equitable treatment in the testing process, equality of outcomes, and an opportunity to learn. Test bias is a component of fairness, as are reliability and validity.

137. **A) Threat of retaliation**
The threat of retaliation often decreases aggressiveness unless paired with provocation. Deindividuation means the bully will act more aggressively due to anonymity. Observation of other bullies leads to the maintenance of the bullying behavior via social learning theory. Stable levels of aggression would not increase or decrease bullying behavior.

138. **B) Reduced recovery time from physical health concerns**
Recovery from physical health concerns and even early death are more probable as a result from ACEs. ACEs are known to increase HPA activity throughout the day. Additionally, cortisol levels tend to increase as cortisol is often associated with stress response. Academic performance is likely to be impacted negatively by these experiences.

139. **C) Microaggression**
Microaggressions are subtle forms of prejudice and discrimination. While this comment is prejudicial, biased, and discriminatory, it is best defined as a microaggression due to its subtlety and unintentional conveyance of hostility toward atheists.

140. **C) The client's possible history of a suicide attempt**
A client's history of attempting suicide is a critical factor in determining current risk. A client's risk for attempting suicide increases significantly if there has been a previous attempt. This is the most important factor for the assessment. Family and friends may serve as a protective factor and are worthy of discussion with the client. Motivation to change and engage are also worthy of assessment. An objective suicide assessment would likely prove useful for the client, too.

141. **B) Resilience**
Higher rates of resilience were negatively associated with PTSD. PE is an evidence-based treatment for PTSD. Increasing its utilization would treat, not decrease, the likelihood of a diagnosis. Tertiary prevention would occur after a diagnosis of PTSD was made. Health promotion efforts may aid in this effort. However, this is a broad term and would have to be crafted to address PTSD directly.

142. **B) Overt aggression**
Overt aggression describes behavior that is physical in nature and aimed at causing harm. Relational behavior includes behaviors focused on manipulation and damaging social relationships. Conventional moral behavior is a Kohlberg term where individuals are concerned with conforming to social norms. Typical childhood behavior may include physical altercations, but this scenario is best exemplified as overt aggression.

143. C) Cognitive dissonance

Cognitive dissonance is unpleasant and may cause someone to incorporate new information, such as possible joint damage, to eliminate inconsistency between attitudes and behaviors. Social proof is engaging in behaviors due to other people doing those behaviors. Communicator credibility occurs when someone argues against their own best interest. Obedience occurs when a person submits to authority. This individual did concur with the physician's recommendation.

144. B) Dishabituation

Dishabituation occurs when a response to a stimulus increases when the stimulus is changed. Habituation occurs when the response to the stimulus decreases after repeated presentation. Ulnar–palmar grasping is the pressing of objects against the palm. While the infant likely has improved visual acuity, it does not account for the sudden new interest in the toy.

145. A) Temporarily assist the students and refer them to child psychologists as soon as feasible.

Psychologists can provide emergency services outside their scope but must discontinue services when the crisis has ended. Lack of competence in child psychology, while not ideal, does not prohibit emergency care to that population. Enrolling in training may prove useful, but waiting for completed training would not allow a psychologist to assist the children in this example. Care should be terminated when appropriate services are available or the crisis has ended, not when the students or guardians choose.

146. B) Ensure the article is marked as an advertisement in the newspaper.

American Psychological Association Code Standard 5.02(c) states that a paid advertisement relating to psychologists' activities must be identifiable as such. Given that the rationale for the article is the advertising dollars the psychologist has spent with the newspaper, the article would qualify as an advertisement. Thus, the article should be identified as such, regardless of the fact that the psychologist did not request it or pay for it. This would not qualify as a multiple relationship as the psychologist is only working with the editor in one capacity.

147. A) Review the steps students may take to perform well on the exam.

Messages appealing to fear are more effective when the speaker provides information on how to avoid the danger. Informing the students that the professor is going to attempt to motivate them to study is known as forewarning. People will be less receptive to messages if they are told in advance the speaker will try to persuade them. Communicators are less credible when speaking about their self-interest. By emphasizing students' past successes, they will perceive themselves as less vulnerable to poor performance and be less receptive to the professor.

148. C) Dr. Jackson acted ethically as long as the former client was not experiencing a mental health emergency.

American Psychological Association Code 6.03 allows psychologists to withhold the release of records for lack of payment unless the records are needed for emergency treatment. The caveat of unless there is a mental health emergency is an important one. Clients do not always have an automatic right to their records; regardless of notice, records must still be furnished in an emergency.

149. C) Belmont Report

The Belmont Report, published in 1979, still guides many institutional review boards in the conduct of ethical research. General Principles are broad and aspirational in nature. Ethical standards are specific and enforceable rules covering many professional practices. The ASPPB Code of Conduct represents the profession's own standards to protect welfare and integrity.

150. **D) Reintegration status**
 Reintegration status attempts to resolve the moral issues stemming from the previous disintegration status. The hallmark of contact status is the lack of awareness of racism. Disintegration status is defined by emotional conflict from an emerging understanding of racism. Pseudoindependence status is defined by a jarring event or events to question one's racist views and appreciate the role White people have in perpetrating racism.

151. **A) Cross-modal perception**
 Cross-modal perception occurs when infants recognize an object with a sense when they have only previously encountered another. Proprioception is the sense of body position and self-movement. Visual perception and sensory development are at play in this vignette; however, this is not an issue of just vision.

152. **A) Nonverbal and primarily nonculturally biased abilities, such as efficiency on novel tasks and new learning**
 Horn and Cattell's definition of fluid intelligence is nonverbal and primarily nonculturally biased abilities, such as efficiency on novel tasks and new learning. An individual's knowledge base or range of acquired skills, which are dependent on exposure to both culture and the specific information value by a given culture, is the definition of Horn and Cattell's crystallized intelligence. The development of the Wechsler scales is defined, in part, by construction that is primarily based on the psychological theories of skill and capacity. An individual's potential to learn and master different skills is the definition of aptitude.

153. **C) An event the child discusses with their parents**
 Children are far more likely to remember events in which they actively participate or that they discuss with their friends or family members.

154. **D) Experiencing anger and resentment of White culture**
 Experiencing anger and resentment indicates the next stage of the Black racial identity development model, the immersion–emersion stage. Low self-esteem is more indicative of the first stage or the preencounter stage. Afrocentrism would be an identity found in the internalization stage. Increasing racial/cultural awareness is an aspect of his current stage encounter.

155. **A) Weschler Individual Achievement Test–Third Edition (WIAT-III)**
 The WIAT-III focuses on reading while still assessing other areas, such as mathematical operations and written expression. The WJ-IV could meet the needs of the psychologist; however, it does not place added emphasis on reading. The Test of Written Language–Fourth Edition and Gray Oral Reading Test–Fifth Edition focus solely on written language and reading skills, respectively. Neither covers other areas of academic functioning.

156. **C) Action**
 Clients in the action stage have a working plan and enact changes based on specific behavioral interventions and plans. The contemplation stage is defined by ambivalence regarding change and weighing the pros and cons of change. The preparation stage is defined by a readiness to enact change behavior and developing a plan to enact behavior. The maintenance stage focuses on working to sustain changes made in the action stage.

157. D) Marginalization
Marginalization occurs when an individual doesn't identify with their own culture or the majority culture. Integration occurs when there is a balance between one's own culture and the majority culture. Assimilation occurs when a person relinquishes their own culture and accepts the majority culture. Separation occurs when a person withdraws from the majority culture and accepts their own culture.

158. B) Neuropsychological Assessment Battery (NAB)
The NAB is used for adults, and the assessment may be used in its entirety or to address specific questions. The Halstead–Reitan functions similarly to the NAB but lacks nearly as many subtests. The Leiter-III is used to assess individuals where language abilities are a concern. The WPPSI-IV is for preschool students and assesses Full Scale IQ across five subfactors.

159. B) Limits of confidentiality
American Psychological Association (APA) Code 8.02 reviews the requirements for informed consent to research. Participants must be briefed on their limits of confidentiality. Given this is not a therapeutic relationship, the potential risks and benefits of a therapeutic relationship are not relevant. The risks and benefits of participation in research should be disclosed. Fees are not explicitly covered in APA Code 8.02, though generally, participants do not pay to participate. Participants are not required to complete the study. They may withdraw at any time.

160. B) "In his past job, our new employee was not allowed to participate in workplace functions due to an outdated office layout. We will modify the office to facilitate that."
Choosing to modify the office to facilitate the employee's participation utilizes language that views disability as a social construct, as it describes disability as a socially created problem stemming from a limitation of physical and social barriers (poor office layout). The other responses use language like "accommodations" and "healthcare concerns/issues," which emphasize the medical model and that disability is a problem caused by disease, trauma, or other healthcare concerns.

161. A) Reality
Reality therapy, developed by Glasser, minimizes environmental impact and states humans have four psychological needs: belonging, power, freedom, and fun. Social cognitive theory focuses on reciprocal determinism, which focuses on the interaction of personal factors, behavior, and the environment. Radical behaviorism is an operant theory that posits behavior occurs when reinforced. Systematic theory is a combination of psychodynamic and cognitive-behavioral theories.

162. B) Benchmarking
Benchmarking is the process of organizations monitoring behavior to promote best practices. This questionnaire does not ask about patient satisfaction; rather, it asks about the implementation of their treatment. Behavioral analysis is the observation and measurement of behavior for an individual person. Accountability may be an aspect of the questionnaire; however, ensuring appropriate protocols are followed is better defined as benchmarking.

163. C) Work with their legal counsel to take appropriate steps to resolve the conflict surrounding the subpoena.
This situation relates to American Psychological Association Code Section 4.01, Maintaining Confidentiality. Psychologists should take reasonable steps to resolve the conflict per the advice of their legal counsel and may ultimately appear in court. Should those reasonable steps not suffice, a judge may compel the testimony. The psychologist will ultimately testify but should provide the minimum information necessary to answer specific questions.

164. C) Autism spectrum disorder (ASD)
ASD is assessed with the Social Responsiveness Scale.

165. A) Dynamic systems theory
Dynamic systems theory postulates a child's mind, body, and physical and social worlds form an integrated system guiding new skills and eventually a return to normalcy. Ecological systems theory may be at play, but this only represents changes to the child's microsystem. Cognitive-developmental theory focuses solely on cognitions rather than social interactions. Sociocultural cognitive theory focuses, again, more on thinking, though it does consider social interaction.

166. B) Contact hypothesis
The contact hypothesis states that prejudice will decrease when contact among members of different groups increases. Implicit bias may be mitigated through busing, but this has not been as clearly demonstrated. Microaggression reduction could be affected, but comparable to implicit bias mitigation, it is not clear this will occur. Social exchange theory relates to attraction occurring after assessing rewards and costs.

167. A) Potential for compromised validity of the assessment results
Emerging research indicates the potential for assessment result data to be less valid when administered by computer. Accuracy, ease of record keeping, and administration time are all benefits of computer-based administration of psychological assessments.

168. D) Ensure the client is aware of the student's training status.
This vignette relates to American Psychological Association Code Standard 10.01(c), which notes that trainees should ensure clients know their supervisory status. Consent (or assent) and payment policies are important to discuss but are important to all, regardless of whether or not someone is licensed.

169. C) Brief
Brief group therapy is a structured form of therapy that focuses on providing interventions. Psychoeducational groups involve teaching skills and providing information. Process groups are likely to be open-ended and involve processing issues of group members. Task groups are highly structured and focus on specific task accomplishment.

170. C) Sublimation
Sublimation is the conversion of libidinal drives from the id into a socially acceptable outlet, such as the gym. Reaction formation is the replacement of an unacceptable motive with its opposite. Projection attributes one's unconscious motives to the motives of others. Displacement is the shifting of energy from an acceptable desire to a possibly unrelated object.

171. C) Written consent may be waived if the potential participant is given all the necessary information, including risks and benefits, prior to their participation.
American Psychological Association Code Standard 8.05, provides that "Psychologists may dispense with informed consent only (1) where research would not reasonably be assumed to create distress or harm." Additionally, Standard 8.02 notes the information that psychologists must provide to potential participants prior to their engagement in a study.

172. C) Scaffolding
Scaffolding is the changing level of support an instructor provides when adjusting to a student's skillset. Educational support is not a term from Vygotsky's sociocultural cognitive theory. ZPD is the task of learning a difficult piece rather than the support itself. Shaping is a Skinnerian term to slowly shame behaviors by rewarding successive improvements toward a target behavior.

173. C) Examine inter-item consistency via the Kuder–Richardson formula.

The Kuder–Richardson formula is useful for a homogeneous scale such as one that measures a single trait (i.e., mania). Split-half reliability may prove helpful when a scale is heterogeneous. A lower reliability coefficient would mean the scale becomes less reliable. Comparing the ability to assess the construct of mania with a well-validated mania scale speaks to construct validity.

174. A) Object permanence

Object permanence is the understanding that objects continue to exist after they cannot be seen, heard, or touched. Primary circular reactions are the coordination of events that initially occurred by chance. In secondary circular reactions, an infant's actions become outwardly intentional and directed. Simple reflexes are rooting and sucking, which are accomplished from birth to 1 month. All four options are terms from Piaget's cognitive-developmental theory.

175. D) The frustration is the transference of frustration with their partner to the psychologist.

Transference is projecting positive or negative thoughts and emotions and driving them onto the psychologist, which the client is doing with their frustrations with their partner. Repression is the rejection of the id's content, such as having no memory of a trauma. Resistance, the inability to access unconscious content, is not evident in this prompt, though it may occur in some instances. The id appears not to be inhibited, as evidenced by the libidinal frustration from the client.

176. B) Thalamus

The thalamus is comprised of nuclei that serve as specific transmission sites to perform this function. The basal ganglia is primarily involved in motor output. The cerebellum is also most often associated with movement. The hippocampus's primary functions involve memory.

177. C) Review the cognitive distortion of dichotomous thinking and examine the evidence for the automatic thought.

Reviewing the cognitive distortion of dichotomous thinking and examining the evidence for the automatic thought appropriately identifies the "all or nothing" thinking. Examining the evidence for thoughts is a key component of cognitive therapy, which is the framework utilized to identify an automatic thought initially. Asking the client to describe what feelings are associated with this thought may prove helpful but does not align with cognitive therapy. A trauma-focused therapy, such as prolonged exposure, would not be appropriate for a breakup. Though emotional reasoning is a cognitive distortion, the automatic thought is an example of dichotomous thinking.

178. B) Learned helplessness

Learned helplessness is an explanation for depression, which states that as people develop a sense that they are unable to escape pain (or depressive symptoms), they feel helpless and reduce efforts to make positive changes. Negative thinking (cognitive distortions) is a thematic term Beck argued would result in depression. Self-defeating thinking is a term coined by Ellis, stating that such thoughts lead to unhelpful behaviors and thoughts. Attributional theory argues that learned helplessness isn't a universal experience.

179. A) Linguistic maturity

Linguistic maturity is predictive of academic achievement. Gender and religiosity are not strongly related to academic achievement in young children. Cultural traditions are generally reinforced through education.

180. **A) Treatment alternatives**
American Psychological Association Code Standard 8.02 outlines what research participants must be told prior to beginning their participation in the study. Providing information on risks and benefits, incentives, and limits of confidentiality are true of any research participant. Treatment alternatives are a specific requirement for participants in a research study that involves experimental treatments.

181. **C) The client has difficulty recalling the trauma due to being intoxicated at the time.**
A core part of PE is the imaginal exposure of recounting the trauma. If the client cannot remember the event, it may prove difficult to complete the PE protocol. A common misconception of exposure therapy is that the distress of recounting the trauma exacerbates the problem when, in fact, it is a well-validated means of treating PTSD. A client's difficulty with cognitive restructuring makes that individual a good candidate for PE as it is primarily behavioral. While a client may be resistant to a manualized protocol, this should be discussed with the client as the most efficacious treatments for PTSD are such protocols (PE and cognitive processing therapy).

182. **C) Millon Clinical Multiaxial Inventory–IV (MCMI-IV)**
The MCMI-IV was developed to support the diagnosis of personality disorder and has numerous personality profiles that aid in diagnosing. The MMPI-3 and PAI may also assist in diagnosing personality inventories; however, they cast a broader net that is less focused on personality disorders. Lastly, the HBQ assesses children's and adolescent's health functioning.

183. **A) Woodcock–Johnson IV Tests of Cognitive Abilities (WJ-IV)**
The WJ-IV is an intellectual battery that is appropriate for use in clients from age 2 to older than 90. The SB-5 is appropriate for use with clients aged 2 to 85 years. The WAIS-IV may be used with individuals aged 16 to 89. The UNIT-2 may be used for those aged 5 to 21 years, 11 months.

184. **C) Ambivalent/resistant**
Ambivalent/resistant caregiver behavior is inconsistent between appropriate and neglectful responses. Secure caregiver behavior is evidenced by appropriate, prompt, and consistent responses to a child's needs. Avoidant caregiver behavior is little or no response to distressed children and encouragement of independence. Disorganized caregiver behavior is frightening and involves maltreatment and communication errors.

185. **D) Work to elicit the client's own internal motivation to address their gambling.**
Eliciting motivation to change is a core component of Motivational Interviewing (MI). MI is efficacious when working with clients struggling with addiction and problematic behaviors. Discussing the financial and relational costs may elicit anger and irritability from the client if they are not ready to change their gambling. Psychoeducation surrounding cognitive distortions would be appropriate in cognitive behavioral therapy (CBT), which is not a first-line treatment for gambling. Confronting existential anxiety would be appropriate in existential therapy, which, like CBT, is not a first-line choice for gambling.

186. **A) Response to intervention (RTI)**
RTI uses regular progress measurement to determine a treatment's efficacy. RTIs are commonly utilized in schools. Behavioral analysis refers to the observation and measurement of a specific behavior. Standardized assessment may prove useful; however, this generalized term doesn't speak specifically to assessing a school intervention. *Relapse prevention* is a term often utilized in substance abuse but speaks to the return to any undesirable behavior.

187. A) Assimilation of new information
By assimilating new vehicles, the child is incorporating new vehicles into the existing schema of cars. Formal operation is a stage of Piaget's theory that begins in adolescence. Accommodation of new information would be the adjustment of one's schema to realize that not all vehicles are cars. While the child may, in fact, be in a critical period of development, this is a broad term that doesn't speak to the specificity of the vignette.

188. B) Complete a genogram.
Nuclear family emotional patterns are emotional styles passed down through generations in Bowen's extended family systems therapy. To understand their genesis, a geneogram will identify extended family and the quality of familial relationships. The family projection process is a Bowenian concept of family members projecting dysfunctional emotions onto a third party. Identifying subsystems is a concept in structural family therapy. Emotional cutoff relates to a family member separating from other family members. It does not speak to the origins of nuclear family emotional patterns.

189. C) Test–retest reliability
Test–retest reliability is obtained by administering a specific test to the same group at different points in time. Reliability refers to the degree to which test scores are consistent. Internal consistency reliability is a coefficient that is derived from inter-item consistency. Interrater reliability is the consistency of results across all examiners.

190. B) Plasticity
Plasticity is sensitivity to the environment engendered by experiences that impact immature systems during development. By changing the environment for vision, the ophthalmologist seeks to strengthen and impact the immature system of vision. The preoperational stage is from Piaget's theory and includes drawing people, imitating the way one speaks or moves, or pretending a stick is a sword. SOC emphasizes conscious decisions regarding changes in life over time. Discontinuity is a term used to describe theories with discreet stages, such as Kohlberg's theory of moral development.

191. C) General cognitive ability
General cognitive ability has repeatedly been shown to be the best indicator of vocational success. Self-efficacy, resilience, and motivation are also factors to success, but to a lesser degree.

192. D) Integrity
Integrity includes not misrepresenting oneself to the public. Fidelity and Responsibility relate to developing trust and upholding professional standards. Beneficence means to do good, while Nonmaleficence means avoiding harm. Justice entails exercising competence and reasonable judgment.

193. B) The child may experience additional guilt.
Children of mothers with depression are more likely to struggle with emotional understanding and may experience more shame and guilt than their peers with nondepressed mothers. Children with parents who have mental health diagnoses are more prone to mental health concerns than their peers, but by no means is it for certain. A child is more likely to prefer the parent who exhibits more positive emotions, which, in this instance, is the other parent. There is a greater likelihood of mental health impacts with one parent experiencing a mental health diagnosis.

194. **D) Cognitive behavioral**
Cognitive behavioral supervisors focus on skill-building and having structure during supervision. Constructivist supervisors assume that truth and reality are in the eye of the beholder. Systemic supervisors emphasize how the supervision process mirrors family dynamics. Supervisors utilizing a parallel process approach to supervision view the supervisor relationship as mirroring the client's problems.

195. **B) Discern if the baby is anemic or if a referral to an endocrinologist is appropriate.**
This vignette describes a failure to thrive (FTT), characterized by the inability of a baby to gain weight. This could be caused by anemia or a thyroid issue warranting care from an endocrinologist. An Apgar assessment is given to an infant immediately after birth, so this would be inappropriate. Teratogens are of primary concern to a fetus. Lastly, a Neonatal Behavioral Assessment Scale would be utilized with a newborn.

196. **A) Engage in program-centered administrative consultation.**
Program-centered administrative consultation provides feedback to improve the program. Consultee-centered administrative consultation emphasizes helping the consultee perform better in a respective role. Advocacy consultation emphasizes big-picture change on a systemic level. Client-centered case consultation focuses on improving the consultee's skills with a particular client.

197. **D) They selectively optimized their behaviors in an effort to optimize.**
Life-span theory postulates a selective optimization with compensation model. A key component is considering the changes that occur over time as one ages, such as physical injuries, and the adjustments or compensations one makes as a result, such as changing career paths. The theory of mind usually occurs in early childhood. It is a child's developing understanding of what the mind is and how it works. The ZPD encompasses tasks that one can't complete on their own but can be learned with guidance from another person. The mesosystem and exosystem stem from ecological systems theory. The mesosystem is a connection between systems in Bronfenbrenner's model. The exosystem includes things like the government, industry, and political systems, which are not at play in this vignette.

198. **B) It forms the muscles, bones, circulatory system, and some organs.**
The mesoderm is responsible for muscles, bones, and some organs. The skin, nerves, and sense organs are the ectoderm. The endoderm is the digestive system, lungs, urinary tract, and glands. Brain and neural development are not represented in one of the layers from the embryonic period.

199. **B) Assent**
Guided by American Psychological Association Code Standard 8, Research and Publication, a researcher should receive assent from a minor prior to participation and consent from their parent or legal guardian. Debriefs occur after the conclusion of the minor's participation. Inducement is something given to aid in the recruitment of research participants.

200. **D) *International Classification of Diseases* (ICD)**
The *ICD* is the standard diagnostic tool for all medicines, not just psychiatry and psychology. The *DSM* is utilized widely in the United States and Canada and strictly speaks to mental health. The WHO oversees the *ICD*. The SCID is a diagnostic interview used by mental health professionals to aid in diagnosis.

201. C) Trauma-focused cognitive behavioral therapy (TF-CBT)
TF-CBT is empirically validated for use with children, specifically those who have experienced sexual abuse. CPT and PE are excellent treatments for PTSD in adults. DBT was primarily developed to treat borderline personality disorder.

202. D) Justice
Justice includes ensuring individuals who may otherwise not have access to services do, in fact, have the ability to see a psychologist.

203. B) Rorschach Inkblot Test
The Rorschach Inkblot Test is scored using the Exner system and is completed in two phases. The MCMI-IV and the MMPI-3 are not scored in distinct phases like the Rorschach Inkblot Test and other projective assessments.

204. C) Identity assumption
Identity assumption is defined as establishing that someone is, in fact, attracted to the same sex. An individual may begin to "come out" or experiment with same-sex physical intimacy. Sensitization incorporates a vague understanding of being different from same-age peers. Identity confusion occurs in puberty when someone experiences arousal for people of the same sex and may feel guilt or a need for secrecy. Commitment is the full integration of one's sexual identity into daily life.

205. A) Criterion-referenced
Criterion-referenced tests are used to assess where an examinee stands regarding a particular skill, status, or functioning. Norm-referenced assessments compare an examinee to a specified population. A standardized assessment is a broad term that covers multiple types of assessments. Criterion-referenced, norm-referenced, and self-report are all examples of standardized tests. Self-report assessments are usually symptom-based questionnaires and surveys.

206. B) Discuss the criticality of common factors in ensuring therapeutic success.
Not feeling heard or understood by a provider is a potential risk to a good, structured intervention such as cognitive behavioral therapy (CBT). Reviewing the importance of common factors and their use in session would be most appropriate. While discontinuing the use of thought records could occur, they are an important tool for completing CBT, which is a well-validated intervention for depression. Additionally, given CBT's efficacy in addressing depression, switching treatments immediately isn't advised. Waiting without providing supervision or feedback to the supervisee would not be appropriate, given the client's concerns.

207. B) Adler
Adler suggested this as a means of psychological well-being and healthy personality. Jung conceptualizes personality because of the unconscious and conscious mind. Rogers emphasized a person-centered approach. Klein emphasized object relations theory, a psychodynamic approach to personality.

208. C) Exosystem
The exosystem includes laws, political systems, and government, which would include important legal decisions such as the legalization of same-sex marriage. The microsystem incorporates family, school, and friends; the mesosystem is the connection between systems and the microsystem; and the macrosystem includes norms and mores of a culture.

12. PRACTICE TEST: ANSWERS   407

209. **A) Lent's social-cognitive career theory (SCCT)**
SCCT comprises these four models. It emphasizes the relationship between the environment and one's cognitions. CCT emphasizes individuals' constructions of their interpretations of the world and environmental adaptations. CIP is modeled as a three-level pyramid. The Gottfredson theory emphasizes individuals' management of available career options while accounting for their social status and personality.

210. **A) Modafinil**
Modafinil is often utilized to address narcolepsy. Diazepam is a benzodiazepine and would increase sleepiness. Methylphenidate, while a stimulant, is more appropriate for attention deficit hyperactivity disorder. Sertraline is a selective serotonin reuptake inhibitor and would not promote wakefulness.

211. **B) Do not let students know when they will or will not receive extra recess.**
Not letting the students know if they will receive a reward or not for their performance is an example of a variable interval schedule. This type of interval schedule is most likely to result in a slow extinction rate, meaning it will be most likely to last for the remainder of the school year. Providing extra recess each time is a fixed interval schedule, which immediately decreases the behavior after the reinforcement is delivered (i.e., a quicker extinction rate). Letting students know beforehand if they would receive a reward would likely result in a lack of the desired behavior when no reward is provided. It is unlikely that a reward would not impact students' behavior.

212. **A) Conscious processing hypothesis**
The conscious processing hypothesis states anxiety increases when performing under pressure, which results in conscious efforts for a task that otherwise occurs with automatic processing. Negative thinking (cognitive distortions) is a thematic term Beck argued would result in depression. Expectancy theory relies on valence, expectancy, and instrumentality to understand motivation. Prospective memory describes an awareness of completing a future action.

213. **B) Investigators may have limited cultural competence or not represent the target population.**
A lack of cultural understanding or representation may inhibit potential participants' willingness to give their time to the study. For a population that is disproportionately distrustful of institutions of power, such as universities, efforts toward recruitment would be disproportionately impacted by further dissonance between researchers and potential participants.

214. **C) Approach–avoidance conflict**
Approach–avoidance conflict occurs when a goal elicits a desire to move toward it and away from it. Approach–approach conflict occurs when a person must choose between two equally positive choices. Avoidance–avoidance conflict occurs when a person must choose between two equally negative choices. Double approach–avoidance conflict occurs when two choices each elicit a desire to move toward and away from them.

215. **B) Conduct a work analysis.**
A work analysis is the process of creating a good job description to guide the hiring process and subsequent evaluation. A work sample or exercise is a situational judgment test to assess problem-solving skills. This would occur after a work analysis. Employee selection would be based on the work analysis. Interviews would be conducted after a work analysis and employee selection.

216. A) Identification
Identification occurs when behaviors change out of a desire to identify with another person. Compliance occurs when someone changes behavior to obtain a reward or to avoid punishment. Internalization is accepting a belief or attitude that is expressed publicly or privately. Social influence is an umbrella term that encompasses identification, compliance, and internalization.

217. D) Culturally prescribed norms, mores, and behaviors associated with biological sex.
The definition of gender is culturally prescribed norms, mores, and behaviors associated with biological sex. A person's sense of self as male, female, or other, while closely related to gender, defines gender identity. How an individual presents as male, female, or other given the culture through physical expression describes gender expression. A person's biological status is assigned before or at the time of birth based on visible characteristics describing sex, which is a biological term rather than a social construct.

218. C) Dialectical behavior therapy (DBT)
Holding two competing thoughts or emotions is a core component of DBT. CPT is a treatment designed to treat posttraumatic stress disorder. REBT postulates that emotions stem from beliefs about situations rather than the situations themselves. CBT focuses on changing maladaptive thinking patterns and behavioral response chains.

219. C) Signal detection theory
Signal detection theory describes the detection of important external stimuli from excess "noise." Hierarchical processing states a perceived stimulus undergoes successive expansions. Attention is a broad term referring to global states or selective processes. Structural interference states that similar tasks compete for attentional resources.

220. C) Conservation of resources
Conservation of resources theory posits that an individual's primary motivation is to build and maintain resources that assist the individual, as well as the social system that supports that individual. Goal-setting theory also describes sources of motivation; however, it does not speak to broad social systems. Conscious processing describes the role anxiety has with performance under pressure. Processing efficiency theory describes the impact of anxiety on the available cognitive resources to complete a task.

221. A) The client has a history of poor relationships with his parents, resulting in basic anxiety.
Feminist psychology pioneer Karen Horney postulated that maladaptive personality development was the result of basic anxiety. If basic anxieties are not appropriately addressed, they are responsible for unhealthy interpersonal functioning. Parataxic distortion is a term coined by Sullivan that aids in explaining the origins of neuroses. Intimacy versus isolation is a stage of psychosocial development put forth by Erickson. A low degree of social interest may be accurate; however, this would be a term utilized in Adlerian, not feminist psychology.

222. A) A failure to retain the null hypothesis
A failure to retain the null hypothesis is considered a Type I error. Type I or II errors are not based on the alternative hypothesis. Therefore, a failure to retain the alternative hypothesis and a failure to reject the alternative hypothesis are not viable answers. A failure to reject the null hypothesis is considered a Type II error in significance testing.

223. **B) Help the client find sources of frustration, such as the number of task completions impacting pay.**
Helping the client find sources of frustration, according to drive theory, states that frustrations can increase motivation more than a continuous reward. Assisting the client in developing intrinsic and extrinsic motivations stems from needs-based theories. Inherent growth tendencies are associated with self-determination theory. Valence and arousal are not related to motivation but rather are models of emotion.

224. **B) The strength of the relationship between variables**
The illusory correlation is a perception that a relationship exists between variables. If a minor relationship exists (i.e., few home break-ins), then this would be the illusory correlation at play. Overvaluing dispositional traits of fellow citizens as dangerous references the fundamental attribution error. Participants attributing their own safety to being vigilant references dispositional factors, vigilance, for success, which is the self-serving bias. While frequency of errors and biases in social thinking may prove to be helpful, it would not specifically lead to the illusory correlation.

225. **A) Establishment**
In the establishment stage (ages 25–44), individuals advance their career trajectory. In the maintenance stage (ages 45–65), individuals maintain their work and adapt to changes as needed. In the growth stage (ages 4–13), individuals accumulate knowledge related to the possibility of work. In the exploration stage (ages 14–24), individuals explore options and initiate a career trajectory.

Index

ABAB design, 256, 388
abbreviated test of intelligence, 66
ability, 169
academic achievement, 368
acceptance and commitment therapy (ACT), 76, 204, 238, 352
acculturation, 96, 105
   categories of, 97
   status, 364
ACEs. *See* adverse childhood experiences
achievement, 169
ACT. *See* acceptance and commitment therapy
active learners, 144
actor–observer bias, 79, 102
ADA. *See* Americans with Disabilities Act
ADDRESSING acronym, 97, 108
adjunctive interventions, 216
Adlerian theory, 101
Adler's individual psychology, 201
adolescent
   mothers, 153
   pregnancy, 139
adverse childhood experiences (ACEs), 132, 133, 152, 360
advertisement, 323, 362
advocacy consultation, 236
affiliation, 81
age-based development, 155
aggression, 82, 83, 135, 152
agraphia, 42
AI. *See* artificial intelligence
"all-or-nothing" period, 114
alternate/parallel forms, 265
ambivalent/resistant caregiver behavior, 403
American Law Institute Test (1962), 175
American Psychological Association's (APA) Ethical Principles of Psychologists and Code of Conduct, 301, 302, 305–307
Americans with Disabilities Act (ADA), 96, 101, 365
amygdala, 14, 34, 72
analysis of covariance (ANCOVA), 278, 279, 352
analysis of variance (ANOVA), 276, 351
ANCOVA. *See* analysis of covariance
Animal Welfare Act, 263
ANOVA. *See* analysis of variance
antidepressant, 19, 337, 339, 368
antipsychotics, 22

anxiety, 354, 355, 357, 360
   related disorders, 170
   screening measure, 357
anxiolytics, 18
APA Ethics Code 7.06, 249. *See also* ethics codes standards
Apgar score, in assessing newborns, 145
aphasia, 27
apparent harm, 331
apraxia, 28
aptitude, 169
aptitude tests, 170
Armed Services Vocational Aptitude Battery, 170
artificial intelligence (AI), 318
assessment, 312
assessment centers, 159, 160, 185, 197, 198
assessment method, selection criteria for, 177, 178
assessment, qualified for military, 340
assessment scores, stability of, 370
assimilation, 106, 404
assumptions, and technical information, 275, 276
Atkinson, Morten, and Sue's minority identity development model, 337
attachment, 133
   classifications, 134
attendance, 389
attention, 45
attentional control, 46
attentional resources, 45
attentional selection, 46
attraction, 81
attribution, covariation model of, 79
attribution of cause, 79
attributions, bias and errors in, 79, 80
attribution theories, 79
attrition, 354
atypical antipsychotics (second- and third-generation), 22, 23, 38
audience characteristics, 86
authorship, 348
autism spectrum disorder, 164
autonomy, 76
availability heuristic, 396
average life span, stages of, 243

BA. *See* behavioral activation
barriers to recruitment, 289

412 INDEX

basal ganglia, 14, 70
basic anxiety, 202
Basic Interest Scale, 173, 356
Beck's cognitive therapy, 203
behavior, 389
behavioral activation (BA), 206
behavioral analysis, 181
behavioral approaches, 91
behavioral assessment, 157
behavioral/educational consultation, 236
behavioral functioning assessment, in children, 164
behavioral theories, 100
Behavior Assessment System for Children–Third Edition (BASC-3), 188
benchmarking, 400
beneficence, 302, 322, 383
Bennett Mechanical Comprehension Test, 170
Bennett Mechanical Reasoning Test, 170
benzodiazepines, 36
BGT. *See* brief group therapy
Binet–Simon scale, 156
bioecological systems theory, 118
biological influences of factors, 119
bipolar II mood disorder, 346
birth complications, 122, 123
Black racial identity development model, 363
Black racial (Nigrescence) identity development model, 93, 99
    stages of, 94
board certification to psychologists, 347
borderline personality disorder (BPD), 204, 205
BPD. *See* borderline personality disorder
brain
    cerebrum, 12
    development, 124
    frontal lobe, 12, 13
    imaging techniques, 335
    occipital lobes, 14
    parietal lobes, 13, 14
    skull and cranial meninges, 12
    stem, 15
    subcortical regions, 14–16
    systems, 57, 58
    temporal lobes, 13
    ventricles, 12
brief group therapy (BGT), 211, 401
broad-based measures of assessment, 164
Broca area, 27, 40
Bronfenbrenner's bioecological model of human development, 118, 374
bully's aggressive behavior, 360

Campbell Interest and Skill Survey, 173
Canadian Psychological Association's (CPA) Canadian Code of Ethics for Psychologists, 301, 302
Cannon–Bard theory, 380
career construction theory (CCT), 225
career counseling theory, 374
career-ending injury, 372

case–control designs, 255
castration anxiety, 199, 200
CASVE cycle, 223
catecholamine, 339
category test, 168
catharsis, 201, 238
Cattell–Horn–Carroll (CHC) theory of intelligence, 189
Cattell–Horn model, 189
CBPR. *See* community-based participatory research
CBT. *See* cognitive behavioral therapy
CCT. *See* career construction theory
CEA. *See* cost effective analysis
central nervous system (CNS), 11
cerebellum, 15
cerebrum, 12, 33
CFA. *See* confirmatory factor analysis
child custody evaluations, 329
childhood events, 363
child's cultural background and age, 154
child's participation, 372
Chi-square tests, 267, 283, 284
cigarette smoke, 343
CIP. *See* cognitive information processing
cisgender, 95
citizenship behavior, 248
classical/Pavlovian conditioning, 50, 51
classical test theory (CTT), 156, 160, 339
    and reliability, 264
client-centered care, 229
client-centered case consultation, 236
client outcomes, factors affecting, 229
client's lack of payment, 362
client's safety, 360
clinical supervision, 229, 230
CNS. *See* central nervous system
cocktail party phenomenon, 64
cognition, emotion, and motivation, interrelationships among, 60–62
cognitive and behavioral theories, 91, 92
cognitive appraisal, 72
cognitive-behavioral model, 232
cognitive behavioral therapy (CBT), 24, 40, 203, 336, 344, 352, 365
cognitive bias, 74
cognitive development, 127, 128
cognitive-developmental theory, 115
cognitive dissonance, 398
    theory, 86
cognitive distortion, 402
cognitive functions, 43, 165, 166
cognitive information processing (CIP), 223
cognitive interference theory, 384
cognitive processing therapy (CPT), 60, 205, 350
cognitive skill, 359
cohort designs, 255, 256
Columbia-Suicide Severity Rating Scale (C-SSRS), 195
Combined Response Inconsistency (CRIN) Scale, 350
common intellectual batteries, 166–168
common therapeutic factors, 213

INDEX

communication, 86, 87, 128, 129
   nonverbal, 101
   theory, 209, 380
community-based participatory research (CBPR), 289, 290
competence, 144, 309, 310, 320, 385
   APA and CPA Ethics Codes, 309
competency, assessment of, 174, 175
compliance, 84
computed tomography, 25
computers, 366
   administered measures, validity in, 182
   use of, 182
concurrent criterion validity, 266
concurrent validity, 188, 357
concussion, 31
confidentiality, 325, 332
confirmatory factor analysis (CFA), 266
conflicts, 375
   between ethics and organizational demands, 316
conformity, 85
Conners Continuous Performance Test–3, 396
consciousness, 338
conscious processing hypothesis, 407
conservation of resources theory, 408
constructivist supervisors, 232
construct validity, 163, 188, 258–260
consultation, forms of, 235, 236
consultee-centered administrative consultation, 236
consultee-centered case consultation, 236
contact hypothesis, 401
contemporary theories, 118
content validity, 162, 265
contingency model, 92
continuity, 114
continuous reinforcement, 68
conventional antipsychotics ("typical" or "first-generation"), 20
"conventional" thinking, 135, 379
convergent validity, 266, 294
conversion therapy, 339
cooperation, 102
correct/incorrect researcher decisions, 273
correlation, 280, 355
correlational studies, 255, 256
correspondent inference theory, 79
cost effective analysis (CEA), 229
courage, 246
COVID-19 pandemic, 5, 10, 119, 182, 222, 227, 286
CPT. *See* cognitive processing therapy
cranial meninges, 12
creative self, 242
criminal responsibility, assessment of, 174, 175
CRIN Scale. *See* Combined Response Inconsistency Scale
criterion-referenced test, 158, 183, 184
criterion validity, 266, 390
cross-cultural psychology, 98
cross-modal perception, 399

C-SSRS. *See* Columbia-Suicide Severity Rating Scale
CTT. *See* classical test theory
cultural/multicultural issues, 311, 312
   APA's multicultural guidelines, 311
culture, 97
   and individual diversity, 92
   sensitivity, 196
curriculum-based measurement, 170, 396

dangerousness, 341
data interpretation, factors influencing, 181
DBT. *See* dialectical behavior therapy
death in family, 139, 140, 153
decision-making, 335, 342
defense mechanisms, 200
dementia, 28–31, 338, 340
departures from normality, 272
depression, 339, 340, 341, 352, 374, 375
   FDA-approved treatment, 18
descriptive statistics, 269
development, 111
   critical period in, 141
   domains of, 121
   models of, 95, 96
   passive or active agents in, 115
developmental science, 111
developmental theories, 115
diagnostic classification systems, 178
Diagnostic Interview Schedule (DIS), 159
dialectical behavior therapy (DBT), 204, 205, 408
diaphragmatic breathing, 206
dichotomous thinking, 240
differential diagnosis, 177
dignity, 304
dimensional/basic emotion models, 57
direct observation, 159
DIS. *See* Diagnostic Interview Schedule
disabilities, 96
   models of, 96
disaster relief effort, 332
discontinuity, 114
discriminant validity, 266
discrimination, 82, 83, 84
   model, 234
dishabituation, 398
disinhibited behaviors, 346
dispositional attribution, 395
dissemination, 290, 347
distal stressors, 110
distribution shape, 272
distributive justice, 106
divorce, 138, 151
domestic violence, 329
doses, to achieve desired high, 387
double approach–avoidance conflict, 102
drive theory, 58, 59
driving exam, 184
DSM-5-TR, 352
dynamic systems theory, 119, 120, 401

ecological assessment, 157
educational opportunities, 154
EEG. *See* electroencephalography
EFA. *See* exploratory factor analysis
effectiveness trials, 254
efficacy trials, 254
ego, 106
electrical–chemical process, 33
electroencephalography (EEG), 26
electronic communication, 87
Ellis' rational emotive-behavioral therapy, 204
emerging self-concept, 129
emotion(al), 54
   development, 130–132
   dysregulation, 152
   experience, theories of, 55, 56
   regulation, 131
empathy, 102, 135
environment, 132
environmental/ecological psychology, 87
environmental influences, 142
environmental models, 113
environment ("nurture"), 112
Erikson's stages of psychosocial development, 137, 202
establishment stage, 409
esteem, 382
ethical decision making, 315, 316
ethical obligation, 328
ethical principles, 302, 323, 362
ethical problem, 346
ethical standards, 304–307, 320, 353
ethical violation, 319, 344
ethics and clinical supervision, 331
ethics and research, 263
ethics codes, 319
ethics codes standards, 307–313
ethics codes, structure of, 301, 302
ethics in research, 313
   APA Code of Ethics, Section 8, 313
   CPA Code research ethics (I.18, I.32, I.39, II.14, II.18), 313
ethics in supervision, 317
   APA Code (3.08 Exploitative Relationships), 317
   APA Code Section 7.06(a), 317
   CPA Code, 317
ethnic and racial identity, development, 214
ethnicity, 92
ethnocentric monoculturalism, 97
event sampling, 184
evidence-based decisions, 181
evidence, levels of, 263
evolutionary theory, 88
exam's impact on students' final grade, 362
executive functions, 46, 47, 63
exercises
   and meditation, 8
   physical, 68
   psychologists, 222
   psychology, 222, 223
   in self-acceptance, 217

existential therapy, 207
exogenous attention, 63
exosystem, 119
exploitation, 324
exploratory factor analysis (EFA), 266
external validity, 258, 262
extra credit opportunity, 356
extrapyramidal symptoms, 341
extrinsic reward, 70

face validity, 265
fairness, 163
family, 136
   stability, 154
FBA. *See* functional behavioral assessment
fear, 340
   of social disapproval, 396
feminist therapy, 208
fidelity, 303, 324
financial hardship, 349
financial security, 154
Finger Tapping test, 169
5-point Likert scale, 159
fixed interval schedule, 68
fluid intelligence, 363
fluid intelligence peak, 344
focus groups, 286
foot-in-the-door technique, 100
free association, 201
Freud's psychoanalysis, 199
Freud's psychoanalytic theory, 105, 106
Friedman Test, 284
frontal lobe, 12
frustration, 368
functional behavioral assessment (FBA), 157, 184, 196
functional magnetic resonance imaging, 27
functional neuroimaging, 26
fundamental attribution error, 100
funding sources, 228, 229
future violence, 191
   risk of, 175, 176

GABA, 16, 19, 23, 36, 382
GADS. *See* Gilliam Asperger Disorder Scale
GATB. *See* General Aptitude Test Battery
gender, 138, 376
   awareness, 130
   consciousness, 130
   constancy, 130
   identity, 95, 130
   and sexual orientation, 94
General Aptitude Test Battery (GATB), 170
general-factor (*G*) theory of intelligence, 156, 161
generalizability theory, 160, 266
generalized anxiety disorder, 335, 352, 354
general occupational themes
   scale, 173, 356
genetics, 123, 124
genotype, concept of, 141

German caregivers, 133
German children's attachment behaviors, 133
Gestalt theories, 91
Gestalt therapy (GT), 207, 208
Gilliam Asperger Disorder Scale (GADS), 164
global psychology, 98
glutamate, 17, 36
Gottfredson's theory of circumscription and compromise, 224, 237
grandparents, 154
grounded theory, 286
group and system processes, 84
group-based randomized experiments, 254
group psychotherapy, 211
group therapy, 237
GT. *See* Gestalt therapy
guilt, 404

halo effect, 247, 248
Halstead Impairment Index, 169
Halstead–Reitan Neuropsychological Test Battery, 168, 357
haptics, 102
harm avoidance, 307, 308
   APA Code, 308
   CPA Code, 307
Hawkins and Shohet model, 234
health behaviors, broad assessments of, 172, 173
health promotion, 225
heredity, moderate level of impact, 396
heuristics, 78
hippocampus, 14, 72, 74, 392
hiring process, 375
historical theories, 115
Holland Code of Artistic, 237
Holland's personality and environmental typology, 238
Holland's theory of vocational interest, 189
Holloway systems approach model, 234, 235
holy trinity, 162
homophobia, 83
human behavior, biological nature of, 11
humanistic and existential theories, 108
humanistic/existential theories, 91
Huntington disease, 16
hydroxyzine, 42
hypothalamic–pituitary–adrenal axis, 124
hypotheses, 253

ICC. *See* item characteristic curve
ICD. *See International Classification of Diseases*
id, 106, 199
identification, 85, 408
identity, 136
identity development, 93
IDM, integrated developmental model
illicit substances, 341
illusory correlation, 377
implicit bias, 82, 83, 84
impression formation, and management, 80, 81
   self-handicapping, 81
   self-monitoring, 81
   self-promotion, 81
independent samples *t*-test, 275
individual diversity, 97
individual ("nature"), 112
industrial psychology, 217–220, 247
inferential statistics, 272
informal action, 395
informal resolutions, 386
informational conformity, 85
informed consent, 228, 310, 327, 364
   APA and CPA codes guidelines, 310
insomnia, 339
institutional review board (IRB), 263, 325, 344, 367
integrated developmental model (IDM), 233, 234, 246
integrity, 303, 308, 309
   APA Code prohibits unfair discrimination, 308, 309
   APA 3.08 state, 308
   conflict-of-interest concern, 309
   plagiarism (APA 8.01[a], CPA III.7), 309
intellectual batteries, 355, 369
intellectual disability, 155
intelligence, 47
   research-based theories of, 47, 48
intelligence tests, 334
   bias in, 50
   psychometric properties and, 49
intent-to-treat analyses, 254
interactional approach, 113
interactional model, 142
interactive communication, 150
Interjurisdictional Practice Certificate (IPC), 228
internal consistency, 161, 264
internal consistency reliability coefficient, 162
internal validity, 258
internal validity, threats to, 261, 262
International Classification of Diseases (ICD), 178, 179, 405
international psychology, 98
Internet, 87, 182
interpersonal and systematic theories, 92
interpersonal functioning, problematic, 377
interrater or interscorer reliability, 162
interrater reliability, 188, 265
intersectionality, 97
interventions, 144
intraindividual conflict, 101
   categories of, 87, 88
IRB. *See* institutional review board
IRT. *See* item response theory
item characteristic curve (ICC), 161
item discrimination, 185
item response theory (IRT), 156, 160, 161, 266

James–Lange theory, 72
Japanese infants, 133
job satisfaction, 84, 247

John Holland's personality and environmental typology (1997), 223
judicial decisions, 314
Jung's analytical psychology, 201
Jung's archetypes, 379
justice, 303, 304, 406
    principle of, 330

Kelly's theory of covariation model of attribution, 79, 103, 104
kinesics, 102
kinship care, 139, 153
knowledge, 129, 331
Krumboltz's two-part learning theory, 224
Kruskal–Wallis Test, 284
Kuder Occupational Interest Survey, 173, 384
Kuder–Richardson formula, 187, 188

language, 128, 150
    acquisition, 144
    development, 144
latent constructs, and observable measures, 264
laws, 314
Lazarus' sophisticated appraisal model of emotion, 345
learning, 50
    theories, 60
learning theory of career counseling (LTCC), 224
Lent's social-cognitive career theory (SCCT), 224
LGBTQIA+ community, 374
libido, 199
life-span theory, 120
linguistic validity, 196
little scientists, 144
Locke's goal-setting theory, 347
Loganbill, Hardy, Delworth model, 233
logistic regression, 282, 389
long-term memory, 394
low-cost smoking cessation services, 329
LTCC. *See* learning theory of career counseling

MacArthur Competence Assessment Tool-Criminal Adjudication (MacCAT-CA), 175
macrosystem, 119
magnetic resonance imaging, 25, 26
major depressive disorder (MDD), 336, 340
malnutrition, 125
mania, 367
manipulate information, 70
Mann–Whitney Test, 284
Maslow's theory of self-actualization, 207
mate selection, 88
MDD. *See* major depressive disorder
measure development, and selection, 267, 268
measurement, 264
measurement error, 267
measurement invariance, 268
measures of central tendency, 270
measures of variability, 270
mediation, 285

medical models, 112
medication, 354. *See also* psychopharmacology; psychotropic medication
memories, 53, 54, 70
    long-term, 394
    procedural, 150
    recognition, 150
    sensory, 394
    short-term, 70
    working, 385
mens rea, 396
mental disorders, diagnostic and statistical manual of, 179–181
mental health, 152, 251, 361
    disorder, 348
    prevention, stages of, 226, 227
mental strategy, 334
mesoderm layer, 372
mesosystem, 119
meta-analyses, 87, 182
MI. *See* motivational interviewing
microaggressions, 397
MID. *See* minority identity development model
midterm performance, 341
Minnesota Multiphasic Personality Inventory (MMPI), 171
Minnesota Multiphasic Personality Inventory–3 (MMPI-3), 348, 350, 351
Minnesota Rate of Manipulation Tests, 170
minority identity development model (MID), 214, 245
minority influence, 85
MMPI. *See* Minnesota Multiphasic Personality Inventory
MMPI-3. *See* Minnesota Multiphasic Personality Inventory–3
models of intelligence
    developmental research on, 48, 49
    structural research on, 48
    tests, applications of research on, 49
moderation, 285
moderators, 285
monoamine oxidase inhibitors, 20
monogamous mating, 104
mood assessment
    in adults, 165
    in children, 164, 165
mood stabilizers, 23, 336
moral development, 135
moral judgment interview, 135
motivation, 54, 375, 376, 377, 403
motivational interviewing (MI), 208, 209
motivation, theories of, 58
motor development, 125, 126, 150
Mullen Scales of Early Learning, 192
multicultural considerations in supervision, 235
multiple baseline designs, 256, 257
multiple-factor theory of intelligence, 156
multiple relationship, 310, 311, 326, 332
    CPA Code state, 310, 311
multisensory stimulation, 63

multitrait–multimethod matrix, 163
multivariate ANOVA, 279
Murray Bowen's extended family systems therapy, 209, 210
musical talent, 141
myelin sheath, 382

narcolepsy, 374
NBAS. *See* Neonatal Behavioral Assessment Scale
need-based theories, 59, 60
Neo-Freudian theorists, 202
Neonatal Behavioral Assessment Scale (NBAS), 145, 146
neuroangiography, 26
neuroimaging, 25
neuron, 15, 33
neuropsychological assessment, 156
Neuropsychological Assessment Battery (NAB), 400
neuropsychological functioning, 168–169
neuropsychological testing, 350
neuropsychology, 156, 184
neurotransmission, 34
neurotransmitter, 16, 335
new therapy clients, ethical method of recruiting, 331
nonmaleficence, 302, 322, 383
nonparametric statistical tests, 283
nonverbal communication, 101
noradrenalin, 16
normal distribution, 270
normal *z*-distribution, properties of, 271
norm-referenced tests, 158
nuclear family, emotional patterns, 370
null hypothesis significance testing, 272

obedience, 85, 100
object permanence, 402
object-relations theory, 202, 203, 334
occipital lobes, 14
occupational scales, 356
Oedipus complex, 199, 200
older age, 106
one-sample *z*-test, 274, 275, 351
 computations for, 275
online administration, 328
open-ended interactions, 158
operant conditioning, 51, 52, 68
opioids (narcotic analgesics), 23
oppression, 246
orbitofrontal cortex, 74
ordinary least squares (OLS) regression, 280–282
organizational justice, 81, 82, 105
organizational psychology, 220–222, 246
organizations encourage behaviors, 182
organizations monitor behavior, 182
outreach strategies, 289
overt aggression, 152, 397

PAI. *See* Personality Assessment Inventory
paired samples, 276

paired samples *t*-test, 392
paradoxical reward effects, 74
paradoxical theory of change, 243
paralanguage, 102
paramedic's license, 373
parametric/nonparametric approaches, 272
paratexic distortions, 202
paratexic mode, 202
parent–child interaction, 119
parent–child relationships, 242
parietal lobes, 13, 34
path analysis, 282, 283
patient, 313
 APA 3.10(b), 313
 CPA I.5–I.8, 313
 Health Insurance Portability and Accountability Act (HIPAA), 313
PE. *See* prolonged exposure therapy
Pearson product–moment correlation *(r)*, 279, 280
penis envy, 199, 200
people's rights, respect for, 304
perception, 44, 45
perfect completion, 374
performance, 338, 375
performance validity tests (PVTs), 174
personality, 89, 107, 374
Personality Assessment Inventory (PAI), 158, 170, 171, 174
personality theory, 113
Personal Style Scales, 356
person-centered supervision models, 231
person schemas, 106
persuasion, 86
PET. *See* positron emission tomography
pharmacodynamics, 17, 36
pharmacogenetics, 25
pharmacokinetics, 17
phenomenology, 286
phenomenology centers, 286
phenotype, 142
physical and motor development, 123
physical disability, 365
physical exercise, 68
physiological responses, 70
Piaget's cognitive-developmental theory, 115–117, 143, 350
Piaget's model, 343
plasticity, 114, 141, 142
pleasure principle, 199
polyadic subsystems, 395
polygynous mating, 104
positively/negatively biased, 341
positive psychology, 216, 217
positron emission tomography (PET), 26
"postconventional" thinking, 135
posttraumatic stress disorder (PTSD), 162, 205, 226, 351, 361, 369, 373
"preconventional" thinking, 135
prejudice, 82, 83, 366
 methods for reducing, 84

Premack principle, 385
premorbid data on intellectual functioning, 344
prenatal development, 121
　environmental impact during, 121, 122
　periods of, 121
primary emotions, 130
probabilistic epigenesis, 147
probability and normal z-distribution, 271, 272
procedural memory, 150
professional consultation, 235
professional development, 316, 317
　APA 2.03, 316
professional standards, 313, 314
　APA guidelines, 314
program-centered administrative consultation, 236
program evaluation strategies, and techniques, 287, 288
progressive muscle relaxation, 206
prolonged exposure therapy (PE), 205, 369
prosocial behavior, 82, 89, 135
prosocial emotions, 89
proxemics, 102
psychiatric pharmacogenomics, 25
psychoanalytic/psychodynamic theories, 89–91
psychodynamic theories, 115, 199
psychoeducational groups, 211
psychological assessment, 155
psychological flexibility, 237
psychological safety, 84, 104
psychological tests, 319
psychologist behavior, 325
psychologist conducting therapy, 312, 313
　APA and CPA guidelines, 312, 313
psychologist research, 356
psychologists, licensed, 321, 329
psychologist's misrepresentation, 371
psychometrics, 155
psychometric theory, 160, 161
psychomotor ability tests, 170
psychopharmacology, 17–24
　combined treatments, 24
psychosexual theory, 200
　of development, 199, 202
psychostimulants, 24
psychotherapy groups, 211
psychotherapy theories, 231
psychotropic medication, 17, 18, 337
PTSD. *See* posttraumatic stress disorder
Purdue Pegboard Test, 170
PVTs. *See* performance validity tests

QALY. *See* quality-adjusted life year
qualitative inquiry
　grounded theory, 286
　phenomenology, 286
qualitative methodology, 286
　focus groups, 286
　in-depth interviews, 286
　uncontrolled case studies, 286
qualitative research, 354
quality-adjusted life year (QALY), 229

quantitative research, 285, 286
　analysis in, 287
　reliability/validity issues in, 287
quasi-experimental studies, 255

race, 83, 92
racial/cultural identity development model (RCID), 93
　stages of, 93
randomized controlled trial, hypothetical outcome plot, 260
rational emotive behavior therapy (REBT), 76
RCID. *See* racial/cultural identity development model
reality therapy, 92, 208
REB. *See* research ethics board
recognition memory, 150
reflexive attention, 63
rehabilitation, 96
　psychologists, 156
reinforcement
　of behaviors, 343
　schedule, 52, 53
related samples t-test, 276
relational aggression, 135
relational functioning assessment, in children, 164
relationship
　strained, 349
　within workplace, 246
relaxation training, 206
reliability, 161, 185
research ethics board (REB), 325
research findings, presentation of, 290
research methodology, 253
reshaping reality, 110
resilience, 114, 225, 244
resistance, 201
respect, 383
respondent-driven sampling, 355
response to intervention (RTI), 182
responsibility, 303
retention issues at company, 345
Rey 15-Item Test, 382
risk, 114
　reduction, 226
RMSEA. *See* root mean square error of approximation
Rogers' person-centered therapy, 207
romantic illusions, 154
Ronnestad and Skovholt model, 234
root mean square error of approximation (RMSEA), 267
Rorschach Inkblot Test, 172, 406
RTI. *See* response to intervention

SADS. *See* schedule for affective disorders and schizophrenia
Salvador Minuchin's structural family therapy, 210, 211
same-sex family, 138, 139, 153
same-sex parents, 335
sample selection, 288

sampling distribution of the mean, 274
scaffolding, 401
SCCT. *See* Lent's social-cognitive career theory
schedule for affective disorders and schizophrenia (SADS), 159
schema, 78, 105
schizoid personality disorder, 369
schizophrenia, 335, 339, 345
   treatment, 372
school psychologists, 156
SCID-5. *See* Structured Clinical Interview for the *DSM-5*
scientific theories, 253
SDS. *See* self-directed search
Seashore Rhythm test, 168
sedation, 38
seizure, 32, 337, 340
selective optimization with compensation (SOC) model, 145, 146
selective perception, 110
selective serotonin reuptake inhibitors, 20–22
self and personal identity, 397
self-concept, 343
   components of, 151
self-defeating cognitions, 357
self-determination theory, 345
self-directed interventions, 216
self-directed search (SDS), 172
self-efficacy, 129, 152
self-esteem, 129, 130, 152, 349
self-evaluation, 129, 152
self-harming behavior, 323
self-knowledge, 223
self-monitoring, 396
self-regulation, 132, 152
self-report, 158
semistructured interviews, 158
sensation, 43
sensitive/critical periods, 113, 143
sensitivity, 162, 188, 284, 285
sensory and perceptual development, 126, 127
sensory memory, 394
serotonin (5-HT), 16
SES. *See* socioeconomic status
sexism, 83
sexual identity, 245, 246
sexual intimacy, 354
sexual minority identity development, 214, 215
sexual orientation, 95, 373
sexual prejudice, 83, 105
sexual relationship, 331
short-term memory, 70, 394
signal detection theory, 75, 408
single-case experiments, 256
   evaluating results in, 257
single-group design, hypothetical outcome plot, 259
situational power imbalances, 263
skull, 12
social behaviors, 88, 89
social categorization, models for, 78

social cognition, 77, 78
social cognitive approaches, 92
social competence, 135
social development, 151
social–emotional assessment in children, 164
social–emotional development, 129
social–emotional features, 112
social–emotional functioning, 164
social–emotional growth, 157
social exchange theory, 104, 349
social impact theory, 85
social influence, 84, 99
social interactions, 342
social judgments, 80
socially inappropriate externalizing behaviors, 360
social media, 317, 318
social networking sites, 87
social power, 85
Social Responsiveness Scale, 365
social role model theories, 234
social skills, 135
society role, in development of personality, 202
socioeconomic status (SES), 149, 150
   of child's family, 129
SOC model. *See* selective optimization with compensation model
somatic marker hypothesis, 56, 57
Spearman–Brown formula, 161
specificity, 284, 285, 354
specific learning disorder, 66
Speech–Sounds Perception test, 168
spinal cord, 11, 33
split-half reliability score, 161
spontaneous speech, loss of, 346, 350
sports
   medicine, 222
   organizations, 223
   performance anxieties, 62
   psychologists, 222, 319
   psychology, 222, 223
      APA define as, 222
SRMR. *See* standardized root mean square residual
standardization, 157
standardized root mean square residual (SRMR), 267
statistical conclusion validity, 258
statistical methods, of measurement, 268, 269
statistical power, 273
statistical significance, 275
   and probability, 272, 273
   supplementing information regarding, 273, 274
statutes, 314
stepfamilies, 138
stimulus-driven fashion, 64
stimulus–response–consequence model, 92
stimulus–response relationship, 206
strabismus (lazy eye), 371
strange situation procedure, 133, 134
strategic family therapy, 211
stress, 132, 151, 152
stroke, 334

structural equation modeling, 283
structural imaging, 25
structural validity, 265
Structured Clinical Interview for the *DSM-5* (SCID-5), 159
student's training status, 401
study design, 254
style of life, 374
subcortical brain regions, 14
sublimation, 238, 401
subpoena, to testify, 365
substance abuse, 327
suicidal risk, 196
suicide
   assessment, 371
   attempts, 355
   evaluation, 176, 177
   risk, 193
super-ego, 106, 200
Super's career and life development theory, 223
supervisee's strengths, 335
supervision, 322
   fundamental components of, 230, 231
   multicultural considerations in, 235
   process, concepts of theories relate to, 233
   sessions, 335
supervisor, 356
   functioning, 335
   relationship, 249
support, 379
SVT. *See* symptom validity testing
symptom validity testing (SVT), 189
synaptic pruning, 147, 148
synaptogenesis, 147, 148
syntaxic mode, 202
systemic supervision, 232
systems/organizational development consultation, 236
systems theory, 209

Tactual Performance test, 168
technology-assisted psychological services, 227, 228, 331
telehealth, 329
   services, 327
telepsychology, 227, 228
   APA's Telepsychology Guidelines, 318
   CPA Code, 318
   services, 243, 349
temperament, 131
temporal, 34
   lobes, 13
teratogen, 147, 148
terminate care/transition, 392
test bias, 163
test fairness, 397
test–retest reliability, 161, 185, 264
TF-CBT. *See* trauma-focused cognitive behavioral therapy
thalamus, 14, 402
theory of mind, 129
theory X orientation, 345

therapeutic
   approach, 107
   attention, 262
   factors, 212, 339
   process, 364
   relationship, 351
   window, 36, 336
therapy services, 353
threat, 356
TIC. *See* trauma-informed care
time-sampling methods, 159
Trail Making test, 169
trainee performance, 250
training in positive self-talk, 76
trait models, 113
trait theory, 92, 108
transactional model, 135
transference, 201
transformational leadership, 88
transition to parenthood, 139, 153
transtheoretical model (TTM), 212, 213
trauma-focused cognitive behavioral therapy (TF-CBT), 205
trauma-informed care (TIC), 206
traumatic encephalopathy, 31
treatment
   alternatives, 403
   contemporary theories of, 199
   planning, pain and depressive symptoms, 357
   plan to address learning difficulties, 370
triangulation, in family systems, 241
tricyclic antidepressants, 20
trinitarian model of validity, 187. *See also* validity
t-scores, 164, 389
TTM. *See* transtheoretical model
two-sided message, 104
Type I error, 377
Type II error, 187

uncontrolled case studies, 257, 258
unipolar mood, 355
unstructured
   interviews, 158
   personality assessment, 172, 189

valence, 387
validity, 162, 185, 265
   concurrent criterion, 266
   construct, 163
   content, 162
   convergent, 266
   discriminant, 266
   external, 258
   face, 265
   internal, 258
   linguistic, 196
   structural, 265
   testing, 174
variable interval schedule, 68, 407
variance, 347

ventricular system, 12
verbal interactions, 143
vocational
 demands, 369
 interest, assessments of, 172, 173
 psychologist, 156
 success, 333
Vygotsky's concept of the zone of proximal development (ZPD), 143
Vygotsky's sociocultural cognitive theory, 117, 118

weight gain, 372
wellness, components of, 243
Wernicke aphasia, 33
Weschler Individual Achievement Test–Third Edition (WIAT-III), 399
Weschler Intelligence Scales, 395

white racial identity development model, 93, 363
 stages of, 94
WHO. *See* World Health Organization
Wilcoxon Signed Ranks Test, 284
Woodcock–Johnson Fourth Edition (WJ-IV) Tests, 161
work analysis, 248
working memory, 385
work performance, 371
work samples, 159
World Health Organization (WHO), 178, 179

Youth Risk Behavior Surveillance System (YRBSS), 173

ZPD. *See* Vygotsky's concept of the zone of proximal development
z-scores, 270, 348
 conversion, 271